HELLENISTIC CULTURE AND SOCIETY

General Editors:

Anthony W. Bulloch, Erich S. Gruen, A. A. Long, and Andrew F. Stewart

The Image of the Jews
in Greek Literature

The Image of the Jews in Greek Literature

The Hellenistic Period

———

Bezalel Bar-Kochva

UNIVERSITY OF CALIFORNIA PRESS

Berkeley   Los Angeles   London

University of California Press, one of the most distinguished
university presses in the United States, enriches lives around
the world by advancing scholarship in the humanities, social
sciences, and natural sciences. Its activities are supported by
the UC Press Foundation and by philanthropic contributions
from individuals and institutions. For more information, visit
www.ucpress.edu.

University of California Press
Berkeley and Los Angeles, California

University of California Press, Ltd.
London, England

Library of Congress Cataloging-in-Publication Data

Bar-Kochva, Bezalel.
    The image of the Jews in Greek literature : the Hellenistic Period /
by Bezalel Bar-Kochva.
        p.   cm. — (Hellenistic Culture and Society ; 51)
    Includes bibliographical references and index.
    ISBN 978-0-520-25336-0 (cloth : alk. paper)
    1. Jews in literature.   2. Greek literature, Hellenistic—History and
criticism.   I. Title.
PN56.3.J4B37   2009
880.9'3529924—dc22   2008035549

Manufactured in the United States of America

19   18   17   16   15   14   13   12   11   10
10   9   8   7   6   5   4   3   2   1

This book is printed on Natures Book, which contains 50% post-
consumer waste and meets the minimum requirements of ANSI/NISO
Z39.48-1992 (R 1997) (Permanence of Paper).

To Bina, Sharon, and 'Irit

CONTENTS

ILLUSTRATIONS

FIGURES

MAP

BT	Babylonian Talmud.
CPJ	V. Tcherikover et al., eds. *Corpus papyrorum judaicarum.* Cambridge, Mass., 1957–64.
DG	H. Diels, ed. *Doxographi graeci.* Berlin, 1879.
D-K	H. Diels and W. Kranz, eds. *Fragmente der Vorsokratiker*⁵. Berlin, 1934.
FGrH	F. Jacoby, ed. *Die Fragmente der griechischen Historiker.* Berlin and Leiden, 1923–69.
FHG	C. Müller and T. Müller, eds. *Fragmenta historicorum graecorum.* Paris, 1840–70.
GGM	C. Müller, ed. *Geographici graeci minores.* Paris, 1855–61.
GLAJJ	M. Stern. *Greek and Latin Authors on Jews and Judaism.* Jerusalem, 1974–84.
Guttmann	Y. Guttmann, *The Beginnings of Jewish-Hellenistic Literature.* Jerusalem, 1958–63. [In Hebrew]
IG	*Inscriptiones graecae.* Berlin, 1877–1926.
Kidd 1	L. Edelstein and I. G. Kidd, eds. *Posidonius.* Vol. 1: *The Fragments*². Cambridge, 1989.
Kidd 2	I. G. Kidd, ed. *Posidonius.* Vol. 2: *The Commentary.* Cambridge, 1988.
LSJ	H. G. Liddell, R. Scott, and H. S. Jones. *A Greek-English Lexicon*⁹. Oxford, 1940.
Niese	B. Niese, ed. *Flavii Iosephi Opera, Editio maior.* Berlin, 1885–95.

OGIS	W. Dittenberger, ed. *Orientis graeci inscriptiones selectae.* Leipzig, 1903–5.
PCZ	C. C. Edgar. *Catalogue général des antiquités égyptiennes du Musée du Caire: Zenon papyri.* Cairo, 1925–31.
PG	*Patrologia graeca.* (J.-P. Migne, ed. *Patrolgiae cursus completus, Series graeca.* Paris, 1857–60.)
PT	Palestinian Talmud.
RE	A. Pauly, G. Wissowa, and W. Kroll, eds. *Realencyclopädie der classischen Altertumswissenschaft.* Stuttgart, 1893–.
Schürer et al.	E. Schürer et al. *The History of the Jewish People in the Age of Jesus Christ (175 B.C.–A.D. 135): A New English Version Revised and Edited by G. Vermes and F. Millar.* (vol. 3 also by M. Goodman). Edinburgh, 1973–86.
SVF	J. von Arnim, ed. *Stoicorum veterum fragmenta.* Leipzig, 1903–5 (vols. 1–3). Leipzig, 1924 (vol. 4, ed. M. Adler).
*Syll.*³	W. Dittenberger, ed. *Sylloge inscriptionum graecarum*³. Leipzig, 1915–24.

ACKNOWLEDGMENTS

Work on this book commenced in the late 1990s as a monograph on Posidonius of Apamea and the Jews. It was later expanded to include all the Greek authors who wrote on the Jews in the Hellenistic period. Over the years my research has been sponsored by the Israel Science Foundation of the Israel Academy of Sciences and Humanities, to which I am greatly indebted. I would also like to take this opportunity to express my gratitude to Mr. Zvi Meitar, M. Jur., of Tel Aviv and London, a man of vision, who introduced me to modern technologies and generously supported my students.

I would like to extend thanks to a number of scholars: the Indologists Professor Klaus Karttunen of the School of Advanced Studies in Helsinki and Professor Ariel Glucklich of Georgetown University, who commented on two chapters and saved me from various mistakes and inaccuracies; and the anonymous readers of the University of California Press and Professor Erich S. Gruen, one of the editors of this series, for their constructive criticism and useful comments.

I had the privilege of frequently consulting Professor John Glucker of the Department of Classics at Tel Aviv University about various problems and issues and benefited greatly from his enormous knowledge of classical philology and the classical heritage. I will always be deeply obliged to this brilliant and most admirable scholar and man of many virtues.

Dr. Ivor Ludlam of Haifa University translated the chapters that had already been published as articles in Hebrew periodicals. An acute and meticulous scholar of the Greek language and philosophy who will make his mark in the world of learning in the future, Dr. Ludlam also helped improve the content of the manuscript and added an appendix on Stoic physics. For all of his contributions, I express my warmest gratitude.

Last but not least, thanks are due to the dedicated editors of the University of California Press—Laura Cerruti, Cindy Fulton, and Marian Rogers—for both their editorial contributions and their remarkable patience in handling my manuscript in the face of my computer ignorance and recurring corrections.

Some notes on my editorial decisions. As the book is intended not only for ancient historians and classical scholars but also for Judaic students, I have tried my best to make its content clear for both disciplines, sometimes at the risk of imparting information that may seem obvious or redundant to one or the other field. For this reason, generally I have transliterated individual Greek words and terms, except in cases where I felt the use of the original Greek was required.

Regarding the use of parentheses and brackets in the translations: parentheses ( ) are used for explanations and Greek or Latin words of the texts; square brackets [ ] for supplementary words required by the context and expression in English; angular brackets < > for letters or words omitted in the original text; curly brackets { } for superfluous letters or words added by mistake during the transmission of the work or for glosses inserted by copyists; and daggers (††) for corrupt versions.

Chapters 2–4, 6–7, 9, 11–12, and 15 of this book were previously published, in 1996–2003, in the Hebrew periodicals *Tarbiz* and *Zion*. The English version of these chapters, however, is considerably expanded and improved and thus replaces the Hebrew articles for all intents and purposes. Finally, the bibliography is current to early 2007.

I dedicate this book to my wife, Bina, and to my daughters, Sharon and ʿIrit, who bravely bore its heavy burden for nearly a decade.

B. B.
Jacob M. Alkov Chair of Jewish History in the Ancient World
Tel Aviv University
Passover 2007

Introduction

Ever since the triumph of Christianity, Jews have drawn much more attention in Western civilization than have most other ethnic groups, as a result of both their central place in the Christian tradition and their dispersal among nations. It is no wonder, then, that opinions about the Jews—whether expressed by Jews or by Gentiles—have rarely been objective or disinterested. The personal circumstances of scholars and current trends of thought and feelings concerning Jews and Judaism have also influenced research in the field of history. The well-known controversy between Theodor Mommsen and Heinrich Graetz, in nineteenth-century Germany, as to the nature and function of the Jews in the Roman Empire, is but one example.

The vast literature on Greek and Roman attitudes toward the Jews produced by modern scholars is no exception. Very often, the conscious or subconscious attitude of the modern scholar—whether Jewish or Christian, philo-Semitic or anti-Semitic, religious or agnostic, Zionist or anti-Zionist—has influenced his or her interpretation of the ancient evidence. Treatment of the subject of ancient attitudes toward the Jews has indeed always been emotionally charged.

It is not easy—in fact, it is extremely difficult—to escape one's background altogether, even for an Israeli born in Palestine, like myself, who has had no personal experience of anti-Semitism. Yet the traditional function of the historian, to describe things as nearly as possible *wie es eigentlich gewesen,* should make him attempt to analyze the material at his disposal with as much detachment as possible. I believe that, despite the inherent difficulties, a strict and consistent application of philological and historical methods to the study of the sources can still lead us toward a better understanding of ancient issues and problems.

This book deals with the attitudes of Gentile authors toward the Jews in the Hellenistic age, a stage in ancient Jewish history that constitutes one of the crucial turning points in the development of Judaism—the time of the religious persecutions by Antiochus Epiphanes and the Maccabaean Revolt and its aftermath, the Hasmonaean state. More precisely, it examines the attitudes of Hellenistic Greek authors and scholars toward the Jewish people, and their religion and customs, over a span of 270 years, from the first real encounters between Jews and Greeks, starting with the Eastern conquests of Alexander the Great (333 B.C.E.), down to the conquest of Syria and the Hasmonaean kingdom by Pompey (63 B.C.E.).

The early Hellenistic age is the starting point of my study. Greek authors of the classical age, who were keen on geographical and anthropological matters, did not refer to the Jews, just as they were late in referring to Rome and actually seem not to have known about the Germans. Even Aristotle, who lived for another eleven years after Alexander conquered Judaea, makes no mention of the Jews and seems not to have known about them. Their obscurity can be explained by the remoteness of Judaea from the coast and from maritime commerce (rightly observed by Josephus, *Ap.* 1. 60). The only exception, a brief allusion to circumcision in Herodotus (2. 104. 3), possibly with the Jews in mind, is of little significance.

The book has two parts, in line with the division observed by Josephus: the first part discusses Greek authors who wrote prior to the religious persecutions by Antiochus Epiphanes (168 B.C.E.), from the time of the Successors (323–301) through the time of Ptolemaic rule in Judaea (301–200) and the time of Seleucid rule there up to the religious persecutions (200–168). The second part deals with authors who wrote at the time of the Hasmonaean revolt (167–142/1), and the Hasmonaean state down to its termination by Pompey (142/1–63). This division facilitates the search for substantial trends and/or fluctuations in the attitudes of Greek authors toward the Jews during the first period by clarifying their motives and sources of inspiration; it also helps to sort out the exact nature and dating of the changes that took place in the attitudes of authors of the second period, each for his own reasons, following the dramatic events of the mid-second century and the developments that accompanied them in Judaea, together with the developments in relations between Jews and Greeks in the Egyptian diaspora.

The book concludes with the Roman conquest of Judaea and the elimination of Jewish independence. The Roman occupation of the East created new conditions for confrontations between Jews and the pagan world, not only in Judaea, but also in the great Jewish diaspora in Egypt and in Rome itself. Although Greek and Roman authors of the period made extensive use of their predecessors' work, which not only served to provide material but also helped to form their opinions regarding the Jews, the events of their own time were the determining factor in their opinions. Therefore discussion of these sources is beyond the scope of the present work. For this reason I have not included separate discussions of Greek and Latin authors from the time of Augustus (Timagenes, Diodorus, Strabo, Pompeius Trogus, and Nicolaus of Damascus), even though they used mostly Greek sources from the Hasmonaean period. Nor is my intention to discuss the so-called ancient anti-Semitism,[1] and its causes and forms of expression in the classical world. The aim of this book is to consider only the treatment of Jews by Greek authors, in the era outlined above.

These terms of reference also mean that the accounts of Oriental authors who wrote on the Jews in Greek (those of Brossus the Babylonian and Manetho the Egyptian are extant) will be considered only when pertinent to the discussion of some of the Greek authors and their sources. Such native non-Greek Hellenistic authors require in-depth examination in their own right, by experts in both the relevant Oriental languages and cultures and classical studies, a combination of disciplines rarely to be found in any one individual today. One may only hope that such scholars will one day enlighten us with regard to the works of these Oriental authors, and especially the much-debated passages attributed to Manetho.

The detailed discussion in this book focuses on twelve authors from whom we have fragments and testimonia referring to the Jews: they are, in chronological order, Theophrastus of Eresus, Clearchus of Soli, Hecataeus of Abdera, Megasthenes, Hermippus of Smyrna, Agatharchides of Cnidus, the anonymous Seleucid scribe(s) who composed the final version of the so-called blood libel, Timochares, the Seleucid court historian, Lysimachus of Alexandria, Posidonius of Apamea, and Apollonius Molon. Authors such as Castor the chronographer and Teucer the ethnographer, about whom we have no more specific information than that they wrote about the Jews, are not included, nor are authors such as Polybius, whose extant references do not allow us to form any idea about their attitudes toward the Jews. A good proportion of the authors discussed are particularly significant. Five were outstanding intellectual authorities in their fields in the Hellenistic age. Theophrastus was the father of ancient botany, Aristotle's successor in the Lyceum in Athens, and the leading Peripatetic of his generation. Hecataeus of Abdera was the father of "scientific" ethnography, and his influence on the whole genre in his time, the early Hellenistic age, extended well beyond the borders of Egypt, where he was active. Agatharchides of Cnidus was the greatest Alexandrian historian of the Hellenistic age. His writing was said to surpass even Thucydides in certain respects, and his views on various political and social issues seem surprisingly modern. Posidonius of Apamea was the dominant

1. For arguments against the use of the term "anti-Semitism" in the context of the ancient world, see Cohen (1986); de Lange (1991); Yavetz (1993); Schäfer (1997a) 197–211. The substitute terms usually applied, however, pose difficulties of their own. The use of quotation marks may be a possible alternative.

intellectual figure of the Hellenistic world in the first century B.C.E. in many fields and was admired by Greeks and Romans alike, not least Cicero, who drew heavily on Posidonian works in his own philosophical writings. Apollonius Molon was the greatest of orators and rhetoricians, according to his admirers Cicero and Suetonius. Both Posidonius and Apollonius were active on the island of Rhodes at a crucial moment in the shaping of Greek views on the Jews—the Hasmonaean state's period of expansion (and perhaps also during its decline).

Not much has survived of Greek writing on the Jews in the Hellenistic age. We have the following at our disposal: two ethnographic accounts included as excursuses in works on other subjects (by Hecataeus and Posidonius); a few reports, some quite detailed, on the political and military developments in relations between Jews and the Hellenistic powers (by Agatharchides, Timochares, and Posidonius); some evaluations and remarks on the uniqueness of the Jews and their characteristics (by Theophrastus, Clearchus, Hermippus, and Apollonius Molon); and three curious stories and episodes demonstrating Jewish features (by Mnaseas, the anonymous Seleucid scribe[s], and Lysimachus). Although a number of monographs in this era were devoted to the Jewish people and their history, almost nothing has survived from these studies. The only exception is a compilation entitled "On the Jews" by Alexander Polyhistor, a Milesian freedman active in Rome. A relatively large number of substantive fragments and testimonia from Polyhistor's anthology are found in the *Praeparatio evangelica* of Eusebius and in later lexicographical sources. In most cases, however, these are no more than extracts from Jewish Hellenistic literature, repeating and developing what the Bible has to say on a few central figures, and pieces of information on Jerusalem deriving from both Jewish and Gentile authors. Since, like other anthologists, Polyhistor wrote on the Romans, Babylonians, Egyptians, and others, it is hard to tell what exactly his own attitude toward the Jews was, although it seems to have been basically positive. We know of two more works on the Jewish people by Greek authors, which also originated in Asia Minor, and were written at the time of the Hasmonaean state or shortly afterward. Apollonius Molon most probably wrote a treatise on the Jews from which a few scattered statements about contemporary Jews have been preserved, as well as one fragment of some sentences on the patriarchs of the Israelites. A great enigma is the six-volume work on Jewish history by Teucer of Cyzicus, who also wrote on the Arabs. The only trace of Teucer's Jewish monograph is the information that he wrote it. Other monographs may well have been written on the Jews, at least in the Hasmonaean period.

It is clear that the material that has come down to us is but a small fraction of what was written on the Jews in the Hellenistic age. Such a state of affairs is far from uncommon in classical studies and, indeed, reflects the state of preservation of ancient literature as a whole. Most of the material written on the Jews has been lost in the same ways that most of ancient literature has disappeared. References to Jews in this period seem to have been no less extensive than references to other peoples; such references were surpassed in number and extent only by references to the major Oriental peoples (Egyptians, Babylonians, Persians, and Indians), the Phoenicians (long well-known to the Greeks because of their maritime and commercial activities), and the Gauls and the Thracians (who were, naturally, due to historical developments, becoming a topic of great interest to Greek and Roman authors alike). The amount of information on the Jews may well have been greater than that on the Arabs, the Lybians, the Ethiopians, the Albanians, and the Scythians, for example, and, if I am not mistaken, even the Illyrians, a people neighboring both the Macedonians and the inhabitants of Italy. The diffusion of the Jews among other peoples may help explain why much has been written about the Jews, as opposed to other groups.

The church patriarchs' interest in preserving the works of Josephus and references to Jews in pagan literature helped some of this material survive. It is no accident that most of the authors discussed in this study, seven in total, survived in Josephus's polemical work *Contra Apionem*. Three of the authors (Hecataeus, Megasthenes, and Timochares) survived through the church patriarchs (Clement and Eusebius) and Photius, the ninth-century patriarch of Constantinople; only one author (Theophrastus) survived through the agency of a late pagan author (Porphyry of Tyre). The exception is Posidonius, whose special standing in the Hellenistic intellectual world ensured that his historical work would be spread over a relatively wide range of secondary sources: pagan authors (Strabo and Plutarch), Photius, Josephus, and probably more.

Although the amount of material that has survived is only a fraction of the total output, the twelve authors discussed in this book provide us with a rather broad cross-section of Greek Hellenistic writing on the Jewish people and their religion. When taken together, the twelve authors form what may be considered a representative sample by virtue of their diverse range with regard to time, origin, centers of literary activity, genres, opinions, and attitudes. The authors were active in the four periods customarily used to describe the history of the Jews in Judaea in the Hellenistic age: (a) the Diadochic period, 323–301 B.C.E. (Theophrastus, Clearchus, Hecataeus, and Megasthenes); (b) the Ptolemaic period, 301–200 (Hermippus and Mnaseas); (c) the Seleucid period, 200–142/1 (the anonymous Seleucid scribe[s] and Agatharchides); (d) the Hasmonaean period, 142/1–63 (Timochares, Lysimachus, Posidonius, and Apollonius Molon). Posidonius of Apamean Syria excepted, these authors were born all over the pre-Alexandrian Hellenic world: Greece (Theophrastus), Cyprus (Clearchus), the Thracian coast (Hecataeus), western Asia Minor (Megasthenes [?] and Hermippus), and Lycia and Caria, in the southwest corner of Asia Minor (Mnaseas and Agatharchides). They were active in four of the most prominent centers of political and/or intellectual life of the Hellenistic world: Athens (Theophrastus and Clearchus), Alexandria (Hermippus, Mnaseas, Agatharchides, and Lysimachus), Rhodes (Posidonius and Apollonius Molon), and Antioch in Syria (Megasthenes, the Seleucid court scribe[s], and Timochares). The genres they used when writing about the Jews was quite varied: first and foremost, of course, ethnography (Hecataeus, Megasthenes, Lysimachus, Posidonius, and Apollonius Molon), philosophical treatise (Theophrastus and Clearchus), historiography (Agatharchides, Timochares, and Posidonius), court chronicle or the like (the Seleucid scribe[s]), mythography (Mnaseas), and biography (Hermippus). Some of their works represent other genres as well, such as memorabilia (Megasthenes), geographical-mythological anthology (Mnaseas), rhetoric (Apollonius Molon), and legal apology (Theophrastus). The wide generic, chronological, and geographical diversity of these authors and works, not to mention the great authority of some of them, allows us to regard the testimonia and fragments as much more than a random collection of material.

· · ·

Various attempts were made in the past to interpret or explain the development of the positions of Greek Hellenistic authors regarding the Jews. Some of these interpretations were more detailed than others; some were only implied. Josephus Flavius made the first attempt, remarking in his *Contra Apionem* on the approach and motives of authors (including Oriental authors) who wrote on the Jews in Greek. It is also possible to learn from his comments about the stages of development as he saw them. In the first book of *Contra Apionem,* Josephus adduces extracts from Greek authors (some of which are actually passages forged by Jews) to prove that ancient Greek (including classical Greek) authors and thinkers appreciated and even admired Jewish belief and virtues (1. 162 ff.). Moreover, he claims that the great Pythagoras learned from the Jews and adopted their views. Josephus goes on to refute the accusations against the Jews, saying that anti-Jewish polemic began with Egyptian authors like Manetho who strove to defame the Jewish nation and its antiquities mainly because of lingering hostility from the time of the Exile in Egypt and the Exodus, and because of the stark contrast between their religion and that of the Jews (1. 223 ff.). In the second book of *Contra Apionem,* Josephus states that two Greek authors, Posidonius and Apollonius Molon, spread the libel according to which the Jews annually sacrificed a Greek/foreigner to their god and "tasted" his flesh, with a view to defending Antiochus Epiphanes against the charge of desecration leveled against him following his incursion into the Jewish Temple (2. 79, 90, 93). The reader would be given to understand that Antiochus had punished the Jews in a manner befitting this crime against humanity. Thus Josephus established the traumatic event of the imposition of the religious edicts of Antiochus Epiphanes (168 B.C.E.) as the turning point in Greek intellectual attitudes toward the Jews. That is to say, up until the persecutions, Greek authors described the Jews positively with great esteem and even admiration; this state of affairs changed when the policies and unprecedented persecutions of the Jews by Antiochus Epiphanes produced a need for justifications.

Josephus's view has been adopted in principle by many modern scholars, who have added to it their own background explanations, emphases, variations, and nuances. Thus in twentieth-century research, scholars proposed two, three, or four stages in the development of relations between Greek intellectuals and Jews in the period prior to the Roman conquest. It will suffice here to survey the main points of these proposals without going into detail about individual scholars, evidence, and sources.[2]

Scholars are nearly unanimous on the state of affairs in the first stage, the early Hellenistic age, or at least the period of the Diadochs, before there were closer contacts between Greeks and Jews. It is held that Greek authors were generally extremely positive about the Jewish people. Not a few scholars characterize the Greek attitude toward the Jews in this period as "admiration" and "wonder"; others speak of "idealization," "great esteem," or at least "sympathy" and "respect," noting the portrayal of the Jews as a community of philosophers, or philosopher-priests, and even claiming that they are described as having a heritage similar or superior to that of the Greeks. Usually this attitude toward the Jews is explained by the Greek tendency at the beginning of the Hellenistic age to wonder at what they regarded as the mysterious and fascinating culture of the Orient, which had recently opened up to them. Some even argue that the Jews were held up as a role model. These scholarly views are based on the accounts of Theophrastus, Clearchus, Hecataeus, and Megasthenes, all of the Diadochic period, and Hermippus of Smyrna, who was active in the late third century. Most

2. When the list is confined to research appearing since the collection by Reinach, the first scholar to attempt to encompass all Gentile literature on the Jews in the Hellenistic-Roman period, useful surveys relevant to our subject are the following, in chronological order: Reinach (1895) viii–xviii; Willrich (1895) 13–63; Stählin (1905); Bludau (1906); Büchler (1910/11); Juster (1913) 1: 31 ff.; Radin (1915) 76–89, 163–209; Meyer (1921–23) 2: 26–35; Luria (1923); Stein (1934); Bickermann (1927); Heinemann (1931) 3–43; Leipoldt (1933); Bickermann (1937) 17–24; Jaeger (1938a), (1938b); Goldstein (1935); Heinemann (1939/40); Zeitlin (1945); Marcus (1946); Baron (1952) 183–99; de Liager Böhl (1953); Raisin (1953); Poliakov (1955) 21–29; Tcherikover (1958); Guttmann 1: 39–114; Lewy (1960) 5–39; Tcherikover (1961) 365–77; Efron (1962) 7–36; Adriani (1965); Gager (1972); Hengel (1973) 464–85; Lebram (1974); Stern, *GLAJJ*, vol. 1; Habicht (1975); Sevenster (1975); Stern (1976); Hengel (1976) 94–115; Momigliano (1978); Daniel (1979); Stern (1980) 226–28; Mélèze-Modrzejewski (1981); Feldman (1983); Gager (1983) 35–112; Wittaker (1984) 35–134; Goodman in Schürer et al. (1986) 3: 594–607; Cohen (1987b); Drodge (1989) 1–12; Bickerman (1988) 13–20; Feldman (1988); Gabba (1989); Mendels (1992) 395–402; Feldman (1993); Stern (1993) 12–15; Yavetz (1993); Giovannini (1995); Rutgers (1995); Amit (1996); Kasher (1996); Schäfer (1997); Yavetz (1997); Schwartz (1999); Labow (2005) 162–216, 316–29; Gruen (2005). This list does not include specific studies on individual authors.

of these authors, apart from Hecataeus, had only the haziest of information about the Jews. Some scholars, though having reservations about including Hecataeus among the Greek chorus of admirers, have still classified him as basically quite positive in his treatment of the Jews.[3] Other commentators have gone so far as to suggest that the myth about the origin of Greek philosophy in Judaism (or "the theft" of Jewish wisdom by the Greeks), well known from both Jewish Hellenistic literature and the church patriarchs, began with early Greek Hellenistic authors like Clearchus, Megasthenes, and especially Hermippus.

Following Josephus, many scholars place the great turning point in relations between Greeks and Jews at the time of the religious persecutions of Antiochus Epiphanes, to which they add the subsequent Hasmonaean state. One or two prominent scholars have suggested that Greek intellectuals lost interest in the Jews beginning around 300 B.C.E., ignoring them altogether until interest picked up again in the wake of the Hasmonaean wars. Others have contested this view, introducing a different intermediate stage: the developments in relations between the two peoples in the third century and the first quarter of the second century B.C.E. They argue that Greeks who settled in the East, especially intellectuals who were close to the seat of government in Alexandria, gradually came to know the Jews, their customs, and their religion more intimately. As a result, these Greeks began to express reservations and even hostility toward the Jews. This new approach can already be discerned in Hecataeus, a courtier of Ptolemy I, and even more clearly in Mnaseas, one of the Alexandrian scholars active in the reign of Ptolemy IV or V at the end of the third century. Hecataeus was the first Greek author to accuse the Jews of *misoxenia,* while Mnaseas was the first to record the libel about the presence of the statue of an ass in the Jerusalem Temple. It is also sometimes claimed that Jewish Hellenistic literature was fighting back already in this period against contemporary hostile tendencies in Greek literature.

It seems to be almost beyond dispute that at least some of the anti-Jewish accusations and libels were not invented by Greeks. There is broad agreement that Greeks found them among many other anti-Jewish materials circulating in Egypt both as a counter to Jewish stories about the Exodus (and their provocative use by Jews) and as a result of prolonged tensions and animosity between the Egyptians and the Jewish population in their midst. The first hostile traditions reported by Greeks are therefore Egyptian in origin and flourished against an Egyptian background. As has already been mentioned, some believe that Greeks had adopted these traditions long before the religious persecutions.

Other scholars adhere to the position of Josephus exactly as it is presented, namely, that the attitudes of Greeks toward the Jews changed only in the aftermath

3. See Mélèze-Modrzejewski (1981), also with regard to Theophrastus, and esp. Schäfer (1997) 15–17, 35–36, 175, and passim with regard to Hecataeus.

of the religious edicts and the Hasmonaean revolt, and argue that there was no prior anti-Jewish Greek literature. In the view of these scholars, this literature came about because of a need to excuse and explain the religious edicts and the subsequent persecutions, which ran counter to Greek tradition. The Greek Hellenistic world, and above all the Seleucid court, sought justification for the drastic measures taken by a ruler who was such a great benefactor of Greek heritage in old Hellas and throughout his own kingdom. The justification was found in the early anti-Jewish Egyptian traditions. To these the Greek authors added new accusations of their own, based on their acquaintance with features of Jewish life. A celebrated scholar, Elias Bickermann, and a few others following him, have insisted that the so-called blood libel, the central axis of the justification for the deeds of Antiochus Epiphanes against the Jews, was essentially a Seleucid invention, and not drawn from Egyptian tradition.[4] In any case, it soon influenced the anti-Jewish attitude of Ptolemaic authors. It is no accident that the first Alexandrian historian to refer to a major Jewish practice—the Sabbath—as a superstition was Agatharchides of Cnidus, a contemporary of the Hasmonaean revolt.

According to the suggested reconstructions, the apologetics on the persecution of the Jews motivating the anti-Jewish literature of the mid-second century B.C.E. were quickly replaced by voices of protest, some would say of fear and anxiety,[5] in the face of the rising power of the Jews in Judaea, and beyond its borders, in the time of the Hasmonaean state (142/1–63 B.C.E.). The Hasmonaean destruction of Hellenistic temples and cult centers in the Holy Land, the conquests and destruction in Hellenistic cities, the annexation of territories to the Jewish state, the exiling of residents or their forceful conversion—including circumcision—all exacerbated the antagonism of Greek enlightened authors toward the Jewish people. Later on, the tension between Jewish and Greek as well as Hellenized Oriental populations in the Hellenistic diaspora worsened, especially in Egyptian Alexandria. This occasionally produced serious local disturbances. In addition, the Jews were unwilling to compromise their religious and social identity and continued to isolate themselves from their surroundings in close communities, exhibiting aversion to social connections with Gentiles. At the same time, many Jews managed to climb the social ladder to positions of influence in the army, administration, and economy, which caused envy and fear. All this, together with the traditional tendency to turn the alien (or an exclusive minority, as in this case) into a scapegoat, led the Greeks to develop "anti-Semitic" reactions of the type familiar throughout history, with the usual symptoms and features.

---

4. See Bickerman (1976–80) 2: 226–45.

5. See Yavetz (1995) and esp. Schäfer (1997a) 198 ff. Leon Pinsker, a precursor of Theodor Herzl, was the first to describe anti-Semitism as Judaeophobia, in the booklet *Auto-Emanzipation: Mahnruf an seine Stammgenossen, von einem russischen Jude,* published anonymously in Berlin in 1882.

Isolated, albeit substantial, voices place the blame on the existence and deeds of the Jewish diaspora in Egypt alone. According to them, anti-Jewish literature reacted to the very Jewish presence in the Diaspora and was directed against that. These scholars do not count the policies and deeds of the Hasmonaean state as a significant factor in the development of anti-Jewish literature, arguing that Gentile literature did not censure the deeds of the Hasmonaeans.

In this context, it is worth noting the "extramural" conception, which is quite widespread among Jews and Christians alike and discernible in the writings of historians working on comprehensive histories of the Jewish people or the history of anti-Semitism. By confusing the different periods and being less than scrupulously accurate with the facts, some assert that from the beginning Greek intellectuals had a negative attitude toward the Jews stemming from the unbridgeable antagonism between the two religions and cultures. Some also go so far as to claim that it was this attitude that led Antiochus Epiphanes to impose the religious edicts on the Jews. Such talk about a cultural gap and inherent hostility is also found, not surprisingly, in the various types of anti-Semitic literature written at the end of the nineteenth century.

Despite differences over the number of stages in the development of the Greek attitude toward the Jews, their chronology, and the factors and causes shaping them, most of the proposals mentioned share a basic assumption. They strive to show that the attitudes of Greek authors toward the Jews developed in a linear fashion in reaction to historical events. This point of view, together with the various opinions and stages that have been suggested, requires reexamination. To underscore the need for such revision, an example from my own personal experience will suffice. The conception that Greeks in the early Hellenistic age displayed exceptional admiration for the Jews is based to a certain extent on the fragments and testimonia adduced by Josephus from the treatise "On the Jews," which has been attributed to Hecataeus of Abdera (*Ap.* 1. 183–204; 2. 43). Their authenticity, however, has been in question since ancient times. My monograph on this subject examined the fragments and testimonia from a historical and literary perspective and compared the material with the entire output of Hecataeus of Abdera.[6] This analysis of what remains of the treatise assured me that it was in fact a Jewish forgery whose errors and many historical incompatibilities and anachronisms can no longer be explained away.

. . .

The obvious methodological conclusion is that a rigorous examination needs to be made of each and every author. The discussion has so far centered on a diachronic examination of the surviving material: a survey of all the material in

6. Bar-Kochva (1996d).

chronological order, which considers how each detail reflects the Greek attitude toward the Jews, referring to the sources of information, exploring the transmission of opinions and motifs from one author to another, and in particular, their connection with contemporary events.[7] In some cases, the examinations are not diachronic, but by subject, considering the reaction of Greek pagan intellectuals to various aspects of Jewish life, such as the Jewish faith, cult practices, observation of the Sabbath, circumcision, dietary laws, and the image of Moses, and the traditions concerning the origin of the Jewish people.[8] Many of these inquiries are of great value to scholarly discourse, especially in clarifying the evolution of the image of Jewish customs from generation to generation, and for various proposals explaining the causes and motives influencing the attitude of pagan authors toward the Jews. All this, however, is still not enough.

Extensive examinations of individual authors per se have been made so far only for the first three Greek authors to refer to the Jews: Theophrastus, Clearchus, and Hecataeus of Abdera.[9] These individual studies, all written by outstanding scholars over two generations ago, made a substantial contribution to the advance of research on the three authors. Yet contemporary events and the personal circumstances of these scholars, together with the sensitivity of the subject itself, frequently prevented them from evaluating the sources in a sober fashion. The attitude of Gentiles toward Jews is rarely discussed dispassionately.

The extensive examination I am proposing here requires first of all a careful philological scrutiny of the written text of each author under discussion, its transmission and versions, with a view to ascertaining its authenticity and, as far as possible, the form and content of the original text. An author's life must be examined before his literary activity is considered. No stone can be left unturned. The hunt is not only for traces of contacts or possible encounters of the author with Jews, but for any motives that may shed light on the author's references to and portrayal of Jews. Even professional rivalry with adherents of another discipline or philosophical school may prove significant. Once the author's life has been examined, we can turn to his literary output and become acquainted with his writings, the genres in which he worked, his methods, and his unique qualities. Our understanding of the author's historiographical and/or ethnographic method and his philosophical outlook, especially concerning state, society, and religion, should help to clarify his aims and approach in writing about the Jews. Our next step is to analyze the work in which each reference or passage about the Jews appears: its genre, the genre's features, the subject of the work, its style, and

7. See, e.g., Stählin (1905); Stern (1976); Conzelmann (1981); Gabba (1989).

8. E.g., de Liagre Böhl (1953); Daniel (1979); Wittaker (1983); Feldman (1993); Schäfer (1997).

9. Bernays (1866); Guttmann (1946), (1958–63); Lewy (1960). On Bernays, see p. 39, note 81 below.

its aims, and of course the context of the references to or passage(s) on the Jews, and their place and purpose in the work as a whole. All this must be considered from the broader perspective of the form and aims of the same or related genres and subgenres in Greek literature over the centuries. The author's references to the Jews also need to be compared with his and other contemporary authors' references to other peoples.[10] In some cases scrupulous source criticism will be necessary, even at the risk of tiring the reader. The need for such analysis arises when the intent of the text is insufficiently clear or is inconsistent with other remarks of the author or with what is known about him, and especially when source criticism can expose the origins and development of certain attitudes and motifs over generations.

Without all these procedures, conclusions based on sporadic references to the Jews, even those providing detailed descriptions, may be premature and ill founded. These rules sound simple and even obvious; but they need to be applied. In addition to all this, we must also overcome—no matter how difficult it may prove—our oversensitivity to any mention of the Jews and step back from the Judaeocentric approach that characterizes research in the field, on both sides of the divide.

. . .

Finally, a note on style, evidence, and methodology. The cautious phrasing of this book and some uncertainties in the sources may puzzle certain readers who may occasionally feel that more conclusive language and decisive source material are required. On this point I refer the reader to the response of the great student of ancient Greece, Martin L. West, at the end of his admirable book *The East Face of Helicon*:

> The testy critic may complain that there are too many 'might haves' and not enough indisputable 'must haves'. But mathematically rigorous demonstrations cannot be expected in these matters. It is a question of defining and weighing possibilities. . . .
> In the final reckoning . . . a corpse suffices to prove a death, even if the inquest is inconclusive.[11]

Investigation of all relevant aspects of the texts and their authors, as well as application of all possible methods (including source criticism), narrows the margin of mistake. The road to historical truth is often rather complicated.

---

10. This last point has been stressed by Bohak (2003). For a collection of stereotypes in the Greek and Roman world, see Isaac (2004).

11. *The East Face of Helicon: West Asiatic Elements in Greek Poetry and Myth* (Oxford, 1997) 629–30.

PART I

From Alexander and the Successors to the Religious Persecutions of Antiochus Epiphanes (333–168 B.C.E.)

1

Theophrastus on Jewish Sacrificial Practices and the Jews as a Community of Philosophers

Theophrastus was the first of the four Greek authors of the early Hellenistic period to write on the Jews.[1] He was born in Eresus on the island of Lesbos in the late seventies of the fourth century B.C.E., and was to spend some decades of his life in the company of Aristotle, first in Assos on the northwest coast of Asia Minor, then in the Macedonian court at Stagira in Chalcidice, and finally in Athens. When Aristotle died in 322, Theophrastus was left as head of the Peripatetic school in Athens, and he lived on there, apart from two years spent in exile in Chalcis, until his death (c. 288). His writings included a great number of works and lecture notes on a wide variety of subjects in philosophy and sci-

---

1. There has been some controversy about whether Theophrastus's passage on the Jews preceded the Jewish excursus of Hecataeus. Stern (1973) proved that Theophrastus was not familiar with the Jewish excursus of Hecataeus (against the view of Jaeger [1938b] 142 ff.; Murray [1973] 163–68 et al.). Stern's comment (162) is worth quoting: "Hecataeus is much more in keeping with the real Jewish situation, as would befit a later composition, and an author who, it seems, knew the Jewish people better than Theophrastus. In Hecataeus, the Jewish people appears as a separate group, with a stable political order, and not as a strange sect of Syrian philosophers, as would be the impression given by the earlier account of Theophrastus." The evidence appears to indicate that the work was composed in the years 319–315/4 B.C.E.; see Pötscher (1964) 124; Stern (1973); Murray (1973) 167. On the composition of Hecataeus's *Aegyptiaca*, in which the Jewish excursus was included, in the years 305–302 B.C.E., see Bar-Kochva (1996d) 15–16.

ence. A number of these works have reached us intact, most notably *Enquiry into Plants* and *On the Causes of Plants* (on the geography and the physiology of plants, respectively). Preserved smaller works include *On Stones, On Fire, On Winds, On Odors,* and *Characters,* a collection of sketches of negative characters such as misers and flatterers and the like. In addition to these treatises, a large portion of Theophrastus's *Metaphysics* has survived, together with fragments of other works, some quite long, and testimonia concerning these and other works. Theophrastus has been regarded essentially as a link connecting classical Greek thought and science with their Hellenistic counterparts, although it must be said that in certain fields his own original contribution was considerable, particularly in his capacity as the "father of botany."[2]

INFORMATION ON JEWS, AND THE WORK *PERI EUSEBEIAS*

Theophrastus's remarks on the Jews do not present a real ethnographic account. They are concentrated in a passage within a long fragment taken from his work *Peri eusebeias.* The passage concerns Jewish sacrificial practice, and it calls the Jews "philosophers by descent," attributing to them a number of characteristics: a preoccupation with theological discussions, stargazing, and prayer. At the same time, there is no reference to the Jews where one might have been expected. Theophrastus's botanical-geographical work, *Enquiry into Plants,* contains a scattering of descriptions of, and references to, the peculiar plant life of the area around Jericho, which in his time was included in the territory of Judaea. However, he mentions neither the Jews nor Judaea, and not even Jericho, making do instead with general geographical terms such as "Syria," "Koile Syria," and "the Valley of Syria."[3] In his other botanical work, the *Aetiology of Plants,* Theophrastus describes the Ascalon onion (7. 4. 7–9; cf. Strabo 16. 2. 29) without indicating the location of Ascalon.

In light of what we know about Theophrastus's life, it is unlikely that he had contacts with Jews or an opportunity for a real dialogue with them. There are no indications that he ever visited the lands of the Orient, or even Egypt,[4] and certainly not Judaea or Koile Syria. In his work *On Laws,* which surveyed the

---

2. On the life of Theophrastus, see Diogenes Laertius 5. 36–57 and the testimonia collected in Fortenbaugh et al. (1992) 1: 20–90; see also Regenbogen (1948) 1357–62; Sollenberger (1985) 61–62. On the extent of Theophrastus's influence and originality much has been written; see the articles by Sorabji, Betogazura, Gottschalk, Glucker, Sedley, and Long in Ophuijsen and Raalte (1998) 203–384.

3. On the flora around Jericho: Theophrastus *Enquiry into Plants* 2. 6. 2, 5, 8; 4. 4. 14; 9. 6. 1–4.

4. The notion that Theophrastus visited Egypt and Cyrene was widely held for many years in the research literature; see esp. Capelle (1956) 173 ff. It has been refuted by Fraser (1994) 169–81, esp. 180.

laws of both Greeks and barbarians (according to Cic. *Fin.* 5. 11),[5] nothing was said about the laws of the Jews or Moses.[6] Theophrastus also wrote a work in three books on "lawgivers" (*nomothetai*—Diog. Laert. 5. 45). Had there been any reference to Moses and his laws in that work, it would surely have been mentioned in some way by Jewish Hellenistic or Christian authors, especially Josephus, Eusebius, and Clement of Alexandria, whose reading, taken together, certainly encompassed the whole of Greek literature. Accordingly, the possibility that Theophrastus had direct contacts with Jews seems even more remote. At the most, Theophrastus may have heard something about the Jews, orally or from letters of veterans of Alexander's campaigns, tourists, and sailors who had traveled about in the Orient,[7] or from Greeks who had visited Egypt during the governorship of Ptolemy, son of Lagos. It was from such sources that he had been informed about the vegetation in the lower Jordan Valley, had he not found it in a written source.[8]

Theophrastus's remarks concerning the Jews were included in his work *Peri eusebeias.* The treatise dealt with the question of proper cultic practice worthy of the gods, and the title might best be understood as *On the Right Way to Respect the Gods,* effectively *On Proper Cultic Practice,*[9] and not *On Piety,* as it is frequently translated. It was composed some time between 319 and 315/4 B.C.E., apparently as an informal literary response to the charge of *asebeia* (lack of respect for the gods

5. Noted by Bickerman (1988) 15. Cicero does not name the work, and it seems that out of the four works by Theophrastus on laws (Diog. Laert. 5. 44–45), the one called *On Laws* is meant.

6. Josephus (*Ap.* 1. 167) states that Theophrastus in his *On Laws* mentioned the Hebrew word *qorban* (sacrifice) in connection with the Tyrian laws prohibiting the use of the oaths of foreigners. Josephus explains that the Jewish sacrifice is intended. The fact that this trivial and mistaken statement is the only one imported by Josephus from Theophrastus in his efforts to find references to the Jews in Greek literature suggests that Theophrastus's *On Laws* included nothing about Jewish laws. For the many testimonia on *On Laws,* see Fortenbaugh et al. (1992) 2: 442. Josephus did not know anything about the passage on the Jews in *Peri eusebeias.*

7. So Bernays (1866) 111.

8. See notes 54 and 55 below on Theophrastus's sources about Egypt. It has been speculated that on his expedition Alexander took with him a group of scientists who, among other things, conducted a botanical survey of the conquered lands and sent the collected information both to the Lyceum in Athens, seat of the Peripatetics, and to a "research center" established in Babylon: see Bretzl (1903) 30–67; Pfister (1961) 39–67; see, however, the skeptical approach of Fraser (1994) 174 ff.

9. *Sebomai* originally meant "respect something exalted," such as gods, the king, or parents; the etymological meaning of *eusebeia,* a word that came to have many definitions in Greek philosophy, was thus "the paying of proper respect and reverence." Pötscher (1964) 127–28 argues that the definition of *eusebeia* preserved by John Stobaeus, the fifth-century C.E. doxographer, reflects the opinion of Theophrastus: Εὐσέβειαν μὲν οὖν εἶναι ἕξιν θεῶν καὶ δαιμόνων θεραπευτικήν, μεταξὺ οὖσαν ἀθεότητος καὶ δεισιδαιμονίας ("*Eusebeia* is a habitual state of administering to the gods and *daimones,* intermediate between atheism and superstition," *Flor.* 2. 147). The terminology and presentation are certainly Peripatetic, and the definition may possibly originate with Theophrastus.

expressed in the performance of cultic duties) for which Theophrastus was put on trial in Athens (Diog. Laert. 5. 37).[10] Within this context, Theophrastus advocated modest and thrifty cultic practice and abstention from animal sacrifice (supporting, indeed, vegetarianism). In order to consolidate his moral (and legal) arguments, Theophrastus attempted to prove that animal sacrifice was not something desired by the gods. This he did in part by offering a comprehensive anthropological theory concerning the development of human dietary habits from their very beginning, and the development of sacrifice to the gods arising from those eating habits.[11] It is in this context that his passage on the Jews appears.

Theophrastus's *Peri eusebeias* has not come down to us, but long extracts from it have been preserved in the second book of περὶ ἀποχῆς ἐμψύχων (*On Abstention from [the Meat of] Animals*) by the third-century C.E. Neoplatonist Porphyry of Tyre. The attribution of these extracts to Theophrastus is based essentially on a number of explicit references in Porphyry's work, which has come down to us in its entirety. This was corroborated with a detailed argument by the celebrated German-Jewish philologist Jacob Bernays in an 1866 monograph in which major parts of *Peri eusebeias* are reconstructed and their content interpreted.[12] The passage on the Jews is included in one of the two main extracts made by Porphyry (2. 26. 1–4). A full if indirect quotation (via Porphyry) from Theophrastus's account of the Jews is also to be found in Eusebius (*PE* 9. 2. 1) and is of some use in determining the formulation of the original.[13]

THE ANTHROPOLOGICAL THEORY

Theophrastus, then, refers to the Jews during his exposition of the development of human dietary and sacrificial habits. It is worthwhile to begin, therefore, with a brief survey of his anthropological theory. Porphyry did not preserve the whole account of Theophrastus, nor do the surviving Theophrastean fragments provide a complete and consistent picture; moreover, the omission of sentences and even

10. On the dating of the work, see above, note 1. On the prosecution brought by Agnonides, Theophrastus's trial, and acquittal, and on the fate of the prosecutor, see the discussion and bibliography in Regenbogen, "Theophrastos," *RE* suppl. 7 (1948) cols. 1359–60.

11. On the general background to the development of such theories, see Uxkull-Gyllenband (1924); Haussleiter (1935); Dierauer (1977); Sorabji (1993). On additional aspects: Cole (1967) 15–46; Feldman (1968b); Brink (1956) 123–45; Drodge (1989) 108–10. See also Sorabji in Ophuijsen and Raalte (1998) 211–21, on the philosophical background.

12. Versions and editions of the text: Bernays (1866) 40 ff.; Nauck (1886) 155–56; Pötscher (1964) 146–86; Bouffartigue and Patillon (1979) 2: 92–93; Fortenbaugh et al. (1992) 2: 405–37. The main parts of Theophrastus's account are concentrated in three sections of Porphyry: 1. 5–9. 2; 11. 3–15. 1; 19. 4–32. 3. On attempts to find additional remains of the book, see Fortenbaugh (1984) 263–67.

13. The text is in Mras (1982) 8: 486.

passages from the fragments is evident.[14] Porphyry himself states explicitly that he recorded only the main points and omitted, for instance, various examples drawn by Theophrastus from many peoples (2. 20. 2; 32. 3). It is therefore necessary to supplement some missing points in order to understand the theory as a whole, and thus clarify the role of the Jews in it. This should be done in accordance with the logic and spirit of the rest of the account, and with the aid of probable parallels.[15]

Theophrastus distinguishes between two stages in the development of diet and cult: the vegetarian and the meat-eating stages. The distinction itself, the chronological priority of the vegetarian stage, and the various elements of the first stage, are not particularly original, based as they are, essentially, on various versions of the myth of the Golden Age, with certain adaptations.[16] There are, however, no known real parallels to the sequence of events of the carnivorous period as it appears in his version.

The development in the first stage is described as follows. In the far distant past,[17] humans ate only plants, proceeding from wild plants to agricultural crops. The Egyptians, the wisest of humans, were the first to sacrifice to the gods (2. 5. 1). Other peoples followed suit. First produce of the season was deemed appropriate to please the gods, and the sacrifice changed with the natural and agricultural development of the types of crops. At first, when there were only wild grasses to eat, they sacrificed their roots and shoots (2. 5. 2). With the appearance of oak trees, men sacrificed a few acorns and many leaves (5. 6). Upon the arrival of fruit trees, they sacrificed fruit. With the development of agriculture, they sacrificed barley and wheat, initially only shoots and seeds, but later also ground corn and cakes (6. 2). At the same time there developed libation rituals: water at first (20. 3); then, by stages, honey, wine, and oil. All these were burnt completely, in honor of the gods (5. 3; 6. 2, 4), the heavenly bodies (5. 1), as a way of imbuing these gifts

14. See notes 19, 49, and p. 33 below.

15. For discussions on the vegetarian period and the development of the eating of flesh according to Theophrastus, see Haussleiter (1935) 237–45; Guttmann 1: 75–78; Dürhauer (1977) 173–77; Obbink (1988) 275–77; Sorabji (1993) 173–75. The survey below differs in various details from these discussions.

16. See the survey of Greek and Roman materials in Haussleiter (1935) 54–79. The most detailed and interesting of these are Hesiod *Works and Days* 108–201 (esp. line 118—the land produces an abundance of crops *automatē*); Prodicus in Sextus Empiricus *Adversus mathematicos* 9. 18; Ovid *Metamorphoses* 1. 101–12, 15. 96–142; *Fasti* 1. 337 ff. Cf. Plato *Respublica* 372b ff.; *Politicus* 272a; and the interesting version of Dicaearchus, one of the most prominent pupils of Aristotle (preserved in Porph. *Abst.* 4. 2), which emphasizes abstention from the killing of animals.

17. On the question of the chronology in light of Theophrastus's view of periodic cosmic disasters that destroyed flora and fauna, see Bernays (1866) 44–51; Fortenbaugh et al. (1992) 2: 272–74; Obbink (1988) 274–75.

with a degree of permanence; fire was considered to resemble most closely the immortal heavenly bodies (5. 2).

Why or when did humans begin to sacrifice animals? On this point there is some disagreement (9. 1). It appears that the turning point occurred at different times in different places, and not always for the same reason. It was believed to have happened mostly because of famine (9. 1; 27. 1), but it could also be caused by other disasters (9. 1), especially wars (7. 2; 12. 1; 22. 1). In some places (such as Athens), it resulted from superstitions, anger, or fear, or an unfortunate coincidence (9. 1–2). The sequence of events from famine to animal sacrifice is elaborated in the passage following the account of Jewish sacrificial practices (27. 1ff.), and unlike the survey of the first stage, it may well have derived at least partly from Theophrastus's own imagination. According to him, humans incurred the wrath of the gods because of their neglect of proper cultic respect. They were punished as a result, by being deprived of their customary means of existence. As they could no longer find plants upon which to feed, they were obliged to begin to eat each other. In an effort to appease the gods, men also began to offer human sacrifice. This custom has survived until this very day in certain places but over the course of time has generally been replaced by animal sacrifice. The new form of sacrifice encouraged humans to begin eating animal flesh as part of the sacrifice ritual, and gradually it came to be a common practice separate from the ritual as well. Humans continued sacrificing and eating animals even when the famine was over and crops were to be had in plenty.[18]

In the passages that have been preserved, Theophrastus does not offer a similarly detailed account of the development of animal sacrifice as a result of war.[19] The preserved account of the development of this custom from other circumstances mentioned above (2. 9. 2, 29–30) does not affect our discussion, and so may be left to one side. I shall return to the "famine" version in due course, referring to it as "the main version."

Theophrastus was opposed to the eating and sacrificing of animals on moral

18. Some links in the anthropological theory are also suggested by modern anthropologists (cannibalism-human sacrifice-animal sacrifice). See, e.g., Meek (1931) 2: 57; Sagan (1974) 52–53; and *contra*: Harris (1977) 5 ff. Putting plant-eating before flesh-eating is typical in myths of the Golden Age. An opposing view, that cannibalism preceded vegetarianism, appeared in Hecataeus of Abdera (in Diod. 1. 14. 1).

19. An abbreviated remnant of this chain of events, taken from Theophrastus, is to be found in Porphyry *On Abstention* 2. 7. 2: During the wars, humans came into contact with blood (αἱμάτων ἥψαντο) and declared it good to sacrifice humans and animals and to eat their flesh. The passage has been shortened by Porphyry, and this has led to a certain lack of clarity. According to the following paragraph (7. 3), the tribes who had begun to perform cruel sacrifices as a result of the wars were punished by the gods with extinction. In the "famine" version, however, the famine itself is the punishment.

grounds (esp. 2. 12. 2–4; 24. 2–5; 25): such acts deprive animals of their soul, that part of animals and humans by which they belong to the same category of living beings;[20] these acts are peformed by force, against the will of the animals; in addition, the animals brought to the altar are not the sort to endanger man or cause him any harm. Indeed, most are actually beneficial, and killing them demonstrates ingratitude; finally, man offers up to the gods a gift that is not his to give. On all these and other counts, animal sacrifice is deemed to be extremely unjust and cruel. The anthropological theory presented above was intended to show that animal sacrifice was nothing more than a substitute for a cruel practice—human sacrifice—which itself originated in a particularly despicable custom—cannibalism—the "necessity" of which was only temporary (during the time of famine). The eating of animals is the result of a development that has little to do with the real dietary needs of human beings in the present. Eating and sacrificing animals must be regarded as not only immoral but also quite unnecessary in the present circumstances where plant life is once again flourishing. Proof of this is the fact that early man lived on plants alone and had no need for meat supplements.

There was nothing new in this advocacy for vegetarianism. Orphics and Pythagoreans (or rather their *akousmatikoi*) had long abstained from eating meat and sacrificing animals because of their belief in the transmigration of souls. They were not alone: Greek poets and philosophers who depicted the Golden Age as a period of vegetarianism were thereby expressing their desire to "return" to vegetarianism in the present.[21] Theophrastus's contribution was the presentation of a coherent anthropological picture in the guise of a historical-practical proof, and the raising of some new moral arguments.

20. See esp. 2. 12. 3–4, and cf. 3. 25. The latter passage expands on those features common to all members of the human race, before moving on to the features common to humans and animals, because of which, violence against animals turns out to be unjust. The passage is explicitly attributed by Porphyry to Theophrastus, but which work is not specified. Fortenbaugh et al. (1992) 2. 350–52 include this passage not in their collection of fragments from *Peri eusebeias*, but in the category of "Ethics," without indicating a particular work (no. 531). This is presumably because the beginning of the passage dealing with humans could have been included in another work by Theophrastus. Bernays (1886) 96 ff. does consider it to be from *Peri eusebeias*, as does Pötscher (1964) 182–83. The reasons Bernays offers for not including the passage in Theophrastus's work περὶ ζῴων φρονήσεως καὶ ἤθους (On the Soundmindedness and Character of Animals") are not decisive. The ideas expressed in the passage could have appeared both in that work and in *Peri eusebeias*. On the question of the moral arguments of Theophrastus and their degree of consistency, see Fortenbaugh et al. (1992) 2: 267–71; 'Amir (1996) 113 ff. Note that Porphyry (*Abst.* 2. 21) indicates that Theophrastus (2. 21. 1–4) quotes Empedocles (D-K 31 B 128, l. 9), who describes a time when men regarded the sacrifice of animals as the greatest abomination. Empedocles seems to have believed in the transmigration of souls, from plants to animals to humans (e.g., Diog. Laert. 8. 77).

21. E.g., Empedocles in Porphyry *On Abstention* 2. 20 (= D-K 31 B 128); Plato *Politicus* 272b–c. On later Greek and Latin authors, see the discussion in Hausleiter (1935) 54–78.

THE PASSAGE ON THE JEWS AND ITS CONTEXT

Theophrastus's passage on the Jews (2. 26) appears at the beginning of the main version (the "famine" version) of the account describing the process by which man first began to eat animals (27. 1–32. 2). It is preceded by a number of paragraphs in which Theophrastus attempts to prove that animal sacrifice is not pleasing to the gods and is entirely rejected by them (25. 1–7). The last paragraph preceding the account on the Jews (25. 7) concludes the arguments with the accusation that humans sacrifice to the gods not because they wish to satisfy them, but because they want to satisfy their own desire for eating meat:

> And we sacrifice, of [animals] fit for sacrifice, not those which gratify the gods, but rather by far those which gratify the desires of men, witnessing against ourselves that we persist in such sacrifices for the sake of enjoyment.

Now comes Theophrastus's account of the Jews (2. 26. 1–4):[22]

> (1) But[23] †of [the] Syrians, [the] Jews†,[24] because of [their mode of] sacrifice from the very beginning, even now, says Theophrastus, perform an animal sacrifice

22. For the various editions of the text, see notes 12–13 above. The Greek text, with the emendations referred to in notes 24, 25, 28, 30, and 31, follows: (1) καίτοι †Σύρων μὲν Ἰουδαῖοι† διὰ τὴν ἐξ ἀρχῆς θυσίαν ἔτι καὶ νῦν, φησὶν ὁ Θεόφραστος, ζῳοθυτοῦσι. εἰ τὸν αὐτὸν ἡμᾶς τρόπον τις κελεύοι θύειν, ἀποσταίημεν ἂν τῆς πράξεως. (2) οὐ γὰρ ἐστιώμενοι τῶν τυθέντων, ὁλοκαυτοῦντες δὲ ταῦτα νυκτὸς καὶ κατ' αὐτῶν πολὺ μέλι καὶ οἶνον λείβοντες ἀναλίσκουσι τὴν θυσίαν θᾶττον, ἵνα τοῦ δεινοῦ μηδ' ὁ πανόπτης γένοιτο θεατής. (3) καὶ ταῦτα δρῶσι νηστεύοντες τὰς ἀνὰ μέσον τούτων ἡμέρας· κατὰ δὲ πάντα τοῦτον τὸν χρόνον, ἅτε φιλόσοφοι τὸ γένος ὄντες, περὶ τοῦ θείου μὲν ἀλλήλοις λαλοῦσι, τῆς δὲ νυκτὸς τῶν ἄστρων ποιοῦνται τὴν θεωρίαν, βλέποντες εἰς αὐτὰ καὶ διὰ τῶν εὐχῶν θεοκλυτοῦντες. (4) κατήρξαντο γὰρ οὗτοι πρῶτοι τῶν τε λοιπῶν ζῴων καὶ σφῶν αὐτῶν, ἀνάγκῃ καὶ οὐκ ἐπιθυμίᾳ τοῦτο πράξαντες.

23. καίτοι: In this context, the word indicates a contrast between Jews and the other humans mentioned in the previous section.

24. The formulation in the MSS of Eusebius—Σύρων μὲν Ἰουδαῖοι—presents two major difficulties. First, the sentence lacks an apodosis to μέν. The particle μέν does not—in this sentence—have an absolute meaning ("certainly," as emphasis; why would emphasis be required here?). The previous passage does not provide any clue, and neither does the following text. The potential reader would not have known who the Jews were in any case. Second, the combination Σύρων Ἰουδαῖοι sounds defective in Greek. Mras (1982), the editor of Eusebius, conjectured that ὧν had dropped out after Σύρων, presumably because of dittography, but the resultant Σύρων ὧν μὲν Ἰουδαῖοι makes even worse Greek. Several words have probably been omitted. The general meaning might have been as follows: the Jews are a community of philosopher-priests of the Syrian people. Cf. Clearchus (in Joseph. Ap. 1. 179): οἱ φιλόσοφοι παρὰ μὲν Ἰνδοῖς Καλανοί, παρὰ δὲ Σύροις Ἰουδαῖοι τοὔνομα λαβόντες ἀπὸ τοῦ τόπου ("The philosophers among the Indians are called Kalanoi, among the Syrians, Jews, taking their name from the place"); this is also implied by Megasthenes' reference to the Jews (in Clem. Strom. 1. 15 (725): "All the [views] which have been expressed about nature among the ancient [Greeks] are also expressed among those who philosophize outside Greece, some [views] among the Indians by the Brachmans (= Brahmans), and some in Syria by the Jews"; and

(ζῳοθυτοῦσι).[25] If someone were to command us to sacrifice in the same way, we would be repelled[26] from the act. (2) For[27] they (= the Jews) do not eat the sacrificed [animals], but burn them completely at night and by pouring on them much honey and wine they waste away[28] the sacrifice more quickly, lest the all-seeing [sun][29] becomes a spectator of the terrible [deed]. (3) And they do these things[30] fasting for the days between these.[31] During all this time, since they are philosophers by descent,[32] they speak to each other about the divine, while at night they observe the stars, looking at them and calling on god through prayers. (4) For these (= the Jews) were the first to sacrifice both of other animals and of themselves (i.e., also human sacrifices), having done this out of necessity and not from desire.

The passage has led scholars to describe Theophrastus's attitude toward the Jews as "positive,", "full of admiration," and even as "idealizing." These scholars place great emphasis on the designation of the Jews as "philosophers" who spend much of their time discussing the ways of the divine, stargazing, and praying. Since

cf. the way other groups of philosopher-priests are presented in Hellenistic literature: the Magi—"the philosophers among the Persians"; the Brahmans—"the philosophers among the Indians"; the Druids—"the philosophers among the Gauls"; the Getae—"the philosophers among the Thracians." See below, note 63.

25. The reading in the MSS of Porphyry is ζῳοθυτοῦντες, while Eusebius wrote ζῳοθυτούντων. The latter form, however, does not agree with the nominative Ἰουδαῖοι, and neither form is a finite verb, which is required here. Bernays (1866) 85 emended to ζῳοθυτοῦσι, which seems to be the right, save the iota subscriptum, which should be omitted (see later in the discussion).

26. The verb ἀφίστημι with the genitive can mean "shrink from" (cf. LSJ s.v. 4B). This negatively charged translation is more appropriate in the context than "abstain from," which is emotionally neutral.

27. On the causal link of γάρ in this sentence and paragraph, see below, note 48.

28. The MSS read ἀνήλισκον. Bernays emended to ἀναλίσκουσι, which is required by his reading ζῳοθυτοῦσι.

29. A similar expression appears in Lysimachus (Joseph. Ap. 1. 306). Stern (GLAJJ 1: 386), in his commentary to Lysimachus, has drawn attention to the parallels in Herodotus 1. 138 (the sun "sees" sins and faults, and punishment comes as a result); Clement Stromateis 5. 7.

30. The MSS reading is τοῦτο, but the sentence requires the plural, ταῦτα.

31. The text reads: καὶ νηστεύοντες τὰς ἀνὰ μέσον τούτων (Eus.; MSS τούτου) ἡμέρας. The formulation is difficult. What are "these" (τούτων)? As the sentence stands, the only possible interpretation is that "these" refer to the nocturnal sacrifices, and that the Jews fasted for the days between the sacrifices. It is a strange statement, even in this imaginative account of the Jews (τούτου is no better). The clause ἀνὰ μέσον τούτων is almost certainly corrupt.

32. φιλόσοφοι τὸ γένος: this can be translated "philosophers by descent," "philosophers from birth," "philosophers due to their nature," "philosophers according to their nature," "philosophers according to their race," and so on. I am inclined to translate the phrase here as "philosophers by descent," which is the literal meaning. A similar phrase—γένη φιλοσόφων—a reference to all the "barbarian" nations wrongly attributed to Plato appears in Clement Stromateis 1. 15 [68. 1]. Guttmann 1: 78 n. 26 suggests translating our phrase as "philosophers in essence." But the parallels he cites from Greek literature correspond to the phrase in Theophrastus neither in context nor syntactically.

sacrifices receive great emphasis, it has been assumed that Theophrastus regards the Jews as a caste or sect of philosopher-priests.[33]

Before turning to a discussion and reevaluation of the account, it may be worth clarifying the connection between the passage and what Theophrastus says before and after it. The passage states that the Jews do not eat the meat of the sacrificial victim, and that they were the first to conduct animal and even human sacrifice, which they did "out of necessity and not from desire" (para. 4). These assertions stand in stark contrast to what is said in the previous passage, according to which humans sacrifice out of a desire to enjoy the eating of animal flesh. The Jews, therefore, are exceptional in their motivation for performing sacrifices. They continue their practice to this very day, but only out of respect for an ancient custom whose reason has long been forgotten. In the past, that reason was "necessity." What, then, was this "necessity"? The following section outlines Theophrastus's main version of his anthropological theory concerning the development of sacrificial customs and the eating of animals: it was a famine, a dearth of the plantation normally used for eating and sacrifice, which obliged humans to sacrifice first humans, and then animals (2. 27. 1–4; cf. 12. 1–2).[34]

In the passages that have come down to us, Theophrastus does not say whether the Jews ate animal flesh; but since he claims that the Jews did not eat the victim's flesh, and in the light of the context and the anthropological theory he is presenting, it seems he assumed that the Jews never reached the stage of eating animal flesh. In other words, the anthropological development of the Jews was arrested at the stage of human and animal sacrifice prior to eating the flesh of the victims. Porphyry knew very well that the Jews ate flesh, and noted that they refrained from eating certain types of meat, particularly pork (*Abst.* 1. 14; 2. 61; 4. 11). He may, therefore, have omitted some statement by Theophrastus concerning Jewish "vegetarianism."

THE ASSESSMENT OF JEWISH SACRIFICIAL CUSTOMS

A reading of the account of Jewish sacrifice, in the context of Theophrastus's anthropological theory, indicates that the author intended to praise two aspects of the practice while condemning the rest. The favorable aspects appear from the context: (1) the Jews do not eat the meat of the sacrificial victim (if not meat by and large), and (2) the animal sacrifice is performed out of respect for an ancient

---

33. See Bernays (1866) 111–15; Guttmann (1946) 156–65; Jaeger (1938a) 359–60; Guttmann 1: 74–88; Stern (1973) 162–63; id., *GLAJJ* 1: 7–8; also Jaeger (1938b) 137 ff.; Hengel (1973) 466–67; Stern (1976) 2: 1105; Mélèze-Modrzejewski (1981) 419; Philhopfer (1990) 202; Feldman (1993) 140, 203–4; Kasher (1996) 157. See also Feldman (1983) 282. For a more sober view, see Gabba (1988) 620 and Mélèze-Modrzejewski (1989) 4–5.

34. Cf. the word ἀνάγκη (necessity), which appears several times, e.g., 2. 12. 1.

custom preserved in its original form. The sacrifice was conducted originally out of necessity and was not an excuse for a feast. Only at a later stage did humans inaugurate a meal to accompany the sacrifice, out of "desire" for meat. Later still, meat was eaten for its own sake, without sacrifice. The Jews, however, remained loyal to the original custom, neither adopting the accompanying meal nor acquiring a desire for flesh. Elsewhere Theophrastus explicitly praises the observation of ancient customs (Porph. *Abst.* 2. 5. 4; cf. Tac. *Hist.* 5. 5. 1). In this respect the custom manifests a certain sincerity in the religious conduct of the Jews, as opposed to the hypocrisy of other peoples who sacrifice only tasty animals (25. 7).

The outstanding negative aspect of the present Jewish practices is the mode of sacrifice. The passage emphasizes in various forms that the practice is exceptionally cruel. The most significant sentence says: "If someone were to command us to sacrifice in the same way, we would be repelled from the act" (2. 26. 1), and in the next paragraph (2) the act is explicitly called "terrible." Even the Jews are said to be ashamed of the deed and to do everything in their power to prevent the sun from finding any traces of it by removing the evidence (para. 2). As far as the practice itself is concerned, the editors of Porphyry read, following the manuscripts, various forms of the verb ζῳοθυτεῖν (ζῷον—animal), meaning that the Jews used "to perform an animal sacrifice" (para. 1).[35] In the following paragraph (2) the Jews are said not to eat of the meat of the sacrifice, but to burn the animal completely (holocaust). Theophrastus has accordingly been understood to mean that the Jews slaughter a victim and burn it completely, in contrast to the familiar Greek custom of partaking of the victim's flesh.

This reading, however, poses an insoluble difficulty. What is so repellent about sacrificing a holocaust? In what way is a holocaust more cruel than a sacrifice in which only certain parts are burnt, while and the other parts are eaten by the participants? After the long and ostensibly objective-"scientific" argumentation against animal sacrifice, this outburst against the practice of sacrificing holocausts is disproportionate and indeed out of place. Moreover, if by the statement "we would be repelled by the act" Theophrastus is referring to those already convinced, namely, he and his supporters, why does he refer to the Jewish sacrifice with much greater severity than he does to the animal sacrifices of other nations? He would surely have perceived Jewish abstinence from eating meat as a mitigating factor making the deed actually less atrocious and disgusting than other forms of sacrifice, inasmuch as human sacrifice was usually regarded as less

---

35. Cf. ζῳοκτονία (the killing of animals); ζῳοφαγεῖν (to live off animal flesh); ζῳγράφος (first, a painter of animals; later, a painter in general); ζῳογονεῖν (to raise animals). Many additional examples can be found in the dictionary of Dimitrakos (1964) 3210–24. Bernays (1866) 83, Pötscher (1964) 173, and Fortenbaugh et al. (1992) 422, all translate ζῳοθυτεῖν as *Tieropfer*, "sacrificial animals."

detestable than cannibalism. If Theophrastus meant by "we" his Athenian audience—and this is the most natural and acceptable interpretation—why would Athenians and other cultivated Greeks recoil from performing a whole burnt offering even if commanded to perform it?

Performing complete burnt offerings was a widely accepted custom and deeply rooted in Greek culture from its beginnings. Sacrifices of this sort were usually called ὁλόκαυτοι (holocausts), and sometimes θυσίαι ἄγευστοι (untasted sacrifices—e.g., Plut. *Mor.* 124B). These sacrifices were generally offered to the chthonic gods, heroes, the dead, and storm winds; they could also serve as a means of atonement and the fulfillment of pledges. The topic has been much discussed in the research of the past 120 years, and many examples have been adduced both from literary and historical sources and from archaeological and illustrative material. The custom was practiced in all parts of the Greek world, including Athens and its immediate vicinity, and spanned the centuries from the time of Homer through the classical age to the Hellenistic age.[36] This widely accepted picture has been modified by Walter Burkert in his general book on Greek religion: he points out that partaken sacrifices were occasionally made to the dead, heroes, and the chthonic gods, while holocausts were also made occasionally to Zeus.[37]

A holocaust, therefore, was "normative" and widely accepted in the Greek world, even if less popular than partaken sacrifices. Bearing all this in mind, it seems that, were Athenians and other cultivated Greeks to be commanded to sacrifice a holocaust, there would have been no reason for them to recoil from the deed. Theophrastus would not have made such an outspoken statement within an argument meant to persuade his audience and judges. What, then, aroused his strong disgust?

The difficulty can be solved by a small emendation of the verb ζῳοθυτεῖν (to sacrifice animals), namely, the removal of the iota subscript. The meaning of ζωοθυτεῖν is "to sacrifice a victim alive" (ζωός = alive),[38] that is, without killing it

---

36. Material on this matter has been gathered and discussed in the following works in particular: Stengel (1880) 737–43; (1883) 361–79; Nilsson (1906) 436–53; Rohde (1907) 205 ff., esp. 235–45; Stengel (1910) 93–95, esp. 126–45, 188–90; (1920) 16, 124–27, 136–39, 141–42; Farnell (1928) 95–96, 309; Meuli (1946) 193, 209; Nilsson (1955) 139–42, 178–82; Rudhardt (1958) 238–39. Of the many examples in the sources I shall mention just *Odyssey* 10. 518–33; 11. 25–46.

37. See Burkert (1985) 63. Similar remarks are scattered in a variety of forms throughout his detailed book on sacrifices: Burkert (1972). Ekroth (2002) argues in a monograph on hero-cult that holocaust sacrifices to heroes were quite rare (being considered as similar to sacrifices to the gods), as were funeral sacrifices (as distinct from ordinary sacrifices to the dead); see also Nock (1944).

38. Cf. the words ζωοτοκεῖν (to give birth to live young); ζωγρεῖν (to take a prisoner alive); ζωάγρια (reward for a life saved); ζωοποιεῖν (to reanimate, keep alive, etc.); ζωοφυτεῖν (to give life); ζωόκαυστος (burnt alive); ζωογονεῖν (to propagate, keep alive); ζωοποός (creator of life)—

prior to burning.[39] In a passage suffering heavily from bad transmission, the iota may have been added for one reason or another by Byzantine copyists,[40] or even by Porphyry, who was well acquainted with Jewish practices,[41] and may therefore have found it necessary to emend the text.

The victim is burnt whole: this is the form of the sacrifice, and this is also the method by which the victim is killed. The burning of the animal, a slow and most painful death accompanied by the horrific anguished cries of the victim, is thus what made the act so appalling. To express this, Theophrastus employs a rhetorical *topos* found most prominently in *Dissoi logoi,* an anonymous sophistic work from about 400 B.C.E.; there, a whole string of actions that would repel or shame a civilized Greek are listed, even including customs of semi-Greeks, and not only those of distant peoples.[42]

Such a form of sacrifice is alien to Athens and other places representative of Greek culture in the classical and Hellenistic ages. From the hundreds of pieces of information we have on Greek sacrificial practices, it is known to have been practiced on a special annual occasion in Aetolian Calydon, whence it passed to

---

Theophrastus *On the Causes of Plants* 2. 9. 6. Dozens of such compounds are to be found in the Greek dictionary of Dimitrakos (1964).

39. The Greek-English dictionary of Liddell-Scott-Jones (s.v.) gives the verb appearing in Porphyry as ζωοθυτέω and translates accordingly, "sacrifice live victims," and this is how it is translated by Stern (*GLAJJ* 1: 10), although he writes ζῳοθυτούντων and follows up this reading in his commentary (cf. Stern [1976] 1104–5). Elsewhere, Theophrastus uses the expression θύειν τὰ ἔμψυχα when describing the sacrifice of animals (2. 3. 11). Interestingly, while the iota subscript appears in the Eusebius edition by Mras, it does not appear in the edition of Eusebius in the *Patrologia Graeca* (21. 681 [404.45]). Considering the general laxity of the *PG*, this should not serve as evidence.

40. The word ζῷον appearing in the passage twice (in the genitive case, para. 4–5) would have been enough to confuse copyists and editors. For the major corruptions in the passage, see notes 24, 25, 28, 30, and 31 above. Theophrastus's books were already damaged in the Hellenistic period and were extensively reconstructed at the beginning of the first century B.C.E., a procedure that introduced many errors (see on this Strabo 13. 1. 54, and see below, note 78).

41. Porphyry viewed the Jews favorably and was well versed in their beliefs, history, and customs, in addition to being familiar with all the writings of Josephus, and at least Genesis from the Pentateuch (on this, see Stern, *GLAJJ* 2: nos. 456b, 466, and a reservation on p. 424 n. 6). His detailed response to the Book of Daniel, large fragments of which are preserved in Jerome, also displays the extent of his familiarity with Jewish sacred literature.

42. See *Dissoi logoi* 2. 14 (= D-K 90. 2. 14 [2: 408]), which refers for example to the custom of the Massagetai, inhabitants of the region between the Caspian Sea and Lake Ural, of eating their deceased parents, saying that their stomach is the best grave (cf. Hdt. 1. 216). The writer adds that if any Greek were to perform such a deed, he would be exiled from his land and "would die miserably as one who had done terrible and shameful deeds." See also *Dissoi logoi* 2. 12–14 and 16 on the customs of various peoples and tribes that cultivated Greeks would not dream of following. The peoples mentioned include the Macedonians, Thracians, Scythians, Persians, and Lydians—and even the Spartans in a small matter.

the Messenians (Paus. 7. 18. 8–13; 4. 31. 7).[43] The Aetolians, residing in a mountainous and almost inaccessible region, were not considered Hellenes by the civilized
and cultivated Greeks. They were generally described as primitive tribes thriving
on war and robbery.[44] The distance between the Athenians and the Messenians,
the helots of the Spartans, was greater, and there was also a geographical barrier
making access difficult. It is quite doubtful whether Theophrastus was aware
of these eccentric local customs: he was based in the Lyceum and did not travel
around Greece, and even then, he used to complain about having no time to
write his books because of the need to check details for his public lectures (*Letter
to Phanias*—Diogenes Laertius 5. 37). A comprehensive, popular geographic-
folkloristic work on Greece, of the sort written by Pausanias centuries later, was
unavailable in his time.

Whatever the case may be, these two isolated but mutually connected instances
could not signify Hellenic acceptance of the custom, just as human sacrifices
in Arcadia, still performed in the time of Theophrastus (Porph. *Abst.* 2. 27. 2),
seemed to him not to represent enlightened Greek culture and Athenian norms.[45]
Theophrastus could, therefore, have stated confidently that had his audience—

43. In the annual ceremony held in Calydon in honor of the goddess Artemis Laphria, birds, wild
boars, deer, bear cubs and fox cubs, and mature beasts of prey were customarily thrown into the fire
on the altar. Pausanias (7. 18. 11–13) adds that this cult was moved to Patrae in Achaea in the reign
of Augustus under special circumstances after the destruction of Calydon. The cult was apparently
adopted much earlier by the Messenians, when they were close to Calydon, after Naupactus was
handed over to them (425 B.C.E.; Paus. 4. 31. 7). Pausanias also tells of a similar cult in a temple of
Eileithyia in Messenia (31. 9). The details indicate that this was a variation of the adopted Aetolian cult.

44. See Thucydides' celebrated comments: 1. 3. 5; 3. 94. 4–5. On the customs and religion of the
Aetolians, see Anthonetti (1990).

45. On the practice of human sacrifice to Zeus Lykaios on Mt. Lykaion in Arcadia, see Hughes
(1991) 96–107, 115–16. The usual interpretation of Theophrastus's statement concerning the customs
of the Arcadians is questioned by Dennis (1988) 213–17. See also Dennis's conclusion concerning
the Greeks' attitude in the classical period toward human sacrifice (364–67). I should add (*contra*
Burkert [1985] 61–62) that other fire cults known from the Greek world do not seem to have included
animal sacrifice without the animal being killed first. The sources, only some of which are adduced
by Burkert, say nothing about throwing live animals into the fire. In these ceremonies human
dummies made of wood were thrown onto the fire, as were bronze statues, work tools, weapons,
ornaments, clothes, booty, etc., but no mention is made of live victims being cast into the flames.
In one case—Hyampolis in Phocis—the aetiological story in at least one version clearly hints at
prior killing of the victim (Paus. 10. 1. 2; see also on this point Nilsson [1906] 223). It is also worth
noting the fire cult in honor of Heracles on Mt. Oita in memory of the legend of his self-immolation
there (see, e.g., Ov. *Met.* 9. 230 ff.). Nilsson (1955) 131, in his discussion of this event, thinks that the
myth was created following the local custom of throwing dummies onto the fire. Archaeological
remains found at the site indicate that tools, weapons, bronze statues of Heracles, ostraca inscribed
with oaths to Heracles, and animals were all burnt there (Nilsson, 131 and 87). However, there is
no evidence or hint in the sources that victims were burnt alive, not even in the relatively detailed
story about the sacrifice in Diodorus 4. 38–39. If there is anything to be learned from the condensed

Athenians and other cultivated Greeks—been commanded to burn victims while they were still living, they would have recoiled from the deed. The reader would also have been able to understand why the Jews were so ashamed of the act, hiding it from the eye of the sun, and making haste to cover their tracks.[46]

Theophrastus states that this form of sacrifice has been performed by Jews since ancient times. The very burning of the animal in addition to the abstention from its flesh indicates adherence to an ancient tradition. Theophrastus stated earlier that plant sacrifices were completely burnt in honor of the gods, and explained that this was done in order to bestow upon the plant sacrifices eternal life such as that enjoyed by the gods—the heavenly bodies similar to fire.[47] It would seem that in his view this was done first, and for the same reason, in the case of human and animal sacrifices. Only later, as a result of the institution of the accompanying feast, were animals killed prior to being burnt. Some of the limbs were burnt on the altar, and the rest were eaten by the celebrants.[48]

. . .

reference to the cult of Heracles on Mt. Oita in the scholion on *Iliad* 22. 159 (ed. Erbse [1977]), it is that the bull (if it was to be sacrificed) was skinned before being burnt, from which we may infer that it was already dead (an inference that may also be made from the line in the *Iliad* that is being interpreted). On the non-Greek origin of the cult on Mt. Oita, and on the main feature, the burning of the image of Heracles, see the approach of Farnell (1928) 166–74. Be that as it may, Mt. Oita was in the "Wild West" of ancient Greece, in northeast Aetolia. On the mountain itself lived a smattering of Aetolians whose links with mainstream Hellenic culture were quite tenuous. The sacrifice of Heracles on Mt. Oita was a local custom and not a Panhellenic event. It is interesting that Pausanias, who made a special effort to provide information on any eccentric type of cult at the sites he visited, made no mention of this cult, although he mentions and describes Mt. Oita in about a dozen places, and despite his obvious inclination to elaborate on Heracles cults in other places.

46. Cf. the removal of traces of human sacrifice by Egyptians: Plutarch *On Isis and Osiris* 380D. In the same case it is explicitly stated that the victim was burnt alive.

47. See pp. 19–20 above.

48. It is worth noting that the location of the particle γάρ (for) at the beginning of paragraph 2 ("for they do not eat sacrificed [animals] but burn them completely at night") does not pose any real problem for the interpretation suggested above. The particle does not refer to the previous sentence, as an explanation of why Greeks recoil from the act. That sentence is an especially strong rhetorical statement that does not need any explanation (in fact, an elaboration would only detract from its force). What follows γάρ serves to give a practical explanation for the basic statement about the Jews, placed two sentences before: they burn the victim alive, since they do not eat the flesh. The reasoning is that eating the victim is what necessitates its being killed prior to burning. The flexible use of γάρ is discernible in the same passage in paragraph 4, where it obviously does not refer back to the previous sentence (the "fact" that the Jews were the first to sacrifice animals and humans cannot be an explanation for their engaging in philosophy and astronomy) but refers to 2. 25. 7 ("having done this out of necessity" [26. 4] as against "for the sake of enjoyment" [25. 7]). Theophrastus is not exceptional in this usage. It was already noticed in the nineteenth century that Herodotus often uses γάρ to refer not to the previous sentence but to a much earlier sentence: see Broschmann (1882)

Greeks would have found more offensive than the reference to the mode of animal sacrifice the statement appearing at the end of the passage, according to which the Jews were the first to perform animal and human sacrifice. It is not stated here whether the Jews continue to perform human sacrifice.[49] The anthropological development itself, described by Theophrastus, is common to some societies; he knows that the Carthaginians, the Arcadians, and the Albanians still perform human sacrifice (2. 27. 2), but he singles out the Jews as the first. He is certainly not attempting to idealize them. If Theophrastus does not apply harsh words against Jewish human sacrifices, this is only because this reference is part of the general survey striving to describe scientifically the anthropological process (unlike the reference to the sacrifice of animals, which is the issue at stake). For this reason Theophrastus does not explicitly condemn the Arcadians and the Carthaginians, who continue to sacrifice humans even in his time.

THE SOURCES OF INFORMATION

Nothing Theophrastus writes fits real Jewish sacrificial customs: the Jews did not sacrifice only burnt offerings; they did not refrain from eating the meat parts of the sacrifice; they did not burn a victim while it was still alive; the sacrifice was not performed at night; the participants fasted neither during the sacrifice nor after it; they did not pour honey and wine over the victim, and the Torah even explicitly forbids the sacrifice of honey (Lev. 2.11).[50] At least two of the other activities that the Jews are said to carry out at the time of sacrifice, in their capacity as "philosopher-priests"—observing the stars and discussing matters divine—did not accompany the Jewish sacrifice; and the first of these activities

---

17–18. Denniston (1954) 63–64, in his classic work on the Greek particles, adduced on this point a list of examples from Attic tragedy, including many examples where the speaker uses γάρ to refer to something he has said earlier, although another character has spoken since. The phenomenon is well represented in historical, ethnographic, and partly philosophical texts, especially where γάρ is preceded by a main statement, followed by secondary ones (as is the case in paras. 1–2).

49. That the Jews are not explicitly mentioned in the following passage (Porph. *Abst.* 2. 27), where Carthaginians and Arcadians are cited as examples of peoples who perform human sacrifice "even now," does not necessarily imply that Theophrastus thought that the Jews had desisted from the practice. The Carthaginians and the Arcadians are only examples, and, furthermore, the continuation of the sentence is cut off: οὐκ ... μόνον ... ἀλλὰ ... ("Not only the Carthaginians and the Arcadians but also ... "). What comes after ἀλλά in the text does not conform with the sentence, indicating a lacuna. In any case, I would have expected Porphyry to omit any reference to the Jews performing human sacrifice (if there were such a reference). He knew very well that the Jews did not sacrifice humans in his own day. That they did it in the past he could conclude from the story of the sacrifice of Abraham in Genesis, with which he was very familiar (see note 41 above).

50. This was known even to some Greeks, in one way or another, at a later time, although it was accompanied by inaccurate interpretations and additions. See Plutarch *Quaestiones convivales* 672B.

was alien to them at that time. The sacrificial rite described by Theophrastus is a dark and somber ceremony that is hidden from the eye of the sun. In actual fact, the Jewish sacrifice was a public ceremony performed with joy and accompanied by music and song;[51] and to argue against the statement that the Jews were the first to perform human and animal sacrifice would be redundant. It is clear, then, that the source for this information could not have been Jewish, not even a Jewish source modified by Theophrastus.[52]

From the second century B.C.E., Greek anti-Jewish writers drew inspiration from Egyptian rumors and written sources. In the early Hellenistic period, when Greek authors had no reason to be hostile toward the Jews, there is all the more reason to regard Egyptian rumors as Theophrastus's sources of inspiration for this sort of information. Indeed, Theophrastus is known to have used Egyptian sources in a number of his works,[53] and received oral reports from Greeks returning from Egypt.[54] It may therefore be suggested that Theophrastus gained from such sources the information concerning Jewish human sacrifice as well as the notion that the Jews sacrificed animals by burning them alive.

Certain details of Theophrastus's anthropological theory indicate application of Egyptian traditions. Theophrastus, like Aristotle and other Greek authors, regarded Egypt as the cradle of civilization, and the Egyptians as the wisest of humans (*Abst.* 2. 5. 1, 26. 5).[55] For this reason he attributes to the Egyptians the institution of the first—the vegetarian—stage of sacrifice (*Abst.* 5. 1). The second stage began, according to the main version (the "famine" version), when men neglected sacred matters and were accordingly punished with famine (*Abst.* 27. 1).

51. The gloomy character of the ceremony in contrast to the joyfulness of the Jewish cult has already been noticed by Bernays (1866) 11; Guttmann 1: 80.

52. Various suggestions based on the assumption that Theophrastus used Jewish sources of information have been offered, esp. by Bernays (1866) 111–14 (a trace of the sacrifice of Abraham; the fasting of the clan of priests on duty [אנשי המעמד]; fixing the end of the day of fasting by the appearance of the stars; the requirement to burn by morning whatever is left of the meat of the victim; and the continual burnt offerings [קרבן התמיד]). These suggestions have been rejected by many and have been replaced by other associations (the story of Cain and Abel; a comparison with the Phoenician-Carthaginian custom, etc.); see esp. the reservations and refutations of Reinach (1895) 8 n. 3; Radin (1915) 82; Jaeger (1938a) 143; (1938b) 135; Guttmann 1: 78–80 (who is inclined to accept some of Bernays's suggestions); Stern, *GLAJJ* 1: 11; Gabba (1989) 619–20; Mélèze-Modrzejewski (1989) 9. See also note 81 below on Bernays.

53. See the references of Theophrastus to lists (ἀναγραφαί) of Egyptian kings and to works on Egyptian kings in *On Stones* 24, 55; and cf. Eichholtz (1965) 9–10.

54. On information Theophrastus received orally on botanical matters in Egypt, see Fraser (1994) 180–81. See also notes 4, 8, and p. 17 above.

55. On Egypt as the cradle of man and civilization see esp. Hecataeus in Diodorus 1. 10 ff. Herodotus reported this in the name of the Egyptians themselves and the inhabitants of Elis in his Egyptian *logos* (Hdt. 2. 160).

This led to the decline of mankind, from human sacrifice to cannibalism, animal sacrifice, and ultimately the eating of animals. The sequence of the second stage is peculiar to Theophrastus, as are the details themselves, being without parallels, so far as we know, in old Greek traditions concerning the stages of the decline of mankind.[56] The causal connection between impiety and famine is well known from classical Egyptian sources, as well as from texts originating in the Ptolemaic period, such as the celebrated "Oracle of the Potter." These elements and cannibalism are to be found separately in Greek traditions about Egypt. Thus, the *Bibliothēkē*, wrongly attributed to Apollodorus of Athens, relates that Busiris, the mythological Egyptian king, established a sacrifice of strangers to appease the god after nine consecutive years of drought (2. 5. 11; followed by a number of later Greek and Latin authors and scholiasts). Pseudo-Apollodorus is to be dated to the first or second century C.E., but the traditions are much earlier. All these have their parallels in anti-Jewish Egyptian stories that were passed on to Greek authors in the Hellenistic age. Jewish disdain for the Egyptian gods is said by Lysimachus of Alexandria to have brought famine upon the land of Egypt,[57] and the second version of the Egyptian blood libel imputes cannibalism to the Jews (Joseph. *Ap.* 2. 95),[58] thus also recalling the statement that the Jews were the first to introduce human sacrifice.

That Theophrastus was inspired by Egyptian oral sources and rumors in forming his theory is thus rather plausible. What still deserves attention is the possible role of the Jews in the theory. Significantly enough, immediately after stating that the Jews were the first to perform human and animal sacrifices (26. 4), at the end of the passage on the Jews, Theophrastus adds the following sentence (26. 5):

> This may be seen in observing the Egyptians, the wisest of all, who refrain so much from killing any animal that they turned the images [of animals] into representations of the gods.

That is to say: the claim that the Jews were the first to perform animal and human sacrifice is corroborated by the fact that the Egyptians refrained from killing animals.[59] What is the connection between the two items? A link in the chain

---

56. Excluding the "neglect" of the gods, which also appears in Hesiod *Works and Days* 136; this, however, is but one of a series of sins perpetrated in the Silver Age, and the punishment is not famine but war.

57. Lysimachus in Josephus *Contra Apionem* 1. 305–6, and see below, pp. 321–24, on the second version, according to which the *dyssebeis* (men disrespectful of the gods and of cultic worship) caused *akarpia* (crop failure). Cf. Hecataeus in Diodorus 40. 3. 1–2, on the neglect of religious duties by the Egyptians themselves, caused by the conduct of the Jews, as the reason for the plague.

58. See below, pp. 259–63.

59. Animal sacrifice and the eating of meat by the Egyptians is well known from Egyptian sources and is described in Greek sources. See, e.g., Herodotus 2. 37–42, 47–49; Hecataeus in

of reasoning is missing. Porphyry may well have abbreviated what he found in Theophrastus, as was sometimes his wont (2. 32. 3–5; cf., 2. 7. 2). Although other possibilities should not be ruled out, the intent may well be that in the distant past, when famine struck the land of Egypt, the Jews turned to human sacrifice, and later to animal sacrifice. The indigenous Egyptians, however, being the wisest of humans (cf. 2. 5. 1), refrained from harming animals, as they continue to do to this day. In this context it is worth mentioning a statement of Hecataeus of Abdera, reported in abbreviated form and not too clearly by Diodorus (1. 84. 1). According to the extant text, there are those who say that in the distant past, when Egypt was suffering from a great famine, many people ate their fellow men, but none of the Egyptians ate the meat of sacred animals. As is usual with Hecataeus, this report is based on Egyptian traditions. Accordingly, the autochthonous Egyptians not only avoided cannibalism but also refrained from eating animals. The cannibals were obviously the foreigners staying in Egypt, but who they were is anyone's guess.

The reference to the Jews fasting (26. 3) may also be ascribed to Egyptian influence. Observing the fast in close proximity to the sacrifice (before and after the deed), and the mention of this immediately after the statement that the act was "terrible," would imply that the fasting was intended as form of purification and atonement.[60] It is not a Greek fast, a rarity in itself, of a purely ritual nature to commemorate events in the lives of the gods. It is a fast along Egyptian lines, with a view to purification and atonement. Greeks knew ever since the time of Herodotus that Egyptian priests would fast before sacrifices and would even whip themselves.[61]

If indeed the Jews played a central role in Theophrastus's anthropological theory, this still does not make Theophrastus anti-Semitic. He had met no Jews

---

Diodorus 1. 70. 4 ff. Theophrastus's remark appears to be a hasty generalization based on information about the abstention of Egyptians from harming species of sacred and certain other animals.

60. The fast could not be related to the subsequent account about Jewish philosophers observing the stars, discussing matters divine, and praying. It is not an act of asceticism intended to distance the participants from the material world and concentrate minds on the divine. The context of the sentence indicates otherwise.

61. See esp. Herodotus 2. 40, and the detailed description by Chaeremon of the Egyptian priesthood (Porph. *Abst.* 4. 6–8). On the fasts of the Egyptian priests, see Lloyd (1976) 182. From the classical Greek world we know only of fasts in honor of Demeter and those in the Eleusinian mysteries, if we exclude mere limitations on food and drink of one sort or another, which occurred in other places and on different occasions. On fasts in classical Greece see Erbsman (1929), where they are discussed indifferently with Roman fasts, according to types of fast; L. Ziehn, *RE* s.v. "Νηστεία," cols. 88–107; Gerlitz (1954); Nilsson (1955) 94–95; Erbsman (1969) 456 ff. Unfortunately, the reference to the time of the Jewish fast is corrupt (see note 31 above), and we cannot ascertain whether the fast precedes the sacrifice or follows it.

and hardly knew anything about them. At best he is a witness to the beginnings of Egyptian anti-Judaism. But he was certainly not an admirer of the Jews.

THE JEWS AS A COMMUNITY
OF PHILOSOPHER-PRIESTS

The second central component of the passage is the description of the Jews as philosophers, and the activities accompanying the sacrifice: conversation on matters divine, observation of the stars, and prayer. All this sounds complimentary; but is it enough to balance the negative impression of Jews created by their sacrificial practices? Let us first trace the sources of information and/or inspiration, and place the classification of the Jews in its historical context.

From the passage as a whole we can learn—and indeed this has been remarked upon by scholars—that Theophrastus regards the Jews as a community of philosopher-priests among (or "of") the Syrians.[62] They are continually engaged exclusively in matters of cult worship and activities to do with the divine. The statement that the Jews are "philosophers by descent" (or "from birth"—para. 3) indicates that their occupation in philosophy is due not to individual but rather to collective hereditary talent and/or inclination. As Theophrastus did not know anything about Jewish beliefs, this portrayal would not have been his invention. It seems to be based on a widespread popular rumor. It is reminiscent of explicit statements made by two younger contemporaries of Theophrastus. Clearchus, the Peripatetic philosopher-author, wrote: "The philosophers are called [...] Jews among the Syrians" (Joseph. Ap. 1. 179); and Megasthenes, who was sent to India as an ambassador of Seleucus I, implicitly compared the status of the Jews among the Syrians with that of the Brahmans among the Indians (Clem. Strom. 1. 15 [72. 5]).

The description of the Jews as a community of philosopher-priests is understandable when considered against the broader background of the general and inexact notions the Greeks of that time had about Oriental peoples, with regard to their beliefs, customs, ethnic relationships, and social structure. Greek authors wrote about the existence of sects, castes, or communities of priests, philosophers, or philosopher-priests throughout the Orient. The most prominent of these were the Egyptian priests, the Magi among the Persians, the Chaldaeans (a misnomer

---

62. This has been noted by Bernays (1866) 111 and repeated by many others using various sociological terms. The objection of Jaeger (1938b) 132 n. 4 is unjustified. Cf. Stern, GLAJJ 1: 10; Philhopfer (1990) 73–75; and note 24 above. In fact, scholars speak about a "caste" or a "sect." Both are wrong. Theophrastus described a group of people of common descent ("philosophers by descent"—para. 3), concentrated around their Temple. "Community" seems to be the appropriate term. Cf. below, p. 81, note 112.

in Greek literature referring to the priests of Mesopotamia) among the Assyrians and the Babylonians, and the Brahmans among the Indians.[63] All of these were entrusted with cult worship, and each had some sort of distinctive feature that caused the Greeks to label them "philosophers," be it particular views on the origin and destiny of the soul, a dualist belief, activities such as observation of the stars, or extreme ascetic conduct intended to increase spiritual awareness, to mention but a few. The rumor that the Jews were philosopher-priests was probably based on a combination of vague information concerning the central status of the Temple in Jewish communal life, and the uniqueness of the Jewish cult and religion, above all their refraining from idol worship, which should have been noticed by curious Greek visitors.[64] The difficulty in distinguishing among the various Syrian ethnic groups may account for the Jews being defined as a Syrian community.

The activities ascribed to the Jews in their capacity as philosophers are discussions about divinity, which are held before and after the sacrifice; stargazing on the nights of the sacrifice; and calling on God through prayers. It was only natural for philosophers who doubled as priests and performed sacrifices to engage in theological discussions at a time of sacrifice. Also, the observation of the stars, the visible gods, was considered a theological activity: it was responsible for the very creation of the faith, constantly strengthening it, and inspiring people to think about various aspects of it.[65] The alleged performance of sacrifices at night inevitably invited the attribution of stargazing to the Jews.[66]

63. These things are known from many sources, both historical and ethnographic. It will suffice to mention the lists of such groups in two late authors quoting or relying upon sources from the beginning of the Hellenistic period: Diogenes Laertius 1. 1–11; Clement *Stromateis* 1. 15–16 (see also Strabo 15. 1. 68, 70; 16. 2. 39; Diodorus 4. 31. 2. 4). Among the additional tribes or ethnic groups appearing in those sources are the Druids among the Gauls, the Getae among the Thracians, and the Samanaioi among the Bactrians. For a description of the Egyptian priesthood as a caste, see, e.g., Herodotus 2. 36ff.; Hecataeus in Diodorus 1. 70. 5–12, 73. 1–5; Chaeremon in Porphyry *On Abstention* 4. 6–8.

64. The first explicit piece of information on the abstention of Jews from anthropomorphism and the worship of idols, and their belief in one god, is to be found in Hecataeus of Abdera (Diod. 40. 3. 4), which appeared some ten to fifteen years after the writing of Theophrastus's account. See in detail pp. 95 and 133 below.

65. See Jaeger (1938b) 132–34 and esp. Guttmann (1956) 159–65; 1: 80–86 (and references there to Plato); Stern, *GLAJJ* 1: 8, 11. See, e.g., the detailed account by Hecataeus of Abdera on the emergence of religious thinking following the observation of heavenly bodies (Diod. 1. 11–13).

66. The three pursuits attributed to the Jews by Theophrastus, stargazing, theological discussions, and praying, are reminiscent of three of the characteristics of the Magi, "the philosophers among the Persians" (Diog. Laert. 1. 6–8, citing authors of the early Hellenistic period). In the preliminary Hebrew version of this chapter (Bar-Kochva [2000b] 54–56), I suggested that Theophrastus was influenced by a contemporary rumor that the Jews descended from the Magi (Diog. Laert. 1. 9; on the source of the rumour, see below, p. 85, note 124). This link now seems to me rather doubtful;

As for prayers, the performers of priestly duties in Greece were skilled both in sacrifices and in prayers (e.g., Pl. *Pol.* 290c-d), and every sacrifice was accompanied by prayer.[67]

THEOPHRASTUS ON "PHILOSOPHERS" AND ETHICS

Now that the classification of the Jews has been set in its historical context, it is time to consider the moral judgment of Theophrastus. Do the epithet "philosophers" and the related activities square with the negative features of the Jewish sacrificial customs? Anyone called a philosopher in the Hellenistic period was obviously assumed to have the knowledge and ability to deal with matters in the fields of philosophy. However, what interests us in the context of the passage as a whole is the moral evaluation of the Jews.

Aristotle argued that anyone who failed to realize ethical principles in his personal life was not worthy of the title "philosopher." Such people could be called at best "philosophizers" (οἱ φιλοσοφοῦντες), or something similar.[68] Theophrastus has his own variation. A testimonium attests to his distinguishing between "philosopher" and "true philosopher." The testimonium survives in Arabic in a commentary on Aristotle's *Categories,* written by Abū l-Faraj ibn al-Ṭayyib, a Nestorian monk and physician who was active in Baghdad in the first half of the eleventh century. He wrote commentaries on several of Aristotle's books and on a work by Theophrastus. The testimonium runs as follows:[69]

> There is another group headed by Theophrastus that claimed (i.e., Theophrastus says)[70] that the beginning [of philosophy] should be in the sciences of values (ethics), and used this reasoning: they thought (i.e., Theophrastus thinks) that a man must above all train his soul and habituate it to good customs and let it act in noble

---

Theophrastus did not need such a rumor, and it is a little too speculative to attribute to him such a combination of issues on a Jewish matter that has no bearing on the arguments of his book. At the same time, I would add that these three features were not standard in the descriptions of groups of philosopher-priests. Particular features and activities were attributed to each group.

67. See Pullegn (1997) 7–14, 161–63.

68. See, e.g., Aristotle *Nicomachean Ethics* 1095a2 ff. On "philosophers," see, e.g., Aristotle *EN* 1098b16–18; cf. the distinction made by Dicaearchus between the wise of the past and the philosophers of his time; see Wehrli (1944) 29, 30 (= Mithardy [2000] frr. 37, 43).

69. See the text in Fortenbaugh et al. (1992) 2: no. 466b. On the translation of Theophrastus into Arabic, see Gutas (1992) 63–102.

70. The source quoting Theophrastus read οἱ περὶ Θεόφραστον, which is a normal way of expressing "Theophrastus himself." The translator understood the expression literally as "those around Theophrastus." Cf. no. 466a in vol. 1 of the collection of Fortenbaugh (1992), taken from another Arabic source. It begins: "As to the family of Theophrastus, they think that a man should begin with the theory of correcting behavior."

things . . . and they (i.e., Theophrastus) also adduce as evidence the words of Plato[71] that the true philosopher[72] is the one who exercises himself beautifully and habituates his soul to worthy customs, and not the one who preserves [in his memory] opinions (of others) or the one who solves doubts.

The distinction inferred from this may be illustrated by two parallels: Posidonius of Apamea, following his predecessors, calls the Druids, who he says are in charge of human sacrifice, "the philosophers among the Gauls" (in Diod. 5. 31. 2. 4, 31. 3);[73] the moral image of the Magi, the "philosophers" among the Persians, was rather low in the Greek world. The story about the conspiracy of the Magi (the rebellion of Smerdis) after the death of Cambyses, made famous by the detailed account of Herodotus (3. 61ff.), attributed to them deceit and cruelty. The Persian celebration in memory of the killing of the Magi (*magophonia*) was also well known in the Greek world.[74] Moreover, Greek authors used the term "Magi" to denote any type of tricksters or charlatans.[75]

To conclude the discussion of the description of the Jews as "philosophers" and of their activities, the question still pending is, why was this description placed in the context of the passage on Jewish sacrificial practices, itself part of the argument against the eating and sacrificing of animals? It has been suggested that Theophrastus wished to say that a nation of philosophers was actually reluctant to sacrifice animals.[76] We have already seen, however, that their shame stems not from the sacrifice itself but from its mode of execution. One does not need to be a philosopher to be ashamed of this. In any case, the term "philosophers" in Theophrastus does not imply proper moral judgment. It seems that Theophrastus, who gave the Jews a certain role in his argumentation and possibly also in his anthropological theory by and large, just wished to give his Greek reader some idea of who these people were.

. . .

71. Such explicit statements were not written by Plato in his dialogues, although they may be deduced from the various comments made by his Socrates. Sayings (*apophthegmata*) of philosophers were brought together in collections and could have reached Theophrastus even by oral tradition. This may even be an apocryphal saying. Similar comments were made by Polemo of Athens (end of the fourth century) according to Diogenes Laertius 4. 18, although they are not directed specifically at philosophers.

72. The original would appear to have read ὁ τῷ ὄντι φιλόσοφος or ὁ ὡς ἀληθῶς φιλόσοφος.

73. On the Posidonian source for the Gallic excursus of Diodorus, see Kidd 2: 308 ff. On the Druids as "philosophers among the Gauls," cf. Diogenes Laertius 1. 1; Clement *Stromateis* 1. 15 [71. 4].

74. The sources are in Clemen (1928) 512–13.

75. See Bickerman and Tadmor (1978) 251, and the sources there. On the Magi in classical literature, see de Jong (1997).

76. So Bickerman (1988) 16.

Theophrastus's account of the Jews is thus morally negative, but intellectually positive. He does not seem to have bothered to acquire accurate information about the Jews but relied on common rumors and hearsay, partly hostile, partly imaginary, mostly coming from Egypt. After all, the role of the Jews was only to serve as an illustration for Theophrastus's anthropological theory, itself intended to help justify his opposition to the sacrificing and eating of animals. Theophrastus had no personal interest in the Jews as such and had no personal feelings toward them. The account well reflects the lack of real knowledge the Greeks of his generation had about the rather isolated community in the Judaean hills.

THE IMPACT OF THE PASSAGE

Because of his high standing in the Hellenistic world of thought and science, and because he is the first author to refer to the Jews in some detail, Theophrastus must have had some influence on the formation of Greek opinion regarding the Jewish people at the beginning of the Hellenistic period. The description of the Jews as philosophers, for example, by Clearchus and Megasthenes may have been influenced by Theophrastus, although they could have been relying rather on the same prevalent rumors as had Theophrastus himself. The Theophrastean Jewish sacrifice may also have inspired the partially preserved reference by Hecataeus to the exclusive and unique nature of the Jewish sacrifice (Diod. 40. 3. 4), if the latter was not directly influenced by Egyptian informers.[77]

However, there is no further echo of Theophrastus's account in references to the Jews until the time of Porphyry, not even in Josephus and Clement, who took such pains to trace references to the Jews in Greek authors. This is to be explained by the transmission of the writings of Theophrastus, on the one hand, and their vast quantity, on the other. His writings were passed from one private collection to another and were even hidden for a long time, so that they were not worked on until the first century B.C.E., when Sulla transferred them to Rome. There they were edited, corrected, and copied and began slowly to circulate.[78] During the two and a half centuries in which the Jewish stereotypes took shape,

---

77. On this matter, see below pp. 117 and 132.

78. See esp. Strabo 13. 1. 51; Plutarch *Sulla* 26; Porphyry *Vita Plotini* 24. The information refers to Aristotle and Theophrastus together. There has been much debate on the accuracy of the detailed information given by Strabo, especially concerning the disappearance of the writings of Aristotle. Some believe that there were still copies available in Athens, albeit unread by philosophers of that period, who preferred to argue with their contemporaries on problems of concern to them. On the fate of Aristotle's writings in that period, see esp. Gigon (1959); Chroust (1962); Moreaux (1973) 1: 20–30; Guthrie (1981) 6: 59–65; Sandbach (1985); Blum (1991) 53–64; Wilker (2002). The subject is also discussed here and there in the collection of articles edited by Fortenbaugh and Steinmetz (1989) esp. 23–73. It is interesting that even Cicero, in the middle of the first century B.C.E., was still not directly

the writings of Theophrastus were virtually unavailable to most writers. Later, the sheer quantity of his literary output seems to have presented an obstacle (see the enormous list of his works in Diog. Laert. 5. 45–50), although *Peri eusebeias* became quite influential at the end of the Roman period.[79] The passage on the Jews (and possibly another reference) was just a drop in the ocean, easily lost to view, and Theophrastus's views on the Jews would have been looked for naturally in his writings on laws.[80] Porphyry was able to trace the passage because he had collected material for his work on vegetarianism, quoting and paraphrasing from *Peri eusebeias,* and besides, was especially interested in Jewish matters. His relatively extensive writing on Jews and Judaism is one of the main factors drawing Eusebius's attention to Porphyry's work. Eusebius in his *Praeparatio evangelica* (9. 1. 3) says explicitly that he found the passage in Porphyry's *On Abstention.* Due to the accidental nature of the preservation of Hellenistic literature, it is impossible to arrive at more definite conclusions.

. . .

The prevailing conception in modern research on Theophrastus's attitude toward the Jews is that he praised and even admired them. This interpretation originated with Bernays and other scholars of former generations who seized upon any thinker in times past who said, or appeared to say, positive things about the Jews. Presumably this is why they overlooked the major negative statement of Theophrastus's account that the Jews were the first to perform human sacrifice, as well as the logical and historical difficulties arguing against the received reading ζῳοθυτοῦσι (sacrifice animals). This reservation is not to detract from the great achievements of these scholars. Their achievements are to be appreciated all the more in view of the political, cultural, and material obstacles and pressures they had to face.[81] Even good old Homer drops off occasionally.

acquainted with the writings of Theophrastus, but only indirectly through the lectures of Antiochus of Ascalon; see Cicero *De Finibus* 5. 1, 8.

79. On which, see esp. Obbink (1988) 273.

80. See pp. 16–17 above.

81. A good example is Jacob Bernays, the scholar who placed research of *Peri eusebeia* on a solid footing. The son of the orthodox rabbi of Hamburg, Bernays adhered to his religious education and faith despite all the pressures put upon him, including his ineligibility for an ordinary university appointment. Considering the internal and external tensions to which he was subject, it is easy to understand the great effort he devoted to squaring Theophrastus's account with Jewish sources, and why this outstanding philologist did not pick up on the negative aspects of the passage. His inclination to square Theophrastus with the Jewish sources may also be explained by his great familiarity with the latter, that degree of expertise that sometimes encourages one to find parallels where they do not exist. On Jacob Bernays, see the biographical articles of Toury, Orbach, and Glucker in Glucker and Laks (1996) 3–56.

2

Aristotle, the Learned Jew, and the Indian Kalanoi in Clearchus

In *Contra Apionem* 1. 177–82, Josephus offers a fragment and a testimonium from a passage about the Jews in a work by Clearchus of Soli, a Peripatetic author and one of Aristotle's pupils, who flourished at the beginning of the Hellenistic period. The passage, taken from Clearchus's lost work *On Sleep*, described an interesting meeting between an intellectual Jew and Aristotle while the great Greek philosopher was staying in Asia Minor (347–345 B.C.E.). The passage included details concerning the origin of the Jews, their abode, and the particular qualities of the Jew who met Aristotle.

Clearchus provides the sole surviving testimony of a Greek concerning a meeting and conversation between a Jew and a Greek philosopher or author of the classical period. Consequently, the story has received much attention in scholarly literature. While the meeting itself has been generally dismissed as unhistorical, the comments attributed to Aristotle have been frequently cited as the most outstanding piece of evidence for the accepted view that Greek authors at the beginning of the Hellenistic period expressed great admiration for the wisdom of the Jews. The account of Clearchus has even been cited occasionally as evidence that elements of the later myth about Greek philosophy originating in Judaism were to be found already in the writings of Greek authors of the early Hellenistic period.[1]

I shall attempt to ascertain whether the passage is indeed enthusiastic about

---

1. See Bernays (1866) 110–11, 187; Labhardt (1881) 19–23; von Gutschmid (1893) 578–89; Reinach (1895) 10 ff.; Radin (1915) 84–87; Silberschlag (1933) 66–77; Jaeger (1934) 116; (1938a) 129–33; (1938b) 138–42; Lewy (1938) 205–35; Festugière (1945) 29–31; Wehrli (1948) 47–48; Lewis (1957) 264–66; Guttmann 1: 91–102; Hengel (1973) 467–69; Stern, *GLAJJ* 1: 47–52; id. (1976) 1109–11; Momigliano (1975) 85–86;

the wisdom of the Jews; what qualities the passage attributed to the Jewish people; why Clearchus regarded these qualities as worthy of emulation; why the author attributed these qualities to the Jews; and finally, what the passage as a whole was intended to convey.

THE LIFE OF CLEARCHUS, HIS WORKS, AND THE TREATISE *ON SLEEP*

Very little is known about the life of Clearchus. No ancient account devoted to him has come down to us, and we must rely on random pieces of information from various sources, and references to personalities and occurrences that are found in fragments and testimonia.[2] From these sporadic data we learn that Clearchus was born in Soli in Cyprus, and that he was a pupil of Aristotle. Another piece of information, found in a scholion on Plato *Laws* 739a, allows us to fix Clearchus's dates with greater precision. The testimonium includes a number of sentences reportedly from *Arcesilaus,* a dialogue by Clearchus.[3] Arcesilaus of Pitane (316/5–241/0) became scholarch of the Academy in 268 or 265. Accordingly, it has been argued that Clearchus continued writing down to the 270s or even a little later.[4] Since he also happened to be a pupil of Aristotle, who died in 322, Clearchus must have been born no later than the late 340s. It follows already from this that Clearchus could not have been an eyewitness to the meeting he attributes to Aristotle (not that he claims that he was). Important biographical information can also be deduced from a fragmentary inscription discovered during the excavation in Ai Khanum (now in Afghanistan), a Greek settlement on the banks of the river Oxus in Bactria, an area settled by Greeks of the generation of Alexander, which eventually became an independent kingdom bordering India. The inscription relates that a certain Clearchus brought to the place proverbs he had copied at Delphi. The proverbs that have survived deal with the life of the individual from adolescence to death. Louis Robert, the great French epigraphist who reconstructed and interpreted the inscription, identified the author with Clearchus of

---

Gabba (1989) 620–21; Feldman (1993) 5, 203, 525; 'Amit (1996) 254–55; Kasher (1997) 164–65. Deviating from the consensus on admiration: Mélèze-Modrzejewski (1989) 10–11. On the later myth, that the Torah was the source of Greek philosophy, see pp. 204–5 below.

2. On Clearchus, see W. Kroll, *RE* s.v. "Klearchos," cols. 580–84; Stein (1930/1) 251–59; Wehrli (1948) 45. The biographical testimonia are scattered throughout Wehrli's collection.

3. Wehrli (1948) 11, 49. On Arcesilaus, see Glucker (1998) 302 ff., and references there to previous literature.

4. Stein and Wehrli find additional support in the passage on the meeting with the Jew from *On Sleep,* which they date to after 292 B.C.E. on the understanding that Clearchus had in front of him Megasthenes' reference to the Jews (Stein [1930/1] 258–59; Wehrli [1948] 46). This supposition fails on several counts; see pp. 81–82 below.

Soli, assuming that he had set out on journeys in the Far East in order to spread Delphic wisdom.[5] Robert's suggestions are quite plausible and have been almost unanimously accepted. The biographical data about Clearchus arising from the inscription have certain ramifications for the issues discussed below, and not only because Clearchus states in his account that the Jews originated in India.

Clearchus was not one of Aristotle's more senior disciples; he was far from the stature of Eudemus, Aristoxenus, or Dicaearchus, not to mention Theophrastus. There is little originality of thought in what has survived of his writings on philosophical matters, and the subjects he chose to discuss were marginal to Peripatetic preoccupations, apparently avoiding important questions such as those concerning logic and ontology. At the same time, Clearchus was quite a prolific author, if we are to judge from the number of works mentioned in the fragments and testimonia. Not a few of his works have some sort of connection with the subjects to be discussed below, and should therefore be surveyed beforehand.[6]

Clearchus devoted two works to Plato: *Encomium of Plato,* and *On the Things Said in Plato's Politeia Concerning Mathematical Matters.*[7] These works demonstrate that this pupil of Aristotle had a special admiration for Plato, which is also reflected in fragments from his treatise *On Sleep,* where the story of the meeting with the Jew is preserved. Plutarch also bears witness to Clearchus's straying from the Peripatetic way (*Concerning the Faces of the Moon Revealed in Its Course* 920F). Fragments from another work by Clearchus, *On Education* (*Peri paideias*), outline those values he considered important.[8] Other works by Clearchus are the following:

1. *On Friendship* (*Peri philias*): a subject and title adopted by several authors of Clearchus's time, including Theophrastus; remains of Clearchus's work by this title are limited to anecdotes concerning symposia and homosexual love
2. *Gergithios* or *On Flattery:* a work on parasites and flatterers and the life of luxury and pleasures
3 *Erotica:* stories of homosexual and heterosexual love and desire, bestiality, and even erotic love for a statue
4. *Sayings* (*Paroimiai*), and *On Riddles* (*Peri griphōn*): collections of epistles, sayings, and riddles, and some humorous material
5. *Lifestyles* (*Bioi*): a wide-ranging work in eight books containing a great deal of material on the ways of life (*diaita*) of peoples, tribes, cities, and famous individuals

5. Robert (1968) 416–57.

6. For more detailed surveys of Clearchus's works, see Kroll (note 2 above); and Wehrli (1948) in various places, and in his collection of passages.

7. See Wehrli (1948) frr. 5–10.

8. A number of scholars regard the information in Diogenes Laertius (1. 9) that the Jews origi-

At least some of these works were arranged in the form of Aristotelian dialogues. The work *On Sleep,* from which Josephus drew Clearchus's passage on the Jews, is of this type. Unlike the more familiar Platonic dialogue, in which the participants argue back and forth as in an ordinary conversation, an Aristotelian dialogue had a formal arrangement in which one participant after another would deliver a speech on a particular subject, while the remaining participants merely added the occasional polite remark, trivial observation, or prompt. No Aristotelian dialogue has survived, but the structure is inferred by comparison with extant Ciceronian dialogues that we know were in the Aristotelian style (Cic. *Fam.* 1. 9. 23. 6). The Aristotelian dialogue form will have some bearing on the discussion later.

Just three fragments have survived from *On Sleep.*[9] One of the fragments contains the description of the alleged meeting between Aristotle and the learned Jew. The other two have been preserved in Proclus, the fifth-century Neoplatonic philosopher. They tell of deeds and events that are said to have taken place in the presence of Aristotle and that are supposed to prove that the unembodied soul has eternal existence.[10] Many readers of the Platonic dialogues, probably including many of his pupils, assumed that this was an opinion held by Plato himself.[11] Whatever the case may be, it was not an opinion held by Aristotle, at least not in his later period and after the death of Plato. Clearchus tried, therefore, to attribute to the later Aristotle this allegedly Platonic opinion. It has consequently been assumed that this was the aim of the work as a whole. As one would expect of an Aristotelian dialogue, however, this was not the only aim. Around the subject of sleep it was possible to develop a discussion on a variety of issues, such as the essence of sleep, the nature of dreams, and so on.

As for the date of the dialogue, we do not have an explicit reference. An estimate can be made from the little biographical data at our disposal, combined with a comparison of what Clearchus and other early Hellenistic authors knew about the Jews. By such means we can place the writing of *On Sleep* in the last decade of the fourth century.[12]

---

nated among the Magi as deriving from Clearchus's work *On Education.* This, however, is unacceptable; see note 124 below.

9. Wehrli (1948) frr. 6–8.

10. Cf. also Wehrli (1948) fr. 38. For various suggestions on the aim of the work, see Wehrli, p. 47.

11. Such sentiments are voiced in various dialogues, including *Phaedo, Phaedrus,* and *Politeia;* but opinions expressed in the dialogues—even by the character Socrates, who is so often regarded as a mouthpiece of Plato—should not automatically be assumed to be the opinions of Plato.

12. See below, pp. 81–82.

THE FRAGMENT AND THE TESTIMONIUM
OF CLEARCHUS IN JOSEPHUS

Josephus cites Clearchus's passage about the Jews for the same reason that he cites passages from other Greek (or allegedly Greek) authors in his *Contra Apionem*: to prove to the reader that the Jewish people is not young, since the Greek world long knew of the Jews. The passage from Clearchus appears immediately after passages from Hermippus of Smyrna, Herodotus, and (pseudo-)Choerilus, the epic poet (*Ap.* 1. 164–75), and before passages from the treatise *On the Jews*, which is falsely attributed to Hecataeus of Abdera, and a passage from Agatharchides of Cnidus (*Ap.* 1. 183–212). Josephus begins by stating that the account of Clearchus testifies that the Greeks not only knew the Jews but also admired them, and that Clearchus was one of the most important of Aristotle's pupils (*Ap.* 1. 175–76). Following this is a fragment from *On Sleep* in which Aristotle is describing his meeting with the learned Jew (*Ap.* 1. 177–81; henceforward, "the fragment"). The fragment does not include everything said in the story about the Jew. It is accompanied by Josephus's own summary of the rest of the story (*Ap.* 1. 182; henceforward, "the testimonium"). Josephus concludes with an invitation to the reader to take another look at the work by Clearchus, from which it may be understood that Josephus (or his aides) used not an intermediate source, but Clearchus's work directly.[13]

Two other ancient sources are of some assistance for understanding the passage from Clearchus: the fragment (without the testimonium) was copied as it appeared in Josephus by Eusebius (9. 5. 1–7). Eusebius's version helps here and there in establishing the correct readings of the Greek text of Josephus.[14] A brief testimonium on the occurrence of a meeting between Aristotle and the Jew, apparently based directly on Clearchus's work and not on *Contra Apionem,* is to be found in Clement of Alexandria (*Strom.* 1. 15 [70. 2]). It is possible to deduce from it (in addition to other considerations) whether the original text does indeed have Aristotle expressing admiration for the wisdom of the Jew.[15]

The following is a literal translation of the passage in Josephus:

(175) It is easy to know that not the most worthless of the Greeks, but those most admired for wisdom, not only were aware of the Jews, but even admired those of them whom they encountered. (176) For Clearchus, the pupil of Aristotle, and sec-

---

13. See the excursus of this chapter, pp. 85–89 below.

14. It is interesting to note in an aside that the corrupt Latin translation of Eusebius led to the mistaken claim in Latin and Hebrew literature of the fifteenth century and later that Aristotle was a Jew; see Wirszubski (1990) 4–6.

15. See below, pp. 52–53, and the text in note 41.

ond to none of the philosophers of the Peripatos,[16] says in the first book of *On Sleep* that Aristotle his teacher related the following concerning a certain Jewish man, and attributes the account to Aristotle. It is written thus: (177) "While it would take a long time to name the many [things this man did], nevertheless it would not be too bad (= "one could do worse than"; that is, it would be appropriate or desirable) to detail as many of that man's [things/deeds] as have a certain wonder and, similarly, a certain philosophy.[17] "Know clearly, Hyperochides," he said, "I shall appear to tell you wonderful things equal to dreams."[18] And Hyperochides discreetly said, "Why, for this very reason we are all asking to hear [the account]."(178) "Well, then," said Aristotle, "according to the precept of the orators, we are to detail first his origin, lest we disobey the teachers of pronouncements."[19] "Say what seems to

---

16. τῶν ἐκ τοῦ Περιπάτου φιλοσόφων οὐδενὸς δεύτερος: See the discussion, pp. 85–89 below.

17. θαυμασιότητά τινα καὶ φιλοσοφίαν ὁμοίως: Von Gutschmid ([1893] 579) proposes reading the two nouns as a hendiadys (= θαυμάσιόν τινα φιλοσοφίαν); however, the presence of ὁμοίως shows that not one but two ideas are being presented. See also the testimonium, and in more detail below, pp. 54, 57–58.

18. ὀνείροις ἴσα: L (Laurentianus, the eleventh-century archetype for most of the extant MSS of *Contra Apionem*) reads θαυμαστὸν ὀνείροις ἴσα, which must be corrupt. θαυμαστόν makes no sense as an adjective (we might at least have expected θαυμαστόν τι), and there is no way to link it with the plural ἴσα. It is also impossible to follow Müller ([1877] 168) in taking it as an adverb, both because of the absence of a verb and because Clearchus is unlikely to have used this form rather than the Attic form of the adverb. The word is absent from the version in Eusebius and is omitted in the editions of Dindorff and Bekker; Niese, however, follows L, and he is followed by Thackeray (1926) and Reinach and Blum (1930), who, respectively, translated the whole phrase "as wonderful as a dream," and "singulières comme des songes." Neither translation is possible. The reading of manuscript S, which represents another transmission tradition, and the *editio princeps* that followed S (see pp. 480–81 below), deserve attention: θαυμαστόν τι καὶ ὀνείροις ἴσα. Since θαυμαστόν appears at first sight so rooted in the MSS tradition, one might be tempted to believe that S and the *editio princeps* have preserved the true reading (as in many other cases; cf., for example, οὐ χεῖρον [S] as against οὐχ εὗρον [L] in the beginning of the same sentence). The difficulty with this suggestion is that the word ἴσα is to be understood as functioning like an adverb; but connecting it with the verbal phrase δόξω λεγεῖν would be forced. For this and other reasons, it seems preferable to accept von Gutschmid's proposed emendation ([1893] 582–83): θαυμαστ', ὀνείροις ἴσα (wonderful things equal to dreams). The corruption to θαυμαστόν can easily be explained when the phrase so emended is considered as one continuous string of letters: θαυμαστονειροισισα. The emendation also has the virtue of explaining ἴσα as an adjective (not an adverb), agreeing with the neuter plural substantive θαυμαστ(ά), which itself agrees with the previous ὅσα.

19. ἀπαγγελιῶν: This word, found in Eusebius's version, is a technical term from the field of rhetoric and literary criticism (as may also be learned from the beginning of the paragraph). It denotes a dry, unornamented report or factual account by the author or speaker concerning events to which he was a witness. If it is likely that the prospective audience is unfamiliar with the personalities or the background to the events, the report is prefaced by an introduction (*prooimion*) in the same style; see, e.g., Aristotle *Ars poetica* 1448a20 ff., esp. 1449b26–27, where tragedy is defined; pseudo-Aristotle *Rhetorica ad Alexandrum* 20–21. The reading of L and S (ἐπαγγελιῶν—"announcements,", "public rebukes," etc.) is wrong.

you,"[20] said Hyperochides. (179) "That man then was by origin a Jew out of *Koile Syria*, but these are descendants of the philosophers in India. The philosophers are called, so they say, Kalanoi among the Indians but Jews among the Syrians, taking their name from the place. For the place they inhabit is called Judaea. The name of their city is quite a tongue twister, for they call it Hierousalēm. (180) This man, then, being entertained as a guest by many, and being in the habit of coming down[21] from the high places to the coastal places, became Greek not only in his language but also in his soul. (181) And then, while we were spending time around Asia, the fellow turned up in the same places and met both us and certain others of the scholastics (members of the school), testing their [and our] wisdom.[22] But as he had been living together with many of those with an education, he was rather imparting somewhat of the things he had [at his disposal]."[23] (182) Aristotle has said this in [the work of] Clearchus, detailing furthermore a great and wonderful steadfastness (*karteria*) and self-control (*sōphrosynē*) of the Jewish man in his lifestyle; it is possible for those who wish, to learn more from the book itself. For I am guarding against setting down more than is sufficient. (183) Clearchus then has said this in a digression; for his subject was something else he mentioned us in this way. Hecataeus of Abdera, however, both a philosophical man and most proficient in practical matters, having reached maturity together with King Alexander, and keeping the company of Ptolemy son of Lagos, he referred [to the Jews] not incidentally, but composed a book on the Jews themselves . . .

20. ὅτι σοι δοκεῖ: Niese followed the reading of L, εἴ τί σοι δοκεῖ, but this makes the speaker appear somewhat impatient or reluctant, and this is surely not the tone expected of an ardent admirer of Aristotle. Furthermore, Hyperochides has already expressed a keen desire to hear about the wonderful deeds of the Jew (end of para. 177). There is a similar difficulty in Eusebius's version, οὕτως εἰ δοκεῖ ("thus, if it seems [to you]"). This version, reflected in the Latin translation (*ita si . . .*) was adopted by Thackeray. It seems, however, that in this, as in a fair number of instances, the reading of S and the *editio princeps*—ὅτι σοι δοκεῖ—is to be preferred. Not only is the tone more in keeping with an admirer of Aristotle, but it is easy to see how ὅτι σοι could be corrupted both to εἴ τί σοι and to οὕτως εἰ. The sentence as a whole concerns the need to follow rhetorical convention by relating some biographical details about the Jew, while leaving the actual choice of details to Aristotle.

21. ἐπιξενούμενός . . . ὑποκαταβαίνων: These participles must be understood as causal. The two clauses are complementary and give two reasons why and how the Jew became Greek. The Jew became Greek both because he was in the habit of being a guest of "many"—clearly Greeks—in "the high places" and in Asia Minor, and learned their language and wisdom, and because he would also come down from the high places to coastal areas. This second point helps to explain how a Jew could become Greek not only in language but also in spirit; his alleged spells of residence in the coastal areas would have exposed him to the cradle of Greek culture, the active and vibrant centers of Greek life where he could meet Greek thinkers of the first rank, and would have exposed him to the Ionian coast and the Aegean Sea, which had contributed so much to the shaping of the Greek character and way of life. Notably, S adds ἐν οἷς ἦμεν εἰς τοὺς αὐτοὺς τόπους, but this seems to be just a gloss.

22. αὐτῶν τῆς σοφίας: αὐτῶν must refer both to the other scholars and to Aristotle and his followers, coming as it does after the linking of these two groups by τε καί.

23. On the translation and interpretation of this sentence, see below, pp. 49–53.

THE AUTHENTICITY OF THE PASSAGE AND
THE QUESTION OF HISTORICAL RELIABILITY

In the early stages of modern research in the eighteenth and nineteenth centuries, scholars suspected the authenticity of the Clearchus passage in Josephus and regarded it as a Jewish forgery. In this context it was even claimed that Clearchus did not write a dialogue *On Sleep* at all.[24] However, in the second half of the nineteenth century it became clear that two other fragments of the work had survived.[25] The other reasons advanced against the origin of the passage have also been rejected for many years.[26] It is worth adding that the claim that the Jews descended from the fictitious Indian Kalanoi (*Ap.* 1. 179) is in itself an argument against a Jewish forgery, as is the note about the difficulty in pronouncing the name *Hierosalēm*.[27] As will become clearer below, the description of the special characteristics of that Jew, and the deeds attributed to him in Clearchus's original work, all corroborate the conclusion that the work is not a Jewish forgery.

Quite apart from the issue of the origin of the passage, the historical reliability of the account has also been questioned. There has been a tendency to regard the story as apocryphal: Aristotle never met any Jew, let alone engage in a philosophical discussion with him. The dialogue *On Sleep* is altogether the product of imagination, and it incorporated many stories lacking historical value. At the same time, some scholars have given more credit to the possibility of a meeting, and to certain other elements of the account.[28] It would therefore be appropriate to dwell briefly on this matter of the historical reliability of the passage as well.

Two anachronisms have been pointed out in the passage. Clearchus dates the meeting to the period of Aristotle's stay in "Asia." He can only mean the few years during which Aristotle was in Assos, on the northwest coast of Asia Minor (347–345 B.C.E.).[29] The Jew from Judaea is said to have spent some time with the learned Greeks in Asia Minor, and is described by "Aristotle" as a Greek not only in his language but also in his soul (*Ap.* 1. 180). It sounds somewhat early for such a description to fit a Jew of Judaea in the time of the Persian Empire when Greek culture did not yet hold sway in the Mediterranean basin. If this argument

24. See Meiners (1716) 98; Ionsius (1781) 212–13; Creuzer (1806) 70–77; Havet (1873) 66–69.

25. See the fragments in Wehrli (1948) nos. 7–8. They were already known earlier, but they were identified with certainty only in the second half of the nineteenth century.

26. See Verraert (1828) 72 ff.; Müller (1840–70) 2: 323–24; Bernays (1857) 190 ff.; Willrich (1895) 45–46; see also Bernays (1866) 110, 187; Müller (1877) 167–70; von Gutschmid (1893) 587–88; Silberschlag (1933) 68–74.

27. The last point is made in a note on the name Hierosalēm by Willrich (1895) 46.

28. See von Gutschmid (1893) 586; Silberschlag (1933) 75–77; Guttmann 1: 101–2; Bickerman (1988) 15; Kasher (1996) 165–66; Millar in Schürer et al. 3: 17.

29. On Aristotle's stay in Assos, see Chroust (1972) 170 ff.

is not yet decisive, the second anachronism is indisputable: "Aristotle" calls the Indian philosophers "Kalanoi," after Kalanos, the Indian gymnosophist who met Alexander and accompanied him on his campaigns in 327.

These points still leave room for the possibility that Clearchus heard about a meeting between Aristotle and a learned Jew, and that he adapted it to the structure and aims of his work, adding contemporary elements anachronistic to the meeting. What settles the matter is a point raised by Werner Jaeger: in the works of Aristotle there is no mention of the Jews.[30] This requires some elucidation. The years between Aristotle's stay in Assos and his death in 322 saw the development of his theology. Had he met the Jew and heard from him about the wisdom of the Jews, he would have referred in some way or other at least to Jewish monotheism. There is no such reference in those writings of Aristotle at our disposal, and no indication that there was any such mention in the works that have not come down to us. In the ancient world these were the better known part of the Aristotelian corpus, and Jewish and Christian writers would have exploited any reference there to the Jews for their own ends. It should also be noted that Aristotle stresses that the "unmoved mover" is one and not many, and that this is called by him "the god" (esp. *Metaph.* 1072b28–30 and 1075b37–1067a3); had Aristotle known about a people in Syria believing in one god, he would certainly have mentioned the fact. This is his practice on less conspicuous occasions. A similar conclusion arises from the remains of a book of Eudemus of Rhodes, apparently called *On the History of Theology*. Eudemus was, unlike Clearchus, one of Aristotle's outstanding pupils (perhaps second only to Theophrastus). He described the religious views of the Babylonians, the Magi, the Sidonians, and the Egyptians, yet there is no reference to the Jews, and it seems from what we have that there was no such reference.[31]

Clearchus, therefore, is not to be used as evidence for a dialogue between Jews and Aristotle and his contemporary sages of the last generation of the classical period, or for any acquaintance whatsoever between them; but rather as

---

30. Jaeger (1938b) 130–31.

31. This was noted by Jaeger (1938b). Kasher, advocating the authenticity of the testimony of Clearchus, overlooks Jaeger's remarks concerning the writings of Aristotle but reacts to the reference to Eudemus: "The writings of Eudemus of Rhodes are themselves fragmentary, and it is consequently difficult to establish decisively that he had no information about it" (Kasher [1996] 165–66 [my translation]). It is, however, not a matter of "writings," but of one book only by Eudemus (*On the History of Theology*), and specifically, one fragment concerning a survey of basic beliefs of Oriental religions between Persia and Egypt (in roughly geographical order), in which the author passes over the Jewish religion; see the fragment in Wehrli (1956) fr. 150, p. 70, l. 20 ff. No less decisive is the fact that Eudemus is cited by none of the many Jewish and Christian authors who were so eager to find evidence that Greek philosophers were familiar with Judaism and based their own wisdom on that of the Jews.

evidence for the opinions and concepts of Clearchus himself, at the beginning of the Hellenistic period. What, then, did Clearchus know about the Jews? What were his sources of information? How did he regard the Jews? In order to answer these questions we must focus on two questions that arise from the passage: How are we to understand "Aristotle's" account of his encounter and those of others with the learned Jew? (b) What are the "wonderful deeds" the Jew is said to have performed?

THE WISDOM OF THE JEW AND
THE WISDOM OF ARISTOTLE

How did "Aristotle" describe the wisdom of the Jew? The answer lies in the content and formulation of the last two sentences of the direct quotation from the dialogue (*Ap.* 1. 181). These sentences have been traditionally read in one variation or another as follows: the Jew tested the wisdom of Aristotle and his circle and taught them more than he learned from them.[32] The wisdom of the Jew thus proved to be superior to that of Aristotle; hence the recurring statements in scholarly literature about the great admiration of "Aristotle" (i.e., Clearchus) for the wisdom of the Jews. But is this really the right way to understand the text?

There is nothing surprising in the "testing" itself. It fits the way the dialecticians set each other questions with a view to rejecting or modifying the concepts and opinions of their interlocutors. It is, however, at the outset hardly credible that a first generation Peripatetic who idolized his master should even hint that anyone, in this case a Jew, might be superior to Aristotle in wisdom or learning. Let us begin with a brief review of the relevant part of "Aristotle's" account:

> (180) This man, then, being entertained as a guest by many, and being in the habit of coming down from the high places to the coastal places, became Greek not only in his language but also in his soul. (181) And then, while we were spending time around Asia the fellow turned up in the same places and met both us and certain others of the scholastics (members of the school), testing their [and our] wisdom. But as he had been living together with many of those with an education, παρεδίδου τι μᾶλλον ὧν εἶχεν.[33]

---

32. See, e.g., Lewy (1938) 206; Guttmann 1: 93; Hengel (1973) 469; Feldman (1993) 5; Kasher (1996)
32. Momigliano (1975) 85 writes: "Having talked to so many sages he was able to instruct Aristotle"; and Stern (1976) 1110 comments: "His cultural level was so high that he had more to tell people he met than to learn from them."

33. (180) οὗτος οὖν ὁ ἄνθρωπος ἐπιξενούμενός τε πολλοῖς κἀκ τῶν ἄνω τόπων εἰς τοὺς ἐπιθαλαττίους ὑποκαταβαίνων Ἑλληνικὸς ἦν οὐ τῇ διαλέκτῳ μόνον, ἀλλὰ καὶ τῇ ψυχῇ. (181) καὶ τότε διατριβόντων ἡμῶν περὶ τὴν Ἀσίαν παραβαλὼν εἰς τοὺς αὐτοὺς τόπους ἄνθρωπος ἐντυγχάνει ἡμῖν τε καὶ τισιν ἑτέροις τῶν σχολαστικῶν πειρώμενος αὐτῶν τῆς σοφίας. ὡς δὲ πολλοῖς τῶν ἐν παιδείᾳ συνῳκείωτο, παρεδίδου τι μᾶλλον ὧν εἶχεν.

The decisive statement appears in the second clause of the final sentence: παρεδίδου τι μᾶλλον ὧν εἶχεν. The word μᾶλλον can be interpreted as a form of
comparison, "more"; or it can have the absolute sense of "rather," introducing a
correction to an impression presumed to have been given by the previous statement. The translators and interpreters who regard "Aristotle" as dwarfed by the
Jew in wisdom treat μᾶλλον as a comparative.[34] Reading μᾶλλον as "more,"
however, does not convey that the Jew had more wisdom than "Aristotle." What
is said is the following: "[The Jew] was imparting somewhat more than the things
he (the Jew) had [at his disposal]" (τι would need to be taken with ὧν as a partitive
genitive). This is a very strange sentence: how could a Jew impart more than he
himself knew? One could suggest the emendation εἴχομεν (we had)[35] instead of
εἶχεν (he had) and understand "somewhat more than the things we had"; that
is, somewhat more knowledge than "Aristotle" had. There is no support, however, for such an emendation in the manuscripts of Josephus or in Eusebius. We
might have expected Eusebius to jump on such a reading had he found it in his
manuscript of Josephus. Nor was this the reading in the manuscript of Josephus
or Clearchus consulted by Clement of Alexandria, who strove to demonstrate
the superiority of Oriental and Jewish wisdom to that of the Greeks (see further
below).

In addition to the difficulty of attributing to Clearchus a statement indicating
that the wisdom of the Jew was superior to that of Aristotle, the context presents
the reader with two further difficulties for such an interpretation. The beginning
of the final sentence (ὡς . . .) explains its end; that is, the Jew was able to provide
his audience with what he provided because he had stayed previously in the
company of many men of learning. How, though, does this explain why he taught
Aristotle more than he learned from Aristotle? Had Aristotle not spent his life in
the company of learned men? Furthermore, the plain text indicates that the first
part of the final sentence refers back to the previous sentences (*Ap.* 1. 180), where
it is stated that prior to the meeting with Aristotle, the Jew had been given hos-

---

34. So, for example, in the old English translation of Whiston (1737) 772: "And as he had lived
with many learned men, he communicated to us more information than he received from us"; and in
the Latin translation of Dindorff (1845) 1: 536: "atque cum plurimis doctrina praestantibus familiar-
iter vixerat, plus aliquanto quam acciperet nobiscum ille communicabat"; Guttmann 1: 93 and n. 39:
"He transmitted something more, from his part, than what he acquired"; Lewy (1938) 206: "He communicated to us rather more of such things as he knew himself"—a hybrid translation open to various interpretations; Simchoni (1959) 29: "But he bestowed upon them more than what he received
from them"; Kasher (1996) 32: "He bestowed [upon us] more than he received [himself from us]." For
exceptions in modern translations, see note 40 below. This interpretation is reflected more than once
in Jewish medieval versions of the old myth on the "theft" of Jewish wisdom by Greek philosophers.

35. I.e., "I had"—"Aristotle" has already used this polite plural form to refer to himself earlier
in the passage.

pitality by many (Greeks), and had thus become a Greek not only in his language but also in his soul.[36] It follows that the Jew's learning and thinking would be Greek. At any rate, there is no hint of Jewish or Oriental wisdom. If that were the case, however, what would be the Jew's advantage over Aristotle, a philosopher who had read almost all that there was to read in Greek? His voluminous reading is evident in his writings, and in his explicit and implicit references to all sorts of written material. Plato is said to have called him "the reader" (ὁ ἀναγνώστης).[37] If this is what Aristotle's teacher thought of him, how much more so one of his junior pupils?

Therefore, the word μᾶλλον in the sentence under consideration is not a comparative ("more") but must have its absolute sense ("rather").[38] The sentence as it stands should be translated as follows: "He (the Jew) was rather imparting something of the things he had [at his disposal]."[39] The previous sentence gives the impression that the Jew only "tested" his interlocutors. The present sentence corrects this impression by asserting that the Jew imparted "something" of his own knowledge, and was able to do so because of his extended stay among learned Greeks.[40] The story may thus be understood in a number of ways; for

36. See note 21 above on the construction and meaning of this sentence as a whole.

37. See *Vita Aristotelis Marciana*, ed. Gigon (1962) para. 6, line 41; the work is an anonymous Byzantine composition based on good sources (Gignon, 11–21). On the sources concerning Aristotle's great private library, see Düring (1957) 337–38; (1966) 607; Platthy (1968) 124–28.

38. The absolute sense of μᾶλλον, which is the common usage in Homeric Greek, appears frequently in Greek prose, including Aristotle and Josephus himself. The ratio between this and the comparative sense in philosophical and rhetorical works seems to be somewhere between 1:2 and 1:1 (in historical works the comparative sense is considerably more frequent). In *Contra Apionem*, for example, out of eleven instances the absolute sense is intended four times (1. 11, 37, 81; 2. 125); in the fragments of Clearchus, twice out of four instances (in the present case, and in the fragment preserved in Ath. 15. 670e; the comparative sense is intended at Ath. 12. 514e; Plut. *Concerning the Faces of the Moon Revealed in Its Course* 920F).

39. The place of the word μᾶλλον in the sentence does not pose any difficulty to the interpretation that it should be understood in the absolute sense. Nor is there a problem with the word order τι μᾶλλον ὤν. It is a variety of hyperbaton, a regular rhetorical figure. In the present case, μᾶλλον is delayed in order to prevent hiatus (τι ὤν) and to provide emphasis. On the various types of hyperbaton and their aims, see Denniston (1960) 47–59. On the prevailing tendency of Greek authors to vary word order, well known to readers of Greek, see generally, e.g., Dover (1960) passim: "pursuit of variety"; "desire to achieve variety"; "deliberate variety of order is as obvious here as variety of vocabulary," etc.

40. Thackeray (1926) 237 (LCL) translates: "It was rather he who imparted to us something of his own." Accordingly, the word μᾶλλον indicates a contrast to what has just been said: the Jew tested Aristotle and his followers, but instead of learning from them, he in fact taught them and imparted to them a little of his own knowledge. However, the formulation of the sentence barely supports Thackeray's emphasis ("It was he") and suffers from the same difficulties already referred to above concerning the apparent eclipse of Aristotle's wisdom by that of the Jew. Above all, would

example, when the fellow conversed with Aristotle and his colleagues, he did not restrict himself to asking questions and listening passively to the answers they gave, but, because he had previously stayed in the company of learned Greeks, he gave in to the temptation to show off in front of the great Greek philosopher and his acquaintances with some of the knowledge he had acquired on the subjects discussed; or he did not wait for them to finish answering, but occasionally jumped in and answered himself; or he was dragged into their conversation as befits one with a Greek soul, and the like. Whatever the case may be, a portrayal of the superiority of Jewish or Oriental wisdom is not intended.

The "report" on the conversation with Aristotle is transmitted in full as a part of an account by Aristotle himself, and, unlike the story about the "wonderful deeds" of the Jew, it seems that it was not abbreviated. Had Clearchus presented the Jew's words of wisdom, there would have been no reason for Josephus (or even for an intermediate source if there was one) to omit them. The conversation itself is not the main point, and it was not for this that "Aristotle" mentioned the Jew. As we shall see in the next section, the conversation is mentioned only by way of introducing the truly significant item—the "wonderful deeds" of the Jew, which illustrated his special virtues.

The conclusion that the account attributed to Aristotle does not impute to the Jew superior wisdom, let alone superior Jewish wisdom, is supported by the testimonium of Clement of Alexandria (second to early third century B.C.E.). He states only that "Clearchus the Peripatetic says that he knew of a Jew who met Aristotle" (*Strom.* 1. 15 [70. 2]).[41] This appears in a chapter where Clement is doing all he can to prove that the source of Greek wisdom is Oriental, and particularly Jewish, wisdom. To this end, he has cited Plato, Democritus, Pythagoras, and Thales. Clement would certainly not have missed an opportunity to show Aristotle claiming priority and superiority for Jewish wisdom had one been provided by Clearchus. His silence suggests that he was unable to interpret the text of Clearchus in front of him in this manner; Clement was quite capable of pushing the interpretation of a text much farther than is reasonable—as in the case of Megasthenes on the Jews[42]—in order to prove that the wisdom of the Jews preceded that of the Greeks, and yet he apparently could not do that here. Clearchus's Greek is straightforward, and Clement of Alexandria, who appears

---

Clearchus, of all people, have even allowed "something" of the Jew's wisdom to be superior to that of Aristotle? An apparently correct translation into Greek Katharevousa is to be found in Bella (1938) 1: 39: κατὰ τὴν συναναστροφὴν δὲ μετὰ πολλῶν διακρινομένων ἐν τῇ παιδείᾳ μᾶλλον μετέδιδέ τι ἐκ τῶν γνωσεών του ("Because of living together with many excelling in education, [he] rather imparted some of his knowledge"). See also Reinach and Blum (1930) 35: "Il nous livrait plutôt un peu de la sienne."

41. Κλέαρχος δὲ ὁ περιπατητικὸς εἰδέναι φησί τινα Ἰουδαῖον, ὃς Ἀριστοτέλει συνεγένετο.

42. Clement *Stromateis* 1. 13 [72. 5]. See below, pp. 142–46.

to have been born in Athens and had an excellent Greek education, was not mistaken in his reading. In the event of any doubt, he would surely have consulted Clearchus's original text (if he had not done it in any case).[43]

At the same time, it should be made clear that "Aristotle's" account of the conversation does appear to contain a certain intimation of praise (mingled with some surprise). This does not arise from any superiority of the wisdom of the Jew, however, but from the very fact that a member of a "barbarian" nation, whose native land was remote and whose language was peculiar, had managed to acquire Greek speech and learning; that he had been able to display his achievement in conversation with learned Greeks; nay, with Aristotle himself; and all this in the period before Greek became widespread in the East. This sort of appreciation resembles that of Germans, for example (or, indeed, modern Greeks), for visitors to their country from distant lands (excluding "guest workers") who display a proficiency in the local language and culture. This is well expressed in the introduction of the Jew: he became a Greek not only in his language but also in his soul. An identical expression is applied by Agatharchides of Cnidus, 150 years later, to Boxus, a Persian living in Athens (Phot. *cod.* 250. 5, 442a-b), which indicates that it was a common turn of phrase with respect to such people. When Josephus talks about the great admiration of Greek writers for Jews (*Ap.* 1. 176), referring to this passage in Clearchus, he does not have in mind the wisdom of the Jew, but their "wonderful deeds" (see next section). Finally, it must be reiterated that there is no claim in Clearchus that the philosophy of the Orient is superior.[44]

THE WONDERFUL DEEDS OF THE JEW—*KARTERIA* AND *SŌPHROSYNĒ*, KALANOS AND THE CYNICS

It had already been remarked by the first scholars to discuss Clearchus's account that the original text contained one or more wonderful deeds attributed to the Jew. Indeed, "Aristotle" emphasizes in his introductory comments that he is about to relate unusual acts ("a certain wonder," "wonderful things similar to

---

43. Considering the vast extent of his reading of Greek literature, it is most likely that Clement was not relying here on secondary sources. He does not quote from *Contra Apionem* in his works, since he did not need it. The only reference to Josephus in Clement's works is found in *Stromateis* 1.21 [147. 2–3], and not to *Contra Apionem* but to the *Bellum Judaicum* (4. 439–41). This concerns the number of years from Moses to David, and from David to Vespasian.

44. It is worth noting in this context the parallel to Aristotle's account that a number of scholars have found in the apocryphal report by Aristoxenus (Wehrli [1948] fr. 53) of a meeting between Socrates and an Indian sage; see Willrich (1895) 46; Lewy (1938) 218–19; Hengel (1973) 469; Stern (1974) 47; (1976) 1110. However, Aristoxenus is not talking about the superiority of Indian over Greek wisdom; he is merely expressing his opinion concerning philosophical priorities, engaging thereby in a purely internal Greek controversy over the matter (see on this below, pp. 74–75).

dreams," *Ap.* 1. 177), and that on this issue he will not refrain from relating details. It is clear that he is not referring to the dialogue he conducted with the Jew. Even had the Jew displayed outstanding wisdom, overshadowing Aristotle himself, it is not to this that the expressions refer; the word *thaumasia* (wonderful things/ deeds), variations of which appear in the passage, refers to deeds and events that cannot be grasped by the mind (*paradoxa*) or are contrary to the laws of nature or experience accumulated over the years, not to the extraordinary intelligence or learning of a particular person. The term was regularly used to denote a certain literary genre that was already in existence in the classical period but flourished particularly in the Hellenistic period, especially in the third century B.C.E. A work of this genre was wrongly attributed even to Aristotle.[45] The statement that in these marvelous deeds of the Jew there is "a certain wonder and, similarly, a certain philosophy" (*Ap.* 1. 177) refers, therefore, to the philosophical approach motivating them, or to their philosophical implications, rather than to any philosophical argument or dialogue.[46]

A. The Identity of the Anonymous Hypnotist in Proclus-Clearchus

The fragment does not contain an account of the wonderful deeds performed by the Jew. Josephus (or his assistants) made direct use of Clearchus's work, rather than an intermediate anthology.[47] The omission, therefore, is Josephus's, and he must have had a good reason for it. What was the nature of these deeds? Why did Josephus omit them? Already in the nineteenth century the omission was being supplied by a story preserved in a commentary on Plato's *Politeia* by Proclus, the fifth-century pagan Neoplatonic philosopher.[48] Proclus quotes a passage from Clearchus's work *On Sleep* concerning a man whose identity and nationality are not mentioned, but who, in the presence of Aristotle and his pupils, took the soul of a sleeping boy by means of a staff, and afterward returned it. In this way, it was demonstrated to Aristotle that the soul is separate from the body.[49] This

---

45. On the part played by *thaumasia* in ethnographic literature of the period, see Trüdinger (1918) 1–44. On works devoted entirely to wonder stories, which were so popular in the Hellenistic period, see Susemihl (1892) 2: 463–86 and the collection of Giannini (1966). On the popularity of wonder stories, see, e.g., Aulus Gellius 6. 4.

46. See further, pp. 77–80 below.

47. See pp. 85–89 below.

48. See Havet (1873) 67; von Gutschmid (1893) 529, 588.

49. Wehrli (1948) fr. 7. A translation of the Proclus fragment follows: "That it is possible for the soul to exit and enter the body is shown also by the man who, according to Clearchus, used the soul-dragging wand on the sleeping youth, and who persuaded the divine Aristotle—as Clearchus says in *On Sleep*—concerning the soul, concluding that it separates from the body and that it enters the body, and that it uses the body like an inn. For he struck the boy with the wand and dragged out his soul, and by means of the wand as it were leading it far from the body he showed the body to be

suggestion has been developed over the years,[50] and has been widely accepted among scholars. [51]

According to the most detailed version of the suggested supplement, that of Hans Lewy, the whole point of the dialogue *On Sleep* is to prove Plato's opinion concerning the separate existence of the soul: the account of the (Jewish) hypnotist has a central place in the work, and it is he who provides the decisive proof that convinces "Aristotle." Why did Clearchus describe the hypnotist as Jewish, of all nationalities? Because of a rumor that the Jews were descended from the Magi (Diog. Laert. 1. 9).[52] Since magical deeds were attributed to the Magi, "the counterparts of the Jews among the Persians,"[53] and a belief in the survival of the soul was attributed to the Jews, Clearchus used these elements in his dialogue, portraying a Jew proving his belief by means of a magical deed. Why, then, did Josephus omit the episode? Because it would detract from the image of the Jews in the eyes of "enlightened Greeks" for whom he wrote the work, and because Jews, too, would criticize this portrayal as witchcraft prohibited by the Torah (Lev. 19.26; Deut. 18.10).

Lewy had to deal with another problem arising from this interpretation: why Proclus failed to mention the name and nationality of the hypnotist, although he does so in other wonder stories appearing in his commentary on the *Politeia*. Lewy explains that the pagan Proclus, living when Christianity was gaining ground in Greece, had no wish to speak in praise of a Jew. For the same reason Proclus regularly failed to mention in his writings Jews and Christians and never cited the holy scriptures. He waged his polemic against the Christians without being too obvious and yet, despite his caution, was still exiled from Athens for a while under Christian pressure.

At this stage, before making a close comparison of the fragment and the testimonium, it should be stated that the link between the hypnotist and the Jew is somewhat arbitrary. Clearchus would have cited many examples in his work to prove his claims. This is clear both from a comparison with fragments from his other works and from the general practice of Peripatetic argumenta-

---

unmoving and to be unfeeling, preserved unharmed like something inanimate, in the face of <the blows of the> lacerators. The soul, continuing meanwhile to be far from the body was led back again close [to the body] by the wand, and after its entrance reported each and every thing. As a result, all those watching such an inquiry, especially Aristotle, were convinced that the soul is separable from the body."

50. Lewy (1938) 209 ff.

51. See Hengel (1973) 468; Momigliano (1975) 85–86; Stern (1974) 52; Troiani (1977) 115; Gabba (1989) 621; Kasher (1996) 170.

52. On this rumor, see note 124 below.

53. See, e.g., Diogenes Laertius 1. 1; Clement, *Stromateis* 1. 15–16, for the description of the Magi as the philosophers among the Persians.

tion. Aristotle's followers for the most part used to collect examples for arguments and particular details under discussion. *On Sleep,* like any Aristotelian dialogue, dealt with one or more central subjects, and a large number of side issues. Examples were cited for all of these, of which only two examples, in addition to the passage on the Jew, have survived; both are preserved by Proclus in his commentary on Plato's *Politeia:* the story about the anonymous hypnotist under discussion here, and another story about the death and resurrection of an Athenian named Cleonymus.[54] Both stories were introduced by Clearchus to demonstrate the separate existence of the soul, which was one of the central issues of the work, if not the central one. Both stories are "wonderful" (the story about Cleonymus is described explicitly by Proclus as *thaumasios*). Indeed, any event proving the independent existence of the soul, apart from the body, is naturally "wonderful." However, we have no guarantee that these were the only examples cited on this subject; nor do we know how many "wonderful" examples were cited to demonstrate or prove other possible central ideas or secondary concepts discussed in the book. Since all this is connected in one way or another with sleep, it is reasonable to suppose that they did not lack "wonder." The reason only two examples concerning the separation of the soul from the body have survived is that they were relevant to Proclus's commentary on the myth at the end of Plato's *Politeia:* the myth tells how Er, son of Armenios, a native of Pamphylia, fell in battle and wandered twelve days in the underworld taking notes, and then came back to life, his memory unaffected.

It should also be observed that Peripatetic authors of the late fourth century B.C.E. insisted that the Magi were not at all acquainted with magic (Diog. Laert. 1. 8).[55] Whether this is true of the Magi, or not, is another matter. What matters is the image of the Magi among the Peripatetics. Furthermore, in light of the scant information Clearchus had on the Jews, it is greatly to be doubted whether he could have known about a Jewish belief in the immortality of the soul; and we still need decisive evidence for the popularity, if not the very existence, of Jewish beliefs concerning the immortality and resurrection of the soul at the end of the classical period and before the religious prohibitions of Antiochus Epiphanes.

Only Yehoshua Guttmann has criticizes the position of Lewy and his predecessors.[56] His reasons are not decisive.[57] Guttman does not himself propose a

54. See Wehrli (1948) fr. 8.

55. Referring to pseudo-Aristotle *Magicos* and to Dinon of Colophon. On this, see Clemen, *RE* s.v. "Μάγοι," cols. 206–10.

56. Guttmann 1: 94–107.

57. To take one example, Guttmann 1: 95–96 argues that Josephus would not have omitted the story had he known it, since magical deeds are attributed by him to King Solomon (*AJ* 8. 45–49; cf. Babylonian Talmud, Me'ila 17b), and stories concerning the separation of the soul from the body and its wandering in the upper regions are known from Talmudic literature (e.g., BT, Pesahim 51a; Baba

plausible alternative. He is merely of the opinion that the expressions "wonder," "wonderful things," and "equal to dreams" should not be understood literally. He claims that Plato in the *Laws* uses the phrase "similar to a dream" even when he does not intend to report "extraordinary" deeds or things, and the adjectives used by Clearchus only express an opinion, in somewhat excessive language, concerning the moral quality of what the Jew said: the Jew described to Aristotle the just political and social regime in the country of the Jews, a society where "just men rule"; this excited the latter, and hence the expressions mentioned.[58] However, the references adduced by Guttman from the *Laws* are not to the point. Plato uses the word "dreaming" in the sense of "imagining" (656b), and the word "dreams" in the sense of "fantasies" or "unrealistic utopia" (746a).[59] In these contexts in the *Laws* there is no mention of "wonderful things" or the like. It is also difficult to understand why Josephus omitted a description either of Jewish society as one in which "just men rule" or of the Jews as role models for an ideal society. Such a quotation would have contributed considerably to the purpose for which Josephus introduced Clearchus in the first place.

B. The "Wonderful Deeds" and the Ability to Withstand Internal and External Pressures

An examination of the testimonium following the fragment reveals that the nature of the wonderful deeds "equal to dreams" needs to be understood differently:

(182) Aristotle has said this in Clearchus, detailing furthermore a great and wonderful steadfastness (*karteria*) and self-control (*sōphrosynē*) of the Jewish man in his lifestyle.[60]

Bathra 10b). Indeed, in the last two generations, mainly in light of material from the Judaean desert and amulets from Jewish cemeteries in Egypt, and in light of references in 1 Enoch, Philo, and Josephus, as well as in rabbinic and Christian literature, there is no longer doubt about the spread of magic practices among Jews of the Second Temple period, both in the Holy Land and in the Diaspora (on Jewish magic and mysteries, see, e.g., the survey of P. S. Alexander in Schürer et al. 3: 347–79; Betz in Faraone and Obbink [1991] 250–51). However, the exorcism of bad spirits or the wandering of the spirit in the upper regions at the moment of death would seem to be of a different order from the expulsion of the soul from the body and its return by means of a staff. The performance of miraculous acts by means of a staff (albeit not of this kind) is indeed attributed to Moses in the Torah, but this paved the way for the portrayal by some Greek and Roman authors of Moses as a wizard and a charlatan. Josephus was aware of these accusations and reacted to them in *Contra Apionem* (2. 145). He had good reason, therefore, not to mention any story about the expulsion of a spirit by means of a staff, if there was any such story.

58. Guttmann 1: 100–102.

59. οἷον ὀνείρατα λέγων, ὀνειρώτων. Guttmann gives another reference (957c), but it is erroneous, and I have been unable to locate what he intended to indicate. Other instances of ὡς ἐν ὀνείρῳ in Plato do not support his position.

60. καὶ προσέτι πολλὴν καὶ θαυμάσιον καρτερίαν τοῦ Ἰουδαίου ἀνδρὸς ἐν τῇ διαίτῃ καὶ σωφροσύνην διεξιών.

Josephus is making a very short summary here of everything he found in Clearchus's account after the part he quotes verbatim, namely, the account of "wonderful deeds" attributed to the Jew. Josephus says in the testimonium that Aristotle detailed (διεξίων) the Jew's unique qualities. This statement is practically identical to what "Aristotle" says at the beginning of the fragment, where he promises to go into detail (διελθεῖν) concerning those deeds of the Jew that have a certain wonder in them, although in the fragment itself the promise is not fulfilled. Josephus uses the adjective θαυμάσιος (wonderful) in the testimonium, and this accords with the two expressions appearing at the beginning of the fragment, θαυμασιότης (wonder), and θαυμαστ', ὀνείροις ἴσα ("wonderful things/deeds equal to dreams"; Ap. 1. 177). The fragment uses the plural "as many of that man's [things/deeds] as have a certain wonder," and later, "wonderful things/deeds." This indicates that the account was not about a one-time event. Nor is the testimonium only about an isolated deed, but rather a series of deeds and situations illustrating the *karteria* and *sōphrosynē* in the lifestyle of the Jew.

Thus the expressions in the fragment—"[things/deeds] as have a certain wonder," and "wonderful things/deeds"—must be understood in the context of the testimonium as pertaining to *karteria* and *sōphrosynē*. Steadfastness and self-control are certainly not at issue in the episode quoted by Proclus, a case of hypnotism. When the fragment and testimonium are taken together it appears that "Aristotle" gave a string of practical examples demonstrating these virtues of the Jew. Josephus, however, omitted these examples. Why? We shall consider this question once we have identified what sort of examples he omitted.[61]

It is worth clarifying here the significance of the term *sōphrosynē*, which underwent many transformations in Greek literature over time.[62] One meaning that came to the fore in Plato and Aristotle is not simply temperance, but self-control, the result of which is temperance. This meaning is particularly clear in cases where *sōphrosynē* occurs together with *karteria*. *sōphrosynē* and *karteria* are actually two aspects of the same characteristic, the ability to withstand pressure, internal and external respectively.

Without going into too much detail, in Plato's *Gorgias*, *sōphrosynē* is contrasted with *hēdonē* (pleasure), and the conduct of the *sōphrōn* (the temperate man) is described as follows: "controlling himself, and ruling the pleasures and desires in himself" (491d10–e1). Aristotle in *Nicomachean Ethics* (1107b4–6; 1117b23–1119a20) regards *sōphrosynē* as a "middle way" (*mesotēs*) with respect to bodily pleasures and desires (food, drink, sex), not spiritual ones. In this sense, then, *sōphrosynē* is the ability to withstand one's own bodily desires (*EN* 1117b30–

---

61. See below, p. 79.

62. On the development of the concept of *sōphrosynē* in the Greek and Hellenistic world, see North (1966) 1–243.

1118a5). The Aristotelian *sōphrōn* is the one who knows the limits of his bodily needs and controls his desires accordingly, indulging them to the extent that they serve his needs, and no more. *Sōphrosynē*, then, like *karteria*, would apply in the account of the Jew not to one particular act but to his whole way of life, or to the series of acts expressed by such a way of life.

The combination of self-control and the ability to withstand external pressures explains the references in the fragment to "philosophy." The deeds of the Jew "have a certain wonder and philosophy." These two characteristics are virtues (*aretai*): *sōphrosynē* is one of the four cardinal virtues, and *karteria* is one prominent aspect of another cardinal virtue, courage (*andreia*); *karteria* itself appears in Aristotle's extended list of virtues (*EN* 1221a9).[63] The Jews are defined by Clearchus as "philosophers" (*Ap.* 1. 179). Therefore, the Jew's way of life, exemplifying as it does both *karteria* and *sōphrosynē*, realizes ethical ideals. Ethics is one of the main pursuits of Hellenistic philosophy. For this reason, then, the deeds of the Jew are said to have "a certain [...] philosophy" (*Ap.* 1. 177).

C. The Jews, the Kalanoi, and the Virtues

The conclusion that *karteria* and *sōphrosynē* are the characteristics of the "wonderful deeds" of the Jew is supported by an examination of the "Indian connection" emphasized in the fragment. The meaning of *sōphrosynē* in this context as "self-control" is also made clearer by this examination.

"Aristotle" in the fragment makes a strange double statement to the effect that the Jews are descendants of the Indian philosophers and that they are called Kalanoi (*Ap.* 1. 179). How Clearchus (or rather his sources) arrived at a connection between the Jews and the Indians is a question to be considered later.[64] Here I shall concentrate on the purpose of the link made between the Jews and the Kalanoi. What led Clearchus to apply this name, which never actually existed, to the Indian philosophers, and what did he think about it? Why did he choose to link the Jews with the Kalanoi when there were so many real groups, sects, castes,

---

63. See also the reference to καρτερία among the characteristics of the "morally good" (*spoudaioi*)—*Nicomachean Ethics* 1145b8. For the definition of *karteria*, see *Nicomachean Ethics* 1150a32; 1221a9. Aristotle defines *karteria* at first as "the opposite of the soft and refined" and later establishes that it is the middle way between *trypherotēs* and *kakopatheia*, all to do with the reaction to emotions concerning temptation and danger, such as pleasure and pain, where the cause of temptation or danger is external. At one extreme, *trypherotēs* is capitulation to every such emotion; at the other extreme, *kakopatheia* is complete insensitivity to any such emotion. The mean, *karteria*, is the possession of one who feels all these emotions and yet struggles and does not give in to them. In this he differs from the *enkratēs*—one who, while aware of the emotions, is serene and has no internal conflict (*EN* 1150b1 ff.). See further below, note 107.

64. See below, pp. 82–84.

and subcastes to choose from? In other words, what is the significance of of the link between the Jews and the Kalanoi?

Kalanos was an Indian ascetic sophist who had gained a great reputation in the Hellenistic world. He was one of those people the Greeks called *gymnosophistai* (naked philosophers; the word "sophist" here having a positive sense).[65] Kalanos appears in the historiography of the reign of Alexander and in ethnographies on India as the person who accompanied Alexander from India back to Persis. Of all the legends and rumors surrounding this man, the most famous was the (real) story of his death. Common to all versions of this story is the report that when the man became ill, for the first time in his life, at the age of seventy-two, he decided to have himself burned to death. He faced his death joyously in front of a great audience comprising Alexander and his troops, climbed onto the pyre, and thenceforth made no movement, not even when he was engulfed by flames.[66] The only other gymnosophist named is Mandamis or Dandamis, described in some of the sources as the wisest of the Indians, and older and more consistent in his way of life than Kalanos, especially in that he refused to join Alexander's expedition back west, staying instead in his own country with his Indian disciples.[67]

In our passage, the name Kalanos has been turned by Clearchus into an epithet for all the Indian philosophers, and now appears in the plural. Such an occurrence is elsewhere unknown in the literature of the Hellenistic-Roman period.[68] Clearchus himself had been in Bactria, in the immediate vicinity of India and had perhaps visited the country. He was aware of the peculiarity of the gymnosophists, of whom Kalanos was but a single individual. In a minute fragment from his work *On Education,* preserved in Diogenes Laertius (1. 9), Clearchus says: "The *gymnosophistai* are descendants of the Magi." The Magi were known as "the philosophers among the Persians."[69] The use of the name Kalanos to designate the Indian philosophers was therefore not accidental. The aim would have been to emphasize all the more strongly the peculiar characteristics of the gymnosophists, singled out by Greeks mainly for their *karteria.* Aristobulus of

65. On the term and its development, see Karttunen (1997) 56.

66. The main sources are Strabo 15. 1. 61 (Aristobulus), 64 (Onesicritus), 66 (Nearchus), 68 (various sources, and Megasthenes); Diodorus 17. 107; Arrian *Anabasis* 7. 2–4, 18 (Megasthenes); Plutarch *Alexander* 64–65 (Onesicritus); Cicero *Tusculanae disputationes* 2. 52; *De divinatione* 1. 47; Athenaeus 10. 437; Aelian *Varia historia* 2. 41; 5. 6; Curtius Rufus 8. 9. 32.

67. Strabo 15. 1. 65; Arrian *Anabasis* 7. 1–2, 5.

68. The *Suda,* in the entry "Kalanos," states: Κάλανος, Ἰνδός, ἐκ τῶν Βραχμάνων. οὕτω δὲ πάντα σοφὸν οἱ Ἰνδοί προσαγορεύουσιν ("Kalanos, Indian, of the Brachmans. Thus do the Indians call every sage"). That is, Indians call every sage a Brahman, not a Kalanos, as the lax formulation might seem to indicate. Whatever the case may be, the tenth-century Byzantine lexicon could well have drawn on Clearchus.

69. E.g., Diogenes Laertius 1. 1; Clement *Stromateis* 1. 15 (71. 4); Cicero *De divinatione* 1. 47.

Cassandreia, a maintenance man close to Alexander, says that the "sophists" who met Alexander in Taxila (Takṣaśilā in the Punjab) taught him a lesson in *karteria* (Strabo 15. 1. 61; cf. Arr. *Anab.* 7. 2. 2), and Onesicritus the Cretan, a "Cynic" sailor who also participated in Alexander's campaign, reports that the king heard that the gymnosophists devoted themselves to *karteria,* and for this reason wished to meet with them (Strabo 15. 1. 63). The acts of *karteria* performed by the gymnosophists were often related in the literature of the time of Alexander and the Successors, and in later authors using these texts as their source; but the reader gets the impression that Kalanos surpassed everyone in realizing this virtue. This impression is reinforced, for example, by Philo of Alexandria, who is here drawing upon his sources:

> Kalanos was an Indian by birth, of the *gymnosophistai.* This man was considered of all his contemporaries the most able in *karteria* (καρτερικώτατος), and was admired not only by his countrymen but also by members of other peoples, and what is most rare, by hostile kings, because he combined good deeds with praise-worthy words. (*Quod omnis probus liber sit* 93)

Philo is not expressing his own impression of what he has read, but is reporting the appreciation of his predecessors. This may be concluded at the very least from what comes after this passage, a (fictitious) letter allegedly sent by Kalanos to Alexander. The letter is not known from any other source, but Philo did not usually invent letters of this sort.

Karteria, then, is the most peculiar characteristic of the gymnosophists, and Kalanos was regarded as the most outstanding of all of them in this respect. The image of Kalanos was established by his dramatic self-immolation in Alexander's camp in the presence of all the army and attendants. This act was recorded for posterity in great detail by various authors, some of whom were eyewitnesses. The modern reader, too, while browsing through the various fragments of Alexander's authors and of contemporary and later ethnographers, is particularly impressed by this act and the ornamental ceremony accompanying it in the sources, such as the procession Alexander organized in honor of Kalanos on that occasion, the magnificent chariot in which Kalanos lay at the top of the pyre, and the fanfare of trumpets accompanying his burning. The image of Kalanos and his acts of *karteria* were deeply engraved on historical memory. The account of his self-immolation, while itself not exactly in accord with Greek taste, drew attention to his other deeds and turned him of all people into a model for *karteria* in its most prominent form.

The portrayal of the Jews as "philosophers" originating from the Kalanoi is also connected with *sōphrosynē,* the second characteristic attributed to them by "Aristotle"-Clearchus. On which, most relevant is the account of Onesicritus on his first meeting with Kalanos. Onesicritus found Kalanos lying on stones in the blazing sun and told him that he had been sent by Alexander to hear from him the wisdom of the Indians. Kalanos burst out laughing at the external appearance of Onesicritus, dressed as he was in an army overcoat, broad-rimmed hat, and army boots, and then told him the following myth:

> In ancient times, all things were full of barley meal and wheat meal, just as now [they are full of] dust; and springs flowed, some with water, others with milk and similarly with honey, some with wine, and certain ones with olive oil; but by plenty and self-indulgence, men fell into arrogance (*hybris*). Zeus, hating the situation, destroyed all things and assigned a life through labor. When *sōphrosynē* and the rest of virtue[70] came into the middle (= became common), there was again an abundance of good things. But the state of affairs is now already near to satiety (insolence?) and arrogance, and a destruction of the things that are is in danger of happening. (preserved in Strabo 15. 1. 64)[71]

The context clearly shows that *sōphrosynē* is self-control, especially concerning food and drink, but also with regard to luxuries. Of all the virtues, only *sōphrosynē* is mentioned explicitly as the one that returned to the world its natural abundance. Onesicritus goes on to say that Mandamis (Dandamis), described as the oldest and wisest of the Indians, asked Alexander to use his position and royal authority to persuade people to acquire *sōphrosynē*—self-control (πειθεῖν σωφρονεῖν). The acts attributed to Kalanos himself in the same passage fall under the category of *karteria*.

Kalanos embodies the ideals of *sōphrosynē* and *karteria*. The unique statement in the testimonium, therefore, that the Jew excelled in *karteria* and *sōphrosynē*, does not stand alone. It is necessarily connected with Clearchus's other unique statements, that Indian philosophers were called Kalanoi, and that the Jews were descended from the Kalanoi. The *karteria* and *sōphrosynē* of the Jew and his wonderful deeds demonstrating these qualities must therefore be understood (and identified) in the light of the customary deeds of the alleged ancestors of the Jews, the Indian Kalanoi. This elucidation will be of use later in this discussion, when we attempt a more precise identification of the "wonderful deeds" (pp. 75–80).

D. Clearchus on the Life of Luxury and Self-Indulgence (Tryphē)

The above conclusion raises the question of Clearchus's interest in such matters. What place did *karteria* and *sōphrosynē* occupy in his writings in general? The answer will provide greater insight into "the Indian connection" that Clearchus

---

70. The expression τῆς ἄλλης ἀρετῆς means "the rest of virtue" (= all the other virtues, which, together with *sōphrosynē*, comprise virtue in general), and not "the other virtue," as if there were only one other virtue in addition to *sōphrosynē*. See, e.g., Aristotle *EN* 1178a9.

71. On the source of the myth, see below, p. 72 and note 94.

attributes to the Jews, and more important, it may enhance our understanding of his aims in attributing these virtues to the Jews.

An examination of the fragments and testimonia on Clearchus's great work *Lifestyles* (*Bioi*) shows that *sōphrosynē* held an important—if not the most important—place in his scale of values in that work. All the material that has been preserved from this work—a quarter of all the fragments of Clearchus—is devoted to a condemnation of *tryphē,* a life of luxury and self-indulgence, particularly an overindulgence in the pleasures of food and drink, all of which constitutes the opposite of *sōphrosynē. Tryphē* is presented as the cause of disaster and destruction, while *sōphrosynē* is offered as a recipe for long life.

All but three of the passages that have survived from this work of Clearchus have come down to us in Athenaeus, the Alexandrian author-excerptor of the second century C.E., as have passages from Clearchus's other works expressing condemnation of the life of luxury (such as his *Gergithios*). Athenaeus's work, the *Deipnosophistai* (*The Learned at Table*), includes many passages on indulging the pleasures of eating and drinking. That almost all the material from the *Bioi* of Clearchus, and not a little from his other works, survived thanks to Athenaeus might incline one to doubt that Clearchus's condemnation of *tryphē* held a central place in his ethical doctrines. Clearchus, however, was not the only one to attack the life of luxury, and his sentiments matched those of other contemporary mainstream authors writing about events of the time. It should be noted that Athenaeus is quite reliable in transmitting his sources and tended to copy them verbatim.[72]

We have twenty-seven fragments from the *Bioi.* The work included a great deal of material on the ways of life of peoples, tribes, cities, kings, political and military leaders, and philosophers. Works with the same title were also written by some of the other early Peripatetics—Theophrastus, Dicaearchus, and Strato of Lampsacus. It was thus an accepted genre in the time of Clearchus, in which thinkers could express their opinions on ethical matters, and in the manner of pupils of Aristotle, particularly by means of practical examples rather than remaining on the theoretical level.

Clearchus describes in the passages that have survived from this work the *tryphē* of various bodies and personalities, and the disasters it brought upon them. Among the peoples mentioned are the Medes, the Persians, the Lydians, the Sicilians, and even the Scythians; among the cities—Miletus, Samos, Colophon, and Tarentum; among the personalities—Dionysius the Younger, tyrant of Sicily; Darius III; Sardanapalus; and the philosopher Anaxarchus. The list of deeds exemplifying *tryphē* is quite varied, including constant gluttony and drinking

---

72. See Brunt (1980) 480–82.

and public indecency (partly forced); the wearing of women's clothes, cosmetics, and wigs by men; and the total removal of body hair. In addition, there is a detailed list of strange acts connected with eating, such as the prior chewing of food by servants, wrapping the tongue in a membrane, and other acts of extreme fastidiousness. To exemplify the wealth of descriptions, three passages preserved in Athenaeus follow. The first describes the way of life of the inhabitants of Tarentum in southern Italy:

> Clearchus says in the fourth [book] of his *Lifestyles* that the inhabitants of Tarentum, having acquired strength and power, advanced to such a great degree of luxury (*tryphē*) that they smoothed the whole of their skin and preceded everyone else in this depilation. He says that they all wore a transparent bordered robe on which [kinds of] things the "way of life" (= fashion) of women now gives itself airs. Later, led by self-indulgence into arrogance (*hybris*), they made a ruin of Karbina, a city of the Iapygoi, gathering out of it children and maidens and women in their prime into the temples of the inhabitants of Karbina, and making an exhibition, they presented the naked bodies to everyone for a day to look at. And anyone who wanted could jump as if into an unfortunate herd and feast with his desires on the blooming youth of the assembled. . . . The divine power (*to daimonion*) was so upset that it blasted all those of the inhabitants of Tarentum who offended in Karbina. (12. 522d-e)

In the second passage, Clearchus describes the behavior of the philosopher Anaxarchus of Abdera (the teacher of Pyrrho the Skeptic), who accompanied Alexander on his campaign:

> About Anaxarchus, Clearchus of Soli in the fifth [book] of his *Lifestyles* writes thus: To Anaxarchus, called *eudaimonikos* (one who regards happiness as the chief good), there fell wealth through the ignorance of his contributors, and his wine was poured by a naked girl nearing puberty, chosen for being superior to the others in beauty, thereby exposing (lit. "drawing toward the truth") the lack of self-control of those using her in this way. The baker kneaded the dough while wearing gloves and a muzzle about his mouth, so that neither would sweat drip nor would the kneader breathe on the lumps of dough. (12. 548a-b)

Athenaeus adduces another exposé by Clearchus of a similar type:

> Clearchus in the fifth [book] of his *Lifestyles* says that Sagaris of the Mariandynoi out of luxury was fed all the way to old age from the mouth of his nurse so as not to exert himself with chewing, and never extended his hand lower than his navel. (12. 530c)

Clearchus repeatedly calls all these practices *tryphē* and regards them as central factors in the decline and fall accomplished either by divine intervention or by human action. Thus at the end of his account of the love of luxury and self-indulgence evinced by Dionysius, son of Dionysius, the tyrant of Syracuse, he says:

We must beware what is called *tryphē,* being an upsetter of lives, and *hybris* †[. . .]
to be considered destructive† of all. (12. 541e)

Lack of self-restraint as a cause of arrogance and destruction we have seen above
in the myth related by Kalanos as told by Onesicritus (Strabo 15. 1. 68). Against the
life of luxury and pleasure Clearchus sets the way of life of Gorgias of Leontini,
the fifth-fourth century rhetor-sophist, who reached a very advanced age without
losing his mental faculties:

> For by how much better than these [was] Gorgias of Leontini, about whom the
> same Clearchus says in the eighth [book] of his *Lifestyles* that through living in a
> self-controlled manner (τὸ σωφρόνως ζῆν—a life of *sōphrosynē*) he lived about 110
> years with his wits about him. And when someone asked him what his regime was
> that allowed him to live for so long so harmoniously and with perception, he said:
> "Never having done anything for the sake of pleasure." (Ath. 12. 548c)

Gorgias's regime (*diaita*) is portrayed as refraining completely from pleasures.
His *sōphrosynē* is self-restraint, the opposite of *tryphē,* the life of luxury.

The motif of *tryphē* as the cause of the degeneration and weakening of individuals, cities, nations, and empires, and consequently of their decline and fall, is
not the invention of Clearchus. It is, in fact, one of the two or three main themes
of the myth of the Ages of Man, the written versions of which begin with Hesiod.
The promotion of a life of simplicity was attributed to Pythagoras by his admirers
(e.g., Diod. 10. 5; Justin 20. 4. 2–10), as was the view that pleasures and excessive desires were the greatest evil in human life, leading to personal destruction
(Iambl. *VP* 77–78; cf. 41–42). Along the same lines, Herodotus had expressed the
opinion that a pampered life of luxury undermines the ability to resist and to
fight (1. 155; 6. 11; 9. 122). There are also places in Plato where "Socrates" expresses
very similar opinions (e.g., *Resp.* 4. 422a). Antisthenes, who flourished in the
first half of the fourth century, and was wrongly regarded later as the father of
the Cynics, was vehemently opposed to the pleasures of the individual,[73] as of
course were the real Cynics. In the second half of the same century there were
others who attacked the self-indulgence of some societies and regarded it as the
reason for the sharp changes in fortune of certain cities and kingdoms. The most
prominent of these critics was Theopompus of Chios, who flourished in the third
quarter of the fourth century.[74] He influenced in one way or another his younger
contemporaries, Timaeus of Tauromenium, and, to a lesser degree, Duris of
Samos (both died around 260), and Phylarchus (died around 200).[75]

Returning to the Peripatetics, Aristotle himself does not discuss *tryphē* as the

---

73. See the fragments in de Cleva Caizzi (1966): nos. 29a, 34, 37a-b, 108.
74. On *tryphē* in Theopompus, see Flower (1994) 67 ff., 150–52, 191, 202–3.
75. See Flower (1994) 166–67; Brown (1958) 44 ff.

reason for degeneration and destruction, and only in one place, referring to the inhabitants of Miletus, does he say that exhaustion and decline were caused by surfeit and self-indulgence.[76] Aristotle's rejection of a life of self-indulgence, however, is a logical outcome of his notion of virtue as the middle way. It is known that two third-century Peripatetic authors wrote works titled *On Ancient Tryphē* (περὶ παλαιᾶς τρυφῆς).[77] Little information concerning the contents of these works has reached us, but judging from the material preserved from Clearchus and other contemporary authors, the main object of interest would have been peoples and cities that declined from former greatness because of overindulgence in a life of luxury. Preaching a life of simplicity was also an objective of a work called *Lifestyle of Greece* (Βίος Ἑλλάδος) by Dicaearchus, one of Aristotle's foremost pupils (unlike Clearchus). This at least appears to be the case from a long testimonium/fragment describing the simple life of "the Golden Age" (preserved in Porph. *Abst.* 4. 2), and from another testimonium contrasting the *tryphē* of the Persians with the simple life of the early Greeks (Ath. 13. 557b).[78] Theophrastus, too, in his work *On Good Cultic Practice*, regards *tryphē* as one of the sick evils of man, clearly referring to his own time (in Porph. *Abst.* 2. 60. 1).

The widespread use of the *tryphē* motif in the second half of the fourth century was a result of events of the time. Greek contemporaries witnessed two impressive developments following the rise of Macedon: Philip II's conquest of the Greek cities, and then the glorious campaign of Alexander deep into the Persian Empire. This was the first time that the Greeks experienced for themselves the consequences of the appearance of a new empire and the collapse of the previous world power. They were naturally occupied with the reasons for these cycles in world hegemony. Theopompus attempted to explain in his *Philippics* what facilitated Philip's domination of the Greeks and other peoples.[79] Clearchus in his *Lifestyles* indirectly explained what led to the collapse of the Persian Empire. Among other things, he elaborated on the life of luxury of the Medes and the kings of Persia, and especially of Darius III, the last of the Achaemenids.[80]

---

76. See Rose (1886) fr. 557.

77. One of these works has been attributed to Aristippus of Cyrene, a contemporary of Socrates and an advocate of a life of pleasure (Diog. Laert. 1. 96); but it was composed by a Peripatetic author in the middle of the third century b.c.e. The second work is the that of Hieronymus of Rhodes. On this, see von Wilamowitz-Moellendorff (1881) 48–54.

78. On the Βίος Ἑλλάδος of Dicaearchus, see Wehrli (1944) 56–64; Schütrumpf (2001) 255–77. On the fragment/testimonium in Porphyry: Saunders (2001) 241–49.

79. Flower (1994) 71–130.

80. See Athenaeus 12. 514d (the Medes); 529d (the Persians); 539b (Darius III). References to Persian luxury already appear in Aeschylus, not, however, as a direct reason for military defeats, but rather for the gods' anger at their hybris—the Persians used silver and gold utensils, which the Athenians believed should be granted only to the gods. See Shefton (1972) 148–49.

These descriptions, and similar accounts by Clearchus on cities, peoples, and other kingdoms, were also intended to serve as a warning about the future. As has been suggested, Clearchus traveled to the new settlements in Bactria in order to promulgate Greek wisdom, and he may well have toured other clusters of Greco-Macedonian settlement. For this reason he was able to sense more than other Peripatetics who had remained at home the risks inherent in the economic prosperity and subsequent life of luxury of Greeks in the East: the conquering class, a minority in the population, acquiring its new high standard of living at the expense of the natives, was liable to sink and degenerate into a life of luxury, while forever on guard against potentially disastrous internal uprisings. As someone who wandered thousands of kilometers to remind the Greeks in the Far East of the fundamental principles of man at the various stages of life, Clearchus regarded it as his duty to warn the Greeks of the peril facing all the Greek settlements. We cannot know whether he was already expressing such sentiments in Bactria, or whether they crystallized only upon his return home. The inscription he left in Bactria has not been fully preserved. Only a few extremely general ancient sayings having to do with the life of the individual remain.

It is worth adding that the motif reappeared in the second century B.C.E. when historians attempted to explain the extinction of the Hellenistic kingdoms. Polybius began the trend, which acquired a notably satirical edge in the *Histories* of Posidonius of Apamea.[81] Later on, it was applied by Livy, Sallust, and others in their sharp criticism of the licentiousness toward the end of the Republican period, which they identified as a reason for the decline of the Roman Republic. There is no need to demonstrate here the recurring use of the motif, in all its possible variations, in literature of the Roman Principate.

Thus in his account of the *sōphrosynē* of the Jews Clearchus delivered a relevant and timely message to all the conquerors and settlers in the East; but this was not Clearchus's only message.

E. Real Karteria: Between Clearchus and the Cynics

Clearchus's opinion about *karteria* has reached us indirectly through his criticism of contemporary Cynics. In order to examine this criticism properly, it should be noted at the outset that many aspects of Cynicism relevant to the discussion are disputed: especially the identity of the first Cynics and the connections between them; the stages of development of the Cynic "ideology" and practice; and the Cynic way of life. Testimonia give conflicting reports, and it is impossible to reach a final conclusion on any of these matters. The traditional picture of a Cynic succession (*diadochē*) has Antisthenes (445–360 B.C.E.) as the

81. See below, pp. 422–31.

father of the "school," which he bequeathed to Diogenes of Sinope (403–321), who in turn passed it on to Crates of Thebes (365–285), who gave it to Zeno of Citium, the founder of Stoicism (335?–263?). It is clear today that this is a late and artificial construction.[82] At the same time, it can be accepted that when Clearchus wrote his book there were already not a few men who were called Cynics, who followed Crates, and who regarded Diogenes' way of life (in reality and in legend) as a role model. It is possible that already at that time Antisthenes was referred to as the founder of this "school of thought."[83]

Since the Cynics were not a "school" in our modern sense of the word and were not students receiving a systematic doctrine from their master, differences of expression in words and deeds were considerable, and not infrequently a Cynic's lifestyle would go to the extreme. It should be allowed, however, that some of the deeds attributed to Cynics may have been no more than figments of their opponents' imagination, and that other instances reported in later literature are no more than reflections of developments characterizing the unrestrained Cynics of the Roman period.

Whatever the case may be, it is clear that *karteria* was a fundamental element in the Cynic way of life from its beginnings.[84] Clearchus reacted to this directly in his work *On Education*, where he addresses the Cynics: "You do not lead a life of *karteria*, and in reality you lead the life of a dog" (in Ath. 13. 611b).[85] Later in the same passage (b–c), Clearchus lists the qualities of a dog and concludes that the Cynics have adopted only the negative ones and added further negative qualities that are the opposite of a dog's positive features. He emphasizes their aloofness from human society, their provocative and hostile behavior, their life on the streets, lacking any purpose or direction, their wantonness and the contempt in which they are held by everyone. Clearchus adds that they eat anything they can get their hands on, and bolt down their food just like a dog. He concludes:

> By reason of all these things you are alien to virtue, and useless with regard to anything useful in life. For there is nothing more unphilosophical than [you self-] styled philosophers. (611d)[86]

82. On the last point, see Mansfeld (1986) 295–382, reprinted in Mansfeld (1990) 343–428.

83. On these issues, see esp. von Fritz (1926); Dudley (1937); Sayre (1937), (1948); Höistad (1948); Pagnet (1975) 29–119; Niehues-Pröbsting (1979); Bracht Branham and Goulet-Cazé (1996) 1–135, 414–15.

84. See, e.g., Diogenes Laertius 6. 2, 15, 23; cf. Cicero *De oratore* 3. 60; Epictetus 1. 24. 8; 3. 22. 58, 24. 64.

85. οὐ καρτερικὸν βίον ἀσκεῖτε, κυνικὸν δὲ τῷ ὄντι ζῆτε.

86. The following sentences—ἐξ ὧν ἁπάντων ἀλλότριοι μὲν ἀρετῆς μάταιοι δὲ <ἐστέ> εἰς τὸ τοῦ βίου χρήσιμον. οὐδὲν γάρ ἐστι τῶν καλουμένων φιλοσόφων ἀφιλοσοφώτερον—were omitted by Wehrli from his collection of fragments of Clearchus (Wehrli [1948] fr. 16), apparently upon the assumption that these were an addition by Athenaeus with reference to all the philosophers in

As mentioned above, *karteria* is a Socratic ideal and one of the Aristotelian virtues. Clearchus's attack on the attribution of *karteria* to the Cynic way of life stems from the vast difference between the assumptions and principles of the Peripatetics and those of the Cynics, and the perceived threat to stable society posed by the Cynic way of life. The Cynics claimed that the life of the polis was opposed to nature. Anyone attempting to live according to nature, according to them, had to remove himself from society. Accordingly, the Cynics cut themselves off from society, contributed nothing to it, mocked and challenged all social conventions and institutions, lived wherever they wished, performed a variety of sexual acts and other bodily functions in public, although such acts were considered obscene, offended and insulted other people, ate like dogs, praised cannibalism, let their hair and beard grow wild, and wandered around in filthy, worn-out rags. For Aristotle, however, *karteria* and its fellow virtues are not opposed to the social order. Indeed, they are virtues that require the existence of a community for their fulfillment. One cannot, for example, manifest justice and magnanimity without social interaction. Aristotle's very definition of man as a "political animal," an animal that lives in a polis, shows that he regards the life of the polis as expressing, rather than oppressing, the nature of man. For Aristotle, then, the Cynic position is opposed to human nature and the virtuous life.

The eating habits of the Cynics were far from expressing *sōphrosynē* as understood by the Peripatetics. The Cynics were indeed opposed to luxuries and sophisticated food, but our sources describe them as eating anything they happened to come across, without restraint or moderation. Clearchus describes them as bolting their food in the manner of dogs. A later example of this is Cynulcus, an imaginary Cynic character participating in Athenaeus's *Deipnosophistai*: in contrast to the other participants, he is impatient with the various speeches delivered during the meal and demands to receive his food at once (4. 156b). The same Cynulcus delivers several fierce speeches against *tryphē* (esp. 15. 687a). Athenaeus (4. 156b-d) also mentions a work called *The Symposium of the Cynics* by Permaniscus of Metapontum, a grammaticus of the second century B.C.E. In the Cynics' "symposium," an unlimited amount of food is served, and the participants are filled to bursting; but the food is simple and crude—lentil soup. The difference between the Cynics and those who indulge in *tryphē* in the matter of food and drink, therefore, concerns only table manners and the quality and variety of food. This has nothing to do with real *sōphrosynē*, certainly not as

---

the context of his discussion (cf. Wehrli's commentary, 50). There seems to be no justification for this omission, however. The sentences sound like an inseparable part of Clearchus's comments on the Cynics.

Clearchus sees it. We shall see below further evidence that the Cynics attributed to themselves *sōphrosynē* in matters of food and drink.

Beyond the ideological dispute there were personal motivations at work: the Cynics used to mock philosophers for their involvement in the life of the polis, particularly offending the Peripatetics, who were always ready to advise kings and write laws. Hence the strong words of Clearchus quoted above. The enmity between Clearchus and the Cynics would also have stemmed from their different attitudes toward Plato, whom Clearchus greatly admired. Antisthenes was already expressing hostile sentiments against Plato, likening him to the male organ (σάθων), and attacking him in a dialogue bearing the same epithet (Diog. Laert. 3. 35; Ath. 5. 220d; 11. 507a). Even if in Clearchus's generation, Antisthenes was still not regarded as the father of the Cynics, Diogenes of Sinope was certainly described as such. Many of the barbs of Diogenes against Plato, together with Plato's own negative remarks about Diogenes, are to be found among the many anecdotes and sayings littering the biography of Diogenes of Sinope in Diogenes Laertius (6. 7, 24–26, 40, 41, 53, 58).[87] We have no way of knowing how many of Diogenes' followers personally abused Clearchus himself during the course of his life and literary activity.

Let us return now to *karteria* and its appearance as a characteristic of the Jew who spoke with Aristotle. *Karteria* is an ethical-philosophical ideal, a virtue whose exact character is debated by Clearchus. In his view, the Cynic model is unacceptable. That is not *karteria* at all. The Jew who met Aristotle, however, more than met Clearchus's expectations for *karteria*. His way of life served as a role model for this virtue. Would it be going too far to suggest that Clearchus's praise of the Jew's *karteria* is in fact a (disguised) continuation of his debate with the Cynics?

This is particularly plausible in light of the connection Clearchus makes between the Jews and the Indian Kalanoi, a link that parallels the attempt made by his contemporary, Onesicritus, to demonstrate a similarity between the Cynics and the Indian sages in his praise of *karteria* and *sōphrosynē*. Onesicritus, a native of the tiny island of Astypalaea in the southern Cyclades, a sailor and author described as a Cynic, took part in Alexander's campaign—at least in its later stages—and served as a "chief navigator" during the advance downstream into India. He also participated in the journey led by Nearchus from the mouth of the Indus along the coast of the Indian Ocean and the Persian Gulf up to the Tigris.[88]

87. For a collection of Plato's alleged comments against Diogenes and Antisthenes, and theirs against him, see Riginos (1976) 98–101, 111–18, 147–49.

88. On Onesicritus, see Fisch (1937) 129–43; Strassburger, "Onesikritos," *RE* 18 (1939) cols. 460–67; Pearson (1960) 83–111; Brunt (1983) 446–47; Pédech (1984) 71–90; and esp. Brown (1949). See also the books and articles mentioned below, notes 91–95.

Activity of this sort does not suit someone who has adopted a Cynic way of life, and the information (attributed to Onesicritus himself) that he was a "pupil" of Diogenes (e.g., Diog. Laert. 6. 34; Strabo 15. 1, 65) is doubtful. For this reason it is supposed that he was an admirer of Diogenes and that his writing, but not his lifestyle, was influenced by the Cynics. His work *How Alexander was Raised* (πῶς Ἀλέξανδρος ἤχθη)—written along the lines of Xenophon's *Cyropaedeia*—was known in the classical period to be unreliable and full of imaginary and amazing stories. It included descriptions of Indian philosophers, their wisdom and their way of life, introduced in the context of actual or fictitious meetings between them and Alexander or his emissaries. There is a striking similarity between many of the opinions and customs attributed by Onesicritus on these occasions to the Indian philosophers—especially concerning *karteria*—and those of the Cynics (see esp. Strabo 15. 1. 63–65; and note the emphatic mention of Diogenes of Sinope in that context, 1. 65; and Arr. *Anab.* 7. 2. 6). For this reason it has been assumed that Onesicritus deliberately described the Indian sages in Cynic guise as a way of bestowing upon the Cynic lifestyle prestige and a glorious antiquity.[89] It does indeed seem likely that he also made explicit in his work a link, real or imaginary, between the opinions and behavior of the Indian philosophers and those of the Cynics. At the same time, Onesicritus must have concealed entirely the antisocial characteristics of the Cynics, particularly their disrespect for others, and the provocative nature of their speech and actions, all completely at odds with the "respectful" way of life of the Indian gymnosophists.[90]

89. Sayre (1948) 40–41; Brown (1949) 4–7, 41, 49, and elsewhere. The approach of these two scholars has been widely accepted and adopted without much modification. For a more detailed account using this approach, see Hansen (1965).

90. On the positive attitude of the gymnosophists toward society, see, e.g., Strabo 15. 1. 59, 64, following Megasthenes and Aristobulus. Descriptions of the Indian gymnosophists appearing in the Greek sources generally fit the "normative" Hindu ascetics—those who enjoyed state funding and provided in return various social services. It is quite likely that these are the people of Alexander's army and other travelers would have met. There were, however, other ascetics (the Aghorīs and the Gorakhnāthīs) among the worshippers of the god Śiva, the Destroyer of Worlds, whose behavior was similar in its antisocial aspects to that of the Cynics (albeit for different reasons). They tried to imitate Śiva in various ways: they lived in disposal grounds for the ashes of the dead or in rubbish heaps; they avoided physical contact with other humans; their external appearance was repulsive; they even used dogs (considered an unclean animal) as companions. Onesicritus did not mention them, judging by the lack of references in surviving sources based upon Onesicritus, Strabo chief among them. It is interesting that Sayre (1937) and those after him who claim an Indian origin for the Cynics (esp. with regard to the way of life of Diogenes), and who are obliged to offer rather forced evidence, are unaware of the groups of ascetics of the god Śiva and other similar groups. Their special relation to dogs, at the very least, should have raised the suspicion of a possible origin for the appellation "Cynic" (although the similarity is most likely purely coincidental). At the same time, it must be said that there is no evidence for Śiva worship, properly speaking, in the fourth century B.C.E. On the ascetics of Śiva, see, e.g., Gonda (1970) 43 ff.; Cross (1979); Hartsuiker (1993).

The tendency to attribute to the Indian gymnosophists some of the characteristics of the Cynics, occasionally mitigated somewhat, and to bestow upon
the Cynics roots or at least parallels in an ancient culture, is also discernible in a
papyrus acquired in Cairo in 1930 and attracting detailed discussion from 1959
onward.[91] This long papyrus contains a number of Cynic diatribes. The first of
these (cols. I–VIII) describes a discussion between Dandamis, the Indian sophist,
and Alexander. Dandamis speaks harshly to the Macedonian king in the Cynic
manner and is highly critical of the moral and social faults of the Greeks. He
advocates a "natural" ascetic life (including vegetarianism) as the remedy for all
of society's ills. The papyrus is dated to the middle of the second century c.e.,
yet it contains material deriving from much earlier sources. This first diatribe
is almost certainly derived from the literature of the early Diadochic period, or
soon after it.[92]

At this point it is worth returning to the passage from Onesicritus (Strabo
15. 1. 64), in which Kalanos narrates the myth of the world cycle of want and
plenty caused by the tendency of humans to live a life of luxury and abandon
sōphrosynē.[93] This myth, as reported by Onesicritus, is an *interpretatio Graeca* of
a well-known Indian myth.[94] In none of the versions of the original myth is there
a term parallel to *sōphrosynē*, and the acts of humans in the age of decline cannot
be described as the opposite of *sōphrosynē*. There is instead a general reference
to an abandoning of the "law" and the existing norms. Since Onesicritus colors
the views and habits of Kalanos in Cynic tones (with all the necessary "improve-

91. The first publications: Martin (1959) 77–115; Photiadès (1959) 116–39.

92. See esp. Hansen (1965) 351–66. On later Christian reworkings, see Hansen, 366 ff., and
Derrett (1960) 64–135.

93. See the text above, p. 62.

94. Various scholars speculate that this myth is Greek-Cynic. See esp. Brown (1949) 41. However, it originates in a celebrated Indian myth. The myth tells of the four or five ages that together
comprise the cosmological cycle of the worlds, with decline occurring from age to age. The variation of the myth reported by Onesicritus-Strabo refers to the second age, the Age of Tretā. The first
age, the Age of Kṛta, was superior to all the succeeding ages in that there was no need of food at
that time. Food became necessary only in the second age, but at least it was abundant. The food
supplies declined during the third and fourth ages, forcing humans to work hard just to survive.
The general decline is ascribed to a gradual drop in respect for, and reliance upon, "the law." In
the third and fourth ages, this development leads to an addiction among the unlearned masses to
luxuries. The cycle ends in a cosmic catastrophe, after which a new cycle begins, and so on forever.
On earlier versions of the myth concerning the second age, see Śatapatha Brāhmaṇa 13. 6. 2, 9–10;
Mahābhārata 3. 188. 9–13; Manu Smṛti 1. 83, 85–86. Later, more detailed versions vary considerably
among themselves. The dating of these versions is rather obscure. However, it is agreed that the first
formulation of the Śatapatha Brāhmaṇa is of the seventh–sixth centuries b.c.e., while the earliest
parts of the Mahābhārata (whichever they may be) are from the early fourth century b.c.e. The same
is true for the Manu Smṛti. See Dimock (1978) 14–20; van Buitenen (1978) XXIII–XXV; Brockington
(1988) 26–27.

ments" this entails), we may conclude from his version of the myth (while ignoring other aspects of the Cynics' gastronomic habits) that contemporary Cynics regarded their abstention from luxuries in food and drink as an expression of *sōphrosynē*.

We do not have direct evidence that Clearchus knew Onesicritus's work or any part of it; but it is chronologically possible. Clearchus's work *On Sleep* was written near the end of the fourth century. The date of publication of Onesicritus's work is disputed. While some have dated it to no later than 310,[95] it has been suggested that the first books of the work could have appeared shortly after Alexander's death, and the fourth book may have appeared only around 305.[96] Whatever the case may be, the work was out before Clearchus wrote *On Sleep*. Since Clearchus went to Bactria, he would have been particularly interested in any Greek work on India and Alexander's travels in that region. It is, therefore, quite probable that Clearchus was aware of the direct or indirect comparisons made by Onesicritus between the Indian sages (especially Kalanos) and the Cynics.

In his treatise *On Education,* which contained the polemics against the Cynics (Ath. 13. 611b-d), Clearchus expressed the view that the Indian gymnosophists originated from the Magi (Diog. Laert. 1. 9). The book may well have described the way of life of the "Indian philosophers" in the context of a survey of different forms of *paideia*. It is not impossible that in this treatise he also hinted at, or even explicitly referred to, the attempts of Onesicritus and others to find a link between the lifestyle of the Indians and that of the Cynics.

• • •

To conclude, we have seen above that Clearchus states that the Jews originate from the Indian philosophers whom he falsely calls Kalanoi. He presents as an exemplary model the Jew with his prominent characteristics *karteria* and *sōphrosynē*, both also characteristics of the Indian gymnosophists, and especially of Kalanos. We have also seen that Clearchus explicitly condemns the Cynic conception of *karteria* as false and similarly dismisses their whole system of virtue. All this when his contemporary Onesicritus has recently (indirectly) praised Cynic *karteria,* and *sōphrosynē,* attributing their origin to the Indian gymnosophists. In light of all of the above, it appears probable that the Jew with his prominent features *karteria* and *sōphrosynē* is portrayed in relative detail, not only to act as a foil to the luxurious way of life of Clearchus's contemporaries, but also in order to serve as an indirect reply to the explicit or implicit comparison made by contemporaries between the Cynics and the gymnosophists. The example of the

95. F. Jacoby, *RE* s.v. "Kleitarchos (2)," cols. 652–53; id., *FGrH* II. D. no. 134, p. 468; Strassburger, *RE*, col. 466 (see note 88 above); Pearson (1960) 85.

96. Brown (1949) 4–7.

Jew allows the reader to see how gymnosophists really behave, since the Jews are descended from the Kalanoi. The wonderful deeds of the Jew exemplify *karteria* and *sōphrosynē* in the Indian style. They are by no means antisocial acts, and in fact the Jew contributes to society in his own way. He respects his interlocutors and humans in general, and he in turn earns their respect. The positive social aspect is emphasized by the fact that the Jew is used to associating with learned Greeks, including Aristotle and his pupils so hated by the Cynics.

Clearchus is not alone in availing himself of an imaginary Indian character through which to express opinions in a debate between rival Greek philosophical groups or schools of thought. Aristoxenus of Tarentum, the *mousikos*, a contemporary of Clearchus and himself a pupil of Aristotle, was antagonistic, if not downright hostile, toward Socrates. He relates an alleged encounter between Socrates and an Indian sage.[97] The Indian mocks Socrates for engaging only in the study of human life and tells him that no one can understand the affairs of men without understanding the affairs of the divine. This order of priorities reflects the Aristotelian conception, which stands in marked contrast to the Socratic tradition. Socrates is attributed with saying that instead of studying the divine, where certainty is impossible in any case, man would do better to discuss human affairs (Xen. *Mem.* 1. 12–16). Platonic writings also reflect the Socratic tradition in this respect, apart from the *Timaeus,* where the speaker is not Socrates but Timaeus. Plato has his Socrates explain in the *Phaedo* when and why he abandoned entirely his interest in nature, a subject that greatly occupied the pre-Socratics (the *physikoi*), and devoted his full attention to human affairs (*Phd.* 95e ff.). Aristotle, however, not only returned to the subject of nature, but also stressed that this study is necessarily prior to understanding the soul of man (*De An.* 402a ff.). Aristoxenus is thus supporting his master, Aristotle, by attacking in this way Socrates' preoccupation with human affairs and his disengagement from matters of nature and the divine.

The use of a fictitious external character was an acceptable device in polemics of the period and in the controversies between the philosophers. This practice resembles, to some extent, the tendency of authors at the beginning of the Hellenistic period to provide descriptions of imaginary peoples, or imaginary descriptions of real peoples, as ideal philosophical models (e.g., *Aegyptiaca* and *On the Hyperboreans* of Hecataeus, the Indian ethnography by Megasthenes,

---

97. Out of the book *Vita Socratis,* quoted by Eusebius *Praeparatio evangelica* 11. 3. 8 (= Wehrli [1948] fr. 53): φησὶ δ᾽ Ἀριστόξενος ὁ μουσικὸς Ἰνδῶν εἶναι τὸν λόγον τοῦτον. Ἀθήνησι γὰρ ἐντυχεῖν Σωκράτει τῶν ἀνδρῶν ἐκείνων ἕνα τινά, κἄπειτα αὐτοῦ πυνθάνεσθαι, τί ποιῶν φιλοσοφοίη. τοῦ δ᾽ εἰπόντος ὅτι ζητῶν περὶ τοῦ ἀνθρωπίνου βίου, καταγελάσαι τὸν Ἰνδόν, λέγοντα μὴ δύνασθαί τινα τὰ ἀνθρώπινα κατιδεῖν ἀγνοοῦντά γε τὰ θεῖα. On the apocryphal character of this story, see Karttunen (1989) 111. On Aristoxenus's attitude toward Socrates, see Wehrli (1945) frr. 51–60.

Sacred Scripture by Euhemerus, and many other works by other authors). The most outstanding work of this type on the Jews, namely, the Jewish ethnography by Posidonius of Apamea, preserved in Strabo's *Geographica* (16. 2. 35–37), was written much later.[98]

Why was a Jew of all people chosen by Clearchus to exemplify the true characteristics of the gymnosophists? A meeting between Aristotle and a Jew in western Asia Minor at the end of the classical age would have been considered plausible by Clearchus's intended audience, a generation after Aristotle, and much more credible than a meeting between Aristotle and an Indian gymnosophist, certainly more than the meeting described by Aristoxenus between Socrates and the Indian sage. Indians, with the exception of auxiliary troops who only occasionally served with the Persian forces in the campaigns against the Greeks (Hdt. 7. 86), reached the Mediterranean basin only later during the Hellenistic period, and not as philosophers, but as mahouts. Jews, on the other hand, were in evidence in Asia Minor already at the end of the classical age, and their permeation throughout the Greek-speaking world increased after the conquests of Alexander.

F. *The Wonderful Deeds and Their Omission by Josephus*

Now that we have considered the meaning of *karteria* and *sōphrosynē*, the virtues Clearchus attributes to the Jews, and his possible motives for doing so, we may try to identify the "wonderful deeds" that Josephus omitted from his testimony. I shall begin with a close examination of an interesting and widely held theory first advanced by Hans Lewy.[99]

Lewy made the link between Aristotle's remark in the fragment about "wonderful things equal to dreams" and the account of the hypnotist in Proclus (n. 49 above); at the same time, taking into consideration the references in the testimonium to the *karteria* and *sōphrosynē* of that same Jew, he suggested separating the wonderful things hinted at in the fragment from the deeds hinted at in the testimonium.[100] Continuing this line of thought, Lewy attempted to find in a passage in Olympiodorus some specific deeds of the type Clearchus must have been referring to, in his opinion, in the testimonium. Olympiodorus, a Christian Neoplatonist of the second half of the third century C.E. and a resident of Alexandria, wrote commentaries on several Platonic and Aristotelian works. In two places in his commentary on *Phaedo*, Olympiodorus relates a story about two wonderful men whom Aristotle met in person. This is what he reports:

---

98. On which see chapter 11, pp. 355–98.

99. Lewy (1938) 222–28.

100. Lewy translates the relevant sentence in the testimonium as follows: "the great and miraculous endurance of the Jewish man in diet and temperament." However, the Greek word *diaita*, that appears in Proclus, means not diet but a way of life in general (diet = *diaitēma*).

That the whole human race should be nourished in this way is made clear by (the case of) the man who was nourished in this way, from the rays of the sun only. Aristotle told about him, having himself seen him. . . . Then Aristotle told about a man both sleepless and nourished by the sunlike air alone. [101]

Olympiodorus does not reveal his source for Aristotle's account. The names and origins of the wonderful men are not reported, but it is clear that in the original account their role was to demonstrate that a human being could dispense with customarily essential bodily requirements and yet remain alive thanks to the separate existence of the soul. For this reason, it is usually assumed that the stories were taken from the young Aristotle's dialogue *Eudemus,* which has not been preserved. In this dialogue, the separation of body and soul was emphasized, a notion that the older Aristotle no longer held. However, Jacob Bernays suggested that the source might be Clearchus's dialogue *On Sleep,* where Aristotle was portrayed as the main speaker. Bernays further suggested emending Olympiodorus' text to read ἄπνουν (breathless = lacking life) instead of ἄϋπον (sleepless).[102] According to this suggestion, Clearchus would have portrayed Aristotle reporting that he had seen a man remaining a long time without any signs of life, nourished apparently from nothing but the sun's rays, who eventually returned to life. Bernays regarded the account as similar in message to the story of the hypnotist in Proclus-Clearchus, both proving in a somewhat similar way the separate existence of the soul.

Lewy accepted Bernays's suggestion in general, but not Bernays's emendation:[103] Aristotle saw a man who survived a very long time without sleep and without food. This feat would have sufficed to demonstrate great stamina. The man in question would have been the Jew whom Aristotle met and conversed with. The qualities of the man were summed up by Josephus, without going into details, as a wonderful feat revealing *karteria.*

Why Olympiodorus failed to mention the man's Jewish origin still needs to be explained. This omission is curious given the strenuous efforts of Christian authors to find evidence for admiration of the Jews expressed by classical authors. Furthermore, if Bernays's emendation is accepted, the man's apparent lifelessness would have nothing to do with either *karteria* or *sōphrosynē* and would certainly

---

101. ὅτι δὲ δεῖ τι καὶ ὅλον γένος ἀνθρώπων εἶναι οὕτω τρεφόμενον, δηλοῖ καὶ ὁ τῇδε ταῖς ἡλιακαῖς ἀκτῖσι μόναις τρεφόμενος, ὃν ἱστόρησεν Ἀριστοτέλης ἰδὼν αὐτός . . . εἰ ἐνταῦθα ἱστόρη-σεν Ἀριστοτέλης ἄνθρωπον ἄυπνον καὶ μόνῳ τῷ ἡλιοειδεῖ τρεφόμενον ἀέρι. See Norwin (1913) 200, ll. 3–6, and 239, ll. 19–21.

102. Bernays (1866) 187, no. 37.

103. Lewy (1938) 225 n. 90. Olympiodorus sets down what he concludes from the case prior to the testimonium, and it indicates that the account concerned not a man "lacking life," but a man "lacking sleep."

not fit the Jew who conversed with Aristotle. If, on the other hand, we agree with Lewy in rejecting Bernays's emendation, the man's abstention from sleep, food, and drink for years on end would also have little to do with *sōphrosynē*. It would be an extreme form of behavior rarely practiced, according to Aristotle's own statement on the matter, and for this reason it lacks a proper term to describe it (*NE* 1107b7–11; 1118b15–20; 1119a6–12). The same may be said about complete and long-term abstention from sleep. The very identification of Clearchus as the source for Olympiodorus is only a guess and has not been accepted by editors.[104] It may equally well be speculated that the source is any one of a whole string of Peripatetic works on sleep, the soul, or other topics, related or not. As mentioned above, it is usually assumed that Olympiodorus drew on Aristotle's *Eudemus*.

To get some idea of the "wonderful deeds" omitted by Josephus, the results of the investigations on the following topics need to be combined: (1) the comparison of the fragment with the testimonium; (2) the meaning of *karteria* and *sōphrosynē* in Greek philosophy; (3) the curious statement about the descent of the Jews from the Kalanoi; (4) the characteristics of the Kalanoi and the Indian gymnosophists by and large in Greek historiography and literature; (5) the ideals and values of Clearchus himself and his part in the "wars of the philosophers." Thus the "wonderful deeds" seem to have been of the sort attributed to the Indian gymnosophists, and which could demonstrate *sōphrosynē* and *karteria,* the abilities to withstand internal and external pressure respectively.

Among the wonderful deeds illustrating *karteria* that were attributed in Hellenistic literature to Indian "sophists" we find lying and sleeping upon rocks come rain or shine, lying upon hot sand, or even floating in midair; standing, sitting, or lying motionless for an extensive period; eating only while standing; standing on one leg for a whole day while holding a heavy log (changing legs only once).[105] In ancient Indian literature there are dozens of examples of various types, such as fasting continuously for twelve days; abstaining from sleep for twelve days in a row; standing on one leg or holding one hand raised for twelve years; obtaining nourishment from milk alone for a number of years, or from one sesame seed a day for a number of months; living in a dark cave without leaving it for years; meditating while sitting in a frozen river (in winter) or surrounded by a circle of fire (in summer); standing erect, barefooted and motionless, for a num-

---

104. The passage was included in the collection of Aristotelian fragments by Rose (1886) 47, fr. 42. Wehrli chose not to include it with the fragments of Clearchus, although he was well aware of Bernays's suggestion. See Wehrli (1948) 7–8.

105. Such examples in a variety of forms are scattered throughout Hellenistic and Roman literature. The greatest collection of earlier sources is to be found in Strabo 15. 1. 59–70, with explicit references, all from the Diadochic period (Aristobulus, Onesicritus, Nearchus, and Megasthenes). On floating in midair, see Philostratus *Life of Apollonius of Tyana* 3. 15. See also Aulus Gellius *Noctes Atticae* 2. 1, on people standing motionless for a day and a night with eyes fixed on one spot.

ber of days on top of an anthill; going on a pilgrimage of hundreds of kilometers, pausing every three paces to fall flat on the face in obeisance; and so on and so forth.[106] Other strange practices characterizing the Indian holy men of today (*Sādhus*) continue a tradition of thousands of years. I should just mention taking a dip in icy water, holding one hand in the air for days, and sleeping propped up against a wall.[107] All these had their variations in duration. Clearchus, who spent some time in Bactria, which bordered India, must have been acquainted with Greek writings of the time about India, and he could have selected and mitigated what he found there so as to record only more moderate Indian customs most suitable for his purposes. Since the title of his work was *On Sleep*, it would seem most likely that he described less extreme activities having to do with sleep, such as abstention from sleep for just a few days, a special asceticism concerning the place or the type of material upon which to sleep, or the sleeping position.[108]

Some of the deeds mentioned above also demonstrate in this context a degree of *sōphrosynē*, the ability to withstand internal pressure. However, since the fragment reports social meetings with learned people, it seems that this quality is

106. Such deeds are scattered throughout the two great Hindu epics, the Mahābhārata and the Rāmāyaṇa, and in the book of laws, the Manu Smṛti.

107. The reader may find a collection of, and sociological and anthropological investigations into, such strange activities in Cross (1992), a dissertation presented to the University of California, Berkeley, later published in India. See also Ghurye (1964); Tripathi (1978). For a short survey and an illustrative collection, see Hartsuiker (1993).

108. Holding up the *karteria* of the Indian philosophers rather than the fake *karteria* of the Cynics as a somewhat counter example to follow raises the question of whether the activities described do not contravene somewhat Aristotle's golden mean (see note 63 above on *karteria*) or his opinion that "pain is an evil to be avoided" (*EN* 1153b1–5). However, we do not know whether Clearchus fully accepted Aristotle's ethical principles, since no theoretical discussion by him on these subjects has come down to us. The Peripatetics, as opposed to the Epicureans, did not treat their master's doctrines as sacred. Just as Theophrastus often diverged from Aristotelian principles, so could have Clearchus, particularly if he met Indian gymnosophists on his travels. We have already seen that he preferred Plato's opinion (or at least an opinion attributed to Plato) to Aristotle's on the major question of the separation of the soul from the body. Certain traits and deeds attributed to Socrates in Plato's *Symposium* bear a mild resemblance to those mentioned above: an ability to enjoy wine without becoming intoxicated, wearing just a simple cloak (ἱμάτιον) and walking barefoot even in deepest winter, going without sleep and standing for a whole day while puzzling out a problem, and so on (*Symp.* 219e5 ff.—the speaker is Alcibiades). This characterization of Socrates was well known to Peripatetics of Clearchus's generation, and he could have served them, as he served others, as the model of a sage. The gymnosophists obviously have completely different explanations for their actions, but these are irrelevant to the present discussion; Greek travelers and authors would naturally have given their own interpretations to what they saw. As for pain, the activity can be presented not as an end in itself, but as a form of exercise to promote the ability of soul and body to withstand external pressures that may come to all men. Furthermore, the realization of *karteria*, a virtue, is itself a good that outweighs the concomitant evil of pain (cf., e.g., the case of a boxer who is prepared to suffer pain for the promise of fame—*EN* 1117b3–9).

treated as pertaining to eating and drinking: certain social events combined philosophical discussion with a meal, where it was customary to eat and drink to excess. The Jew would have eaten moderately, just to satisfy his minimal bodily requirements, while also observing certain strict table manners, as is expected of a good Brahman.[109] Perhaps Clearchus had reported how the Jew was satisfied with just an olive a day, or with milk or strange herbs, in the way of Indian ascetics. This would not exactly correspond with Aristotelian *sōphrosynē,* but neither is it complete abstention. Furthermore, we do not know where Clearchus, a pupil of Aristotle, placed the limits of *sōphrosynē.*

Whatever the exact identity of the wonderful deeds, such *karteria* and *sōphrosynē* are not Jewish features, and certainly not the sort of things that a Greek author at the beginning of the Hellenistic period could observe in practice. Parallels drawn either from later Jewish sages advocating the need for self-restraint in food and drink or from accounts of Jewish martyrology (which occurred later, in any case),[110] are hardly relevant to the issue. Clearchus attributed to the Jews features that were known to him as particularly characteristic of the Indian gymnosophists, the most famous of whom was Kalanos.

Considering the drift of everything said above, we can understand why Josephus thought it better not to include a detailed account of the deeds of *karteria* and *sōphrosynē:* he must have sensed that these examples were drawn from another culture, and that the model was not of a Jew but of one of the Indian Kalanoi. Various references in the works of Josephus show that he was reasonably well read on the inhabitants, customs, and beliefs of India.[111] Such descriptions would not have contributed to the image Josephus was trying to present of the Jews. They would certainly not have furthered his main purpose of proving that Greek authors knew Jews and met them; a knowledgeable, intelligent reader would have realized that these examples only prove the opposite. Such considerations may have been at the back of his mind when Josephus wrote at the end of the episode: "I have taken care not to add more than is necessary" (*Ap.* 1. 182), presumably a slip of the pen, not surprising for a rather negligent historian.

109. Given the mediocre quality of knowledge the Greeks had about the Indians, the suggestion is not affected by the fact that in India one refrains from eating while talking philosophy; or that Indian "table manners" have much more to do with purity than with *sōphrosynē.* These customs appear in various versions in the law books of the Brahmans. See, e.g., the Apāstamba (1. 6. 18. 4), apparently from the fourth century B.C.E., where there also appear strict instructions pertaining to "table manners" (1. 6. 17–18): location, participants, body posture, purification, defilement of the dead, the acquisition and preparation of foods (and limiting the time), a complex "hand-washing" ritual, guttural hygiene, the way to chew, and so on and so forth.

110. Suggested by Lewy (1938) 214–15.

111. Esp. *Bellum Judaicum* 7. 351–57; *Contra Apionem* 2. 144; and cf. *Antiquitates Judaicae* 1. 38, 147.

This reconstruction of the contents and purposes of the account may be concluded with a consideration of its context in the treatise *On Sleep*. I would surmise that Aristotle was mentioning principles concerning one problem or another arising from the phenomenon of sleep (not necessarily the question of the separation of body and soul, from which discussion came the episode surviving in Proclus). He may have prefaced his remarks with some general comments praising the gymnosophists or Kalanoi, then mentioning his meeting with one of their descendants, a Jew, and given an eyewitness account of characteristic wonderful deeds relevant to the topic in question. Since the meeting was social, he would have mentioned not only the Jew's marvelous abilities regarding sleep, but also his wonderful eating habits, thereby underlining the Jew's virtues of *karteria* and *sōphrosynē*, which were so characteristic of the Kalanoi. Aristotle's enthusiastic eyewitness account of these features gave validity and authority to the opinion of Clearchus on three subjects: (1) matters of sleep; (2) the life of *tryphē* adopted by his Greek contemporaries occupying the East; (3) the Cynics' claim that their way of life realizes genuine *karteria* and *sōphrosynē*, and their supporters' claim that they are related to the Indian gymnosophists.

CLEARCHUS AND THE JEWS—
SOURCES OF INFORMATION

Although the original passage in which Clearchus described the meeting between the Jew and Aristotle was quite long relative to other references to Jews in surviving Hellenistic and Roman literature (excluding ethnographic excursuses), his real information about the Jews is scant in the extreme. All that he knows is that they reside in Judaea, that their city is Jerusalem, and that they are singled out from the other ethnic groups in Syria (without knowing actual details).

In contrast to these snatches of real information, Clearchus states that the Jews originate from the Indians, and that their position as philosophers among the Syrians is similar to that of the Kalanoi among the Indians. He further elaborated on their unusual ability and great willingness to withstand external and internal pressures of the type associated with the Indian gymnosophists. The Hellenistic name "Hierosolyma" for Jerusalem is unknown to him, and he makes no mention of the Jewish monotheistic religion or the Jews' abstention from any material representation of the divine. It is a matter of speculation whether he had heard about these things or not. On the one hand, his statement that the Jews are the descendants of Indian philosophers might indicate that he knew nothing substantial about the Jewish cult or Jewish beliefs. With all the knowledge about India that he acquired at least in Bactria, Clearchus must surely have known about the polytheistic nature of the religion of the Brahmans and about their great variety of religious statues. On the other hand, the same Clearchus states that the gymnosophists are descended from the Magi (Diog. Laert. 1. 8), although the Magi, according to our many testimonia, refrained from making images and believed in dualism (e.g., Diog. Laert. 1. 6). On this argument, then, it is impossible to decide whether Clearchus knew anything of substance about the Jews' basic religion.

How did Clearchus come to claim that the Jews are a community[112] of philosophers, originating in India, and holding the same position among the Syrians as that of the Kalanoi in India? What is the connection between all this and the descriptions and other references pertaining to the Jews that have reached us from the period of the Successors? The notion that the Jews constitute a community of Syrian philosopher-priests is first encountered in Theophrastus. It appeared in his work *On Good Cultic Practice,* which was written between 319 and 315 B.C.E.,[113] and it is probably based on a widespread rumor.[114] Clearchus, a pupil of Aristotle, must have been aware of this work by Theophrastus, Aristotle's heir to the Peripatetic school, all the more so since it conveyed a practical significance for the members of the school; it was written as a philosophical-anthropological defense against the charge of *asebeia*—disrespect toward the gods—for which Theophrastus was standing trial in Athens. Clearchus at the time of the trial was still a young man, probably in his twenties, and the Indian features in his work suggest that he wrote *On Sleep* only after his return from the Far East. A reasonable amount of time between the death of Aristotle in 322 and the composition of this work is required not only because of the story of the fictional meeting between Aristotle and the Jew but all the more so because Clearchus attributes to Aristotle the Platonic opinion that the soul can exist without a body, a view not shared by the mature Aristotle. At the same time, Clearchus's "information" to the effect that the Jews were a group of philosophers could equally well be based on popular rumor. Be that as it may, Clearchus's Jewish account is later than that of Theophrastus.

It can be determined with a high degree of certainty that Clearchus did not know the Jewish excursus by Hecataeus of Abdera (in Diod. 40. 3. 1–6). There

---

112. I have preferred to use in this context the word "community," rather than terms such as "caste," "class," "sect," "nation," each of which is problematic in its own way. Clearchus was aware that the Jews were an ethnic group concentrated in its own territory. This does not accord with any of the four (or rather five) ancient Indian social divisions, nor with the position of the gymnosphists who were outside or beyond this system and had no territory of their own. Terminological confusion prevails in the writings of Greek authors (even those who stayed in India) attempting to define the various Indian castes, sects, and groups (see Karttunen [1997] 55–64, 82–87). The vague *meros* ("part"; e.g., Strabo 15. 1. 39, 40) was the Greek substitute for the Sanskrit *varṇa*. Confusion by outsiders is only to be expected, and Clearchus was no exception.

113. See p. 15 note 1 and pp. 30–34 above.

114. On the background to the creation of the rumor, see above, pp. 34–36.

is nothing in his account that depends on Hecataeus. Clearchus includes none of the relatively detailed report on the Jewish faith and Jewish customs to be found in Hecataeus,[115] and Clearchus's statement about the strangeness of the name Hierousalem (Joseph. *Ap.* 1. 179) should be contrasted with Hecataeus's reference to the settlement of the Jews in Hierosolyma (Diod. 40. 3. 3), a name no longer alien to Greek ears.[116] Hecataeus inserted his Jewish ethnography as an excursus within his great work on Egypt, written between 305 and 302 B.C.E.[117] The position of Hecataeus in the Egyptian court and the topical aims of his work would most probably have ensured fair circulation among Greek intellectuals soon after its publication, as appears from the significant influence it had on the writings of Megasthenes, Hecataeus's contemporary, who lived far from Alexandria. Clearchus, therefore, seems to have written his work in the last decade of the fourth century or close to it.

THE DESCENT OF THE JEWS

How did Clearchus arrive at the strange link between the Jews and the Indians? It has been speculated that he was influenced by Megasthenes' reference to the Jews (Clem. *Strom.* 1. 15 [72. 5]).[118] Envoy of Seleucus I to the court of the Indian king, Chandragupta, Megasthenes wrote a comprehensive ethnographical work on India and its peoples, presumably in the nineties of the third century.[119] Even allowing for the chronological difficulty, however, it is hard to see how Megasthenes' reference could have been a source of information for Clearchus. There is nothing in it to suggest that the Jews originated from the Indians, nor that they had similar views. Indeed, the phrasing of Megasthenes even indicates that the theological opinions of the Jews differ from those of the Brahmans.[120] Moreover, Megasthenes elsewhere described Kalanos as "lacking self-restraint"

115. There is no connection between the Jewish *karteria* in Clearchus and that in Hecataeus of Abdera (Diod. 40. 3. 6). The latter is referring only to fighting ability, in the context of his description of Moses' military preparation of the younger generation.

116. The similarity between -salem and the name Solymi elicited the form Solyma and a later legend about the descent of the Jews from the Solymi (Manetho in Joseph. *Ap.* 1. 248; Tac. *Hist.* 5. 2. 5). The Lycian Solymi are mentioned in Homer (*Il.* 6. 184, 204), but they had disappeared by the classical age. References to them are to be found mainly in the works of the grammarians writing commentaries on Homer, in etymologies, or in accounts of origins of the sort mentioned. The name Hierosolyma first appears in Hecataeus and was probably invented by him, in line with his tendency to give his material Greek connotations to make it more easily digestible.

117. See Bar-Kochva (1996d) 15–16.

118. Jaeger (1938a) 132 n. 14; (1938b) 141–42; Lewy (1938) 220; (1960) 27–28; Hengel (1979) 467; Conzelmann (1981) 56; Karttunen (1997) 99; but see Stern (1976) 1110–11. See also note 4 above.

119. On the date of composition, see pp. 141–42 below.

120. See below, pp. 156–58. This was the only reference to the Jews in the work of Megasthenes.

(ἀκόλαστος, ἀκρατής), since he joined Alexander's entourage and was for this reason sharply criticized by the Indian "sophists" (in Arr. *Anab.* 7. 2. 4; Strabo 15. 1. 68). The description of the Jew in Clearchus, however, emphasizes self-control. Megasthenes is even explicitly critical of Kalanos's voluntary self-immolation (Strabo 15. 1. 68).[121] Since Clearchus uses Kalanos as a general name for a group noted for Kalanos's qualities, it appears that his main source of information about India praised Kalanos unreservedly as the very essence of an Indian philosopher. This was how Kalanos was described, for instance, by Onesicritus (see Strabo 15. 1. 63–65), and probably also by Nearchus, the commander of Onesicritus.

It only remains to repeat the suggestion already raised in the past, that the attribution of Indian descent to the Jews was inspired by the similarity between the names Indoi and Ioudaioi.[122] Thus the descent of the Jews was explained by a practice well known in Greek and Roman literature, namely, that of identifying genealogical links and origins of peoples simply on the basis of a similarity—real or imagined—between the names of peoples, individuals, countries, and also geographical features, social structures, customs, and beliefs.[123] At the same time, a genealogical link between the two groups was explicitly suggested by the rumor mentioned by Clearchus himself, that "the gymnosophists are descendants of the Magi," combined with a second contemporary rumor, that "the Jews originate from the Magi" (both rumors appear consecutively in Diog. Laert. 1. 9).[124]

I would not rule out the possibility that the creation of the genealogical link was aided by some vague and general rumor about the Jewish abstention from

---

121. On Megasthenes' position regarding the self-immolation of Kalanos, see Brown (1960) 133–35; Hansen (1965) 359–60; Karttunen (1997) 62, 63.

122. So, e.g., Feldman (1993) 463 n. 1.

123. See note 116 above on the connection between the Jews, Jerusalem, and the Solymi; cf. also Tacitus *Historiae* 5. 2. 5, suggesting that the Jews originate in Crete (based on the similarity between Judaea and [Mt.] Ida). For the rumor about the common ancestry of the Jews and the Spartans, based probably on their exclusiveness, see 1 Maccabees 12.7, 21; 2 Maccabees 5.9; Josephus *Antiquitates Judaicae* 12. 225–27. For the motives behind the invention of common ancestries in Greco-Roman literature, see the detailed bibliography in Isaac (2004) 110 n. 197.

124. Κλέαρχος δὲ ὁ Σολεὺς ἐν τῷ Περὶ παιδείας καὶ τοὺς Γυμνοσοφιστὰς ἀπογόνους εἶναι τῶν Μάγων φησίν. ἔνιοι δὲ καὶ τοὺς Ἰουδαίους ἐκ τούτων εἶναι ("Clearchus of Soli in his work *On Education* says that the [Indian] gymnosophists are descendants of the Magi. Some [say] that the Jews too originate from them"). As appears from the formulation in this context, the intermediate source for the remark on the Jews is not Clearchus (*contra* Robert [1968] 451). It was taken from a source dating from the end of the classical period and the beginning of the Hellenistic period. This is suggested by the references to the sources in the detailed description of the Magi and the other groups of priest-"philosophers" woven into Diogenes Laertius's introduction. The Jews and the Magi had one outstanding common feature: consistent abstention from any depiction of the divinity, be it in sculpture or painting (e.g., Hdt. 1. 131; Diog. Laert. 1. 6). The Greco-Macedonian conquerors who came to Judaea could not but notice the absence of statues.

certain foods (a naturally prominent feature of Jews in their first meetings with Greeks, indicated, if not explicitly mentioned, by Theophrastus[125]), which would have brought to mind the various codes of dietary restraints and original customs of Indian priests and groups of ascetics.[126] Notably, the geographical distance imposed no obstacle, nor would there have been a difficulty with the tradition (as perhaps explicitly reported by Theophrastus) that the Jews originated in Egypt. The Ethiopians, for example, were usually presented alongside the Indians and the Egyptians as exemplifying an autochthonous nation, but they were also occasionally portrayed as originating from India (Philostr. *VA* 3. 2). Hellenistic ethnography went wild in genealogical matters. Josephus was aware of this but in the given context had no reason to argue with Clearchus.

The link between the Jews and India was not invented by Clearchus but was a rumor that he picked up and exploited to his own ends. He states that the name Ioudaioi originates with the land Ioudaia. As for the Indian connection, Clearchus is responsible for the invention of the Kalanoi, a group that never existed, named after the Indian whom Greeks most identified with steadfastness and self-control. It is this fictitious Indian group whom Clearchus equates with the Jews in order to use them as a model for true *karteria* and *sōphrosynē*, contrasting them with the Cynic way of life, on the one hand, and decadent hedonism, on the other.

. . .

The apocryphal episode about a meeting between Aristotle and the Jewish sage contributes nothing of substance to our knowledge of the Jews in the Diadochic period, save for the confirmation that Greeks outside Egypt knew very little about them. The account is valuable because it sheds light on the priorities of an author who belonged to the first generation of the Peripatetics, his concern for social and moral problems and values, and his stance in the "war of the philosophers." In this, Clearchus was no different from other contemporary writers. Hellenistic literature is replete with imaginary information on people bearing little correspondence to the facts, designed to exemplify philosophical ideas and the like. Certainly, this episode in no way indicates Greek assent to the notion of any superiority of Jewish or Oriental wisdom to that of the Greeks.

125. See p. 24 above.

126. On the dietary restrictions of the Brahmans, see, e.g., the long and varied list in the fifth chapter of the book of laws, Manu Smṛti (55–56). Here are just a few examples: garlic, onions, and mushrooms; cow's milk ten days after calving, sheep's milk, milk of wild beasts; dishes of corn mixed with butter, milk, and sugar, if they are not sacrificed to the gods (and likewise dishes of a certain rice); meat of animals with uncloven hoof (!); all birds of prey, all fish-eating birds; almost all types of fish and choice meat in general (meat is allowed only as part of a sacrifice). On "table manners," see above, note 109.

EXCURSUS: JOSEPHUS'S DIRECT SOURCE FOR
CLEARCHUS'S PASSAGE ON THE JEWS

Throughout the discussion in this chapter of the wonderful deeds of the Jew described by Clearchus, I work on the assumption that Josephus was directly acquainted with Clearchus's book *On Sleep*. Two prominent scholars have speculated that Josephus was not directly acquainted with this work but availed himself of an anthology on Jews or other subjects.[127] The patchiness of the report could then be attributed not to Josephus but to the excerptor-editor of the collection.

Neither possibility, an anthology on Jewish subjects or a general anthology on subjects and personalities, conforms with what Josephus himself says. Concluding his compressed testimony, Josephus says that anyone who wants to know more about the issues discussed can peruse Clearchus's book. Josephus even explains that he refrained from citing more than was necessary in order to prove that the Jews were known to, and even admired by, the greatest of the Greek thinkers and authors. A similar reference is to be found in Josephus concerning only one other passage, out of the many passages he adduces from other authors (passages occasionally gleaned from intermediate sources). This reference is found at the conclusion of the passage in which he adduces a fragment and testimonia from *On the Jews*, which was attributed to Hecataeus of Abdera (*Ap.* 1. 205). In this instance, there is no reason to doubt that Josephus had the whole work in front of him. It would not be surprising that Josephus managed to locate a passage on the Jews in the work of a prolific but fairly unimportant author such as Clearchus. Just as he used assistants in the writing of *Bellum Judaicum* (*Ap.* 1. 50), so he must have used assistants later on for locating references to the Jews in Greek literature.[128]

---

127. See Guttmann 1: 97; Stern, *GLAJJ* 1: 47–48.

128. However, it is worth noting the article by Luz (1982), which may seem to entertain the view that Clearchus was an immediate source for Josephus. Luz tries to prove that the second speech attributed to Eleazar, the commander of the zealots in Massada (Joseph. *BJ* 7. 341–88), is partly based on Clearchus's *On Sleep*. I, however, find it difficult to accept his arguments. As other scholars have already demonstrated, what is written about sleep in that speech (*BJ* 7. 349–50) is identical to what Posidonius writes about dream prophecy (ap. Cic. *Div.* 1. 63, 64, 115, 129–30). The actual (if partial) parallels Luz adduces for the subject of sleep are from Aristotle's dialogue *On Philosophy*, and Luz only speculates that these points were also expressed in Clearchus's *On Sleep*. Furthermore, it might be asked why Josephus or his assistants could not then have taken these points directly from Aristotle, whose works were far more widespread. When Josephus wrote the *Bellum Judaicum*, the Aristotelian "acroamatic" corpus that we know today had been in circulation (after having been rediscovered) for some 150 years, alongside the more popular "exoteric" writings, now lost. Finally, the contrast in the speech between the attitude of the Indians regarding death and the fear of death evinced by the zealots of Massada bears no similarity to the comparison made by Clearchus between the Jews and the Kalanoi. Why

The only proof offered for the use of an intermediate source is Josephus's comment in his introduction to the passage, in which he describes Clearchus as "second to none among the philosophers of the Peripatos" (*Ap.* 1. 176). Clearchus is similarly presented by Athenaeus as "second to none of the pupils of Aristotle the wise" (15. 701c).[129] Athenaeus wrote his voluminous work *Deipnosophistai* some 130 years after Josephus's *Contra Apionem*. The work, essentially a compilation of quotes from various authors, never mentions Josephus, although Athenaeus could find ample material for his purposes in Josephus's works. As it may well be that Athenaeus availed himself of anthologies in the compilation of his work,[130] one could conclude that both Athenaeus and Josephus took their estimation of Clearchus from an anthology that contained quotations from his works or from an anthology devoted to a certain topic. However, the anthologies known to us from the classical world were devoted to subjects, not authors; and if there were anthologies on authors, we might suppose that they would have been devoted to authors of the stature of Plato rather than Clearchus. As for the second possibility, the passage in Josephus is taken from *On Sleep*, while Athenaeus quotes from "sayings" (*paroimiai*) of Clearchus. There is no connection or similarity between the contents of the two passages: the meeting with the Jew in Josephus; in Athenaeus, the origin, nature, and significance of the compound exclamation ἰὴ παιών (according to the account it can be traced to a myth in which Letho warns her son Apollo to beware of a predatory animal). It is therefore unlikely that the two passages were to be found in the same thematic anthology.[131] It is

---

should Josephus have relied on Clearchus of all people for something as well known in Hellenistic and Roman literature as the Indian attitude toward death? In any case, we have no evidence that Clearchus referred to this in his work *On Sleep*, and in the speech of Eleazar no mention is made of the Kalanoi.

129. Remarked upon by Guttmann 1: 97 and n. 40*; Troiani (1977) 115; repeated by Kasher (1996) 164. Josephus writes: Κλέαρχος γὰρ ὁ Ἀριστοτέλους ὢν μαθητὴς καὶ τῶν ἐκ τοῦ περιπάτου φιλοσόφων οὐδενὸς δεύτερος; and Athenaeus: Κλέαρχος ὁ Σολεὺς οὐδενὸς ὢν δεύτερος τῶν τοῦ σοφοῦ Ἀριστοτέλους μαθητῶν.

130. Athenaeus quotes Clearchus seventy-two times, and in each case names the work cited; there are sixteen works in all. The quotations are concentrated on a small number of topics, particularly anecdotes about pleasure and luxury (*tryphē*) taken from a number of works of Clearchus. Such quotations could have been found in one or more anthologies. Thus among other topics treated in the quotations from Clearchus is suicide (4. 157c). The subject is treated, for instance, by Favorinus, the Gallic philosopher-compiler and contemporary of Hadrian, who devoted to it a chapter in his twenty-four-book anthology *Miscellaneous Inquiry* (παντοδαπὴ ἱστορία). In this work were grouped together anecdotes about famous people according to topics such as suicide, old age, the death penalty and the preceding trial, and the first person to do or invent something. Favorinus himself used previous anthologies and biographies, and later compilers of anthologies (e.g., the fifth-century John Stobaeus) used his. See Ludlam (1997) 141–44. See also the end of note 131.

131. Guttmann 1: 97 n. 40* compares Josephus referring the reader to the whole book of Clearchus ("Those who wish to can learn more out of the book itself," *Ap.* 1. 182) with Athenaeus's statement

also unlikely that the sentences derived from a biography of Clearchus (no such biography is known to us), if only because the meeting between Aristotle and the Jew has nothing to do with Clearchus himself. In any case, Clearchus was not an outstanding author of the sort who attracted biographers. Even were there a *gnomologion*—collection of opinions—of the Peripatetics of the generation after Aristotle, Clearchus would have been overshadowed by Theophrastus and other outstanding Peripatetic figures. The episode, in any case, hardly fits that genre.

It would seem, therefore, that the similar (not identical) presentations of Clearchus in Josephus and Athenaeus are purely coincidental. The expression "second to none" does not mean "first," but "of the first rank."[132] It appears only rarely in classical Greek literature (e.g., Hdt. 1. 23) but becomes quite common later, appearing hundreds of times in Hellenistic and Byzantine sources. Clearly, the expression lost much of its force over the generations, becoming more of a general commendation and no longer indicating only the first rank.[133] We cannot trace this process accurately, but the use of this expression by Josephus in another place (*AJ* 1. 11) indicates that in the present passage he intends the later meaning.[134] Josephus portrays Clearchus as a writer of the first rank in accordance with his

---

("So said Clearchus; and if, my friend, you do not believe this, since I have the book, I shall not keep it from you: from it you will learn much, and will acquire [an undiscovered treasury] of questions," 7. 276a). There is, however, no justification for seeing here traces of a common source or any influence whatsoever. Not only is the phrasing of the sentence completely different, but the passage quoted in Athenaeus is taken from *On Riddles* (περὶ γρίφων), which is concerned with the etymologies of names of holidays and so forth. Furthermore, the sentence in Athenaeus is spoken by Cynulcus, one of the fictional participants in the banquet, who on this occasion describes Clearchus only as "a pupil of Aristotle, and from Soli in origin." I would add that this declaration is still not evidence that Athenaeus used Clearchus directly; the claim to have the whole book is put in the mouth of one of his imaginary participants in a fictional symposium. The reference in Josephus is a different case. Josephus must have been aware that his polemical statements were bound to be challenged by curious, suspicious, or downright hostile readers.

132. A good example of this can be found in the comparison between Pompey and Caesar made by Dio Cassius in his Roman history: γνώμη μὲν γὰρ τοσοῦτον ἀλλήλων διέφερον ὅσον Πομπήιος μὲν οὐδενὸς ἀνθρώπων δεύτερος, Καῖσαρ δὲ καὶ πρῶτος πάντων εἶναι ἐπεθύμει ("In opinion they differed from each other to the extent that Pompey desired to be second to no man while Caesar desired to be the first of all," 41. 54)

133. On the weakening of the expression, see the examples from Athenaeus below, note 135. It appears in Polybius only six times (7. 10. 1–2; 12. 3. 3; 31. 27. 10; 32. 8. 2; twice in quotations in the *Suda*—A no. 3744, and Π no. 1295), but since only about a quarter of his *Histories* has survived, we may assume that he used it much more. Galen, the second-century C.E. physician, uses it more frequently, as do philosophers such as Alexander of Aphrodisias (second–third centuries), Themistius of Constantinople (fourth century), and John Philoponus of Alexandria (fifth century).

134. Josephus writes in the introduction to *Antiquitates* about the High Priest Eleazar, known from the *pseudo-Aristeas* as "second to none of the High Priests in *aretē*." Josephus knew very well that Eleazar's brother, Simon the Just, was the embodiment of perfection. He mentions Simon and his *aretē* explicitly in the historical exposition (*AJ* 12. 43, 157; cf. Siracides 50. 1–29), while Eleazar,

declared aim of showing that the Jews were known and admired not by the most worthless (οἱ φαυλότατοι) of the Greeks, but by "those most admired for wisdom" (*Ap.* 1. 175). In view of his declared aim, Josephus may have described Clearchus as belonging to the first rank without knowing his real status among the successors to Aristotle (and there is no reason to suppose that Josephus was an expert on such matters).

As for Athenaeus, the expression in his time was already well worn. He uses it in two other places, where it is clear that the people referred to are not the best in their profession.[135] A common and unexceptional expression in the passages from Josephus and Athenaeus thus does not prove a source common to both.

Finally, the context of the reference in Athenaeus should noted. Two of the many references to Clearchus in Athenaeus describe him as one of the Peripatetics (4. 160c; 7. 285c), and one as "a citizen of Soli, one of Aristotle's pupils" (6. 234f). That Clearchus is one of Aristotle's most prominent pupils appears only from the reference under discussion (which is the last one), in the context of a speech by one of the (fictional) participants at the meal, Democritus of Nicomedia. This character makes frequent use of superlatives and flattering epithets when introducing the authors upon whom he rests his claims,[136] even when these authors have been cited earlier by the other participants. Thus, for instance, when Democritus introduces Theopompus of Chios,[137] a degree of exaggeration is clearly discernible. This is one way in which Athenaeus attempts to put some life

---

who is also mentioned several times, is not praised, and Josephus makes do with the factual description of his cooperation in the initiative of Ptolemy Philadelphus to translate the Torah into Greek (*AJ* 12. 44–85, and 127).

135. See Athenaeus 1. 1c on Masurius Sabinus, the Julio-Claudian Roman lawyer, called ἀνὴρ καὶ κατὰ τὴν ἄλλην παιδείαν οὐδενὸς δεύτερος, which means no more than "having an excellent general education." In 9. 402c, it is said about Clitomachus of Carthage (187–110 B.C.E.): οὐδενὸς δεύτερος τῶν ἀπὸ τῆς νέας Ἀκαδημείας κατὰ τὴν θεωρίας ὤν ("being second to none of the [members] of the New Academy regarding 'theory'"). Clitomachus was certainly not in the first rank of philosophers of the "New Academy" (whether this term refers to the period from Arcesilaus to Philo of Larissa [159–84 B.C.E.], or only to the two generations between Carneades and Philo). Clitomachus was no more than the faithful pupil who recorded the lectures of Carneades (214–129 B.C.E.), not necessarily understanding every point made by Carneades, and certainly lacking his master's analytic and innovative ability (see Carneades' own estimation in Cic. *Orat.* 51; *Luc.* 78, 139). Carneades stood head and shoulders above everyone else in his generation, and, according to Cicero, he valued Charmades (and apparently Metrodorus) much more highly than Clitomachus. Athenaeus lived in a period when information on the "New Academy" was still available. His comment on Clitomachus must, therefore, be understood to mean that he was one of the best, and no more than that.

136. E.g., 3. 85a; 6. 269d; 15. 671e, 696a. On the characterization by Athenaeus of the participants in the feast, see Mengis (1920) 23–45, although he says little about the special characteristics of Democritus.

137. "A lover of truth who spared no expense for the sake of examining historical accuracy" (3. 85a).

138. There is an interesting parallel in Synesius of Cyrene, a fourth-fifth century Christian

into his characters, who are really no more than a literary device upon which to hang numerous quotations from previous periods of Greek literature. An exaggerated estimation of one pupil or another of Aristotle by later sources is not all that rare.[138] It seems therefore that Athenaeus himself added the complimentary description of Clearchus and did not take it from an older source.

The case of Theopompus raises another possible explanation for the praise bestowed upon Clearchus: this historian (c. 378–320 B.C.E.), whom many contemporary and later authors criticized for his way of writing and his unreliability, bestowed compliments upon himself in his introduction to his *Philippica* and often praised himself in other works. These enthusiastic comments were copied independently by authors and compilers as if they gave an objective appraisal of Theopompus. It may well be that Athenaeus drew upon this introduction for his inspiration when his Democritus came to praise Theopompus.[139] The *Philippica* was famous even before Alexander's death,[140] and it was known to Clearchus: Contemporary authors, possibly Clearchus, were greatly influenced by Theopompus's opinion regarding the cause of the decline and fall of individuals, cities, and countries.[141] Clearchus may also have been influenced by Theopompus in the way he wrote his own introductions, among other things, by giving himself encomia. These would have influenced both Josephus (or his assistants) and Athenaeus.

who engaged in rhetoric and philosophy. In his book on Dio Chrysostom he cites the second-third century Flavius Philostratus as naming, in a list of philosophers, Eudoxus of Cnidus, the astronomer, as "the first among Aristotle's pupils" (ἐν οἷς ἀριθμεῖ καὶ τὸν Εὔδοξον ἄνδρα τὰ πρῶτα τῶν Ἀριστοτέλους ὁμιλητῶν). See Lassere (1966) p. 9. However, the original passage of Philostratus is known to us from his book *Lives of the Sophists* (484a), in which Eudoxus appears without any accompanying description at all. In fact, Eudoxus was not a pupil of Aristotle. Synesius, therefore, added the description himself, although he had a thorough philosophical training (unlike Athenaeus). His motives are unclear. It is possible that he just wished to give a general compliment.

139. On the encomium of Theopompus in the introduction to his *Philippica*, see Flower (1994) 18–19. The relevant testimonia are Dionysius of Halicarnassus *Epistle to Pompey* 6; Strabo 1. 2. 35; Photius (see *FGrH* II. B, no. 115, f. 25 [p. 540]); and the words of Athenaeus. A parallel to Athenaeus is to be found in the *Suda*, s.v. "Theopompus." Among the writers who expressed particularly negative opinions about Theopompus, we might mention Speusippus (Plato's nephew and heir to the Academy), Duris of Samos, Phylarchus, Polybius, Cornelius Nepos, Aelian, and Lucian. See Flower (1994) 52–53, 167, 217. The value of Theopompus as a historian is still a controversial issue.

140. See Flower (1994) 32.

141. See above, p. 65.

3

The Jewish Ethnographic
Excursus by Hecataeus of Abdera

The first Greek author to leave us a relatively extensive description of the Jewish people is Hecataeus of Abdera. The description, included in an excursus worked into his monumental ethnographic work on Egypt, constituted a mini-ethnography on the Jewish people and is one of the most detailed surviving accounts on Jews and Judaism in Greek and Roman literature. Its position as the first Jewish ethnography, coupled with the fame of the Egyptian ethnography of which it was a part, and the reputation of Hecataeus as a trailblazer in the ethnographic genre, all contributed to making it a sort of vulgate on which later authors drew for information on the Jews.[1] Even later authors whose approach to Judaism differed—for better or worse—depended to a certain extent, directly or indirectly, on Hecataeus, despite the availability in their time of more detailed, up-to-date, and reliable information.

---

1. This applies especially to the explanation of Jewish exclusivity as a reaction to their expulsion from Egypt, the accusation against the Jews of a hatred toward foreigners (*misoxenia*), their *apanthrōpia* (perceived as *misanthrōpia*), and the attribution to Moses of the settlement in Judaea and the establishment of Jewish institutions and practices, and the absence of any reference to the kings of Judaea of the First Temple period. See, e.g., Diodorus 34/35. 1. 1–2; Lysimachus in Josephus *Contra Apionem* 1. 309–11; Pompeius Trogus in Justin 36. 2. 11–15; Tacitus *Historiae* 5. 3. 1, 4. 1, 5. 1–4; and the unique version of Posidonius of Apamea, preserved in Strabo 16. 2. 35–36. In contrast, there is no doubt that Josephus was unfamiliar with the excursus of Hecataeus, since he quotes nothing from it in *Contra Apionem* when he was desperate to show that Greek authors were aware of the antiquity of the Jews. The evidence he adduces refers to the Persian period at the earliest, while quoting Hecataeus would have allowed him to refer to the exile in Egypt and the occupation of the land of Judaea.

For these reasons—and especially because it was the first of its kind—
Hecataeus's excursus has also been the subject of much research, attracting far
more attention than the writings on the Jews of any other Greek or Roman author
(apart from Tacitus).[2] This said, however, there still remain a number of topics
requiring examination or reconsideration: recent challenges to the authenticity
of the excursus; the transmission of the original text; the composition of the
excursus: namely, how, and from what sources, Hecataeus collected his material
and how he worked up his information; where exactly the Jewish excursus was
located in Hecataeus's work; and to what end. To these basic subjects may be
added further issues dealing with details such as the absence of a reference to
circumcision, kosher food, and the Sabbath in the list of customs characterizing
the Jews; the unique character of Jewish sacrifice, according to Hecataeus; his
strange assertion that the Jews never had a king; and the meaning of the reference
to Jewish *apanthropia* and hatred of strangers. A consideration of these subjects
and others is required in order to answer the main question: what after all was
Hecataeus's attitude toward the Jews?

WORKS ON THE JEWS ATTRIBUTED TO HECATAEUS

More than one Jew in the ancient world attributed their own enthusiastic works
on the Jews to Hecataeus on the supposition that the reader would not detect
a forgery. These authors wished to take advantage of Hecataeus's reputation to
promote their own ideas and provide them with an air of authority. Indeed,
one work from these pseudonymous compositions has succeeded in misleading
many modern scholars: Josephus adduced in his *Contra Apionem* quotations
and paraphrases from *On the Jews*, a treatise attributed to Hecataeus, in order
to prove the antiquity of the Jews and the admiration he claimed was expressed
toward them by Greek authors (1. 183–205; 2. 43). Josephus adds that the book is
accessible (1. 205), from which we may infer that it was catalogued and kept in

2. Discussions on various aspects of the excursus may be found in Reinach (1895) 14–20; Willrich (1895) 48–51; (1900) 86–91; Radin (1915) 92–96; Meyer (1921–23) 2: 28–30; Engers (1923); Jaeger
(1938a) 143–44; (1938b) 139–41; Dornseiff (1939) 52–66; Jacoby, *RE* s.v. "Hekataios (4)," col. 2765; id.,
FGrH IIIa, no. 264, pp. 39–52; Nock (1944) 174, 179; Walton (1955); Guttmann 1: 49–66; Tcherikover
(1961) 56–59, 119–25; Denis (1970) 263–64; Murray (1970) 158–59; (1973); Gager (1972) 26–37; Hengel
(1973) 464–65 and passim; Stern (1973); id., *GLAJJ* 1: 29–35; (1976) 1105–9; Lebram (1974); Wacholder
(1974) 85–93; Diamond (1974), (1980); Momigliano (1975) 84–85; Wardy (1979) 638–39; Konzelmann
(1981) 56–58; Mendels (1983); Will and Orrieux (1986) 83–92; Bickerman (1988) 16–18; Gabba (1989)
624–29; Mélèze-Modrzejewski (1989) 6–14; Sterling (1992) 75–78; Feldman (1993) 8–9, 46, 149–50,
234–36; Schäfer (1997a) 15–17; Hansen (2000) 11–17; Schwartz (2003). The current discussion is a
much expanded and adapted version of my previous survey on the Jewish excursus in Bar-Kochva
(1996d) 18–43.

at least one public library in Rome. Neither Gentile nor even Jewish literature, however, provides unambiguous evidence that the treatise was used or read. The only quotation from it adduced by Eusebius (*PE* 9. 4. 2–9) is taken directly from Josephus. The authenticity of the book was seriously doubted by the first-second century pagan author Philo of Byblos (Origen *C. Cels.* 1. 15), but his familiarity with the work may only have been secondhand, through Josephus. Like Philo of Byblos, other authors and grammarians would surely have doubted its authenticity, since the Jews are treated there overenthusiastically, while the beliefs and customs of Gentiles are mocked and despised. Were the work widely regarded as a forgery, this would explain why it had little influence and why it was almost entirely ignored in ancient literature. Or it may have been entirely unknown, since it had been intended for a Jewish readership.

Ever since the "northern" Renaissance the question of the authenticity of the book has aroused controversy among scholars. Already at the beginning of the seventeenth century, Joseph Scaliger, one of the greatest classical scholars of all time, determined categorically that the work was a forgery. In 1730, the Hamburg scholar Peter Zorn wrote a monograph that tried hard to prove the book's authenticity. The development of classical source criticism and increasing anti-Semitism caused the negative view to prevail. The German scholar Hugo Willrich published a book in 1900 summarizing all the claims for inauthenticity raised until then, and adding still more (in his markedly anti-Jewish manner). This consensus was maintained almost universally until the thirties of the twentieth century, when Hans Lewy published his article on Hecataeus. The burgeoning of Jewish studies after the Second World War, together with the desire to remove at any price the taint of anti-Semitism frequently accompanying earlier research, brought about a gradual acceptance of the treatise *On the Jews* as authentic. Some negative voices were still to be heard: a small if distinguished minority of classical scholars.[3]

I studied the treatise in a monograph published sometime ago. Through a detailed analysis of the text I attempted to show that almost all the statements and pieces of information in the work are anachronistic or contradict reliable information at our disposal, or cannot be attributed to Hecataeus. Besides that, there is no real, positive evidence that the passages originated with Hecataeus or even in his period.

As regards the composition of the work, I suggested that the treatise was written at the end of the second century B.C.E. by an Alexandrian Jew belonging to the moderate "orthodox" stream of Egyptian Jewry, for whom it served as a kind of manifesto. Its main purpose was to legitimize and justify the continued

---

3. For bibliographical references, see Bar-Kochva (1996d) 4–6, esp. nn. 5–15.

Jewish residence in Egypt, which was actually forbidden by the Pentateuch, at a time when Judaea was an expanding independent Jewish kingdom desperately short of experienced Jewish manpower. Legitimation, as so often in such cases, was religious: the initiative for Jewish settlement in Egypt allegedly came from the highest religious authority of the nation, the High Priest in Jerusalem. This imparted authoritativeness to the move, just as the alleged role of the High Priest in Jerusalem in the translation of the Torah into Greek was intended by the author of *pseudo-Aristeas* to make the Septuagint appear legitimate and desirable. The ultimate purpose of the settlement—to aid the Jewish state—justified the initiative. Now that the Jews had taken root and had integrated into the Ptolemaic governmental system, filling senior positions in the army and administration, and playing a major role in economic life, they could and did exercise influence at court on behalf of their brethren in Judaea. One such intervention by senior Jewish army officers on behalf of the Jews in Judaea is reported (Joseph. *AJ* 13. 353–55): in the year 103/2 B.C.E., around the suggested time of the composition of *On the Jews,* Alexander Jannaeus was severely beaten by Ptolemy IX Lathyrus and watched helplessly as the Ptolemaic internal conflict between mother and rebellious son played itself out on the soil of the Holy Land. In this situation, Cleopatra III contemplated annexing Judaea to the Ptolemaic kingdom, but her Jewish supreme military commanders threatened to abandon her if she did so. Their argument carried the day; Cleopatra desisted, and the Jewish state thus spared continued to enjoy independence.[4] This was not the only instance of such intervention.

A work called *On Abraham and the Egyptians* is also wrongly attributed to Hecataeus of Abdera. Some half dozen Christian authors, beginning with Clement of Alexandria (*Strom.* 5. 14 [1. 113]), quote nine verses said to have been found in a work by Hecataeus called *On Abraham and the Egyptians*. The verses themselves were presented in that work as Sophoclean. A work bearing a similar name (*On Abraham*) and attributed to Hecataeus, presumably the same work, was already mentioned by Josephus (*AJ* 1. 159). The quoted verses express an absolute faith in only one god, who formed the universe and who administers it constantly. Furthermore, they strongly criticize and even mock the worship of idols and the public rites associated with them.

As the verses could not have been written by Sophocles, modern scholars, both classical philologists and Jewish historians, from the eighteenth century onward, have unanimously proclaimed the work a Jewish forgery.[5] This common view has recently been challenged by a leading scholar in the field of Jewish mysticism.[6]

4. See in detail Bar-Kochva (1996d) 54–142, 182–254; (2000/1). See also p. 107 and notes 50 and 51 below for further evidence for the falsification.

5. For bibliography, see Bar-Kochva (2001b) 327–28 nn. 1, 3.

6. Liebes (2000) 85, 95, 294–98.

His arguments, however, do not stand up to scrutiny.[7] The following discussion, therefore, will deal only with the Jewish excursus of Hecataeus, which comprised part of his Egyptian ethnography.

HECATAEUS OF ABDERA AND HIS WORKS

Hecataeus of Abdera appears to have served in various capacities at the court of Ptolemy I.[8] His major work and literary masterpiece was the ethnography on

---

7. See Bar-Kochva (2000/1b), and the response of Liebes (2001/2). Liebes does not actually answer the basic claim that the verses could not have been written by Sophocles. First, the verses have the tone of a sermon, and the references to cult and religious festivals are outspokenly ironical and mocking, reminiscent of 2 Isaiah on paganism. They present an absolute and uncompromising monotheism, leaving no room for any other belief system (εἰς ταῖς ἀληθείασιν, εἰς ἐστὶν θεός, "one in truth, one is God"). Sophocles, above all other Greek authors (more than all the Athenians, as Dicaearchus says), was renowned for reverence to the gods and devotion to their cult and would not have written such things, with such force, in any literary framework, context, or intention. The examples Liebes adduces from Aristophanes and Euripides (252) are irrelevant for the pious Sophocles, who is so different from them in his approach to religion and tradition, and besides, the examples referred to by Liebes pertain to atheism and not to belief in one god, the creator and manager of the world, as expressed in the verses under consideration. Second, whence would Sophocles have acquired the revolutionary views expressed in the verses? Of all of them, only the opposition to anthropomorphism and idol worship are known from pre-Socratic writings. Yet Xenophanes, whom Liebes quotes, does not believe in one god only. He is not a monotheist but a henotheist, one who believes in a god of gods, the lord of the other gods, who are subject to him (what else could be the meaning of his celebrated verse "There is one god, and he is greater than gods and men"?); moreover, the pre-Socratic god does not create the cosmos. Liebes mentions Pherecydes (sixth century) and Plato, but Pherecydes (who besides is very different from other pre-Socratics) talks of a continuous creation of the world at the hands of a succession of gods (among them, offspring of Kronos), and not by one god alone (the fragment: Kirk, Raven, and Schofield [1983] 56), while Plato's account of the *demiourgos* is half a century later than the death of Sophocles (the *Timaeus* was written probably around 360), quite a long time in a period of dynamic progress of ideas; finally, the pre-Socratic god does not conduct the world's day-to-day affairs. This last idea is first found in Stoicism, that is, not before the third century B.C.E. Now, are we to believe that, of all the Greek authors of the fifth century, the devout polytheist Sophocles gave vent to each and every one of these revolutionary ideas? Early acquaintance with the Jewish people and its religion, actually suggested by Liebes (263–64), is impossible in view of the absence of any reference to their unique religion in classical Greek literature, especially in Aristotle; and Liebes's argument that the Jewish excursus quoted by Photius was taken from Hecataeus of Miletus (sixth–fifth century B.C.E.) does not make sense (see note 43 below). As for Liebes's remarks on the "monotheistic" tendencies of Hecataeus of Abdera and his enthusiasm for the Jewish religion (258 ff.), see below, pp. 132–34. At any rate, once the forgery of the verses has been established, the forgery of the work *On Abraham* is also proved. Hecataeus would not himself have forged the verses attributed to Sophocles, and Jewish forgers of classical literature were not yet active in his generation.

8. For circumstantial evidence gleaned from *Contra Apionem* 1. 183, 189, and 191, Diodorus 1. 46. 8, and the contents and apparent aims of Hecataeus's *Aegyptiaca*, see Murray (1970) 143–44; Sterling (1992) 74 ff. (and n. 8); Bar-Kochva (1996d) 7–8 nn. 1–2, *contra* Diamond (1974) 117, 139, 140–41.

Egypt (*Aegyptiaca*), written in the years 305–302 B.C.E.[9] Thanks to his high position at court, he was able to avail himself of a variety of oral and written sources
for the ethnography and history of Egypt.[10] Since the Egyptian ethnography
was, for the Greek reader, quite original and comprehensive, and its author of
high official rank, it was widely recognized in the Greek world—along with the
Egyptian *logos* of Herodotus—as a major authority on Egypt and its customs and
was regarded as a model for ethnographical writing.[11]

This great work on Egypt has not come down to us, but an abbreviated version
of it does exist, made by Diodorus Siculus and constituting a substantial portion
of the first book of his *Historical Library*.[12] This version is supplemented by some
testimonia of Plutarch and other authors. The work of Diodorus begins with
the origins of man and civilization, setting the scene in Egypt. His first book
is consequently an Egyptian ethnography, elaborating on the autochthonous
origin of the Egyptians and the geography of their land and presenting a history of Egyptian rulers and Egyptian customs. Most of the book is based on
Hecataeus of Abdera, apart from the section on geography (paras. 30–41), which
is taken from another source, Agatharchides of Cnidus, and certain passages
toward the end of the book, composed by Diodorus himself, and based on his
personal knowledge. Diodorus adheres to the structure and order of the original
Hecataean ethnography, including all the topics common in Greek ethnography.

In addition to this major work, we know of a utopian exercise by Hecataeus
called *On the Hyperboreans,* an account of the mythical Hyperboreans that
combines Hecataeus's vivid imagination and his notion of an ideal society. The
Hyperboreans according to legend were living somewhere in the far north,
"beyond the dominion of Boreas" (e.g., Hdt. 4. 32–36). What little has survived
of this work is also to be found for the most part in Diodorus's *Library* (2. 47.
1–6).[13] Beside these works, Hecataeus wrote one or more philosophical treatises,

9. Bar-Kochva (1996d) 15–16. Add to the testimonia Diodorus 1. 47. 7–8 (the 118th Olympiad,
i.e., 308–304 B.C.E.). For different dating: Murray (1970) 143; (1973); Stern (1973); Gabba (1989) 625;
Sterling (1992) 76–77.

10. Diodorus 1. 21.1, 26.1, 43.6, 69.7, 86.2, 96.2.

11. See esp. Murray (1970) 166–69; (1972) 208; Fraser (1972) 504–7.

12. See Schneider (1880); Schwartz (1883) 223–62; Leopoldi (1892); Susemihl (1892) 1: 312–14;
Schwartz, *RE* s.v. "Diodorus," cols. 669–772; Jacoby, *RE* s.v. "Hekataios (4)," cols. 2759–60; id., *FGrH*
IIIa, 75–76; Murray (1970) 145, 148–49, 151–52, 164, 168–70; (1972) 207 ff.; Fraser (1972) 1: 496–509,
2: 1116; Lloyd (1974) 287–88; Griffiths (1976) 122; Hornblower (1981) 23 ff.; Sterling (1992) 61–64;
Bar-Kochva (1996d) 289–90. The attempts to deny or minimize a Hecataean origin for Diodorus's
Egyptian ethnography have been rightly refuted. For such attempts, see Spoerri (1959), (1961); Burton
(1972) 1–34; cf. Sacks (1990) 206; but see Sachs, *OCD²*, s.v. "Diodorus (2)," col. 472. On this, see Bar-
Kochva (2000/1) 125–30.

13. On this work, see esp. Jacoby, *RE* s.v. "Hekataios (4)," cols. 2755–58; id., *FGrH* IIIa, no. 264,
pp. 52 ff.; Guttmann 1: 42–45.

whose titles are unknown, and grammatical discussions on Homer and Hesiod, of which nothing has survived.[14]

Hecataeus of Abdera opened a new era in the field of ethnography,[15] just as Thucydides before him had started a new era of historiography. Sea voyages and other journeys undertaken by Greeks, the Greek colonization movement with its demand for written guides, and the advance of the Persian Empire westwards all contributed to the rise of classical Greek ethnography, beginning with Hecataeus of Miletus in the sixth century, and consolidated by Herodotus. In the classical age, Greek ethnography explicitly aimed at collecting and arranging any available scraps of information within a previously determined scheme, with no attempt at selection (e.g., Hdt. 2. 118, 123; 7. 152). The basic scheme was as follows, and usually in this order: *origo*—an account of the origin and development of the people under discussion (mostly through migration, but sometimes through autochthonous development); geography—the land and its features (mainly climate, flora, and water sources); *nomima*—laws and customs; history—usually the achievements of the rulers/kings (as might be expected, military victories, long-range expeditions, and monumental building enterprises, and less frequently the establishment of customs and institutions). In some cases the geography section changed places with the *origo* or the *nomima*.[16]

The new Greek ethnography, which was motivated in particular by the conquests of Alexander, and appeared in the form both of independent monographs and of excursuses in ethnographic and historiographic works, owed much to the work of Hecataeus of Abdera. While preserving the basic sections in their usual order,[17] Hecataeus strove to filter out or at least distance himself from pieces of information that seemed to him unreliable. Accordingly, he rebukes Herodotus explicitly for his lack of selectivity and criticism (Diod. 1. 37. 4, 69. 7). In addition, Hecataeus would omit insignificant information, preferring "useful" data (1. 69. 2, 72. 6), particularly such as might be consistent with his aims. However, for the sake of popularity, he was also inclined to report "extremely strange customs" (Diod. 1. 69. 2; cf. 30. 4).

Another great innovation in Hecataeus's writing was the fairly consistent

14. *Suda* s.v. Ἑκαταῖος. See Jacoby, *RE* s.v. "Hekataios (4)," cols. 2753–54; id., *FGrH* IIIa, no. 264, p. 32; Bar-Kochva (1996d) 8–9, and there, n. 5 on the question of whether Hecataeus was a Pyrrhonian.

15. On Hecataeus as an ethnographer, see Jacoby, *RE* s.v. "Hekataios (4)," cols. 2755 ff.; Guttmann 1: 42 ff.; Murray (1970); (1972) 207; Fraser (1972) 1: 496–505; Mendels (1983); Sterling (1992) 61–78; Bar-Kochva (1996d) 13–18.

16. On the ethnographic genre in the classical period, see Jacoby (1909) 4 ff.; Trüdinger (1918); Dihle (1961); K. E. Müller (1972–80); Fornara (1983) 1–15; Sterling (1992) 20–102; Bar-Kochva (1996d) 10–13, 191–219.

17. See the discussion in Bar-Kochva (1996d) 194–99.

addition of causal links between the various components of the information he provided. He exploited the sequence of four sections of the ethnography to this end, using one section to explain features in another. Thus customs were explained as mainly a reaction to, or result of, events referred to in the *origo* section, the account of the origins of the people under discussion. Alternatively, or additionally, customs were frequently explained as the result of special geographical, particularly climatic, conditions in the people's country of residence. Not a few pieces of information, individually or together, also receive their own causal explanations. Egyptian animal cults, for example, considered ridiculous and despicable by most Greek authors, are explained by Hecataeus positively, as an expression of gratitude for the ecological benefit brought by certain animals to Egypt, such as the elimination of pests (Diod. 1. 86 ff.), for example. Even the belief in the divinity of crocodiles (which according to Hecataeus himself arouses the astonishment of everyone, considering that crocodiles prey upon humans) receives an explanation: it is an expression of gratitude for the protection the crocodiles provide Egypt against the robbers from Arabia and Libya who do not dare cross the Nile for fear of being eaten (1. 89. 1–2; cf. the additional explanation, 3). The Egyptian custom of incest, especially of brother marrying sister (rejected, according to Hecataeus, by all humanity), is explained by Hecataeus as influenced by the successful marriage of Isis to her brother Osiris, her refusal to remarry after his death, and her resolute persecution and punishment of the murderers of her husband/brother (1. 27. 1). The explanations and causal connections often diverge from the reality of the people being described, influenced as they are by Greek experience, historical tradition, and typical ways of thinking, and often by the original thinking and inventiveness of Hecataeus himself.

Similarly, Hecataeus added his own touch to the ethnographic data, adapting them to Greek literary-historical conceptions and schemes, and modifying them with Greek concepts, terms, and names from all fields. This also did not always conform with the history, reality, and beliefs of the people concerned. In many instances, deviations from historical truth do not result from the very act of writing in Greek, but from the way in which Hecataeus interpreted the information he had at hand, either because this was how he understood it, or because of his endeavor to make it intelligible to his Greek readership.

The selection of the data and the causal explanations give the work a scientific air. They were imitated by other authors already in Hecataeus's own generation, evidently by Megasthenes, for one.[18] Hecataeus's *Aegyptiaca* was not, however, an impartial history-ethnography. It had two objectives: to raise the

18. On Hecataeus as a model for imitation by later ethnographers, see Jacoby, *FGrH* IIIa, no. 264, pp. 37–38; Murray (1970) 150, 166–69; (1973) 166; Fraser (1972) 1: 497, 504–7. For his influence on Megasthenes: Murray (1972) 208; (1973) 166.

prestige of Ptolemy, the successor of the kings of Old Egypt, in the eyes of Greco-Macedonians living under other Hellenistic rulers, in an attempt to attract to Egypt competent manpower and the intellectual elite of the Greek world by glorifying the pharaonic past; and internally, to avoid violent confrontations between the Greco-Macedonians settled in Egypt and the natives, particularly the strong priesthood, by emphasizing the royal policy of respecting Egyptian traditions and customs (see, e.g., Diod. 1. 83. 6–8).[19]

In order to achieve these aims, Hecataeus adduced in great detail the account of the Egyptians concerning the beginning of the human race in the land of Egypt, the identity of the Egyptian world of gods with that of the Greeks, the first development of human civilization in Egypt, and a whole list of inventions of the Egyptians that promoted the material and spiritual life of mankind. Hecataeus reports all this with hardly any reservation, and occasionally with explicit consent (more such agreements may well have been in the original work), while emphasizing now and then that he does not adduce Egyptian sources just as they are if they are unsupported or implausible (1. 29. 5–6, 69. 7). Moreover, he gives an idealized portrait of the pharaonic kingdom and regime, which appears akin to a constitutional monarchy, run according to old laws and under the supervision of the priesthood.[20] He even goes so far as to attempt to remove stigmas concerning Egyptians and their lifestyle commonly found in Greek literature. His efforts extended not only to rationalizing Egyptian animal worship. Thus he attributes the notorious Egyptian hostility toward foreigners to the Egyptian kings of old,[21] saying that there had been an extreme change for the better in the treatment of foreigners, due to a royal initiative on the part of King Psammetichus (1. 67. 9–10).[22]

19. See Bar-Kochva (1996d) 16–17. For the point of the work, see the various suggestions in Schwartz (1885) 233–62; Wendland (1912) 116–19; Jacoby, *RE* s.v. "Hekataios (4)," cols. 2757–65; Meyer (1928) 529 ff.; Jaeger (1938b) 136–37; Welles (1949) 39–44; Kienitz (1953) 49 ff.; Guttmann 1: 45 ff.; Murray (1970) 1–2, 157–69; Fraser (1972) 1: 497–505; Drews (1973) 126–32, 205 n. 157; Mendels (1983) 95–96; Sterling (1992) 73–75; Stephens (2003) 32–39.

20. The main source is Diodorus 1. 70–72. See Jacoby, *RE* s.v. "Hekataios (4)," col. 2763; Murray (1970) 159. Murray explains that Hecataeus could offer programmatic strictures to the Ptolemaic monarchy because he was writing during the formative stages of the Ptolemaic regime, when the main concern was to appease the Egyptian priesthood. I would add that a Greek thinker would still have been able, or would at least have tried, to influence the shaping of the new monarchy without risking punishment. The unhistorical description of the decisive influence of the Egyptian priests on the pharaoh, according to which he is no more than a pawn in their hands, is the result of Hecataeus's overreliance on Theban priests, who presented him with supposedly ancient sources; see Murray (1970) 152–57, and for sources, 151 n. 3.

21. See, e.g., Plato *Laws* 953e; Strabo 17. 1. 6, 19 (taken from Eratosthenes); ps.-Apollodorus *Bibliotheca* 2. 5. 11.

22. Influenced by Hdt. 2. 154. Hecataeus's version, however, is an idealization of Psammetichus's treatment of foreigners; see Burton (1972) 203–4.

THE JEWISH EXCURSUS—PRESERVATION,
CONTEXT, TEXT, AND TRANSMISSION

Hecataeus's Jewish excursus had been inserted into the fortieth book of Diodorus. The book has not survived, but certain parts of it have been preserved in Byzantine anthologies, and the Jewish excursus has reached us through the similarly named *Bibliotheca* of Photius, the ninth-century patriarch of Constantinople (*cod.* 244, 380a–381a). This passage is preceded by Diodorus's version of the account of the siege of Jerusalem by Antiochus VII Sidetes in 132 B.C.E. (34/35. 1. 1–5), in which serious accusations were launched against the Jews (including the ass libel).[23] The two passages are quoted by Photius in order to prove his assertion that Diodorus spread "lies" about the Jewish people.

Photius states in his introduction to this passage that it comes from the fortieth book of Diodorus, and Diodorus's introduction to the excursus states that it preceded the account of the war of the Romans against the Jews, namely, Pompey's conquest of Judaea (63 B.C.E.). All the signs suggest that the excursus followed a passage, surviving in a Byzantine anthology (*Excerpta de sententiis*), about the alleged appearance of an embassy of Jewish notables before Pompey.[24] It is told there that they expressed opposition to Hasmonaean rule, pointing out that monarchy was alien to the Jewish people and that in the past the Jews were ruled only by the High Priests (2. 1–3 in the reconstructed fortieth book of Diodorus). The excursus, as Diodorus himself says explicitly at the outset (3. 1), serves as a necessary introduction to the main features of the Jewish people prior to the accounts of the first confrontations between the Jews and the Romans, that is, the clashes between Aristobulus II and Pompey. These accounts, which have not reached us, would originally have followed the Jewish excursus. The features attributed to the Jews contributed to a better understanding of the stubborn opposition in certain Jewish circles to the Romans, and their military strength. The excursus was also used to illustrate the main historical claim attributed to the alleged Jewish embassy, for it states that "the Jews never had a king" (40. 3. 4). I suspect that this connection is why Diodorus preferred to place the Jewish excursus in this context, and not beforehand as an introduction to one of the earlier confrontations between the Jews and the Hellenistic monarchies.[25]

23. On this account, see p. 441ff.

24. On the embassy and the contents of the complaint, see Bar-Kochva (1977) 179–81.

25. Diodorus did not use the excursus to introduce his account of the siege of Jerusalem by Antiochus Sidetes (34/35. 1. 1–5), because it contributes nothing to the reader's understanding of the events, and in any case does not conform with the description of the Jews given in that account in great detail by the advisers of Antiochus Sidetes. Why did Diodorus not use the excursus as a preface to the story of the conflict between Ptolemy I and the Jews in 301, or to the story of the great and proctracted confrontation with Antiochus IV? These stories are not to be found in the fragments

The version of the excursus of Hecataeus with the introductory note of Diodorus and the conclusion added by Photius (Phot. *Bibl. cod.* 244, 380a–381a; Diod. 40. 3. 1–6) follows:[26]

(*Photius's opening remark*)
From the fortieth book around the middle.

(*Diodorus's introduction*)
[3.1] Being about to write up the war against the Jews, we consider it appropriate to narrate beforehand in main points (ἐν κεφαλαίοις),[27] both the foundation [*ktisis*] of this nation from the beginning, and the customs [*nomima*] among them.

(*The excursus*)
In ancient times (τὸ παλαιόν), when there was a pestilential circumstance throughout Egypt, the many began to ascribe the cause of their troubles to divine power; for with many and varied strangers dwelling [there] and practicing different customs concerning the holy and the sacrifices, it turned out that their own ancestral acts of worship of the gods had lapsed. [3.2] Because of this the natives of the land understood that unless they removed the foreigners, there would be no resolution of their troubles. Straightaway, therefore, the foreigners were banished, of whom the most outstanding and active (ἐπιφανέστατοι καὶ δραστικώτατοι), having banded together, were cast out, as some say, into Greece and certain other places, having notable leaders, of whom Danaus and Cadmus, being most outstanding, led the others; but the great multitude (πολὺς λεώς) was driven out into what is now

---

preserved from the lost books of Diodorus, and one cannot know whether the description of these events was extensive enough to justify a long ethnography, or whether the details of the descriptions were in the spirit of the excursus.

26. The marking of the paragraphs of the extract follows the edition of Vogel and Fischer (1888). The edition of Photius: Henry (1959–77) 6: 132–37.

27. The expression ἐν κεφαλαίοις means "in heads," "in topics," "in main points/issues," "summarily," etc. The level of detail here, the numerous explanations, and the sparse use of the participle are unusual for a typical summary. Diodorus means, therefore, that he is reporting the main issues touching on the foundation story and the Jewish customs relevant to his purpose, while omitting everything else. Within these points he omitted, as usual, some relevant details (see below, p. 103). On a similar use of the expression ἐν κεφαλαίοις, cf. Diodorus 1. 9. 4 in the introduction to the Egyptian ethnography: "We would not make exact distinctions concerning the antiquity of each, and which nations antedate which of the others and by how many years, but we shall write up the main points (ἐν κεφαλαίοις), aiming at proportion, what has been said among each concerning their origin and ancient deeds." From what follows, it would appear that Diodorus intends to copy select passages rather than consistently summarize his source in its entirety. Cf. also Porphyry *On Abstention from [the Meat of] Animals* 2. 32. 3: " . . . the main points (τὰ μὲν δὴ κεφάλαια) for it being necessary not to sacrifice animals, these are from Theophrastus, apart from the few inserted stories added and shortened by me." Porphyry adduces from Theophrastus select passages, which he copies with some omission, and does not intend to provide a summary of *Peri eusebeias* in its entirety (see pp. 18–19 above).

called Judaea, which while lying not far from Egypt was nevertheless utterly desolate (παντελῶς δὲ ἔρημον) in those times. [3.3] The man called Moses led the colony (*apoikia*), [he being] greatly superior both in prudence and in courage (φρονήσει τε καὶ ἀνδρείᾳ). On taking possession of the land, this man founded, besides other cities, the one that is now the most outstanding, called Hierosolyma. In addition he built the temple most honored among them, established the offices and rites for the divinity, codified and arranged the things relating to the constitution (*politeia*). He also divided the people into twelve tribes on account of this (διὰ τό) being regarded as the most perfect number and corresponding to the number of months making up the year. [3.4] But he constructed no image at all of gods, through (διὰ τό) not believing the god to be man-shaped; but [believing] only the heaven, holding all around[28] the Earth, to be god and master of all. He established sacrifices and modes of conduct for everyday life differing from those of other nations;[29] for as a result of (διὰ γάρ) their own expulsion (*xenēlasia*) from Egypt he introduced a [way of] life that is somewhat (= quite?) removed from [the society of] men and [somewhat?] hostile to strangers.[30] Having picked out the men of most refinement and the most able to head the entire nation, these he appointed as priests; and he ordered their occupation to be concerning the temple, and the offices and sacrifices for the god. [3.5] These same men he also appointed to be the judges of the greatest disputes, and entrusted to them the guardianship (*phylakē*) of the laws and customs. And for this reason (διὸ καί) [there] never [has been] a king of the Jews, but the leadership of the multitude (*plēthos*) is always given to whichever of the priests appears to excel in wisdom (*phronēsis*) and excellence (*aretē*). They call this man high priest and believe him to become a messenger to them of the commandments of the god. [3.6] They say that this man proclaims the commands in the assemblies and other gatherings, and that the Jews are so obedient on this point that they immediately fall to the ground and make obeisance to the high priest interpreting [the laws] to them. There is appended even to the laws, at the end: "Moses having heard these things from the god says [them] to the Jews." The lawgiver gave much forethought to military deeds and used to force the young men to practice both bravery and steadfastness, and in general, the endurance of every hardship. [3.7] He made military expeditions into the neighboring lands of the nations and, having acquired much land, apportioned it out to private citizens, assigning equal allotments (*klēroi*), but to the priests greater ones in order that they, by receiving more ample revenues, might be undistracted and attend continually to the offices of the god. It was not possible for the common people to sell their individual allot-

28. On the meaning of περιέχειν in this context, see in detail pp. 161–62 below.

29. τὰς δὲ θυσίας ἐξηλλαγμένας συνεστήσατο τῶν παρὰ τοῖς ἄλλοις ἔθνεσι, καὶ κατὰ τὸν βίον ἀγωγάς. It is clear from the subsequent sentence that not only the sacrifices but also the Jewish way of life mentioned in the second clause differed from those of other nations. See also para. 8 on Jewish marriage and burial practices.

30. διὰ γὰρ τὴν ἰδίαν ξενηλασίαν ἀπάνθρωπόν τινα καὶ μισόξενον βίον εἰσηγήσατο. On the ambiguity of the qualifier τινά and its connection with μισόξενον βίον, see p. 131 below.

ments, lest there be some who, through [a desire for] having more [than their fair share], should buy them up, and, by oppressing the poorer, bring on a scarcity of manpower. [3.8] He forced those on the land to rear their children; and since (καὶ δι᾽) offspring were brought up with little expense, the nation (*genos*) of the Jews was always populous. He made both the [matters] regarding marriages and the burials of the dead differ greatly from the [same matters] of other men.

(*A concluding note by Diodorus*)[31]
But during the [foreign] rules that happened later (κατὰ δὲ τὰς ὕστερον γενομένας ἐπικρατείας), out of mingling (*epimixia*) with men of other nations— both under the hegemony of the Persians and of the Macedonians who overthrew this [hegemony]—many of the traditional customs of the Jews were distorted.

(*The comment added by Photius*)
So he (Diodorus) says also here (as in his account of the advice of the "friends" given to Antiochus Sidetes: Diod. 34/35. 1. 2–5) about customs and laws common among Jews, and about the departure of those same people from Egypt, and about the holy Moses, telling lies about most things, and going through the [possible] counterarguments, he again distorted the truth, and using a cunning device as a

---

31. It is rightly accepted by many scholars that this last sentence of the Diodorean excerpt was added by Diodorus himself (see, e.g., Jacoby, *FGrH* IIIa, no. 264, p. 62). It records changes during the Hasmonaean period and is connected with the alleged complaints of the Jewish notables to Pompey against the Hasmonaeans for their deviation from the ancient style of government approved by the Jews. The reference to the "rule . . . of the Macedonians who overthrew the Persians" indicates that it was written long after the end of Persian rule in Judaea, that is, long after the time of Hecataeus. A similar note, which has escaped the attention of scholars, was supplemented by Diodorus at the end of his *epitomē* of Hecataeus's Egyptian ethnography (1. 95. 6): "In later times many of the customs regarded as good were removed, when the Macedonians conquered and finally destroyed the kingdom of the locals." Hecataeus, who was eager to point out the Ptolemaic continuation of Egyptian tradition and style of kingdom, would not have described the Macedonian occupation as a final destruction of the kingdom of the locals. The expression "in later times" also shows that the sentence was not written by Hecataeus. Jacoby (52) argues that the concluding sentence on the Jews was written by Diodorus under the influence of the Jewish excursus of Posidonius, which reports the decline of Jewish customs and religion in the later period (preserved in Strabo 16. 2. 37). This seems reasonable, given Diodorus's extensive use of Posidonius's *Histories*. The remark about the Egyptians, however, is probably based on Diodorus's own impressions when he visited Egypt and saw the change that had taken place as a result of foreign influence on Egyptian laws and customs (at least in Alexandria). The attempt of Willrich (1895) 51 and (1900) 89 to explain that the sentence reflects Hecataeus' opinion of the Jews whom he met shortly after Persian rule does not hold water; likewise the explanations of Diamond (1974) 118–28. See also Gabba (1989) 628 (without explanation). A considerable part of Hecataeus's account actually reflects specific Jewish customs of the Persian period and the beginning of the period of Macedonian rule (paras. 4–6). He would certainly have seen no revolutionary change, according to his view, in Jewish *apanthrōpia*, *misanthrōpia*, and the exclusive customs.

refuge for himself, he attributes to another [author] the above said things, which are contrary to history. For he (Diodorus) adds: "As concerns the Jews, this is what Hecataeus of Miletus[32] relates about the Jews."

Some comments on the transmission of the text and its preservation are required. In view of Photius's declared purpose to expose Diodorus's "lies" and considering the typically Diodorean style and turn of phrase, it has rightly been assumed that Photius faithfully transmitted the text of Diodorus in full.[33] This is supported by Photius's practice in the transmission of extracts from *codex* 238 onward.[34] As far as Diodorus is concerned, even a cursory reading of the excursus reveals that the Hecataean text was not transmitted by Diodorus in its entirety.[35] The abbreviations are clear in two paragraphs. Diodorus omitted details about the rites of Jewish sacrifice (3. 4), marriage, and burial (3. 8).[36] He appears to have been interested mainly in the system of the Jewish regime, as well as Jewish preparations for war, which were all relevant to the context in which he inserted the excursus—Jewish internal strife and the imminent confrontation with the Romans. Consequently he abbreviated and omitted details irrelevant to his purpose. The account of Jewish belief was recorded chiefly due to its relevance for the Jewish theocratic system of government indicated by the delegation to Pompey.[37]

Apart from the abbreviation of some customs and the possible omission of others, the references to the Jewish *origo* and *nomima* by Diodorus seem to represent the contents of the original text. In three cases there is a striking similarity of content between the excursus and references to Egyptians and Jews in Hecataeus's *Aegyptiaca*.[38] Most notable is the prolific use of causal explanations reminiscent

32. Hecataeus of Abdera is meant, as is almost universally accepted; see pp. 105–6 and note 43 below.

33. For a possible (but insignificant) exception, see Diamond (1974) 10–11.

34. Photius adheres to his sources in these codices, apart from slight and insignificant linguistic improvements. Abbreviations were made only to avoid duplications and stylistic awkwardness, or with regard to redundant details that detract from the main issue. See Palm (1955) 16–26, 29 ff., 48 ff.; Hägg (1975) 9 ff. and 197–203, esp. 201–2. Treadgold (1980) 129 is probably mistaken in assigning Diodorus's excerpts in *cod.* 244 to what he calls class IIc; it should be class IIIc (see Treadgold's classification, 82–83, 86, 90–91).

35. See Jaeger (1938b) 150–51; Murray (1970) 144–46; (1973) 168; Stern, *GLAJJ* 1: 34; Diamond (1974) 111–17. On ἐν κεφαλαίοις used by Diodorus (para. 1), see note 27 above.

36. The feeling that the reference to marriage and burial customs was abbreviated, or that the beginning of this new topic was omitted, can perhaps be further supported by stylistic observation: the new topic is introduced with the conjunction καί, which in the previous sentences has been used only to connect ideas within a topic; new topics have regularly been introduced with the particle δέ.

37. See p. 99 above.

38. See Diodorus 1. 73. 7–9, 80. 6. Cf. Diodorus 40. 3. 7–8 (the Egyptian agrarian arrangement and the encouragement of births). See further pp. 127–28 below.

of Hecataeus's method. These parallels in content and form indicate that even if some of the statements and explanations were abbreviated by Diodorus, and the phrasing may here and there sound clumsy, the original meaning and tone were preserved. Significantly, Diodorus was not tempted by the hostile libels about Jewish origins and the sharp remarks about their attitude toward strangers that he included elsewhere in his work (34/35. 1. 1–4),[39] nor was he tempted by his own prejudice (40. 2. 2, "lawless behavior of the Jews"): the Jews expelled from Egypt are not described as lepers, and the reason given for their expulsion is not insulting; the Jewish lifestyle is actually described as *apanthrōpos* (para. 3. 4) and not *misanthrōpos* (as in Diod. 34/35. 1). This suggests that *apanthrōpos* is Hecataean. The question whether, and to what extent, Diodorus adhered to Hecataeus's vocabulary and syntax is more problematic. It can only be said that there are not a few traces of the Diodorean style in the excursus.[40]

As for the sequence of the two components, the *origo* and the *nomima*, there is no reason to doubt that it generally adhered to that of Hecataeus. The internal sequence of the *nomima* section more or less accords with what is customary in foundation stories.[41] Only the remark concerning marriage and burial customs actually closing the account (para. 8) appears to be out of place. It was misplaced by Diodorus in the process of its drastic abbreviation. The original location would have been somewhere in paragraph 4, as an illustration of the contrast between Jewish daily customs and those of the Egyptians and other nations. The remark was transferred to its present location to serve as a bridge to the concluding sentence of the excursus added by Diodorus concerning the change in Jewish customs following the Persian and Macedonian conquests.

Hecataeus's original excursus thus opened with the *origo*, in this case the expulsion of Jews from Egypt, followed by the *nomima* section, containing institutions, provisions, and customs introduced and initiated by Moses. For a reason that still has to be clarified, the excursus did not contain a geographical and historical section, which was common in Greek ethnographies. However, as became customary in the new, Hellenistic ethnography, the author uses one section to explain another, indicating a causal relationship between them. Here he stresses the influence of the *origo* on the development of Jewish customs. The expulsion explains the *apanthrōpia* and "hatred of strangers" (3.4), as well as the striking difference between some Jewish daily customs, such as those of sacrifice, marriage, and

---

39. On the Posidonian source for this passage, see p. 412 below. Posidonius quotes the advice of the "friends" of Antiochus VII to the king, but he disagrees with the libels and the hostile portrayal of the Jews; see pp. 444–55 below.

40. See the detailed discussion of Diamond (1974) 13 ff.; cf. Fraser (1972) 2: 1116.

41. See pp. 120–22 below.

burial, and their foreign counterparts.[42] Jewish beliefs, governmental institutions, and social provisions are similarly not just listed but given a causal reasoning.

THE ATTRIBUTION OF THE EXCURSUS
TO HECATAEUS OF ABDERA

The excursus is identified with Hecataeus because of the statement by Diodorus at the end of the account that "this is what Hecataeus of Miletus narrated." It has long been unanimously accepted that the statement should be emended to read "Hecataeus of Abdera."[43] The slip is the error of a copyist who knew about the great pioneering work of Hecataeus of Miletus, the sixth-fifth century B.C.E.

42. The references to Jewish marriage customs probably stressed Jewish incest prohibitions as opposed to Egyptian permissiveness (mentioned by Hecataeus, Diod. 1. 27. 1), and the Jewish rejection of mixed marriages. It is possible that Hecataeus's account of the different sacrificial customs of the Jews included the rumor that the Jews burn their sacrificial victims alive (see pp. 25–30 above).

43. See, e.g., Reinach (1895) 20 n. 1; Willrich (1900) 89; Jaeger (1938a) 135; (1938b) 139; Jacoby, *FGrH* IIIa, no. 264, pp. 34, 46–48; Guttmann 1: 50; Henry (1971) 137; Gager (1972) 28 n. 8; Diamond (1974) 128–30; Stern, *GLAJJ* 1: 34–35; Gabba (1989) 626; Sterling (1992) 76 n. 86; Hansen (2000) 12 n. 2. The view of Dornseiff (1939) 52–65 (supported recently by Liebes [2001/2] 263), that the reading "of Miletus" should be retained, does not hold water. A Greek of Asia Minor who flourished at the beginning of the Persian period, in the first generation of the Return to Zion, could not have had such detailed knowledge of the Jewish people, or quote a verse from the Pentateuch. The following should be added to the arguments of Jacoby. First, Hecataeus of Miletus was well known in the Greek world, certainly to Herodotus, who mentions him, and to Aristotle, "the reader" (see p. 51 above); however, there is no indication that any Greek historian or philosopher of the classical period was acquainted with the excursus, even when dealing with unique religions and beliefs, when expressing somewhat similar opinions in any field, or elsewhere when such a reference is naturally to be expected (cf. pp. 16–17 and p. 48 above on Theophrastus and Aristotle). Second, the selective nature of the information and the consistent tendency to offer causal explanations are characteristic of Hecataeus of Abdera, but not of the *Periēgēsis* by Hecataeus of Miletus (of which we have over three hundred extracts), which is proposed by Dornseiff as a source for the excursus. Indeed, the work of Hecataeus of Miletus was adjudged by an ancient critic acquainted with it in its entirety to have the opposite characteristics (Dion. Hal. *Thuc.* 5). Third, the account of the Jewish agrarian and child-rearing laws is too similar to Hecataeus's description of the cultivation of the status of warriors in ancient Egypt (see below, p. 127). Liebes (263) argues that Hecataeus of Miletus described the distant land of the Ethiopians and could therefore have known about the much closer land of Judaea. But what did Hecataeus of Miletus (though he visited Egypt) really know about the Ethiopians? And what did Herodotus (who also visited Egypt) and other Greek authors of the fifth–fourth centuries really know about the Ethiopians? How can this be compared with the knowledge reflected in the Jewish excursus of Hecataeus? The first worthwhile information on Ethiopia reached the Greeks only during the reign of Ptolemy II Philadelphus (283–247 B.C.E.) as a result of his expeditions to the south (see Diodorus 3. 11; cf. 1. 37. 5, 37. 10–39. 13) and was first recorded in literature—at least as far as we know—only by Agatharchides of Cnidus, who flourished around 160–145 B.C.E. Even Hermippus, the late third-century B.C.E. Alexandrian scholar, could still report that a dog was the ruler of an Ethiopian tribe and barked out its orders (Ael. *NA* 7. 40).

father of the popular ethnographic genre. Diodorus, who often quoted from the *Aegyptiaca* of Hecataeus of Abdera, could hardly be responsible for the error,[44] although he may have contributed to it by failing to mention his provenance here as in other places (1. 46. 8; 2. 47. 1), thereby allowing a later copyist (Photius?) to make the wrong identification. It was quite easy to confuse the names, as at least one ancient author quoting Hecataeus of Abdera was well aware (Ael. *NA* 11. 1).[45]

The attribution to Hecataeus of Abdera is considered suspect by a few scholars who have claimed the excursus is a Jewish forgery. One of these argued that the excursus was written by a Jewish contemporary of John Hyrcanus (135–104 B.C.E.) who wished to present the Hasmonaean reign as an ideal one, to extol Jewish exclusivity, and to portray the Hasmonaean leader—who embraced the roles of priest, prophet, and ruler (Joseph. *AJ* 13. 299)—in the image of Moses, the founder of the nation.[46] Another scholar has further argued that the excursus was taken from the treatise *On the Jews,* attributed to Hecataeus, while accepting that the treatise as a whole was a forgery composed by a Hellenistic Jew living in Egypt in the Hasmonaean period.[47]

Any claim that the excursus is a forgery should be backed up by weighty evidence and strong arguments. In the present case, the difficulties raised in order to challenge the accepted view are nonexistent or resolvable.[48] Although this should suffice to uphold the claim of authenticity, given the importance of the excursus,

---

44. Jaeger (1938b) 139 n. 37; Diamond (1974) 10; Gabba (1989) 626.

45. Aelian feels obliged to clarify from whom exactly he took his information: "Hecataeus, not the Milesian but the Abderitan" (Ἑκαταῖος, οὐκ ὁ Μιλήσιος ἀλλ' ὁ Ἀβδηρίτης). Diodorus mentions Hecataeus of Miletus once with his place of origin (10. 25. 4) and once without (1. 37. 3).

46. Lebram (1974) 244–53; cf. Meyer (1963) 364.

47. Schwartz (2003).

48. Difficulties of this type are adduced in Schwartz's article: (a) according to the epitome of the *Aegyptiaca* by Diodorus, the Jews were Egyptians who left their country because of overpopulation (1. 29), while according to the excursus, they were foreigners who were expelled from Egypt (on this matter, see below, pp. 111–14); (b) the excursus cannot be placed anywhere in Diodorus's summary-epitome of Hecataeus's work on Egypt, from which it is to be inferred that it was not part of that work; in fact, the excursus would have been at home in the Egyptian ethnography (see below, pp. 109–15); in any case, failure to locate a certain passage in a Diodorean-style epitome of a monumental work is hardly a valid argument; (c) the excursus fails to mention the custom of circumcision, while the epitome mentions it twice in connection with the Jews (1. 29. 2, 55. 1) (on this matter, see below, p. 115); (d) Schwartz points out that Photius (ninth century C.E.) doubted that the source of the excursus was Hecataeus; however, there is no proof, no hint of a check having been carried out, nor is any authority referred to; by and large, Photius never claimed to be engaged in source criticism and philology as we know it; on the errors of Photius in such matters, and his aims, see Treadgold (1980) 67–110; (e) the excursus concludes with the statement that the customs of the Jews changed under Persian and Macedonian control, which could not have been written by Hecataeus of Abdera; this sentence, as has already been recognized by many, is an addition by Diodorus (see note 31 above); (f) the excursus appears as an introduction to the description of the occupation of

it may be worthwhile to examine some of the assumptions of the proposed falsification theories. First, the conjecture that the excursus was included in the forgery *On the Jews*. Josephus used passages from this work in his *Contra Apionem* in order to prove from Greek sources the antiquity of the Jewish people (1. 183).[49] The passages adduced, however, prove only that the Jewish people was already mature in the time of Alexander and the Diadochs. Josephus declares with undisguised pride: "It is therefore clear that our nation was at its peak in his (Ptolemy I's) time as well as in that of Alexander" (1. 185). Now, the Jewish excursus in Diodorus gives a detailed account of the Jewish sojourn in Egypt and the establishment of Jewish settlement in Judaea, conducted by Moses. What better evidence could Josephus have supplied to demonstrate the antiquity of the Jews had the excursus been in his possession? He certainly would not have failed to exploit it had it been part of the work *On the Jews*. Nor was Josephus acquainted with the work of Diodorus, and he never mentions him.

Scholars have already remarked upon the difference between the glorification of the Jews and enthusiasm for their actions in the passages from *On the Jews*, and the rather detached treatment of them in the excursus.[50] Much emphasis has been placed on pseudo-Hecataeus's praise for the destruction of foreign cult, as against the reservation concerning Jewish *misoxenia* in the excursus. I would add that the passages from *On the Jews* contain not even one causal explanation for the information provided, even when this is badly needed,[51] as opposed to the large

---

Judaea by Pompey; Schwartz, following others, considers the source for the account of the conquest to be a work of Theophanes of Mytilene on Pompey; applying the widespread (and correct) "one source" theory concerning the books of Diodorus ("Diodorus normally followed the same source for a long segment for his history"), Schwartz suggests that the excursus was taken by Diodorus from Theophanes, who took it from the forgery *On the Jews*; this argument is neither here nor there so far as the claim of forgery is concerned, since Theophanes could have drawn from Hecataeus; as for the way Diodorus composed his work, it is worth quoting Jacoby on a similar point: "Es ist Diodors art kleinere partieen aus seinen Hauptquellen herauszunehmen, um sie in späteren Büchern und für einen anderen Zusammenhang zu verwenden" ([1943] 46). Examples abound. We are, after all, concerned with an excursus, not a continuous historical description.

49. Cf. 1. 2–5, 72, 161, 162, 166, 168, 172, 176.

50. On Hecataeus's balanced and unbiased evaluation of the Jews, see below, pp. 129–35. Even one who believes that Hecataeus admired the Jews and treated their institutions and practices as models for imitation must admit that the tone of the work is significantly different from the sweeping enthusiasm of *On the Jews*; see, e.g., *Ap.* 1. 191–92 on Jewish martyrology; 193 for the statement that "it is just to admire them (the Jews)" for destroying temples and altars of foreigners; 196 for the enthusiastic description of Jerusalem; 201–4 for the Mosollamus story, in which the wisdom and rational thought of the Jew is contrasted with the idiocy and superstitious nature of the Greeks. Is it conceivable that the author of all this in *On the Jews* could have portrayed the Jews as inferior to the descendants of Danaus and Cadmus (Diod. 40. 3. 2)?

51. The absence of causal explanations can be added to the many arguments against the authenticity of *On the Jews*. For a Jewish practice that necessarily required explanation, see, e.g., Josephus

number of causal explanations, explicit or implied, accompanying the statements in the excursus (in line with Hecataeus's practice in the *Aegyptiaca*).[52]

As for the suggestion that the excursus was a Jewish forgery, the contents of some parts of the excursus remove the possibility that they were written by a Jew. A Jew would not have given a description of the Exodus that is so at odds with the traditional Jewish account (1. 1–2). After all, this is not a marginal detail that may not have been known to a Jewish author, nor would a Jewish author have felt free to distort a cornerstone of Jewish tradition and identity; a Jew would hardly have described the Jewish way of life as *apanthrōpia* and *misoxenia*, even to a minor degree of severity.[53] Nor is it likely that any Jew, let alone pseudo-Hecataeus, would have presented the Jews as inferior to the followers of Danaus and Cadmus (para. 2). One may doubt whether any Jew (apart from an apostate), not to mention an admirer of the Hasmonaeans or the orthodox author of *On the Jews*, would have failed to include circumcision among the main Jewish customs seen by Jews as characterizing their identity.

In addition to the rejection of the theories about a Jewish falsification, there is positive comparative evidence—if such is still needed—that the excursus is indeed Hecataean: the prominence of the Hecataean innovations in ethnographic literature in the Jewish ethnography (the strict selection of the material and the consistent use of causal explanations); the general scheme of the excursus, containing unusually only the *origo* and *nomima* (without the geography and history sections), like Hecataeus's Babylonian excursus, which was adduced by Diodorus in a particularly abbreviated form (1. 28. 1);[54] the similarity to the choice of subjects and the sequence of information in this truncated Babylonian ethnography—the emigration from Egypt under the leadership of Belus (the eponymous father of the Babylonians), the foundation of Babylon by Belus, and the arrangement of institutions and social activities by him (Diodorus preserves the appointment of priests and the functions and special privileges of the priests); and finally, the striking identity of subject matter between Hecataeus's detailed account concerning the agrarian laws of the pharaohs and the increasing natural birth rate among the Egyptians, including the rationale for both, and what is said

---

Contra Apionem 1. 198 (on the construction of the altar in the Jerusalem temple from unhewn stones; see further Bar-Kochva [1996d] 149–50). A Greek, used to his ornamental marble altars, would certainly have wondered why the Jews had such a wretched altar, especially considering that their Temple was so magnificent, and that in the same context there was a detailed reference to the incense altar made of gold. The complete absence of causal explanations may be added to the many arguments against the authenticity of *On the Jews*.

52. See below, pp. 125–26.

53. On the two possible interpretations of τινα in the sentence, see p. 131 below.

54. See the text of the Babylonian excursus below, pp. 109–10, and the explanation of the abbreviated structure, pp. 114–15.

in the Jewish excursus about the parallel laws and customs instituted by Moses, with accompanying causal explanations.[55]

THE ORIGINAL LOCATION OF
THE EXCURSUS AND ITS PURPOSE

In which work of Hecataeus of Abdera did Diodorus find the Jewish excursus? Was it located within the Egyptian ethnography of Hecataeus, as several scholars think? And if so, where exactly? The answer affects a number of major questions pertaining to this chapter.

At least one scholar has suggested that Hecataeus dedicated a monograph to the Jews, and this was abbreviated either by Diodorus or by an intermediate source in the form and size of an excursus.[56] This is a fairly remote possibility. The forger of *On the Jews* who aspired to gain credibility would hardly have attributed to Hecataeus a monograph on the Jews (as opposed to a treatise on a single affair or character, such as *On Abraham*) had Hecataeus already written an extensive work on the same subject. Furthermore, a full work on the Jews by Hecataeus would have had to contain a geography section and another section on history. These sections are absent from the excursus for reasons stemming from the context in which the excursus was placed by Hecataeus.[57] Such sections would have been highly relevant to the context in which Diodorus placed the excursus (the future arena of war between Pompey and the Jews, and the undermining of the legitimacy of the Hasmonaean monarchy). Diodorus would not have omitted them had they existed.

We are left, then, with the accepted view that the excursus was taken from the Hecataean Egyptian ethnography. As for determining its exact location, most significant is the reference to the Jews in the first paragraphs of what we may call the appendix to the Egyptian *origo* section, adduced in summary form by Diodorus (1. 28–29).[58] After elaborating on the adventures and settling achievements of the Egyptian god-kings of the mythological period (such as Osiris, Isis, and Horus), Hecataeus writes (28. 1–3):

> (28. 1) At any rate, the Egyptians also say that after this (the mythological period) very many colonies were scattered throughout the inhabited world out of Egypt. Belus, for instance, believed to be the son of Poseidon and Libya, led colonists to Babylon. Having established himself on the river Euphrates, he instituted priests who, like those in Egypt, were exempt [from paying taxes] and absolved from

55. See pp. 125–28 below.
56. Guttmann 1: 49–50.
57. See pp. 114–15 below.
58. On the *origo* section and its "appendix," see Bar-Kochva (1996d) 195–96.

shouldering public expenses; these the Babylonians call Chaldaeans, and they observe the stars, mimicking the Egyptian priests and "physicists" and astrologers. (2) And they (the Egyptians) say that the followers of Danaus similarly went out (ὁρμηθέντας) from there (Egypt) to settle Argos, almost the oldest of the cities of the Hellenes, and that also the people (*ethnos*) of the Colchi made settlements in Pontus and that of the Jews made settlements between Arabia and Syria, [both nations] being [originally] certain [people][59] who left them (the Egyptians); (3) for this reason, among these nations, it has been passed down from of old the [custom of] circumcising the boys at birth, this custom being brought out of Egypt. *(Next follow the Egyptian arguments for the Egyptian descent of the Athenians.)*

Following Werner Jaeger, a number of scholars have accepted that the Jewish excursus of Hecataeus was adduced in its entirety after this reference to the Jews, and thence passed into the fortieth book of Diodorus.[60] Felix Jacoby, however, asserted that it was impossible to know where the Jewish excursus had been located in Hecataeus's Egyptian ethnography. He noted the incompatibility between the statement that the Jews were autochthonous Egyptians who emigrated, apparently voluntarily,[61] to set up their own settlements (28. 2), and the opening of the excursus, where the Jews are described as foreigners in Egypt who were expelled.[62] To these apparent difficulties it should be added that, according to the passage quoted above, Egyptians prove that the Jews and the Colchi originated in Egypt by referring to the Egyptian custom of circumcision (28. 3). Circumcision, however, is entirely absent from the detailed list of Jewish customs in the excursus.[63] Considering all the other allegedly negative features of the Jews that he had emphasized, Diodorus, living in Rome, would hardly have omitted a custom that the Romans found so deplorable.

59. τινὰς ὁρμηθέντας παρ' ἑαυτῶν. Reading τινάς (certain men/people) as in apposition to the two nations just mentioned (the Colchi and the Jews), we are given to understand that in these cases the people who left Egypt were autochthonous Egyptians, and they became nations separate from Egypt only when they settled. See further below on the Colchi.

60. Jaeger (1938a) 146; (1938b) 137; Walton (1955) 256; Murray (1970) 146–47; Denis (1970) 263; Gager (1972) 28–29; Bar-Kochva (1996d) 208–11.

61. This can be understood from the use of the verb ὁρμηθέντας (see also note 59 above on τινάς), and from the reference to the Jews in close proximity to the Colchi, who Hecataeus states elsewhere were, according to the Egyptians, native Egyptians settled by the Maeotian Lake (the Sea of Azof) during an Egyptian expedition (Diod. 1. 55. 4). Moreover, in the last reference the Jews are mentioned once more in the context of the evidence provided by the Egyptians for the Egyptian descent of the Colchi (5. 5. 5). The introduction and the ending to the appendix (28. 1, 29. 5–6) explicitly state that the Egyptians regarded the nations and tribes mentioned in the appendix as a part of a settlement initiative instigated by their forefathers.

62. Jacoby, *FGrH* IIIa, no. 264, pp. 49–52; Guttmann 1: 49–50; cf. Gager (1972) 28–29; Conzelmann (1981) 57; Sterling (1992) 76–77; Hansen (2000) 16.

63. Noted by Schwartz (2003) 186.

Was the excursus originally located not in the appendix but somewhere in the section on the history of the kings of Egypt? It might, for instance, be suggested that the excursus formed part of the history of Bocchoris (Diod. 1. 65. 1, 79. 1–3; cf. 94. 5–95.1), who appeared in Egyptian traditions as the king who expelled the Jews (Lysimachus in Joseph. *Ap.* 1. 305–11), or another king believed to be the pharaoh of the Exodus/expulsion. This possibility, however, is not supported by the use of the general and vague term τὸ παλαιόν (long ago) at the beginning of the excursus (3.1) to date the expulsion, instead of a reference to a particular Egyptian king (cf. 1. 28. 3 and 69. 4).

However, a close examination of the Egyptian *origo* of Hecataeus and the accompanying "appendix" shows that the Jewish excursus was indeed part of the original "appendix" of Hecataeus and served there as a reaction to the Egyptian-origin reference to the Jews now surviving in Diodorus (1. 28. 3). That is, the excursus was a different version of Jewish descent that Hecataeus adopted as being more trustworthy than the one he had just recorded. A brief survey of the Egyptian *origo* in the Egyptian ethnography and its "appendix" will elucidate this matter.

Some preliminary remarks are in order. Hecataeus accepted, or at least did not question, the Egyptian theory that the human race originated in Egypt (Diod. 1. 10. 1–2), as well as the Egyptian tradition that the human race, almost destroyed by the Flood, began yet again in Egypt (10. 4–5). For the sake of the discussion it should also be added that, following Egyptian tradition, Hecataeus divided Egyptian history into two eras: the mythological era up to Horus (son of Isis and Osiris), when god-kings ruled (13.1–5, 44. 1), and the historical era from the time of Menas onward, when human kings reigned (45.1). Yet in the conclusion to the appendix he does not accept the sweeping Egyptian theory, sometimes accompanied by specific stories and/or arguments, that many tribes, peoples, and cities of the inhabited world are no more than Egyptian settlers (*apoikoi*) sent out of Egypt on the initiative of the kings, some in the mythological era and others in the historical era in order to solve the problem of overpopulation.[64] What remains of the appendix allows us to conclude that Hecataeus regarded the stages of the spread of civilization and the generation of nations and cities throughout the inhabited world as much more complex and varied.

Let us now turn to the appendix itself. Judging from its opening and ending (28. 1; 29. 5–6), its purpose was to discuss the Egyptian theory with regard to the hisorical period. The appendix opens with a statement of the Egyptian theory about the spread of humankind from Egypt in the historical period (28. 1). Then

---

64. 29. 5–6 (presented below). However, Hecataeus seems to have accepted the Egyptian tradition regarding the mythological period only in the case of certain settlements, such as in India and Macedonia. See Diodorus 1. 19. 6–8, 20. 1–3, 27. 5. On the disagreement between the Egyptians and the Greeks concerning the source of settlements in the mythological period, see 23. 8.

come the remains of a Babylonian mini-ethnography (28. 2), demonstrating the Egyptian descent of the Babylonians through their *origo* and *nomima*. This is followed by rather short references to the Egyptian tradition about the Egyptian descent of the Danaoi, Colchi, and Jews (28. 3; the proof—the latter two nations preserve the Egyptian practice of circumcision). Then we find the evidence cited by the Egyptians for an Egyptian descent of the Athenians (28. 4–29. 4). The arguments comprise a detailed comparison of Athenian and Egyptian terms, names, sociopolitical classes, mythological traditions, customs, and the like. Hecataeus rejects this claim as an Egyptian attempt to build upon the fame of the celebrated Greek city (29. 5). The appendix closes with a general statement regarding the Egyptian theory as a whole (29. 5–6):

> (5) . . . In general, the Egyptians say that their forefathers sent out very many settlements to many parts of the inhabited world through the superiority of those who reigned among them[65] and through the excess of abundant population; (6) but since no evidence has been provided and no historian worthy of trust has witnessed [these things], I have decided that the things said are not worth writing.

The conclusion thus repeats the sweeping Egyptian claim, supplemented by the historical-economic background provided by the Egyptians themselves (29. 5). Hecataeus states that there is no point in referring to specific Egyptian tradition about many people where no evidence is provided (29. 6). Hence it appears that he rejects the theory in its comprehensive Egyptian version, and that the appendix comprised Egyptian arguments with regard to some other nations and settlements, accompanied by Hecataeus's specific response. This is clearly seen in the negative reaction concerning the alleged descent of the Athenians.

The appendix has been drastically and clumsily reduced by Diodorus, as happens not infrequently in his books.[66] The abbreviation is evident in the first paragraphs (28. 1–3): no evidence is quoted for the Egyptian descent of the Danaoi, while Hecataeus had said that he would not mention nations for which no evidence had been brought; Hecataeus's comment on the Egyptian claim with regard to the Jews and the Colchi is missing altogether, and even with regard to the Danaoi, where the Greek reader would naturally expect Hecataeus to react;[67]

---

65. ὑπεροχὴν τῶν βασιλευσάντων. The world in the historical period was already inhabited by people who had gone out of Egypt in the mythological period.

66. On the negligence of Diodorus in abbreviating his sources, even to the extent of omitting, without any apparent reason, the most important details and accounts (such as an account of the decisive stage of a battle, while other stages are described in detail), see below, p. 411, esp. note 33.

67. On the mythological background to the connections made by Greeks and Egyptians between Belus and Danaus and the eponymous father of the Egyptians, Aegyptus, see Jaeger (1938a) 134–35; Burton (1972) 118–21.

the claim for an Egyptian descent of the Colchi is considered in much greater detail later in the Egyptian ethnography in the context of the expeditions of King Sesoösis (55. 4–5; cf. Sesostris in Hdt. 2. 104); and there is no reference to the alleged Egyptian descent of Cadmus and his followers, although the name shared by the Greek city of Thebes and the Egyptian city of Thebaid-Thebes suggested his connection with Egypt. Hecataeus explicitly mentions the Egyptian version elsewhere in great detail (1. 23. 4 ff.), while in the Hecataean Jewish excursus the Danaoi and the people of Cadmus are described as foreigners who were expelled from Egypt.

Taking the remains of the original appendix together with Hecataean references elsewhere, it seems that Hecataeus accepted the Egyptian claims so far as the Babylonians and the Colchi were concerned. The insertion of what appears to be a Babylonian excursus, written in the spirit of the Egyptian claims, and the recurring, unreserved reference later on to the descent of the Colchi in the account of the reign of Sesoösis (55. 4–5; Sesostris in Hdt. 2. 104), indicate his positive attitude toward the Egyptian claims in these two cases. In other cases, however, namely, with regard to the Athenians, the Jews, and the people of Danaus and Cadmus, Hecataeus rejected this version. His reaction to the Egyptian tradition about the Athenians has survived in the Diodorean appendix (29. 5). His response to the alleged Egyptian descent of the rest appears in the Jewish excursus (1–2): they are described as foreigners who practiced their own cults, and for this reason were expelled from Egypt.

The Jewish excursus thus finds its proper place in the appendix, following the reference to the Jews' alleged Egyptian descent, and the proof adduced by the Egyptians—the practice of circumcision. Hecataeus responded to this Egyptian tradition with his Jewish ethnographical excursus, which not only explicitly states that the Jews are not originally Egyptian, but also argues that their practices differ from the Egyptian ones. As a matter of fact, Hecataeus's account of the expulsion of the Jews is also basically Egyptian. The multiplicity of theories about the link between the Jews and the Egyptians is known from Egyptian traditions preserved in Hellenistic literature.[68] Besides the portrayal of the Jews as autochthonous Egyptians, and the Exodus as an expulsion or flight or the result of an agreement, there are the descriptions of the Jews who resided in Egypt as foreigners and were expelled for this or that reason, or accompanied foreign conquerors who withdrew to their own lands.

The version of the excursus speaks for itself. At the same time, an explicit statement prior to the Jewish excursus, rejecting the Egyptian tradition concerning the Jews and the followers of Danaus and Cadmus, may well have disappeared

---

68. Manetho in Josephus *Contra Apionem* 1: 89, 229, 235–38, 248, 251; Lysimachus, 306; Chaeremon, 288–92.

when Diodorus lifted the Jewish excursus from the original context and planted it in the fortieth book of his *Library*. As a matter of fact, a negative particle or the like would have sufficed to contrast the excursus with the preceding Egyptian argument.

How, then, did Hecataeus perceive the origin of the Jews and the Hellenic elements mentioned with them? Their anthropological origin was Egypt, like that of other peoples, families, and groups that migrated in one way or another from Egypt in the mythological period and coalesced into nations and cities beyond the bounds of Egypt.[69] They later returned to Egypt for various reasons as separate ethnic groups and were considered foreigners. Their different cults caused friction with the Egyptian populace, for which they were expelled. Then they settled in the lands that they now occupy.

The relative length of the Jewish excursus poses no problem to its inclusion in the appendix. We do not know how long the Babylonian excursus was, but it could not have been short. The comparison between the Athenians and the Egyptians is only a little shorter than the Jewish excursus (and allowances must be made there too for Diodorean omissions). The inclusion of the Jewish excursus by Hecataeus in his appendix is not surprising. Of all the ethnic groups reported to have originated or dwelt in Egypt, the Jews were the only people to emphasize an Egyptian connection in their own *origo* traditions. Furthermore, as a rapidly developing religious-ethnic group in Egypt of Hecataeus's time, they obviously attracted his attention. The ethnographic excursus, surveying the origins both of the people and of their practices, was the most scientific and ostensibly objective method of presenting them and producing evidence and arguments for his reaction to the Egyptian theory. Hecataeus devoted an excursus to the Babylonians and another to the Jews, possibly also one to the Colchians. In the case of the Athenians and the people of Danaus and Cadmus, there was no need to introduce them to the Greek reader, and a direct reference to the Egyptian evidence would have sufficed.

The conclusion concerning the original location of the excursus is corroborated by its structure. As already mentioned above, the excursus comprises only an *origo* section and a *nomima* section and lacks the sections on geography and rulers characterizing ethnographical accounts and compositions (including the *Aegyptiaca* of Hecataeus) since the inception of this genre. The same deficient

---

69. Hecataeus was aware of various rumors about Jewish descent. He was probably himself responsible for the invention of the name Hierosolyma for Jerusalem, which suggested Jewish descent from the legendary Solymi, or some other genealogical connection between them (see p. 82 note 116 above). He could also have been acquainted with the rumors of Jewish descent from the Indians or the Magi known in his time (see p. 83 and note 124). The latter rumor may have inspired Hecataeus in shaping his version of the Jewish religion according to the Herodotean account of Persian belief (see pp. 125–26, 133 below). With regard to the descent of the men of Cadmus and Danaus, there was a variety of Greek traditions, the best known being Cadmus's Phoenician connection.

structure is discernible in the extremely truncated remains of the Babylonian excursus. The absence of a geographical and historical section is due to the original context. Hecataeus was interested in proving his view of the Egyptian theory and saw no point in distracting the reader's attention by elaborating on irrelevant geography and later history. He was therefore content with writing mini-ethnographies containing only the *origo* and *nomima* sections, the latter one providing evidence for the real descent. In the case of the Jewish ethnography, there was also no room for a section on Jewish rulers in light of the description of the Jewish theocracy in the *nomima* section, and the statement that the Jews never had a king.

The absence from the excursus of the custom of circumcision is explicable when the purpose for introducing the Jewish *nomima* in the given context is considered. Circumcision is mentioned in the context of the Egyptian theory, where the Jews and Colchi are described as formerly autochthonous Egyptians who left Egypt; their observance of the Egyptian custom of circumcision is offered by the Egyptians as the only evidence for their alleged Egyptian descent (28. 3; cf. 55. 5). The excursus description of the Jews as foreigners whose customs and lifestyle (*bios*) were deliberately different from those of the Egyptians prevented this practice from being listed among the Jewish *nomima*. Hecataeus carefully screened the ethnographical material at his disposal, utilizing only what he regarded as "useful" (1. 69. 2, 72. 6), namely, interesting and/or serving his goals. After all, neither he nor his readers regarded circumcision as peculiarly Jewish. Herodotus had already reported that circumcision, originating and practiced in Egypt, had been adopted by various nations, such as the Colchi, the Ethiopians, the Phoenicians, and some Syrian people (Hdt. 2. 104. 1–3), while Aristophanes mocks the Egyptians and Phoenicians for practicing circumcision (*Av.* 465–69). Hecataeus, therefore, could have omitted the practice of circumcision without feeling that he was thereby depriving the Greek reader of a feature that distinguished the Jews from all other nations.

Hecataeus had a similar reason for passing over the Jewish dietary restrictions. Egyptian abstinence from the flesh of many types of animals, and its influence on Egyptian exclusivity and aversion to dining with aliens, are explicitly mentioned by Herodotus (2. 41) and were therefore well known in the Greek world. At the same time, the restrictions may have been omitted by Diodorus, who could be content with the general statement about Jewish *apanthrōpia*.

EGYPTIAN AND JEWISH SOURCES OF INFORMATION

We shall begin with the source of the *origo* story (paras. 1–2), called by Diodorus *ktisis* ("the foundation story," para. 1), the appropriate, specific Greek classification for this sort of *origo*. The Jewish departure from Egypt is portrayed as part of the expulsion of all the foreigners. A plague had broken out in Egypt, and the Egyptian masses attributed it to the gods, who had become angered by the neglect of the autochthonous Egyptians in matters of cultic practice. The masses defended themselves by blaming their neglect on the bad influence of the presence of foreigners in Egypt, who worshipped their own gods in their own cults. Consequently they decided that they could best return to their traditional customs and appease the gods by expelling all the foreigners. A minority of the foreigners, "the most outstanding and active," headed by Danaus and Cadmus, landed on the coasts of Greece and neighboring lands, while the vast majority turned to nearby Judaea (paras. 1–2).

This version, designed to counter the Egyptian opinion about the origin of all nations from Egypt, is by itself nothing but a reworking of Egyptian stories—surviving in later Hellenistic and Roman literature—concerning the expulsion of the foreigners as punishment for the foreigners' (especially the Jews') disrespect for the Egyptian gods, which brought disasters upon the country.[70] In citing and reacting to the Egyptian theories on the origin of peoples, Hecataeus mentions explicitly, and several times, that he used Egyptian sources.[71] Influence of Egyptian sources of information can also be detected in what has survived of Hecataeus's account of some Jewish customs.[72] In the account we have, it is the autochthonous Egyptians, not the Jews, who neglected their cults. This change was made by Hecataeus not necessarily for the sake of the Jews, but for the Greek tribes. The xenophobic Egyptian version would not have served Hecataeus's aim of improving relations between the Egyptian and the Greek population at the beginning of Macedonian rule in Egypt. Whatever the case may be, such an account could not allow Moses a prominent role in this section, and it would have been out of place to narrate the marvels of Moses that Hecataeus would have heard from his Jewish informants. Furthermore, the addition of insults to the Egyptians would have detracted from the idealization of the Egyptian people and its customs, the motif running through the Egyptian ethnography.

70. See Lysimachus in Josephus *Contra Apionem* 1. 305–6; Diodorus 34/35. 1. 1–3; Tacitus *Historiae* 5. 3. 1; and see pp. 321–24 below. Willrich (1895) 48; Reinach (1895) 15 n. 1; Jaeger (1938b) 144–45; Gager (1972) 28; Will and Orrieux (1986) 83 and Bickerman (1988) 17 rightly claim that the information derives from hostile Egyptian sources, but they overlook the inversions and the softening of the material; cf. Reinach (1895) 15. Gabba (1989) 627 argues that Hecataeus added the expulsion story, which he found in Egyptian sources, to the Jewish tradition of the Exodus and the Greek tradition about Cadmus and Danaus bringing Egyptian culture to the Greeks.

71. Explicit references to written sources (ἀναγραφαί): 1. 26. 1, 31. 7, 44. 4, 45. 1, 46. 7, 8, 69. 7, 73. 4, 81. 4, 92. 2, 6, 96. 3, 98. 1. As for oral sources, the formulae "the Egyptians say," "they claim," etc., appear many times in the Egyptian ethnography and serve to indicate oral sources (although elsewhere such phrases often indicate written sources).

72. See p. 132 and notes 73, 122 below.

In the more detailed and more extensive section called by Diodorus *nomima* (para. 1), Moses plays a central role (paras. 3–8). He is described as a leader outstanding in his wisdom (*phronēsis*) and courage (*andreia*, para. 3). Hecataeus attributes to him the establishment of the Jewish settlement in Jerusalem and the land of Judaea, the Jewish constitution, and all types of Jewish institutions and customs. Moses' activities as a founder include the following:

1. Guiding the Jews to a desolate land (later called Judaea), after their expulsion from Egypt (para. 3)
2. Founding Jerusalem and other cities (para. 3)
3. Building the Jewish Temple and establishing the cult there (para. 3)
4. Dividing the Jewish people into twelve tribes (para. 3)
5. Determining the fundaments of the peculiar Jewish religion: a belief in one god, identified with the sky, and a cult devoid of statues and images (paras. 3, 4)
6. Transmitting the laws to the Jews (the laws are considered by the Jews to be of divine origin, passed to them through the mediation of Moses) (para. 3)
7. Introducing a way of life differing from that of other nations, described as "somewhat (or quite) removed from [the society of] men and hostile to strangers"—all because of the trauma and ordeal of the expulsion from Egypt (para. 4)
8. Entrusting the future leadership of the Jews to the priests, who were chosen on the strength of their qualities (not their descent) and whose duties included not only the sacrifice of victims but also judicial functions and supervision of observance of the laws (paras. 4–5)
9. Determining that the priests would be headed by a High Priest, a position to be filled by the most gifted of the priests (in certain cases, the High Priest receives guidance directly from God) (paras. 5–6)
10. Organizing the army, training the youth for war, and instituting special rules toward this end (para. 6)
11. Leading campaigns against the neighboring peoples and distributing their lands equally among the Jews, with bigger lots for the priests, to enable them to perform their public duties (para. 7)

Of Jewish laws and customs, the only ones detailed are agrarian—the prohibition on the permanent sale of land, and the inducement to bear many children and keep them alive (paras. 7–8). Other laws and customs (as opposed to institutions) are mentioned by Diodorus in passing, especially those concerning sacrifices, marriage, and burial. It is only emphasized that they differ from parallel laws of other peoples (paras. 3, 8).

One hardly needs to be a biblical or a classical scholar to realize that we have here a Greek reworking of information drawn indirectly from the Bible and from

Jewish life at the time of Hecataeus. Most obvious is the reflection (despite the substantial differences) of biblical stories from different periods: the wandering from Egypt to the Promised Land; Moses' role as legislator, receiving the Torah from God on Mt. Sinai; the invasion of Canaan, its conquest, and settlement; the central status of Jerusalem and the Temple in Jewish life; the belief in one God and the prohibition against anthropomorphic images of the divine entity; the division of the nation into twelve tribes; the role of the priests as interpreters of the Torah, both overseeing its enforcement and acting as judges;[73] the appointment of a High Priest who counsels with God (namely, with the help of "innocents");[74] the existence of mass ceremonies in which the words of the Torah are transmitted to the people by the High Priest or someone of similar authority;[75] the reference to obeisance before the High Priest, which seems to be an inaccurate reflection of the practice of falling upon the ground and bowing before the Lord on such occasions;[76] the prohibition against the permanent sale of land;[77] the command to be fruitful and multiply, and the high birth rate, as appears from the stories of the Patriarchs and the Exodus. The text even includes a paraphrase of biblical verses saying that Moses received the Torah from God (para. 6).[78] To this can be added information based on Jewish life in the time of Hecataeus, such as the provision of greater lots for the priests (para. 7), an interpretation reflecting Second Temple reality when large estates were held by priestly families.[79] The same also applies to the relative density of the population in Judaea proper in the time of Hecataeus.[80] Even the mistaken definition of the Jewish God reflects Jewish terminology of that period: Hecataeus says that the Jews regard heaven as "god." He was obviously misled by the forms of address

73. Deuteronomy 17.8–12, 19.17, 21.5. Cf. Malachi 2.7; 2 Chronicles 17.8–9, 19.5–10, which reflect the Persian period. See also Stern, *GLAJJ* 1: 31; Will and Orrieux (1986) 85–86. Some of the Jewish priesthood's functions and rights parallel those of the Egyptian priesthood as described by Hecataeus (Diod. 1. 73. 2–5). Hecataeus emphasizes that in Greece there is no priestly class (5).

74. Numbers 27.21; 1 Samuel 28.6; Ezra 2.63; Nehemiah 7.65. Walton (1955) 255 and Mendels (1983) 106 refer to Malachi 2.7. See also Reinach (1895) 18 n. 1.

75. Apart from the ceremony on Mt. Sinai, it is worth mentioning Deuteronomy 27.9 ff., 31.10–13; Joshua 8.31–35, 24.1 ff.; Ezra 3.1–13, 10.9–17; Nehemiah 8.1–8; 2 Chronicles 29.4 ff., 34.29 ff.

76. Nehemiah 8.6. Cf. Sirach 50.18: the kneeling of the people at the Temple on the Day of Atonement.

77. See Leviticus 25.25–34; cf. Numbers 26.54; 1 Kings 21.3–4; and the word גורל (lot), which recurs in Joshua. See further Guttmann 1: 56. Tcherikover (1961) 122–23 drew attention to Nehemiah's social reform.

78. Leviticus 26.46, 27.34; Numbers 26.13; Deuteronomy 28.69, 32.44 (LXX).

79. Gager (1972) 33; Stern, *GLAJJ* 1: 32–33; Mendels (1983) 106. Cf. Willrich (1895) 51.

80. On overpopulation in the Judaean mountains, see Stern, *GLAJJ* 1: 34; Bar-Kochva (1977) 169–71; (1989) 56–58; Rappaport (1986); Applebaum (1986); (1989) 9–29; Safrai (2000) 70, 78.

for God—"heaven" and "God of heaven"—common among Jews in his time as a substitute for the Tetragrammaton.[81]

Hecataeus wrote his account before the translation into Greek of the Torah, not to mention the other books of the Bible. Ptolemy I ruled for some spells of time over Judaea (320–316, 312 B.C.E.), the last approximately a decade before the composition of the *Aegyptiaca*. The court must have been acquainted with Jewish life not only in Egypt but also in Judaea. This knowledge could have served a court official like Hecataeus. However, the bulk of the information referring to remote periods, and detailed internal information (however adapted to Greek tastes it may have been), indicate personal consultation with local Jews. We may therefore accept the suggestion proposed by many that Hecataeus consulted Jewish informants—perhaps with a priestly background—resident in Egypt.[82]

SOURCES OF INSPIRATION,
OR THE GREEK SLANT ON THE INFORMATION

As a result of the reworking of the information into a Greek mold, Hecataeus's account differs significantly from that provided by his sources. It would be redundant to list all the basic errors, many of which are self-evident. It will suffice to note that Moses did not enter the Promised Land, did not found Jerusalem, and did not build the Jewish Temple; and the mainstream biblical tradition describes an extremely violent conquest of Canaan.

A good number of scholars in the past have noted the Greek coloring of the excursus, or its being an *interpretatio Graeca*.[83] However, the principles of the Greek reworking of the material, as well as the many details, still have to be properly and fully identified. At the same time, it must be said that many of the parallels drawn with Greek tradition do not stand up to criticism. The Greek world embraced a variety of regimes, societies, customs, and traditions both mythological and historical, which developed over centuries, acquiring and discarding guise after guise. For this reason, it is not difficult to find some Greek counterpart to almost every clause in the excursus, while it is to be doubted

81. Rightly noted by Mélèze-Modrzejewski (1989) 6–7, referring to the Cyrus decree, two of the Elephantine papyri, and 1 Maccabees. Hecataeus's misconception may also have been influenced by the reference to the divinity of Heaven in Herodotus's account of the Persian religion (1. 131), which seems to have been the general inspiration for Hecataeus's causal explanation for the features of Jewish belief (see pp. 125, 133 below).

82. Suggested by Willrich (1895) 50; Jaeger (1938a) 146; (1938b) 139–40; Jacoby, *FGrH* IIIa, no. 264, p. 51; Guttmann 1: 51; Nock (1959) 9; Murray (1970) 158; Gager (1972) 37; Diamond (1980) 81, 87; Mendels (1983) 98–110; Will and Orrieux (1986) 91–92 and passim; Gabba (1989) 627.

83. See, e.g., Jaeger (1938a) 140–43; Guttmann 1: 50–66; Hengel (1973) 465–67; Diamond (1974); Mendels (1983).

whether some of them really influenced its design. A sense of proportion needs to be employed, therefore, when tracing the influence of Greek terms and concepts and assessing the degree to which they played a part in the reworking of the information Hecataeus had at his disposal.

Even more problematic is the effort of a number of scholars to find a common denominator for all the items in the excursus in one or another Greek tradition or doctrine. Thus some have described the excursus as a "Platonic ideal,"[84] while others have regarded it as a "Spartan model" or an "Egyptian Sparta."[85] One scholar views the excursus as a hybrid Platonic-Spartan constitution,[86] and another has even suggested profound Peripatetic influence.[87] The range of proposals itself speaks against the exclusivity of any one of them. In fact, each model could explain only a small number of the items and assessments in the excursus, while a large portion of the text would fall far outside that model's embrace or oppose it completely. The excursus of Hecataeus was not written according to a uniform model, for there was no Greek theocracy. Sorting out the details and considering them together with what has been said above about the Jewish and Egyptian sources will enable us to understand how the excursus was composed.

The Greek coloring is the result of the following features of the excursus: (a) the telescoping of central events in Jewish history and their attribution to the "founder," (b) the use of Greek terms and concepts, and (c) the influence of Greek institutions, beliefs, and values in the description of Jewish ones.

A. Telescoping of the Central Events in Jewish History and Their Attribution to the "Founder"

The account of Moses' deeds telescopes the events and developments of three phases in Israelite and Jewish traditional history: the wandering in the desert, the early settlement of the country, and Hecataeus's own time.[88] Hecataeus telescoped all his information into one generation, concentrating everything around the personality of Moses. In so doing, Hecataeus upheld a well-developed literary tradition. Already in the late thirties of the twentieth century, Werner Jaeger had observed that Moses was portrayed as the classical figure of the founder of a Greek polis.[89] This basic comment requires elucidation, amplification, and qualification.

84. Jaeger (1938a) 151–52; (1938b) 141–42; Guttmann 1: 73–79; cf. Gager (1972) 36; Hengel (1973) 465; Bickerman (1988) 17. But see Jacoby, *FGrH* IIIa, no. 264, p. 52; Diamond (1974) 236 ff.

85. Ginsburg (1934) 117–22; Murray (1970) 158–61; Will and Orrieux (1986) 86–88.

86. Mélèze-Modrzejewski (1989) 6.

87. Diamond (1980) 82–92.

88. That the excursus reflects Jewish life in the Persian period was stressed by Radin (1915) 92–95; Tcherikover (1961) 56–59, 119–25; and particularly Mendels (1983).

89. Jaeger (1938b) 140 is content with the following comment: "This sequence is in harmony with the Greek scheme typical for such a historical development: first comes the emigration of the

The excursus is clearly influenced by the foundation literature (*ktisis*) that was widespread in Greek culture following the colonization movement of the seventh and sixth centuries B.C.E. This literature tended to attribute to the legendary founder (*ktistēs*, *oikistēs*) of the city, settlement, or tribe the activities essential to the setting up of a new community, and used to regard him as responsible for the features and customs for which the place was later famous.[90] Some or all of the following activities were attributed to each founder: the actual initiative to emigrate; leading the expedition; building the city and the temple; organizing the cult; establishing the constitution; instituting the governmental authorities; setting up the army; campaigning and conquering neighboring territory, with the subsequent division of the lands. The sequence of undertakings attributed to Moses the founder follows that of foundation stories in the main. The prohibition against selling land and the requirement to rear children in order to increase the population also have their parallels in foundation stories.[91]

The basic design led Hecataeus to add information that had not been supplied by his Jewish informants but was typical of many foundation stories. The following are just a few examples: the Jewish settlement was established in a desolate area (para. 2);[92] the founder—Moses—prepared the younger generation for war by developing their stamina through exacting exercises (para. 6); after the con-

---

settlers, then the struggle with the people whose land they conquer, then the foundation of a city (πόλις), and finally the legislation. Thus if Hecataeus was told that Moses was the legislator of the Jews, all the other steps had to be put before this final act. He may even have corrected on his own account what the Jewish theologians told him, since this was the normal and natural order." The editing of material according to the scheme of foundation stories has been noted by Jacoby, *RE* s.v. "Hekataios (4)," col. 2765; Lebram (1974) 248–50; Stern, *GLAJJ* 1: 21; Gabba (1989) 627–28; Bar-Kochva (1996d) 26; cf. Reinach (1895) 16 n. 1. Mendels (1983) 101–7, while accepting the influence of foundation stories, regards the order and attribution of all the activities to Moses as originating in trends and developments in the Persian period, and in its unique view of earlier Jewish history. For an interesting comparison between colonization stories in the book of Joshua and Greek foundation stories, see Weinfeld (1987).

90. On this trend in foundation literature in general, see Schmid (1947) 178–80; Virgilio (1972); Graham (1962) 25–39, 151–52; Leschhorn (1984) 85 ff., 106 ff.; Dougherty (1993) 22. For an earlier parallel, see *Odyssey* 6. 7–10.

91. On the equal distribution of lands, and literary tradition concerning their inalienability in Greek colonies, see Graham (1962) 151–52; Asheri (1966) 5–24, 108–21. Cf., for Rome, Dionysius of Halicarnassus 2. 7. 4. The most detailed literary reference to the demand to rear children: 2. 15. 1–3.

92. See, e.g., Dougherty (1993) 4. The attempts by several biblical scholars to find in Hecataeus support for their view that the settlement of the Israelites in Canaan was—at least in part—peaceful and directed toward the empty territories are fundamentally flawed. Hecataeus did not conduct research in biblical criticism and archaeology before writing his account. For such an attempt, see, e.g., Weinfeld (1993) 209 n. 53; cf. the counterarguments of Stern: *GLAJJ* 1: 29–30. It is worth adding to the sources mentioned by Stern *Odyssey* 9. 116–24; Plato *Laws* 704b. Diamond (1976) 246–49 gives another explanation for the source of this statement.

quest of lands beyond the original settlement, Moses divided the plots among the settlers (para. 7).

Hecataeus even attributed to Moses the invention of the Jewish religion (paras. 3, 4), although no Greek founder ever invented a new religion, remaining faithful to the gods and cult of the metropolis, the mother city. The unusual religion, however, was one of the most prominent features of Jews mentioned by him, and Hecataeus would have been led, by the format he had chosen, to attribute it to the founder.

There is a clear lacuna in the telescoped chain of historical events, namely, the kings of the biblical period. Hecataeus even states explicitly that since the executive powers were invested in the priests, the Jews never had any need for a king (para. 5). Had Hecataeus heard such a thing from his Jewish informants? It has been suggested that Hecataeus's informants were Egyptian Jews opposed to the renewal of kingship in Judaea, and for this reason they covered up its previous existence.[93] I have my doubts, especially since there are no real traces of Jewish opposition to kingship either in the Persian period or in the time of Hecataeus, in Judaea or in the Diaspora, nor was there any reason for it. Quite the contrary: the prophets, including Second Temple prophets, clearly pine for the House of David, a sentiment shared by other books of the Persian period.[94] This said, it is not known what undercurrents of thought circulated through Egyptian Jewry, particularly during the period in which the Egyptian priesthood was adopting and propagating new concepts about the authority and personality of the ideal ruler,[95] and at the same time that the Hellenistic world was seesawing between the two traditions of the Greek polis and Macedonian kingship. The possibility cannot therefore be ruled out that certain Egyptian Jews, perhaps of priestly origin, who regarded the First Temple monarchy as the source of all the evils visited upon the Jewish people, provided Hecataeus with this piece of mistaken information.

There exists another possibility: the sentence as a whole is actually formulated in a way similar to the causal sentences of the excursus, the statement about the absence of kinship among the Jews being in fact the result of the role of the high priest, previously described in much detail. Here, however, the prepositions indicate that the cause is a historical fact, while the result is the author's own conclusion.[96] The statement as a whole should therefore be regarded as Hecataeus's own interpretation, and not a summary of what was told him by his Jewish infor-

93. See Mendels (1983) 100–101.

94. See Liver (1959) 1109–10; Japhet (1977) 334–412. Cf. the doubts of Gruen (1998) 54 n. 46. Willrich (1895) 50 (cf. Reinach [1895] 19 n. 3) notes the similarity to the description of the Jewish theocracy in Josephus Contra Apionem 2. 184, 187, but Josephus's account does not reflect the Persian period.

95. See note 20 above.

96. See para. 3: διὰ τό; para. 4: διὰ τό and διὰ γάρ; para. 8: καὶ δι', as against para. 5: διὸ καί.

mants. Yet how did Hecataeus arrive at the conclusion that the Jews never had a king? I would suggest that the omission is due to the writing scheme Hecataeus devised from the outset, together with his method of collecting information: when he gathered data from the Jewish informants—a miniscule fraction of the vast research effort that preceded the composition of the Egyptian ethnography— he concentrated only on collecting material pertinent to the *origo* and *nomima* sections, the only sections that would appear in the mini-excursus. Hecataeus, then, would not have asked his informers about the kings, nor, even if told about them, would he have noted it down. When editing the collected information and writing the final version—possibly after quite some time—things he may have heard incidentally about the Jewish kings would have been forgotten amidst the myriad of other details he had acquired for his Egyptian ethnography. He was thus in a position to link the facts at his disposal concerning the position of High Priests both Mosaic and of his own time and the Persian period, and deduce that the Jews never needed any kings, since they had always had priests with executive powers to lead the people. Hecataeus may have inclined to this conclusion because of his general aim to demonstrate the great difference between the practices and lifestyles of the Jews and the Egyptians.

The vast amount of information collected for the *Aegyptiaca* as a whole, and the length of time between the collection of material and the actual writing of the excursus, might explain the absence of any reference to the Sabbath, a Jewish custom that more than almost any other could have helped Hecataeus to emphasize Jewish exclusivity. Even assuming some mishap in the registering or preservation of the information by Hecataeus, however, the omission of any reference to the Sabbath by the author could have occurred only at a time when Greeks were still not fully aware of the strangeness of the Jewish day of rest. The Hecataean ethnography was published around 305–302 B.C.E., before Ptolemy I's capture of Jerusalem on the Sabbath and his expulsion of many of its residents to Egypt (Joseph. *AJ* 12. 6–8; *Ap.* 1. 205–11). It was only after this expulsion that the Jewish community in Alexandria and the Egyptian *chōra* became a distinctive factor in everyday Egyptian life, and Jewish recruitment into the Ptolemaic army began probably after that. No author of the caliber of Hecataeus would after all that have forgotten to mention the Sabbath in a Jewish ethnography. It is still possible, however, as noted above with regard to the Jewish dietary laws, that the omission of the Sabbath was due to Diodorus. Whatever the case may be, as a result of the absence of the Sabbath, Jewish exclusivity is exemplified only by the customs of sacrifice, marriage, and burial (paras. 3.4, 8); and here it is certainly Diodorus who omitted the details.[97]

---

97. To anticipate some alternative suggestions, it is worth pointing out that although the condensing of the events is strongly influenced by the genre of foundation stories, the Jewish excursus

B. The Use of Greek Terms and Concepts

Hecataean coloring is evident in the casual use of Greek terminology and even data pertaining to personalities, institutions, and the Jewish way of life. The word *apoikia*, for example, is used to denote the settlement in Judaea (para. 3). It meant literally "a settlement away from home," usually signifying a volunteer, organized settlement, but it was also occasionally applied to exiles.[98] Over time, the word came to mean simply "a settlement," without reference to a preexisting metropolis (e.g., Dion. Hal. *Ant. rom.* 2. 2. 4). The expulsion of the Jews from Egypt is described as *xenēlasia* (para. 4), a term usually denoting specifically the Spartan practice of expelling foreigners.[99] The Jewish Torah is called simply *politeia* (para. 3)—literally, "the constitution of the *polis*"—apparently for want of a suitable term denoting a divine constitution (*nomoi* would have been more fitting; *theokratia* first appears in Josephus's *Contra Apionem* [2. 165]). The Jewish settlements founded by Moses are called simply *poleis* (para. 3), "independent city-states," and there are many other Greek terms far from Jewish tradition and reality.

C. The Influence of Greek Institutions, Beliefs, and Values

Beyond the casual use of Greek terminology, Greek elements of government are included in the characterization of Moses and among the institutions established by him. Moses is presented as a man who excelled in the virtues of *phronēsis* (prudence) and *andreia* (courage). There is no mention here of his moral and religious qualities. One might have expected him to be called, for instance, *eusebēs*, a pious respecter of the god, but he is not.[100] The qualities ascribed to him are only those required and typical of a Greek founder-leader-legislator. The priests draw their authority not from noble descent but from those personal qualities that make them fit for public service. Hecataeus calls them "the men of most

---

as a whole is not of this genre. The second part of Diodorus's introduction, which may well reflect the presentation of the elements of the excursus by Hecataeus himself, states that he is about to narrate the *ktisis* and the *nomima*. These are the first—and primary—sections of the ethnographic genre. The excursus also refers explicitly to the customs of later Judaism (paras. 5, 6, 8), something referred to only implicitly or in concealed fashion in foundation stories. It is also worth noting that unlike the case in foundation stories, Moses is described not as leading the Jews out of Egypt, but only as founding the settlement in the new land.

98. In Sinope and Barca, see Graham (1982) 143; in Elea, see Schmid (1947) 171.

99. Noted by Ginsburg (1934); Guttmann 1: 108–11; Murray (1970) 158–59.

100. Noted by Bidez and Cumont (1938) 1: 241; Jacoby, *FGrH* IIIa, no. 264, pp. 51–52; Diamond (1974) 228–29; (1980) 83–84.

refinement (most civilized?) and the most able" (para. 4: τοὺς χαριεστάτους καὶ μάλιστα δυνησομένους),[101] which reflects the ideal of the aristocratic state, where the good are those with superior abilities (e.g., Arist. *Pol.* 1279a34, 1293b1–6, 1294a9) and are not necessarily the wealthy. The High Priest is superior to the other priests in his prudence (*phronēsis*) and his excellence (*aretē*). At this point, Hecataeus is not drawing on philosophical terminology, where *phronēsis* and *aretē* would hardly be treated as two discrete entities, but is adopting a more popular usage of the terms. These are characteristics the average Greek would expect a leader to have. There is no trace of the biblical tradition according to which the priests and the High Priest were appointed by Moses by virtue of their family descent, their outstanding religious devotion, and their unreserved belief in the one God, when put to the test. The requirement of the young "to practice both bravery and steadfastness . . . the endurance of every hardship" (para. 6) is typical of the Greek *paideia*.[102] The mistaken notion that the Jews regarded heaven as god, originating in a misunderstanding of the common contemporary Jewish usage of "heaven" and "God of heaven,"[103] may have been inspired by Herodotus's causal explanation of the Persian religion and cult: he says that the Persians call "the whole circle of heaven" Zeus (1. 131).[104]

THE APPLICATION OF LITERARY FEATURES AND AIMS PECULIAR TO HECATAEUS

Hecataeus's innovations in ethnographic writing are prominently displayed in the Jewish excursus, and these too contributed to the departure of his account from the information he had obtained from his Jewish informants. I shall consider here the two most important innovations: causal explanations and messages for society.

A. Causal Explanations

The excursus abounds in causal links and explanations, some inspired by Greek tradition and thought, some the product of Hecataeus's inventiveness. The Jews settled in their land because it was desolate (3. 2). Jewish exclusivity and hatred of foreigners are explained as a reaction to the unpleasant experiences suf-

---

101. Cf. Aristotle *Nicomachean Ethics* 1095a18–19, b22; *Politica* 1267a40, 1297b9, 1320b7 (see Diamond [1980] 94; Feldman [1993] 235).

102. Noted by Jaeger (1938a) 152; see, e.g., Plato *Laws* 704b–c. Stern, *GLAJJ* 1: 32, referring to Polybius 6. 48. 3 ff., sees here a Spartan feature.

103. See note 81 above. For the reference of Herodotus, see p. 133 below.

104. See further below on the avoidance of anthropomorphism; cf. pp. 159–60 below.

fered by the Jews after their expulsion from Egypt (para. 3.3); the same applies to Jewish sacrificial practices, and most probably marriage and funeral rites (paras. 3.4, 8). The Jewish prohibition against worshipping idols and images is explained by the Jewish belief that God is not anthropomorphic (para. 3.4); this idea is mistaken, at least for the time of Hecataeus,[105] but it is a logical conclusion inspired by the explanation given by Herodotus (1. 131) for why statues of the divinity are not made by the Persians.[106] The Jews believe in Heaven as the "god and master of all," since it "encloses" the earth on all sides (para. 3. 4). Hecataeus explains the division into twelve tribes by noting that twelve is the most perfect number and agrees with the number of months in a year (para. 3. 3); this explanation has no parallels in early Jewish tradition, but it echoes remarks made about the number twelve in Plato's *Laws* (745b-d).[107] The Jewish priests receive greater lots to provide them with enough leisure to perform their public duties (para. 7),[108] while according to the Bible the Israelite priests were not allotted lands. The detailing in Greek dress of the qualities of Moses, the High Priest, and the priests (paras. 3-5) is in fact a causal explanation for their status. There are traces of additional causal explanations, which were either abbreviated by Diodorus or only implied in Hecataeus's account. Causal explanations were also given for Jewish laws and customs relating to landownership and child-rearing.

105. Biblical texts and Second Temple literature of most types are replete with anthropomorphic descriptions of the divinity. Only Jewish Hellenistic allegorical literature and its forerunners escape this tendency. Despite all attempts to interpret the texts as metaphorical, or as opposing anthropomorphism, it is impossible to explain away so many varied references. Indeed, in the last generation, archaeological evidence has been unearthed proving the existence of anthropomorphism with regard to the Israelite god among the inhabitants both of Samaria and of the southern kingdom. It will suffice to refer the reader to just a few bibliographical items. For the biblical and postbiblical period: Kaufmann (1960) 1: 226-44; for the literature of the sages: Lorberbaum (2000) 3-54; (2004) 62-104. For recent archaeological evidence: Meshel (1978); Olyan (1988) 22 ff.; Dietrich and Loretz (1992) 94 ff. The absence of images in Judaea in the Persian period (see E. Stern [1999] 245-55) testifies to strict observation of the prohibition against pictures and idols, but not necessarily to a change in the old anthropomorphic perception.

106. Suggested by Gager (1972) 31. Cf. Hecataeus (διὰ τὸ μὴ νομίζειν ἀνθρωπόμορφον εἶναι τὸν θεόν) with Herodotus (ὡς μὲν ἐμοὶ δοκέειν ὅτι οὐκ ἀνθρωποφυέας ἐνόμισαν τοὺς θεούς). Herodotus himself indicates that the causal explanation is his own. Hecataeus found it ready made. On Hecataeus's "dialogue" with Herodotus's *Histories*, see Murray (1970); cf. p. 96 and note 22 above.

107. See in detail Guttmann 1: 53-54; more references in Stern, *GLAJJ* 1: 30; Diamond (1974) 81-83.

108. Cf. Aristotle *Politica* 1269a35, 1273a34; for Egyptian influence, see Diodorus 1. 72. 2-3. Cf. also Euhemerus's utopian treatise on the Panchaeans, where the priests are given, for the same reason, a double share of the produce (Diod. 5. 45. 5).

B. Messages for the Hellenistic Society
of Hecataeus's Time

Hecataeus seems to have developed information he had acquired concerning the high Jewish birthrate and the prohibition in the Torah against the sale of land in perpetuity. According to Hecataeus, Moses made sure that the division of land was equal, and he prohibited the sale of land in order to prevent a concentration of land in the hands of a few, which eventually would have led to the oppression of the poor and the subsequent scarcity of manpower (para. 3.7). This is followed by the statement that Moses demanded from the Jews a high birthrate, and that they should raise all their children, a requirement made economically possible by the private ownership of land sufficient for each farmer (para. 3. 8). The passage as it is formulated sounds somewhat incoherent and confused, but this may be the result of unintelligent cutting or reformulation on the part of Diodorus. It becomes more comprehensible when considered alongside the detailed parallel in the Egyptian ethnography, where Hecataeus explains how the ancient Egyptian kings secured a continuous and stable supply of qualified and loyal manpower for their armies (Diod. 1. 73. 7–9): ownership of lands by the warrior class (*machimoi*), besides ensuring their loyalty and fighting spirit, was meant first and foremost to enable high birthrates (cf. 80. 5–6 on the low cost of child maintenance) and to encourage members of the warrior class to send their offspring willingly to the army, being highly motivated both to defend their country and to add to its territory. The final demand that Hecataeus attributes to Moses, to raise the children, is a veiled criticism of the Greek custom of killing "superfluous" children (*ekthesis*), widespread because of the scarcity of resources in mainland Greece of the classical age.[109] To drive the point home, Hecataeus praises the Jews for being a populous nation (para. 3. 8). The Egyptians receive praise for the same reason (1. 80. 6).

Hecataeus's explanation for the agrarian laws and child-rearing both of the pharaohs and of the Jews seems to be inspired by Greek foundation literature, alleged Spartan practices, and especially social theories found scattered throughout philosophical literature.[110] All these were adapted so as to convey a message to the Ptolemaic authorities and the Greek-Macedonian population in Egypt. The settlers of "European" extraction suffered from a serious shortage of manpower and were a small minority in the midst of the native Egyptian population, which was in part hostile. Hecataeus was outlining a plan of action designed to reduce as far as possible the demographic gap, and to ensure a continuous

---

109. See Stern, *GLAJJ* 1: 33; Kraemaer (1993) 108. On this practice, see Patterson (1985).

110. See references in Guttmann 1: 56–57; Gager (1972) 34; Stern, *GLAJJ* 1: 33; Diamond (1974) 105–8; (1980) 88–90. See also note 102 above.

supply of efficient manpower ready to fight, if need be, against the Egyptian population and the nomads of the west and south, as well as against the rival Macedonian powers. Indeed, the lesson with regard to child-rearing seems to have been learned, at least in part. There are indications that over time efforts were made in the Ptolemaic kingdom to improve the demographic balance by increasing the birthrate and investing in child welfare. This trend is noticeable in Ptolemaic Egypt, for instance, in the relatively frequent appearance of images of children in the plastic arts (as children, not miniature adults, as was the case in classical Greek sculpture). As for the agrarian regulations, the Ptolemaic military settlement may be regarded as the (unsuccessful or partial) realization of such plans. Hecataeus seems to have been motivated by the topical significance of the above messages to ignore for a short while the main aim of the excursus, the refutation of the Egyptian theory regarding the origin of the Jews by emphasizing the difference between the customs and traditions of the Jews and the Egyptians.

· · ·

Having traced the sources and analyzed characteristics of the various elements of the excursus, let us try to picture the process by which the *nomima* section was constructed. In line with the purpose of the excursus and the context in which it was to be inserted, at the stage of collecting material Hecataeus was looking for information for the *origo* and *nomima* alone. He was especially interested in data about the real connection between the Jews and the Egyptians. For this he used oral sources, both Jewish and Egyptian. After sorting through the material, he placed Moses at the center of this section, making him responsible for all the important initiatives and activities pertaining to the beginning and the development of the Jewish people, as well as for the characteristic features of the Jewish people. Yet in the *origo* section the role of Moses was omitted for reasons connected with the special portrayal of the expulsion and its extent. The accumulated data for the *nomima* section were arranged according to the usual sequence of the genre of Greek foundation stories, Jewish concepts were reformulated in Greek terms, and the information as a whole given Greek coloring and adapted to the new way of writing ethnographies, causal explanations being appended to items of information. Since the excursus was after all based on information pertaining to the Jews, the Greek features integrated in it do not represent a single, uniform Greek political or philosophical system but are eclectic. In addition, particular Jewish laws and practices relating to agrarian ownership and birth were applied and adapted to serve as a message to the contemporary Greek reader. This technique in one variation or another is not essentially different from that used in the construction of any other excursus or ethnographic account of a people, Oriental or otherwise, by Hecataeus or Greek writers who followed in his footsteps.

THE ATTITUDE OF HECATAEUS
TOWARD MOSES AND THE JEWS

The discussion above allows us to assess Hecataeus's attitude toward the character and practices of the Jewish people. Scholars, with a number of exceptions, have tended to regard the excursus as a conscious idealization of Judaism and a model for imitation. Some have even gone so far as to portray the excursus as "enthusiastic" and "most favourable," and the attitude toward Moses as "admiration."[111] The historical explanation for this has been that in the time of Hecataeus there were as yet no confrontations between Jews and Greeks, and the Greeks were still inclined to wonder at the newly revealed Eastern cultures. It would, however, be nearer the truth to regard Hecataeus as an author who strives to be, or at least to appear to be, unbiased, objective, and balanced. The excursus was intended at the outset to refute the sweeping theory of the Egyptians that all nations originated in Egypt. Hecataeus's argument with this required him also to elaborate on the descent and practices of the Jews. He found it especially appropriate to do so because he was naturally interested in this minority community living in Egypt. For him, the Jews were no less worthy of attention than other Oriental peoples encountered by Greeks after the conquests of Alexander, which were described in detail by him and his contemporaries. Their religion and system of government aroused curiosity, and there were also a few Jewish laws that could be usefully adopted by contemporary Greeks and Macedonians in Egypt: the agrarian laws and those relating to the birthrate and rearing of children, all essential for the maintenance of an effective army and for the survival of the Greek settlement in Egypt.

Yet the Jews also had some less savory characteristics. Hecataeus does not overlook them. Everyday Jewish customs (τὰς κατὰ τὸν βίον ἀγωγάς, para. 4) differ from those of every other people. Hecataeus cites as examples sacrificial, marriage, and burial customs, all of which—so he says—differ entirely from those of other peoples. Diodorus may well have omitted other examples offered by Hecataeus. The author goes on to explain that Moses introduced a way of life (*bios*) that is characterized as "somewhat (= quite?) removed from [the society of] men and [somewhat?] hostile to strangers" (ἀπάνθρωπόν τινα καὶ μισόξενον,

---

111. Willrich (1895) 50–51; (1900) 59, 89; Jaeger (1938a) 149, 151–53; (1938b) 140–43; Walton (1955) 255–57; Isaac (1956) 59; Guttmann 1: 53–68; Schalit (1969) 747–48; Gager (1972) 33–37; Murray (1970) 149, 158–59; (1973) 167 ff.; Hengel (1973) 564 ff.; Stern, *GLAJJ* 1: 21, 30; (1976) 1109; Diamond (1980) 85–86; Will and Orrieux (1986) 87–92; Bickerman (1988) 17–18; Gabba (1989) 628–29; Mélèze-Modrzejewski (1989) 12–13; Liebes (2001/2) 258–60; Kasher (2003) 62; Schwartz (2003) 192. In contrast to these views, see Jacoby, *FGrH* IIIa, no. 264, pp. 48 ff.: "es ist ganz deutlich, dass er (Hekataios) das jüdische wesen nicht als vorbildlich, sondern nur als fremdartig empfunden hat"; cf. Tcherikover (1961) 367; Sevenster (1975) 189; Conzelmann (1981) 58; and esp. Schäfer (1997a) 16–17.

para. 4). It should be emphasized that the evaluation as it stands refers to the Jewish way of life in its entirety.

Both concepts—separateness from men and hostility toward strangers—are opposed to mainstream Greek thought and tradition. *Misoxenia,* hostility toward strangers, attributed especially to the Egyptians and the Spartans ever since the classical period, and deplored in the case of the Egyptians by all authors referring to it, in the case of the Spartans by most of them, needs little elaboration.[112] It was later imputed to the Jews and singled out by many pagan authors as their most annoying defect. Hecataeus himself indicates his negative attitude toward hatred of strangers elsewhere in the *Aegyptiaca* (Diod. 1. 67. 8–11; cf. 69. 4), praising hospitality toward Greeks, as he also does in his utopian exercise *On the Hyperboreans* (Diod. 2. 47. 4–5). As for *apanthrōpia,* separateness from men, it not only stands in contrast with what is said by most Greek philosophers, especially the Peripatetics, concerning the nature of man and the proper order of state and society, but it is also often portrayed in comedy, biography, and historiography as the stage before degeneration into misanthropy, the hatred of men—and sometimes these two terms are used interchangeably.[113]

I would advise against sweeping Hecataeus's evaluation under the carpet on the strength of the appended causal explanation ("as a result of their expulsion"), as quite a few scholars have done.[114] It has already been noted that Greek and Roman authors used to explain various personalities' misanthropy as the result of disappointments and travails that beset them.[115] The causal reasoning does not legitimize hatred of strangers and *apanthrōpia.* Hecataeus used such explanations to mold the ethnographic material and provide it with a scientific veneer. Thus, for example, he explains the ancient Egyptian custom of sacrificing redheaded humans as a sort of revenge on Typhon (or an imitation of the pun-

112. See, e.g., the references and comment by Lewy (1960) 148 n. 146; Sevenster (1975) 89–144; Berthelot (1999) 192–93.

113. Examples abound at least from the beginning of the Hellenistic period. It will suffice here to look briefly at the comedy *Dyskolos* by Menander, a contemporary of Hecataeus. In the opening speech, Knemon, the hero, is presented emphatically as *apanthrōpos* (line 6—ἀπάνθρωπός τις ἄνθρωπος). In the course of the play he is seen to be a misanthrope in every respect. In line 32 he is even described explicitly as μισῶν ἐφεξῆς πάντας ("forever hating everyone"). In lines 156–59 he declares that he would be happy were he able to turn everyone into stone. In lines 442–53 he curses the worshippers in the temple of Pan, accuses them of deceiving the gods, and wishes them to perish. And so on. On misanthropy attributed to the Jews and others, see the sources and comment in Stern, *GLAJJ* 2: 93; Feldman (1993) 125–31; Schäfer (1997a) 173–79.

114. Meyer (1921–23) 2: 30; Jacoby, *FGrH* IIIa, no. 264, p. 49; Gager (1972) 35; in effect, also Stern, *GLAJJ* 1: 30; Diamond (1980) 85–86; Will and Orrieux (1986) 93; Gabba (1989) 629; Schwartz (2003) 192; Kasher (2003) 77.

115. See Lewy (1960) 148 n. 146, who mentions Plato *Respublica* 620b; Cicero *Tusculanae disputationes* 4. 27; Pliny *Natural History* 7. 80; Plutarch *Antonius* 69; Kern (1922) fr. 115, p. 34.

ishment inflicted by Isis on the murderer of her husband, Diod. 1. 88. 4–5). Does this mean that Hecataeus approves of human sacrifice? Moreover, it is implied by evidently anti-Jewish authors that the Jewish hatred of strangers resulted from the trauma of their expulsion from Egypt;[116] are the versions of these authors as well to be regarded as sympathetic or apologetic? A broken home might explain a youth's decline into crime, but the explanation does not legitimize such behavior or turn the deed into something positive.

It has also been argued that the enclitic pronoun *tis*, qualifying the adjectives of censure, *apanthrōpon* and *misoxenon*, tones down the criticism.[117] Linguistically, this is true in many cases; but the qualifier is also often used in an opposite sense, as an understatement reinforcing the terms it qualifies.[118] Furthermore, *tis* does not necessarily refer also to *misoxenon*; if so, the characteristic, standing alone and unqualified, is presented extremely negatively and without any softening. An examination of the context cannot decide among the various possibilities. One can only be sure that the original Hecataean meaning, if not wording, has been transmitted by Diodorus.[119] Be this as it may, the statement was certainly not intended to be understood as praise. An admirer of Moses wishing to present his deeds as worthy of imitation would not have described the Jewish way of life instigated by Moses as tainted with misanthropy and *apanthrōpia*, whether to a larger or lesser extent; and misanthropy is hardly praiseworthy, even if accompanied by only a certain amount of *apanthrōpia*.[120]

116. Lysimachus in Josephus *Contra Apionem* 1. 303; Diodorus 34/35. 1. 15 (reflecting anti-Jewish views of Seleucid court historians). The causal connection appears from the sequence. A nuance of this reasoning is indicated by Tacitus (*Hist.* 5. 3. 1): *Moysen unum exulum monuisse ne quam deorum nominumve opem exspectarent utrisque deserti* ("Moses, an exile, exhorted them not to expect any help from gods or men, having been abandoned by both"). Cf. the curious explanation of Pompeius Trogus (who was not hostile to the Jews) in Justin 36. 1. 15. In this case, the connection is explicitly stated.

117. E.g., Gager (1972) 35; Schwartz (2003) 192 et al.

118. See, e.g., Smyth (1956) 310, para. 1268, and examples there. It is also worth adding an example from Diodorus (5. 39. 1): "We shall now turn to the Ligyes. These occupy land [which is] rough and entirely wretched. Because of toils and the continuous ill effects of hard work they have a quite laborious and unfortunate life (ἐπίπονόν τινα βίον καὶ ἀτυχῆ ζῶσι)."

119. This in view of the much harsher anti-Jewish accusations and their wording elsewhere in Diodorus (34/35. 2. 1–4).

120. The desire to regard Hecataeus's account as an idealization and a model for imitation has led scholars to extremes, as may be seen in the case of Guttmann's comment on the sentence under discussion: "All the paragraphs in the description of Hecataeus testify to the idealizing treatment of all the details of the regime of life in Israel, of the constitution of the People of Israel, and even of the customs which in his opinion distanced the People of Israel from other peoples, and hence his account . . . was not intended to rebuke the People of Israel but to explain the factors preserving the religious and social regime of the people in its purity for many generations" (1: 63); similarly, Kasher (2003) 192 and Liebes (2002) 260. Where, however, does Hecataeus say anything about the connec-

The implied criticism of Jewish customs and the Jewish way of life contrast markedly with Hecataeus's determination to justify or explain away every deplorable or strange aspect of Egyptian life. His exaggerated recurring rationalization of the Egyptian animal cult is just one example. He also took pains to expunge from the Egyptians unfavorable characteristics attributed to them by Herodotus. Thus, for instance, the notorious Egyptian rejection of strangers is removed to the distant past and said to have been completely reversed by King Psammetichus (1. 67. 8–9), and the powerful absolute Egyptian monarchy is described as restrained, almost constitutional (1. 70 ff.), which is far from the historical truth. Moreover, Hecataeus claims that not a few of the Egyptian customs had long been "admired" by the Greeks (Diod. 1. 69. 2), and the greatest Greek statesmen, poets, and philosophers came to Egypt to study the Egyptian laws and way of life with a view to utilizing them. Hecataeus emphasized in various ways throughout his work the profound contribution of the Egyptians to human culture (e.g., Diod. 1. 69. 1–7). He did not invent all these, but this is how Hecataeus idealizes his subjects when he wants to.

The negative reference to the Jewish *bios* was not necessarily entirely inspired by hostile Egyptian rumors; it may reflect Hecataeus's own impressions formed by some personal acquaintance with Jews.[121] At the same time, it may well be that part of the information on Jewish sacrifice, marriage, and burial customs, emphasizing the negative aspect of Jewish life, was based on Egyptian sources. In the absence of any detailed account of these customs, one can only guess at their contents and aims.[122]

Some scholars, emphasizing the description of the Jewish religion in Hecataeus

---

tion between Jewish separateness and preserving the "religious and social regime of the people in its purity"? This reason was actually given in the Jewish ethnography of Posidonius (Strabo 16. 2. 35; and see chapter 11 below), but not in Hecataeus. Hecataeus is generous with his explanations for every custom, and Jewish separateness is explained by him as the result of the trauma incurred on the departure from Egypt. And would preserving the "religious and social regime of the people in its purity" require hatred of strangers? It would have sufficed to adopt *amixia*, nonmixing with foreigners (e.g., Jos. *AJ* 13. 247; see p. 432 below on the Posidonian source). Kasher even tries to find support for his view in Josephus's praise for the separateness of the Spartans (*Ap.* 2. 257–61); but what connection is there between the Josephan forced defense against the charge of Jewish misanthropy and an account by an early Hellenistic author such as Hecataeus who reflected Hellenic sentiment in his negative view of the Spartan attitude toward foreigners (as may be seen, for example, in the unflattering use of the Spartan term *xenēlasia* in connection with the Egyptian kings preceding Psammetichus [Diod. 1. 69])?

121. Suggested by Sevenster (1975) 189; Gabba (1989) 629; Schäfer (1997a) 16.

122. See, on Jewish sacrifice practices, pp. 24–34 above. In this context it is noteworthy that, contrary to modern scholars, Photius, who preserved the Hecataean Jewish excursus for us, deplored the account of Diodorus-Hecataeus as a tissue of lies about the Jews. Was he referring to the telescoping of events or to the attribution of negative characteristics and customs, or to both?

(4. 3), see in it a central element in the idealization of the Jewish people.[123] It is, however, no more than mere wishful thinking on the part of readers who regard the features described as ideal. Hecataeus was far from monotheistic in his outlook, explicitly praising worship of idols, and even justifying Egyptian animal cults.[124] For his version of the Jewish faith and cult, Hecataeus drew on Jewish informants and just added a causal explanation. There is a striking resemblance, even verbally, with the Herodotean account of the Persian religion (Hdt. 1. 131. 1–2):

> I know that the Persians have such customs: it is not in their custom to erect statues, temples, and altars, and attribute folly to those who do because, as it seems to me, they, unlike the Greeks, do not regard the gods as having human nature. (2) They go up to the tops of mountains and make sacrifices to Zeus, calling Zeus the whole circle of heaven.

The causal explanation used by Herodotus reappears in Hecataeus. Did Herodotus also intend to present the Persian faith and cult to the Greeks as an ideal and model for imitation? Did Herodotus also think that the gods were not anthropomorphic? One does not have to identify with one's theological explanation for a custom. Furthermore, in his blunt excursus on the Jewish people, Tacitus makes similar statements about the cult and faith of the Jews (*Hist.* 5. 5. 4):

> The Jews with their intellect alone understand that there is one divine power; and that wicked are any who make images of the god out of perishable materials and in the form of men; that [divine power] is the highest and eternal, it cannot be imitated and will not perish. Therefore they set up no statues in their cities, let alone in their temples; not for kings this worship, not for the Caesars [this] honor.

Are we to infer that Tacitus admired the beliefs of the Jews? Did he intend to justify the Jews' refusal to participate in the emperor cult?

What about the Jewish form of government? Was it the ideal form of government aimed at by Hecataeus? The Jewish regime is actually described by Hecataeus as a theocracy, and he stresses that the Jews never had a king (para. 5). Yet Hecataeus earned his keep at the court of Ptolemy I. His account of the pharaonic kingship (Diod. 1. 70–75) is an idealization meant to set a precedent and example for the new Macedonian kingdom of Egypt to imitate. Are we to see

---

123. See, e.g., Guttmann 1: 58–62; Liebes (2001/2) 259–60. On the other hand, Schäfer (1997a) 17 went so far as to suggest that Hecataeus has a negative view of Jewish religion, since he sets the description in the context of the Jewish "misanthropic" customs. However, the reference to these customs and their negative characterization, as well as the accompanying explanation concerning the ordeal of the expulsion from Egypt, appear only afterward and *separately* from the account of Jewish religion.

124. See Bar-Kochva (1996d) 98–99; (2000/1) 344–46.

in the Jewish theocracy a model for Ptolemy and his Greco-Macedonian settlers to follow, with hints in the direction of abolishing the monarchy?

The Jewish account by Hecataeus should be seen in its proper place and perspective. Despite the Greek "coloring" and adaptation, there is no need for us to get carried away by notions of conscious idealization in every detail and in the description as a whole. Hecataeus was doing little more than making the information he had at his disposal palatable to a Greek readership (perhaps even to himself), and this also included tailoring it to the strictures of the ethnographic genre, made more rigorous by himself in his own writing. Thus the explanation for the division of the Jewish people into twelve tribes on the grounds that twelve is the perfect number was not intended to make the Jewish people appear perfect or better than they were (nor does it make it so), but was simply more comprehensible to a Greek; and the characteristics attributed to Moses the "founder," and to the priestly leaders and judges, are no more than what might be expected of a Greek author relating an old, unbiased foundation story. The Jewish excursus was not the only ethnography to be given the Greek touch by Greek ethnographers, and only a few of them were interested in idealizing their subjects and setting an example. Nor should we forget that the basic aim of Hecataeus in writing the Jewish ethnography was after all just to examine (or rather, respond to) the alleged descent of certain nations and ethnic groups from Egypt, presented in the Egyptian ethnography itself as the cradle of humanity.

One should not be misled by the ostensibly restrained style of presentation of the text into believing that Hecataeus was not averse to some of the phenomena he was reporting. The absence of emotion stems in part from a deliberately detached reporting of the facts, and in part from the attempt to provide causal explanations for them. These are two major features that give the writings of Hecataeus a veneer of scientific objectivity. Causal reasoning *per se* is not an expression of consent, certainly not of admiration; and one or two positive messages for the benefit of his Greek readers should not be taken as proof that the excursus as a whole was intended to idealize the Jews and set them up as a general model for imitation.

At the same time the intentions of Hecataeus must be distinguished from the perception of the excursus by Jews, who would have regarded the account as a source of pride. From their point of view, here was a famous Greek author relating the Exodus without putting the Jews in a negative light, and even mentioning them in the same breath with the followers of Danaus and Cadmus, fixing the time of the settlement in Judaea and the establishment of Jewish rule as contemporaneous with the settlement of mainland Greece by Hellenic tribes, a point proving Jewish antiquity and their affinity with the Greeks. The causal explanations would certainly have been considered by Jews as a form of praise: the reason for the division of the Jewish people into twelve tribes; the reasoning for belief in one god and opposition to idolatry; the considerations that guided Moses in forming a Jewish system of government; the virtues of Moses, the High Priest, and the priests he appointed; Moses' concern for the welfare of all layers of society, especially the poor farmers. The average Jewish reader could not have been unaware that the description was far from accurate and dissimilar to biblical traditions, but this would not have detracted from his sense of pride. The account would necessarily have appeared to him to be a great compliment in the spirit of the period. Some characteristics and deeds that by their nature a Greek would have condemned, a Jew would have accepted without question: being a seclusive people shunning human society (i.e., pagan society) was something the Jews did not deny and some actually took pride in. The statement about hatred of strangers would seem to be more problematic. Some Jews denied that they hated, for example, Egyptians, or pagan inhabitants in the Holy Land (in the distant past and in the present). Yet other Jews in the Hellenistic age did not regard such hatred as a vice and even brought it to prominence in their writing.[125]

At least two Egyptian Jews jumped at the chance of using the name of Hecataeus as a pseudonym, one for a "biography" of Abraham, the other for a kind of ethnography of the Jewish people in his time. The anonymous orthodox author of *On the Jews* certainly did not consider *misoxenia* to be a blot on the Jewish character: he mocks the beliefs of the Greeks and relishes reporting the acts of destruction of Hellenistic cult worship in the Holy Land and states that these deeds were worthy of praise (Joseph. *Ap.* 1. 193, 200–204).[126]

. . .

Many scholars have rightly used the Jewish ethnography of Hecataeus of Abdera as their starting point for any discussion of the attitude of the Greek and Roman world toward the Jewish people. It is also considered to be of great value as a main source for the history of the Jews at the beginning of the Hellenistic period and is consulted as an authority on various points pertaining to the development of religion and cult, and especially social life and government, in the Second Temple period. However, many of Hecataeus's statements, adduced to support general and specific theories and conclusions, lose much of their authoritativeness after careful inquiry into Hecataeus's sources of information and inspiration and the role of every detail in each particular context. Notwithstanding, the general concept of Jewish political system as a theocracy (four centuries before the term was first used [Jos. *Ap.* 2.165]) is well verified by the sources to Hecataeus's days.

125. See, e.g., *pseudo-Aristeas* 128–84; *Sapientia Salmonis* 11–19; many examples are to be found in Josephus and Philo regarding both the hatred of Egyptians and distancing from idolators.

126. See Bar-Kochva (1996d) 57–71, 97–101.

4
———

Megasthenes on the "Physics" of
the Greeks, Brahmans, and Jews

Alexander's campaign in India and the subsequent unification under one rule of
the lands from the Mediterranean to the Indian subcontinent for various periods
during the third century B.C.E. greatly facilitated communication and accessibil-
ity between Greece, the Near East, and India. This necessarily led to an exchange
of cultural influences. A number of authors and professionals accompanying
Alexander on his Indian campaign or who were in the area at the time wrote a
great deal about the land of India, its wonders, and the customs of its peoples.
Later authors copied from them, with occasional improvements from their own
imaginations. This wealth of material was augmented by writings of authors who
had visited India or its neighborhood at the beginning of the Seleucid kingdom.

Modern scholarship, acknowledging the possible implications of the new circumstances created in the Hellenistic period, and being aware of the openness of
Greek and Macedonian emigrants to Oriental traditions, has proposed a number
of speculative theories concerning the degree to which Indian thought and ways
of life may have influenced Greek thought. The alleged connection of the Jews
with India and the Indians has to be considered in this context.

INTERPRETATIONS OF
MEGASTHENES' REFERENCE TO THE JEWS

Two fragments of the early Hellenistic authors Clearchus and Megasthenes have
been interpreted as showing, at the very least, that there was a widespread rumor
at the beginning of the Hellenistic period that the Jews originated in India, and,
more importantly, that there was a striking similarity between the views and

136

customs of the Jews and those of the Brahmans. Since these ancient authors had special connections with India or its neighbors, and Megasthenes was considered the leading expert on Indian affairs, some scholars have supposed that the statements of Clearchus and Megasthenes concerning the Jews were accepted as authoritative and greatly influenced the way the Jews were perceived at the time. Clearchus's curious statement that the Jews are of Indian descent, and the implications of this alleged genealogy for his account of some features of Jewish behavior, have all been discussed above in chapter 2.[1] Megasthenes, the second source, is the subject of the present chapter.

Megasthenes was a Greek diplomat and author who wrote a four-book ethnography on India and its peoples. This work, called *Indica,* was for the knowledge of India what the *Aegyptiaca* of Hecataeus of Abdera was for the study of Egypt throughout the Hellenistic and Roman periods. In a single sentence fragment taken from the third book of *Indica,* Megasthenes compares the opinions of the Greeks, Brahmans, and Jews on "things concerning nature" (τὰ περὶ φύσεως— i.e., "physics," a broad subject including theology).[2] The fragment has been preserved by Clement of Alexandria (*Strom.* 1. 15 [72. 5]; repeated by Eus. *PE* 9. 6). Clement himself sees in Megasthenes' statements evidence for his opinion that the written philosophy of the Jews predated that of the Greeks.

Since so few sources have survived, and because generations of Jews and Christians have been so eager to seize upon any early reference to the Jews, much has been read into this one sentence. Some scholars, influenced by Clement's introductory remarks, have regarded Megasthenes' sentence as claiming that philosophical works containing opinions considered Greek were written by Jews, or were at least current among them, long before such things were written by Greeks.[3] Others, in the wake of some church patriarchs, have gone so far as to interpret Megasthenes' statement as indicating that the Greeks took their wisdom from the Jews,[4] which would mean that he was one of the sources for the celebrated myth about the Greek "theft" of Jewish wisdom. Still others have attributed to Megasthenes the view that Jewish opinions on "physics" are similar or identical to those of the Brahmans,[5] the Indian priestly caste considered in ancient literature to be the most elevated of the Indian castes. It

1. Pp. 82–84 above.
2. *Physika* is the area of philosophy concerning questions pertaining to what is in the universe, why, and how. Theology from the Hellenistic period onward was treated as a part of "physics," until it was split off by the Neoplatonists, and methodically so, beginning with Proclus of Athens in the fifth century C.E.
3. See Guttmann 1: 90; Feldman (1993) 7–8; Kalota (1978) 119; and, somewhat hesitantly and obscurely, Gabba (1989) 622.
4. So Gabba (1989) 622 (implicitly); Feldman (1993) 7–8.
5. See Radin (1915) 86; Guttmann 1: 89–90; Hengel (1973) 144; and implicitly, Feldman (1993) 551.

has been suggested that this view is reflected in what remains of the writings of Numenius of Apamea, the Pythagorean philosopher and the forerunner of Neoplationism, who lived in the time of the Bar Kohba revolt.[6] There are also those who have seen in the sentence a hint of a shared origin between Jews and Indians,[7] and others have inferred that Clearchus was influenced by Megasthenes' mention of Jews alongside the Brahmans when he made his strange statement that the Jews originated from the Indian Kalanoi.[8] As for the original formulation of the sentence, it has been suggested that Clement abbreviated his source, and that Megasthenes wrote additional things about the Jews.[9] Some have even speculated that the theological-physical views of the Jews were presented by Megasthenes in a Stoic coloring (or were so understood by him).[10] Concerning the sources for Megasthenes' statement, it has been supposed that it is independent of earlier Greek authors writing on the Jews (e.g., Hecataeus of Abdera),[11] and that it drew on Jewish informants.[12] Of all the different interpretations and suggestions, only one is acceptable: Megasthenes considered the Jews a community of priestly philosophers similar in their occupation to the Indian Brahmans.[13]

In order to interpret the sentence and its intent properly, we must first become acquainted with Megasthenes, his life, and the time and places of his residence (and, accordingly, his possible contacts with Jews); then get to know his *Indica*, the literary genre he chose, the model he was following, its characteristics and structure, and his motives for writing; and finally locate the sentence exactly as possible in the original work and define the characteristics of the chapter in which it appeared. In addition, we must determine why this sentence was quoted by Clement, as well as its original formulation and whether it contains everything Megasthenes wrote about the Jews. Only then may we turn to Megasthenes' treatment of the Jews, try to understand its meaning and purpose, and trace its sources of inspiration.

6. So implies Feldman (1993) 551.

7. Feldman (1993) 8; (1983) 282; Kasher (1997) 144.

8. See p. 82 note 118 above.

9. Guttmann 1: 89–90; Hengel (1973) 467. Both believe that Megasthenes detailed the main characteristics of the Jewish religion.

10. Hengel (1973) 467, following the view of Stein, the author of the entry on Megasthenes in *RE*, concerning Stoic influence in the comparison Megasthenes makes between the "physics" of the Greeks and that of the Indians (Strabo 15. 1. 59).

11. Hengel (1973) 467; Gabba (1989) 614.

12. Jaeger (1938a) 132 n. 14; (1938b) 141–42; Guttmann 1: 89; Conzelmann (1981) 56; Gager (1972) 79.

13. Rightly inferred by Jaeger (1938a) 132 n. 14; Guttmann 1: 89; Gager (1972) 79; Gabba (1989) 622; Feldman (1993) 8; Kasher (1997) 144; Stern, *GLAJJ* 1: 43; Mélèze-Modrzejewski (1989) 5. On the use of "community" in this context and elsewhere, see p. 81 note 112 above.

MEGASTHENES' LIFE AND WORKS

Megasthenes' life is shrouded in obscurity. He was a Greek, perhaps from western Asia Minor,[14] who first served Sibyrtius (Arr. 5. 6. 2), the satrap appointed by Alexander to rule over Archosia, Gedrosia, and the Oreitae (within present-day Afghanistan and Pakistan). This satrap actually became independent after Alexander's death and held office until at least 316 B.C.E. (Diod. 19. 48, drawing on a contemporary, Hieronymus of Cardia).[15] We do not know whether Sibyrtius was then deposed by Antigonus Monophthalmus, or only by Seleucus I after the reconquest of Babylon (312 B.C.E.), or whether Megasthenes continued to serve in these places under other satraps. Be that as it may, at some point he transferred his services to Seleucus I (Clem. *Strom.* 1. 15 [72. 5]).[16] This transition must have occurred after 312, when Seleucus reestablished control over Babylon and began his expansion toward India. The expansion came to a halt with his campaign against the Indian king Sandracottus (Candragupta), who founded the Maurya dynasty and the first Indian empire (324/321). In the peace treaty of 304/303, Seleucus gave up most of his conquests along the Indian border and in return received, among other things, a large number of elephants that participated in his wars,[17] and won the day at Ipsus, where the fate of Alexander's empire was finally decided:[18] the former satraps Seleucus, Lysimachus, and Cassander defeated Antigonus Monophthalmus, who had been attempting to unify the whole empire under his regime (301 B.C.E.).

It has been widely accepted that Megasthenes served as an ambassador of Seleucus I at the court of Sandracottus. Some have suggested that he stayed for most of the time in India in this capacity from 312 B.C.E., while others have suggested 304/3 for the start of his office.[19] Though these assumptions and suggestions lack textual evidence, they have been taken for granted, and the sources

14. See Witkowsky (1898/9) 22–24; Reuss (1906) 304–5; reservations in Stein, *RE* s.v. "Megasthenes (2)," cols. 230–31.

15. On Sibyrtius, see Berve (1926) 2: 353; Stein, *RE* s.v. "Megasthenes (2)," col. 231; Brown (1957) 13–15.

16. Μεγασθένης ὁ συγγραφεὺς Σελεύκῳ τῷ Νικάτορι συμβεβιωκώς ("Megasthenes the author who lived with Seleucus Nicator").

17. On the agreement and questions pertaining to it, see in detail Schober (1981) 155–93; Tarn (1940) 84–89; (1951) 100; Mehl (1986) 153–93; Grainger (1990a) 107–12.

18. On the number of elephants and their role in the battle of Ipsus, see Bar-Kochva (1976) 76–77; Grainger (1990a) 107–12. For additional details, see Will (1979–82) 1: 89; Mehl (1986) 153–93.

19. For the accepted opinion, see Susemihl (1891–92) 1: 547; Bevan (1902) 1: 271, 297; Stein, *RE* s.v. "Megasthenes (2)," col. 232; Brown (1955) 18; Dahlquist (1962) 9–10, 35; Seibert (1967) 48; Altheim and Stiehl (1970) 284 ff.; Müller (1972–80) 1: 245–47; Olshausen (1974) 127; (1979) 292; Zambrini (1982) 71–75; Seibert (1983) 146–47; Karttunen (1986) 84–86; (1997) 70–72 (with reservations).

have not infrequently been misquoted. Some elaboration on the available information and the circumstantial evidence is therefore required.

We know from Arrian (*Anab*. 5. 6. 2) that Megasthenes went on a diplomatic
mission (or missions) to Sandracottus while serving Sibyrtius.[20] The other references to his missions to India do not mention Seleucus or any other master
(Strabo 2. 1. 9; Arr. *Ind*. 5. 3). Nor is there any explicit indication about their
duration. In addition, sending envoys to foreign states was quite common in the
Hellenistic period, but there is no parallel for a long, permanent ambassadorial
mission.[21] These arguments, however, cannot be taken as decisive, given the scarcity of information and the state of preservation of Megasthenes' fragments.[22] We
can assume that Megasthenes' mission to India was not confined to one isolated
and short visit. He must have been sent there several times or have stayed at least
once for a lengthy period. It is explicitly stated that he had close connections
with Sandracottus (Arr. *Ind*. 5. 3),[23] and his detailed accounts of the Indian court,
army, and society, as well as of the capital Palimbothra (Pāṭaliputra) and its surroundings, are evidently the testimony of an eyewitness.[24] Now, as such accounts
are likely to have been written soon after the termination of the mission, and
the work of Megasthenes could not have been written before the 290s,[25] he was
probably sent to India by Seleucus as well. It is also hardly credible that Seleucus
would have failed to send the man, who "assisted him" (Clem. *Strom*. 1. 15 [72. 5])
and was formerly in a close relationship with Sandracottus, to the Indian court
at a time when peace negotiations were being held and a settlement was vital.
These considerations are not compelling, but they seem to tilt the balance in favor
of the accepted hypothesis. We can therefore assume, with all due caution, that
Megasthenes served Seleucus in one or more lengthy missions, or in several visits
to the Indian king, from 312 or 304/3 B.C.E. Megasthenes' diplomatic career seems
to have terminated no later than the death of Sandracottus (estimated at 296/292

20. ὃς συνῆν μὲν Σιβυρτίῳ . . . πολλάκις μὲν λέγει ἀφικέσθαι παρὰ Σανδράκοττον. The second part of the sentence can be interpreted to mean either that Megasthenes was sent often to
Sandracottus or that he often refers to his visit to the Indian king. The sentence as it stands seems
to refer only to the period in which Megasthenes was in the service of Sibyrtius. For other questions
involved, see Karttunen (1997) 71.

21. See Olshausen (1979) 291–309. On this and other considerations, Karttunen (1997) 70–71.

22. See, e.g., Strabo 15. 1. 36: καθάπερ τὸν Σανδρόκοττον, πρὸς ὃ ἧκεν ὁ Μεγασθένης πεμφθείς
("like Sandracottus, to whom Megasthenes came, having been sent"). Information about the sender
(ὑπὸ . . .) may have been lost at the end of the sentence.

23. [Μεγασθένης] συγγενέσθαι γὰρ Σανδροκόττῳ λέγει ("[Megasthenes] says that he socialized
with Sandracottus").

24. E.g., Strabo 15. 36, 53, 57; Arrian *Indica* 10. 5–7. See Kalota (1978) 61–70; Karttunen (1997) 71,
76–81, 88–92.

25. See p. 142 below.

B.C.E.): Strabo states (2. 1. 9) that Daïmachus, who also wrote a book on India, was sent to Allitrochades, the son and heir of Sandracottus.[26] Whether Megasthenes retired to Antioch, or to Babylon, the parallel Seleucid court, or moved to a nearby office, he had enough opportunities to meet Jews if he so wished.

We know that Megasthenes wrote an ethnographic work of four books called "Indian Affairs" (Indika). The work has not come down to us, but it served as a main source for the surveys of India written between the first century B.C.E. and the second century C.E. by such authors as Diodorus, Strabo, Curtius Rufus, and Arrian; it also influenced other authors, such as Pliny the Elder. Consequently, a good number of fragments and testimonia (some quite extensive) have been preserved.[27] An examination of the material indicates that the work included the four basic sections of a Greek ethnographic composition of the classical and Hellenistic periods, in the following order: geography, origo, customs, and history of the rulers.[28] Just as Hecataeus of Abdera did in his work on Egypt and its people, Megasthenes collected material selectively in accordance with his aims, provided explanations for various phenomena, and rationalized the beliefs and strange practices of the peoples he dealt with by pointing out causes and effects both between the basic sections of his composition and between the various details pertaining to each section. Likewise prominent is his wish to idealize the political and social institutions of the natives, described together with their customs and internal divisions. [29]

Consequently, it has been suggested that Megasthenes' Indian ethnogaphy was planned as a Seleucid response to Hecataeus's Ptolemaic-sponsored Egyptian ethnography.[30] The Aegyptiaca does seem to have been written in order to boost

26. On Daïmachus, see Olshausen (1974) no. 124.

27. See the collection of fragments in Schwanbeck (1846); Müller (1841–70) 2: 397–439; Jacoby, FGrH IIIC, no. 715 (pp. 603–39). See the survey of Karttunen (1997) 73–74.

28. See the discussions in Trüdinger (1918) 75–80; Stein, RE s.v. "Megasthenes (2)"; Dihle (1961) 211–13, 222; Müller (1972) 1: 245–52; Derret (1975) 1150–54; Sterling (1992) 95–104; Bar-Kochva (1996d) 200–205, and there on the inclusion of wonder stories (θαυμάσια) within the description of the castes, and not as an independent element. Megasthenes' Indian ethnography began with a geography, as was more customary concerning autochthonous peoples, and not with an origo, the starting point for ethnographies on immigrant peoples.

29. See Brown (1955), (1957); Murray (1972) 207–8; (1973) 166; Zambrini (1982) and (1985) passim; Bar-Kochva (1996d) 200; Karttunen (1997) 73.

30. See Murray (1970) 141–71; (1972) 207–8; (1973) 163–68. It is worth quoting two of Murray's statements: "The work . . . was a direct reply to Hecataeus, and modelled on the method, form and contents of his work . . . it is an attempt to show that India is an even better land than Hecataeus' Egypt, a Platonic ideal state with a rigid caste system and philosophers on top, and that all civilization springs from India not Egypt" ([1972] 208); "Each of the Hellenistic kings wished to be persuaded of the cultural superiority and great antiquity of his own kingdom and so of the special importance of himself and his task" ([1973] 166).

the prestige of the Ptolemaic regime, by idealizing Egypt's past and portraying Ptolemy as the legitimate successor to the glorious pharaonic monarchy. Megasthenes, however, could not have performed a similar service for Seleucus I: Seleucus I did not rule India; and Syria, the center of his kingdom, was thousands of kilometers away from the land of Sandracottus. A proper "Seleucid response" would have taken the form of an ethnography of Babylon. At the same time, a Hecataean influence is quite certain, given Megasthenes' similar approach to the ethnographical material. As Hecataeus's ethnography was composed in the years 305–302,[31] Megasthenes' work would have been composed no earlier than the nineties of the third century.[32] If Megasthenes was indeed on an extended embassy that terminated in 296/292, he may only then have turned to writing the Indian ethnography, which also served to some extent as his memoirs.[33]

THE QUOTATION IN CLEMENT: ITS PURPOSE, ORIGINAL LOCATION, AND AUTHENTICITY

Megasthenes' comment on the Jews has survived in Clement of Alexandria, the Athenian who converted to Christianity and flourished at the end of the second century C.E. Clement, well versed in all genres, quoted or paraphrased extensively from almost all branches of classical and Hellenistic literature to support his various claims. In his work Stromateis, or "Miscellanies," Clement's aim is, among other things, to prove the philosophical nature of the Christian and Jewish religions and its antiquity by pointing out similarities between the ideas of those religions and Greek philosophy and showing that the Greeks drew their great ideas at least from the Old Testament.[34] In chapter 15 of book 1 of his Stromateis Clement claims that thinkers of "barbarian" nations influenced Greek philosophers, in particular, Pythagoras, Democritus, and Plato. The "barbarian" nations mentioned include even the Scythians, Thracians, and Galatians, but most prominent are Oriental nations, such as the Egyptians, Persians, Medes, and Indians. Clement goes so far as to claim that some of the more important Greek philosophers (Thales, Pythagoras, and Antisthenes) were of "barbarian" origin. Greek poets are similarly treated, with an Egyptian origin being claimed even for Homer. In this context there also appears the argument concerning the Indian

---

31. See Bar-Kochva (1996d) 15–16.

32. See also Jaeger (1938a) 142, esp. n. 1 for other reasons; as opposed to Stein, RE s.v. "Megasthenes (2)," col. 232.

33. Cf. Strabo 2. 1. 9 fin.: ὑπομνήματα τῆς ἀποδημίας ("memoirs from a foreign land"). Strabo is referring to the ethnographies of Megasthenes and Daïmachos, and the actual formulation may derive from them.

34. On the aims of the work, see Lilla (1971) 9–59; on the "theft" of wisdom by the Greeks, see Bosset (1901) 205–18; Molland (1936) 57–85; Drodge (1989), and pp. 204–5 below.

influence on the religious conceptions of the Greeks and Romans. Clement develops this argument at great length in chapters 17 and 20–24 of book 1 and in later books of *Stromateis*. In chapter 15 he even raises the claim—perhaps directly or indirectly inspired by Varro, the great first-century B.C.E. polymath—that Numa Pompilius, the second king of Rome, was influenced by the laws of Moses (71. 1–2).[35] Later, he emphasizes that the Jewish people is more ancient than the other "barbarian" nations he mentions (72. 4–5). Clement goes on to claim unambiguously that Philo "the Pythagorean"[36] and Aristobulus "the Peripatetic"[37] showed that "the written philosophy of the Jews preceded that of the Greeks."[38] Clement may well have felt the need to support his claim not only with Hellenistic Jewish authors such as these (whose descent he does not mention) but also with a pagan Greek author, and it would be for this reason that he quotes Megasthenes. Here is what Clement says about the precedence of the Jews and their wisdom, followed by the fragment of Megasthenes (1. 15 [72. 4–5]):[39]

> (72. 4) That [both] the oldest of all these by far, the people of Jews, and their philosophy which came to be written down, preceded the philosophy among the Greeks, the Pythagorean Philo proves by means of many [proofs], and not only he but also Aristobulus the Peripatetic and—so as not to waste time going through every one by name—many others. (72. 5) [Of these] Megasthenes, the author who lived in the company (συμβεβιωκώς) of Seleucus Nicator, writes most clearly (φανερώτατα) in the third [book] of [his] "Indian Matters" the following: "However (μέντοι) all the [views] which have been expressed (εἰρημένα) about nature (τὰ περὶ φύσεως) among the ancients (i.e., ancient Greeks) are also expressed (λέγεται) among

35. The claim is based on the tradition concerning early Rome, according to which the early Romans did not worship idols, and Numa explicitly prohibited the practice. See on this below, pp. 510–11, and references there.

36. Philo is also called "the Pythagorean" by Clement in *Stromateis* 2. 19 (100. 3). On the background for the use of the term, see Runia (1993) 54–76.

37. Additional sources in which the Jewish philosopher Aristobulus is called "Peripatetic," as well as doubts concerning the reliability of this statement, may be found in Holladay (1983–96) 3: 72–73, 204–5.

38. On Philo's comments concerning the Greek "theft" of wisdom, see p. 205 note 176 below. On references by Aristobulus to Jewish sources for Plato, Pythagoras, and Aristotle, see below, pp. 197–99.

39. The most up-to-date edition of the text is that of Stählin (1960) 46: (72. 4) τούτων ἁπάντων πρεσβύτατον μακρῷ τὸ Ἰουδαίων γένος, καὶ τὴν παρ' αὐτοῖς φιλοσοφίαν ἔγγραπτον γενομένην προκατάρξαι τῆς παρ' Ἕλλησι φιλοσοφίας διὰ πολλῶν ὁ Πυθαγόρειος ὑποδείκνυσι Φίλων, οὐ μὴν ἀλλὰ καὶ Ἀριστόβουλος ὁ Περιπατητικὸς καὶ ἄλλοι πλείους ἵνα μὴ κατ' ὄνομα ἐπιὼν διατρίβω. (72. 5) φανερώτατα δὲ Μεγασθένης ὁ συγγραφεὺς ὁ Σελεύκῳ τῷ Νικάτορι συμβεβιωκὼς ἐν τῇ τρίτῃ τῶν Ἰνδικῶν ὧδε γράφει· ἅπαντα μέντοι τὰ περὶ φύσεως εἰρημένα παρὰ τοῖς ἀρχαίοις λέγεται καὶ παρὰ τοῖς ἔξω τῆς Ἑλλάδος φιλοσοφοῦσι τὰ μὲν παρ' Ἰνδοῖς ὑπὸ τῶν Βραχμάνων, τὰ δὲ ἐν τῇ Συρίᾳ ὑπὸ τῶν καλουμένων Ἰουδαίων. The formulation in the MSS of Eusebius is identical, except for insignificant differences in one MS (the thirteenth-century Parisinus).

those who philosophize outside Greece, some [views] among the Indians by the Brachmans (= Brahmans), and some in Syria by those called Jews.

It may be appropriate to consider, first of all, the immediate context and the book in which this fragment would have been found in Megasthenes' work, and in light of these findings assess its degree of authenticity and accuracy. The formulation and general background of the quotation recalls a testimonium in Strabo in the context of a survey of the Brahmans (15. 1. 59). The testimonium gives a relatively detailed comparison of the opinions of the Greeks and the Brahmans on "physics." Preceding the comparison is the following sentence:

> Concerning "physics" [Megasthenes] says that in some things they (the Brahmans) display simplicity, for they are stronger in deeds than in words, being persuaded in many things through myths; but in many [other] things they think similarly to the Greeks (i.e., share the same or similar opinions). [E.g.,] those too say that the cosmos is created and perishable . . . *(the detailed comparison follows)*[40]

The difference between this testimonium from Strabo and that from Clement, apart from the reference to Jews in Clement only, is the degree of detail and example. Clement's fragment is short and schematic, without examples. It includes everything Megasthenes said about the Jews. Had there been other comments about them, or a comparison between their opinions and those of the Greeks, Clement would have jumped at the chance of quoting them in his effort to prove his claim in the introductory sentences to the short testimonium (72. 4) that the philosophy of the Jews preceded that of the Greeks,[41] all the more so as this claim does not accord with the content of the testimonium itself.[42]

In view of the content and formulation of the comparison between Greeks and Brahmans, and Strabo's introductory remarks on the detailed testimonium, it seems that the Megasthenes' fragment on the Jews, which contains only a brief statement about similarities between the "physics" of the Greeks, Jews, and Brahmans, was the conclusion to the comparison between Greeks and Brahmans (following para. 59). At the end of the detailed comparison there would have been a point in concluding that opinions expressed by the Greeks concerning "physics" were popular in part with the Brahmans and in part with the Jews. The sentence did not survive in Strabo, who adduced Megasthenes in indirect speech and as usual abbreviated his report (as well as adding here and there).[43]

A major factor linking the fragment in Clement with the testimonium in

---

40. See the translation and discussion on p. 147 below.

41. *Contra* Guttmann 1: 89–90 and Hengel (1973) 467, who think that Megasthenes elaborated about the Jews.

42. See p. 157 below.

43. See below, pp. 151–53.

Strabo (and enhancing its authenticity) is the identity of the Greek philosophers. The fragment equates the opinions of the Jews and the Brahmans with those of the "ancients" (*archaioi*), a common epithet in the time of Megasthenes for those philosophers we now call pre-Socratics.[44] We shall see below that the comparison in Strabo between the Greek philosophers and the Brahmans comprises Greek opinions on "physics" taken (or deemed taken) from the pre-Socratics. Some of the opinions are even unique to the pre-Socratics.

The suggestion that Megasthenes' comment on the Jews appeared in such a context is also supported to some extent by Clement's previous discussion (1. 15 [71. 5]). Clement mentions the Indian "gymnosophists" (the "naked philosophers") among the other "barbarian" peoples and groups of philosophers who, according to him, anticipated the Greeks in developing philosophical thought. He distinguishes between two types of "gymnosophists," the Brahmans and the Sarmans, and notes incidentally some ascetic habits of the Hylobioi, a group of the Sarmans. His report generally agrees with the information on this caste provided by Strabo, who is using Megasthenes in the passage following the comparison between the Greek and Brahman philosophers (15. 1. 59 fin. ff.).[45]

Clement tells us that the fragment comes from the third book of the *Indica*. An examination of other fragments and testimonia pertaining to this work reveals that it comprised four books and was divided into four sections: the geography was in book 1; the *origo* may have begun in book 1 and certainly ended in book 2; the *nomima* spanned books 2 and 3 (book 3 should be seen as a sort of appendix to the *nomima*, describing the castes); book 4 contained a history of rulers.[46] Our fragment, therefore, was included in the "appendix" on castes, and this corroborates in general the suggestion concerning its location.

To sum up, the Jews were mentioned by Megasthenes only incidentally, by way of association, as a people who also had certain opinions similar to those of the Greeks, and this in the context of a concluding note to the presentation of the "physical" views of the Brahmans. There was no detailed account in Megasthenes of the opinions of the Jews here or elsewhere.

---

44. See Aristotle *Metaphysica* 1069a25; *De generatione et corruptione* 314a6 (noted by LSJ s.v. ἀρχαῖος II. 1). Cf. the expressions οἱ ἀρχαῖοι φιλόσοφοι ("the ancient philosophers"—Arist. *Cael.* 271b3); οἱ πρῶτοι φιλοσοφήσαντες ("the first philosophizers"—Arist. *Metaph.* 983b14); οἱ πρῶτοι φυσιολογήσαντες ("the first investigators of nature"—*Metaph.* 983b30); and see also οἱ ὕστεροι τῶν ἀρχαίων ("the later among the ancients"—Arist. *Ph.* 185b27, concerning Lycophron and others). Clement (*Strom.* 1. 15 [61. 1]) uses the expression τῶν παρ᾽ Ἕλλησι πρεσβυτάτων σοφῶν τε καὶ φιλοσόφων ("the oldest wise men and philosophers among the Greeks"), intending the pre-Socratics.

45. On Megasthenes as the source, see Strabo 15. 1. 60 init. (the reading "Garmans" is mistaken; see Karttunen [1997] 59). On the Sarmans and Hylobioi, see Karttunen 57–59.

46. See Bar-Kochva (1996d) 200–205.

We are now in a position to further confirm the authenticity and accuracy of the reference. Had it been a forgery, we would have expected to find in it at least some points of similarity between the "physics" of the Jews and the Greeks. Furthermore, a Jewish or Christian forger may also have stated explicitly that the opinions of the Greek philosophers on "physics" derived from the Jews, or that the Jews were already engaged in philosophical activity before the Greeks, or some other claim along similar lines. If Clement has interfered in the content of the quotation, it is only in his identification of the Brahmans as Indians, something that would have been redundant in Megasthenes' work, but necessary for Clement's argument, where he is making comparisons with a number of Oriental peoples.

It does not tell against authenticity that Josephus, who twice mentioned Megasthenes (*AJ* 4. 227; *Ap.* 1. 144), did not avail himself in the first book of *Contra Apionem* of this particular comment in order to help prove his main thesis in that book: the antiquity of the Jewish people and the positive esteem with which they were regarded by Greek authors. Josephus uses Megasthenes both times for matters pertaining to the Babylonian king Nebuchadnezzar, and there is good reason to suppose that Josephus drew here not on Megasthenes directly, but on an intermediate source.[47] Whatever the case may have been, he mentions only the fourth book of the *Indica*,[48] while, according to Clement, the fragment comes from the third book. Josephus, or rather the assistants he sent to collect information on the Jews,[49] could easily have overlooked this short and marginal sentence, even if they had access to the original work of Megasthenes, including its third scroll.

THE "PHYSICS" OF THE BRAHMANS AND THE "PHYSICS" OF THE PRE-SOCRATICS

As I have stressed in the introduction to this book, no reference to the Jews in Hellenistic literature should be interpreted in isolation from its context if we are to have any chance of arriving at a proper understanding of it. This testimonium is no exception. The detailed comparison between the opinions of the Brahmans and the Greeks that Strabo adduces in the name of Megasthenes, which in the original preceded the sentence quoted by Clement, may provide some insight into

47. See the philological reasons given in the unfinished commentary on *Contra Apionem* by von Gutschmid (1893) 529; see also Bar-Kochva (1996d) 201 and n. 67.

48. For corroboration of the statement as it is in Josephus, and rejection of proposed emendations, see Bar-Kochva (1996d) 201–2.

49. See *Ap.* 1.50 with regard to *Bellum Judaicum*. This was the usual practice for writers of Josephus's standing, all the more so in compilations such as *Contra Apoinem*.

Megasthenes' approach and disclose his sources of information and inspiration for the "physics" of the parties concerned. Following an examination of all of this, we may be in a position to identify the source(s) for Megasthenes' general comment on the Jews, and consequently be able to explain its meaning. I shall, therefore, digress now from the discussion regarding the "Jewish" fragment and examine in detail the comparison Megasthenes makes between the opinions of the Brahmans and those of the Greek philosophers. To the best of my knowledge, a detailed examination of Megasthenes' comparison has never been undertaken. I will begin with a translation of the passage in its entirety (Strabo 15. 1. 59 [713]), which includes footnotes on specific details, clarifying terms, identifying Greek philosophers whose thoughts are reflected in the passage, and, wherever appropriate, also indicating Indian parallels.

> Concerning "physics"[50] [Megasthenes] says that in some things they (the Brahmans) display simplicity, for they are stronger in deeds than in words, being persuaded in many things through myths; but in many [other] things they think similarly to the Greeks (i.e., share the same or similar opinions). [E.g.,] those too say that the cosmos is born and is perishable,[51] and that it is spherical (σφαιροειδής),[52] and that

50. τὰ δὲ περὶ φύσιν ("things concerning nature"). In the context, the expression may appear to be a prefatory remark added by Strabo, but it is more likely that it was already present in Megasthenes; cf. the fragment referring to the Jews adduced by Clement—τὰ περὶ φύσεως. In any case, despite the gap of three centuries between Megasthenes and Strabo, the expression had not changed, and continued to mean the same as τὰ φυσικά; cf. above, note 2.

51. γενητὸς ὁ κόσμος καὶ φθαρτός. The cyclical theory involving cosmic conflagration, a familiar feature of Stoic philosophy, had already appeared in Heraclitus (sixth–fifth cent.; see Simplicius in D-K 22 A 10, ll. 18–21; Diog. Laert. 9. 8) and Empedocles (fifth cent.; Simplicius in D-K 31 A 52, ll. 12–18). Variations on the cyclical theory that do not involve conflagration are to be found, for example, in Xenophanes (flood) and Anaximander (drought). Plato implicitly expresses his opposition to the cyclical theory (Ti. 32b5–35a3; 37c2–38b5), and Aristotle adduces the views of Heraclitus and Empedocles as reflecting a widespread conception and concerns himself with its opponents (Cael. 279b4–16, 289b14; Metaph. 984a27). He expresses his own unambiguously negative view of it (Cael. 279b17, 280a24), supplies refutations (279b18–283b20), and discusses various aspects of the problem (in his Gen. corr.). We have here, therefore, a pre-Socratic theory, still well-known in the generation of Megasthenes. As for the Brahman opinion on the subject, the belief in the cyclical nature of the cosmos was then, as now, a central feature of Hindu cosmology. It was already in existence long before Megasthenes (see, e.g., Śvetāśvatara Upaniṣad 6. 1–3; cf., e.g., Manu Smṛti 1. 68–74, 79–86; and Mahābhārata 12. 232. 12–31, 233. 4–7, both of which contain earlier sections from the fourth century B.C.E.).

52. This conception may be found in Greek thought already in Xenophanes (sixth cent.; Simplicius in D-K 21 A 31, ll. 10–11; albeit the testimonium is late and rests on Alexander of Aphrodisias), in Parmenides (sixth–fifth cent.; D-K 28 B 8, ll. 42–44; and cf. Diog. Laert. 9. 21), and later in Empedocles (Simplicius in D-K 31 B 35, ll. 13–17), Plato (Ti. 33b, 34a, 44d4 ff.), and Aristotle (e.g., Cael. 279a11, 286b10–287a30, 297a8–30). On the Brahman view that the world in which we live (one of many worlds) is shaped like a sphere (literally, "egg" [anda]), see Kirfel (1920) 4–5, and 55 for sources.

the god[53] who manages (διοικῶν)[54] and makes (ποιῶν)[55] it (i.e., the cosmos)[56] [again and again, (or "continually")][57] wanders [58] (διαπεφοίτηκεν) [59] [all the time] through

53. θεός, the reference to "god" in the singular. This and the form τὸ θεῖον (the divine) are frequent in Greek thought and literature, and their Sanskrit equivalents are not uncommon in the polytheistic world of the Hindus. Versions of the Hindu myths tend to describe the cosmology in terms of one god; for the Brahmans, this god is Brahma.

54. The original etymological meaning is "to manage a household"; hence by extension "to manage a polis" and "to manage the world." Thus, e.g., Plato's *Phaedrus* (246c1–2), Psyche flies everywhere and manages the cosmos (διοικεῖ τὸν κόσμος). Yet the Greek creator god of the heroic and classical ages does not "manage" the world; he leaves this job to other gods. This is true both of Hesiod's Zeus and Plato's *demiourgos* in the *Timaeus*. Aristotle's god—who from the outset is not a creator—keeps out of the business of managing the cosmos, while all things aspire to this god. Only the Stoic god not only creates but also "manages" the cosmos. On the implications of this, and for an analysis of the transmission of the text of Megasthenes, see below, pp. 151–53. It may be worth pointing out that the verb διοικεῖν, which appears in pre-Socratic testimonia concerning the divine power (e.g., on Heraclitus [Marcus Aurelius in D-K 22 B 7, l. 10], Anaxagoras [Simplicius in D-K 59 A 64, l. 35], and Empedocles [Hippolytus in D-K 31 B 131, l. 11]), is a later construal of whatever was in the original, or simply an addition: Marcus Aurelius was inclined to give everything a Stoic coloring (on this tendency of his, see Marcovich [1978] 14–15, fr. 4), while Simplicius and Hippolytus lent their testimonia respectively a Neoplatonic and a Christian tone (note, e.g., the Neoplatonic νοητὸς κόσμος in Simplicius's testimonium).

55. In conjunction with the cosmos (referred to by the pronoun αὐτόν), the participle ποιῶν necessarily means "creating" (see, e.g., the testimonium on Heraclitus mentioned in the previous note). One might have expected the order of the participles—"managing" and only then "creating"—to be the other way round. Strabo might be responsible for the present order; in Stoic philosophy, these two activities were two aspects of the god's continual manifestation, and the order of presentation would not have mattered.

56. When Megasthenes mentioned a creator god (in Greek terms, not *ex nihilo*, but the bringer of order out of chaos), he could only have had in mind Plato's *demiourgos*, the "artificer," who appears in Plato's popular dialogue *Timaeus*. There is no such creator god in pre-Socratic thought. The cosmos—the ordered universe—owes its order not to a creator god, and sometimes clearly never was unordered to begin with (see, e.g., the explicit statement of Heraclitus, in D-K 22 B 30, and similar views expressed by other prominent pre-Socratics). The only apparent exception is Pherecydes (sixth cent.), who asserts that three elements were born of Chronos, but there is no cosmic creation or ordering as such (see note 66 below). The Aristotelian god, the unmoved mover, is also not a creator god, and there is no creation. The universal order is eternal, and the cosmos is unborn and incorruptible. After Plato, the Stoics were the first to speak of a creator god, but Megasthenes could not and would not have referred to their doctrine (see below, pp. 151–52). A parallel to the description in *Timaeus* of a *demiourgos* creating the world out of preexisting material was available in Brahman beliefs: the world was not created out of itself, but by god, acting rather like the *demiourgos*; nor was it created *ex nihilo*. This belief, of which there are many versions, appears already in the earliest texts of the Hindu religion, the hymns of R̥g Veda, orally composed in the period 1200–1000 B.C.E. (e.g., 10. 72, 81–82, 90, 121, 129, 190). See also the clarification in Chāndogya Upaniṣad 6. 2. 1–2.

57. The present participle form (ποιῶν) is to be interpreted as frequentative, referring to the cyclical creation (or rather, ordering and organization) of a new cosmos after the destruction of the old. Megasthenes combined Plato's *demiourgos* with the pre-Socratic theory concerning the cyclical nature of the cosmos. Such a combination is not surprising considering the eclectic nature of Megasthenes' account as a whole.

the whole (δι' ὅλου)[60] of it. And while the principles (*archai*, i.e., elements)[61] of all the things differ from each other,[62] the principle of the creation of the cosmos

58. The verb διαφοιτάω has two possible meanings in this context: "to pass through/to penetrate" or "to wander." The first sense must be rejected. This would suit the activity of the Stoic god in his capacity as *hēgemonikon* of the cosmos, controlling the world by penetrating all of it, also expressed in another aspect as the active *pneuma*, penetrating all things and holding them together. However, the Stoics used a different verb to denote this activity—διήκω. The verb διαφοιτάω is used in this Stoic sense only in Alexander of Aphrodisias (third cent. C.E; see *SVF* 4: pp. 40–41). The second sense, "to wander," is used in Greek with or without the prefix δια- (this is a common addition already in literature earlier than Megasthenes; without δια-: e.g., Hes. *Op.* 255, concerning envoys of Zeus wandering around the world on his business; with δια-: e.g., Hdt. passim, concerning envoys of humans). With reference to the activity of god himself, the verb appears in this sense in Marcus Aurelius (8. 54) and refers to the νοερὰ δύναμις ("mental ability"), a part of god, which according to Stoic thought is wandering around everywhere and is available to anyone who wishes to take advantage of it. It seems that Marcus Aurelius drew on earlier Stoic sources (LSJ's interpretation [s.v. διαφοιτάω] of this use of the verb by Marcus Aurelius—"permeate"—is wrong, as is that of Farquharson [1944] 781–82; the comparison with air, which does not permeate but is everywhere available to those who breathe it, makes the point quite clear). The second sense, like the first, when referring to the creator god who also manages the cosmos, is thus necessarily Stoic. This once again has implications for the transmission of the text of Megasthenes.

59. Unlike the last two participles in the sentence, which convey the continuous aspect, this word represents the perfect aspect. In light of the context, and of the appearance of the verb in an identical form and referring to the present in Marcus Aurelius (see note 58) and Alexander of Aphrodisias (see *SVF* 2: p. 308, fr. 1044, l. 3), the form must be regarded as *perfectum tantum,* serving instead of a present (cf. *SVF* 2: p. 155, fr. 473, l. 34, where the subject under discussion is not god).

60. δι' ὅλου: Megasthenes would not have used such an expression, but rather διὰ παντός, which in his time would have meant "through everything," "throughout the universe." Early Stoics, beginning with Zeno and Cleanthes, initiated a distinction between τὸ ὅλον, "the whole," which is our material world, and τὸ πᾶν, "the all," which is the material world and the limitless surrounding void (cf. *SVF* 4: pp. 103, 111). The void is empty of, and not controlled by, God. What God does control is the world enclosed by the void, hence he "wanders" throughout "the whole," but not "the all." Here, then, is another instance of Strabo's interference with the transmission. In this context, it should be noted that LSJ s.v. ὅλος II is mistaken in presenting Aristotle as contrasting τὸ ὅλον, the whole universe, with τὸ πᾶν, the universal order, or cosmos. At this point in his discussion, Aristotle is referring to accumulations of material in nature: an accumulation whose parts are like it in their nature is a ὅλον, while an accumulation whose parts are dissimilar to it is a πᾶν. This distinction is not cosmological. On the shortcomings of LSJ regarding philosophical terms, see H. J. Jones in his introduction to the revised edition of 1940, pp. viii-ix, and, generally, Chadwick (1996).

61. The pre-Socratics referred to elements mainly with the word ἀρχαί (see the index in D-K 3: 75–76), and so it appears from Aristotle's remarks on Anaximander, Anaxagoras, and Empedocles (*Ph.* 204b5; *Metaph.* 992b19, and esp. 1014a26 ff.; *Gen. corr.* 314a19 and passim). Aristotle himself uses the term στοιχεῖα (e.g., *Cael.* 302a30; *Metaph.* 992b19, esp. in the definition at 1014a26; *Gen. corr.* 314a19 and passim). The two terms appeared in Theophrastus's doxography on "physics"; see Fortenbaugh (1992) 408, 410, 412. It is no accident that Megasthenes used the older of the two terms.

62. The Hindus discerned in the world four material elements: earth, water, fire, and wind. Some of the references are very old. See, e.g., Brihadaranyaka Upaniṣad 2.3.1–3. On Buddhist variations, see Sadakata (1988) 20–21. The clear parallel to all this is the theory of Empedocles, whose four

is water.[63] In addition to the four elements (*stoicheioi*) there exists a fifth nature (*physis*),[64] from which [are made] the heaven and the stars. And the earth is set at the center of everything (τοῦ παντός, i.e., of the universe).[65] Also concerning seed (*sperma*)[66] and soul[67] there are said similar things [among the Brahmans and the Greeks] and concerning many other [things]. They (the Brahmans) also combine [their views] in myths, as does Plato concerning the immortality of the soul and the sentences in Hades and other such things.[68] This is what he (Megasthenes) says about the Brahmans.

An examination of this passage yields a number of conclusions, all of which have direct or indirect implications concerning the reference to the Jews.

---

elements (or "seeds"—ῥιζώματα—in his poetic language) are earth, air, fire, and water (see D-K 31 B 6; Diog. Laert. 8. 76). This view was attributed later to Pythagoras as well (Diog. Laert. 8. 23). The four elements are to be found together also in Plato (*Ti.* 31b4 ff.). Aristotle accepted the four-element theory of Empedocles and refers explicitly to Empedocles as its author (e.g., *Gen. corr.* 314a15 ff.; *Cael.* 302a30 ff.; *Metaph.* 984a9–11, 985a30–b4), but not without criticism (*Gen. corr.* 333a16 ff.; *Metaph.* 989a21–30).

63. According to the version appearing already in Ṛg Veda (10. 121. 1, 124. 7–8), and more clearly in the later Manu Smṛti (1. 8–11), God created the world by means of elements of his body; first water, and later seeds mixed in it, resulting in a golden egg from which the earth and the sky were separated. Also according to the early Upaniṣads, which preceded the Ṛg Veda and the Manu Smṛti, the beginning of the universe was water, from which was created the divine power of Brahma. The view that the beginning of creation was water appears in Greek literature in effect with Homer, who says at various places in the *Iliad* that Ocean and Thetis are the "parents of creation" (Aristotle points this out at *Metaph.* 983b30 ff.). The doxographical tradition attributed to Thales (early sixth cent.) the opinion that water was the "first cause" (πρώτη αἰτία—Arist. *Metaph.* 983b20–984a5; *Cael.* 294a28–30; Simplicius following Theophrastus, in Fortenbaugh [1992] 406, fr. 225, ll. 1–10; Diog. Laert. 1. 27). This view was shared by Hippo, the "atheist" of Samos, a negligible thinker from the end of the fifth century (Arist. *Metaph.* 984a4–5; Simplicius, in Fortenbaugh [see above]). Other pre-Socratics were opposed to this view; e.g., Heraclitus, who argued that fire was the "first cause"; Anaximenes, who preferred air (Arist. *Metaph.* 984a6–8; Simplicius in Fortenbaugh [1992] 406, 408); and Empedocles, whose theory of the four elements was adopted by Aristotle (note 62 above). The view of Thales is hinted at in Plato (*Cra.* 402b1–d2), but it is difficult to see from the context what Plato himself thought about it.

64. Aristotle mentions a fifth element (usually called πέμπτη οὐσία) in several places (e.g., *Cael.* 269b14–270b31, 289a11–35), and it is clear that this is not Aristotle's own invention; cf. *De caelo* 270b15–25, which attributes this principle to "the ancients" (οἱ ἀρχαῖοι)—namely, the pre-Socratics. Likewise, alongside the more accepted Hindu opinion that the sum of all things, including the heaven, was composed of four elements, there was also a widespread view that the outer sphere was made of a fifth element, aether (*ākāśa*), more pure and refined than the other four.

65. The location of the earth at the center of the universe is first mentioned in pre-Socratic sources by Parmenides (mid-fifth cent. B.C.E.; Diog. Laert. 8. 48 [following Theophrastus's doxography], 9. 21), and by his younger contemporary, Democritus of Abdera (Aëtius in Diels [1879] 380). This opinion is expressed in Plato (*Ti.* 40b; cf. Arist. *Cael.* 293b30–32) and by Aristotle (*Cael.* 296a24–297a8). The location of the earth in the universe is discussed in preserved Hindu texts from no earlier than the third century C.E., where it is established that the earth is at the center to the Jews (see the

A. *The Reworking of Megasthenes' Account*

A distinction must be made between Megasthenes' original account and the additions made by Strabo. The additions concern the activities of the god. The text describes this god as one who continually "makes" and manages the cosmos, and wanders through the whole of it.[69] The first Greeks to describe such a god were the Stoics: for them (as for any ancient Greek thinker) the cosmos is not created *ex nihilo* but is formed from already existing material; the Stoic god is constantly shaping the material and governs the cosmos at each and every moment.[70] The Stoic coloring of the text is discernible not only in the traits attributed to the god,[71] but also in two distinctively Stoic terms, and even in the order of the words.[72] On chronological grounds, it is implausible that Megasthenes, living in

---

detailed survey accompanied by sources in Kirfel [1967] 9–15). It is generally recognized that these texts preserve older material, and it seems that this opinion is older too; Megasthenes has some value here in testifying to the existence of this opinion in Hindu "physics" in his period. At the same time, with all the many and various Hindu opinions on "physical" matters, it is not surprising to find the opinion that the sun was at the center of the universe (e.g., Chāndogya Upaniṣad 3. 19. 1).

66. Pherecydes (sixth cent. B.C.E.) says (probably in response to Hes. *Theog.* 176 ff.) that Chronos created the three principles (ἀρχαί)—fire, breath, and water—out of his own seed (ἐκ τοῦ γόνου ἑαυτοῦ), whence came the rest of his divine offspring (Damascius *De principiis* 124 = Kirk, Raven, and Schofield [1983] fr. 49). Cf. the *sperma* of Chronos in Hecataeus of Abdera (Diod. 1. 27. 5). Indian parallels appear in several early cosmogonies, starting with the Ṛg Veda (e.g., 10. 123). There are many such myths at the beginning of Manu Smṛti and later in the Purāṇas.

67. This refers to the well-known Indian beliefs regarding the ability of the soul to exist apart from the body, the soul's immortality, rewards and punishments after death, and reincarnation. All of these have parallels in Pythagoras's doctrines (following the Orphics), although it must be stressed that the testimonia are all late, partly because of the secrecy of the early Pythagoreans. The immortality of the soul is discussed in Plato's *Phaedo*. On Pythagorean influence on theories of the soul presented in Plato's dialogues, see Burkert (1962) 364 ff.

68. In the context of the sentence, the reference to myths in Plato seems specifically directed at the myth of Er, whose soul briefly departs its body and sees what befalls other disembodied souls (*Resp.* 614 ff.), and the myth of the judgment of souls in Hades (*Grg.* 522 ff.).

69. See above, notes 54–60.

70. More precisely, the cosmos is the ordered state of what is—namely, substance (ἡ οὐσία)—when the latter's active aspect (τὸ ποιοῦν)—namely, god—works on its passive aspect (τὸ πάσχον)—namely, matter.

71. The Stoic tone of the passage has already been remarked upon by Stein, *RE* s.v. "Megasthenes (2)," cols. 259 ff., esp. col. 262, followed briefly by Hengel (1973) 467. While Hengel ascribes this Stoicizing to Megasthenes himself, Stein says that it is difficult to decide how far Megasthenes is responsible for the present formulation. Stein's comparison itself rests on a number of mistaken assumptions: he describes, for example, the cosmic cycle in the passage as Stoic, ignoring the pre-Socratic references (see note 51 above), and interprets the word διαπεφοίτηκεν as "penetrates" (see note 58 above).

72. See above, notes 55, 58, and 60.

the Orient, managed to absorb Stoic influences from his younger contemporary Zeno, the founder of Stoicism, who was active in Athens,[73] and inconceivable that Megasthenes would go on to present what were then new and eccentric views as opinions current among the Greeks. Besides, Zeno was not Greek. He was proud of his Phoenician origin and even declined Athenian citizenship in favor of retaining the citizenship of his native city, Citium, in Cyprus.[74]

The Stoic coloring is provided by Strabo, who is reworking Megasthenes' description of god, itself based on a combination of the *demiourgos* of Plato's *Timaeus* and the cyclical theory of some of the pre-Socratics. In the *Timaeus* the god creates the world (once) out of primary matter. He does not manage the world or wander through it, but, once his work is completed, goes about his own business and leaves the control of the world to other gods. There are numerous Stoicizing interpretations such as that of Strabo in later introductions to Plato, where distinctively Stoic terminology is used.[75] Many examples of later additions to the Platonic writings, organically woven into the fragments and testimonia, are to be found, for example, in Simplicius, who gives them a Neoplatonic tone, and in Hippolytus, whose presentation has a predominantly Christian tone.[76]

The likes of Simplicius and Hippolytus had clear reasons for reworking their material as they did. What, however, motivated Strabo to rework in Stoic terms that part of the original comparison by Megasthenes concerning the creator god? Strabo presents himself in his work as a Stoic, and may well have considered himself a Stoic, but his education was of a more general, well-rounded sort, as would have befitted a gentleman of the time. We know, for example, from what

---

73. Megasthenes' work was written in the first decade of the third century B.C.E. (see p. 142 above). Zeno seems to have been born in 335 and came as a youth to Athens to learn with the Cynics, and later with Polemo in the Academy. Only around 300, or later, did he begin to publicize his own philosophical ideas. Even if his novel views on "physical" matters were already widely known at the beginning of the third century—and we do not know what they might have been, in this doubtful event—it is unlikely that they would have caught the attention of Megasthenes, let alone influence his writing of the Indian ethnography.

74. Plutarch *De Stoicorum repugnantis* 1034A; cf. Diogenes Laertius 7. 12. All this despite the great honor and expressions of admiration bestowed upon Zeno by the Athenians, particularly the erection of a public statue of Zeno and the passing of a special ψήφισμα in his honor (Diog. Laert. 7. 6–12). It seems that the honor had less to do with his opinions—his *Politeia* was scandalous—than with his personal moral behavior, which made him a positive role model for the young men who associated with him (Diog. Laert. 7. 10).

75. See, e.g., the *prooemia* and scholia concentrated in Hermann (1902) 109–12, 147 ff. These are but a drop in the ocean of interpretative literature now lost. We know about this literature from Proclus, Photius, the *Suda*, and other philosophical, ethnographical, and doxographical sources and lexicons; see further Dörrie and Baltes (1993).

76. Cf. note 54 above on Simplicius's and Hippolytus's additions and terminological modifications of the opinions of some pre-Socratics.

he tells us, that he studied with a Peripatetic.[77] He had no Stoic axe to grind, but he was reasonably acquainted with the main principles of Stoicism, as would have been most of his educated readership. It seems that in the present case, associations with Stoic views in some of the previous points of comparison led Strabo to expand and interpret his source in a way that would have been intelligible to his audience, who would have been familiar with at least the basic tenets of Stoicism. What was originally an eclectic blend of features that were not peculiarly Stoic—namely, the cyclical nature of the cosmos, its spherical shape, the making (frequentative or continuous) of the cosmos[78]—when taken together, to a first-century mind, described nothing but the Stoic universe, and Strabo was led quite naturally to expand on the description of the creator god in general and well-known terms from Stoic "physics." It should be borne in mind that the earlier parallels to all these views were not familiar to the average educated man of Strabo's generation, except those authors and thinkers who bothered to look at doxographies. Strabo, like most ancient authors, had little historical perspective (as a cursory look at his *Geographica* suffices to show),[79] and would not have wondered how Megasthenes could have known about Stoic philosophy, or could have considered Stoic philosophy and terminology widespread at the time that it was just being started in Athens.[80]

B. The Selection of Greek Views and Their Dating

Allowing for the Stoic coloring by Strabo, it can be said that all the views attributed to the Greeks were held (or were thought to have been held) by the pre-Socratics.[81] Taken together, they do not reflect the philosophy of any particular thinker, nor even of a particular school of thought. Megasthenes presented instead a selection of views that he could equate with Indian conceptions. These were controversial pre-Socratic views, some explicitly rejected by the leading authorities of Megasthenes' time, others simply neglected, while just a few found favor.

The endeavor to find Greek parallels to Brahman conceptions led Megasthenes to look for every possible pre-Socratic equivalent. This is most obvious in the statement that the "first principle" of the cosmos is water, an opinion expressed

77. On this subject, see pp. 535–36 below.

78. See above, notes 51, 52, and 55–57. Strabo naturally tended to regard the verb ποιῶν as pertaining to continual creation.

79. See, e.g., p. 362 note 15 below.

80. The only other theoretical possibility is that one of the pre-Socratics, whose work has not survived, expressed similar views; but such exceptional notions concerning the divine would certainly have been adduced by later Greek philosophers discussed by Aristotle, and summarized in doxographies.

81. See above, notes 51, 52, 56, 57, and 61–67.

by Thales, considered by many to be the first Greek philosopher (early sixth century B.C.E.). It was certainly not an opinion held by Greeks by the time of Megasthenes.⁸² Some of the opinions in the list look Aristotelian, but they also originate with pre-Socratics.⁸³ The latest opinion to appear in the list concerns the *demiourgos*-creator god in Plato's *Timaeus*.⁸⁴ Plato's creation myth, however, is presented in the dialogue as delivered by Timaeus, portrayed as a follower of Pythagoras, and the average reader (and Megasthenes), just like the first two successors to Plato's Academy, his nephew Speusippus and Xenocrates, as well as other interpreters of this work, would have regarded Timaeus as expressing the opinion of Pythagoras.⁸⁵ Most decisive in this assessment is the absence of any peculiarly Aristotelian or Peripatetic opinion, although, as we shall see, Megasthenes drew most of his information from the doxography of Theophrastus, Aristotle's successor. Hence he could justifiably define the collection as the views of the "ancients."⁸⁶

C. Megasthenes' Sources of Information on Greek "Physics"

The fragments and testimonia pertaining to Megasthenes' work on India indicate that he had no proper philosophical training, to say the least. The medley of views from incompatible systems that he adduces as if part of a consistent and widely held Greek doctrine also testifies to this. Unlike many contemporary authors, including ethnographers, he did not write a philosophical work, or anything approaching a philosophical work; at least, we have no evidence that he did. If Megasthenes is typical of his age, he would have had a lay interest in philosophy and would have read popular philosophical books when so inclined. We should not expect such a person to have gleaned the pre-Socratic opinions he mentions in his comparison from original works (difficult and obscure texts, regularly in poetical language and meter). On the other hand, Plato's work was popular and widespread. One of the most popular dialogues, in that period as in any other, was the *Timaeus,* and indeed, Megasthenes draws from that dialogue the notion

82. See above, note 63.

83. See above, notes 52, 61, and 62.

84. See above, note 56.

85. On this view, held by Speusippus and Xenocrates (and later by Posidonius of Apamea), see Burkert (1962) 64–65. On authors who reported that a book by the Pythagorean Philolaus served as a source for Plato's *Timaeus,* see Diogenes Laertius 8. 85 (following one of the philosopher biographies by Hermippus of Smyrna).

86. Megasthenes' reference to Plato, concerning myths about the separate existence of the soul and the judgment in Hades, is irrelevant in this context, since he does not refer to the content of the myths as parallels to Greek views but to the very use of myths to express philosophical ideas. The opinions expressed therein were held by Pythagoreans long before the time of Plato, and before them by the Orphics (see note 67 above).

of the creator god.[87] The popular *Politeia* and *Gorgias* relate ancient Greek myths pertaining to the separation of the soul from the body and trials in the underworld, myths referred to at the end of the testimonium.[88]

Megasthenes' source of information for the pre-Socratics seems to have been an epitome of the monumental sixteen-book doxography by Theophrastus called either "Opinions of Physical Inquirers" (φυσικῶν δόξαι) or "Opinions Concerning Physics" (φυσικαὶ δόξαι).[89] The doxography and its epitome have not survived, but we do have fragments and testimonia informing us mainly of opinions of pre-Socratics and Plato, and summaries of the writings of Aristotle.[90] In addition to his many books on certain pre-Socratics (Anaxagoras, Anaximenes, Democritus, and Empedocles), Theophrastus wrote summaries of some Platonic and Aristotelian works and even composed his own work on "physics" and on the gods (the list is given at Diog. Laert. 5. 43–50). All these provided the material for the doxography that gained great popularity already in his own lifetime. It may not have been the first of its type,[91] but it became a model and primary source for the extensive doxographic tradition that was to develop in the Greek and Roman world. Theophrastus's work is often mentioned explicitly by later doxographers as a source.[92] That Megasthenes drew his information on Plato from a doxography seems unlikely, seeing that his emphasis is on Plato's use of myths. Doxographies, by their nature, emphasize the definitions and opinions given by philosophers, which are presented in a dry and concise style, grouped according to person or according to topic. The doxography of Theophrastus, and certainly its epitome, either would have ignored the myths altogether or would have extracted from them Platonic opinions, without mentioning that they originated in Platonic

87. See note 56 above.

88. On the great popularity of *Timaeus*, see Reydams-Schils (1999). Plato himself made a second edition of *Gorgias* (see Dodds [1951] 34 ff.), which indicates how influential and widespread this dialogue was, as further testimonia also corroborate (e.g., the story of a Corinthian who sold his estate and devoted himself to philosophical pursuits after reading *Gorgias*). The popularity of *Gorgias* was due to its calling rhetors to account, its attack on two figures greatly admired by the Athenians—Pericles and Themistocles, its attempt to explain the failure of Athens in the Peloponnesian War, and its conclusion that the drive to satisfy the desires of the mob, by establishing an empire, necessarily led to the corruption of morals and to decline. As for the immense reputation of the *Politeia*, little needs to be said; its influence may be judged by the stream of works bearing the same title (in one language or another) that it has provoked ever since antiquity.

89. On the original title, see Mansfeld (1992) 64–65.

90. See the collection of fragments in Fortenbaugh (1992) 402–37.

91. See Mansfeld (1986), (1992) passim, and many of his other publications. For the original purpose of writing *Doxai*, see Mansfeld (1992) 67–70.

92. See the references to the many quotes from Theophrastus's doxography in the index to the collection of Diels (*DG*). The point is made by Diels many times in his introduction; e.g., when talking about Cicero: *DG*, pp. 119–32; and cf. 102–18, 132–44.

myths.[93] No wonder Megasthenes does not refer to the similarity between the Orphic "cosmic egg" and the parallel Indian stories.[94] The Orphic views, being expressed in myths, would not have found their way into the Theophrastean doxography.

D. Megasthenes' Information on the Brahmans

Almost all the opinions Megasthenes attributes to the Brahmans concerning "physics"—once Strabo's additions have been accounted for—are indeed such as were popular among the Hindus (and in part among the Buddhists), although not all of them may be located in the materials that have survived from the time of Megasthenes or the periods preceding him. The general accuracy of the opinions allows us to regard Megasthenes as a reliable witness, whether he knew the main native tongue or not. In some cases, his evidence can establish the antiquity of certain conceptions.[95] At the same time, considering the vastness of the Indian subcontinent, the great number of castes, sects, groups, and sub-groups, and the extensive literature that had been developing for generations, the views he presents in his work could not be the only ones widely held on the subjects mentioned. Various opposing theories were current concerning cosmological and theological questions, and development was not uniform or systematic. The picture Megasthenes presents of Indian "physics" is as eclectic as his picture of Greek "physics." It would seem, however, that the Indian picture he presents was in accord with that held by his Indian contemporaries around the capital of Sandracottus at the very least.

SIMILARITIES AND DISSIMILARITIES BETWEEN
THE JEWS, THE "ANCIENT" GREEKS, AND THE BRAHMANS

Even a cursory reading of Megasthenes' remark concerning the Jews negates the interpretations mentioned at the beginning of this chapter.[96] There is no intimation in the fragment that the philosophy of the Jews preceded that of the Greeks, but only that opinions concerning "physics" such as those voiced in the past by the "ancients" are current at the time of author, some among the Brahmans and

---

93. See, e.g., the formulation of the opinions of Plato in Theophrastus's doxography as transmitted through the testimonium of Simplicius, in Fortenbaugh (1992) 422, fr. 230. In Diels's collection of doxographies there appears as the opinion of Plato a remark concerning the immortality of the soul, without any reference to the myth (e.g., *DG* 205, in the testimonia of Plutarch and Tertullian, and elsewhere in *DG*).

94. See the sources in Kirk, Raven, and Schofield (1983) 39–48. Cf. Guthrie (1935) 92 ff.

95. See, e.g., above, note 65.

96. See above, pp. 137–38.

some among the Jews. Megasthenes is certainly not claiming that the Greeks took their wisdom from the Jews, nor is he comparing the opinions of Jews with those of Brahmans. Quite the opposite, in fact. It may be inferred from the text that the opinions of the Jews differ from those of the Brahmans, and hence are not to be compared.[97] The fragment does not indicate, or even imply, a common origin for the Jews and the Indians.

The first particle of the fragment—μέντοι—indicates that the point now being made was a reaction to the preceding point in Megasthenes' original work. The fragment says that the ideas concerning "physics" that had already been expressed in the past by the "ancients" were now current in part among the Brahmans and in part among the Jews.[98] To what was Megasthenes contrasting this statement? In light of the tenses used here, it would seem that the passage preceding this, but following the detailed comparison between the physical opinions of the "Greeks" (in fact, the pre-Socratics) and the Brahmans, raised the point that the Greeks claim that the important physical opinions have always been the exclusive property of the Hellenes. Megasthenes replies in the fragment that this is not the case, since some of these opinions of the "ancients" (i.e., the pre-Socratics) are at present held by Brahmans, and others by Jews. He does not respond to the implied claim of Greek primacy, presumably because he did not have, and could not have had, hard information about the beginnings of "parallel" opinions among the Brahmans. While Greek philosophers had already admitted that Greek astronomy (as opposed to other branches of physics) was greatly influenced by Oriental astronomy,[99] they did not locate its origin in India, but in Babylonia or Egypt. Nor does Megasthenes make such a claim. Clement, however, who had the original preceding claim in front of him, may have understood, especially since this would accord with his purposes, that Megasthenes was reacting also to the claim of Greek primacy, and in his reply giving precedence to the Indians and the Jews. It would not be the first time that Clement interprets (or even modifies) his sources to suit his own purposes.[100]

In this context it is worth noting that the Jews are mentioned after the Brahmans in a reference made by Numenius of Apamea who is quoted by Eusebius

---

97. Had Megasthenes been interested in saying that the Jews and the Brahmans shared views, he might have written, e.g., τὰ μὲν ... ὑπὸ τῶν Βραχμάνων, τὰ δὲ ... ὑπὸ τῶν Ἰουδαίων, τὰ δὲ ὑπ' ἀμφοτέρων.

98. For the benefit of the nonexpert reader: the perfect participle (εἰρημένα) refers to a present state affected by a past, completed act.

99. E.g., Epinomis (wrongly attributed to Plato) 986e; Aristotle De caelo 292a8; cf. Diodorus 2. 30.

100. See, e.g., the "improved" quotation from Plato's Symposium in Clement Stromateis 1. 15 (67. 2), and another supposedly Platonic quotation not found in Plato's writings, in Stromateis 1. 15 (68. 3). The latter may have been drawn from Hellenistic interpretative literature on Plato, such as the commentary on Timaeus by Plato's pupil Xenocrates of Chalcedon, who later became head of the Academy.

(*PE* 9. 7. 1). Numenius greatly admired the law of Moses and even called Plato "the Attic-speaking Moses" and the like.[101] The quotation warns against attempting to understand the divinity through Plato's writings alone and advises turning to Pythagoras, and to the cults, views, and customs of peoples of good repute, these being "the Brahmans and the Jews, the Medes and the Egyptians." The mention of Medes and Egyptians in the same breath with Brahmans and Jews indicates that Numenius too is not implying that there is a similarity between the "physical" conceptions of the Indians and the Jews.

THE SOURCE OF INSPIRATION REGARDING THE JEWS

The Jews are mentioned in parallel with the Brahmans, and the formulation explicitly balances one with the other, as "those who philosophize" within their respective societies. Both, then, are seen as groups of philosophers.[102] This comparison might seem to be influenced by the description of the Jews as a community of priest-philosophers in Theophrastus's *Peri eusebeias* and Clearchus's *On Sleep*.[103] Theophrastus's work was written in 319–315/4 B.C.E., and Clearchus's a few years later,[104] more than a decade before the composition of Megasthenes' *Indica*, which has been dated to the 290s.[105] However, it would be unlikely that Megasthenes had at his fingertips, or that he bothered to consult, an esoteric work such as that of Clearchus, and the same goes for *Peri eusebeias*, from a philosophical point of view one of the least important of the numerous works of Theophrastus. There was in fact no need for Megasthenes to rely on a written source in order to present the Jews as philosophers. This image of the Jews was already in the air a generation earlier and had influenced Theophrastus and Clearchus themselves.[106]

Yet this image of the Jews as a community of philosophers would not by itself be sufficient to suggest that any of their opinions on "physics" are similar to those

---

101. See the passages in Stern, *GLAJJ* 2: no. 363a-e. For the fragments of Numenius, see des Places (1973), and useful remarks there.

102. Megasthenes calls the Jews and the Brahmans οἱ φιλοσοφοῦντες (the philosophizers), and not οἱ φιλόσοφοι (the philosophers). While Aristotle does distinguish between philosophers and philosophizers, with the latter failing to live up to their avowed principles (e.g., *EN* 1093a1 ff., 1098b16), it is clear from Megasthenes' description of the high morals of the Brahmans that he does not make this distinction. He uses the two terms indiscriminately, as indeed was common not only in general literature, but also in philosophical writings.

103. On the Jews as a community of philosophers in Theophrastus and Clearchus, see above, pp. 34–36, 81.

104. On the dating of the composition of these books, see p. 15 note 1, and pp. 81–82 above.

105. See above, p. 142.

106. See above, pp. 34–36.

of the pre-Socratics. Megasthenes' responsible approach to preparing a detailed preliminary survey comparing the "physics" of the Brahmans with the "physics" of the "Greeks" prior to determining a partial similarity between them shows that his account of the Jews is not given on the spur of the moment or based on superficial first impressions, but rather grounded in specific details that he knew about Jewish "physics." What, then, would have led Megasthenes to such a conclusion? Did he interview Jews in his immediate vicinity for this purpose? Or was he closely acquainted with Jews at some stage of his life? Both are possible, given his mobility and keen interest in ethnographical matters.

At the same time, Megasthenes may well have been inspired by the Jewish excursus of Hecataeus of Abdera. He was significantly influenced by Hecataeus's celebrated ethnography, *Aegyptiaca*,[107] which contained the excursus. Megasthenes would have acquired this work after returning from his Indian missions. Hecataeus's version of the "physics" of the Jews accords well with the general evaluation of Megasthenes, that there is a resemblance between a few of the opinions held by the Jews and the (Greek) ancients. The Jewish views on "physics" adduced by Hecataeus are indeed unlike those of his contemporary Greek philosophers, but similar to those of some pre-Socratics.

This is not to say that Hecataeus himself drew upon pre-Socratic sources for his description of Jewish belief, cult worship, and physical concepts. We have seen in chapter 3 that Hecataeus's perceptions regarding Jewish religion are due to a misconstrual of the information obtained from Jewish informants, together with his own interpretation and causal explanations based on Herodotus's account of Persian belief and cult (1. 131).[108] The *Histories* of Herodotus were well known to Hecataeus (who occasionally argued against that work), probably much better known than the cosmological poetry of the pre-Socratics. What interests us, however, in the present discussion is not Hecataeus's sources of inspiration, but Megasthenes' perception of Hecataeus's account. Let us now take another look at the "physics" of the Jews as reported by Hecataeus (Diod. 40. 3. 4):[109]

> But he constructed no image at all of gods, through not believing the god to be man-shaped (μὴ νομίζειν ἀνθρωπόμορφον εἶναι τὸν θεόν) but [believing] only the heaven holding around (περιέχοντα) the Earth to be god and master of all.

This account recalls pre-Socratic assumptions and theories on three basic points: (1) idol worship/anthropomorphism, (2) heaven as divinity, and (3) the shape of the cosmos (heaven and earth).

107. See above, p. 97 and note 18.

108. See p. 119 note 81, p. 125, and, for the text of Herodotus, p. 133 above.

109. ἄγαλμα δὲ θεῶν τὸ σύνολον οὐ κατεσκεύασε διὰ τὸ μὴ νομίζειν ἀνθρωπόμορφον εἶναι τὸ θεόν, ἀλλὰ τὸν περιέχοντα τὴν γῆν οὐρανὸν μόνον εἶναι θεὸν τῶν ὅλων κύριον.

An absolutely negative view of anthropomorphism was known in the Greek world in the sixth century B.C.E., starting with Xenophanes,[110] and there is more than a hint of it in Heraclitus.[111] However, from what survives of Greek texts of the fifth and fourth centuries B.C.E., there seems to have been no thinker associated with the field of Greek "physics" whom Megasthenes could regard as a consistent supporter of this negative view of anthropomorphism. We must discount the few atheists, such as Diagoras, the fifth-century poet from Melos, who demonstrated his negative attitude toward the belief in the existence of gods by, among other things, throwing a statue of Heracles onto a fire, and escaped a death sentence only by running away.[112] Plato often used myths in which god is described anthropomorphically. It does not matter for our purposes whether Plato himself accepted what he wrote, or whether it was only a vital component in the dramatic structure of certain dialogues. The Platonizing reader would have regarded Plato as describing god anthropomorphically, and would not have considered him to be a supporter of the views of Xenophanes (despite the elegant criticism in *Critias* 107b-e). Aristotle is usually careful to the point of elusive, even talking occasionally about gods in mythological terms, despite having at the heart of his "physics" an unmoved mover that is god without human form.[113] It is only in the generation after Hecataeus and Megasthenes that we find a central Greek philosopher—the third-century B.C.E. Stoic Chrysippus—openly critical of anthropomorphism.[114] The interpretation offered by Hecataeus, therefore, was perceived by Megasthenes as equivalent to pre-Socratic views.

As regards heaven as divinity, in two similar testimonia deriving from the doxography of Theophrastus, it is said that Pythagoras was the first to identify heaven with the "cosmos"[115]—a universal order of one sort or another assumed by

110. See D-K 21 B 11, 12, 14, 15, 16, 23, 24; and testimonia such as Diogenes Laertius 9. 19. The general parallel between the accounts of Hecataeus and Xenophanes was observed by Guttmann 1: 60.

111. See Clement *Stromateis* 5. 116 (404. 1 = D-K 22 B 32).

112. See the testimonia in Winiarczyk (1981) 10–11 nn. 27–33.

113. With exceptions: *Metaphysica* 997b10, 1074b3 ff.; *Politica* 1329b25–33.

114. See *SVF* 2: frr. 1057–60 (pp. 311–12).

115. Diogenes Laertius 8. 48: "[Favorinus] says that [Pythagoras] was also the first to call heaven 'cosmos' and the earth a sphere; according to Theophrastus it was Parmenides" (D-K 28 A 44). Favorinus (second cent. C.E.) took his doxographies from Theophrastus, as in the present instance (the testimonium is rightly included in the collection of fragments of Theophrastus in Fortenbaugh ([1992] 416). The reference to Theophrastus as the one who considered Parmenides to be the first pertains not to the first part of the testimonium (heaven-"cosmos"), but only to the second part (earth-sphere). This distinction becomes apparent from the continuation in Diogenes Laertius, according to which Zeno (the founder of Stoicism) considered Hesiod to be the first; neither Zeno nor anyone else would claim that Hesiod was the first to call heaven "cosmos." There is a similar testimonium in Aëtius, reconstructed by Diels from two sources (*DG* 327). Diels shows in his long *praefatio* that Aëtius drew a great deal of his doxographical information from the doxographical

many pre-Socratics in their theories. "Heaven" indeed was also one of the meanings of "cosmos" in fourth-century literature,[116] but many of its original connotations were lost. Plato presents a different conception: while not identifying the *demiourgos*-creator god with heaven, he writes that heaven, which he describes as a material and tangible body, has in it something divine (*Ti.* 28b2 ff.). Aristotle goes farther: the "divine" is in the outermost sphere (e.g., *Cael.* 278b14–15), but not identical with it, since the unmoved mover is not material.

As for the shape of the cosmos, Hecataeus uses the verb *periechein* to describe the connection between heaven and earth. The verb has two senses: "to hold/limit/grasp round about" and "to contain."[117] The intent of the text, therefore, is either that the ends of the earth are "held" by heaven, implying that the earth is actually flat, or that it is spherical, with the heaven an outer sphere "containing" it. There is no hint in the Bible that the earth is spherical. From a combination of references it appears that the earth was usually imagined as a circular tablet with protrusions on its surface, and limited from one horizon to the other by heaven covering it like a tent or a dome (e.g., Isa. 40.22). As far as Hecataeus is concerned, there is no reason to think that his Jewish informants presented a cosmological picture in which the earth is spherical. The verb περιέχειν, therefore, is to be understood in this context as "to be held all around" (i.e., without the held object having any chance of escape). The earth is a sort of rounded plateau held on all

---

work of Theophrastus (*DG* 99 ff.). On Theophrastus as a source for both the testimonia, see Gigon (1935) 54; Finkelberg (1998) 108. See further the anonymous work *On the Life of Pythagoras* preserved by Photius, paras. 11 and 15; and in Iamblichus *De vita Pythagorica* 32 (216): μετὰ δὲ τοῦτο ἐμάνθανε (Abaris) παρ' αὐτοῦ (Pythagoras) περὶ τοῦ οὐρανόθεν ἠρτῆσθαι καὶ οἰκονομεῖσθαι πάντα ("After this Abaris learned from Pythagoras about the fact that all things depend on, and are administered by, heaven"). It is generally accepted that Iamblichus took this sentence from Heraclides of Pontus (fourth cent. B.C.E.): see the bibliographical survey in de Vogel (1966) 304–6.

116. See the collection of examples in Finkelberg (1998) 122, 124. Not all the examples are valid, and in some instances they show how the distinctions between the meanings of the word "cosmos" became blurred, and how the original meaning lost its force. For a detailed, but less accurate, discussion on the identity of *cosmos* and *ouranos* see Herschensteiner (1962) 32 ff., 49 ff., 69 ff., 160 ff., 226, 228 ff.

117. Both meanings are common in Greek. Sufficient for our purposes are two examples attributed to pre-Socratics. Anaximenes, who believed that the world was flat, says: οἷον ἡ ψυχή, φησίν, ἡ ἡμετέρα ἀὴρ οὖσα συγκρατεῖ ἡμᾶς, καὶ ὅλον τὸν κόσμον πνεῦμα καὶ ἀὴρ περιέχει (D-K 13 B 2, ll. 17–19: "[Anaximenes] says: 'Just as our soul, being air, holds us together, so *pneuma* and air hold the whole cosmos from all sides"). The parallel between the two verbs (συγκρατεῖ and περιέχει) indicates that the latter means "holds from all sides," and not "surrounds." This example may be contrasted with an admittedly problematic testimonium attributed to Pythagoras, where περιέχοντα means "surrounding": καὶ γίγνεσθαι ... κόσμον σφαιροειδῆ, μέσην περιέχοντα τὴν γῆν καὶ αὐτὴν σφαιροειδῆ (D-K 58 B 1, ll. 7–8: "And the cosmos is spherical, surrounding the earth—itself spherical—at the middle"). See also, e.g., Aristotle *Metaphysica* 1074a38 ff.; *Physica* 2036b (Anaximander).

sides by heaven. Megasthenes may well have applied this sense to accord with the more primitive (or "ancient") view.

The flat earth view was indeed widely held among pre-Socratics, such as Xenophanes and Anaximenes in the sixth century B.C.E., and Anaxagoras and Democritus in the fifth century.[118] Parmenides, in the middle of the fifth century, appears to have been the first to maintain that the earth is spherical,[119] and Empedocles may well have followed him, as he frequently does, on this point as well, although no testimony has survived,[120] while some others offered a varied range of geometrical shapes.[121] Plato writes in the *Timaeus* that the earth is located at the center of the universe (40b),[122] and from the continuation of the argument, which is open to many interpretations, it may be inferred that the earth is considered similar to the universe in being spherical.[123] Aristotle was unambiguous in his support for the view that the earth is spherical,[124] and he was followed in this by his pupils. Megasthenes, therefore, belonged to a generation whose leading philosophers regarded the earth as spherical. The view of a flat, circular earth was now attributed to "ancients" (i.e., pre-Socratics), and was mentioned as such by Aristotle and in doxographies such as that of Theophrastus.

We have already seen that when the formulation of the passage adduced by Clement is examined, far from indicating a parallel between the views of "phys-

118. On the opinion of Anaximenes, Anaxagoras, and Democritus, see Aristotle *De caelo* 394b14; on the opinion of Xenophanes, D-K 21 B 28; on the opinion of Xenophanes that the depth of the earth is limitless, see Aristotle *De caelo* 294a24. For a summary of the various opinions, see Aristotle *De caelo* 293b32–294a10.

119. As mentioned above, in note 115, Diogenes Laertius (8. 48) indirectly quotes Theophrastus from his doxography on matters concerning nature, according to which Parmenides was the first to call the world a sphere; but Diogenes Laertius, in the same sentence, has already mentioned that Favorinus claims this honor for Pythagoras. Because of the hazy nature of the origins of information concerning Pythagoras, especially in light of the later apocryphal literature that grew up around him (and Favorinus dates to the second century C.E., when this literature began to flourish), it seems better to follow Theophrastus here. See also Diogenes Laertius 9. 21. Another piece of information apparently deriving from Favorinus states that Anaximander thought that the earth was spherical (Diog. Laert. 2. 1), but this contradicts the testimonium of Hippolytus (see note 121 below).

120. All that remains is his view that the universe is spherical (see above, note 52), and his criticism of the theory of Xenophanes and others concerning the unlimited depth of the earth (Arist. *Cael.* 294a25–26).

121. Such as the view of Democritus that the earth is concave (see the testimony of Aëtius in D-K 68 B 94), and the theory of the wavy shape of the earth deriving from Anaximander (see Hippolytus in D-K 12 A 11, ll. 6–8; cf. the reasoning of Aristotle, *Cael.* 295b16 ff.). Leucippus (last quarter of the fifth cent.) states that the earth is shaped like a drum (Diog. Laert. 9. 30).

122. Cf. the reference in Aristotle *De caelo* 293b30–32 and Plato *Phaedo* 112e (if indeed what is written is to be so understood).

123. On the shape of the universe according to Plato, see note 52 above.

124. Aristotle *De caelo* 287a30–b21; 293b32–294a11; 297a8–b17; 297b30–298a20.

ics" held by Brahmans and Jews, it reveals a clear difference. The basic theological principles of the Jews, as presented by Hecataeus and understood by Megasthenes, do indeed differ from what Megasthenes knew about the Brahmans. In his time gods were certainly thought of in India in anthropomorphic terms (although probably there were still no images); heaven was not regarded as divine, and certainly not as the "god and master of everything"; and it was the ocean, rather than heaven, that was described as surrounding the earth.[125]

125. On the last point, see Kirfel (1920) 9–10, and on heaven, 37–45.

5

Hermippus of Smyrna on Pythagoras, the Jews, and the Thracians

At the head of the passages from Greek literature that Josephus adduces in *Contra Apionem* to support his claim that the Jews were of great antiquity and were always admired by Greek authors, there appears an excerpt from a biography of Pythagoras written by Hermippus of Smyrna. Hermippus, a late third-century B.C.E. Alexandrian scholar and biographer, was for five centuries considered by Greek and Roman authors alike to be a significant and respectable source for the history of the philosophers. Josephus regards the excerpt as evidence for the great influence Jews had on the customs Pythagoras established for his disciples (*Ap.* 1. 162–65), known as *akousmata* ("commands heard") or *symbola* ("symbols"). This testimonium is supported by a more general observation concerning Jewish influence on Pythagoras, attributed to Hermippus by Origenes (*C. Cels.* 1. 15 [334]).[1]

Were every detail in the two testimonies of Josephus and Origen to be accepted as authentic, it would seem that, even in the days of Hermippus, one hundred years after the first daily contacts between Jews and Greeks, Greek authors continued to view Jews as a nation of philosophers, regarding Jewish philosophy

---

1. On Hermippus and the Jews, see Freudental (1875) 192; Müller (1877) 161–63; Gutschmid (1893) 4: 558–60; Willrich (1895) 59–60; Reinach (1895) 39–40; Schürer (1901–9) 3: 625–27; Radin (1915) 89; de Böhl (1953) 475–77; Guttmann 1: 151–52, 181; Cardini (1969) 109–11; Burkert (1972) 172–73; Hengel (1973) 469; Wehrli (1974) 57–59, 91–92; Stern, *GLAJJ* 1: 93–96; id. (1976) 1118–19; Sevenster (1975) 184; Jacobson (1976); Troiani (1977) 110–12; Gorman (1983) 32–42; Goodman in Schürer et al. 3: 695–96; Bickerman (1988) 230–31; Gabba (1989) 623–24; Philhopfer (1990) 201; Feldman (1993) 201–2, 224; Sansone (1993); Momigliano (1993) 79–80; Kasher (1996) 151–56; Bollansée (1999a) 108–13, 233–49; (1999b) 48–51; Labow (2005) 162–64.

as having had a significant influence on Greek philosophers, and this at a very early stage of Greek philosophy. Hermippus's testimonium as phrased in Origen even appears to reveal an early version of the myth about the Jewish origin of Greek philosophy, a myth well documented in Jewish-Hellenistic literature, the church patriarchs, medieval and even later texts, including rabbinic literature.[2] Thus the testimonia would appear to indicate that the myth originated among the Greeks rather than the Jews.

HERMIPPUS ON THE JEWS,
AND MODERN APPRAISAL OF HIS STATEMENT

The Josephan passage on Hermippus (*Ap.* 1. 162–65) follows:

(162) Indeed, Pythagoras of Samos, being ancient, and considered to have excelled those who had philosophized in wisdom and respect for the divine [entity], clearly not only knew our affairs, but also was a very great admirer of them.[3] (163) Well then, no composition is agreed [to be his], but many have investigated the things about him, and most outstanding of these is Hermippus, a man careful with regard to all research. (164) He, then, in the first [of his books concerning] Pythagoras, says that he (Pythagoras), after one of his[4] pupils died, by name Calliphon, in origin a Crotonian, used to say that that man's soul spent time with him both at night and during the day;[5] and that he (Calliphon)[6] recommended not to traverse a place wherever[7] an ass sinks to its knees,[8] and to abstain from drying water,[9] and to refrain from all blasphemy.[10]

2. The myth of the Jewish origin of Greek philosophy and its development in late antiquity has received considerable scholarly attention. It will suffice here to refer to Drodge (1989). There is, however, no comprehensive work on the development of the myth in medieval and modern literature.

3. I have translated *zēlotēs* as "admirer," since it would be too much to expect Josephus to claim that Pythagoras was an emulator of the Jews; Hermippus elsewhere uses the word in the sense of "admirer" (Diog. Laert. 8. 56).

4. Reading with S, αὐτοῦ. L, αὐτῶν ("when one of the pupils *themselves* died" or "when one of *their* pupils died").

5. S and the *editio princeps* read καὶ νύκτωρ καὶ μεθ' ἡμέραν—"both by day and by night," with the connotation that there were a number of full days, and not just one whole day. L reads καθ' ἡμέραν, which usually means "day by day"; Niese, who was not acquainted with S, emended to μεθ' ἡμέραν, which means "in broad daylight" as opposed to the adverb νύκτωρ, "by night" (as, e.g., in Aeschin. 3. 77). This is obviously the right reading.

6. On the question whether the prohibitions are to be attributed to Calliphon or Pythagoras himself, the conclusion is unambiguous; see below, p. 184.

7. ἐφ' ὃν ἄν. L has a subjunctive in the subordinate clause (ἐφ' ὃν ὄνος ὀκλάσῃ). S and the *editio princeps* rightly include the necessary particle ἄν.

8. On the meaning of ὀκλάσῃ, see below, pp. 186–87 and note 103.

9. On the meaning of διψίων ὑδάτων, see below, pp. 187, 189.

10. In this context *blasphēmia* refers to offense against divinity only; see pp. 187–89 below, and note 108 on the meaning of "all."

(165) Then (Hermippus) adds after this the following as well: "And (Pythagoras) used to do and say these things imitating and transferring to himself the opinions of the Jews and the Thracians." For that man is in fact said to have transferred many of the customs among the Jews to his own philosophy.

Origen's remark is quite similar to the final sentence of the passage in Josephus, although it is much more comprehensive (*C. Celsum* 1. 15 [334]):

It is said that Hermippus as well, in the first [book of] *On Lawgivers,* has stated that Pythagoras brought his own philosophy from Jews to Greeks.

The excerpt from Josephus may be broken down as follows: after the opening in which Josephus presents Hermippus and his work (163), there comes the testimonium from Hermippus (164; henceforward "the testimonium"), which includes a story spread by Pythagoras himself, in which the soul of Calliphon, his dead student, accompanied him for some time and left him three prohibitions. Following the testimonium comes a fragment (165; henceforward "the fragment") in which Hermippus states that while Pythagoras attributed to Calliphon the prohibitions he followed, in fact it was Pythagoras himself who introduced them, imitating Jewish and Thracian customs. The final sentence (165 fin.: "For that man" etc.) claims that many Jewish customs were transferred to the "philosophy" of Pythagoras. The testimonium adduced by Origen goes even farther, claiming that the "philosophy" of Pythagoras in its entirety originated with the Jews.

There is no reason to dispute the attribution of the testimonium and the fragment in Josephus to Hermippus. As will be seen below, the image of Pythagoras portrayed in the testimonium well matches the approach of Hermippus toward him in the passages that have survived from the biography. The fragment is clearly not a Jewish forgery, since Jewish influence on Pythagoras is presented there as equal to that of the Thracians, hardly a byword for high culture in the Hellenistic world.[11] However, the final sentence is controversial. Some regard it as an additional testimonium of Hermippus or as a continuation of the fragment, while others attribute it to Josephus himself, be it his own interpretation or a paraphrase of a statement by Aristobulus, the mid-second-century B.C.E. Jewish Hellenistic author, concerning Jewish influence on Pythagoras.[12] The testimonium adduced by Origen is also controversial, with some denying its attribution to Hermippus.[13]

---

11. *Pace* Müller, *FGH* III. 32; see Stern, *GLAJJ* 1: 93. Cf. also Goodman in Schürer et al. 3: 696.

12. See the discussion below, pp. 196–200.

13. See below, pp. 200–202.

All scholars have regarded Hermippus's remarks on the Jews as praise, except one, who goes to the other extreme, calling Hermippus "anti-Semitic."[14] Opinions are divided over the exact nature of the praise. When the concluding sentence is taken as part of the fragment from Hermippus, and the testimonium in Origen is regarded as authentic, then this may serve to show that at the end of the third century B.C.E., or even earlier, Greek authors believed that there had been overwhelming Jewish influence on Pythagoras's entire philosophy. When the last sentence in Josephus is not attributed to Hermippus and the authenticity of the testimonium in Origen is denied, then it may be claimed only that some Greeks believed that there had been some Jewish influence on just a few Pythagorean customs. This would also be considered praise for the Jews, although to a lesser extent.

The assumption that Hermippus's statement is actually complimentary to the Jews needs to be examined. It takes for granted that any comparison between Jews and Greek thinkers, especially a philosopher of the stature of Pythagoras, can indicate only great admiration toward the Jews, or even adulation. However, the Greek intellectual arena was a battleground steeped in controversies and passions. Barbed and poisonous attacks were the norm, and esoteric sects would have suffered from all sides. An evaluation of Hermippus's image of the Jews requires a prior investigation into his attitude toward Pythagoras. Other relevant questions requiring preliminary treatment include the origin of both the final sentence in Josephus and the testimonium in Origen, and the identification of the prohibitions mentioned, a tricky subject that is also a matter of controversy. Prior to all these is the question of the general literary approach of Hermippus, and above all, the specific character and aim of his work *On Pythagoras*. It is worth emphasizing that the question occasionally raised concerning the influences of Oriental cultures on Pythagoras is irrelevant when the issue is the image of Pythagoras in the third and second centuries B.C.E., rather than the historical-intellectual processes at the time of Pythagoras, in the sixth/fifth century B.C.E. Similarly, the Pythagorean question by and large—namely, Pythagoras's real historical personality and teaching—does not concern us here.

HERMIPPUS'S LITERARY BACKGROUND
AND CHARACTERISTICS OF HIS WORKS

We possess none of Hermippus's works. All we know about him is gleaned from about one hundred testimonia and fragments preserved mainly in Plutarch, Ath-

14. See the bibliography in note 1 above. On anti-Semitic sentiment, see Gorman (1983) esp. 33, 36. Gorman's article, learned as it is, contains serious errors in Jewish matters.

enaeus, and Diogenes Laertius.[15] A number of surveys have been written over the years on Hermippus and his works,[16] and recently there has appeared a most comprehensive and detailed monograph accompanied by a voluminous commentary.[17]

Hermippus was born in Smyrna.[18] He earned the nickname Kallimacheios,[19] which is significant for determining his era and sources of influence. It has been rightly concluded that Hermippus was one of the pupils of Callimachus,[20] the poet, scholar, and bibliographer active in Alexandria around the middle of the third century B.C.E. Callimachus was a phenomenally prolific writer on a wide range of subjects and may well have been the greatest poet of the Hellenistic period. He was also famous for his learned publications, such as anthologies on many and various subjects, and particularly for the catalogues that he produced for the Great Library of Alexandria. Hermippus was not only Callimachus's pupil but also continued his work as a scholar-excerptor. He may have helped Callimachus in collecting material for the catalogues,[21] and he seems to have made use of Callimachus's archive and the catalogues themselves,[22] which included at the very least information on the origins, dates, center of activity, and even sources of each author, and the date of publication of each work.[23] Whatever the case may be, it appears that Hermippus used Callimachus's work as the basis for the bibliographical lists he included in the biographies of his subjects.[24] There is no reference to the Jews in the surviving material of Callimachus, and most probably no such reference ever existed. It is scarcely credible that Jewish and Christian authors failed to take notice of a reference to the Jews—however trivial it may have

15. The fragments and testimonia have been collected by Müller (1855); Wehrli (1974) 11–41; Bollansée (1999a) 1–93. The fragments and testimonia referred to below follow the numbering in Bollansée.

16. Müller, FGH III. 35–36; Susemihl (1893) 1: 492–95; Leo (1901) 124–28; Diels and Schubart (1904) xxxvi–xliii; J. C. Heibges, RE s.v. "Hermippos (2)," cols. 845–52; Drerup (1923) 72–75; von der Mühll (1942) 89–102; Moraux (1951) 221–26; Steidle (1963) 142–43; Pfeiffer (1968) 129, 150–51; Burkert (1972) 102–3; Fraser (1972) 1: 453–54, 780–81; Wehrli (1974) 7, 102–6; Blum (1991) 60–61, 188–89; Momigliano (1993) 79–81; Flower (1994) 48–49.

17. Bollansée (1999b); subjects not appearing in his monograph are dealt with in his detailed commentary on the fragments (1999a).

18. Fr. 55, and cf. Bollansée (1999b) 8–7.

19. Three testimonia, T2a–c.

20. See the detailed discussion in Bollansée (1999b) 1–7, and bibliography there. Three additional Alexandrian authors were called Callimachean; see Bollansée, 3–6.

21. As Bollansée (1999b) 2–3 speculates.

22. Thus Pfeiffer (1968) 120; Fraser (1972) 1: 781; Momigliano (1993) 80; Bollansée (1999b) 4–7. For bibliographical information, see T20, fr. 37a.

23. Fragments of the catalogues have been collected in Pfeiffer (1949–53) frr. 429–53; cf. Pfeiffer (1968) 128–34; Blum (1991) 150–60.

24. Thus correctly Bollansée (1999b) 179–80, pace Wehrli (1974) 78.

been—by a poet and scholar of the standing of Callimachus. His concentration on topics and motifs drawn solely from Greek heritage has already been widely acknowledged.

Hermippus was also called *peripatetikos*.[25] This epithet was given to several scholar-compilers active in Alexandria who were not philosophers, let alone Aristotelians, such as Satyrus, a biographer and younger contemporary of Hermippus, and Heraclides Lembus, a high official in the Ptolemaic court (c. 170–150 B.C.E.) who also summarized biographies of philosophers. For this reason it has been concluded that the epithet referred generally to scholars who worked in Alexandria,[26] and particularly to those who worked on subjects of special interest to Peripatetics, such as biography. This conclusion fits Hermippus well: he was no philosopher and seems not to have expressed his own opinion on philosophical matters, judging from what remains of his writing. His account of Aristotle and Theophrastus shows no indication that he followed in their footsteps. On Aristotle he related somewhat unflattering episodes (beside positive and unbiased accounts), while he mocked the personality and mannerisms of Theophrastus. The epithet *peripatetikos* cannot help us assess the attitude of Hermippus toward the Jews.

The literary activity of Hermippus has been established as spanning the late third century and early second century B.C.E.: Callimachus died in the 230s B.C.E.,[27] and in one of the fragments Hermippus described the death of Chrysippus the Stoic, who died in the 143rd Olympiad,[28] 208/204 B.C.E. Hermippus would have been in his fifties or sixties when Chrysippus died, and his biographical writing would not have continued long into the next century. It is unknown whether his work *On Pythagoras,* in which he mentions the Jews, predated or antedated the settlement lexicon of Mnaseas of Patara, in which appeared the story of the statue of the ass in the Jerusalem Temple (Joseph. *Ap.* 2. 91–96). In fact it does not matter either way, since their references to the Jews have little in common. The reference to the ass in one of the three prohibitions mentioned by Hermippus bears no relation to the story told by Mnaseas.[29] Besides, when Hermippus reported the Pythagorean prohibition against traversing a place where an ass had sunk to its knees, he did not necessarily have in mind a Jewish custom.[30]

Hermippus wrote many biographies, a work on the Magi, a commentary on

25. T1, fr. 19b.
26. Leo (1901) 118; Brink (1946) 11–12; see also Bollansée (1999b) 9–14, and the comprehensive bibliography there. The minority opinion of West (1974) is unacceptable.
27. On the dating of the death of Callimachus, see the discussion in Bollansée (1999a) 351.
28. Fr. 76 (Diog. Laert. 7. 184), and see Bollansée (1999b) 14–15, who develops previous comments.
29. See below, note 122.
30. See below, p. 193.

Homer, and a didactic poem on astronomical matters (*Phaenomena*). Since his reference to the Jews is located in his work *On Pythagoras,* it will be of advantage to consider only his biographical writings, in particular their extent and general character. They fall into four groups: (a) a compilation titled *On the Seven Sages,* or *On the Sages,* which contained biographies of the seven classical sages[31] (Pythagoras is not one of the sages in Hermippus's version of the list, although he is mentioned by Hermippus as one of the seventeen personalities who appeared on various other lists of the seven sages);[32] (b) a compilation titled *On Lawgivers,* with biographies of such people as Lycurgus and Triptolemus;[33] (c) biographies of philosophers and orators, including certainly Pythagoras, Aristotle, Theophrastus, Gorgias, Isocrates, and Epicurus, and probably others mentioned in the fragments, such as Socrates and Plato;[34] (d) *On Those Who Converted from Philosophy to < . . . > and the Exercise of Power,*[35] an collection of brief descriptions of philosophers or their pupils who became tyrants or advisers to tyrants.

On the question of the exact source for Hermippus's remark on the Jews in Josephus and Origen, it should be noted that an Oxyrhynchus papyrus informs us of an epitome made by Heraclides Lembus of *On the Seven Sages, On Lawgivers,* and the biography of Pythagoras.[36] It has been suggested that Josephus and/or Origen used the epitome,[37] but Josephus explicitly states that he is drawing on the first book of the biography of Pythagoras, while Origen claims to have cited the first book of *On Lawgivers.* It is worth adding that Heraclides Lembus also composed epitomes of *diadochai* (successions) of philosophers by Sotion and for biographies by Satyrus, both contemporaries of Hermippus. In both these epitomes he also included an abbreviated biography of Pythagoras.

The epitomizing of the biographical works of Hermippus testifies to the interest in them in the second century B.C.E. This was particularly the case with the biography of Pythagoras, the only one of the many Hermippean biographies to be treated separately in the epitomes of Heraclides Lembus. Hermippus was almost completely forgotten after the time of Diogenes Laertius, the second-third century C.E. biographer of philosophers, when it was then possible for readers to find more extensive and orderly biographies of famous people.

31. Frr. 9–20.

32. Fr. 10.

33. Frr. 2–8.

34. Frr. 20–55.

35. Frr. 39–40: περὶ τῶν ἀπὸ φιλοσοφίας εἰς < . . . > καὶ δυναστείας μεθεστηκότων. See also Bollansée (1999a) 355–62; (1999b) 72–81; and see below, pp. 177–78 on the political-social theory of Pythagoras, as presented by his opponents.

36. T5, fr. 9a.

37. Werhli (1974) 91.

The works of Hermippus, although entitled *Bioi,* were not as sophisticated as those biographies written by such an outstanding scholar as Aristoxenus, a pupil of Aristotle, already at the beginning of the Hellenistic period,[38] or in the way that the genre was conceived by later Greeks and Romans (following Nepos, Plutarch, and Suetonius). The works of Hermippus contained basic biographical details (including a bibliography), accompanied by random statements and episodes stitched together into an apparent whole. These anecdotes generally spoke for themselves, but Hermippus would occasionally add a comment or an interpretation.[39] From this point of view the works were no different from the *Bioi* written by Aristotle and his pupils Theophrastus and Dichaearchus, but the same cannot be said for their character and degree of reliability.

From the middle of the nineteenth century, many scholars have observed that the biographical episodes and comments of Hermippus are unreliable, and that his writing inclines toward the sensational and the satirical.[40] This tendency is reflected in the material surviving from his contemporaries Sotion and Satyrus, but it is most noticeable in Hermippus. The claim for sensationalism is based mainly on fragments describing the death of the subjects of biographies, or even of secondary characters.[41] These deaths are unnatural and unexpected and include suicides, brutal executions, natural disasters, and some connected with excessive eating and drinking; they all inspire wonder, and may raise a laugh, or at least a smile. Not a few of the descriptions are historically unfounded and are clearly invented, either by Hermippus or by his sources. Some deaths are demonstrably adapted (or opposed) to the character or doctrine of the victim.[42] The death of Pythagoras is one such case.[43]

---

38. The fragments of Aristoxenus are in Werhli (1945) frr. 11–68. See esp. Momigliano (1993) 73–89.

39. For such comments, see pp. 176, 178, 184–85 below.

40. All the scholars mentioned in note 16 above (except von der Mühll, discussing Hermippus's relatively temperate biography of Solon), to whom should be added Rohde (1871) 562; Delatte (1922) 221–23; Lévy (1926) 37–39. Bollansée, attempting to attribute to Hermippus's account some historical value by referring to the bibliographical and prosopographical information to be found there (e.g., T20, fr. 37a), summarizes thus: "Hermippos appears to have presented his readership with an odd mix of 'fun and facts', . . . depictions of anecdotal scenes interlaced with a plethora of picturesque, obscure, memorable and/or sensational elements" ([1999b] 185–86).

41. Writing on strange deaths, and even anthologies devoted to the subject, were no novelty. Phaenias of Eresus, for example, a pupil of Aristotle, had written a work on the death of tyrants; see Wehrli (1957) frr. 14–16. This work was used by the first-century C.E. Titinius Capito in his work *Exitus illustrium virorum* (Death of Famous Men). Nor was this the only Latin work of its kind.

42. See the exhaustive discussion in Bollansée (1999b) 153–41, 227–32. The most instructive example is the description of the death of Heraclitus, which hints at his physical theories and actually ridicules them (fr. 64; and see Bollansée [1999a] 462–69, following Guthrie [1963] 469 n. 3).

43. See p. 180 below.

The prurient nature of Hermippus's work is discernible in a good number of the episodes he writes about. Two examples will suffice, and these are drawn not from the descriptions of strange deaths—usually the preferred illustrations in research on Hermippus—but rather from pieces of everyday information. Additional examples will be adduced below from the biography of Pythagoras.

Aelianus writes as follows in his *De natura animalium* (7. 40):

> I have ascertained that there is also a tribe of Aethiopians in which there rules a dog, and they obey its impulse; they know that if it whimpers it is not impassioned, and if it barks they are aware of its anger. If Hermippus is able to bring this as evidence to someone, adducing Aristokreon as his witness, let him convince. Not having escaped my attention it then came to mind at an opportune moment.

Hermippus took this account from a work by Aristokreon, a geographer who wrote on Ethiopia.[44] Hermippus chose this fictional account because he was looking precisely for this sort of material. Since the expeditions to Ethiopia and the development of the "elephant stations" in the reign of Ptolemy II Philadelphus, Greeks living in Egypt had a great deal of information about their Ethiopian neighbors. Had Hermippus made the effort, he would have found a more plausible report. Only a generation later, Agatharchides of Cnidus included in his work *On the Red Sea* a great deal of information on the diversity of the Ethiopian population and its way of life. While there are still a fair number of baseless rumors and exaggerations in his account, he does not stoop to such absurdities as Hermippus was only too eager to do.

To take another example, this time from the recent history of Athens, Hermippus describes the flamboyant behavior of Theophrastus when performing in front of an audience in the Lyceum (Ath. 1. 21a-b):

> Hermippus says that Theophrastus used to appear in the Peripatos at a regular time, splendid in his prime. He would sit down and deliver his speech without refraining from any gesture or pose; once, while imitating a gourmet, he stuck out his tongue and licked his lips.

The passage is a greatly reduced version of the account originally produced by Hermippus, since it has been preserved in the epitome of the first book of Athenaeus.[45] These features of Theophrastus would undoubtedly have been described in more detail. Even as it stands, there is no support for such a portrayal of Theophrastus as either a teacher or an orator in the relatively many testimonia we have on him. It is, for example, difficult to see in Hermippus's version the man

---

44. See Bollansée (1999a) 91 and n. 49. His attempts (592) to render Hermippus's account reliable or of historical worth are unsuccessful.

45. Rightly noted by Bollansée (1999a) 333.

whom Aristotle dubbed Theophrastus ("divine speaker") or the teacher who, while wanting many pupils, still complained that preparing lectures consumed time better spent writing his books.[46] Hermippus's description is not only unsupported, but it is actually at odds with the rest of the tradition.[47]

ON *PYTHAGORAS* AND THE IMAGE OF PYTHAGORAS

Hermippus's biography of Pythagoras has reached us in the threadbare form of eight fragments and testimonia, including those transmitted by Josephus and Origen. The remainder are preserved in Diogenes Laertius and Athenaeus.[48] The work comprised at least two books (Diog. Laert. 8. 41), and the publication of an epitome just a generation or so later by Heraclides Lembus may suggest that the work included additional books.

The discussion in the previous section concerning the biographical writing of Hermippus already suggests that the biography of Pythagoras may not have been written with historical truth in mind but tended instead toward the sensational and the prurient. A comparison of all the biographical fragments shows that not only was the biography on Pythagoras as sensational as could be expected, but also that the subject of the work was treated with undisguised hostility and bias. Hermippus's negative attitude toward Pythagoras was not unusual. The image and doctrine of Pythagoras were controversial in the ancient world: there was admiration, even adoration, on the one hand, and contempt, hatred, scorn, and mockery, on the other hand, including bitter personal attacks on him and his activities. The pious image of Pythagoras has prevailed in Western culture thanks to the Christian and Neoplatonic heritage.

In 1871, the German scholar Erwin Rohde published an article on the sources of the second-third century C.E. Neoplatonist Iamblichus for his enthusiastic biography of Pythagoras. In the article, which was to become a classic on the stages of transmission of the Pythagorean tradition,[49] Rohde gave short shrift to the biography on Pythagoras by Hermippus, which he identified as nothing but "eine giftige Satire" ("a venomous satire") inspired by satirical motifs and hostile remarks against philosophers to be found in Greek comedy.[50] Rohde provided no evidence for his assertions, apart from a reference to the story

---

46. Bollansée (1999a) 333–37 makes strenuous, if unsuccessful, efforts to find a kernel of truth in the description of Theophrastus. He too concludes that it originates in a source hostile to the Peripatetics (337).

47. See the collection of bibliographical items on Theophrastus in Fortenbaugh (1992) 20–87.

48. See the passages in Bollansée (1999a) F21–27 and T1.

49. See Rohde (1871). On the great influence of the article, see Philip (1959) 185–87. The author does not disagree with Rohde over Hermippus, but on other statements made by him.

50. Rohde (1871) 562. It may have been said already before: see the references in Müller (1877) 162.

about Pythagoras hiding underground in Croton. He may well have assumed that the other fragments of the biography on Pythagoras spoke for themselves. His interpretation was adopted by many scholars in surveys of the works of Hermippus and in other contexts.[51] However, it did not reach the attention of scholars (apart from two[52]) commenting on Hermippus's reference to the Jews, either because of their eagerness, inspired by Josephus and others, to find praise for the Jews in Greek literature or because they were misled by the extravagant praise that Josephus himself expressed for the quality of Hermippus's work. Josephus may have been taken even more seriously here because of his manifest caution, following many others, with regard to the authenticity of works attributed to Pythagoras (163).

Rohde's assessment has been challenged recently by the Belgian scholar Jan Bollansée, who published a large volume in 1999 containing a collection of the fragments and testimonia of Hermippus with detailed commentary, as one of the sequels to the monumental *Fragmente der griechischen Historiker* by Felix Jacoby. Shortly afterward Bollansée also published a comprehensive monograph on Hermippus.[53] Bollansée maintains that Hermippus is not responsible for any bias or hostility in his biography of Pythagoras, and claims Hermippus's intention was only to choose passages that provide "a good story," as he did in his other biographies, where he simply sought to interest readers, and sometimes shock them. According to Bollansée, Hermippus found his material in earlier authors and invented nothing. Bollansée even goes so far as to state that Hermippus copied his sources without any modifications.[54] Bollansée interprets the "Jewish" passage according to these basic premises, with Hermippus taking his account from a Jewish-Hellenistic source. Thus the customs and beliefs described do actually reflect Jewish customs and beliefs of the time. The passage, in Bollansée's view, does not belittle Pythagoras but praises the Jews. Bollansée concludes by calling the passage "pro-Semitic."[55]

As Bollansée has devoted over nine hundred pages to a comprehensive and meticulous analysis of Hermippus's writings, his opinion deserves special attention. While Hermippus clearly did incline toward the "interesting" or prurient, this in itself is insufficient reason to conclude that he was indifferent to the deeds

---

51. See the comprehensive bibliography in Bollansée (1999b) xi–xv, and 50 n. 91.

52. Gorman (1983) and Bollansée (1999a) 233–49. Both fail to make the necessary conclusions concerning the nature of the biography, each for his own reasons. Against the usual assumption that Hermippus intended his words to praise Pythagoras and the Jews, see Bar-Kochva (1994) 461–62 and n. 8, paraphrased by Kasher (1996) 155.

53. Bollansée (1999a), (1999b).

54. Bollansée (1999a) 233–297; (1999b) 50–55, 118–41, 154–63, 182–83.

55. Bollansée (1999a) 243–46; (1999b) 48, 50–51.

and characters of the subjects of his biographies. In some cases his personal attitudes can easily be detected. As for Bollansée's approach to the biography of Pythagoras as a whole, it suffers from a number of obvious weaknesses:

1. Two of the eight passages, to be adduced later in the discussion, present Pythagoras as a deceitful charlatan (the *katabasis* story), and his doctrine and politics in general as advocating tyranny and despotism and encouraging treason and extreme violence against opponents (a note in the Athenion account). It would be rather strange to claim that Hermippus took all this from his sources only in order to present "a good story," without his personally having an extremely negative opinion of Pythagoras. A biography containing such grave accusations would not have been written in this way solely to entertain. Any work on the highly controversial character of Pythagoras would have been regarded, at least in the third/second century B.C.E., as taking sides. Hermippus was not an automaton who contributed to the demonization of Pythagoras only by chance.

2. One of these two passages even shows that Hermippus blatantly stated his own strongly negative attitude toward Pythagoras's political theory and his personality, calling him sarcastically "the fine Pythagoras."[56]

3. The Jewish fragment testifies to the active involvement of Hermippus in the content of the episodes, with him expressing his completely negative view of one of the fictional stories spread by Pythagoras. As with the *katabasis* story, Pythagoras is actually presented as a liar who tried to convince his disciples using fictitious tales.[57]

I would add that in not a few cases it was difficult for Bollansée to find evidence for the existence of similar stories, concerning Pythagoras or anybody else, in literature prior to Hermippus, yet he hypothesized that there were such stories.[58] Furthermore, Bollansée himself praises (rightly) the narrative skill of Hermippus.[59] The notion of a "hands-off" storyteller with narrative skill is difficult to comprehend. There must have been some editorial interference, to say the least.

---

56. The testimonium is extremely brief and shared with the historian Theopompus, who preceded him; see pp. 177–78.

57. See pp. 184–85 below.

58. See, e.g., Bollansée (1999a) 150–53 (the prohibition against the use of cypress wood in the manufacture of coffins); 257–58 (the profession of the father of Pythagoras); 285 (the death of Pythagoras); 264–67 (the descent of Pythagoras under the earth); (1999b) 134 (the story of the soul of Calliphon); and so with episodes concerning other biographies (e.g., p. 71 on the appearance of Theophrastus).

59. Bollansée (1999b) 118–41, stating at the outset: "He (Hermippus) must have been a gifted storyteller with an unerring sense of the picturesque and/or memorable (often sensational) scene and a keen eye for the intimate and/or obscure detail."

The basic evaluation of Rohde would therefore seem to be fairly sound. Because of their importance to the general assessment of Hermippus's attitude toward the Jews, and in order to remove any doubt with regard to his attitude toward Pythagoras, it might be worth presenting here the two most hostile passages from the biography.

Here, first, is the description of Pythagoras's rise to a position of influence in Magna Graecia, the Greek regions of settlement in southern Italy:

> Hermippus says something else about Pythagoras. [For he says] that on coming to Italy he made a little house under the earth and ordered his mother to write the happenings on a tablet, indicating also the time, then send down to him until he should come up. This the mother did. Pythagoras after a time came up, thin and skeletal. Going to the assembly he claimed that he had arrived from Hades, and indeed he read out to them the things that had happened. They cringed at what was said and wept and wailed and believed Pythagoras to be someone divine, so that they even handed over to him their women to learn some of his [doctrines], and these women were called "Pythagoraeans." Hermippus [says] these things. (Diog. Laert. 8. 41)

The story of the *katabasis* (descent) has been much discussed. It was thought in the past that it was merely an intentional inversion made by Hermippus to the story well known from Herodotus (4.95) and Hellanicus (*Suda* s.v. Ζαμόλξις) about Zamolxis, Pythagoras's slave.[60] According to that story, on his journey from Ionia back to Thrace, Zamolxis tried to persuade the Thracians that they would gain eternal life. To this end, he suddenly disappeared and remained for three years in a subterranean structure. The inhabitants mourned for him as one dead, so that when he finally reappeared they considered his claim proven. It is not certain nowadays which story came first, and it may be that the two stories existed basically in parallel perhaps already in the pre-Socratic era (apart from accretions of later generations).[61] Be that as it may, apart from Bollansée, no one disputes the evaluation that the Pythagoras story is mocking and hostile in intent.[62] The story speaks for itself, and an author including it in his biography of Pythagoras as a vulgate in the floruit of Alexandrian scholarship, when the image of Pythagoras was strongly disputed, could not be indifferent to it.[63]

---

60. So have many claimed since Rohde (1871) 557 n. 1. See the bibliography in Bollansée (1999a) 265 n. 104.

61. Bollansée (1999a) 265–74; (1999b) 192–33, following Burkert (1972) 147–62; but see Gottschalk (1980) 117–18.

62. See, e.g., Burkert (1972) 156: "The mocking tone of this account of a journey to the underworld is of course unmistakable."

63. Contrary to Diogenes Laertius, the much later, uncritical, and often senseless compiler, who was committed, if at all, only to the Epicureans. In any case, Diogenes Laertius attributed the *katabasis* story explicitly to Hermippus.

As regards the political doctrine and activity of Pythagoras, Athenaeus (second century C.E.) quotes a report from the "Histories" of Posidonius (published 84 B.C.E.) about the "Peripatetic philosopher" Athenion, culminating in his rise to a brief tyranny in Athens during the anarchy accompanying the Mithridatic War of 88 B.C.E. (Ath. 5. 211d–215b).[64] The report, in fact a powerful sarcastic satire, describes in detail the rise of Athenion from the gutter, his deceitful manipulation of the Athenians by which he was finally elected *stratēgos,* his betrayal of their faith in him when he declared himself a tyrant, and especially his reign of terror over the city: the meager rationing of food to inhabitants, his immediate disposal of "sensible inhabitants," a night curfew, confiscation of property and money of innocent citizens, executions without trial, torture, scourging to death, show trials, persecutions and elimination of his opponents in exile, and so on.

Immediately after describing Athenion's seizure of the city and the first murders of potential opponents, Athenaeus continues thus: [65]

> After not many days, when the philosopher (i.e., Athenion) had revealed himself a tyrant and had demonstrated the dogma of the Pythagoreans concerning the plot and what that philosophy wished for them that the fine (kalos) Pythagoras had introduced, as Theopompus reported in book 8 of the Philippics, *and Hermippus, the Callimachean,* immediately he removed from his path the sensible ones of the citizens—against the dogmas of Aristotle and Theophrastus, as if the proverb saying "Don't [give] a sword to a child" were true—[and] set guards at the gates, in order [that] at night many of the Athenians, wary of the future, would let themselves by ropes and flee. Athenion [then] sent calvary [to catch them]. (Athen. 5.213f.)

The story goes on to describe the acts of cruelty that Athenion visited upon the escapees. Athenaeus included the sentence from Hermippus in order to characterize Athenion's actions: the man put into practice the political doctrine of Pythagoras and followed the advice to be found there, in his betrayal of the trust of the Athenians, in the establishment of a tyranny, and in his cruel deeds against the populace. The testimonium is clearly only a summary of the details Hermippus would have given concerning the political doctrine and career of Pythagoras. It squares with the hostile traditions accusing Pythagoras or his

---

64. On the passage, its context, and background, see esp. Malitz (1983) 346–55; Kidd 2: 863–87, and esp. 864 for a detailed bibliography.

65. It is already well established that Posidonius himself had not included the testimonium of Hermippus in his story, but that this was done by Athenaeus. Posidonius treated Pythagoras with respect: see Kidd 2: 870–80; Bollansée (1999a) 292 n. 196, and many bibliographical references there. Bollansée (1999b) 79 attributes the fragment of Hermippus to the composition *On Those Who Converted from Philosophy to < . . . > and the Exercise of Power,* but would such a significant statement (and possibly accompanying stories) have been left out of the biography?

adherents of setting up, or intending to set up, a tyranny in Croton,[66] and relating the activity of certain Pythagoreans throughout the centuries who had become cruel tyrants in southern Italy.[67] The message of the testimonium stands in stark contrast to the position of the supporters of Pythagoras, such as Aristoxenus, who claimed that Pythagoras deplored tyranny and worked toward a regime of freedom.[68] It is quite possible that Hermippus's statement was also accompanied by descriptions of, or at least references to, Pythagorean tyrants notorious for their cruelty.[69] The sarcastic epithet "(morally) fine" or "noble" (*kalos*) applied to Pythagoras in the testimonium well underlines the attitude of the writer toward his subject.[70] Hermippus, then, not only reworked or invented "a good story" but also made his own position clear.

Hermippus thus had an extremely negative attitude toward Pythagoras, quite in keeping with the general lines of the anti-Pythagorean traditions. In three out of eight surviving passages Hermippus explicitly or implicitly sharply censures Pythagoras. If the other five passages—now removed from their original context—may be perceived by modern readers as either complimentary or "neutral," this is only because it has always been the practice of satire to let the actions speak for themselves. The ancient literati, familiar with the traditions and rumors on the lifestyle of the philosophers and their doctrines, and aware of the tone of the biography by and large, would hardly have missed the jibes and sarcasm. The real intent of these five passages can therefore be reconstructed by recalling the characteristics of similar types, well known from the history of all periods.

To summarize the discussion so far, the portrait of Pythagoras drawn by Hermippus may be reconstructed as follows: the man was nothing but a cheat and a charlatan. It was a clever trick that convinced the people of Croton, his new city, of his supernatural powers.[71] Recognition of his special abilities had

66. E.g., Diogenes Laertius 8. 39, 40, 46; Dicaearchus in Porphyry *Vita Pythagorae* 56–57; Pompeius Trogus in Justin 20. 4.

67. On the political activity of Pythagoras in Magna Graecia, see von Fritz (1940); Minar (1942); Dunbabin (1948) 359–73. Particularly well-known is the harsh charge of Appian, *The Mithridatic War* 28, that the Pythagorean tyrants were more cruel than usual tyrants. Burkert (1972) 118 n. 57 even speculates that Hermippus was the source for Appian on this point.

68. See the references in Bollansée (1999a) 294 n. 201, to which may be added Porphyry *Vita Pythagorae* 7, 9, 16, 21; Diogenes Laertius 8. 22.

69. Suggested by Bollansée (1999b) 80.

70. In this context it does not matter if the epithet was originally invented by Theopompus or by Hermippus. It was certainly not supplemented by Athenaeus.

71. Pythagoras is said to have presented himself as Apollo the Hyperborean, Heracles, or the son of Hermes (Aristotle in Rose [1886] fr. 191; Porphyry *VP* 2, 20, 29; Iambl. *VP* 28 [140], 30 [178]; Diog. Laert. 8. 4, 11). On the wonderful deeds attributed to him, see Aristotle in Rose (1886) fr. 191; Porphyry *Vita Pythagorae* 23–24, 27, 28–29; Iamblichus *De vita Pythagorica* 28 (142–44); and there too (favorably, of course) on the use made of marvel stories to reinforce his authority. Among other

married women flocking to him (details may well have attracted the attention of Hermippus).[72] The same trick also persuaded citizens to accept his theory that the soul is immortal.[73] Pythagoras reinforced his claim with fictional tales such as that of the soul of Calliphon keeping him company night and day for a time (*Ap.* 1. 164).[74] In addition to novel beliefs, Pythagoras issued strange, even ridiculous, commands and prohibitions, like the one against using cypress wood for coffins.[75] The three prohibitions referred to in the Josephan fragment are of this type (see below). The reader is made to see that these beliefs and customs, and the veil of mystery around Pythagoras for his followers, all served to reinforce his control over them. Pythagoras was thus considered the sole possessor of knowledge of right and wrong, of the secrets and the reasons for the precepts. In his drive to power he did not even hesitate to impose arbitrary prohibitions that harmed the livelihood of his parents.[76] In fact, the customs and beliefs are unoriginal: the charlatan is also a plagiarist, having stolen his doctrine from various peoples,

---

things, Pythagoras was said to have bitten a huge snake in Sybaris, Sodom of the Hellenes, and thus freed the inhabitants from terror, and calmed storms on rivers and at sea. See also the sources collected in D-K 14. 7 (including Aristotle), and the discussion in Burkert (1972) 142–44.

72. Bollansée (1999a) 274–76 seems to regard this detail of the story as an innocent and incidental reference to the community of women in Pythagorean society. On the duty of loyalty in marriage much has been said in Pythagorean literature. Yet it is doubtful whether this is the intention, coming as it does at the end of such a venomous story. It is worth noting that the men of the city do not themselves come to study with Pythagoras, but send their wives to him in the belief that he is a divinity. The text differs from the positive version of Dicaearchus, which spoke of separate assemblies of young men, children, and women on the orders of the archons (in Porph. *VP* 18; cf. Pompeius Trogus in Justin 2. 4. 8–12). The author thus seems to be mocking yet again the stupidity of the inhabitants, while also hinting again at the deviousness of Pythagoras. Imposters claiming to have supernatural powers who exploit naive women are a well-known phenomenon not confined to any one period. The comedy on the Pythagorean woman (see below, note 87) may well have contained such insinuations, thus imputing hypocrisy to the Pythagorean conservatism in family affairs. Anti-Pythagorean tales to this effect would hardly have passed through the screening of the Christian church.

73. The literature on Pythagoras described the course of the wanderings and cycles of the soul (see, e.g., Dicaearchus in Werhli [1944] fr. 36 = Mithardy [2001] fr. 42; Heraclides Ponticus in Diog. Laert. 8. 4). On the great lengths Pythagoras went to to persuade his followers of the transmigration of souls, see Diodorus 10. 5. 2–3; Porphyry *Vita Pythagorae* 26, including evidence close to the genre of wonder stories (*thaumasia*).

74. See pp. 184–85 below; cf. p. 182 below on Pythagoras and the shield of Menelaus.

75. Fr. 22 (Diog. Laert. 8. 1). For other *akousmata* known from ancient literature, see below, note 100.

76. Fr. 23 (Diog. Laert. 8. 41) describes Mnesarchus, the father of Pythagoras, as a gem engraver, while other sources have him in maritime commerce. There is a barb in the fragment: one of the prohibitions attributed to Pythagoras was against the wearing of rings bearing the images of gods (Clem. *Strom.* 5. 5 [28. 4]; Iambl. *VP* 18 [84]; Diog. Laert. 8. 17). His father's occupation, therefore, would have suffered from this prohibition. The barb is noticed by Bollansée (1999a) 257–62, and he compares the tactic with the innuendo behind the strange death descriptions in Hermippus (esp. the death of Heraclitus, fr. 64). It should be added that the Pythagoreans urged the respect of parents (see, e.g., Porph. *VP* 38) and old people in general (Diog. Laert. 8. 22).

none counted among the wise nations, and some actually on the fringes of the Hellenistic world.[77]

Pythagoras regarded his close followers as an instrument in gaining power and political control. His political doctrine encouraged treason and justified the use of any means, including mass murder, torture, and the obstruction of justice, while advocating tyranny. Hermippus may well have stated explicitly that Pythagoras attempted to realize his doctrine in Croton.[78] Such ignoble deeds would have merited the sarcastic epithet *kalos* ("fine, noble").

Pythagoras dies in a ridiculous manner, proving the folly of his commands and prohibitions: when his enemies, the Syracusans, were pursuing him and his supporters, Pythagoras avoided taking a shortcut through a field of beans and was thus captured and killed.[79] Hermippus hints here at the well-known Pythagorean prohibition against eating beans,[80] and expands it in a way that is not known from any other source, probably to make the prohibition even more ridiculous. Pythagoras, as often happens to such men, is thus portrayed as eventually believing in the fictions he fed to his adherents, and even treating them with extreme devoutness. The strangeness of the Pythagoreans only increased in the following generations: they grew their hair long and wild (apparently with a shaggy beard), wore filthy rags, and walked barefoot, like the Cynics.[81] The

77. Many authors wrote about the influence of the Egyptians, Persians, Babylonians, Indians, and Phoenicians on Pythagoras: e.g., Isocrates *Busiris,* 11 [28]; Porphyry *Vita Pythagorae* 6; so too Callimachus, the guide and mentor of Hermippus (in Diod. 10. 6. 4). In the *Epinomis* attributed to Plato (987d) it is explained that the Greeks who were influenced by "barbarian" peoples greatly improved what they received thanks to the good weather that affected their character; and see in detail the anonymous work on Pythagoras preserved in Photius *Bibliotheca* 249, para. 21. Many Greek authors saw no wrong in plagiarism, but many others regarded it as a serious offense. Charges of plagiarism were leveled against Plato and other philosophers, but particularly, it seems, against Pythagoras (cf. pp. 310–11 below).

78. Diogenes Laertius 8. 40; cf. 8. 39; Porphyry *Vita Pythagorae* 51; Iamblichus *De vita Pythagorica* 31 (191); and see Bollansée (1999a) 276–85.

79. Fr. 25; cf. Iamblichus *De vita Pythagorica* 31 (191). On the bizarre nature of the story, see Burkert (1972) 103 n. 29.

80. The prohibition against eating beans is one of the most famous of the Pythagorean prohibitions and is mentioned in every ancient list of *akousmata,* beginning with that of Aristotle (Diog. Laert. 8. 34). It was an easy target for mockery and was also the subject of much interpretation in the ancient world (see, e.g., the discussion in Markovich [1984]), and in the modern world, by medical researchers (see, e.g., Brumbaugh and Schwartz [1979/80], and references there to previous medical articles). Aristoxenus presented Pythagoras positively in his biography and therefore felt obliged to state that Pythagoras actually liked to eat lentils (Wehrli [1953] fr. 25).

81. Fr. 26 (Ath. 4. 163e); and see Bollansée (1999a) 282–92, and esp. Burkert (1972) 202–5, on the existence of a Pythagorean offshoot in fourth-century B.C.E. Athens similar in external behavior to the Cynics; and there too on Diodorus of Aspendus, mentioned in the fragment. However, Hermippus treats the Pythagoreans as a whole.

major Pythagorean elements noticeable by their absence in Hermippus are the isolationism of Pythagorean groups and the veil of secrecy. It is unlikely that they were overlooked in Hermippus's biography of Pythagoras.

This portrayal of Pythagoras might surprise, even annoy, modern readers who have been accustomed to regarding the man as a model of morality and of scientific learning. Readers in the ancient world, however, would have taken it in stride, since Hermippus's portrayal was well within the mainstream anti-Pythagorean tradition. To clarify the point, it would be helpful to give a sketch here of this prevailing trend in contemporary literature.

Mockery, accusations, gossip, and libels against philosophers were hardly new in Greek literature. They were all familiar to the pre-Socratics and intensified in the "wars of the philosophers" of the succeeding centuries. They were especially popular in Middle Comedy and rhetoric.[82] The most notorious example is Aristophanes' wild satire of Socrates in *The Clouds*. Such criticisms were made not only against Socrates, but also against other major figures, such as Plato and Aristotle, and many relatively minor philosophers, such as Heraclides Ponticus and Demetrius of Phaleron, who suffered particularly harsh criticism, as appears from the later biographies of the philosophers by Diogenes Laertius. The attacks increased in severity against closed and/or eccentric sects, such as the Pythagoreans, who aroused basic fears and suspicions among ordinary people, and against social dropouts such as the Cynics and would often fail to distinguish between them. An outstanding example in the Hellenistic period of an attack against all the dogmatic philosophers is the *Silloi* (Lampoons), a three-book collection of verses by Timon, a pupil of the Skeptic Pyrrho, active in Athens in the third century B.C.E. Each philosopher received individual attention, and some—like Pythagoras—suffered particularly harsh treatment (Diog. Laert. 8. 37). Such material was grist for the mill of the biographers, and similar material had already made its way into the biographies written by the first Peripatetic philosophers.

An impression of the image of Pythagoras in negative and satirical works of the generations preceding Hermippus can be gained from a review of some of the material known to us. Of the pre-Socratics, Heraclitus called Pythagoras "leader of blabbers" (κοπίδων ... ἀρχηγός),[83] while Xenophanes mocked the Pythagorean belief in the transmigration of souls (Diog. Laert. 8. 36).[84] Hippasus of Metapontum, a disciple whom Pythagoras banned from his company on the charge of "revealing the secrets," was attributed with a poetic work called *On the*

---

82. See the general discussion in Owen (1983) and the sources in Cardini (1969) 3: 334–40 and note 87 below.

83. D-K 22 B 81 (from the scholion on Euripides).

84. See further Diogenes Laertius 9. 1, which includes Pythagoras in a list of learned men lacking understanding; cf. Athenaeus 13. 610b: "senseless".

Mystical, which launched a violent attack on Pythagoras (Diog. Laert. 8. 7). In the second half of the fourth century, Heraclides of Pontus (a pupil of Speusippus, the nephew of Plato who inherited the Academy), himself portrayed by Hermippus as a charlatan (Diog. Laert. 5. 91), recorded fictional stories in which Pythagoras said that he originated from Hermes, and related the strange transmigrations of his soul up to the last birth (Diog. Laert. 5. 4–5).[85] These are not hagiographic traditions, but gossip of adversaries ridiculing the megalomania of the *guru*. Prominent is the story that Pythagoras, in one of his previous incarnations, recognized the shield dedicated by Menelaus to Apollo, despite its advanced state of decay; he remembered seeing it when he had participated in the Trojan War (cf. Diod. 10. 6. 1–3, where it is the shield of Pythagoras himself, with which he fought at Troy; Porph. *VP* 26). This story is essentially of the same type as one of the apocryphal additions to the stories of Baron Münchhausen according to which he possessed a copy of *Oedipus Rex* that Sophocles himself had given to him with a dedication. Similar symptoms occur in another story from an anonymous source: Pythagoras flies on an arrow of Hyperborean Apollo and thus manages to see on the very same day his friends in Italian Metapontum and distant Sicilian Tauromenium (Porph. *VP* 27, 29). As Pythagoras is said in the same context to have identified himself with Hyperborean Apollo, among others (29), the reader may well have been given to understand that the arrow on which he flew was shot by Pythagoras himself. One cannot help recalling the stories about the flight of the Baron into the Turkish fortress on a cannonball and his remarkable escape from the swamp by pulling himself up by his hair while still mounted on his horse. Dicaearchus, a pupil of Aristotle, also wrote a biography on Pythagoras containing negative elements, including the story of the disturbances Pythagoras and his followers caused everywhere they went, and that Pythagoras was the last reincarnation of a prostitute named Alco.[86]

Two fourth-century comedians, Alexis and Cratinus, wrote comedies entitled *Pythagorizousa* (The "Pythagorean" Woman; Ath. 4. 161c–d), and their contemporary Aristophon wrote a venomous comedy called *Pythagoristēs* (A Pythagorean).[87] Intellectuals, therefore, not only mocked Pythagoras in philosophical and biographical writings but devoted comedies to him that exposed him to the ridicule of the masses.

Biographies and lampoons of Pythagoras were still being written throughout

---

85. See also Wehrli (1953), frr. 40–41, 44, 87–89. Gottschalk (1980) 106, 111–27, 143–44, on the contrary, thinks that Heraclides regarded Pythagoras as "a mythical figure, larger than life" (143). This is debatable.

86. See Wehrli (1944) frr. 32, 35a, 36 (= Mithardy [2000] frr. 38, 41A, 42).

87. The material on Pythagoras in Middle Comedy is to be found in D-K 1: 478–80; for a survey, see Burkert (1972) 198–201.

the third century and in the time of Hermippus, along with general appearances in other works such as Timon's *Silloi,* mentioned above. Satyrus, for example, who was active in Alexandria, wrote a biography of Pythagoras that seems to have been especially critical in nature. Sotion may have done the same in his *Succession of the Philosophers,* where he reports, among other things, on Pythagoras's arrogance and his disdain for his young followers (Diog. Laert. 8. 7; cf. 8. 10).

Hermippus may have written his biography of Pythagoras as, among other things, a reply to the positive biography of Pythagoras written by Aristoxenus "the Musician,"[88] a pupil of Aristotle who had previously studied with the Pythagorean Xenophilus.[89] This biography was the fullest source of information on Pythagoras in the generation of Hermippus, and it was only a question of time before a response to it appeared. Aristoxenus's biography itself may have been a reply to previous criticism and mockery in the literature on Pythagoras.[90] "Counter-biographies" were nothing new in literature of the period. The possibility has been raised, for example, that the *Encomium* of Plato by Clearchus of Soli was written as a reply to the criticism of Aristoxenus in his biography of Plato, where, incidentally, Plato (together with Aristotle and others) is accused of having stolen ideas from Pythagoras.[91] Demetrius of Phaleron may also have written *On Socrates* as a reply to the attack of Aristoxenus on the personality of Socrates.[92]

Hermippus, therefore, did not compose his biography of Pythagoras in a vacuum. He necessarily took a position on the subject. It would have been well understood by his readers, accustomed as they were to satire, that his aim was to mock and criticize even if explicit comments on the stories were few and far between. Only people who had read just one or two isolated passages could have missed the point. It is no coincidence that Hermippus is not cited or even mentioned by positive, not to say admiring, biographers of Pythagoras, such as Porphyry and Iamblichus in the third century C.E. Their biographies have survived whole and contain an abundance of citations, including quotations from authors who criticized Pythagoras, such as Dicaearchus.[93] Porphyry and Iamblichus, who searched for every piece of information about Pythagoras, should have been familiar with

---

88. Not only because of the intense Pythagorean interest in music and its influence on the soul and its elements, as claimed by Susemihl (1892) 1: 499.

89. Wehrli (1967) frr. 11–41a; and see fr. 26, in which Pythagoras talks about the function of music in healing the soul. On the complex attitude of Aristoxenus to Pythagoras, see Burkert (1972) 106–7.

90. As Burkert (1972) 200 suggests.

91. See Porphyry *Vita Pythagorae* 53. According to Hermippus, Plato stole the *Timaeus* from Philolaus, the successor-pupil of Pythagoras (fr. 69).

92. See Momigliano (1993) 77–78.

93. See Porphyry *Vita Pythagorae* 56–57.

the biography of Pythagoras by Hermippus, quoted by Diogenes Laertius. Whatever the exact dating of the latter might be, he seems to have lived close to their
time.

THE STORY OF PYTHAGORAS:
THE SOUL OF CALLIPHON AND THE THREE PROHIBITIONS

Some points in the testimonium and its connection to the fragment of Hermippus
require elucidation, to help in correctly assessing the background and the intent
of Hermippus's reference to the Jews.

To whom are attributed the three prohibitions of the fragment? According to
some, it is Pythagoras;[94] according to others, the soul of his pupil Calliphon.[95]
The story as formulated indicates that Calliphon is the one who "recommended"
the prohibitions. Furthermore, it is inconceivable that the live Pythagoras should
give orders to the dead Calliphon, especially about behavior relevant to the living.
The rationale behind the story is that Calliphon provided Pythagoras with some
new prohibitions on subjects he had experienced in the afterlife, where he had
been exposed to the truth.

In view of Hermippus's general attitude to Pythagoras and as appears from
his reaction, the episode about the soul of Calliphon, said to have been spread by
Pythagoras himself ("used to do and say"), was probably adduced by Hermippus
as an example, like the *katabasis* story, of the underhand way Pythagoras proved
the immortality of the soul (or rather the continuous existence of the dead as
daemons), a belief that Hermippus appears to have rejected.[96] Another aim of the
Calliphon story would have been to provide three of the Pythagorean prohibitions with the stamp of supernatural authority.

Hermippus responds by providing a more earthly source of the prohibitions:
he notes that Pythagoras "used to do and say these things imitating and transferring to himself the opinions (*doxai*) of the Jews and the Thracians." *Doxai* are
literally "what appear" to be right, both theoretically and practically. The verb
ἔπραττεν ("used to do") and the participle μιμούμενος ("imitating") in the sentence show that these opinions touched upon practical matters. The verbosity of
the particles ("imitating and transferring") suggests the connotation "attributed
to himself." Whatever the case may be, the connection between the testimonium
and the fragment is unambiguous: Pythagoras misled his supporters about the
real source of the prohibitions. Hermippus thus treated the story as an all-around

---

94. Cardini (1958) 1: 109; Wehrli (1974) 57–58; Gorman (1983) 32; Bollansée (1999a) 235–36.
95. Sansone (1993) 58–59; Bollansée (1999a) 235.
96. Cf. Diogenes Laertius 8. 69 with the parallel in Heraclides Ponticus (Wehrli [1969] fr. 76); cf.
Burkert (1972) 103 n. 30.

fiction about Pythagoras's connection with the World of the Dead, characterizing the man's deceitful methods.

To sum up, according to the sequence of the text, Pythagoras narrated how the soul of his dead pupil Calliphon stayed by his side night and day and left him three pieces of advice. Hermippus then adds in the fragment that Pythagoras observed the new prohibitions and passed them on to his disciples, but notes that in truth these prohibitions come from the Jews and the Thracians, according to the Greek conception—"barbarian" people. I would add that there is no room for the suggestion voiced here and there that the testimonium and the fragment were not linked to each other, but appeared in different contexts of the biography, and that only Josephus put them in one sequence. This would mean that the fragment does not refer to the Jews and the Thracians. However, the connection between the two is not artificial, and there is no sign for a "stich"; moreover, the testimonium does not mention the Jews or the Thracians; why then was it introduced as an opening to the fragment? And above all, presenting the fragment alone would have served Josephus's aim much more efficiently: it would naturally have been interpreted as referring to all deeds and doctrines of Pythagoras (as is indeed stated by Josephus in the concluding sentence, explicitly attributed to someone else, not to Hermippus), while the inclusion of the testimonium minimizes the Jewish influence on Pythagoras.

Another proposal in same vein, to the effect that Hermippus also intends to imply in the fragment that Pythagoras's belief in the immortality of the soul was influenced by the Thracians and the Jews,[97] is not supported by combining the testimonium and the fragment, despite the well-known belief of the Getae-Thracians in the immortality of the soul (though free association may have led to the Thracians being mentioned in this passage as one of the two sources for the customs).[98] It follows that the passage should not be used in the debate over when the immortality of the soul and resurrection became widespread and acceptable beliefs among major sections of the Jewish population in Judaea.[99]

How did Hermippus evaluate the three prohibitions? They are no different in type from the many Pythagorean *akousmata* known to us: some strange, some explicable, although the reason is often forced. To anyone hostile to the Pythagoreans, the commands and prohibitions shared some common features:

---

97. Suggested by Lewy (1960) 36; Bollansée (1999a) 241–43.

98. See p. 194 below.

99. While it is not impossible that the Jews in Egypt adopted the belief in the immortality of the soul from their Egyptian neighbors some time before the Hasmonaean revolt, and that it quickly spread in Judaea following the religious persecutions, proof is lacking. It is worth mentioning that Pythagoras combined the belief in the immortality of the soul, which he had adopted from the Egyptians or the Thracians, with the concept of the transmigration of souls, which would have reached him from the Far East.

they were arbitrary, pointless, and smacked of superstition and were ridiculed by comedians.[100] Hermippus in other fragments implicitly mocks two Pythagorean commands.[101] There is no reason to suppose that the fragment under discussion presents the prohibitions in a positive light. A definitive conclusion, however, requires an examination of the prohibitions themselves.

THE THREE PROHIBITIONS: THEIR IDENTIFICATION AND NATURE

Those scholars who have discussed or referred to Hermippus's statement regarding the Jews assumed that he intended to say that all three prohibitions were common to Pythagoras, the Jews, and the Thracians. Being unaware of the true nature of the Hermippean biography of Pythagoras, they also believed that the customs were rational, being based on sound moral or practical principles. Accordingly they sought to identify the prohibitions with rational Jewish customs, sometimes at the cost of emending the text or perverting its sense. In order to identify the customs correctly, the text of the fragment must first be read carefully.

The prohibition regarding the ass has usually been translated and interpreted as forbidding passage over a spot where an ass has fallen and died.[102] Yet the text talks about an ass sinking to its knees.[103] An ass sinks to its knees (bending its forelegs) not when it falls over or collapses and dies, but rather performs this

---

100. For the benefit of readers who are not at home in the ancient world, here are some examples from the dozens of Pythagorean commands and prohibitions mentioned in the sources: "Do not stay in a room that a swallow has passed"; "Do not talk in a dark room"; "Place yourself on the battlefield in such a way that if you are wounded, you will be wounded in the chest"; "Copulation should be avoided in the summer"; "Do not plant a date palm"; "Always place salt on the table"; "Do not eat with the left hand"; "Wash the left leg first"; "Enter a temple with the right leg, and exit with the left"; "Do not fry food already cooked"; "Do not gather crumbs from the table"; "Do not stop on the threshold"; "Do not look back when leaving your house"; "Do not retrace your steps next to the boundary"; "Do not sing unaccompanied by a lyre"; "Do not look at yourself in the mirror with the aid of artificial light"; "Do not sleep at noon"; "Do not leave bedclothes unfolded." For collections of fragments (by no means exhaustive) listing Pythagorean *akousmata*, see: D-K 1: 462–66; Cardini (1969) 3: 243–71. Over the generations, the strange commands received allegorical and religious-cultic interpretations, while the plausible ones were explained rationally. Some of the Pythagorean commands are strikingly similar to examples of superstitions adduced by Theophrastus in his *Characters* (sec. 16). By way of further illustration, Porphyry (*VP* 44), recording a Pythagorean superstition, states that if a lentil flower is plucked in season, planted in a flowerpot, and then the flowerpot is covered in earth, after ninety days one finds not lentils but the head of baby or a vagina.

101. Frr. 23, 25; and see above, note 76 and pp. 179–80 (the prohibition against engraving images on seals and the story about Pythagoras's death).

102. See, e.g., Thackeray (1920) 229: "not to pass a certain spot, on which an ass had collapsed." An accurate translation only by Goodman in Schürer et al., 3: 696.

103. There are many verbs in Greek that could denote the falling of an ass. The verb ὀκλάζω

action of its own volition when it is tired and wishes to rest (whether burdened or not), when it is oppressed (e.g., by humiliation or cruelty), when suffering from cold, and sometimes in order to express a refusal to continue on a certain course. Furthermore, the prohibition is not concerned with a place where an ass has been in the past, but wherever an ass may at that moment be bending its knees.[104]

The term δίψια ὕδατα, "dry water," can also mean "drying water." As "dry water" does not make sense, the meaning must be "drying water"—namely, thirst-making water and the like.[105] Emendation is unjustified.[106] The prohibition obviously refers to drinking.

Blasphēmia can mean offensive speech against either gods or men.[107] The sentence itself does not allow a decision either way.[108] A Pythagorean parallel might be of assistance. We do not have a Pythagorean prohibition against cursing humans; but there is one Pythagorean source enjoining *euphēmia* ("good speech," the opposite of *blasphēmia*) toward the gods, daimons, heroes, parents, and benefactors (Porph. *VP* 38), without mentioning men in general. Pythagoras himself is said to have observed *euphēmia* toward the gods, and that this was one of the commands he gave to his disciples.[109] Hieronymus of Rhodes, an eclectic philosopher contemporary with Hermippus, relates that Pythagoras saw on his visit to Hades the souls of Homer and Hesiod, one hanging from a tree and encumbered by snakes, the other bound to a post and muttering incomprehensibly, punishments for their utterances against the gods (Diog. Laert. 8. 21). Thus Hermippus probably has in mind *blasphēmia* against the gods, and not against men.[110]

A prohibition against cursing the gods seems to us a natural and positive command. The Greeks did not take this for granted, however, and for them, such a command would have seemed strange. It is worth digressing on this point at

---

refers not to collapsing but to sinking to one's knees, as correctly interpreted by Müller (1871) 162; Gutschmid (1893) 559.

104. καὶ ὅτι παρεκελεύετο μὴ διέρχεσται τόπου ἐφ᾽ ὃν ἂν ὄνος ὀκλάσῃ. Cf. note 7 above.

105. See Gutschmid (1893) 4: 559. Gutschmid rightly compares δίψιος with διψώδης and διψητικός, which mean both "thirsty" and "thirst-making."

106. *Pace* Sansone (1993) 52.

107. On curses against the gods as a common practice, see below. Similarly, *blasphēmia* against humans, common in comedy and tragedy, was not considered a transgression among the Greeks and could not be the pretext for a lawsuit. It was, however, commonly believed that a curse upon a fellow human would call up a harmful demon. On curses against Pythagoras, see Iamblichus *De vita Pythagorica* 30 (178).

108. Müller (1871) 162–63 (cf. Bollansée [1999a] 237) suggests that not only gods were intended, pointing to πάσης in the sentence; but it is the type, not the object of the insult, that is intended.

109. It seems that these two parallels were first noted by Gorman (1983) 36–37; cf. Aristotle in Ross (1888) 134, fr. 5; Iamblichus *De vita Pythagorica* 2 (55), 28 (149); Bollansée (1999a) 237. Both parallels concern clean language toward the gods only.

110. *Pace* Bollansée (1999a) 237.

the risk of rehearsing matters known to scholars of ancient Greek religion and literature. The typical Greek would often curse or mock the gods. He would have found good reasons for doing so already during his youth, in which he would have been heavily influenced by Homer, and then by Greek literature in general, steeped as it was in stories of gods irredeemably adulterous, unfair, scheming, and partial, whose own factions provoked wars among men. It is not surprising that in such an atmosphere Greeks would curse and mock the gods, and thus relieve themselves of everyday frustrations. This was well summarized by Dionysius of Halicarnassus, the first-century B.C.E. historian of the beginnings of Rome (*Ant. rom.* 2. 18–20): he praises the Roman prohibition of *blasphēmia* as opposed to the Greek lack of respect. He says that Romulus rejected myths containing *blasphēmia* against the gods, in the form of stories describing them as wicked, harmful, and shameless; he even details the ugly (in his opinion) Greek myths about the immoral gods and the events that serve to commemorate them.

A classical or early Hellenistic Greek would not have worried about *blasphēmia*. The basic assumption was that the gods neither heard nor saw what went on in the world, and that if they happened to be present, they had no idea what was happening. There are very few contemporary texts that present a different view, and even some of these regarded the notion of continual divine supervision as a successful invention by wise men to guarantee justice in the world.[111] For the average Greek, to attract a god's attention, one would go to a place devoted to that god, usually a temple; to gain favor with that god there would be a ceremony in which cursing and mocking the god was prohibited. This was the only time that a typical Greek would observe *euphēmia*. Indeed, the priest would precede the sacrifice with the command *euphēmein*, requiring the assembled host to refrain from saying all but the sacred words of the ceremony, and a "sacred silence" would fall.[112] The Pythagorean prohibition extended this sacred silence

---

111. The view that gods were a human invention is well exemplified by a fragment from the tragedy *Sisyphus*, attributed to Critias (D-K 88 B 25). The speaker declares that humans invented laws in order to stop mutual harm and to promote cooperation; but transgressions were found to be profitable when there were no witnesses. Therefore, a wise man invented a story about gods who could see everything humans did, and know everything humans thought. The gods, then, are portrayed as merely a fiction invented to compel humans to observe the law at all times. Such a claim would have been dangerous to its advocate, since it denied the very existence of the gods (as opposed to cursing existing gods). It has been suggested that Critias, an Athenian citizen, could get away with this daring speech if the speaker in the tragedy were Sisyphus, who would later in the tragedy be portrayed receiving—or being told that he will receive—fitting punishment in Hades for this crime.

112. On the "sacred silence," see Menching (1926) 101 ff. It is worth noting two exceptions: the "curse cult" during the sacrifice to Apollo at Anaphe, and the sacrifice to Heracles at Lindus; see Callimachus *Aitiai*, fr. 7, ll. 19–21 (in the collection of Pfeiffer [1949–53] 1: 15–16); pseudo-Apollodorus *Bibliotheca* 2. 5. 11. 8.

well beyond the confines of the ceremony, and it must have been perceived as expressing a superstition that the gods see and hear all, at all times, everywhere.[113]

The prohibition against "drying water" seems to parallel the Pythagorean command to drink only simple water (λιτὸν ὕδωρ—Diod. 10. 7. 2; Diog. Laert. 8. 13),[114] which was ridiculed by outsiders.[115] "Drying water" is not simply salty water, as has been speculated.[116] Refraining from salty water was and still is obvious, requiring no prohibition for its enforcement, and thus was not considered abnormal behavior. The fifth century B.C.E. saw an authoritative work by Hippocrates detailing the various types of water according to source, content, advantages and disadvantages (mainly to health), and climatic influences (including winds) upon them (*Aer.* 7–11). It advised which types were worth drinking and which types should be avoided (including spring water of all types and molten ice, which was not always recommended). Seawater was described as particularly harmful to health. Hippocrates, however, does not advise what to do about thirst-making water, and it is not even mentioned.

It seems that Hermippus refers to drinks causing dryness, that is, dehydrating, and/or to drinks increasing the feeling of thirstiness. In view of the drinking habits of the ancient world, one can think about sweetened water, which usually contained a great quantity of astringent materials (tannin and the like), for example, grapes (actually their skin), pomegranates, and dates. Likewise, water containing alcohol, mainly beer or date beer, which were more widespread than any other type of drink in the lands of the north and in the Fertile Crescent, respectively (e.g., Diod. 1. 34. 10, pertaining to Egypt, which is relevant to our discussion); or even wine might be intended (wine was generally drunk mixed with water). There may be some connection between this and the Pythagorean *akousma* not to plant palms—dates were the main sweetener in the Orient. The diet of Pythagoras described by Porphyry does not include wine (contrary to the Greek habit), but grasses and roots preventing thirst are mentioned (*VP* 34). There may be circumstances where drinking sweet water might be disadvantageous, but the sweeping prohibition against drinking "drying water" would have appeared ridiculous and superstitious to the Greeks, and not only to hedonists and alcoholics, despite later attempts to explain it away as conforming with the drive toward an ascetic life (e.g., Diog. Laert. 8. 13).

113. For the different opinion of later Pythagoreans, see Iamblichus *De vita Pythagorica* 30 (174–75).

114. Already noted by Müller, *FHG* III. 162; see also Wehrli (1974) 58. Müller would seem to believe that the aim was to forbid the drinking of wine, while Wehrli thinks that "simple water" means "flowing water" (i.e., spring water) as opposed to still water.

115. E.g., in Middle Comedy, Alexis and Aristophon, D-K 1: p. 479, ll. 13, 21–22; p. 480, l. 28.

116. Gutschmid (1893) 4: 559 (seawater); Schürer (1901–9) 3: 626 n. 205; Stern, *GLAJJ* 1: 96; Feldman (1993) 524 n. 5.

The prohibition against crossing a place where an ass happens to bend the knees of its forelegs seems more than anything to derive from a superstition. The lists of Pythagorean customs that we now possess contain many strange acts and prohibitions, but they are by no means exhaustive, since the whole system was oral and very extensive, touching on virtually every aspect of daily life.[117] That Hermippus, therefore, of all our surviving sources, is the only one to mention this particular *akousma*, should not surprise us. It may be understood in light of the special position of the ass in Mediterranean beliefs and folk literature, or the Pythagorean contempt for asses.[118] The special situation of the ass kneeling on a public road could have been seen, for example, as a bad omen. It echoes to some extent the Pythagorean prohibition against walking on main thoroughfares (Diog. Laert. 8. 17). However, this prohibition certainly remains open to other interpretations.

The Pythagorean parallels and the general approach of the anti-Pythagoreans to the *akousmata* indicate that the prohibitions mentioned were generally regarded as superstitions. Hermippus lists them because they conform to his portrayal of Pythagoras as a manipulative leader who uses deceit and various devices to acquire authority over the innocent. In this case, Pythagoras uses strange and counterintuitive prohibitions whose rationale only he appears to understand, thereby increasing the dependency of his supporters on him. It has long been noted that the Pythagorean commands and prohibitions were incomprehensible to his simpleminded followers, who merely heard and obeyed the *akousmata* (following Porph. *VP* 37); hence the followers are called *akousmatikoi*. Hermippus heightens the mocking criticism of the three pointless prohibitions by even denying Pythagoras any originality and describing them as imitations of superstitions of two "barbarian" peoples.

No attempt has so far been made to find a Thracian parallel for any of the prohibitions. The chance of finding one is slim, since classical literature rarely mentions Thracian daily life, and Thracian literature (as distinct from inscriptions), if there was any, has not reached us. If there is any hope of finding a parallel, it may come from an illustrative archaeological find. Many Jewish parallels have been offered, however. The simplest parallel is the prohibition against *blasphēmia* toward God: "Thou shalt not revile God" (Exod. 22.28; Lev. 24.15–16).[119] The prohibition was interpreted in the Septuagint and by some of the Jewish Hellenistic authors as concerning the gods of other nations.[120] As for the other two prohibi-

---

117. On the *akousmata*, see esp. note 100 above.

118. On attitudes toward the ass, see Krappe (1946), and there too on the ass in Thrace; and see below, pp. 226–29. On Pythagorean scorn for the ass, see note 125 below.

119. Müller (1877) 163; Gutschmid (1893) 4: 560.

120. The Hebrew word for "God" is actually in plural form (*'Elohim*). In the Septuagint, Exodus 22.27: θεοὺς οὐ κακολογήσεις; see also Philo *De specialibus legibus* 1. 81; *De vita Mosis* 2. 205;

tions, none of the proposed parallels has matched the text, which has led to a few forced emendations. Proposed parallels with the ass prohibition include the following: the command in the Torah to assist an ass lying under its burden (Exod. 23.5);[121] a connection with the ass libel, that is, the alleged cult of the ass in the Temple;[122] a reference to the story of Balaam, whose ass stopped its journey at the sight of the angel of the Lord (Num. 22.21–34);[123] "excessive piety . . . from

Quaestiones in Exodum 2. 5; *Hypothetica* ap. Eusebius *Praeparatio evangelica* 8. 6–6-7; Artapanus ap. Eusebius *Praeparatio evangelica* 9. 27. 4, 9, 10, 12.

121. See mainly Jacobson (1976) 146. This extraordinary scholar's article deserves special attention. Yet there is nothing in Hermippus in common with the biblical verse—no burden, no need to assist, and no personal enemy; there is only a prohibition to cross that place, which is in direct contrast to the verse. Jacobson would supplement the prohibition in Hermippus with the second part of the verse, but it stands on its own. He also points to the Pythagorean prohibition "Do not help unload a burden (for there must not be a reason for not toiling), but take part in loading" (Iambl. *VP* 18 [84]; Porph. *VP* 42, *Protrep.* 21i; Diog. Laert. 8. 17). However, here it is not the ass, as in the Torah, but the owner or ass-driver who is to be helped. Jacobson then cites some of the Aramaic translations, the Mishnah in Baba Mezia 2. 10, and the parallel discussion in Babylonian Talmud Baba Mezia 23a-b to reinforce his claim for a similarity between the biblical precept and the Pythagorean prohibition. Yet the halachic debate is only about whether the command includes loading in addition to unloading (so Jonathan's translation, and some of the disputants in the Talmud) or just unloading (so Uncelus and in the Mishnah). Thinking in the opposite direction appears in the Pythagorean command to assist, which pertains only to loading. The underlying motive for the very rabbinic distinction between loading and unloading was the sages' concern for the animal's welfare: the loader should not be assisted if the mule appears to be already overloaded and suffering. The Pythagoreans, however, would not have cared about the suffering of the ass, which they despised (see note 125 below), but would have concerned themselves rather with the welfare of its owner. Be this as it may, would reductive explanations and fine points of *halakha* such as these already be widespread among Egyptian Jews, and would Hermippus or his source have been aware of such subtle interpretations? It should be added, merely as an observation, that in the Septuagint translation of the verse (regarded by Jacobson as Hermippus's source of inspiration), the animal mentioned is a "beast of burden" (ὑποζυγίον), and not an ass, as in Hermippus; and it is described as "having fallen" (πεπτωκός), rather than merely bending its knees. In sum, the biblical verse and Pythagoras in Hermippus give opposite injunctions: the biblical instruction to cross such a place and help the ass-driver is countermanded by the Pythagorean prohibition against crossing such a place at all, let alone helping the ass. Any further attempt to explain the Exodus verse as the source of inspiration for Hermippus would require too much textual emendation and/or problematic speculation to be acceptable.

122. Thackeray (1926) 228, n. b; and on his translation, see note 102 above. Cf. Labow (2005) 163. He seems to mean that Hermippus was talking about a prohibition against crossing a place where a divinity has fallen, been hurt, or died. Cf. the priests of Dagon jumping over the threshold where their god had collapsed (1 Sam. 5.1–5). The present instance, however, concerns merely a resting ass; and when did the Pythagoreans believe in the divinity of the ass? Did their enemies ever attribute to the Pythagoreans such a belief? The Pythagoreans had only contempt for asses (see below, note 125).

123. Gutschmid (1893) 4: 559; Troiani (1977) 111; and see the response of Jacobson (1976) 146. Why would Jews refrain from crossing a place where their enemies met with a bad event (even according to the logic of Hermippus)?

fear that it [the ass] is a defiling carcass";[124] a polite way of saying that the ass was relieving itself, thus interpreting the prohibition as against stepping on a place where an ass has relieved itself.[125] The main proposed parallels with the "drying water" prohibition are the following: the prohibition against drinking מים מגולים (exposed water),[126] lest it has been drunk by a snake and has become contaminated with venom;[127] a reference to the search for water during the wanderings of the Israelites in the desert (Exod. 17.1–7; Num. 20.1–12);[128] and more far-reaching, an allegorical interpretation,[129] and a rather sophisticated explanation finding connections with Greek mythological stories.[130]

I would note in passing that it seems far-fetched to attribute to Hermippus (or his Greek sources) expertise in esoteric biblical stories or a profound knowledge of Jewish oral law,[131] when Greek authors centuries later were still unfamiliar with the basic biblical stories forming the Jewish identity and tradition. This reservation is all the more cogent with regard to Greek authors of the generation

124. Kasher (1996) 153. Why the ass, of all animals and living creatures? Its corpse was not regarded by the Pharisees as polluting (Mishnah Yadayim 4. 6), and the ass is not mentioned in the Torah among the defiling animals, so that at least some sections of Sadducees (in contrast to others referred to in the Mishnah) shared the opinion of the Pharisees. Notably, the verse "And every firstling of an ass thou shalt redeem with a lamb" (Exod. 13.13) does not demonstrate "great concern about pollution," as Kasher believes, but a practical consideration arising from the importance of asses in everyday life. According to a Talmudic midrash it just betrays a prejudice in favor of the ass (see below, p. 249).

125. Gorman (1983) 33–34 translates ὀκλάσῃ as "relieve itself" and connects this with the Pythagorean contempt for asses because they relieve themselves with their hindquarters facing the sun (according to Ael. NA 10. 28, and there also additional explanations for the negative attitude of the Pythagoreans to asses). That is to say, it was prohibited to step on a place where an ass had relieved itself. Naturally, there is no need for such a prohibition. In any case, the verb ὀκλάζω does not mean "to relieve oneself," not even as a euphemism for human behavior, let alone that of domestic animals, which do not practice genuflection in such a position (asses relieve themselves while standing). Gorman links the Jews to this injunction by referring to the modest evacuatory habits of the Essenes (e.g., Joseph. BJ 2. 8–9), supported by the additional Pythagorean prohibition against urinating while facing the sun (Iambl. Protrep. 106. 18). He assumes that the Essene customs, through the agency of the parallel community in Egypt, the Therapeutai, were known to the Jews of Alexandria, and hence to Hermippus. Quite apart from the lack of similarity, the chronology is completely awry.

126. The interpretation "exposed" appears in Gardini (1958) 110; Liberman (1934) 1: 49.

127. Liberman (1934) 1: 49. See also Albeck (1959) 390. Liberman (quoting D. Saliternik) suggests emending to διψάδων ὑδάτων ("snake water"), which he interprets as water with which snakes have come into contact, recalling the Talmudic prohibition against waters that are מגולים—i.e., uncovered—and must not be drunk, in case of contamination by snake venom, etc. (e.g., Trumoth 8.5, 45c). Yet this word combination is not found in Greek.

128. E.g., Gorman (1983) 35–36; and see the response of Bollansée (1999a) 239 n. 22.

129. Jacobson (1976), accepted by Bollansée (1999a) 239–40.

130. Sansone (1993).

131. As was actually done by Hengel (1973) 446 n. 11; Bollansée (1999b) 50–51.

of Hermippus: unlike the first generation of Greeks in Egypt, such as Hecataeus of Abdera, the Alexandrian scholars of the late third and early second centuries B.C.E. seem to have shut themselves up in their ivory tower in the Mouseion and ignored what was going on around them, concentrating their efforts nostalgically on the preservation of the ancient Greek tradition.[132]

Did then Hermippus really intend to compare all three Pythagorean prohibitions to Jewish precepts (as most scholars have believed)? Not necessarily.[133] He may have intended to say that Pythagoras adopted foreign opinions and customs, partly from the Jews and partly from the Thracians. There is, therefore, no need to insist on three Jewish parallels for the three prohibitions. The discussion above seems to support the latter alternative.

Thus the comparison with the Jews may be confined to the prohibition against blasphemy, a prohibition that found expression in Jewish daily life, in contrast to the Greek tendency routinely to curse the gods in public. The Jews' style in everyday discourse (Greek in this case) would have acted as an ethnic-religious identifier, easily grasped even by one who had no special interest in the Jews. At the same time, I would not completely dismiss the possibility that this parallel is purely coincidental, and that the reference to the Jews and the Thracians as the source of the Pythagorean customs does not rest on specific information regarding these prohibitions. Ethnic characteristics and stereotypes were quite fluid in ethnographic literature, and such customs would migrate from one people and group to another. In fact, Hermippus was able to find these customs quite easily in his teacher Callimachus's work *Barbarian Customs* (Βαρβαρικὰ νόμιμα—namely, of "barbarian" people),[134] in the same way that he took motifs and material from many sources to create his stories and adapt them to the subjects of his biographies.

Why did Hermippus attribute the source of the customs to the Thracians and the Jews, of all the barbarians? It might be thought that he wished to place the source as far away as possible from the center of the Greek world in order to emphasize the eccentricity of such customs. Were this so, however, he could have named peoples far more remote, such as the Scythians, or the Iberians and the Gauls, on the one hand, and one of the peoples of Bactria and India, on the other, as indeed is often the case with regard to Pythagorean sources of inspiration in literature on Pythagoras.[135]

132. See below, pp. 233–35.

133. Jacobson (1976) 145 has noted the lack of clarity on this matter.

134. See the collection of fragments of Callimachus: Pfeiffer (1949–53), fr. 405.

135. E.g., Alexander Polyhistor, in his compilation of Pythagorean commands, stated that Pythagoras was a pupil of the Celts and the Brahmans in addition to the Assyrians (in Clem. *Strom.* 1. 15 [70. 1]). Such assertions found their way even into a treatise written by Iamblichus, who admired

The mention of the Thracians is actually not surprising. There was a tradition that Zamolxis, Pythagoras's slave, conveyed Pythagoreanism to the Getans-Thracians (Hdt. 4. 94–95; Strabo 7. 3. 5). Hermippus or his source(s) may have overturned the tradition entirely by portraying Pythagoras as the recipient of Thracian customs, perhaps explicitly through the agency of Zamolxis, who would no longer have had to go home to bestow Pythagoreanism upon his fellow barbarians. It does not concern us here whether the belief in the immortality of the soul, which served as the only evidence for Pythagorean influence on the Thracians (already in Hdt. 4. 95), really did reach Pythagoras from Thrace rather than Egypt, whether by means of the Orphics or not. What counts is the development of traditions and images. The narrative background to the origin of the prohibitions—the soul of Calliphon informing Pythagoras of them—would have been enough to produce an association with the Thracians, as they were known to believe in the immortality of the soul. Furthermore, the well-known connection between the Orphics and Thrace, on the one hand, and Pythagoras and the Orphics, on the other (e.g., Iambl. *VP* 146), would have sufficed to suggest a connection between the customs of Pythagoras and the Thracians. Since Orpheus was at times considered to be a Thracian god, it would also have been possible to claim with some justification that it was Pythagoras who borrowed from the Thracians.

As for the Jews, since Hermippus probably intended to attribute to the Jews just the origin of the prohibition of *blasphemia,* and the difference between Jews and Greeks in this respect was prominent in the life of these closely connected communities in Ptolemaic Egypt, no wonder Hermippus related this *akousma* to the Jews. However, scholars who think that Hermippus regarded the three prohibitions as originally Jewish speculated that Hermippus took as a source of inspiration the Jewish excursus of Hecataeus of Abdera, which would have served naturally as a basic source of information on the Jews for the scholars of Alexandria. Hecataeus stated that the customs of the Jews and their way of life differed from those of other peoples (Diod. 40. 3. 4).[136] It would have been easy to conclude from this that Jewish customs were very strange, and they could therefore have been identified with Pythagorean customs by anyone wish-

---

him. He states that "others say (φασί)" that Pythagoras included in his doctrine things that he had learned from the Orphics, the Egyptian priests, the Eleusinian Mysteries, the inhabitants of Samothrace and Lemnus, the Celts, and the Iberians (*VP* 28 [151]; cf. Porph. *VP* 6). However, the Thracians and the Jews are not mentioned. Iamblichus consistently avoided using information that he found in Hermippus because of the latter's blatant hostility toward Pythagoras. In the present case he had an additional reason: Pythagoras of Hermippus is misleading his followers with regard to the real origin of the three prohibitions.

136. See above, p. 129. Wehrli (1974) 59 mentions Hecataeus as a source of inspiration but does not then reach the correct conclusion regarding the nature of the prohibitions, since he fails to grasp the general aim of Hermippus in his biography.

ing to ridicule Pythagoras. Theophrastus, who was the subject of a biography by Hermippus, could also have encouraged the latter to regard Jewish customs as strange.[137] Furthermore, the similarity between Pythagoreanism and some Jewish customs, real or alleged, such as the abstention from all or certain types of meat, must have been known already to the Greeks, and this too would have led Hermippus or his source to make use of the Jews in his attack on Pythagoras.[138]

Contrary to claims made in the past, it should be emphasized that there are no ancient testimonia of substance for traditions maintaining a genealogical link between the Jews and the Thracians, of the sort that would have caused Hermippus to mention them in the same breath.[139] Even the summary of the (imaginary) rumors concerning the origin of the Jews in Tacitus (*Hist.* 2. 2. 1–3. 1) makes no mention of such stories. All this despite the image of the Getae or the Thracians as refraining from the eating of meat. In addition, the contemporary Jewish belief in the immortality of the soul described by Tacitus would have induced him to report a story about the common origin of the Jews and the Thracians had there been one.[140]

The generalizing tone of the concluding sentence written by Josephus himself (see the next section) indicates that he believed that the fragment compared all the customs mentioned to Jewish customs. It is not difficult to understand why he failed to observe that at least two of the prohibitions had no real Jewish paral-

137. For Theophrastus on the peculiarity of Jewish sacrificial practices, see above, pp. 24–30.

138. On the similarities in matters that were unlikely to have been known in the generation of Hermippus, see below, note 156. On the belief in the immortality of the soul, see above, note 99.

139. Willrich (1895) 59–60 observed that the Jewish god was identified with Dionysus Sabazius, the Phrygian-Thracian god, as appears in Valerius Maximus (Stern, *GLAJJ* no. 147a) in the context of the expulsion of the Jews from Rome in 139 B.C.E. (following Livy). Willrich speculated that it was this identification that led to Hermippus mentioning the Jews together with the Thracians (and see also Stern, *GLAJJ* 1: 359; Bollansée [1999a] 246). However, it is unlikely that Hermippus would have been aware of such remote identifications; nor would the circumstances making this link (see the discussion in Stern) necessitate the existence of traditions concerning a common origin.

140. My late friend, Daniel Gershenson, drew my attention to a possible Thracian context in a statement by a Jewish Babylonian sage, that Abraham's mother was Amthalai Bar Carnebo (Babba Bathra 91a; *variae lectiones:* Carnbi, Barnebo, Bar Nebo). If Carnebo were to be preferred to Bar Nebo (although the latter would fit with Abraham's Mesopotamian origin), or is not the common Babylonian eponnym *Ka:r-Nabū*, it would be worth looking for a Greek parallel. A fragment from *Triptolemos*, a lost tragedy of Sophocles (Nauck [1964] fr. 547; see also Hyg. *Astr.* 2. 14) concerns a certain Charnabon (Χαρναβῶν), king of the Getae. This tribe appears more than once in Greek literature as representing the Thracians. It has already been conjectured that Amthalai (also the mother of Haman in the same context) is Amalthea, the nymph who protected the baby Zeus in the cave in Crete. At the same time, the Babylonian sage may have arrived at this name from the proximity of the constellation Carnabon to the constellation Amalthea (Hyg. *Astr.* 2. 14 and 2. 13). All in all, it would be best to avoid jumping to conclusions based on the wild associations of Babylonian Talmud sages.

lel, and that the ass prohibition was no more than a superstition. Josephus was concerned with exploiting any text by a Greek author that could provide evidence for the priority of the Jews and for Greek admiration of the Jews. It was not in his interest to deflect attention from this by criticizing details in the text he adduced, thus undermining the credibility of his source. Josephus is usually consistent in this treatment of his Gentile Greek sources, as is clear in cases where we may be sure that he knew that his sources were in error. [141]

PYTHAGORAS AND THE JEWISH TORAH:
JOSEPHUS, ARISTOBULUS, AND ORIGEN

The examination of the testimonium and fragment in Josephus has shown that the Jewish influence on Pythagoras, referred to by Hermippus, was actually marginal, pertaining as it did to three esoteric customs at most. This conclusion does not conform with the closing sentence of Josephus, or with the testimonium in Origen. Josephus writes (*Ap.* 1. 165):

> For that man (Pythagoras) is in fact said to have transferred many of the customs among the Jews to his own philosophy.[142]

The sentence appears as a continuation and conclusion to the fragment of Hermippus. It is, however, clearly not of a piece. Could it be an additional testimonium taken from Hermippus?[143] The opinion of those who attribute it not to Hermippus but to Josephus himself is the correct one.[144] Yet their argument that the sentence merely repeats what has been said in the fragment is problematic, since it does not remain specific, but generalizes. More significant is the absence of the Thracians, although this may of course be ascribed to an omission by Josephus. Decisive is the term used for Pythagoras: "that man" (ὁ ἀνὴρ ἐκεῖνος), when "he" (αὐτός) would have been more than enough;[145] the understood subject, Pythago-

---

141. For example, he has no hesitation in repeating Livy and Strabo's false contention that Pompey conquered Jerusalem on a day of fasting, although the event happened "in the third month." There is no fast day in the third month, and at most Jerusalem may have been taken on the Sabbath (Joseph. *AJ* 14. 66; cf. Strabo 16. 2. 40; Dio Cass. 37. 16. 4). This is but one of many available examples.

142. λέγεται γὰρ ὡς ἀληθῶς ὁ ἀνὴρ ἐκεῖνος πολλὰ τῶν παρὰ Ἰουδαίοις νομίμων εἰς τὴν αὐτοῦ μετενεγκεῖν φιλοσοφίαν.

143. As appears from the location of the quotation marks in Niese's edition, and proposed, e.g., by Wehrli (1974) 16, 91, who also included the sentence in his collection of fragments of Hermippus (fr. 22). Cf. Bickerman (1988) 230; Gabba (1989) 624.

144. See Schürer (1901–9) 3: 626; Thackeray (1926) 229 n. e; Walter (1964) 56 n. 1; Stern, *GLAJJ* 1: 93; Gorman (1983) 32; Goodman in Schürer et al. 3: 969 ; Bollansée (1999a) 233, 248–49.

145. Pythagoras has just been referred to with oblique forms of αὐτός at *Contra Apionem* 1. 164: ἑνὸς αὐτοῦ τῶν συνουσιαστῶν (where Calliphon is referred to as ἐκείνου), and συνδιατρίβειν αὐτῷ.

ras, is sufficiently clear without a pronoun, in this as in the previous sentence. We might have expected οὗτος ("this man," "the latter") to refer to Pythagoras, since he is the last subject mentioned. Were Josephus merely recapitulating, his use of ἐκεῖνος ("that man," "the former") would refer confusingly to Hermippus, the previous subject, the one reporting the information about Pythagoras. Clearly, Josephus has taken this final sentence from another source.

Josephus begins his presentation of the testimonium with the word λέγεται ("He [Pythagoras] is said"). Had Josephus been using a Gentile Greek source, he would have been only too pleased to mention his name. The notion that Josephus is using a Jewish source has long had its supporters, and the name of Aristobulus is often mentioned in this regard.[146] Aristobulus was a mid-second-century B.C.E. Jewish Hellenistic author active in the Alexandrian court during the reign of Ptolemy VI Philometor, that is, in the generation of the Hasmonaean revolt.[147] Aristobulus wrote *Commentaries on the Torah of Moses*, which contained discussions on the philosophical significance of various issues appearing in the Pentateuch. On Pythagoras he writes (ap. Eus. *PE* 13. 12. 4):[148]

> As also Pythagoras transferred many of our [ideas? beliefs?] to his belief system (*dogmatopoiia*).[149]

There is a close verbal and grammatical similarity between the sentence in Josephus and that of Aristobulus. It is especially worth noting the use in both of the verb μεταφέρω (transfer) and the adjective πολλά (many).[150] The differences are slight and understandable: Josephus added νομίμων (of customs) to clarify what exactly was "many," a noun being lacking in Aristobulus's statement. Josephus was obliged to do so to connect this sentence explicitly with the customs mentioned just before in the fragment of Hermippus. He also replaced "belief system" with "philosophy," which is more understandable. The remaining differences are minimal and mainly due to a change in the sentence structure made by Josephus to incorporate the

146. Thackeray (1926) 229 n. e; Walter (1964) 56 n. 1; Gorman (1983) 32–33, who also raises the possibility that Josephus was using other Jewish Hellenistic authors.

147. Much has been written on Aristobulus: see esp. Guttmann 1: 186–220, and the monograph on Aristobulus by Walter (1964); for exhaustive up-to-date surveys of the various suggestions concerning his personality, date, sources, and methods, see Goodman in Schürer et al. 3: 579–87; Holladay (1983–96) 3: 113–43, and extensive bibliography there.

148. The edition of Mras: ὡς καὶ Πυθαγόρας πολλὰ τῶν παρ' ἡμῖν μετενέγκας εἰς τὴν ἑαυτοῦ δογματοποιίαν κατεσχώρισεν.

149. Clement *Stromateis* 1. 15. [22. 3] (ed. Stählin) also has a version of the sentence from Aristobulus: καθὼς καὶ Πυθαγόρας πολλὰ τῶν παρ' ἡμῖν μετενέγκας εἰς τὴν ἑαυτοῦ δογματοποιίαν. The version presented in the previous note is to be preferred: see Mras (1944) 222; Walter (1964) 118–19. The sentence in Clement has been reworked to fit its context.

150. Noted by Gorman (1983) 32–33.

introductory addition of "[Pythagoras] is said . . .".[151] There is in all this nothing out of the ordinary for a Josephan paraphrase or citation.

It is true that Josephus does not mention Aristobulus anywhere in his writings. Josephus was, however, familiar with at least the Jewish ethnography of Alexander Polyhistor (*AJ* 1. 240), which cited many Jewish Hellenistic authors by name, yet Josephus consistently refrained from naming in support of his claims those whom he thought were Jewish (except for cases when he is mistaken about their origin). Furthermore, there is evidence to indicate that Josephus was acquainted with the work of Aristobulus.[152]

The possibility that Aristobulus could have used some statement of Hermippus as the basis for his own comment must be rejected.[153] Had Hermippus provided such a statement, Josephus would have used it directly from him, while naming him explicitly. Indeed, Aristobulus would have done the same. The church patriarchs would not have remained indifferent, especially Clement, an Athenian born and bred who, now in Alexandria, was determined to find any possible evidence of Jewish influence on Greek philosophers. The passage from Hermippus in Josephus would surely have sent Clement back to Hermippus's biography of Pythagoras, whom he would have quoted extensively on this issue had he found there anything more.

The statement in Aristobulus is his own original invention, or at the most a reworking of a rumor or material he found in earlier Jewish Hellenistic literature.[154] It was an obvious conclusion to be made from the Jewish fake Orphic literature, which contained among other things Pythagorean elements. Aristobulus himself adduced one Jewish "Orphic" poem without questioning its authenticity.[155]

The link between Pythagorean doctrine and Judaism was made by Hellenistic Jews such as Aristobulus (who, unlike earlier Greek authors, were familiar with Jewish law) first and foremost because they noticed certain similarities between the two doctrines and their customs.[156] They ventured to portray Pythagoras as taking his doctrine from the Jews, being aware that he had already been portrayed

151. The structure in Aristobulus is "As . . . having transferred . . . he placed," while in Josephus it is "He is said . . . to have transferred."

152. See the discussion in Walter (1964) 52–58; Holladay (1983–96) 3: 63–64, both with references to previous work. Walter (1964) 56 n. 1 notes a string of parallels between Aristobulus and Josephus in *Contra Apionem* 2. 168, 255–86, to which a few more could be added.

153. Hinted at by Gorman (1983) 33.

154. Walter (1964) 156–58.

155. Eusebius *Praeparatio evangelica* 13. 12 (664d–666b); and see Guttmann 1: 155–61; Walter (1964) 202–58; Holladay (1983–96) 3: 164–71, and the accompanying notes.

156. These Pythagorean similarities or associations with Jewish customs and beliefs include belief in the immortality of the soul (it should be borne in mind that Aristobulus was active at the

in the classical period as borrowing from various sources, especially Egyptian and other Oriental cultures, a notion that only grew more widespread in the Hellenistic period.[157] If the Greeks themselves attributed Oriental influence to Pythagoras, why should the Jews not take advantage of this when their customs bore some similarity to those of the Pythagoreans? Oriental peoples, especially the Egyptians, were quite keen on exploiting for their own ends Greek legends about visits of Greek sages and scholars to the East, where they learned from the natives; Hellenistic Jews could not allow themselves to lag behind. They struggled with the Egyptians and the Greeks over their image and status. One device that suggested itself was the portrayal of the Torah of Moses as a source of inspiration for Greek philosophy, a side effect of which would have been the strengthening of the self-confidence of Hellenistic Jews in the rightness of their special way of life in the face of the otherwise overwhelming power of the dominant pagan culture. It stands to reason that the myth of stolen wisdom had been utilized by the various allegorists in the internal Jewish controversy to legitimize the application of Greek methods in their interpretation of the Torah, and if we can learn from later rabbinic literature, the myth also allowed conservative groups to draw from Greek heritage, as if it were a wisdom returning to its original owners.

Pythagoras was not the only one portrayed by Aristobulus as taking his ideas from the Jews. Of Plato he went so far as to say that it was clear that he followed Jewish law and that he "worked hard" on everything included in it (Clem. *Strom.* 1. 22 [150. 1]; Eus. *PE* 13. 12). In the same context, he wrote that Socrates, Plato, and Pythagoras learned from the Torah of Moses the concept of the voice of God. On Homer and Hesiod, he said that they learned from the Torah of the Jews about the holiness of the seventh day (Clem. *Strom.* 1. 22 [150. 1]; Eus. *PE* 13. 12). What he says about Pythagoras is therefore just as far-fetched as his references to other Greek thinkers and poets, and just as Aristobulus had no Gentile source telling him about the influence of the Jewish Torah on Homer, Hesiod, Socrates, and Plato, he had no source informing him of such influence on Pythagoras.

It might be worth adding that Aristobulus was almost certainly not an esoteric

---

time of the Hasmonaean revolt and during the reigns of the Hasmonaean brothers, when belief in the resurrection of the dead was already known among Jews in the Holy Land and in the Egyptian diaspora); the prohibition against eating carrion; abstention from meat or certain types of meat or body parts (the sometimes conflicting versions of this Pythagorean prohibition are due to the splintering of the Pythagoreans into different groups); baptism and purification; the rules of pollution caused by death, birth, etc.; the prohibition against burial in woven wool; the prohibition against yoking a bull with a ram for plowing; modesty in relieving oneself; the prohibition against harming fruit trees; the reclusive life of the sect and its daily routine, resembling the habits of the Essenes (as already observed by Josephus in his survey of the Essenes [*AJ* 15. 371]); and the apparent link between the Sabbath and the Pythagorean theory regarding the perfection of the number seven.

157. For later sources, see above, note 77.

personality, but someone who at one time taught Ptolemy VI, as mentioned in 2 Maccabees (1. 10), an identification widely accepted by the church patriarchs as well as by modern scholars.[158] Aristobulus's account, then, is most likely to have been known to Greek authors at some point or other, and some of them could have adopted and adapted it in various ways, according to their attitude toward the Jews and the Pythagoreans.[159] The links between the Jews and the Pythagoreans would have developed over time, given the Pythagorean influences on Philo (who is even called "Pythagorean" by Clement: *Strom.* 2. 19 [100. 3])[160] and perhaps some scraps of information on exclusive Jewish sects, and it all comes together prominently in the writings of Numenius of Apamea, living at the time of the Bar Kohba revolt.[161]

Now to the testimonium in Origen's *Contra Celsum* (1. 15 [334]). In the context of his refutation of the claim made by Celsus that the Jews, being neither an ancient nor a wise people, had contributed nothing to humanity, Origen writes:

> It is said that Hermippus as well, in the first book of *On Lawgivers,* has stated that Pythagoras brought his own philosophy from Jews to Greeks.[162]

This is not a fragment from Hermippus,[163] but a testimonium about Hermippus that Origen must have found elsewhere.[164] The content of the testimonium looks like a paraphrase of the concluding sentence of Josephus.[165] While that sentence (deriving from Aristobulus) has Pythagoras incorporating many Jewish customs

158. Eusebius *Praeparatio evangelica* 8. 9. 38 (375d). This identification is supported by the statement appearing both in Clement and in Eusebius that Aristobulus dedicated his composition on the Jews to Ptolemy VI Philometor. Elsewhere, Clement sets him in the reign of Ptolemy II Philadelphus (*Strom.* 5. 15 [145]).

159. The sole survivor of all these is that of Diogenes Antonius, apparently of the first century B.C.E., which mentions the influence of the Jews on Pythagorean dream divination (in Porph. *VP* 11 = Stern, *GLAJJ* no. 250); but it also mentions in the same breath the influence of the Egyptians, the Babylonians, and even the Arabs, who are never mentioned in Greek and Latin literature as one of the "wise peoples."

160. Cf. p. 143 note 37 above.

161. See the fragments in Stern, *GLAJJ* nos. 363a–369; and the collection of the fragments of Numenius by des Places (1973).

162. Ed. Marcovich (2001): λέγεται δὲ καὶ Ἕρμιππον ἐν τῷ πρώτῳ περὶ νομοθετῶν ἱστορηκέναι Πυθαγόραν τὴν ἑαυτοῦ φιλοσοφίαν ἀπὸ Ἰουδαίων εἰς Ἕλληνας ἀγαγεῖν.

163. *Pace* Gutschmid (1893) 4: 557; Wehrli (1974) 91–92, who includes the sentence in his collection of "fragments" of Hermippus (33, fr. 81); Stern, *GLAJJ* 1: 93; Bollansée (1999a) 110–11.

164. Correctly observed by Goodman in Schürer et al. 3: 696; Bollansée (1999a) 108; (1999b) 114.

165. Noted by Schürer (1901–9) 3: 626, who observed that in the very same section (15) Origen mentions the passage attributed to Hecataeus of Abdera in *Contra Apionem,* and in the following section (16) Origen refers the reader to Josephus for other Greek authors who served as evidence for the antiquity and/or wisdom of the Jews. Goodman in Schürer et al. 3: 696 believes that Origen used a Jewish source (not Josephus) purportedly citing Hermippus.

into his philosophy, the present claim is more sweeping, with the whole of his philosophy coming from the Jews. The change is due to Origen's aim in this passage, namely, to prove through the writings of Greek authors that the Jews were among the wisest of peoples in the ancient world, and that the great sages of Greek philosophy borrowed their basic principles from them.[166] It should be noted that Pythagoras was particularly admired by the church patriarchs.

Furthermore, Origen reports that Pythagoras brought his philosophy from Jews to Greeks. The sentence itself is ambiguous. It might appear to mean that Pythagoras brought his philosophy first to the Jews, and then from the Jews to the Greeks. Origen's overall aim tells against this interpretation. Rather, Pythagoras served as a middleman who brought Jewish thought to the Greeks. Origen is not exact in his formulation of the sentence because he is trying as far as he can to remain faithful to the text of Josephus (which he regarded as a testimonium from Hermippus), while at the same time conveying the message that the Torah of the Jews was accepted by the Greeks already in ancient times. Of the nine words in Origen's sentence, six are indeed to be found in Josephus's last sentence, two with slight changes. As for the degree of Jewish influence, Origen could well have been influenced by the work of Aristobulus, which was known to him (C. Celsum 4. 51).

Origen was very familiar with the writings of Josephus (apart from the Life of Josephus) and cited them explicitly four times in Contra Celsum, referring the reader twice in that work to a close reading of Contra Apionem ("the composition in two books on the antiquity of the Jews," as he calls it)[167], and that is not to mention additional Josephan references and quotes in Origen's monumental commentaries on the books of the Old Testament (especially, as might be expected, Lamentations and Jeremiah). It has already been demonstrated that Origen slightly modified his quotations from Josephus in order to adapt them to his theological views.[168]

---

166. Origen's misreading of the text may be compared with translations and interpretations of Clearchus's account of the meeting between Aristotle and the wise Jew that betray much wishful thinking (see above, pp. 49–53). Another example, close to the present subject, is the translation by Joshua Guttmann, a scholar well versed in Greek language and literature, of Eusebius Praeparatio evangelica 8. 9. 38 (375d): ὁ δὲ Ἀριστόβουλος καὶ τῆς κατ᾽ Ἀριστοτέλην φιλοσοφίας πρὸς τῇ πατρίῳ μετειληχώς ("Aristobulus, who took from the philosophy of Aristotle in addition to his ancestral [philosophy]"). Guttman translated: "Aristobulus, who attributed part of the philosophy of Aristotle to that of the Torah of the Jews" ([1958] 1: 278). Aristobulus mentions no such thing, or anything remotely like it, in the rest of the fragments and testimonia that we have. This reservation, however, does not detract from my admiration for the scholarship and research achievements of the late Joshua Guttmann.

167. The quotes: 1. 16, 47; 2. 13; 4. 11. On Origen's use of Josephus, see de Lange (1976) 64–78; Mizugaki (1987); Feldman (1990).

168. See especially Mizugaki (1987) 328–36.

Origen understood (or wanted to understand) that the final sentence of Josephus was a continuation of Hermippus. He regarded the agent of the first word of the sentence, λέγεται, to be Hermippus ("[Pythagoras] is said [by Hermippus] . . ."). Origen then began his own paraphrase with the same verb, but naturally made Josephus the agent of it ("It is said [by Josephus] that Hermippus . . . has stated that . . .").

The obvious objection to these arguments is that although Josephus had earlier cited the first book of Hermippus's *Life of Pythagoras,* Origen refers to Hermippus's work *On Lawgivers,* as if he has taken his statement directly or indirectly from it. However, *On Lawgivers* dealt with personalities other than Pythagoras.[169] The epitome of Heraclides Lembus also contained *On Pythagoras* and *On Lawgivers* as separate works. Origen may have made the misattribution either by relying on his memory or by glancing at Josephus's introduction to the passage while writing the sentence: the reference by Josephus to the first book of *On Pythagoras* comes a few lines earlier than the concluding sentence that Origen adduces; the word *nomimōn* ("of customs") in that final sentence may have caused Origen to believe that he saw an attribution to Hermippus's *Peri nomothetōn* (*On Lawgivers*). It is not surprising that Origen, despite his sharp mind, could make such a mistake, given his vast literary output as well as his ecclesiastic commitments and many journeys. And after all, Pythagoras was praised by the Christian Patriarchs as a lawgiver.

The sentence, therefore, passed from Aristobulus to Josephus to Origen. The story about the Jewish origin of Greek wisdom first appeared in the work of Aristobulus the Jew and was probably invented by him, if not by Jews a little earlier.

HERMIPPUS'S ATTITUDE TOWARD THE JEWS

Hermippus mentioned the Jews in a statement that Pythagoras incorporated in his peculiar system of commands (*akousmata*) one Jewish custom, or at the most three customs (two of them marginal ones). The references appeared in a work portraying Pythagoras as a charlatan with an unrestrained thirst for power and influence, spreading among his followers arbitrary, unjustified customs based in part or entirely on superstitions, in order to reinforce his rule and the secretive character of his sect. The charlatan is also described as a plagiarist: a number of customs were taken from other peoples, but Pythagoras presented them as his own, or as his disciples', commands.

---

169. *Pace* Wehrli (1974) 91; Bollansée (1999a) 113; (1999b) 27, 46; both try to explain that Hermippus's remarks on the Jews were to be found both in the biography on Pythagoras and in the composition *On Lawgivers,* or in the summary of Heraclides of both works. However, Hermippus, who regarded Pythagoras as advocating tyranny and undermining laws, would hardly have included his biography of Pythagoras in a collection of lawgivers.

This cannot be taken as a compliment to the Jews. At the same time, one should not conclude that Hermippus has a negative attitude toward the Jews. Although Hermippus hints at some arbitrary, pointless, and superstitious customs, this is quite normal in anthropological discourse of the Greek classical and Hellenistic world: many customs of close neighbors, distant peoples, and even of certain Greeks were explicitly portrayed as *deisidaimoniai* (*superstitiones* in Latin). The term's primary meaning in the singular was "fear of the gods or of *daimones*," leading to strange behavior. The term's meaning broadened over time to denote superstitions in general.

Hostility toward a particular people would be obvious if all or most of their main customs, or their religion by and large, were treated explicitly or indirectly as superstitions, and for the most part with scorn, sarcasm, condemnation, mockery, or anger. Judaism was indeed so described by some Greek authors, and to an even greater extent by Romans of later periods.[170] Hermippus, however, referred at most to three isolated and marginal customs. If this passage is the only reference to the Jews in all the writings of Hermippus—as it seems to be, in light of the fact that Josephus and the church patriarchs cite no other passages on the Jews from Hermippus—it would appear that Hermippus had no special interest in the Jews and knew about them only from the account by the celebrated Alexandrian author Hecataeus of Abdera and some hearsay. In this, Hermippus was no different from other contemporary Alexandrian scholars in their ivory tower, interested only in preserving the classical Greek tradition.

These conclusions necessarily raise the question of how Josephus failed to see that Hermippus was extremely hostile toward Pythagoras, and that being linked with Pythagoras brought no credit to the Jews. Moreover, Josephus praised Pythagoras as the greatest of the philosophers (*Ap.* 1. 162), while heaping praise on Hermippus for the accuracy of his writing (163).[171] He even introduces Hermippus as the finest author to have written on Pythagoras.

Josephus clearly had not read the work of Hermippus, nor the epitome by

170. Cf. p. 305.

171. Two later authors also heap praises on Hermippus: Dionysius of Halicarnassus in *Isaeus* 1. 2, having read his biography on the pupils of Isocrates; and Aelian, in *De natura animalium* 7. 40, as an introduction to one of the most absurd stories of Hermippus (see above, p. 172). The judgment of Aelian is not surprising, as he himself was obsessed with wonder stories, but it is difficult to comprehend the positive attitude of Dionysius of Halicarnassus. He would certainly have been impressed by the long bibliographies accompanying the biographies of Hermippus, which gave a veneer of seriousness to the works, and not a few ancient authors err in their compliments to other historians (e.g., Pliny, pref. 25 on Diodorus Siculus), but that still does not satisfactorily explain how a historian of his stature and ability could have been unaware of the true nature of Hermippus's works. The recommendations and reports of prominent contemporary scholars are occasionally also a cause of embarrassment.

Heraclides Lembus. He seems to have relied on the summaries and quotations that his assistants, burrowing through libraries in search of Greek sources for Jewish references, presented to him out of context.[172] Such a scenario seems more probable than that Josephus used an anthology.

Josephus was so mistaken in understanding the fragment that in his concluding sentence he overemphasized the Jewish influence on Pythagorean customs. The sentence was inspired by Aristobulus, the Jewish Hellenistic author, who was, as far as we know, the first scholar to speak of extensive Jewish influence on Pythagoras, Socrates, and Plato (in addition to Homer and Hesiod). Origen regarded the final sentence of Josephus as continuing the fragment of Hermippus and copied it with a few modifications as evidence that great Greek philosophers took their doctrines from the Jews.

. . .

Finally, some concluding remarks regarding the beginnings and development of the myth about the Jewish origin of Greek philosophy, and the place of Hermippus in its development. Hermippus, bridging the third and second centuries B.C.E., referred not to Jewish "philosophy" but at most only to a few marginal customs and their connection with Pythagoreanism; in this he hardly approached the spirit of the myth, *pace* the opinion of many scholars. Just as Clearchus of Soli, reporting on the meeting of Aristotle with the Jew, did not say that the Jew was wiser than Aristotle or that Aristotle learned from him,[173] and just as Megasthenes in his comparison of the Jewish and Indian doctrines on "nature" did not say that Jewish teachings were chronologically prior to the Greek,[174] so Hermippus did not say that Pythagoras took his doctrine from the Jews, or anything similar to that. The myth was created by Hellenistic Jews in Egypt, and not by Greeks. Movement in this direction is already discernible in the Jewish forgery of the Orphic poems. The first author whose explicit account on this subject has reached us, and who may have been its originator, was Aristobulus the Jew, active in the generation after Hermippus. This mythmaking was one of the tactics that Hellenistic Jews could use to bolster their self-confidence in the face of the overwhelming force of Hellenism and strengthen the image of Judaism among their neighbors and the major powers.

Later on, the myth was also used in the internal Jewish discourse to legitimize the use of Greek wisdom for the understanding of the Torah. The position of Aristobulus in the court of Ptolemy VI helped in promoting his writings in

172. See further, p. 146n.49 above.
173. See above, pp. 49–53.
174. See above, pp. 156–58.

literary circles, first of all among Hellenistic Jews. Artapanus the Jew,[175] who lived in the second century B.C.E., wrote that Moses was the teacher of Orpheus (Eus. *PE* 9.27.4), probably as a response to the legend that Orpheus learned from the Egyptians (Hecataeus, *ap.* Diod. 4.25.3 and elsewhere). The myth echoes more than once in Philo's writings,[176] whereas Josephus was influenced by it to a limited extent when he summarized Aristobulus's account as if reflecting Hermippus's view, although elsewhere he took the myth at face value (*Ap.* 2.257, 281). According to Clement it was adopted by many other authors (*Strom.* 1. 15 [72.5]). If he does not have in mind Jewish authors, this statement sounds rather exaggerated; had it been correct, Clement would not have failed to quote, or at least name, these authors. Clement mentions only Megasthenes and Numenius, who explicitly referred to Aristobulus, and formutated the myth in various ways ("Who is Plato if not Moses speaking Attic?").[177] The myth was eagerly exploited by the church patriarchus, beginning with Justin the martyr in Rome and Clement in Alexandria (first half of the second century C.E.) to serve their ends.[178] Pagan authors consequently began to deny the myth and struggled against it (e.g., Celsus in the late second century C.E.). At least from the time of Origen in the third century, the spirit of the myth was associated also with Hermippus. Origen was not directly familiar with Hermippus's work and adopted the concluding sentence of Josephus as evidence. The myth took many forms in Jewish and Christian thought at the end of the classical period, in the Middle Ages, and in the modern age, until at least the eighteenth century, with Pythagoras playing a role (especially in the writings of Johannes Reuclin and Rabbi Moshe Isserlisch—the Ram'a). Thus, for instance, he was described by Menaseh ben Israel as a disciple of the prophet Ezekiel. At the same time, Aristotle—for obvious reasons—occupied center stage.

175. The accepted opinion that Artapanus was Jewish has recently been challenged by Jacobson (2006). Unfortunately, the brilliant discussion by Guttmann (2:109–39) escaped his notice. It actually responds to the doubts raised later by Jacobson.

176. See, e.g., *Quaestiones in Genesin* 3. 5, 4. 152; *De specialibus legibus* 4. 16. 61; *De mutatione hominum* 167–68; *De somnis* 2. 244; *Quis rerum divinarum heres sit* 214; *De aeternitate mundi* 19. Philo explicitly accuses Heraclitus of stealing from the wisdom of the Jews and from their Torah, and actually uses the same accusation (though more delicately) against Plato and the Greek legislators. On the depiction of Moses by Philo as the "father" of philosophy, see Gager (1972) 69–69.

177. See Clement *Stromateis* 1. 22 (150.4); Eusebius *Praeparatio evangelica* 9. 10.146 (410d); Suda, s.v. Νομήνιος.

178. See the discussion in Lilla (1971) 27–41.

6

The Diachronic Libels and Accusations (A)

Mnaseas of Patara and the Origins and Development of the Ass Libel

The libel that a statue of an ass was to be found in the Jerusalem Temple (and Jewish onolatry by and large) is considered by scholars (following Josephus) to be one of the three most humiliating charges leveled against the Jews in ancient times (the two others being the leper libel and the blood libel). The present chapter concentrates mainly on the story of the theft of an ass head from the Jewish Temple, adduced by Mnaseas of Patara in Lycia (third–second century B.C.E.), the first Greek author known to have reported the ass libel. I shall attempt below to clarify how Mnaseas and contemporary Greeks regarded the story. Then I will discuss the four versions of the libel in later Greek and Roman authors, and its Egyptian origins.

THE STORY OF MNASEAS:
CONTENTS AND TRANSMISSION

Mnaseas's racy story tells how an Idumaean of the city of Dora (Adorayim) tricked the Jews. Disguised as the god Apollo, he entered their Temple, took the head of the ass on display there, and carried it off to his city. This, then, is evidence for the existence of the ass libel at a time prior to the great confrontation between the Jews and the Hellenistic world, which began with the crisis in relations between the Jews and Antiochus Epiphanes, a crisis later exacerbated by the Maccabaean Revolt, the territorial expansion of the Hasmonaean state, and the escalating conflict between Jews and Greeks in Egypt from the last quarter of the second century B.C.E. onward. Upon reading the story, the question arises whether Mnaseas treated it as historical fact and/or intended to use it as a vehicle for discrediting the Jews. Many scholars who take the latter for granted describe Mnaseas as the first "anti-Semitic" Greek author.[1] And Mnaseas was an author not without influence: he was one of the most outstanding students of the Alexandrian scholar Eratosthenes of Cyrene, himself an exceptionally learned, versatile, and prolific scholar, known in Alexandria as "the second Plato" or "the new Plato." The story under discussion appeared in a work of Mnaseas that enjoyed a relatively wide circulation.[2] If we accept that Mnaseas was "anti-Semitic," we shall have to conclude that Greek authors began to express explicit and extreme hostility toward Jews as they became better acquainted with the Jewish way of life, already before the stormy events of the Hasmonaean period. Some scholars have even suggested that these early expressions of animosity influenced the hostile attitude of Antiochus Epiphanes and his counselors toward the Jews.

What we have of Mnaseas's story has not reached us directly. A somewhat abbreviated version has survived in Josephus *Contra Apionem* 2. 112–14. Josephus argues against Apion's citation of the episode in Mnaseas as supporting evidence for the truth of the story Apion related earlier about the entry of Antiochus Epiphanes into the Jewish Temple, where he saw the "golden (ass) head" (*Ap.* 2. 80). Josephus attempts to refute both the account of the spectacle allegedly encountered by Antiochus (2. 81–89) and the account of Mnaseas concerning the theft of the ass head (2. 113–20). The first part of the story of Mnaseas, a description of the background and preparations for the theft (112–13), has survived only in the Latin translation of *Contra Apionem* instigated in Sicily by Cassiodorus, the sixth-century scholar and head of the secretariat of Theodoric the Great.[3] The second part, on the theft itself (114), has been preserved in the Greek manuscripts as well. A translation of the entire story follows:

(112) Again, as if he is most pious, [Apion] mocks [us] by adding Mnaseas to his story. For [Apion] says that [Mnaseas] related that while the Idumaeans were waging a war

1. For references to studies on Mnaseas's account of the Jews, see Stern, *GLAJJ* 1: 98; Goodman in Schürer et al. 3: 598. See also notes 65 and 69 below. I retract my earlier conclusions concerning Mnaseas and the development of the libel (Bar-Kochva [1996a]).

2. See Müller, *FHG* III. 149. The popularity of the work may be inferred from the variety of authors of different periods and genres who provide testimonia for it; see the passages in Mehler (1846); *FGH* III. 149–58; the story about the theft of the ass head is reported in neither collection.

3. On the Latin translation, see Niese (1896) xiv ff., xxii–xxiv; Schreckenberg (1996); the latest edition of the Cassiodorus translation: Boysen (1898).

against the Jews[4] for quite a long time,[5] in a certain town of the Idumaeans,[6] called Dora,[7] one of those who in it worshipped Apollo[8] came to the Jews. He (Mnaseas) says the name of this man [was] Zabidus, who then promised them (the Jews) that he would hand over [to them] Apollo, god of the Dorians, and that he (Apollo) would come to our temple if all kept away. (113) And all the multitude of the Jews believed. But Zabidus made a certain wooden device and placed it around himself and fixed on it three rows of lights and thus walked so that he appeared to those standing at a distance as if stars were making their way through the land.[9] (114) The Jews, on the one hand, struck by the strangeness of the sight [and] remaining at a distance, held their peace; Zabidus, on the other hand, with great calm entered the temple and tore off (ἀποσῦραι) the golden head of the pack-ass (κάνθων)[10]—for so he (Apion) has wittily written—and returned to Dora[11] as quickly as possible.

4. The MSS reading of the Latin translation is *Iudaei contra Iudaeos*. Hudson (1720) 2: 1371 emends *Iudaeos* to *Idumaeos*. The terms "Jews" and "Judaea" are frequently interchanged with their counterparts "Idumaeans" and "Idumaea" both in Greek and in Latin. Indeed, the Idumaeans must have been mentioned in light of the details of the story and the refutation of Josephus in paras. 115–120. The story, however, being Idumaean in origin, one would expect the order *Idumaei contra Iudaeos*, all the more so as the story appears to have been included in Mnaseas's work under an entry on the city of Dora-Adorayim (see below, pp. 219–20).

5. The awkward Latin phrase *longo quodam tempore* ("for a certain long time") may be an attempt to translate the Greek χρόνον μακρόν τι ("for quite a long time").

6. Hudson (1720) 2: 1371 rightly emends *civitate Iudaeorum* to *civitate Idumaeorum* (cf. the refutation of Josephus, para. 116). This does not, however, correct the impression that the war took place within the town. The author surely wished to indicate the origin of Zabidus, and not the war zone, but the nature of the corruption is unclear. It may result, for example, from an error in translation or transmission, involving the misconstrual of a word or the omission of several words. The following sentences are also somewhat cumbersome. An attempt at emendation in these circumstances, therefore, would be inappropriate.

7. The received text reads *qui Dorii nominantur*, but one of the Latin MSS reading *quae Dorin nominatur* is certainly preferable. In the refutation of Josephus the city is twice called Δῶρα (para. 116), which is also the name used for it by other Greek sources (along with Ἀδῶρα and Ἀδωραίμ). The Greek original, therefore, probably read ἥ Δῶρα ὀνομάζεται: cf. para. 116: Δῶρα πόλις ὀνομάζεται. The Latin version became corrupted by a faulty reading of the place-name (cf., a little later, *deum Doriensium*), and by the attempt to make the relative pronoun and the verb agree with the Idumaeans rather than the city itself. For the origin of the version *Dorii* and *Dori*, see below, note 11.

8. Reading *quendam eorum qui in ea Apollinem coleba<n>t*. The relative pronoun, referring to the preceding plural pronoun, must itself be plural; hence so too the verb.

9. *quasi stellae per terram* τὴν πορείαν ποιουμένων. The Greek text is preserved from this point on.

10. The Greek MS L (Laurentianus), from which most of the other MSS of *Contra Apionem* derive, reads τοῦ ἀκανθῶνος ("of the thorny [thing]"). The Latin translation has *asini* ("of the ass"). Hudson (1720) 2: 1371 accordingly emended to τοῦ κάνθωνος ("of the pack-ass").

11. L reads εἰς Δῶριν. In S and the *editio princeps*, rightly, εἰς Δῶραν (see above, note 7). On the high value of S and the *editio princeps*, see below, pp. 480–81. The error in L is reflected in the Latin translation in the reading *Dorin*, corrupted into *Dorii*.

The story transmitted by Josephus, as appears from his own words, was based on Apion's version. There are no indications that Josephus was directly acquainted with Mnaseas's book.[12] The story is presented in indirect speech, and Apion may already have reported the story in this way. Apart from the changes made during the conversion to indirect speech, Apion and Josephus also introduced modifications in formulation and in the abridging of the material. This involvement is discernible— as is usual in such cases—in the "seams" joining this story to the rest of the work of Josephus, namely, at the beginning and the end of the story, and in the remaining references to Apion and Mnaseas inserted at various points. Certain abridgments of details within the story may also be traced.[13] In one instance the involvement of Josephus is particularly clear.[14] Furthermore, the process of abbreviation and reformulation in reported speech has adversely affected the flow of the story, and a number of sentences are awkward (112b in particular). The task of reconstructing the original text is made far more difficult by the disappearance of the Greek text of the first part of the story, which has survived only in Latin translation, as is also the case with the blood libel and the ass libel in Apion's account (2. 80, 90–96). This is most obvious with regard to the corruptions in the ethnic denotations "Jews" and "Idumaeans" and the place-name "Dora." Some of the errors are due to the textual transmission either of the Latin translation or already of the Greek original. The surviving Greek text of the second part of the story contains proper readings that assist our reconstruction of the first, Latin part. Further aid is at hand in the subsequent passage preserved in Greek, where Josephus tries to refute the story (2. 115–20).[15]

12. Mnaseas is mentioned twice more in Josephus, but these references do not allow us to infer that Josephus knew his works at firsthand. In *Contra Apionem* 1. 216, Mnaseas appears in a list together with other Greek authors mentioned by name, and "many other" (unnamed) Greek historians whose incidental remarks on the Jewish people, according to Josephus, suffice to demonstrate the antiquity of the Jews. Josephus even hints that he had not read their accounts, and this conforms with the fact that he nowhere quotes them in his work, although they could have supported his position. Mnaseas is grouped with them presumably because of the reference to the war between the Idumaeans and the Jews. Just as Josephus had adduced (pseudo-)Hecataeus's account of the activity of the Jews at the time of Alexander and the Successors (*Ap.* 1. 183–85) to demonstrate the antiquity of the Jews, he would also have regarded as evidence Mnaseas's reference to a protracted and apparently distant war, long before the Idumaeans' forced conversion to Judaism. Mnaseas is again mentioned in the *Jewish Antiquities* (1. 91) as one of the authors who referred to the Flood and/or the ark. Josephus numbers Mnaseas on the same occasion with authors who wrote histories of "barbarian" peoples. The context and the other authors mentioned indicate that Josephus meant authors of non-Greek origin. To the best of our knowledge, Mnaseas did not write histories. Josephus, therefore, does not seem to have known Mnaseas's work except indirectly through Apion and references in other authors.

13. See below, pp. 219–22.

14. Para. 112: *nostrum templum;* cf. para. 90: *nostro templo,* with regard to another version of the ass libel, also taken from Apion.

15. See above, notes 4–11; on the abundance of errors in the translation, see Niese (1896) xiv ff.,

MNASEAS, THE MAN AND HIS WORK

Mnaseas's account is strange and unusual. It is a complete fantasy, suffused with a remote and marvelous mythological atmosphere. In order to understand the story properly, prior to drawing conclusions about the attitude of Mnaseas toward the Jews, it is necessary to examine who Mnaseas was and his methods of work.[16]

Mnaseas is mentioned by the *Suda*, the tenth-century Byzantine lexicon, in its entry on Eratosthenes, the scholar, poet, and scientist who headed the Library of Alexandria in the last quarter of the third century B.C.E. The *Suda* states that Mnaseas was one of Eratosthenes' pupils. The mention of Mnaseas at the head of the list, together with only two other pupils, suggests that he was one of Eratosthenes' more outstanding students, if not the most outstanding (Aristophanes of Byzantium, who succeeded Eratosthenes as head of the Mouseion, was not his disciple). Thus Mnaseas, a native of Patara in Lycia, must have spent at least some time in Alexandria, and would have been deeply influenced by the scholars active in the Library, and by Eratosthenes in particular. The dates of Mnaseas's life and literary activity are far from certain and depend upon the dating of the death of Eratosthenes, who may have died in 190, or some twenty years earlier, around 210.[17] The exact chronology is relevant to establishing the background to the creation of the story about Zabidus and the ass, and to the dating of its composition.

Mnaseas wrote two works: one was a collection of oracles delivered to petitioners in Delphi, and the second contained information and stories about settlements. Too few testimonia have survived from the first work to be of help here.[18] One may learn from them that Mnaseas had a tendency to write poetry, but then his oracular material would have required him to do so. The story about the ass head must have been taken from the second work. That work had three parts—*On Asia, On Europe,* and *On Libya*—each comprising several books.[19] The ass-head

---

xxii-xxiv; Schreckenberg (1996). On the many errors in the translation of the blood libel, see below, pp. 254–56, notes 4–16.

16. Only brief surveys have been written on Mnaseas, hardly exhausting the problems arising from an examination of the surviving material. On Mnaseas, see Müller, *FHG* IV. 659–60; Susemihl (1891–92) 1: 679–80; Laqueur, *RE* s.v. "Mnaseas," cols. 2248–52; Fraser (1972) 1: 524–25, 781–82. References below to the testimonia follow the numbering of the collection in *FHG* III. 149–58.

17. See Pfeiffer (1968) 153–54, 172.

18. *FHG* IV frr. 46–50.

19. *On Europe:* frr. 1–25b (see the references in frr. 7, 12, 15, 17); *On Asia:* frr. 26–37 (reference in fr. 26); *On Libya* (= Africa): frr. 38–42 (reference in fr. 40). *On Europe* comprised at least eight books (fr. 19 clearly concerns Europe), *On Asia* at least two (fr. 32), and *On Libya* probably more than one (fr. 40). The structure may be compared to that of Callimachus's work Κτίσεις νήσων καὶ πόλεων καὶ μετονομασίαι (Foundations of Islands and Cities and Name Changes), mentioned in the entry

story, centering around the successful trick pulled off by an Idumaean from the city Dora-Adorayim in Mt. Hebron, would have been included in *On Asia*. As for the work as a whole, the introduction to two testimonia describes it as a *periplous* (circumnavigation),[20] which scholars have indeed accepted as its title. This was the title usually given to guides for seamen, ever since the time of the sixth-century Scylax of Caryanda; but it does not seem to have been the title of Mnaseas's work. Not a few of the testimonia concern settlements that lay far from the coast.[21] Furthermore, as we shall see, the emphasis and contents of the compilation were entirely different from the genre mentioned above. We cannot know what title was given to the work by Mnaseas. Librarians and later copyists in antiquity often provided false, inaccurate, or misleading titles based on superficial impressions. At the same time, the incorrect name does shed light on some elements of the basic structure of the work, since they are what led to the mistake. The work was, therefore, a collection of information and stories on settlements arranged according to some geographical scheme in which each settlement would be the subject of an individual entry or would be referred to in a continuous description of a journey. Information and stories about the settlement would follow.

---

on the author in the *Suda*. No information has reached us concerning the parts and books of this great work, but Philostephanus of Cyrene, a pupil of Callimachus, produced a compilation, which, as was often the case, seems to have been no more than a revised version of his master's work, and it contained parts such as *On the Cities of Asia*, *On the Cities of Europe*, *On Islands*, *On Cyprus* (presumably a subsection of *On Islands*), and *On Wonderful Rivers*. The division may well reflect that of the compilation by Callimachus. See the references to sources concerning the compilation of Philostephanus and its division in Fraser (1972) 2: 752–53, nn. 21–28, and the discussion in Fraser (1972) 1: 522–23; Bollansée (1999b) 4. See also note 22 below on Callimachus's work on marvels and wonders, and *On the Rivers of the Oikoumenē*.

20. Fr. 6 (Athenaeus), 39 (Photius). In fr. 13 (Stephanus of Byzantium) we find "Mnaseas in the third book of the *periēgēseis* (travel guides)." Since the testimonium is concerned with the identification of an Illyrian tribe, the context has rightly been considered to be the part on Europe (so Müller in his collection). The testimonium has also been taken to mean that *periēgēsis* was the title of the whole work (Müller, *FHG* III. 149, followed by others), or of each part of it, with the whole composition being called *periplous* (Laqueur, *RE* s.v. "Mnaseas," col. 2251). The formulation of the reference, however, is manifestly in error, and it is also clear from frr. 12 and 15 that Illyria appeared in the second book of *On Europe*. Stephanus may have relied on his own memory for the reference to a very brief testimonium. Be this as it may, the characteristics of works called *periēgēsis* (at least down to the second century C.E.) were essentially no different from those of the *periplous* genre. They were factual and concentrated on geographical, topographical, and economic data. Mnaseas, therefore, could not have called his work (or regarded it as a) *periēgēsis*, just as it was not called *periplous* (see below). On the oscillation of ancient authors between the names *periplous* and *periēgēsis*, see Pliny *Naturalis Historia* 1. 5, referring to the work of Posidonius of Apamea ("Περίπλουν aut Περιήγησιν"); cf. Athenaeus 7. 278d. Not a few scholars believe that the real name of the work referred to by Pliny was neither of these, but Περὶ Ὠκεανοῦ (On Ocean).

21. Frr. 1, 4–6, 8, 14, 20, 21, 25, 26. So too the story of Apollo and the ass.

We now have forty-four testimonia and one fragment from the work. These, considered together with the incorrect title, allow us to piece together more precisely the general characteristics of the work: its genre, structure, content, features, and aims. The reconstruction is assisted by considering what may be salvaged of the titles and general structure and contents of compilations by Alexandrian authors of the generation preceding Mnaseas, especially the many works of Callimachus of Cyrene, the celebrated poet-scholar who was traditionally regarded as the teacher of Eratosthenes. In this connection the later editions or imitations of Callimachus's scholarly works published by his pupils and others can provide us with some valuable information.[22] No such reconstruction of the work of Mnaseas has so far been attempted, but it is required to put the episode concerning the theft of the ass head in the right perspective.

The one fragment we have from the lexicon is sufficient to establish that the work was written in prose,[23] and not in verse, the medium used for many scholarly works of the same period (such as those of Aratus of Soli, Callimachus, and even Eratosthenes). In light of the contents of the surviving passages and all the relevant factors mentioned above, the work in all its parts and books appears to have been a lexicon (in the late Byzantine sense of the word), with a separate

22. On the compilations of Callimachus, see Susemihl (1891–92) 1: 366–67; Pfeiffer (1968) 134–35; Fraser (1972) 1: 454–55, 523–24, 776–78; and see the fragments in Pfeiffer (1949–53) 1: frr. 403–60. Of particular interest to us is the apparent arrangement of his work Ἐθνικαὶ ὀνομασίαι (Ethnic Names; see Ath. 7. 329a) according to books on individual subjects such as On Fish, On Birds, On Winds, On Nymphs, and On Stones. The subject order was alphabetical (like, for example, the Homeric Glossai of Zenodotus, the first head of the Library of Alexandria), and the internal arrangement of each subject was according to peoples and cities, apparently following a geographical order. The internal order—essentially relevant to our consideration of Mnaseas—may be inferred from the title of a book from that work, devoted to the months of the year, which is given as μηνῶν προσηγορίαι κατὰ ἔθνους καὶ πόλεις (Names of Months According to Peoples and Cities) on its own (without reference to the whole composition) in the entry "Callimachus" of the Suda. As for the contents of entries, from the stories surviving from the book περὶ ὀρνέων (On Birds; Pfeiffer [1949–53] 1: frr. 414–28), the work Ethnic Names seems to have included not just etymologies and definitions of words, but also aetiological stories that would have served as illustrations or explanations for local names of birds, fish, winds, etc. It is also worth noting another work by Callimachus whose full title, preserved in the Suda, indicates its arrangement: θαυμάτων τῶν εἰς ἅπασαν τὴν γῆν κατὰ τόπους ὄντων συναγωγή (Collection of Wonders throughout the Whole World [Arranged] According to Places). One part of this, or of an earlier version of it, is known, from the entry mentioned above from the Suda, to have been called Περὶ τῶν ἐν Πελοποννήσῳ καὶ Ἰταλίᾳ θαυμασίων καὶ παραδόξων (On the Wonders and Marvels in the Peloponnese and Italy). Another work of Callimachus is also instructive: On the Rivers of the Oikoumenē, which is divided into On the Rivers in Asia and On the Rivers in Europe (see Pfeiffer [1949–53] 1: frr. 407–11, 457–59). See also note 19 above on Callimachus's Foundations of Islands and Cities and Name Changes, which may have served partially as a model for Mnaseas's work.

23. Fr. 32 (Ath. 8. 346d).

entry for each of the various settlements, rather than a continuous description of a journey containing accounts of settlements along the way. The general aim of the work was to present readers with engaging and highly readable folklore material, both mythological and semimythological, in an accessible form, with the arrangement facilitating the location of information. The material was unlikely to be known to the average reader, but it was of the sort that would raise associations and connections with the Greek literary and mythological tradition. In accordance with this aim, the settlements chosen were mainly small or almost unknown,[24] and not the famous cities or sites that were blessed with many celebrated mythological stories. Most of the material was taken from esoteric, often old, or mostly forgotten Greek sources, or from oral traditions.[25] Part of the material was reworked to a greater or lesser extent by Mnaseas. Thus it would have been a selective geographical-mythological lexicon that chose to present for the entertainment of readers relatively unfamiliar settlements about which the little mythological material available was novel and/or stimulating.

As mentioned above, the lexicon contained three parts, one for each continent adjacent to the Mediterranean. Each part comprised a number of books, and these were arranged and divided according to large geographical units, countries, or regions. The entries within each unit may have been arranged alphabetically or presented in geographical order, probably according to a circular route, as was common in Hellenistic literature. Each entry included stories, anecdotes, or statements on one or more of the following subjects: the foundation of the city,[26] its customs, public events and ceremonies,[27] unusual natural phenomena in the city or its environs,[28] personalities—the founder(s), inventors, discoverers, the first to do a particularly celebrated deed, and famous people from that city.[29] The entries, presumably, had an identical internal order, beginning with the name of the city and the foundation story. The stories and statements on every subject, be it the foundation or natural phenomena or wonders, often derived from etymological explanations for the name of the settlement, the people, or local personalities. Sometimes they are even derived from complex genealogical connections between personalities and mythological heroes and deities with a direct

24. Frr. 3, 5, 8, 9, 12, 17, 20–22, 25, 27, 28, 38–41. Some better-known cities do make an appearance, however, if they are not too well-known and if the associated story is sufficiently piquant (e.g., Ascalon, fr. 32).

25. Frr. 19, 21, 25, 29, 49. See further Laqueur, *RE* s.v. "Mnaseas," col. 2252. Xanthus the Lydian (fr. 32), who appears in Herodotus, is the only relatively well-known author mentioned. But one cannot say to what extent he was known in the generation of Mnaseas.

26. Frr. 8, 12, 17, 19, 21, 22, 28, 38, 39.

27. Frr. 18, 25, 27, 32, 43.

28. Frr. 5, 6, 11, 41, 42.

29. Frr. 1–5, 7, 40, 43, 44.

or indirect connection, real or imaginary, to the settlement that is the subject of the entry.[30] The stories were not infrequently based on accidental linguistic similarity. The testimonia, however, do not indicate any reference to dry and technical geographical details, such as the exact location of the settlement, distances, way stations, prominent landmarks, fortresses, anchorages, regional storms, imports and exports, and other details of practical topography—features typical of works bearing the generic title *Periplous*.[31] At most, there are general statements concerning the region in which a settlement is located (e.g., "Dardanos, a city in Troas").[32]

From this it may be deduced that Mnaseas was not writing for sailors, merchants, or tourists, but for readers who wished to locate as quickly as possible interesting and entertaining information and stories about a remote settlement whose name had been encountered by chance, or for armchair tourists who wished to travel effortlessly through distant lands in pursuit of the unusual. Such readers were not interested in distances and other technical details, but in stories to spark the imagination. Mnaseas provided his readers with stories either new and interesting, or that could be found only with great effort in the works of his predecessors. His readers could dip in at their leisure, since there was no continuity of content between one entry and the next. The text could be read without too much intellectual effort, although there were many associations to delight anyone acquainted with the classical Greek tradition, as indeed most of Mnaseas's contemporary readers would have been.

In his desire to attract, engage, and entertain readers, Mnaseas emphasized all that was different, strange, and amazing. Hence, for instance, the story about talking fish in a river in Arcadia, appearing in that part of the work dedicated to "Europe."[33] Another story in the same part tells of temple chickens in the service of Heracles, and temple hens in the service of his wife, Hebe. Only a channel separated the two temples, but the two groups of poultry came together only in the mating season, and their offspring were in due course separated according to sex.[34] Mnaseas does not balk at telling such stories even when some of his readers can check their reliability, and his Alexandrian colleagues were likely to compare his accounts with opposing views of other authors.[35] The deliberate emphasis on wonder blurs the distinction between history and mythology, the world of

30. Frr. 5, 7–9, 12–14, 17, 19, 21, 24, 26, 28, 31, 33, 36, 37, 40.

31. See the remains of the genre in *GGM* and additional collections, and the discussions in Güngerich (1950).

32. Fr. 28. At the same time, since the location prefaced the entry in the lexicon of Stephanus of Byzantium, it would seem to have derived from the title rather than the entry itself.

33. Fr. 6 (Ath. 8. 331d). Pausanias VII. 21. 2 should also be mentioned. It is no wonder that a story in a similar spirit concerning another river appeared in Callimachus (Ath. 8. 331e).

34. Fr. 11 (Ael. *NA* 18. 46).

35. So, for example, the story of the speaking fish runs against an explicit statement by Aristotle

gods and the world of men, and everything is thrown into the mix. Classical
Greek gods and local "barbarian" deities walk among mortals and even share
family trees with them. They appear at times as mortals or as representations of
physical objects such as heavenly bodies. One can find in Mnaseas variations—
indeed, reversals—on the Euhemerist interpretation of the world of gods that
began a century earlier.[36] While Euhemerus regarded the gods as none other
than mortals who had contributed to humanity and earned deification, Mnaseas
follows those who identified some gods with personalities who invented things of
benefit to humanity (such as Zamolxis, the Getan-Thracian legislator, identified
by Mnaseas with Cronus[37]), and others with eponymous heroes unknown to
readers and hence of interest. These identifications contributed to the blurring of
the distinction between gods and men, as did the other stories presented in the
same context.

Despite the "Euhemerist" features, the content of each story was reported in its
naive form, without reservation or criticism. This is not surprising. Mnaseas was
simply following in the footsteps of his highly influential master, Eratosthenes.
That strict scientist could distinguish between fact and fiction, mythology and
scientific data, and in this spirit criticized those interpreters of Homer who had
tried to rationalize the stories of the *Iliad* and the *Odyssey*. In his own poetry,
however, Eratosthenes acted rather differently. He developed a theory of poetry
that aroused much controversy and a variety of commentaries in his and succeeding generations. Eratosthenes declared that the aim of the poet was to delight
and not to educate,[38] and he practiced what he preached.[39] For example, in his
poetic work *Erigone*, Eratosthenes presents in the most naive fashion the old
legend of the maiden Erigone. She is said to have hanged herself out of grief for
her father Icarius, an old Athenian; and Zeus, admiring her devotion, fixed her
in the heavens, along with Icarius and his cart, and her faithful dog, Maera, the
whole group making up one constellation.[40]

Eratosthenes adhered to his own rule in his work *Katasterismoi* ("Placing
among the Stars"), which is especially relevant to the Apollo-ass story. This treatise, though popular at the time, is now lost, and its reconstruction is the subject

---

(Ath. 8. 331d; and see Fraser [1972] 2: 1043 n. 212); and see fr. 5 on the development of dietary
customs from the meat-eating to the vegetarian stage, contrary to the anthropological theory of
Theophrastus (pp. 19–20 above).

36. Noted by Müller, *FHG* III. 149; see, e.g., frr. 1, 2, 40, 44, and elsewhere.

37. Fr. 23 (Photius, *Lex* s.v. Ζάμολξις).

38. Quoted by Strabo 1. 2. 3: ποιητὴν γὰρ ἔφη πάντα στοχάζεσθαι ψυχαγωγίας, οὐ διδασκα-
λίας. On the debate, see Pfeiffer (1968) 166.

39. See esp. Pfeiffer (1961) 168–70.

40. The latest edition of the remains of *Erigone* is Rosokoki (1995). The story is known mainly
from Ovid *Metamorphoses* 10. 450, Nonus *Dionysiaca* 47. 235–55, and Hyginus *Astronomia* 2. 4.

of debate.[41] However, the name of the work, the testimonia, and what is known of similar works of scholar-poets before and after Eratosthenes all indicate that this work was actually a collection of mythological legends concerning the generation of the stars, entirely free of science, despite the fact that the author also happened to be keen on astronomy. The novelty of this compilation lay in the collection and arrangement of the mythological-narrative material around the subject of the generation of the stars in a way that enabled readers to follow the text while observing the stars and in its use of a very rich vocabulary and liberal inclusion of associations of a more sophisticated and complex nature than was previously known. Eratosthenes, then, made a clear distinction between his scientific and his poetic writings. The former were intended to educate, the latter to entertain. Even if some earlier Alexandrian compilers may occasionally have taken some marvel stories, folklore, and other such material more seriously, Eratosthenes certainly did not.

THE SOURCE FOR THE STORY
OF THE THEFT OF THE ASS HEAD

Mnaseas did not invent stories but merely preserved and reworked what he found elsewhere. Scholars have already noted that the story about Apollo and the theft of the ass head is of Idumaean origin.[42] Indeed, the hero of the story, Zabidus-Zabidos, bears a typical Aramaic-Arabic-Nabataean name (Zabid) well known throughout the East in the first millenium B.C.E., when Aramaic gradually displaced the Canaanite dialects. We know that the name was widespread among the Idumaeans beginning from the middle of the Achaemenid period. The city to which the ass head is brought is Dora-Adorayim, one of the two main cities of the Idumaean eparchy (Joseph. *AJ* 13. 256). The second largest city of the eparchy, Marisa, was located in the hills of the southern Shephela, nearer the coastal plain, and was inhabited by many Phoenicians (though the Idumaeans seem to have been the dominant ethnos). Adorayim was at the heart of the Idumaean settlements on Mt. Hebron. It was, therefore, for all intents and purposes, the central Idumaean city.[43] Mnaseas explicitly calls Dora "city of the Idumaeans." The connection of Phoibos Apollo with Helios inspired the Idumaeans, at least

41. See the attempted editions of Robert (1878); Olivieri (1897); Powell (1925) nos. 58–68; and the discussions of Knaack, *RE* s.v. "Eratosthenes," cols. 377–81; Solmsen (1942) 204 ff.; Keller (1946) 18–25; Martin (1956); Keydell (1956). On the popularity of the work, see Pfeiffer (1968) 168.

42. Bickerman (1976–80) 2: 253, followed by others. Reinach (1895) 50 suggests that the story was based on an old Philistine legend (according to 1 Sam. 4–5 and the Phoenician story of Mnaseas in fr. 32). See also Willrich (1895) 52–53.

43. Further references to the place in the Hellenistic period: *PCZ* 59006; 1 Maccabees 13.20; Jubilees 38. 8; Joseph. *AJ* 13. 207, 257, 396; *BJ* 1. 63, 166.

those in the Egyptian diaspora, to identify Apollo with Qos, their national god.[44] The only aspect of the activity of Qos (apart from his aid to believers) known to us from inscriptions and ostraca is his function as the god of light (Qwsnhr or Qwsnhor),[45] and this characteristic is utilized in the story narrated by Mnaseas, with "Apollo" on his way to the Jewish Temple radiating starlight. We are also told the background to the episode, a war between the Idumaeans and the Jews (2. 112). The tension between the Idumaean population on Mt. Hebron and the Jewish settlements on Mt. Judaea had been growing ever since the return of many Jews from Babylonia in the last third of the sixth century, reaching its peak during the Hasmonaean revolt, when the Idumaeans collaborated with the Seleucid authorities, and came to an end only with the conquest of Idumaea and the forcible conversion of the Idumaeans at the hands of John Hyrcanus (112/108 B.C.E.). There is every indication, therefore, that the basic story was Idumaean, and it probably developed through an oral tradition.

Since Mnaseas was living in Egypt around the year 200 B.C.E., it has been rightly surmised that he heard the story from Idumaean settlers in Egypt.[46] Indeed, in addition to the statement, founded on an Egyptian libel (see below), that a statue of an ass was to be found in the Temple, other considerations may be advanced to support the view that the story was composed in Egypt, and not in Mt. Hebron-Idumaea. First, the old Egyptian and Oriental practice of accumulating votive offerings and statues of foreign deities to symbolize surrender was still valid and very frequent in Hellenistic Egypt, the Ptolemies boasting about such achievements just as the pharaohs used to.[47] Second, the name Apollonios was common and evidently popular among Idumaean military settlers in Egypt, replacing names composed with Qos, the name of their national deity;[48] there is, however, no evidence for the frequent use of the name Apollonios among the Idumaeans of Mt. Hebron and Marisa; nor is there any substantial evidence for a widespread cult of Apollo in the area of Idumaean settlement.[49]

---

44. See, e.g., Vriezen (1970) 330–53. On the identification in Egypt, see esp. Zucker (1937) 3–63.

45. See the inscription in Eph'al and Naveh (1996) 175. 8; cf. Porten and Yardeni (1986–89) 2: B 2. 8. l. 13 (p. 38).

46. Stern, *GLAJJ* 1: 100–101, followed by others.

47. See, e.g., the Cairo stele of year 311, ll. 17–19 (the text: Roeder [1959] 100–106; Kaplony-Heckel in Kaiser [1983] 1: 613–19), and a "reverse story" (Antiochus III being blamed for violating and taking away Egyptian gods from their temples) in the Raphia decree, ll. 18–19, 22, 28, the Egyptian practice being indicated in l. 14 (the text: Gauthier and Sottas [1925] 30–31; Thissen [1966] 19, 60, 63). Cf. Daniel 11.8

48. See the list of names in Zucker (1937); Launey (1949–50) 1: 556–58, 2: 1236–41; cf. Rappaport (1969); Fraser (1972) 1: 281, 2: 438–39.

49. There are as yet no Aramaic inscriptions or pottery sherds that testify to an identification of Qos with Apollo. On the abundant Aramaic and Greek ostraca discovered in Marisa there are hun-

As for the dating of the composition of the Idumaean story: according to the text, the event occurred during a protracted war between the Idumaeans and the Jews (para. 112). The story's origin in the Idumaean diaspora in Ptolemaic Egypt and Apollo's central role oblige us to date it to the Hellenistic period. Any time down to the Persian period, as proposed by some scholars,[50] is therefore too early. Other scholars have suggested that the story came about in the wake of the confrontations between the Jews and Idumaeans at the time of Judas Maccabaeus,[51] but it is doubtful whether Mnaseas was still alive by then.[52] Moreover, the atmosphere of the story hardly reflects conditions of that time. The story actually reflects the weak position of the frustrated Idumaeans in their struggle against the Jews, while in the time of Judas Maccabaeus they received active and aggressive support from the Seleucids, who even invaded Mt. Judaea several times from the direction of Mt. Hebron-Idumaea. Once, in the battle of Beth-Zechariah (162 B.C.E.), the Seleucid troops shattered the army of Judas Maccabaeus and nullified his previous military and territorial achievements. Nor is there any reference in the story to active third-party control of the Temple, the city of Jerusalem, or the surrounding area. Despite the legendary character of the story, one might have expected some allusion to this detail. Furthermore, there would naturally have elapsed a suitable amount of time between the invention of the story and its use by Mnaseas, especially in light of the remote mythological atmosphere of the episode. Even if Mnaseas is dated a little later, we would be hard pressed to date the origin of the story to the Hasmonaean revolt. For all these reasons, it would seem that the story was invented at some time between the consolidation of the Idumaean diaspora in Egypt in the third century B.C.E. and the religious persecutions and the Hasmonaean revolt, but at a reasonable distance in time before Mnaseas, that is, well before the end of the third century B.C.E., probably around

---

reds of names, and Qos is mentioned dozens of times, but the name of Apollo either as a theophoric component or as a direct reference to the god is absent. On the other hand, among the fifteen names appearing on weights, Apollo appears as a component in three. This is still a low rate compared with weights discovered in other places, such as Gaza. In Greek inscriptions from the Sidonian settlement of Marisa, which were discovered at the beginning of the last century, the names Apollophanes and Apollodorus appear twice, but the name bearers are Phoenicians (on the inscriptions, see Peters and Tiersch [1905] 37–72, nos. 1, 23, 24, 29). As for the image of Apollo, findings from recent excavations have produced only one terra-cotta piece upon which Apollo may be seen, playing a stringed instrument. The figure of Apollo is completely absent from coins. I am grateful to the archaeologists and epigraphists in charge of the excavations in Marisa for the information they provided me concerning the relevant archaeological find: Prof. Amos Kloner, the director of excavations; Dr. Esther Eshel and Dr. Eva Kozikova, in charge of publishing epigraphic material; and Dr. Ala Kushnir, who interpreted the inscriptions on the weights.

50. Troiani (1977) 170; Kochman (1981) 194–95.

51. Müller (1877) 270; Jacoby (1927) 281.

52. See p. 210 above and note 17.

the middle of the century, while the two peoples were struggling over territory for their subsistence, and the Jews were pushing back the Idumaeans in the area of Mt. Hebron and the southern Shefela. This struggle, protracted as it was, led to the development of a deep hatred, attested in literature of the period, and was not just a one-time event.[53]

MNASEAS'S ACCOUNT
AND ITS TRANSMISSION BY APION

Now to the reconstruction of the details in Mnaseas's account as it reached Apion. It has already been mentioned that the text was reworked and abbreviated throughout, whether to adapt to different aims or for technical reasons. The remains of Mnaseas's work are adequate for tracing the outline of the account.

The city of Dora is presented at the beginning of the story as if this is the first time it is referred to. The hero of the story is described as an Idumaean who lived in "a certain (*aliqua*) city of the Idumaeans called Dora" (*Ap.* 2. 112). We recall that Mnaseas's work comprised entries of place-names, and every entry began with an etymological and/or aetiological explanation of the origin of the name. It is unlikely that this story would have been included in an entry on another esoteric settlement than Dora, since this would have offended against the design of the work, which was to make the stories easily accessible to readers. The story would not have appeared in an entry on Jerusalem, since that city would have been too famous in the Greek world at that time to qualify for an entry. Its special status was already emphasized by Clearchus of Soli and Hecataeus of Abdera, at the end of the fourth century B.C.E., and its fame increased in the middle of the third century in the wake of the Diadochic wars and the "Syrian Wars." Also, the very content and development of the story, with the protagonist Zabidus being an Idumaean, one of the citizens of Dora who worship Apollo, and setting out from Dora, to which he then returns, indicates that the far less famous city of Dora, rather than Jerusalem, was the subject of the entry.

It appears that already Apion modified the beginning of the ass story. This was necessary in order to integrate the story into the new context. Readers had to be told where Dora was, and what its connection was to the war between the Idumaeans and the Jews mentioned in the first sentence as background to the event. Josephus, however, had no need to introduce the Idumaeans themselves. His involvement in the opening is felt in the verbal similarity between the formulation of the sentence in which Idumaean Dora is presented in the context of the story and the presentation of Dora (Dor) on the coast by Mt. Carmel in the

---

53. Kasher (1996) 407 dates the episode to the Fourth Syrian War (219–217) and the Fifth (202–200). This still seems a little too late.

context of his subsequent refutation.[54] It is also worth noting the scorn communicated in both sentences by the use of the qualifiers τινι and *aliquo* ("a certain"). Josephus may be hinting that the Idumaean city does not even exist, which indeed is something he tries to prove at the start of his refutation (para. 116).[55]

The story as it appeared in the lexicon did not need to begin by informing readers that the city of Dora was Idumaean. This had already been done at the beginning of the entry, where the foundation story would have appeared. The name Dora would have invited a story about the (Hellenic) founder who named the city after himself. It is most likely that the founder was said to be Doros, or some variation on the traditional name of the legendary Dorian eponymous ancestor. This explanation, like the other frequent etymological explanations in the lexicon, would have been the contribution of Mnaseas himself, rather than something he heard from Idumaeans in Egypt. At the same time, there is nothing to prevent the Idumaean narrator from being the one who added the etymological connection in order to prove the common origin of the Idumaeans and the Hellenes, and perhaps also to counter the tradition that developed among the Jews in the Hellenistic period that they were related to the Lacedaemonians, a branch of the Dorians.[56]

As for the body of the story, one detail possibly omitted is that Zabidus returned to his city when the night was exceptionally dark. Again, Josephus may well have omitted the name of Jerusalem, since only he of the three authors responsible for the transmission would have found the name redundant. A more significant omission is the portrayal of the statue in the Temple. Readers of the present version might gain the impression that only an ass head was on display, for this is what Zabidus the Idumaean steals and takes back to his city. The original story, however, seems to have described a complete statue of an ass, since Zabidus is said to have torn off (ἀποσῦραι) the head of the ass—that is, torn the head off the body of the ass.[57] According to the internal logic of the story, Zabidus the Idumaean could not have carried the whole statue and hastily returned with

---

54. Para. 112: *in aliqua civitate Idumaeorum quae Dora nominatur* (= ἐν πόλει τινὶ Ἰδουμαίων ἣ Δῶρα ὀνομάζεται); para. 116: τῆς μέντοι Φοινικῆς . . . Δῶρα πόλις ὀνομάζεται.

55. Josephus is not being entirely honest and fair in para. 116, where he refutes and personally attacks anti-Jewish, or purportedly anti-Jewish, authors. Josephus knew very well that Mnaseas meant the Idumaean city of Adorayim, called "Dora" by the Greeks. He mentioned it eight times in his other works, usually in the form Adōra. Josephus behaves in a similar fashion in his personal attacks in the *Jewish War* and *Vita Josephi*, as well as in *Contra Apionem* (see pp. 473–74 on his attack against Apollonius Molon). His dishonesty, however, is no greater than that of other contemporary authors (and not only rhetors).

56. 1 Maccabees 12, 7, 21; 2 Maccabees 5. 9. Cf. Josephus *Jewish Antiquities* 12. 226, 13. 167.

57. Noted by Bickerman (1976–80) 2: 253. It stands to reason that the author had in mind a statue made not of one piece but a composite, perhaps of different materials.

it to Dora without detection. And indeed Tacitus preserves a version of the story that reported the existence of a statue of a complete ass in the Temple (*Hist.* 5. 4. 2). Apion's account of the visit of Antiochus IV to the Temple, to which Mnaseas's story was attached in support, referred not to a whole ass, but only to a golden (ass) head (*Ap.* 2. 80). Hence it must be concluded that already in the reworking of the story of Mnaseas by Apion a description of the statue of an ass was missing, and only the head of an ass was mentioned.[58]

Did the original Idumaean story mention explicitly that the ass represented the Jewish god? It may well have been said, and omitted by Josephus, but it may not have been. At any rate, this would have been the original intention of the Idumaean storyteller who wished, in accordance with Oriental tradition, to describe the mutual attempts to kidnap the god of the enemy, thereby depriving the opposition of defense, and the success of the Idumaeans in this struggle, or rather the victory of the Idumaean Apollo over the Jewish god (cf. 1 Sam. 4–5).[59] However, if this was not stated explicitly, Mnaseas may have understood the statue of an ass to be a votive offering (*anathēma*) connected to the past of the Jews, just as votive offerings (including statues of asses) were set up in Greek temples in order to commemorate a particular event. Tacitus—in view of his open hostility, certainly following his sources—explicitly interpreted the nature of the ass in the Jerusalem Temple in this way.[60]

At the same time, the statement that the head was of a pack-ass (*kanthōn*)—a type of domesticated ass recognizable mainly by its height and size—and not simply an ass raises the possibility that the Idumaean storyteller (followed

---

58. "The head of a pack-ass" is mentioned in Josephus's refutation (para. 115), but this does not by itself prove that Apion referred to anything more than the head of a pack-ass. The ease with which such a mistake could happen may be illustrated by Tertullian's argument against the libel: in the same passage he deplores Tacitus for saying that "our God is an ass head", and that the Jews "venerated the likeness of a beast of this kind" (*Apol.* 16. 1–3). Neither description properly reflects Tacitus's statement (*Hist.* 5. 4. 2; see pp. 242–43 below). It seems that references to the head of an ass in *Contra Apionem* came up while Tertullian was writing. Apion, however, was not mistaken and made the change deliberately (see note 59 and p. 241 below).

59. Apion certainly understood the matter (and wished to be understood) in this way, since his version of the "visit" of Antiochus Epiphanes to the Temple is reported by Josephus as follows: *In hoc enim sacrario Apion praesumpsit edicere asini caput collocasse Iudaeos et eum colere ac dignum facere tanta religione* (*Ap.* 2. 80: "For in this temple Apion presumed to declare that the Jews had placed the head of an ass and were worshipping it and making it worthy with such great cultic behavior"). Yet Apion's version is no evidence for the formulation in Mnaseas. Apion, at a much later date and with his Egyptian background, was well aware that the Egyptians identified the Jewish god with Seth, and consequently with an ass. The interpretation of the statue may have been his own invention, just as he turned the ass into the head of an ass and cited as his authorities for the information about Epiphanes seeing the head of an ass in the Temple both Posidonius and Apollonius Molon (*Ap.* 1. 79), although both in fact referred to a statue of Moses riding an ass (see below, pp. 239–41).

60. See below, p. 242.

by Mnaseas) referred not merely to the statue of an ass but also to its burden. Indeed, in the hostile version of the Seleucid court scribes concerning the entry of Antiochus Epiphanes into the Temple, it is stated that he saw a statue of Moses riding an ass (Diod. 34/35. 1. 3). If this is the case with Mnaseas's story, however, its main motif would not be a war between the gods; but since other explanations may be offered for the mention of a pack-ass rather than an ass,[61] caution dictates as our working hypothesis that Mnaseas described the statue of an ass only, and not of a man riding an ass.

The end of the story may also be missing. A number of testimonia on entries in Mnaseas's work report or indicate ceremonies celebrated to mark events in the life of the city.[62] It might not be too far-fetched to speculate that the story of the ass head ended with a remark to the effect that the inhabitants of Dora hold an annual ceremony to mark the event, a ceremony in which, for example, the ass head is displayed in a carnival procession through the streets of the town. Enemy idols and votive offerings kept in temples were put on display in processions to mark victories or popular festivals both in the ancient East and in Hellenistic Egypt. It might further be conjectured that on the night of the carnival the inhabitants dressed as Apollo, in a wooden structure decked with lights, rather like the spectacular "costume" worn by Zabidus, the hero of the city, and that they held a procession of images of Apollo decorated with shining stars, similar to the torch-light processions so common in the Hellenistic world. The remote mythological atmosphere of the story further suggests that some mention may have been made of an ass head preserved in the temple of Apollo in Dora "up to this day," or some similar formulation. The same applies to annual victory celebrations.

Let us look again at the plausible structure of the entry on Dora in Mnaseas's work. The entry would have begun, as did others in this lexicon, with a foundation story and/or information about the legendary founder, the eponymous ancestor who lent his name to the city. The main part of the entry was the stimulating legend concerning the local god Apollo, his temple, and his involvement in the struggles of the Idumaean inhabitants with their Jewish neighbors. The story would have ended with a reference to the festival marking the event. The entry may have contained other marvelous and unusual stories.

---

61. One could argue, for example, that the "pack-ass" in the Idumaean story would have added a nuance to the insult, emphasizing that the ass worshipped by the Jews in their Temple was good only for the humble and humiliating task of carrying burdens. Josephus might have this in mind when he remarks upon the wit of Apion in referring to the animal as a pack-ass (para. 114 fin.). Other explanations are also possible. For instance, the version identifying the statue of the ass with the Jewish god is a variation of an earlier version about a statue of Moses riding an ass, whence the depiction of the animal as a "pack-ass."

62. See note 27 above.

Did Mnaseas integrate elements of his own into the original Idumaean story? There are certainly well-known Greek motifs in it. The use of a wooden contraption in order to gain entry into the Jewish Temple recalls the wooden Trojan horse. The theft of the ass head echoes the episode in which Odysseus steals the Palladion, the statue of a maiden (identified with Athena) who protected Troy—a "reversed" version of that story also appears in Mnaseas's collection.[63] These motifs, however, are so essential to the plot that they must already have been adopted by the Idumaean storyteller. If he aspired to integrate into Egyptian Greek or Hellenized society, he may have been familiar with Greek culture; alternatively, he may have derived the motifs from ancient Eastern traditions. Thus, for example, the motif of the Trojan horse is known to us from the Harris papyrus, which tells of the capture of Jaffa by Tutmosis III, using Egyptian soldiers who were hidden in two hundred baskets sent to the besieged city (probably as a gift to the gods).[64] The kidnapping of statues of gods of the enemy and their installation in friendly temples in order to deprive the enemy of their protection was, as has already been mentioned, a ploy well known in Oriental literature and alluded to in the Bible (1 Sam. 5.2).

Whatever the case may be, the story is incredible, marvelous, and at times illogical. The Jews blend into the mythological fabric of the story. The vague dating of the event allows readers to assume that it took place in the distant past, when gods still mingled among men. The Jews fall into a well-set trap by pagan-mythological conventions. The distant onlookers recognize Apollo, the Idumaean god of light, when they see lights like stars proceeding from Dora to the Jewish Temple. The stars are not set in the sky but are close to the ground, as indeed might be expected when the god in mortal form is walking among men. The Jews believe in the power of Apollo and want to neutralize him by confining him in their Temple and thereby depriving the Idumaeans of their power. It is for this reason that they are ready to go so far as to leave their Temple unguarded at the height of a war. Readers are not made privy to the cunning reason given by Zabidus that persuaded the Jews to abandon their Temple and distance themselves from the course traversed by Apollo. (Was it out of respect for Apollo or so that Apollo might not suspect his imminent capture? Neither option is satisfactory.) It is also unclear how the Idumaean managed to return to his distant city through a dense, hostile Jewish area, weighed down by the golden head of the pack-ass; but a legend should not be pressed too hard; and the narrator, being aware of it, chooses to tell only what is required for the enjoyment of the reader.

63. Fr. 28; cf. Herodotus 5. 83–86 (possibly also 6. 134); Macrobius 3. 9.
64. See the text in Pritchard (1955) 22–23.

MNASEAS AND THE JEWS

Scholars mentioning Mnaseas in passing or in more detail have usually called him anti-Semitic, a Jew hater, and the like, who is intent on conveying anti-Jewish messages.[65] A proper appreciation of Mnaseas's intentions requires drawing a clear distinction at the outset between him and the Idumaean narrator, their motives, and the perception of their respective audiences.

The Idumaean narrator, who dwelt in Egypt and invented or adapted the original story, certainly intended to portray the Jews as gullible and their religion as farcical, while vaunting the superiority of the Idumaeans. As many scholars since the nineteenth century, and possibly even earlier, have noted, the libel about the existence of a statue of an ass in the Jerusalem Temple originated in Egyptian culture, where the god of evil, Seth (Typhon to the Greeks), was portrayed as an ass, among other things. The god of the Jews, who in Jewish stories was the bane of the Egyptians, was identified by the Egyptians with Seth; hence the description of the god of the Jews as an ass.[66] The Idumaean narrator, a permanent resident in Egypt (perhaps descended from Idumaeans who had immigrated already in the Persian period), wove around the basic libel that he heard from Egyptian natives a story inspired by popular motifs from Greek literature and/or Oriental folklore. The narrator and his Idumaean audience would have found relief in the story for their frustrations resulting from the increasing pressure of the expanding Jewish settlers on their brethren in Mt. Hebron, the Idumaeans who had arrived there during the Jewish Babylonian exile. It is this pressure that presumably prompted the Idumaean emigration to Egypt.

As for Mnaseas, did he have anti-Jewish intentions? In light of all the above concerning the literary circle in which Mnaseas moved and the structure, features, and aims of the collection in which he included the story, it seems at the outset that calling Mnaseas anti-Semitic would be somewhat of an exaggeration. There is no particular reason to suppose that the story was adduced by Mnaseas in order to express any personal position or that Mnaseas consciously intended to convey through the medium of the story anti-Jewish messages. Contemporary circumstances surrounding the relations between Jews and Greeks in Alexandria fail to support such a view.[67] He may well have wished only to delight readers

---

65. Stählin (1905) 14–15; Radin (1915) 168; Heinemann, *RE* s.v. "Antisemitismus," suppl. 5, col. 28; Guttmann (1929); de Liagre Böhl (1953) 123–25; Tcherikover (1961) 365; Efron (1962) 13–14 (rather carefully); Fraser (1972) 1: 525; Stern (1976) 1119; Bickerman (1976–80) 2: 253–54; Conzelmann (1981) 45–46; Gager (1983) 40–41; Bickerman (1988) 225–31; Gabba (1989) 643–44; Kasher (1996) 406–7; Bar-Kochva (1996d) 311; van Henten and Abush (1996) 286–87; Schäfer (1997a) 55–56.

66. See below, pp. 244–45.

67. See note 100 below.

with a stimulating and intriguing story that he had heard, a story—as we shall see—full of entertaining mythological associations, just like many other stories in his work. He had come across a fantastic, unreal story about a little-known city in Idumaea, and precisely because of this, he included it in his lexicon. An outstanding pupil of Eratosthenes is hardly likely to have treated such an unrealistic and internally inconsistent story seriously, or any differently from other such stories that he collected. Mnaseas would clearly have been able to distinguish between scientific criticism and entertainment. In this he would not only have been following in the footsteps of Eratosthenes and previous writers in the Library of Alexandria, but would also have been part of a longer tradition most familiar to us from Herodotus, who preserved in his work many stories that he did not consider to be true, but to which he added no reservations whatsoever. The collection of mythological material for anthologies without critical notes is not unknown to scholars, and the same may be said about modern anthologies of legends concerning geographical sites.

Furthermore, Mnaseas would have known some basic facts about the Jews. Greeks of his caliber knew already by the beginning of the Hellenistic period that the Jews believed in only one god—certainly not Apollo—and that they refrained both from making graven images of their divinity and from idol worship. An accessible and detailed account of the Jews was available—certainly to anyone working in the Library in Alexandria—in the Egyptian ethnography of Hecataeus of Abdera, which, judging from its impact on Megasthenes, was influential even in the Seleucid kingdom, and elsewhere far beyond the borders of Egypt.[68] Nor should it be forgotten that that work referred to the most prominent features of the Jewish community in Alexandria where Mnaseas studied and published his books.

Would Mnaseas, while not believing the story, still have utilized it in order to discredit the Jews? Before turning him into an "anti-Semite," it might be worth considering how Mnaseas and contemporary Greeks regarded the ass, the animal at the center of the story.[69] It is similarly worth considering the attitude of Mnaseas and contemporary Greeks toward the deception itself, and toward the naivety of the Jews, in light of typological parallels from Greek literature and the lexicon of Mnaseas.

---

68. See above, pp. 141–142, 159–63.

69. Feldman (1993) 145–46, 499–501; (1996b) 201–3, touching in a general fashion on the ass libel, mentions some positive expressions and references to the ass in Greek Hellenistic and Roman literature and concludes: "No one will doubt that Apion was malicious in his intent, but that does not mean that he was necessarily read in that light by others" ([1996b] 235). As for Mnaseas, Feldman regards his story as "an attempt to mock Jewish credulity" ([1993 170–71). It is to Feldman's great credit that he has drawn attention to the fact that the image of the ass in the Greek and Roman world was often positive. My conclusions, however, differ (except in connection with Apion himself).

A. The Attitude toward the Ass

The ass is treated differently from culture to culture, place to place, and period to period. Agricultural societies, especially those in hilly areas, often valued the ass for its usefulness and advantages over the horse, including the ass's stamina, its ability to climb and carry loads, its cheap maintenance, and its mild temperament, together with its patience, persistence, and reasonably good health. In other societies, especially those on plains, the horse was obviously more useful and valuable than the ass, and the latter was often mocked, by both the nobility and the common people, because of its sluggish movement and reactions.[70] Consequently, while some societies attributed loyalty, diligence, shrewdness, and even holiness and divination to the ass, others attributed to it negative, sometimes contradictory, characteristics: servility and stupidity on the one hand, and pollution, devilry, and wickedness on the other.[71] Individual authors or compilators (such as Homer or Aesop) are often ambiguous in their attitudes toward the ass, as are entire cultures (such as the Jews of the Hellenistic-Roman period). The popular image of the ass today as a symbol of stupidity (zoologists beg to differ) is irrelevant to the issue at hand, as is the lowly image of the ass in the *Lucius or Ass* attributed to Lucian and in the *Metamorphoses* of Apuleius, a story that begins—hardly coincidentally—in Thessaly, a flat region renowned for its horses. More to the point is the Greek and pre-Greek literary and mythological heritage, and other popular traditions that were well known to Mnaseas and his Greek contemporaries.

Over half a century ago, Alexander H. Krappe, the extraordinary scholar of Western folklore, published an article entitled "Apollo the Ass," in which he adduced a great deal of material showing how the ass was favorably viewed, and even worshipped, in the Aegean world, Anatolia, and the Balkans.[72] Some

---

70. All this has been well explained by the ancients themselves; see, e.g., Plutarch, who praises the hare as the antithesis of the ass, although having the appearance of a "reduced ass" (*Quaest. conv.* 670E).

71. The latter qualities were presumably attributed to the ass not only under the influence of mythological and religious traditions, with their gradually developing motifs, but also with logical and associative connections (as in Egypt: Seth rides an ass; Seth is the source of all evil; Seth is identified with the ass; the ass then symbolizes evil). The ancients would have regarded the ass as a symbol of evil and cruelty because their daily proximity to the animal exposed them to the various types of extreme violence perpetrated by asses among themselves, such as the killing by dominant males of newborn asses. The diabolical image of the ass would no doubt have been intensified by observing the great sexual appetite of the male ass, and the attraction that female asses exerted over men inclined to bestiality.

72. Krappe (1948). The article is listed in the bibliography for Mnaseas's account of the Jews in Stern, *GLAJJ* 1: 90, although it does not mention Mnaseas or the story about Zabidos, Apollo, and

pertinent conclusions may be drawn from the sources cited by Krappe, and from other sources and considerations that escaped his attention:

1. The ass was described as, among other things, an animal sacrificed to Apollo. That is to say, the ass was considered to be sacred to Apollo. Sources for this attribute of the ass include Pindar, Callimachus and Sammias of Rhodes.[73] Callimachus greatly influenced Eratosthenes; and Sammias was a contemporary of Mnaseas and a native of the island off Patara, the birthplace of Mnaseas.

2. The ass was one of various animals (e.g., wolf, swan, crow) that often represented Apollo.[74] Krappe reaches this conclusion through an examination of mythological links and anthropological models, among other factors. The epithet *Killaios*, used for Apollo especially in Mysia, Troas, and Lesbos (Strabo 13. 1. 62–63), and the statement of the second-century lexicographer Pollux of Naucratis that the word *killos* in the Dorian dialect means "ass," offer more direct evidence of this association.[75] The latter explanation is supported by the testimony of the fifth-century Alexandrian lexicographer Hesychius.[76] Pollux was not one of Hesychius's sources, as both the entry for *killos* and Hesychius's introduction to his lexicon make clear.

3. Strabo (13. 1. 62) mentions the temple of Apollo Killaios in Mysia. As this name means "Apollo the ass-like," the main statue displayed in the temple would have been that of Apollo in the form of an ass.

4. The ass is associated variously with certain gods, satyrs, and daemons in Asia Minor (mainly Phrygia), and with some of the same in Greece, Crete, and Thrace. The ass is consecrated and/or sacrificed to these figures and/or used as a means of transport by them. Some of these figures are even occasionally described as an ass (e.g., Dionysus, Midas, Marsyas, Silanus, and Priapus, who was also identified, at least in Lampsacus, with Apollo).[77] A fragment from the *Katasterismoi* of Eratosthenes reports that some of the stars that Dionysus fixed in the sky "are called asses." Another

---

the ass. Stern does not, however, refer to the article or its findings in his introduction or in his notes to Mnaseas's story of the theft of the ass head. His reticence is understandable. The same may be said of Goodman in Schürer et al. (1986) 598.

73. Pindar *Pythian* 10. 32–35; Callimachus frr. 187, 188 (ed. Schneller); Sammias in Antoninus Liberalis *Metamorphoses* 20 (ed. Martin); see Krappe (1948) 223–24.

74. See Krappe (1948) 223–24.

75. Pollux 7. 50: Κίλλον γὰρ τὸν ὄνον οἱ Δωριεῖς καὶ Κιλλακτῆρα τὸν ὀνήλατην λέγουσιν ("For the Dorians call the ass *killos,* and the mule driver *killos*-driver").

76. Hesychius, s.v. Κίλλαι· ἢ ἀστράγαλοι ἢ ὄνοι ("Killai: either knucklebones or asses") and s.v. Κίλλος· ὄνος καὶ τέττιξ πρωινὸς ὑπὸ Κυπρίων ("Killos: [So are called] ass and dawn cicada by the Cypriots").

77. Krappe (1948) 225–32, and references there.

fragment from the same work relates that the asses ridden by Dionysus, Hephaestus, and the satyrs alarmed the Giants with their braying, thus winning the day for the gods in their celebrated mythological battle with the Giants. In a gesture of gratitude, the gods honored the asses by setting them in the heavens as the constellation of Cancer.[78] Another version of the story about the fixing of an ass in the sky, also related by Eratosthenes, was preserved by the second-century Latin mythographer Hyginus (or possibly pseudo-Hyginus), who wrote a book on astronomy.[79] In this version, Priapus killed the ass of Dionysus in a struggle that erupted between Priapus and Dionysus after a verbal altercation over whose organ was longer. Dionysus fixed the ass in the sky as one of the stars in the same constellation of Cancer.[80] It is not surprising that Tertullian (second–third century B.C.E.) mentions, as something well known and obvious, an ass cult observed by contemporary pagans (*Apol.* 16. 5).

5. Pausanias, a native of Asia Minor like Mnaseas, reports (10. 18. 4) that the inhabitants of Ambracia (in northwest Greece) erected a bronze statue of an ass in the temple of Apollo at Delphi in gratitude to the ass whose braying gave warning and saved them from a night raid by their Molossian neighbors.[81] This account appears in Pausanias's survey of prominent artifacts in the temple at Delphi and is not to be doubted. Pausanias's work, which was intended to serve as a travel guide, among other things, was based mainly on autopsy and placed particular emphasis on the description and mention of artistic items.[82] Pausanias spent an especially long time on his visit or visits to the temple at Delphi and recorded in great detail what he saw there. There is no reason to suspect him of fabricating a statue that never existed or was never situated in the most sacred and most visited temple in the Greek world. Furthermore, Pausanias is, as usual, precise in his description of the location of the statue: it is displayed next to the statue of Apollo, which was erected by the inhabitants of Lindos; and the statue of Apollo is next to one of the statues of Athena, a gift of the Achaeans; and this is next to the statue of a horse taken as booty in the Persian Wars, and so on and so forth.

---

78. *Katasterismoi* 11, pp. 15, 16 Olivieri (= pp. 90, 92 Robert).

79. That he derived most of his information from Eratosthenes is shown by Robert (1878) 1–34, 220–36; Martin (1956) 58 ff.; Fraser (1972) 2: 1021–22; see also Fraser for further references. The latest edition is Viré (1992).

80. *Astronomia* 2. 23 (ed. Viré); and cf. Robert's synoptic edition of *Katasterismoi*, pp. 88–91. More references on the connection between Priapus and an ass in Krappe (1948) 225.

81. This report has been cited by Lewy (1960) 121 n. 36 and others as a parallel to the explanation of Tacitus for the presence of a votive offering in the form of an ass in the Jerusalem Temple.

82. On the autopsy of Pausanias, see Frazer (1900) 1: LXVI–XCVI; Habicht (1985) 165–75; Arafat (1996) 16–21.

The peculiarly positive attitude toward the ass, apparent from the information above, would have been only natural and understandable on the part of Greeks in most regions of mainland Greece and in the hilly lands of Asia Minor. In these lands, the ass was even more vital than vehicles are for us today. The urban (and even modern rural) reader is generally not aware of the great range of activities performed by this animal. It is therefore worth emphasizing that the ass not only conveyed goods of all kinds and served as transport for the household but also drew and transported water, plowed the fields, operated the mill and the olive press, cleared land of thorns and weeds, provided dung, which was used for fertilizer, building, and heating, and the she-ass supplied milk that has special qualities, and so on. People came to depend on the ass, developed a sense of obligation toward it, and subsequently regarded it as sacred, and even as a manifestation of the good and beneficial god.

This was the case, perhaps even more so, in the native land of Mnaseas. Lycia is a belt of precipitous mountains (the western Taurus range) that sweep steeply down toward the sea, leaving a narrow, heavily indented coastal plain, which in many places is almost impassable. Settlement in such a region would have been impossible without the aid of the ass. Traditions that portrayed Apollo in the form of an ass are known to have been prevalent in the regions neighboring Lycia (mainly Mysia and Phrygia). Such traditions are not (as yet) known about Lycia and its vicinity, but the Lycians were the quickest and most ardent adapters of Greek tradition in Asia Minor. They were influenced early on by the Doric alphabet and in the Hellenistic period abandoned their own language in favor of the Doric dialect. The Greek settlers in Lycia would probably have adopted the Doric epithet *Killaios* ("pertaining to an ass," "ass-like") affixed to Apollo in western Asia Minor. Whatever the case may be, Mnaseas would certainly have been familiar with the traditions about Apollo in Asia Minor. Mnaseas was after all a native of Patara, which had a rival claim to Delos as the birthplace of Apollo and boasted an oracle to that god.

The choice of Apollo, the embodiment of physical beauty and harmony, to represent the deification of the ass, a symbol of ugliness, is not all that surprising. Apollo, unlike most of the gods in polytheistic religions, is portrayed in literature and the plastic arts as a multifaceted character full of contradictions. Even his name illustrates the point: Ἀπόλλων means "destroyer," but he is also a healer, known not coincidentally as the father of Asclepius. Kind and gentle characteristics and deeds are frequently attributed to him, and he is a patron of fine arts. Yet his bow lets loose evils of all sorts, such as the plague at Troy in answer to the prayer of his priest (on many another occasion his barbs are arbitrary and without purpose), and he can indulge in unrestrained brutality, occasionally displaying undisguised glee. Thus in an outburst of fury, Apollo flayed the skin off the living body of the satyr Marsyas, who had dared to compete with him in flute playing (a gentle art in itself; Diod. 3. 58. 2–5 et al.); in the guise of an attractive youth he joyfully kills a lizard and displays its corpse for all to see by pinning it to a log.[83] Other adventures and acts of heroism that illustrate Apollo's diverse attributes are too numerous to mention.

As has been remarked above, Mnaseas's lexicon was full of allusions to mythological traditions, enriching the associative imaginations of readers and thus increasing their enjoyment. Setting Apollo, the god of Zabidus and the Idumaeans, against the ass would conjure up interesting mythological associations, such as the conflict between Priapus and the ass, the victory of Priapus, and the setting of the ass as a star in the firmament. The first part of the Mnasean story was connected to a war between a god and an ass, and readers would recall that in other places Priapus was identified with Apollo. Here, then, is a struggle between Apollo himself and an ass. Likewise, Marsyas, who competed against Apollo and was killed by him, was described as an ass, among other things; and just as Priapus cut off the head of the ass, so too the Idumaean Apollo tore off the head of the ass in the Temple. Readers would have recalled the story of Priapus and the ass yet again when they reached the account of the strange device intended to represent Apollo, a group of stars shining in the dark making its way from Dora to the Jewish Temple; the ass, after its defeat at the hands of Priapus, was set as a star in the sky by its owner, Dionysus. Establishing asses as stars in the heavens out of gratitude also appeared in traditions about Dionysus, and in the legend about the war between the gods and the Giants. Intelligent readers would have enjoyed the notion that the Temple ass was stolen by walking stars that were none other than fellow asses set in the heavens. Moreover, the stars over the head of the wooden construction that seemed to the Jews to represent Apollo would have reminded readers of stories about mythological heroes such as Heracles who were placed in the heavens with stars over their heads, as portrayed more than once, for instance, in Eratosthenes' *Katasterismoi*.[84]

Imaginative association could suggest even more convoluted combinations (as is the way of mythological stories), such as the idea that Zabidus had gone to fetch (or to bring back) the image of Apollo from the Jerusalem Temple, disguised as Apollo in another form; that Apollo, the multifaceted god, who exerted himself in the defense of Troy, appeared in Judaea as "the wooden horse," the bane of the Trojans; or that Apollo, the traditional protector of sacred places, tricks his way into a temple and steals from it; and so on and so forth. Some Greeks from the

---

83. Praxiteles of Athens, the fourth-century B.C.E. sculptor of the Cnidus Aphrodite, produced a statue of this scene (copies in the Vatican and the Louvre); photograph in Lippold (1950) pl. 84, no. 3, and in many other scientific and popular publications.

84. ἔχει δ' ἀστέρας ἐπὶ τῆς κεφαλῆς λαμπρούς; see, e.g., chapters 3, 4, 8 (ed. Olivieri, pp. 4, 5, 11 = ed. Robert, pp. 62, 64, 80), and elsewhere.

regions of Asia Minor may even have understood the point of the story as a covert portrayal of a war between two asses. Educated Greeks, steeped in mythology and mythological thought from childhood, would have made such connections with ease, much more so than modern scholars of mythology, who frequently give their imaginations free rein in their pursuit of connections between characters, places, and stories. Greek readers were also acquainted with far more mythological and folkloristic material than what is available to modern scholars. Mnaseas himself made such wild connections, especially in the many genealogies and etymologies that have survived in the testimonia.

B. The Portrayal of the Trick and Other Considerations

Turning now in the story from the role of the ass to that of Zabidus: would Mnaseas, and would his Hellenistic readership, upon hearing the Idumaean story, have been likely to interpret the trickery of Zabidus over the Jews as evidence of Jewish inferiority and stupidity? The tale of trickery was not necessarily intended to mock the Jews, just as the tale of the wooden horse, in all of its versions in antiquity, was never intended to make fun of the Trojans or belittle them, but rather to celebrate the exceptional cunning of Odysseus, particularly emphasized in the *Iliad* and *Odyssey*. In the semimythological atmosphere where gods mingle with mortals, the trick played by Zabidus could have been understood in the same way as the stratagem that led to the fall of Troy, namely, as a successful ploy of one side and an unfortunate lapse of the other. A striking parallel to the cunning use of a divine disguise is to be found in an anecdote told by Herodotus (1. 60): when Pisistratus returned to Athens, a tall and comely woman arrived in a chariot, presented herself as the goddess Athena, and ordered the Athenians to receive Pisistratus back into their midst. Did Herodotus intend to pour scorn on the Athenians and present them as gullible? In the same passage Herodotus declares explicitly that the deed was despicable but effective against the Athenians, the wisest of the Greeks, the people who were always superior to the "barbarians" in wisdom.[85]

It is also worth considering other fictional stories about Oriental peoples that have survived from Mnaseas's work. Two examples feature the Phoenicians, a people the Greeks admired for their skills, and who enjoyed a respectable position in Hellenic genealogical tradition. The stories focus on Atargatis (in Aramaic, the name is a combination of 'Ashtoreth and 'Anath), the all-powerful goddess of fertility throughout the northwestern Semitic region. One story portrays Atargatis as a hard queen who forbade her subjects from eating fish because of

---

85. It has already been suggested that Mnaseas's story was intended to contest the notion, widespread in the Greek world at the beginning of the Hellenistic period, that the Jews were a wise people (i.e., a nation of philosophers); see Radin (1915) 168.

her own appetite for fish. For this reason she was brought votive offerings of silver and gold fish, while her priests daily brought her gifts of live fish in festive attire, fish that were finally boiled and eaten by the priests themselves (Ath. 8. 346e). The story is no more than an embellishment of the aetiological explanation for the prohibition against the eating of fish in the cult of Atargatis, a prohibition well known to the Greeks.[86] Did Mnaseas report it with the intention of mocking the beliefs of the Phoenicians, whose priests also exploit their naivety and stupidity?

Mnaseas continues with another story:

> Atargatis, as Xanthos the Lydian says, was captured by Mopsos the Lydian and submerged with her son, Ichthys (Fish), in the lake at Ascalon,[87] on account of [her] hybris, and was devoured by the fish.

Mnaseas states that he took the story from Xanthos of Lydia, a fifth-century B.C.E. author who was also a source for Herodotus. The story was probably found in Xanthos's main work, *Lydiaca,* which contained most imaginative mythological stories. The connection between Atargatis and fish stems from her role as the goddess of fertility: the fish was a symbol of fertility in the Orient (and in the Bible as well). Indeed, in the fragment the son of Atargatis is called Ichthys (Fish), and Greek sources (following Oriental sources) describe the goddess herself as having the head of a woman and the body of a fish.[88] What does the story tell us? This same fish-tailed goddess so adulated by the Phoenicians as the goddess of fertility, aquatic mother to a son called "Fish," was thrown by Mopsos the Lydian into the lake at Ascalon, where she was devoured by fish. The story does not express fertility and life, as one would expect from symbols of fertility and reproduction, but rather the opposite: destruction and death coming to the symbols of fertility themselves, in ways and places they would least expect.[89] Would anyone seriously wish to claim that Mnaseas adduced the story in order

---

86. See *Syll.*³ III. 997, and Diodorus 2. 4. 3.

87. On the lake, "broad and deep and full of fish" near Ascalon, see Diodorus 2. 4. 2. Since the source for the testimonium of Mnaseas is Xanthus of Lydia, the mistake seems to have been widespread already in the fifth century B.C.E., but its origin cannot be satisfactorily explained. Cumont (1929) 100 speculates that a pool in the temple of Atargatis is intended; but this is not what the text states. The error may have originated in an unsuccessful attempt to interpret the name of the place (or the harbor) "Maiumas of Ashkelon." At the same time, this name is mentioned only in Christian sources, and we do not know when the Maiumas festivals were introduced (if they were indeed the origin for the name of the site).

88. See, e.g., the myth of Derceto in Ascalon, in Diodorus 2. 4. 3. Derceto was identified with Atargatis (Strabo 16. 4. 27, citing Ctesias; cf. Pliny *HN* 5. 81). The name is based on a phonetic corruption that became rooted in Ascalon alongside the name Atargatis. On the Derceto cult, see van Berg (1972) 13–36.

89. A combination of the two stories reveals, among other things, the inclusion of well-known ironic-macabre statements or even desires of sailors and fishermen utilized in the formation of

to mock the beliefs and cults of the Phoenicians and present the Phoenicians as fools? The Greeks used to accuse the Phoenicians of cruelty, dishonesty, and greed, but they never doubted the Phoenicians' cunning and alertness and even praised their varied skills. Negative moral stereotypes were also foisted on the Egyptians despite the Greek appreciation of them as among the wisest of races.[90] The testimonia and fragments of Mnaseas and his contemporaries include a number of stories with a mythological or semimythological background, which modern readers might regard as disrespectful toward the gods or their worshippers, including the Greeks themselves.

Despite everything said above, did Mnaseas report the story of the ass with hostile intent in order to mock the Jews, having been influenced by the Egyptians' negative attitude toward the ass and its identification with Seth-Typhon? We would need to accept that Mnaseas was so steeped in Egyptian culture that he could forget or overlook the many Greek-Anatolian associations of the story. This would hardly be expected of a Greek author of that generation working in the Library of Alexandria (possibly just for a limited period), particularly when addressing Greek readers throughout the Aegean world. Notably, in the passages surviving from Mnaseas there is only one reference to Egyptian religion and mythology, and there is nothing in it to indicate any profound familiarity with either;[91] indeed there Mnaseas links Epaphus—namely, Apis (Hdt. 3. 27), known in fifth-century Greek literature as the son of Zeus and Io—with Dionysus and Osiris, the best-known figure in the Egyptian pantheon and long identified with Dionysus (Hdt. 2. 144), and likewise with Serapis, a Greek-Egyptian hybrid divinity, who was the patron god of Alexandria and the dynastic god of the Ptolemies. All this is in accordance with Mnaseas's tendency to invent genealogical connections and etymologies or collect them from any source available.

At this juncture it is worth mentioning the generally accepted notion that authors of the Alexandria library lived in cultural-literary seclusion, hardly touched by the local languages and untainted by the Egyptian heritage, as happened often in history to elites of colonial societies. Accordingly, Greek tradition and literature alone formed the cultural background of these authors and shaped their ideas and values. This seemingly lofty approach may have been adopted mainly out of their determination to devote their time and energy to the preservation of the Greek heritage in the exclusive, inviting environment of the Museum, and possibly also because of a certain disdain on their part

---

the story (e.g., fish eaters desire, or have a tendency, to be eaten by fish), and the embodiment of opposites—here in the actions and fate of the goddess—as so often happens in pagan religion.

90. On Greek and Roman stereotypes of Phoenicians and Egyptians, see Berthelot (1999) 185–90; Isaac (2004) 324–35, 352–70.

91. See fr. 37 (Plut. De Is. et. Os. 365F).

toward the basic manners and habits of the native population. This is just one aspect of the comprehensive "Ivory Tower" conception of quite a few prominent historians, who describe a strict social separation of the ethnic communities in Alexandria, and the political, religious, and cultural seclusion of the Greeks from the native population.[92] This disassociation from the natives' life and heritage commenced sometime around 300 B.C.E., in the second half of Ptolemy I Soter's reign.[93] Hecataeus's *Aegyptiaca,* composed sometime between 305 and 302, is a striking example of the initial positive perception and handling of the Egyptian heritage, which can be distinguished already in the first steps of Alexander in the land of the Nile.

This sweeping conception has been challenged in the last two decades by a number of classical philologists who have argued persuasively for broad acquaintance with Egyptian myths, literature, and practices reflected in the poems of some Greek Alexandrian authors[94]—although usually in a veiled form.[95] It has also been pointed out that Ptolemaic festivals and parades were heavily influenced by the old pharaonic traditions, and this applies as well to other Ptolemaic practices and arrangements.[96] The valid evidence, though, pertains only to the times of Ptolemy II Philadelphus (283–246 B.C.E.; see the poems of Theocritus, Callimachus, and Apollonius Rhodius on the new festivals and other practices and institutions). The Ptolemaic scholars and poets at this stage had an agenda motivated by the obvious necessities and policies of their royal patron. The Greek-Egyptian ceremonies and celebrations were initiated at this point, and, as is customary with such public events, they were there to stay. Most of the other new arrangements are no more instructive with regard to the "Ivory Tower" conception than is the apparent Hellenistic influence in Judaea for the assessment of the extent of the seclusion of devout Jews in the age of the Mishnah and Talmud. Later

---

92. See, e.g., Fraser (1972) 1: 189 ff., 2: 784; and with regard to Callimachus, e.g., Green's extensive book on the Hellenistic period, where he states: "The attacks [of Callimachus; B. B.] on popular or accessible literary forms tended to be not just elitist, but also xenophobic. At the end of Hymn 2 Callimachus makes Apollo tell Envy (who has been supporting poetic prolixity): 'The Assyrian river (i.e. the Euphrates) has a broad stream, but carries down much dirt and refuse on its waters'. Polyglot, cosmopolitan, above all Oriental influences are to be deprecated ... stick to the pure unsullied spring of the Greek Muses" ([1990] 172).

93. On the change see Murray (1970) 142; Bing (1988) 134–35.

94. The latest contribution to this subject is the stimulating monograph of Stephens (2003) 20–237, which includes many references to the contributions of her predecessors (esp. p. 18 n. 47). Although not every piece of evidence is valid (e.g., pp. 99–100, 107, 242–44), the conclusion is certainly acceptable with regard to the times of Ptolemy II. Notably, the editor of the remains of Callimachus (Pfeiffer [1949-53]) rejected the "Ivory Tower" conception long ago; see Pfeiffer (1968) 108.

95. To the explicit references mentioned by Stephens (2003) 8–10 and elsewhere, one may add the information that Callimachus wrote on the legend of Isis and Osiris (Pfeiffer [1949-53] fr. 811).

96. See Stephens (2003) 13–16, 245–47.

material gives the impression that the policy of openness introduced by Ptolemy II was reversed sometime after his death in 246, and the Greeks of Alexandria (and especially of the Museum) gradually retreated to seclusion and alienation from their Egyptian neighbors.[97] This trend would have gained momentum (if it did not begin) with the long revolt of the autochthonous population after the battle of Raphia (217 B.C.E.), a revolt that lasted about thirty years. However, in view of the uncertainty about the time of the turning point, the pace and extent of the changes, and the precise dating of Mnaseas's literary activity, it would be somewhat rash to determine that Mnaseas was entirely ignorant of the Egyptian religious heritage.

The development of Greek knowledge about Typhon and Typhon-Seth is relevant to one aspect of this inquiry. Typhon himself appeared from the very beginnings of Greek literature as the cause of lethal storms who was overcome by Zeus after a protracted struggle and was described as an enormous monster in the shape of a man, or an animal, with flaming eyes and a mouth spouting lava, with a hundred dragon heads and wings. This image of Typhon prevailed in the Hellenistic and Roman age as well (e.g., pseudo-Apollod. *Bibl.* 1. 6. 3). Typhon was already identified with Seth in Herodotus (2. 144, 156) because of Seth's destructive nature and his struggle with Osiris. However, the link between Typhon-Seth and the ass does not appear in what we now have of Greek literature before the end of the first century C.E., not even in Hecataeus of Abdera, who describes the adventures of Typhon-Seth in great detail, dwelling on his struggles with Osiris and how he is avenged by Isis (Diod. 1. 1. 17–27. 6).[98] The similarity of Typhon-Seth to an ass is first mentioned in Plutarch (*De Is. et Os.* 362F), some three centuries

97. Without attempting here to present the relevant material, which is well known to scholars (but which can be ambiguous and the bulk of which is still disputable), I would just note that there is no trace of Egyptian influence in Eratosthenes' extant writings, even where it might be expected. Thus he makes no attempt in his *Katasterismoi* to connect the sign of Taurus with the bull Apis, although Apis was well known to Greek literati after Herodotus, and chose instead to explain the sign's origin only according to Greek tradition (see *Katasterismoi* 14: Oliveri [1897] 18–19; cf. Robert [1878] 106–7).

98. Callimachus's poem on Isis and Osiris (see note 95 above) certainly made no mention of Typhon's external appearance as an ass or the like. The *testimonium* on the poem came from the fifteenth-century John Tortellius, first head of the Vatican Library, and is quite complicated. Tortellius, referring to the story of Isis and Osiris summarized in the commentary on the *Aeneid* by the fourth-century C.E. grammarian Servius (6.154), appears to have had access to the later and fuller version of that commentary, which is no longer extant. Tortellius's remarks, based on the fuller commentary, indicate that the story in Servius derives from Seneca, who took it from Callimachus. The story that appears in full in the extant version of Servius is detailed yet makes no mention of Typhon's external form. There is no reason to think that it was mentioned in the extended version of Servius or in the original poem by Callimachus. It would have been very unusual to miss such a piquant piece of information.

after Mnaseas, when Egyptian culture had already made a considerable impact on the Greek and Roman world. This is no surprise, since for Greeks it would have been difficult to imagine a god identified with the colossal and frightening Typhon as such an ordinary and peaceful animal as the ass. Moreover, because of the great variety in the depiction of Seth in Egyptian iconography, the identification of the animal representation of Seth with the ass was not necessarily obvious to a Greek of Asia Minor,[99] let alone the negative connotations associated with it. The same holds for the Egyptian identification of the God of the Jews with an ass. None of these aspects could be counted among the fundamental elements of Egyptian culture divulged to foreigners who came into contact with it. Beliefs, legends, and images of similar weight in Jewish, Christian, and Islamic cultures are known to only a few members of the other cultures, even if they live in neighboring ghettos or on the same street. It should be stressed that the relations in that generation between Jews and Greeks in Alexandria were not the sort to motivate the scholars of Alexandria to hunt down Egyptian anti-Jewish traditions, let alone adopt them.[100] Whatever the case may be, even were we to suppose that Mnaseas was aware of the image of the ass in Egyptian tradition

99. The common figure of Seth familiar from Egyptian texts and iconography is zoologically unclassifiable. Furthermore, in the second millenium B.C.E., Seth was often variously described as a pig, an antelope, a hippopotamus, a goat, a crocodile, a snake, and even a fish, as well as an ass. Seth was also identified with and depicted in the form of other gods, such as Toth and Ammon, and even his rivals, Epophis and Horus, or Semitic gods such as Baal. Seth in the form of an ass was indeed widespread in the first millenium B.C.E., but the early iconography of Seth was still to be seen in temples and inscriptions. If Greeks had to fall back on writing the names of even central Hellenic gods (apart from Athena) in order to identify them, even on monumental projects (e.g., above the reliefs of the great altar in Pergamum), there is no reason to suppose that they were well versed in the subtle variations in form of the Egyptian gods and their consorts. On the various forms of Seth and his identification with other gods, see te Velde (1977) 7–26, 140; and see the popular summary in Wilkinson (2003) 193–98.

100. To avoid misunderstandings, it should be pointed out that there is no longer any question about the unreliability of the story in 3 Maccabees about the failed attempt of Ptolemy IV Philopator to enter the Holy of Holies in the Jerusalem Temple, and his subsequent attempt to avenge himself upon the Jews in Egypt by herding them into a hippodrome to be trampled by elephants. 3 Maccabees was written much later than the time of Ptolemy IV, and the book artfully makes use of events of later periods (such as the attempt of Heliodorus to enter the Jerusalem Temple in the reign of Seleucus IV, together with the persecution of Egyptian Jews, the elephant affair, and the festival instigated to commemorate the event, all reflecting developments in the time of Ptolemy VIII Physcon). The details of the story are also touched up and exaggerated (under the influence of 2 Maccabees and the book of Esther). The few attempts to prove the historical reliability of the stories about Ptolemy IV have not been successful. They rest upon a shaky familiarity with the history of the Ptolemaic kingdom and the trilateral Greek-Egyptian-Jewish relations. A sober and exhaustive summary of the research is found in Goodman in Schürer et al. 3: 537–42, and see there a detailed bibliography. See also Huss (2001) 449–50; Johnson (2004) 129–41.

and its ramifications, there would be no reason to assume that he would have preferred the Egyptian representations to the Greek concepts he had grown up with, especially as he and his Alexandrian contemporaries were alienated from the Egyptians and their cultural heritage.

. . .

The question of Mnaseas's attitude toward the Jews needs to be considered with reference to Greek culture, especially that of Asia Minor, and in terms of contemporary Greek concepts, not those of later generations. Several factors speak for themselves: the positive and grateful regard for the ass both in the mountainous regions of Asia Minor, where Mnaseas came from, and in the writings of Callimachus and Eratosthenes, Mnaseas's guide and mentor; the identification of the ass with Apollo, in particular the cult of "Apollo the ass-like" in the countries near Lycia, Mnaseas's native land; and the presence of statues of asses in Greek temples, especially the main statue in the temple of Apollo in Mysia, and as a votive offering in the Panhellenic temple of Apollo at Delphi. To these should be added the genre and character of Mnaseas's lexicon; the nature of other folkloristic stories in the same lexicon; the adaptation into the story of motifs known to be unbiased from Greek literature; the relative isolation of contemporary Alexandrian writers from Egyptian culture. All these factors tip the scales against the common view that Mnaseas was "anti-Semitic" and intended to discredit the Jews. This would be the case if we assumed that Mnaseas himself understood that the ass represented the Jewish god, and certainly if we assumed that Mnaseas regarded the ass merely as a votive offering, and even more so if the original story referred to a statue of Moses riding an ass.

We would be hard put to explain why Mnaseas and his Greek readers would be surprised by the statue of an ass in the Jewish Temple when another statue of an ass was on display in the Delphic temple of Apollo, the most authoritative and prestigious temple-oracle in the Greek world; and when the statue of an ass would have been the most sacred object in the temple of Apollo Killaios in Mysia, not far from Mnaseas's native city. We are not mind readers and must therefore make do with the facts and data available. The accumulated evidence would suffice in any fair court of justice to acquit Mnaseas of the charge of "anti-Semitism" and malicious intent. Our appraisal of the position of Mnaseas and his contemporaries must be free of deep-seated modern negative connotations associating the ass with stupidity. Together with this, care must be taken not to be influenced by the negative aims of the original Egyptian libel and its variations and developments in later generations, or by the subjective feelings of Jews reading the story.

The dubious honor of being the first Greek "anti-Semitic" author should be awarded to the anonymous Seleucid court historian of the mid-second century B.C.E. who adapted the Egyptian blood libel to the time of Antiochus Epiphanes (see chapter 7). However, the first Greek "anti-Semitic" author among the literati in Alexandria would seem to have been Lysimachus of Alexandria, who, a century after Mnaseas, collected all the hostile Egyptian traditions concerning the origins of the Jewish people and even supplemented them. He did so at a time when there was real concern among the Greeks in Egypt at the growing power of the Jews in the Ptolemaic court (see chapter 9).

THE DEVELOPMENT OF THE LIBEL

The conclusions reached above apply only to Mnaseas and his Greek contemporaries, and not to later Greeks in the times of the great confrontations between Jews and Greeks, and when a greater intimacy with Egyptian heritage was more common, indeed gradually becoming to some extent part of the cultural tradition of the Hellenistic world. Each author and every source transmitting the ass libel must be individually examined. Some rejected the libel; others used softer or harsher versions, each according to his educational background, personal experiences, contemporary events, and own aims. What follows is an account in general terms of the development of the ass libel in classical literature. The evolution of the libel in the later polemics between pagans and Christians will not be discussed here, since it is actually irrelevant to the present survey.

The anecdote in Mnaseas concerning the theft of the ass contained the earliest known explicit reference to the ass libel. The Idumaean-Egyptian narrator who was Mnaseas's source for the anecdote utilized a slander developed in Egypt to the effect that the Jews worshipped an ass. The libel originated in the Egyptian identification of the Jewish god with Seth (Typhon), the Egyptian god of evil, who was occasionally portrayed in the form of an ass.[101] In the original Idumaean story, if not in Mnaseas's account as well, the ass was a beast of burden with a golden head. The identification of the ass with the Jewish god seemed obvious to the Idumaean narrator but was not necessarily so understood by Mnaseas, who may well have regarded the sculpture as a votive offering representing an event from the formative past of the Jews, as Tacitus and his sources interpreted it.

A different account of the discovery of an image of an ass in the Temple was recorded in the first century B.C.E. by Posidonius of Apamea and Apollonius Molon. The former rejected it, while the latter accepted it as historically reliable.[102] According to this version, when Antiochus Epiphanes entered the Temple, he saw a statue of Moses riding on an ass and holding a scroll containing the laws of the Jews. The account, as preserved by Diodorus Siculus (34/35. 1. 3–4), was taken by Diodorus from Posidonius, who drew on Timochares, a Seleucid

101. See pp. 243–45 below.
102. See pp. 431–55, 451–55, 490–91, and 515 below.

court historian active in the thirties and twenties of the second century B.C.E.[103] Timochares' own source was a previous Seleucid court historian of the genera-tion of the Hasmonaean revolt.[104] This version is a great deal softer than that used by the Idumaean storyteller, since the ass does not represent the Jewish god but serves only as Moses' means of transport. The composite statue could be regarded as an expression of the founder or leader cult so popular elsewhere in the Hellenistic period. The Seleucid authors availed themselves of this account rather than the ass-god version either because the latter was unknown to them or because the former was more credible, but in any case because it was more suit-able to the needs of their story about Antiochus Epiphanes entering the Temple. The account is apologetic, intended to explain why Antiochus imposed his edicts against the Jewish religion (cf. Joseph. *Ap.* 2. 90). First, the Jews refused both to practice the cult of the king, accepted by other peoples in the Seleucid empire, and to set up a statue of Antiochus in their Temple on the grounds that they practiced no cult of any man, and there were no images in their Temple; but lo and behold, Antiochus found in this very Temple a statue of Moses, proving both Jewish claims to be false and exposing the Jews as disloyal to the government, and indeed rebels against the crown. Second, Moses holds the Jewish book of laws, laws that contravene the accepted norms of mankind. In the original story, there immediately followed the notorious blood libel. Antiochus on the same occasion meets the captured Greek whom the Jews intend to sacrifice to their God and "taste" of his flesh (*Ap.* 2. 91–96). The nature of the laws in the book held by Moses are thereby well illustrated. This cruel act of human sacrifice and cannibalism obviously required firm intervention on the part of the authorities. The Seleucid account thus justified stamping out the Jewish religion and stamp-ing on its symbols.[105]

As may be clearly seen, the account of the discovery in the Temple of the statue of Moses seated on an ass was artificially inserted, along with the blood libel, into the story of the visit of Antiochus Epiphanes to the Temple prior to the imposi-tion of the religious edicts.[106] The artificial nature of the insertion indicates that the libels were not invented by the Seleucid court scribes. The Moses-ass account must have been known earlier, as was the ass-Jewish god version. This earlier version may not have mentioned the Jewish book of laws, an element peculiarly suited to the apologetic requirements of the Seleucid court historians, who could

103. On Timochares as Posdionius's intermediate source, see pp. 462–64 below.

104. That the story was invented in the circles surrounding Antiochus IV in order to explain the unprecedented steps taken by Antiochus IV against the Jewish religion was first suggested by Graetz (1872), and developed by Bickermann (1937) 22–23; (1976–80) 2: 245–55.

105. See further, pp. 276–77, 443 below.

106. On the artificial insertion of the blood libel, see below, pp. 265–67 and 277–79.

thereby justify persecuting the Jewish religion by referring to the "misanthropic" laws of Moses (Diod. 34/35. 1. 3–4).

A philological examination of references to Moses suggests that the version of Moses seated on an ass also has an Egyptian origin. The story employs the Egyptian form *Mōysēs*,[107] instead of the regular Greek *Mōsēs,* applied in the Posidonian Jewish excursus (Strabo 16. 2. 35) that preceded the story about the ass in the Temple.[108] Elsewhere, Diodorus uses both *Mōsēs* and *Mōysēs,* in accordance with what he finds in his sources.[109]

Septuagint usage corroborates this point. The translators of the Pentateuch, conventionally dated to the third century B.C.E., consistently avoid the use of the word ὄνος (ass) when it is connected with Moses, and introduce instead various substitutes. Thus the Hebrew version of Exodus 4.20 reads: "And Moses took his wife and children, mounted them on an ass, and set out for Egypt with the staff of God in his hand"; but the Septuagint replaces "ass" with τὰ ὑποζύγια (beasts of burden). In Numbers 16.15, Moses justifies himself against the accusations of Korah and his followers: "I have not taken from them so much as a single ass; I have done no wrong to any of them"; the Septuagint has ἐπιθύμημα (a desirable object) instead of "ass." These two verses are mentioned in an ancient Beraita of the Babylonian Talmud among fifteen cases where the legendary translators of the Septuagint deliberately changed the original meaning (BT Megillah 9b). Although one may argue that the present Septuagint readings may have been a later alteration of an earlier translation, the testimony of the Beraita, counting the two readings among the few deliberate and original mistranslations, carries considerable weight; the list is after all but a minute fraction of the multitude of deliberate modifications in the translation of the Torah (as of the word "ass" itself).[110]

The legend about the statue of Moses seated on an ass, like the libel about the Jewish god in the form of an ass, was thus known in third-century B.C.E. Egypt. It drew upon the legends of Seth (Typhon). The ass is the animal used by Seth as his mode of transportation. In this version, Moses, not the Jewish god, was

---

107. See Bar-Kochva (1996d) 314; cf., e.g., Artapanus in Eusebius *Praeparatio evangelica* 4. 7.3 ff.; Artapanus made much use of Egyptian sources, in which he was thoroughly at home. On the form *Mōysēs,* see Nestle (1907) 111–21; Diamond (1974) 37–38; Nikiprowetzky (1984).

108. See pp. 448–51 below.

109. In the Jewish excursus taken from Hecataeus, who drew on Jewish informants, Diodorus writes *Mōsēs* (40. 3. 3); but, toward the end of his Egyptian ethnography, in a passage not taken from Hecataeus (unlike most of the work), Diodorus writes *Mōysēs* (1. 94. 2; see the mention of Iao, the Egyptian form for the tetragrammaton). For an argument that the latter paragraph was not taken from Hecataeus, see Murray (1970) 146.

110. For a survey of the LXX translation for חמור (ass) in other verses, see Geiger (1857) 360, 439; Neher-Bernheim (1963) 113–16. Most of the material is, however, irrelevant to the present discussion.

identified with Seth.[111] Did the Seleucid court scribes also intend an additional jibe at the Jews by hinting at an identification between Moses and Typhon? Were they aware of the identification?[112] Was the reference to an image of an ass in the Temple—even treating the ass as Moses' mount—intended as an insult? We cannot know. Our acquaintance with the Seleucid court scribes is virtually nonexistent, unlike the information we have about the circle of scholars in third-century B.C.E. Alexandria to which Mnaseas belonged. All that can be said is that, 250 years later, at the end of the first century C.E., Plutarch is engaged in polemics with a number of unnamed authors who identified the father of the Jews (clearly referring to Moses) with Typhon riding an ass.[113] It is unfortunate that we do not know the names of these authors or their dates. Plutarch himself knew the Typhon legends and mentioned them in various forms in his work *On Isis and Osiris*. In any case, it is quite doubtful whether Seleucid court scribes were aware of a link between the Typhon legends and the libel.

A third version of the libel, where the Jewish god is represented by a golden ass-head, appeared in the writings of Apion (Joseph. *Ap.* 2. 80) and Damocritus (Suda, s.v. Δαμόκριτος), an unknown author who lived after the destruction of the Second Temple.[114] Damocritus used Apion's account, as may be learned from his treatment of the blood libel.[115] Apion claims to have found the story of Antiochus entering the Temple in Posidonius and Apollonius Molon. In his version, however, the Jews worship not a statue of Moses seated on an ass, as appears in Diodorus-Posidonius, but only the head of an ass. This is an original modification by Apion himself, inspired both by the Egyptian identification of the God of the Jews with an ass and by his own paraphrasing of Mnaseas, where he mentions only the snatching of the head of the ass, without reference to the body. The change to just the head of an ass seems to have been made deliberately in order to magnify the mockery and absurdity of the Jewish belief.

The ass-head version, then, first appeared in the first half of the first century C.E. Apion, who seems to have been half-Egyptian,[116] was intimately acquainted with

111. See pp. 245–49 below.

112. In this context it is worth noting that the adoption of the blood libel by these Seleucid court scribes does not indicate a familiarity with all the legends of Seth-Typhon. The ultimate source of inspiration for the libel was indeed these legends, but the libel itself was created as an independent anti-Jewish slander, devoid of all reference to Seth. In this form it spread throughout Egypt and beyond; and thus it reached the attention of the Seleucid scribes, presumably through ethnographies or histories written in Greek by authors of Egyptian origin.

113. Plutarch *De Iside et Osiride* 363C–D; see further, pp. 245–46 below.

114. On the testimony of Damocritus, see below, pp. 259–63.

115. See below, pp. 262–63.

116. Josephus presents Apion as an Egyptian pretending to be a Greek (*Ap.* 2. 28–29), and this is accepted by most scholars who think that the name Apion derives from Apis, the Egyptian

Egyptian mythology, and in his writings conveyed Egyptian myths to his Greek readers. Given the Egyptian contempt for donkeys, which was gradually becoming known also in Greek literature of the late Hellenistic period,[117] this extreme adaptation was well suited to Apion's purpose of ridiculing the Jewish faith. He would not have achieved the same effect on Greco-Egyptians of his generation, who were accustomed to *princeps,* king, and founder cults, by referring to a statue of Moses seated on an ass. Apion's strong drive to ridicule the Jews, manifested in his presentation and elaboration of more than one story about the ass in the Jewish Temple, obviously derived from events of his generation: Caligula's command to place his statue in the Jewish Temple, the Jewish protest, and the delegations to Rome following the intercommunal riots in Alexandria in which Apion himself participated (40 C.E.). There could not have been a more effective argument to refute the Jewish claim that their god forbids placing statues and images in his temple, and thereby expose their disloyalty to the emperor.

A fourth version, perhaps softer than the second, reported the existence of the statue of an ass (and not just its head) in the Temple as a votive offering. The account is preserved in the form it had acquired by the end of the first century C.E. in Tacitus (*Hist.* 5. 4. 2), having passed through centuries of development. Tacitus's account does not say whether the ass head was made of gold or decorated with gold, presumably because such a detail was irrelevant for his purposes. More significantly, the ass is not portrayed as the Jewish god, but as a votive offering (*votiva*) commemorating an event that occurred when Moses and the Jews were wandering in the desert and exposed to drought; Moses noticed a herd of wild asses making their way to a water source, followed them, and discovered abundant springs. This account, known also from Plutarch (*Quaest. conv.* 4. 5. 2 [570D-E]),[118] provides an aetiological explanation that had been attached at some stage to the rumor of an ass in the Temple, an explanation essentially no different from the one given by Pausanias (10. 18. 4) for the presence of a statue of an ass at Delphi, where it is a votive offering of the Ambracians to express their gratitude toward the ass that saved them from an attack by their neighbors. There are similar explanations in classical literature for votive offerings of statues of animals erected in temples to commemorate their help in showing lost people

---

god-bull, and therefore would rather have been carried by a native Egyptian. "Apion," however, was a respected Greek name, originating in classical Greece, and meaning simply "a pear tree." A connection with Apis is linguistically problematic, although popular etymology might have taken advantage of the similarity between the names Apion and Apis. This still does not turn Apion into an Egyptian. Notably, Apion's father was named Posidonius and Apion was reputed as a Greek throughout the Greek and Roman world. Given Apion's birthplace in an oasis, he may well have been only half-Greek.

117. E.g., Plutarch *De Iside et Osiride* 31. 363 B-D.

118. This has been rightly stressed by Spooner (1891) 461; Bickermann (1937) 104 and n. 1; Lewy (1960) 121 and n. 26; Stern, *GLAJJ* 2: 37.

the way to a water source.[119] It is in keeping with the aetiological explanation that Tacitus portrays the asses as "a herd of wild asses," not just asses or pack-asses. Considering Tacitus's hostility toward the Jews, he cannot be considered the one who softened the libel. We cannot say when this version came about or who was responsible for it. From what Tacitus reports in this context on the completely negative stance of the Jews toward animal cult, and on the nature of the Jewish divinity (*Hist.* 5. 3–5), it appears that he at the very least did not regard the ass statue as the idol of a cult, but as no more than a memorial.[120]

This reconstruction of the development of the libel has been based on the premise that Mnaseas, following the Idumaean story, reported the presence in the Temple of the statue of just an ass. However, it is still possible that the statue reported was of Moses riding an ass.[121] In such a case, the reconstruction would differ slightly: the Idumaean narrator accepted the Egyptian rumor about the existence in the Temple of a statue of Moses riding on an ass, and this was copied by Mnaseas. Mnaseas's work was written some two generations before the Hasmonaean revolt, and, enjoying a wide circulation, it eventually reached the Seleucid court, where the "information" about a Temple statue of Moses riding an ass was eagerly exploited for the Seleucids' apologetic purposes. In his version of the same affair Apion referred, for the reasons mentioned, to only the head of an ass.

Whatever the case may be, it should be emphasized that the first Greek written source now in our possession explicitly identifying the God of the Jews with an ass, and reporting the ass cult in the Temple, is relatively late and was not written by a real Greek. Apion was probably half-Egyptian and was active mainly toward the end of the first half of the first century C.E., some 250 years after Mnaseas.

THE ORIGIN OF THE LIBEL

The Mnaseas story and the Septuagint show that the mid-third century B.C.E. is the *terminus ante quem* for the invention of the Moses-ass and the ass versions. When and why were these two versions invented, and what were their sources of inspiration? Of the many theories proposed to explain the source of inspiration for the libel, all but one must be rejected on philological, historical, or chronological counts.[122] The popular explanation pointing out a similarity between the tetragrammaton and the Egyptian word for "ass" must also be rejected.[123] The

119. See Lewy (1960) 145 n. 136, referring to Apuleius 2. 1.

120. A different reconstruction of the development of the ass libel is offered by Bickerman (1976–80) 2: 225 ff.; Bickerman argues for a Syrian origin. This and the following section should serve to refute his suggestion.

121. See pp. 221–22 above.

122. E.g., Zachariah 9.9, noted by Neher-Bernheim (1963) 107, 116, and Feldman (1993) 499, about the Messiah appearing on an ass, could not have been known to Egyptians in the third century

similarity is phonetically rather dubious,[124] and other factors also argue against such a connection.[125] In any case, it fails to explain the origin of the Moses-ass version.

The most acceptable explanation is also the simplest: both versions originated in one way or another from the Egyptian Seth (named Typhon by the Greeks) traditions. This explanation has been accepted by a good number of scholars.[126] However, as the connection between the Seth-Typhon legends and the ass libel has not always been properly explained, and the process of development not yet established, a review of the links in the chain connecting the Egyptian and anti-Jewish traditions will not be out of place here.

In pharaonic Egypt, at least from the time of the Assyrian occupation (670

B.C.E.; there cannot be any connection with the biblical story of Balaam and his ass (*pace* Neher-Bernheim, 113; Feldman, 499), nor with the name Ḥamor (Ass), the father of Shechem (Gen. 34.2; cf. Halévy [1903]); the legend could not have been inspired by the resemblance between the Greek word *onos* (ass) and Onias (indicated perhaps by Apion: Joseph. *Ap.* 2. 49), since the libel preceded the emigration of the Oniads from Jerusalem to Egypt (*pace* Bouché-Leclerq [1907] 2: 58 n. 1); the identification of the Jewish god with Dionysus, suggesting a connection with Dionysus's ass, is known only from the Roman period (*pace* Perdrizet [1910] 243 ff. et al.). The suggested connections with the *'even shetiyah* of the Temple, as if the libel originates in the visit of Antiochus IV to the Temple (Graetz [1872] 196–97; Rösch [1882] 523; Friedländer [1903] 377 ff.), are too fanciful; and the same applies to the suggestion (Goldschmidt [1935–36] 175–78) that the phrase *'ir ha-qodesh* ("the holy city") was changed by somebody to *'ayir ha-quodesh* ("the sacred young ass"). There are several other suggestions that are even more fanciful (e.g., Zipser [1871] 114–15; Müller [1877] 258–59).

123. First noted by Bochart (1663) 2: 181. See also Pellegrini (1874) 17 ff.; Simonsen (1912) 298; Heinemann (1919) 120 n. 1; Jacoby (1926) 270 ff., and many others. See Stern, *GLAJJ* 1: 98; Feldman (1993) 500; van Henten and Abush (1996); Bar-Kochva (1996d) 318–23; Kasher (1996) 380–82.

124. The word "ass" in classical Egyptian, Ramesite, and Demotic is *i'a'a*; in Coptic, *eio*. The tetragrammaton first appears in pharaonic inscriptions as *yhw*. In the Aramaic documents from Elephantine it is *yhw*, transcribed in Greek as *Iao* (Diod. 1. 94. 2). The two words would hardly have sounded similar to an Egyptian ear used to short words composed of vowels.

125. For example, one might ask how it was that Egyptian and Hellenistic-Roman authors did not mention it explicitly as evidence for the ass libel (cf. the etymologies by Varro and Herennius Philo for the name Iao according to the Babylonian and Phoenician languages—ap. Stern, *GLAJJ* 1: no. 75; 2: no. 324). Furthermore, had such a similarity been noted by Egyptians, their Jewish neighbors would have been consistent in replacing the name of Iao by the many known substitutes ("heaven", "the place," etc.). However, the use of Iao by Egyptian Jews is well documented from the Persian as well as the Hellenistic-Roman period (see the references in Stern, *GLAJJ* 1: 172). It was probably also written in the versions of the Septuagint current in the period of the Second Temple, the substitute *kyrios* being a Christian innovation (see the summary by Jellicoe [1968] 270–72). Later magical texts are irrelevant to the question of the origin of the libel; see Griffiths (1970) 409 and Jacoby (1926) 271 for two contrary views.

126. See, in several variations, Movers (1841) 297; Müller (1877) 263; Stählin (1905) 15–16; Meyer (1921–23) 2: 33; Bousset and Gressmann (1926) 76; Tcherikover (1961) 365–66; Neher-Bernheim (1963) 109 ff.; Gabba (1989) 643–44; Feldman (1993) 500–501; Bar-Kochva (1996a); Schäfer (1997a) 55–62; (1997b).

B.C.E.),[127] the old Egyptian deity Seth gradually acquired the character of the "devil," the bad deity, the source of all evils and misfortunes besetting the Egyptians and their gods. The list of disasters brought about by Seth includes darkness, mass deaths, diseases, and storms.[128] He was also regarded as the god of the wilderness and nomads, of foreign countries, and of aliens resident in Egypt, especially the Semites,[129] and was explicitly identified with Baal and other foreign deities.[130] It was therefore only natural for the Egyptians, who were at least annually reminded by their Jewish neighbors about the stories of the Exodus, to identify the Jewish god or Moses with Seth. It is clear from their anti-Jewish accusations that the Egyptians were well acquainted with the Exodus traditions, since they reversed them in order to defame the Jews.[131] The hostile Egyptians in their creativity could hardly ignore the evident similarity between some of the plagues in the Jewish tradition and the disasters brought about by Seth.

Seth was frequently described in the first millenium B.C.E. as having the form or the skin of an ass, or as being disguised in the form of an ass, and in art he appears as a human figure carrying what may be interpreted as the head (or a mask) of an ass. The ass was also regarded as one of Seth's sacred animals and as his personal mount.[132] The ass was ridiculed by the Egyptians, in contrast to their veneration of a number of animals. What better animal for their enemies to worship than an ass? Or what better mount for Moses? Furthermore, the Jews claimed that there was no statue in their Temple, but they prohibited Gentiles from entering the shrine, and only the High Priest was allowed access to the "Holy of Holies"; it would have been only too natural to spread rumors that a statue of an ass—the most contemptible of animals, the god of evil or that god's mount or the mount of their founder—was being secretly exhibited in the place most sacred to the Jewish people.[133]

Indeed some sources indicate that Moses was at least connected, if not identified, with Typhon. A number of scholars quote the following passage from Plutarch as the most important evidence for the origin of the Moses-ass version in Seth's legends:[134]

127. See te Velde (1977) 139–40, 145–46, 148–49.
128. Te Velde (1977) 91–94, 118, 128.
129. Te Velde (1977) 109–11, 115–16, 150.
130. See te Velde (1977) 109, 119–20, 124, 126–29.
131. See, in more detail, pp. 331–33 below.
132. See Griffiths (1966) 409–10, 412, 418; te Velde (1977) 8, 14, 26. See, e.g., Plutarch *De Iside et Osiride* 362F ff. For details on the earlier form of Seth, see note 99 above. For the following analysis of the sources, cf. Bar-Kochva (1996a), with some substantial differences.
133. On the last point, see Friedländer (1903) 376; Gabba (1989) 643; Feldman (1993) 499.
134. See esp. Rösch (1882) 523 ff.; de Liagre Böhl (1953) 125; Tcherikover (1961) 365.

Those who say that Typhon fled from the battle on an ass for seven days, and having been saved produced sons, Hierosolymus and Judaeus, are at this point clearly
dragging Jewish issues into the story. (*De Is. et Os.* 363C-D)

The passage clearly combines two traditions. The first derives from the old Seth
myth, while the second represents a fragment of an eponymic tradition about
Moses, Judaea, and Jerusalem (see Tac. *Hist.* 5. 2. 3). The two have been stitched
together rather roughly by a later author of unknown date, and the reference to
"seven days" would have been integrated as an indication of the origin of the
Sabbath (cf. Tac. *Hist.* 5. 2. 6; Justin 36. 2. 14). As it stands, the passage shows
that a story about Seth finding refuge in the desert and using an ass as transport
existed, and that some source did indeed connect it with Moses.

A so far unrecognized identification of Moses with Seth-Typhon is implied
in Artapanus, a Jewish-Egyptian author of the third or second century B.C.E.
Artapanus describes Moses as πυρράκης ("fiery red"; Eus. *PE* 9. 37). Typhon's color
was also believed to be fiery red (πυρρόχρους).[135] Artapanus's description of Moses
is no more surprising than other astonishing statements found in his literary
remains. He drew this description, along with many other details, from Egyptian
sources, which he consistently reformed and interpreted in a positive fashion.[136]

Scholars have noted a connection between Moses and Typhon not only in
Plutarch's passage but also in Manetho's *Aegyptiaca*,[137] written about 270 B.C.E by
an Egyptian priest who was well versed in Greek. The evidence is well known, but
it is indirect and open to interpretation, and so deserves some elaboration here.

According to the first excerpt (Joseph. *Ap.* 1. 75-90), the "shepherds"—Hyksos—
withdrew from Egypt, wandered in the desert, and finally settled in Judaea, where
they founded the city of Jerusalem. This in itself indicates some connection, at
least, with the Jews. The Hyksos were elsewhere described by the Egyptians as worshippers of Seth.[138] The "shepherds" are also linked with Typhon in this excerpt:
having been repulsed from all regions of Egypt, they are said to have concentrated
in the region of Avaris and fortified it (*Ap.* 1. 86-90). Avaris in Egyptian tradition
was the city of Seth.[139] The second excerpt recounts a story about the revolt of the
lepers employed in the stone quarries (*Ap.* 1. 229-50). Their leader was Osarseph, a

---

135. Diodorus 1. 88. 4-5; Plutarch *De Iside et Osiride* 364B. For Egyptian sources, see Rochemonteix and Chassinat (1897-1934) 6: 213-19.

136. See esp. Guttmann 1: 109-35; Holladay (1977); (1983) 189-244. The fragments are from Eusebius
Praeparatio evangelica 9. 18. 1, 23, 27.

137. Variously suggested in almost all the references mentioned in note 126 above.

138. Te Velde (1977) 121, and n. 2.

139. See te Velde (1977) 122, and n. 5, on the Egyptian sources concerning Avaris and Seth; and
see further below on *Contra Apionem* 1. 237.

priest of Heliopolis. The name sounds like a combination of Osiris and Joseph. In what appears to be an interpolation toward the end of the story, it is said that the priest changed his name to Moses. Osarseph, in any case, is in effect portrayed as Moses.[140] The leper-rebels found refuge in Avaris, the deserted city of the "shepherds." This time Avaris is explicitly presented as the city that, "according to the theology, is Typhonian from the beginning" (*Ap.* 1. 237). The successful revolt of the lepers was assisted by the "shepherds" who dwelt in the city called Jerusalem (241), later identified as the Solymitai (248), who came to their aid. The Egyptian king and his followers found refuge in Ethiopia for thirteen years. Osarseph, the leader of the rebels, is said to have introduced laws and practices extremely hostile to the Egyptians, and directed especially against Egyptian religion and cult (239–40, 244, 248–50), and ordered "that they should have contact with none save with their comrades to the oath" (239). The connection of Moses with Typhon is thus suggested in the second excerpt, while the first indicates only a connection between Typhon and the Jews in general.

It is frequently disputed whether Manetho was at all anti-Jewish or had the Jews in mind when he wrote his account. Not a few scholars have suggested that some or all the passages preserved in Josephus are a later reworking of Manetho's account. Some have even gone so far as to suggest a Jewish reworking.[141] This is not the place to discuss all these opinions, but it may be said that the various arguments raised so far—in most cases without any extensive Egyptological or Manethonian research on the text—fail to demonstrate conclusively that Manetho cannot be the author of most of the passages in question (apart from one or more interpolations). In any case, the link between Typhon and the elements that caused trouble for the Egyptians, elements that Manetho and/or his contemporary Egyptians would easily have been able to identify with the Jews, is principally based on sections of the excerpts that can hardly be suspected of not being authentically Manethonian.

The tendency of Egyptians in the Persian period to connect their enemies with Seth is well illustrated by the Egyptian identification of Cambyses with Seth. The Egyptians also called the hated Artaxerxes III Ochus an ass (Ael. *VH* 4. 8; cf. Plut. *De Is. et Os.* 362F, 363C). Egyptian Jews cooperated with the Persian oppres-

---

140. See Tcherikover (1961) 361–64; Fraser (1972) 1: 509; Kasher (1974) 69–84; Stern, *GLAJJ* 1: 63–64; Conzelmann (1981) 78–79.

141. See, e.g., Müller, *FHG* II. 514; Meyer (1904) 71–79; Laqueur, *RE* s.v. "Manethon," cols. 1064–80; Heinemann, *RE* s.v. "Antisemitismus," cols. 26–27; Braun (1938) 27; Jacoby, *FGrH* III.C, no. 609, p. 84; Waddell (1940) XVII–XIX; Gager (1972) 113–17; Sevenster (1975) 184–88; Aziza (1987) 49–55; Bickerman (1988) 224–25; Gabba (1989) 633–34; Mendels (1990) 94–95; Schäfer (1997b); Gruen (1998) 56 ff.; Labow (2005) 53–58. The authenticity of the passages is argued for by Stern, *GLAJJ* 1: 63–64; Kasher (1974).

Moses Seated on an Ass
(Egypt: Persian Period)

The Jewish God in the Form of an Ass
(Egypt: Persian Period)

The Idumaean Story
(Egypt: c. 250 B.C.E.)

Mnaseas
(Alexandria: c. 200 B.C.E.)

The Visit of Antiochus IV Epiphanes
to the Temple
(Seleucid Court scribe[s], Syria: c. 163 B.C.E.)

Timochares
(Antioch: c. 129 B.C.E.)

Posidonius
(Rhodes: C1 B.C.E.)

Apollonius Molon
(Rhodes: C1 B.C.E.)

Diodorus
(Rome: C1 B.C.E.)

Ass Head
Apion
(Alexandria: C1 C.E.)

Damocritus
(C1 C.E.)

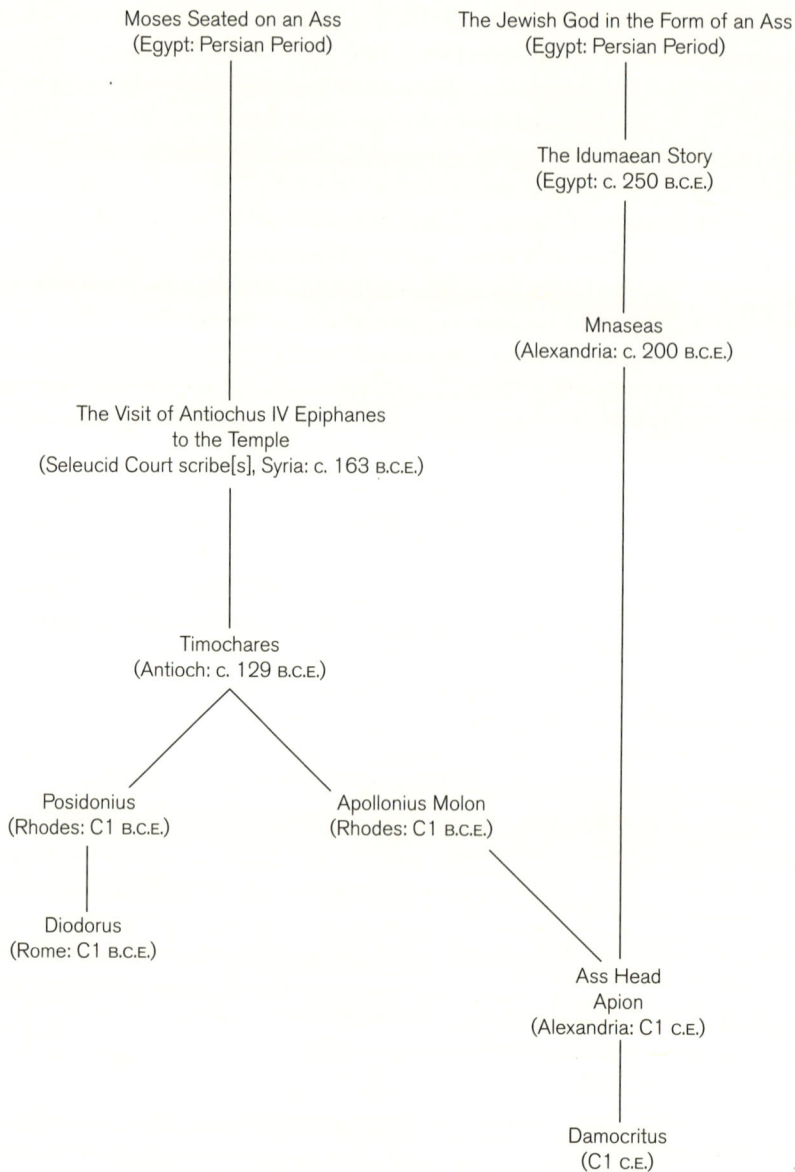

FIGURE 1. The Transmission of the Ass Libel

sors, and religious tension between Jews and Egyptians was as unavoidable in that period as in others.[142] In light of all this, would it be rash to suggest that the identification of Moses and the Jewish god with Seth originated before the third century, in Egypt of the Persian period? The same applies to the connection of Moses and the Jewish god with ass riding and ass cult respectively.

The account portraying Moses seated on an ass could have gained additional support from Jewish traditions. Apart from the stories about the wandering of the Israelites in the desert, Moses is also said to have once escaped from Pharaoh to the desert (Exod. 2.15). The ass was a regular pack animal and mount for ordinary people in Egypt and its deserts (rather than the camel).[143] The Torah relates how Moses once put his wife and children on an ass in the desert (Exod. 4.20). Similar inspiration could have been drawn from oral or written traditions about the Exodus that were circulating among Egyptian Jews. The existence of such Midrashim is attested (though for a later period) by the tragedy on the Exodus written by Ezekiel, the Jewish-Hellenistic poet, and by the unique version of the Ten Plagues in Wisdom of Solomon (16–19).

A typological parallel to the role of asses in Exodus Midrashim is presented by a Midrash in the Babylonian Talmud. The Talmud discusses why, of all unclean animals, only the firstborn asses have to be redeemed and should not be used for work (Exod. 13.13). The law of the firstborn appears in the Pentateuch subsequent to the Passover regulations and is explained by the plague of the firstborn: those who were not killed have to be redeemed in the future (Exod. 13.11–15; esp. 15). The question is, therefore, why the asses were also spared. The Midrash answers:

> For they (the asses) supported Israel in the time of the Exodus, for there was not even one in Israel who did not take with him ninety Lybian asses loaded with the silver and gold of Egypt. (BT Berakhot 5b)

As we can see, the Midrash actually applies to its purposes another biblical verse: "And the Israelites had done as Moses had told them, asking the Egyptians for jewelry of silver and gold and for clothing . . . in this way they plundered the Egyptians" (Exod. 12.35–36; cf. 11.2). This Midrash, late though it is, demonstrates how stories connecting asses with the Exodus events could be invented. Egyptian Jews, who expanded upon the Exodus traditions, may have created similar explanations and midrashim. After the invention and development of the ass libel, these interpretations were obviously suppressed by Jews and almost disappeared from their traditions. This is why we do not find more of them.

142. See pp. 330–31 below.
143. See *Encyclopaedia Biblica* (1955–82), s.vv. "Camel," "Donkey," "Horse."

PART II

The Hasmonaean Period

From the Jewish Revolt to the Roman Conquest
(167–63 B.C.E.)

7

The Diachronic Libels and Accusations (B)

The Seleucid Court Scribe(s) and the Blood Libel

The Hellenistic blood libel against the Jews does not refer to the murder of children, nor, apparently, to the actual drinking of blood or the use of blood for cultic purposes. Such stories, prevalent in the medieval blood libel, were well documented in Greek and Roman ethnographic literature (e.g., Hdt. 3. 11) and were even used by the Jews themselves as a justification for expelling the Canaanites from the Holy Land (*Sap. Salmon.* 12.5); yet they were not aimed against Jews and indeed were, for much of the Roman period, directed mainly against Christians.[1] This said, the Hellenistic blood libel against the Jews was even more cruel than the later libels. It is called a blood libel, as the term regularly denotes a slander concerning ritual murder of any kind, and it is in this sense that the expression will be used here.

The blood libel, like the ass libel, underwent a number of incarnations, the most detailed of which is the combined version created in the wake of the confrontation between Antiochus Epiphanes and the Jews. Our knowledge of it derives mainly from Josephus (*Ap.* 2. 91–96). Josephus reports the combined version of the libel that appeared in Apion's work, and subsequently provides arguments in an attempt to refute the charge. Apion had claimed that he found the libel in the writings of no lesser authorities than the leading lights of philosophy and rhetoric of the first century B.C.E., Posidonius of Apamea and Apollonius Molon. The thorny issues of the attitude of these intellectuals toward the Jews in general, and the subsequent question of whether Apion did indeed find the blood

---

1. On blood libels against Christians, see esp. Justin *Apologia* 2. 10; *Trypho* 10; Origen *Contra Celsum* 6. 27; Eusebius *Praeparatio evangelica* 4. 7, 11; 5. 1. 4.

libel in their writings, will be discussed in chapter 13 of this book. In the present chapter I shall attempt to reconstruct the contents of the libel itself, establish its original sources, and trace its development during the turbulent changes in relations between the Jews and their surroundings.

THE LIBEL IN "*CONTRA APIONEM*"

The historical framework for the account of the libel is the visit of Antiochus Epiphanes to the Temple in 168 B.C.E., a visit that ended in the desecration of the Temple, after which religious restrictions were imposed on the Jews. The blood libel does not appear on its own; it is preceded by the ass libel. Apion relates how Antiochus Epiphanes discovered that the Jews worshipped in the Temple the golden head of an ass, and there follows the blood libel. Apion's account is composed of two parts: the framework story about the meeting between Antiochus and the Greek victim in the Temple (*Ap.* 2. 91–94a, 96); the details of the libel itself, purportedly told to the Greek by the Jews themselves (94b–95).

Neither the account of the two libels nor the framework story has reached us in its original Greek form. Some pages of the second book of *Contra Apionem* (paras. 52–113) have survived only in the sixth-century Latin translation, called the Cassiodorus translation. It would not be too bold to surmise that the pages containing the two libels were destroyed at some stage of the transmission in line with the utter rejection of the libels by Photius (*Bibl.* cod. 244, 381a) and possibly also by other Byzantine authoritative figures. The Latin translation of the blood libel suffers from numerous defects, much more so than that of the ass libel.[2] Some errors are manifestly the result of the translator's misinterpretation of the Greek text; there are also omissions and significant differences in formulation among the various Latin manuscripts.[3] The framework story and the libel run as follows (Joseph. *Ap.* 2. 91–96):

> (91) Apion said that Antiochus found in the Temple a couch and a man lying on it, and placed before him a table full of dishes maritime, terrestrial, and of birds, and the man had become numbed by them. (92) But he soon honored the king's entrance as if it would afford him the greatest relief, and falling prostrate at his (the king's) knees with extended right hand he begged release. And with the king commanding him to have faith and to say who he was or why he was living there or what the reason was for his dishes, then he (Apion) says that the man, with a

---

2. See pp. 207–8 above and notes 3–11 above; cf. Niese (1888) 5: xiv–xvii; Bickerman (1976–80) 2: 225 n. 1; Kidd 2: 949.

3. On the omission of the oath according to Josephus *Contra Apionem* 2. 121, see p. 256 below. The attempt of Shutt (1987) to reconstruct the Greek text of the two libels is not successful; cf. Schreckenberg (1996) 78.

groan and tears narrated sorrowfully his enforced circumstances. (93) [He] said that he was actually a Greek, and that while he was wandering about the province for his livelihood he was suddenly snatched away by foreign men and led away to the Temple and shut up there, and he was being observed by no one but was being fattened by the entire preparation of dishes.[4] (94) And actually at first these unexpected favors had deceived him and had brought happiness, then suspicion, afterwards numbness, and finally consulting the servants attending upon him[5] he had heard the unspeakable law[6] of the Jews, for which he was being fed, and this they (the Jews) did every year at a certain established time, (95) and actually[7] seized a Greek foreigner[8] and fattened him for a year and having led him down to a grove[9] actually killed this man[10] and sacrificed his body according to their rites and tasted[11] of his flesh[12] and made a vow in the sacrificing of the Greek, that they

4. The words *cuncta dapium praeparatione* literally mean "with the whole preparation of meals," which makes little sense. In the context, one might have expected a description of food. The Latin translator probably understood this but had some difficulty with the Greek formulation. The source probably read παντοδαπῇ παρασκευῇ, literally, "with all sorts of preparation," where "preparation" denotes the food prepared rather than the preparation of the food (cf. LSJ s.v. παρασκευή II). The translator made the wrong choice and was left with the problem of finding in παντοδαπῇ a reference to food, which the context requires. He would have translated the first part of the word correctly (παντο = *cuncta*, "all," to agree with *praeparatione*) but rendered the second part falsely due to its superficial resemblance to the Latin word for a meal (δαπῇ—*dapium*, "of meals").

5. *ministris ad se accedentibus:* literally, "servants coming near to him." It is possible that *accedo ad* translates προσπολέω = "attend," "serve."

6. *legem ineffabilem; lex* translates νόμος ("law," "custom"). In this context, not necessarily a law.

7. *et compraehendere quidem Graecum peregrinum: quidem* ("actually") strengthens the previous word ("seized") for no apparent reason. There are many cases in the Latin translation of *Contra Apionem* where *quidem* appears to strengthen the verb, and most cases may be explained as an attempt to translate a Greek particle such as γέ or δή. In this case, however, the text may be corrupt and should be emended to read *quendam* (= τινα, indefinite—"a"), agreeing with *Graecum peregrinum*. On *quandam*, see note 13 below and note 10 for a reversed corruption. The abduction is not planned to catch a specific, select individual, but any casual foreigner (Greek).

8. *peregrinum* is most probably a translation of ἀλλόφυλον, perhaps a misreading of the term used in the Greek formulation of the secret oath, ἄλλον φῦλον (a person belonging to another race—para. 121; see note 16 below). ξένος would be best translated as *alienus* or *alienigena* (but see Damocritus, note 27 below).

9. *ad quandam silvam: silva* may mean "a wood" as well as "a grove." Given the Egyptian origin of the libel (see discussion on pp. 271–76 below), "grove" is preferable. On the translation of *quandam*, cf. note 13 below. The indefinite *silva* indicates that the scene of the crime was not determined beforehand. The participants, trying to hide the crime, turned into the first grove on their way.

10. *occidere quidem eum hominem:* in this case, *quendam* would be impossible, and *quidem* is clearly intended to strengthen the force of the previous verb (cf. note 7 above).

11. Thackeray (1926) translates *gustare* as "partake," which is admissible if each portion is understood to be very small. The verb also appears in para. 100.

12. *ex eius viscera:* the word *viscera* may denote the important internal organs, such as entrails, or more generally, flesh. In the present circumstances, where the participants were the Jewish people

would have unfriendly relations with the Greeks, and then they threw away the remains of the dead man into a pit.[13] (96) Then [Apion] reports that he (the man) said that there were now [only] a few days left for him to live and asked that, blushing at (= respecting) the gods of the Greeks †he would both overcome† the plots of the Jews against his lifeblood, and free him from the evils surrounding him. [14]

Josephus omitted the end of the story, but it can be reconstructed from his subsequent refutation of the libel, together with Diodorus's account of the advice of the "friends" of Antiochus VII (34/35. 1. 3–4):[15] upon the discovery of the abhorrent practice, Antiochus decided to defile the Jewish Temple and persecute the Jews and their religion. The text of the libel itself also requires completion: the wording of the oath of hatred has not been preserved in the extant Latin translation, but the Greek original is quoted in Josephus's response (Ap. 2. 121):

> We swear by the god who made the heaven and the earth and the sea to show goodwill to no other race, and especially not to Greeks. [16]

---

or rather a representative crowd, and each portion was in any case small, just enough to be "tasted," the author seems to intend the second meaning. Parallels to the eating of only entrails or of the whole body are to be found in Greco-Roman literature, notably in references to Egyptian practices (see pp. 261, 271–72 below).

13. *quandam foveam* suggests ὄρυγμά τι. It is clear that the pit is indefinite; hence the translation "a pit." The ceremony is thus performed in haste.

14. *ut erubescens Graecorum deos et superantes in suo sanguine insidias Iudaeorum de malis eum circumstantibus liberaret*: *sanguis* in this context obviously means "lifeblood," and the story of the cannibalistic feast also does not refer to blood; the text of the sentence is corrupt. Thackeray (1926) 330 suggests emending so that Antiochus is the subject of *superans*, reading "respecting the gods of Greece, and overcoming this Jewish plot against his lifeblood, to deliver . . .". But this interpretation requires *in suo sanguine* to take on the meaning of *in suum sanguinem* "against his lifeblood," and the logic of the sentence is suspect; surely it is by delivering the man from his ills that Antiochus would overcome the plot, and not vice versa. I would suggest reading *ut erubescens Graecorum deos, et superantes in suo sanguine insidias Iudaeorum <devinceret (destruet, vel sim.), et> de malis eum circumstantibus liberaret*, meaning "that, respecting the gods of the Greeks, he would both destroy the plots abounding in his blood and free him from the evils encompassing him." The clause *superantes in suo sanguine insidias* is understood here as a translation of τὰς ἐν τῷ αἵματι αὐτοῦ περισσευούσας ἐπιβουλάς. For περισσεύω + ἐν + dat. as equivalent to Latin *supero* + *in* + abl., see Vulgate 1 Corinthians 15.58; 2 Corinthians 8.7a; 7b; Colossians 2.7. For ἐπιβουλαί as *insidiae*, see Acts 20.19.

15. See pp. 455–57 below on the omission by Posidonius of the blood libel, which was included in the original story.

16. Reading ἄλλῳ φύλῳ ("to any other race") rather than ἀλλοφύλῳ ("to a stranger"); cf. ἄλλῳ ἔθνει ("to any other race" in Diod. 34/35. 1. 3) and ἀνθρώπων τινί ("to anyone of men" [= "any man"] in Lysimachus [Joseph. Ap. 1. 309]).

REMARKS ON EARLIER RESEARCH

In the discussion of the ass libel, I already had occasion to refer to Elias Bickerman's celebrated article of 1927 on the ass and the blood libels.[17] While his suggestion that not only the framework story but also the ass libel originated in Syria has gained little support, his literary analysis of the blood libel has been unanimously applauded, with his suggested origin and dating for it being widely accepted.[18] It would, then, be appropriate to summarize Bickerman's conclusions, and discuss each in turn.

Bickerman argues that the blood libel, as it appears in Apion, is a combination of two different versions. He finds shoddy stitching between the two accounts in the sentence "having led him down to a certain wood actually [they] killed this man || and sacrificed his body according to their rites." With his typical irony, Bickerman comments: "Einen schon Toten zu opfern, ist etwas zu spät."[19] His assumption is that cult sacrifice necessarily included the killing of the victim, and indeed it was a mark of disrespect toward the gods to sacrifice a dead animal. In most cult sacrifice ceremonies known to us, the killing is part of the ceremony, and it is performed on the altar itself or at its foot.

This statement requires some elaboration, as Jewish sacrificial practice appears to challenge it. Jewish ritual slaughter, in contrast to the usual Greek sacrifice, was not performed exclusively on the altar or at its base. According to Leviticus (chaps. 1–9), the slaughter was performed, as were the prior ceremonial activities of the laying on of hands and waving (סמיכה ותנופה), and the subsequent activities of skinning, carving, and washing, at the "entrance of the tabernacle." Sources referring to the time of the Second Temple (especially Mishna Zebachim) reveal that all these activities were performed in the Temple Court (עזרה), each type of victim in a different place, and it was only after this that the blood and the organs were brought to the altar. It might therefore be

---

17. See p. 243, note 120 above, and elsewhere. The article was published unchanged in the collection of Bickerman's papers (1976–80). I refer henceforward to the collection, which is readily available.

18. See, e.g., Flusser (1949) 105; Tcherikover (1961) 366–67; Lewy (1960) 151; Stern, *GLAJJ* 1: 412; Gabba (1989) 644–45; Feldman (1993) 127. Tcherikover and Stern differ from Bickerman with regard to the identification of the inventors of the libel. For further criticism, see Bar-Kochva (1996c); Schäfer (1997a) 60–62, 236–37.

19. "To sacrifice someone who is already dead is somewhat too late": Bickerman (1976–80) 2: 238. The overall rejection of Bickerman's analysis of the sentence by Schäfer (1997a) 63–64 is unsubstantiated. The distinction between two stories integrated in the sentence is inevitable and appears also from a good number of indications and considerations detailed below. Cf. also notes 9 and 13 above on the haste in turning to the grove and getting rid of the victim's remains in a nearby pit.

argued that, although all the elements together constitute the sacrifice (and this is explicit in Lev. 1.3–4), the author of the existing version of the libel, aware of Jewish procedure, wrongly conceived of the slaughter as an activity separate from, and prior to, the sacrifice.

In response to such an argument, it must be said at the outset that the very possibility that the author knew the rules of Jewish sacrifice in such detail is unlikely in the extreme. Were he to have had even the most basic information about Jewish sacrifice, he would have known that the Judaean Jews sacrificed only in the Jerusalem Temple, and the imagined sacrifice in the grove could not have been described by him as "according to their rites." And had he been at all conversant with Jewish sacrificial law, he would have known that the remains of a victim were not thrown into a pit, since "that which remaineth . . . ye shall burn with fire" (e.g., Exod. 12.10; Lev. 7.17). Above all, Greek and Roman authors had only a rather general, often even vague, notion of Jewish customs and law, all the more so with regard to strictly technical matters such as sacrificial law. The descriptions of Jewish rites of sacrifice that have reached us from the literature of the period are purely figments of the imagination.[20]

Bickerman's basic distinction, therefore, between a story of the killing and the story of the sacrifice, stands up to criticism. The same cannot be said of his detailed reconstruction of the two versions, their dating, their sources, and their literary genre. Bickerman sees the two versions as simply placed back to back and connected at the clumsy join already mentioned. It is therefore easy for him to separate them. The first version (up to the words "actually killed this man") describes the kidnapping of the victim, his fattening up for a year in the Temple, and his subsequent removal to the grove where he is killed. The second version describes the victim being sacrificed in the Temple to the Jewish God and the audience tasting of his flesh and swearing an oath of unfriendly relations with foreigners, especially Greeks.

Bickerman regards the first version as a variation of the "king of Saturnalia" celebrations popular in the Greco-Roman world as well as in remote cultures.[21] In such a festival, a man would be crowned for the duration of the celebrations, would enjoy his temporary status to the utmost, and would be executed at the conclusion of the ceremonies.[22] The second version, on the other hand, is based on the *topos* of "conspiratorial gatherings": the conspirators meet secretly, usually

20. See pp. 30–31 above on Theophrastus. On Plutarch *Quaestiones conviviales* 672B, see Bar-Kochva (1997b) 405 n. 62.

21. Bickerman (1976–80) 235–38. The connection with the "king of Saturnalia" was first suggested by Müller (1877) 263 ff., and repeated by Friedländer (1903) 385. They, however, do not distinguish between the two versions.

22. See, e.g., the survey of Frazer (1913) 9: 306–411.

commit a horrible crime that serves to reinforce their mutual bonds of loyalty, and may indulge in a cannibalistic feast.[23]

Bickerman goes on to identify the inventors of the libel, and determines their purpose, accepting Josephus's comment that the libel was designed "to vouch for Antiochus and cover up his infidelity and sacrilege, which he perpetrated on our people because of a lack of funds" (*Ap.* 2. 90; cf. 97). Bickerman attributes the invention of the story (and the two versions of the libel) to Seleucid court historians, who aspired to excuse the unprecedented measures of Antiochus Epiphanes.[24] The libel helped to justify his persecution of the Jews by demonstrating their inhuman character and religion, and by exposing their conspiracy against the whole of humankind, especially the Greeks.[25] The blood libel was, then, according to Bickerman, a Greek-Seleucid invention, adapting European folklore material.

Bickerman's analysis, attractive as it sounds, cannot be accepted in its entirety. However, its two most significant elements stand up to criticism: the suggestion that there were two versions of the libel (but not Bickerman's reconstruction); and the conclusion (following Josephus and Heinrich Graetz) that the story about Antiochus's visit to the Temple (not the libel itself) originated in one way or another in Seleucid propaganda. In the following section, I shall try to reconstruct the two versions, and find out whether the libel (as distinct from the framework story) was indeed invented by the Seleucid court historians, and, finally, attempt to trace the ultimate origins of the two versions, and their combination into one.

THE PARALLEL IN DAMOCRITUS
AND THE EXECUTION

Before going into the questions just raised, it would be appropriate to consider another reference to the blood libel. It appears in the *Suda,* in an abstract of a monograph on the Jews by Damocritus, an unknown Hellenistic author probably in the period after the destruction of the Second Temple.[26] The entry, brief as it is, may help us in reconstructing the full account in Apion and the two versions of the libel integrated into his story (*Suda* s.v. Δαμόκριτος):[27]

---

23. Bickerman (1976–80) 2: 227–31.

24. Bickerman (1976–80) 2: 238–39. First suggested by Graetz (1872) 199, and repeated by Müller (1877) 263 ff.; Friedländer (1903) 385–86. The reservations of Schäfer (1997a) 74–75 are unjustified.

25. Bickerman (1976–80) 2: 243–44.

26. On Damocritus, see Müller, *FHG* IV. 377; Susemihl (1891) 2: 387 n. 227; Reinach (1895) 121; Flusser (1949) 104 ff.; Stern, *GLAJJ* 1: 530–31. On his dating, see Stern, who draws attention to the recurrent imperfect form.

27. Δαμόκριτος, ἱστορικός. Τακτικὰ ἐν βιβλίοις β′. Περὶ Ἰουδαίων· ἐν ᾧ φησιν ὅτι χρυσῆν ὄνου κεφαλὴν προσεκύνουν καὶ κατὰ ἐπταετίαν ξένον ἀγροῦντες προσέφερον καὶ κατὰ λεπτὰ τὰς σάρκας διέξαινον, καὶ οὕτως ἀνήρουν. Cf. the shortened version s.v. Ἰούδας καὶ Ἰουδαῖος.

Damocritus, historian. *Tactics* in two books. *On Jews,* in which he says they used to worship the golden head of an ass, and every seventh year,[28] being idle,[29] they would bring [to the altar][30] a stranger, and bit by bit cut his flesh, and in this way destroy him.

We are mainly interested in the penultimate sentence of the passage: κατὰ λεπτὰ (bit by bit) τὰς σάρκας (the flesh) διέξαινον (they cut). The verb ξαίνω (and διαξαίνω) basically denotes combing wool with a toothed instrument, wire brush, or the like. This may at first sight recall later Jewish and Christian traditions (in Hebrew, Aramaic, and Syrian) concerning Roman tortures and executions of martyrs in Caesarea Maritima in which an iron comb is used to lacerate the flesh of the victim.[31] It is, however, impossible to effectively card the flesh bit by bit into small pieces, so as to provide for a "taste" of a great crowd. Another meaning of διαξαίνω is "to tear asunder." Accordingly, the sentence has been interpreted as describing the dismemberment of a living man in the sort of frenzied Dionysiac orgy known from Asia Minor and certain Greek islands.[32] Tearing asunder, however, is no more successful than carding at producing small pieces.

Greek medical literature provides us with another meaning for διαξαίνω: "to cut in the context of small organs and even sinews." Such cutting would clearly require a delicate surgical knife.[33] Execution by cutting into small pieces would

---

28. According to the full entry, once in seven years; according to the short version, once in three years. The logic of the first version is quite understandable (see below), and therefore it seems preferable. For anthropological parallels for "three years", see p. 268 below.

29. ἀργοῦντες ("being idle") is my emendation to the MSS reading ἀγρεύοντες ("hunting"). The idea that the Jews first hunted and then brought a victim to the altar would require the aorist participle ἀγρεύσαντες. The MSS reading as it stands has the victim being brought to the altar, yet being hunted at the same time. The use of the verb ἀγρεύειν in the given context in an entry of a lexicon is in itself rather strange. The emendation involves only a slight change. The sense would be that while the Jews were idle (every seventh year), they had nothing better to do than bring a foreign victim to the altar (see below for more details). A later copyist may not have understood the reference to idleness and may have "corrected" the word to ἀγρεύοντες, reasoning that the Jews were not idle but "hunting" foreigners.

30. προσέφερον: the verb προσφέρω (offer) is used here elliptically in the sense of "offer a sacrifice to a god." See LXX Amos 4.25, where προσφέρω is a literal translation of the Hebrew להגיש (הזבחים ומנחה הגשתם-לי במדבר ארבעים שנה) = μὴ σφάγια καὶ θυσίας προσηνέγκατέ μοι ἐν τῇ ἐρήμῳ τεσσαράκοντα ἔτη). Cf. Matt. 5.23; Heb. 9.4.

31. מסריקי דפרזלא, סקרא, and מסרקות של ברזל: see, e.g., BT Berakhot 61b; Eusebius *On the Martyrs of Palestine* 6. 6 et passim. Cf. BT Gittin 57b; Sanhedrin 96b; and see the synopsis in Reeg (1985) 70*–71*.

32. Flusser (1949) 104 ff.; and see Porphyry *De abstinentia* 2. 55; Clement *Protrepticus* 36P; cf. Plutarch *Themistocles* 3. Stern, who accepts Flusser's interpretation, translates: "They used to kill him by carding his flesh into small pieces" (*GLAJJ* no. 247).

33. See LSJ s.v. διαξαίνω, with references to Galen and Rufus Medicus (both second century C.E.)

be feasible with such a knife, and indeed we have an account of one such incident recorded by Juvenal, which arose from the animosity between two Egyptian villages (Juv. *Sat.* 15. 75–83):

> They expose their backs to swift flight with the Ombians pursuing,
> They who inhabit neighboring Tentyra of the shady palm.
> Here slips one from too much fear, his course
> Hastening headlong, and is captured. And him, cut into very many
> Bits and small pieces (so that one dead man for many people
> Might suffice) entire—with bones devoured—do eat
> The victorious crowd. Nor did they cook in blazing bronze
> Or on spits; to such an extent they thought it long and tardy
> To wait for fires, content with a corpse uncooked.

The precise point at which the victim dies is not indicated. It does not seem that he is being lynched, but rather prepared for the cannibalistic ceremony by being cut into many small pieces while still alive. He is diced so that his flesh might suffice for many people.[34] Note that the Jews are said by Apion to have tasted, not eaten, the flesh of the victim. Since the Jewish people (that is, a significantly representative sample of it) is supposed to have made up the audience, one might suppose that the pieces were too small to afford much more than a taste.[35] We may infer that Damocritus also had in mind some cannibalistic feast.

and the philosopher Alexander of Aphrodisias (third century): διαξαίνω νεῦρον εἰς ἴνας, διαξαίνω ἔντερον. Paulus Aegineta (sixth-seventh century) uses the verb to denote the cutting of flesh. On surgical knives in the classical world, see Milne (1907) esp. 32 on knives for delicate surgical operations such as the opening of veins, the removal of moles, etc.

34. A parallel for this is to be found in a midrash about the prophet Samuel's execution of Agag, the king of Amalek: "He was cutting olives (i.e., tiny pieces) of his flesh and feeding them to נעמיות (a type of large fowl) ... (He) chose for him (Agag) a bitter death" (Pesikta De-Rav Kahana 3. 6; cf. Peskita Rabbati 12. 13 [55b]). Medieval midrashim like the Pesikta usually draw on earlier ones. It may echo some form of Egyptian execution recorded in the Roman period (see p. 271 below), perhaps preceding a cannibalistic ceremony, replaced in the Jewish legend by a reference to feeding fowls. I am not aware of this mode of execution occurring in the period when the medieval midrash was edited.

35. This also appears from one of Josephus's rhetorical questions following the libel: "How indeed is it possible that all gathered for these victims and the flesh sufficed for so many thousands to taste, as Apion asserts" (*Ap.* 2. 100). The reference to Apion does not necessarily prove that he explicitly mentioned the participation of many thousands of Jews. In view of Josephus's debating techniques, the assertion could have been inferred from the words "the Jews," which may have preceded the sentence about the "cannibalistic feast," or from the general sense of the story. There is an interesting anthropological parallel in a Polynesian ceremony. All members of the tribe, including small children, were obliged to test the victim when he was the chief of an enemy tribe. The herald would even repeat the cry "Has everyone tasted?" See Turner (1861) 426–27. On "tasting" the flesh of murdered people as a form of vengeance, see also Clearchus in Athenaeus 12. 541e.

It would seem, then, that Damocritus drew ultimately on Apion.[36] Apion's works were, by and large, quite famous in the Roman and Greek world, and Josephus's countertreatise considerably increased his reputation as the most aggressive Jew-hater. Apion's detailed account was therefore the most natural source for an author like Damocritus to consult, as he evidently aspired to present an extremely negative picture of the Jews. Damocritus's version of the ass libel was indeed identical to Apion's: the entry refers to "a golden ass head," which was an "improvement" by Apion, and not, as in other sources, to the statue of an ass, or of Moses riding on an ass.[37] It mentions a sacrifice and an execution and implies a cannibalistic feast, indicating that Damocritus's work contained the two versions of the blood libel as well. It appears that Damocritus (like many modern readers) did not notice the internal contradictions in the combined story, to the extent that he even wrote about the sacrifice before the killing; at the same time, it is possible that he tried to harmonize both versions (the sacrifice and the killing) by using the word προσέφερον—"brought [to the altar]"—instead of, for example, ἔθυον—"sacrificed."

It has been argued that Damocritus was using another source, since he refers to a frequency of once in seven years, while Apion speaks of an annual event.[38] This, however, looks like an "improvement" by Damocritus upon Apion, in line with the contemporary merging of the seventh year with the Sabbath, the increasing interest in, and negative attitude toward, the Sabbath, and the tendency to explain its origin by the events in the Exodus.[39] The line of reasoning went like this: Jewish misanthropy was caused by the expulsion from Egypt; the Sabbath (and likewise the sabbatical year) was established by the Jews to commemorate their salvation in the wilderness after six days of sufferings;[40] and

---

36. Reinach (1895) 121; (1930) 74 n. 1; Jacoby, *FGrH* III.C, no. 730, p. 691.

37. See p. 241 above.

38. See Flusser (1949) 105–6; Stern, *GLAJJ* 1: 530. Nor do Flusser's other contentions stand up to criticism. Cf. Feldman (1993) 127. On the reference to "a stranger" alone, see note 44 below.

39. See the survey of Gentile sources on the Sabbath by Whittaker (1984) 63–72. On the seventh year as a year of rest, see Nicolaus in Josephus *Bellum Judaicum* 1. 60; *Antiquitates Judaicae* 13. 234; Tacitus *Historiae* 5. 4. 3.

40. On the origin of the Sabbath: Apion in Josephus *Contra Apionem* 2. 23; Pompeius Trogus in Justin 36. 2. 14; Plutarch *De Iside et Osiride* 363C-D; Tacitus *Historiae* 5. 3. 2, 4. 3. On Jewish "misanthropy" as a reaction to the expulsion and subsequent suffering, see Diodorus 34/35. 1. 2; Pompeius Trogus in Justin 36. 1. 15; Lysimachus in Josephus *Contra Apionem* 1. 309; Tacitus *Historiae* 5. 3. 1. The remark by Damocritus that the ceremony was held every seventh year may have arisen from reflecting upon the connection between the origin of the Jews and Saturn, with all that that entails. This connection is mentioned in Tacitus (*Hist.* 5. 4. 4) and appeared in earlier sources. The indolence of the seven-year sabbatical was adduced as evidence for this connection, with astrological explanations being given for it involving the movements of Saturn (*Hist.* 5. 4. 4). Saturn-Kronos was believed to have eaten (or swallowed) his sons (Hes. *Theog.* 453–506 and later sources).

by extension the seventh year was chosen for the most vicious expression of Jewish misanthropy. The connection between the sabbatical year and the blood libel added a new abhorrent dimension to the already deplorable "indolence" of the Jews on the Sabbath: the author explicitly links their "being idle" (i.e., not doing useful work) in the seventh year with their perpetration of the appalling crime. As the elder Cato reportedly remarked later, *diuturna quies vitiis alimenta ministrat* ("Extended rest provides nourishment to vices," or in more modern parlance, "The Devil finds work for idle hands"). After all, one would not expect Damocritus, who devoted a monograph to the Jews, to always repeat verbatim his generally well-known source, without contributing something of his own.

The conclusion that Damocritus drew on Apion helps us in reconstructing the two versions of Apion. There is a conspicuous lacuna in Apion's story as quoted by Josephus: the "killing" version does not specify how the victim was actually killed. One may assume that some description of the execution would have been present in a libel that strove so diligently to demonstrate the inhumanity of the Jews. The version of Damocritus allows us to complete the text of Apion in this regard: the victim was killed by cutting his flesh into small pieces by means of a special cutting implement, and the pieces were then distributed to the crowd for tasting (being too small to qualify for eating). The cannibalistic version of the libel was therefore more shocking and monstrous than the account as preserved in Josephus. The omission of the description of the execution may be attributed to the Latin translator: the text of the story about the visit of Antiochus IV to the Temple is evidently abbreviated in places, as appears from the absence of the text of the oath. At the same time, a deliberate omission by Josephus, in order to soften the forcefulness of the libel, seems even more likely.

THE SACRIFICE OF THE VICTIM AT THE ALTAR

The extraordinary form of execution imputed to the Jews in one version of the libel reflects on the sacrificial technique in the other version. Would the inventors of this version have missed the opportunity to illustrate the cruelty of the Jews afforded by the method of sacrifice? The reference as it now stands is vague: "sacrificed his body according to their rites (*secundum suas sollemnitates*"; *Ap.* 2. 95). What then were "their rites," according to this version in its original form? What did Gentiles know or imagine about Jewish sacrificial practices?

The only Greek or Hellenistic description of Jewish sacrifice survived in the fragment of Theophrastus on the Jewish people (Porph. *Abst.* 2. 26). As we saw in the analysis of this fragment, Theophrastus reported that the Jews sacrificed animals by burning them alive until they were completely consumed by the flames

(2. 26. 1–2).[41] Theophrastus even adds that the Jews were the first to practice human sacrifice (2. 26. 4); it is not clear whether he added that they continue to do so to the present day.[42] Whatever the case may be, the statement in the blood libel account that the sacrifice of a Gentile was performed "according to their rites" suggests that the author intended sacrifice by burning alive. This interpretation receives indirect support from a conspicuous parallel in the sources of inspiration for the libel (see p. 274 below).

In principle, the method of killing in both versions of the libel is thus similar: the miserable foreigner finds his death in a slow, cruel, and most painful way. The form of execution and sacrifice, therefore, was exploited to illustrate further the hatred of the Jews toward foreigners. We shall see later (pp. 266–67 below) who omitted the sacrifice version's description of burning the victim alive from the combined version in the story of the visit of Antiochus IV to the Temple.

A RECONSTRUCTION OF THE TWO VERSIONS: THE TEMPLE SACRIFICE AND THE CANNIBALISTIC FEAST IN THE GROVE

Let us return now to Bickerman's suggested reconstruction. Relying on the position of the reference in Apion to the sacrifice following mention of the killing of the victim, Bickerman distinguishes between two versions, one of which, in his view, follows the other: (1) the fattening of the victim in the Temple and his killing in a grove; (2) a sacrificial ceremony (in the Temple) that included a cannibalistic feast and the taking of an oath of hatred. However, the killing of the stranger bit by bit, as preserved by Damocritus, obviously preceded the cannibalistic feast, not the sacrifice. Moreover, why would a man be led to a grove and killed there if he has just spent time in the Temple, a place dedicated to slaughter (and sacrifice)? Again, the account implies a conspiratorial secrecy (hiding the man in the Temple; killing him in a grove of all places; efforts to remove all traces of the crime); yet although temples had plenty of hidden chambers, it is precisely at the commencement of the crime that the man is removed from his seclusion in the Temple and transported through the city and then beyond, to a grove, where at last the extreme secrecy can be resumed.

These and previous observations suggest a few points that should be considered in a reconstruction of the two versions. The elements in each of the following pairs cannot belong to the same account: (1) the incarceration in the Temple; the abduction to a grove; (2) the Temple sacrifice; the killing of the victim in a grove; (3) the holocaust sacrifice; the cannibalistic feast; (4) the complete burning of the victim in the Temple; the disposal of the remains in a pit. In other words, the killing in the grove, the cannibalistic feast, and the disposal of the remains in a pit all belong to the "killing" version, not the "sacrifice" version. The reference to an oath, as it stands in the present text ("and made a vow in the sacrifice of the Greek"), certainly belongs to the sacrifice version; but this does not preclude a similar oath in the original "killing" version.

The fattening in the Temple is problematic if it took a whole year (*Ap.* 2. 95). The opening sentence to the libel states that the practice was repeated annually "at a certain established time." However, the foreigner (a casual merchant or the like—cf. 91), might not be available for capture exactly one year before his planned sacrifice. One of the two sentences under discussion, therefore, seems to be an addition, probably by the author of the story about Antiochus IV's visit to the Temple. The reference to the fattening of the victim in the Temple might well be the suspected interpolation, as it would help integrate the libel into his account. Instead of Antiochus arriving improbably exactly at the time of the sacrifice, he enters the Temple at any time during the year preceding it, learns the details of the sacrifice at his leisure, and manages to save the victim to boot. The fattening also lends to the story a tragic character: the perks following the kidnapping come as a pleasant surprise to the Greek, who at first ignores his confinement and enjoys being showered with all sorts of good things. When at last the bitter truth begins to dawn on him, he sinks into a deep depression.[43] The comparison of literary and anthropological parallels, which follows, corroborates the hypothesis that the fattening of the victim is an addition to the original "sacrifice" libel.

That the author of the framework story intervenes here and there may be seen in the reference to the descent of the victim. In the sentence referring to the abduction (95), obviously common to both versions, the victim is awkwardly described as a "Greek foreigner" (*Graecus peregrinus*). The expression is not merely an accidental verbosity or the result of the combination of two versions, but rather a later addition of the epithet "Greek" to the original "foreigner." This appears in the wording of the oath, "to show goodwill to no other race (ἄλλῳ φύλῳ), and especially not to Greeks" (121), where the final clause is certainly an addition: the parallels in Lysimachus (*Ap.* 1. 309) and Diodorus (34/35. 1. 3) state only that Moses instructed his people "to show goodwill to no man" and "not to share table with any other nation, nor to show [them] any goodwill at all," respectively. The additions "Greek" and "Greeks" were required in the context of the story about Antiochus Epiphanes, where the kidnapped man is naturally described as a Greek (*Ap.* 2. 93) and is said to have appealed to the "gods of the Greeks" (96).[44]

---

43. The tragic shaping of the story is indicated by Josephus (para. 97: "huiusmodi ergo fabula non tantum omni tragoedia plenissima est . . . "). See in detail Flusser (1949) 116–18.

44. Damocritus refers only to a *xenos* (stranger); a writer living in the Roman period, after the

The text of the two versions can now be reconstructed. In the following, square brackets indicate my supplements to Apion's text based on Damocritus and Theophrastus; curly brackets indicate interpolations made by the author of the framework story; angular brackets indicate a supplement derived from the refutation by Josephus in *Contra Apionem* 2. 122; and parentheses indicate possible supplements:

VERSION A. THE "HUMAN SACRIFICE" (TEMPLE SACRIFICE, OATH)

The practice was repeated annually at a certain established time. They seized a {Greek} foreigner {and fattened him for a year} and sacrificed him {his body} [by burning it alive] according to their rites ... and made a vow in the sacrificing of the foreigner {Greek}, that they would have unfriendly relations with foreigners {Greeks}: <"we swear by the god who made the heaven and the earth and the sea to show goodwill to no race {and especially not to Greeks}>.

VERSION B. THE "CANNIBALISTIC FEAST"
(IN A GROVE, KILLING, FEAST DISPOSAL)

They seized a {Greek} foreigner, and having led him down to a certain grove killed this man [cutting his body into small pieces] and tasted of his flesh (and vowed to have unfriendly relations with foreigners {Greeks} <"we swear ..." etc.>), and then they threw away the remains of the dead man into a certain pit.

The Antiochus author combined the two versions, holding as far as possible to the natural order of subjects. Where they were more or less identical he would quote only one version, as he would also do in the case of any subject appearing in one version only. Where the two versions differed, he would copy both versions, one after the other, for that particular information. The following outline may illustrate his method:

1. Timing: A once a year, at a fixed time; B once a year
2. "Selection" and identity of the victim: A, B kidnapping a foreigner
3. Crime and scene of crime: B killing in a grove; A sacrifice in the Temple
4. Accompanying ceremonies: B cannibalistic feast, oath(?); A oath of hatred
5. Disposal: B remains thrown into a pit; A complete burning of victim

In this way, the Antiochus author incorporated all the components of the two versions of the blood libel. He was anxious not to lose any piece of vicious rumor imputed to the Jews, in order to magnify the abhorrent impression of the alleged Jewish practices. However, the reference to the victim's being burned alive ("sacrifice" version) had to be omitted, because this did not square with the more hor-

destruction of the Second Temple, would prefer to portray Jewish hatred as directed against all strangers, not just against Greeks. Be that as it may, we have just an extremely short entry.

rific cannibalistic version: there would have been nothing left to kill by cutting into pieces, or to "taste" once the victim had been burned alive. To many ancients (and to medieval Christians), cannibalism was much more repulsive than the act of burning alive, and it was even conceived as a crime against humanity. This patchwork method of blending two different versions into one account was quite common in Greek and Roman literature, and it is well known to scholars of ancient Judaism from Josephus's *Jewish Antiquities*.[45]

LITERARY AND ETHNOGRAPHICAL PARALLELS
AND THE TYPOLOGY OF THE STORIES

Bickerman classifies the two versions (as he sees them) as types of the "king of Saturnalia" and "conspiracy" (*coniuratio*) stories. He further argues that while there are no parallels to these versions in the Orient, one can find a good number of literary and anthropological equivalents in the Greco-Roman world and in remote cultures. Consequently, he reaches the conclusion that these "northern" materials inspired the two versions of the blood libel, and that they were invented in the same circle of Seleucid court historians that composed the framework story of Antiochus IV's visit to the Temple.

As a matter of fact, the typological parallels cited by Bickerman bear only a vague similarity to the two versions as reconstructed by him. The identification of the "sacrifice" version as belonging to the "king of Saturnalia" type is certainly mistaken: the Saturnalia celebrations were cheerful events, aimed at recalling nostalgically the Golden Age, while the motivation of the Jews is clearly to instill and perpetuate animosity toward strangers; the "king of Saturnalia" enjoyed a period of pseudo-rule, taking part in public celebrations, feasts, and a variety of pleasures, but the victim of the Jews is confined in the Temple ("shut up and observed by no one"), and his only pleasure is excessive food in solitude; the Jews' victim was chosen just because he was a "foreigner," while the "king of Saturnalia" could be a prisoner, convicted criminal, prisoner of war, poor local man, or one of the community chosen by lot—but not, so far as I know, a casual foreigner;[46] the execution of the "king of Saturnalia" was never performed by sacrifice on the altar, but by stoning, hanging, beheading, crucifixion, or even having the victim cut his own throat.

Let us turn to literary or anthropological parallels to the two versions as

---

45. See, e.g., pp. 401–9 and cf. p. 324 below.

46. The Albanian human sacrifice (Strabo 11. 4. 7), in which a foreigner is fattened for a year and then executed, does not contain the features of the "king of Saturnalia" feast (*pace* Bickerman [1976–80] 2: 236–37), nor does it present a real parallel to the first version as reconstructed by Bickerman. See the text, p. 269 below.

reconstructed above. In order to distinguish between apparent and real parallels, we need to separate the elements of "human sacrifice" stories and practices and list the many variations.[47] The following list, which is not exhaustive, presents the common components:

1. Frequency of the event: annually at a fixed date (feast of Thargelia [May], Easter, Fourteenth of March, February, June); occasionally, in response to a misfortune (plague, drought, famine); once every three years[48]
2. Choice and identity of the victim: child; beautiful lad; prisoner of war; foreigner; slave; slave, well proportioned, without any fault or blemish; temple servant who went into a frenzy; sinner; criminal; prisoner; convicted prisoner; man sentenced to death; ugly and deformed person of the community; village idiot; degraded and useless man of the community; man of the poorer classes who offers himself as a scapegoat; citizen or soldier chosen by lot
3. Preparations: a whole year, the victim being fed on "choice and pure food"; one year of fattening, the victim bound with fetters; excommunication six days before execution[49]
4. Place of execution: outside the city; a remote and isolated temple; a cliff; a seashore; the stairs of a temple; inside a temple; outside a temple[50]
5. Form of execution: burning alive; killing by a spear thrust before burning; stoning; drowning in the sea; opening the chest and taking out the heart; beheading; beheading and impaling the head; cutting the throat; committing suicide in one way or another; flogging to death; hanging; crucifying; throwing from a cliff; sacrificing on the altar to a god; striking a lance through the side into the heart; burying alive up to the neck in sand
6. Accompanying or preliminary ceremonies: a procession in which the victim is led through the streets and beaten with long white rods; the victim, dressed in sacred garments and bedecked with holy branches, is led through the whole city, accompanied by prayers that all the evils of the people might fall on him; the victim, wearing a string of black or white figs around his neck,

---

47. See esp. Frazer (1913) 9: 170–305; Schwenn (1915); Loeb (1927); Hogg (1958); Shankman (1969); Sagan (1974); Tannahill (1975); Harris (1977); Hughes (1991). And there are many more. Most of the studies and collections concentrate, naturally, on anthropological material from the continents of Africa and America. These have not been included in the summary above.

48. Outside of Europe: once in half a year; once in three, five, or seven years.

49. Outside of Europe: a year or six months in which the victim is worshipped as a god, ornamented accordingly, delicately nurtured (to keep a slim figure), strolling through the streets playing the flute, dancing and singing; the victim is part of the community for five years, receiving the weapons, clothes, and even the wives of a fallen hero, for which he pays the price in due course.

50. On the origins and purposes of the story and the reference to Iphigenia, see Griffiths (1948a) 413–14.

is led around the city; the victim eats a meal of dried figs, a barley loaf, and cheese, then is beaten seven times upon his genitals with squills and branches of wild trees while the flute plays a particular tune; a complex and extremely lengthy series of tortures

7. Purpose of the ceremony (usually only implied): the victim is a scapegoat; to expel evils, demons, evil spirits; to overcome witchcraft; to appease a certain deity; to remove plagues, pestilence, drought, scarcity, and other misfortunes; to atone; the victim is a substitute for a ruler (so that he might not be hurt); to promote fertility or healthy crops; to symbolize the death of a deity and the birth of a new one; to divine the future; to purify; to inaugurate a new temple or house

The combinations are many and various, but there is no single case that presents more than one feature identical to the "human sacrifice" version in Apion. The only case I could track down that refers to the sacrifice of an abducted Greek or foreigner is the story in Herodotus about the practice of the Tauri residing in the Crimea (4. 103):

> For [the Tauri] sacrifice to the virgin both those shipwrecked and whichever seafarers of the Greeks they might capture, in this sort of way: having begun, they smite the head with a club; some say that they push the body down from the cliff (for the temple was founded on a cliff), but the head they impale; others agree about the head but say that the body is not pushed from the cliff but buried in earth. The Tauri themselves say that this daemon to whom they sacrifice is Iphigeneia, the daughter of Agamemnon.

All the elements of this story differ from those of the report of human sacrifice in Apion, apart from the kidnapping of a foreigner (a Greek was not mentioned in the original report, as we have noted above): the event is not seasonal or annual but takes place whenever a suitable victim is captured; there may be several victims, and not just one individual; the victim is not sacrificed upon the altar but killed by striking his head with a club; his body and head are not dealt with as in ordinary sacrifices; finally, the motivation does not seem to be to perpetuate hatred toward foreigners or other nations, but to appease a goddess. Other references to the story about the Tauri (esp. in Apollod. *Epit.* 6. 26; Diod. 4. 44. 7) offer no closer similarities.

Another case worth quoting refers to human sacrifice by the Albanians (Strabo 11. 4. 7):

> There officiates a man most honored (after the king, of course), being in charge of the sacred land, plentiful and well populated, (in charge) both of this and of the temple slaves, many of whom are possessed and utter prophecies; whoever of these becomes possessed too much wanders alone in the woods, and this man the priest

arrests, binds with a sacred chain, nourishes sumptuously for that year, then, having been led forth to the sacrifice of the goddess, having been anointed, is sacrificed
along with other victims. The way of the sacrifice is this: someone holding a sacred
lance, with which it is the custom to perform human sacrifice, approaches out of
the multitude and smites through the side into the heart, not inexperienced in such
a thing; when [the victim] has fallen, some divinations are indicated from the fall
and are made common knowledge; the body is brought to a certain place, and they
all walk upon it, treating it as a means of purification.

The only certain similarity with the "human sacrifice" version in Apion is the
fattening of the victim for one year, and this may take place in a temple. It has
been observed above, however, that the fattening element in Apion's account had
been introduced by the author of the framework story.[51] No other similarity is
to be found: the timing, the identity of the victim, the motivation, the place and
form of execution, the accompanying ceremonies, are all different.[52]

Next, the second version of the libel in Apion, the story about the killing and
the cannibalistic feast. This may certainly be considered a "conspiracy" story, as
indicated by Josephus himself in his criticism: "Who of these (i.e., Egyptians, and
many others apart from Greeks) does not happen to wander sometimes about us,
that we should act only against <Greeks > when the conspiratorial oath (*coniuratio*) is renewed through the pouring out of blood?" (*Ap.* 2. 99). Bickerman quotes
as parallels three notorious cases of "conspiracy" stories from Hellenistic and
Roman literature: the supporters of Tarquin, the last king of Rome (Plut. *Popl.* 4);
Apollodorus of Cassandreia, the hated tyrant from the period of the Successors
(Diod. 22. 5); and the notorious assembly imputed to Catiline.[53] The two latter
stories are very similar: the victim was a youth (in the case of Apollodorus, one
with whom the tyrant had had intimate relations); he is slaughtered; the conspirators eat his entrails and drink of his blood mixed with wine. The Tarquin legend
provides less information. It tells of catching or touching the entrails, of blood
being poured, of a "great and terrible" oath being sworn by the conspirators.
Except for the general principle of the secret assembly, the details differ from the
"cannibalistic feast" in Apion's account: the crime scene is a darkened chamber,
not a grove; the victim does not represent the hated enemy (quite the reverse);
he is killed in a more conventional manner than having his flesh cut into small
pieces; his entrails, not his "flesh," are given to the conspirators; being few, they
do not just have a taste, but enough of a portion to warrant the use of the verb "to
eat"; they even drink of the blood (which does not appear in Apion's version). In

51. See p. 265 above.
52. Cf. pp. 264, 267 above with regard to Bickerman's suggested reconstruction of the first version.
53. Sallust *De Catilinae coniuratione* 22; Plutarch *Cicero* 10; Dio Cassius 37. 30. 3. See Bickerman
(1976–80) 2: 228–29.

only one case, that of Tarquin, do we find the oath that figures in Apion (in the presented text, only in the "human sacrifice" version).[54] This survey shows that there are no convincing parallels to the two versions of the blood libel in Greco-Roman and other European practices. Only the general principles are occasionally similar—the execution of a Greek to a daemon (but a Greek one) in one case, and murder and cannibalistic activity to strengthen the bonds of conspiracy in a few others. The specific details are different, except for the fattening of a victim for a year, which appears more than once in European traditions. But the last feature is an addition made by the author of the framework story.

EGYPTIAN SOURCES OF INFORMATION

Now to the Egyptian material, where the parallels are much closer to the blood libel. The "cannibalistic" version of the libel recalls Juvenal's account of the execution of a captive captured by Egyptian farmers (*Sat.* 15. 75–83):[55] the victim is an enemy and is killed by being cut "into many bits and small pieces," and these are eaten (or rather tasted) by the great crowd. The "sacrifice" version of the blood libel resembles an annual ceremony carried out in Egypt in which a foreigner is sacrificed by being burned alive (Diod. 1. 88. 4–5; Plut. *De Is. et Os.* 380D; see further below).

Only Egypt provides a possible parallel for the two versions of the blood libel in one account (obviously separated). This is to be found in an episode that occurred in Egypt at the time of Marcus Aurelius (*Epit.* Dio Cass. 72. 4. 1):[56]

> Those called Bucoli (= "shepherds"; worshippers of Dionysus?) created unrest throughout Egypt and, under a priest, Isidorus, caused the other Egyptians to revolt. At first, arrayed in women's garments, they had deceived the centurion of the Romans, as if they were wives of the Bucoli and about to give him gold on account of their husbands, and had cut him into pieces (κατέκοψαν—perhaps "cut down") when he approached them. They also sacrificed his companion, and they swore an oath over his entrails and these they devoured.

The sacrificial victim in this case, the companion of the centurion, would himself have been a Roman soldier, thus representing the hated enemy. He is first sacrificed and then devoured. The rebels, Egyptian peasants, are led by a priest, and the victim is sacrificed to a certain god; and the rebels swear an oath, presumably of

---

54. The resemblance to the second version of Bickerman's reconstruction (sacrifice in the Temple, cannibalistic feast, oath of hatred, the throwing of the remains into a pit) is no closer.

55. For the text, see p. 261 above. The description of the cannibalistic sacrifice of Leucippe by Egyptian robbers in Achilles Tatius (3. 15) may well have been of European origin and therefore will not be discussed here.

56. Mentioned by Bickerman (1976–80) 2: 229–30 as an illustration of the "conspiracy" *topos*.

hatred toward the enemy. The religious features indicate that the episode echoes an ancient Egyptian practice. The killing of the Roman centurion also deserves attention: the verb used to describe it is κατέκοψαν (either "they cut into pieces" or "they cut down"). Does the eleventh-century epitome of Dio Cassius hint at a story about another cannibalistic feast involving the Roman centurion himself?

These striking parallels and the origin of the ass libel, related in the same context, in the Egyptian identification of the Jewish god with Seth-Typhon suggest that the blood libel also has an Egyptian origin.[57] There are indeed parallels to the two versions of the blood libel in the Seth-Typhon legends.[58]

One cannot ignore the similarity between the "cannibalistic feast" version and the traditions about the murder of Osiris by Seth-Typhon. From Egyptian and Greek sources, it appears that there were two main versions.[59] According to the first, preserved in its Hellenistic form by Plutarch, Osiris was tricked into being locked in a chest and was then drawn into the Nile. Later on, his body was dismembered by Typhon into fourteen pieces.[60] This dismemberment is at some remove from the killing. The second version, more relevant to the present discussion, reports the killing of Osiris, his immediate dismemberment into twenty-six pieces, and a cannibalistic feast to strengthen the bonds of fidelity. The most detailed record of this version has survived in Diodorus's précis of Hecataeus's *Aegyptiaca,* itself written in the first years of Ptolemaic rule (Diod. 1. 21. 2–3):

> For they say that Osiris, lawfully ruling Egypt, was destroyed by Typhon, his brother, who was violent and impious. He divided the body of the murdered into six and twenty pieces and gave to each one of his fellow attackers a part, wishing all to share the pollution, and by this believing that he would have secure fellow strugglers and guards for his kingdom.

57. See pp. 243–49 above.

58. See in detail Bar-Kochva (1996d) 366–72, summarized accurately by Kasher (1996) 391.The link was first suggested, and in a general way, by Yoyotte (1963) 141, without mentioning Typhon, and treating the libel as all of a piece: "Des détails glanés chez les auteurs d'époque romaine confirment l'origine pharaonique d'une bonne part de la thématique antijuive. Les juifs sont censés se livrer au meurtre rituel (avec démembrement de la victime). Bien que des récits de cet ordre aient figuré dans la littérature antiperse à l'encontre des mercenaires grecs d'Amasis [...] on ne peut s'empêcher de déceler là un cas de l'assimilation de l'étranger abhorré à Seth, qui tua Osiris et le coupa en morceaux." Publishing my article in 1996, I was still unaware of Yoyotte's note and have to apologize for not crediting it at that time.

59. On the two versions, see Griffiths (1960a) 5–6; te Velde (1977) 84. To the later sources should be added the interesting version of Firmicus Maternus in *On the Errors of Pagan Religion* 2. 1–3. It is unanimously agreed that this version reflects early Egyptian traditions.

60. Plutarch *De Iside et Osiride* 356B-C, 357F-358A; cf. 368A. It is unanimously agreed that this version reflects early Egyptian traditions. The much-discussed allegorical meanings in the account are irrelevant to our discussion.

This version is discernible in Egyptian explanations for the names and nick-names of the heroes of this mythological drama, and in the application of the "tit-for-tat" principle in Egyptian traditions concerning the punishment of Seth. There was, for example, an Egyptian pseudoetymology for the name Seth as "the splitter," and Osiris, his victim, is sometimes referred to as "the dismembered one."[61] There is another legend about the dismemberment of Seth himself by his rival, Horus.[62] Two inscriptions boast about the cutting of Seth and his followers into pieces.[63] Pyramid texts treat as a sacred vendetta ritual the cutting of the flesh of animal sacrifices symbolizing Seth.[64] In the Persian period, when hatred of Typhon, the god of the foreigners, grew as a result of the occupation, there was a daily ritual in the temple of Osiris in Abydos and in other Egyptian temples, in which there was a call to "overthrow Seth and his gang," followed by a symbolic vengeance against Seth: a figure of Seth, made of red wax or wood or drawn on paper, was abused, pierced by a spear, cut into pieces with a knife, and then thrown onto the fire.[65] Here may be detected the two elements of the vengeance against foreigners in the composite blood libel against the Jews: cutting into pieces and burning.

The main features of the cannibalistic version of the Osiris murder resemble those of the "cannibalistic feast" version of the blood libel: a secret assembly of conspirators; a murder; the murder has a religious significance; the victim is a rival/enemy; he is cut into pieces; each of the conspirators is given a portion of the flesh (not just the entrails); the ceremony is meant to reinforce the loyalty and mutual commitment of the conspirators and unite them in their hatred of a common target. The identification of Seth with the Jewish god and/or Moses would have inspired Egyptian storytellers in their development of the "cannibalistic feast" version of the blood libel.

The dissimilarities may be put down to a difference in background, while there are two additional features peculiar to the anti-Jewish libel that may have appeared in the original Osiris legend but have not survived. The victim of the Jews is cut into small pieces, and his flesh is only tasted; this is due to the great number of participants implied, while Typhon's gang numbered only twenty-six conspirators. The Egyptian crime scene is not mentioned in the abbreviated story of Diodorus, but it could well have been described in the fuller account in Hecataeus (or in his sources) as a grove, the safest open air refuge available for a group of conspirators on the sandy and flat Egyptian landscape. The absence in

61. See te Velde (1977) 5–6.
62. See Griffiths (1966) 7.
63. Te Velde (1977) 4, and nn. 5–6.
64. Griffiths (1966) 38, 148–49.
65. See te Velde (1977) 150–51.

Diodorus of any references to the way Osiris was killed is not necessarily a result of abbreviation: Egyptian texts say only that Seth "threw Osiris on the ground" or "on his side," which simply means that he killed him.[66] For some religious reason they refrained from going into detail.[67] The dismemberment of Osiris into twenty-six parts afterward indicates a killing technique differing from that imputed to the Jews. In the absence of an explicit reference, the inventor of the anti-Jewish libel could have taken the liberty of foisting upon the Jews an exceedingly monstrous mode of execution. He did not have to exert himself to find it: this cruel method of killing was known to him from Egypt (cf. Juvenal and Dio Cassius, quoted above).

A clear parallel to the "human sacrifice" version appears in the traditions referring to a symbolic punishment of Typhon himself (Hecataeus in Diod. 1. 88. 4–5):

> It was agreed to sacrifice flame-red oxen, since such a one, because of the color, was thought to have become Typhon, who had plotted against Osiris and had received his punishment from Isis because of the murder of her husband. Among men too, they say, in ancient times, those of the same color as Typhon were sacrificed by the kings at the tomb of Osiris. So few of the Egyptians are to be found red-headed, but many of the foreigners. For this reason there prevailed among the Greeks the story about the foreigner killing of Busiris, not the king named Busiris, but the tomb of Osiris having this name in the dialect of the locals.

The Busiris tradition in the first or second century C.E. contains an explicit reference to the sacrifice of foreigners in Egypt (ps.-Apollod. *Bibl.* 2. 116):

> Busiris, son of Poseidon and of Lysianassa, daughter of Epaphus, was king of [Egypt]. He sacrificed the foreigners on Zeus's altar according to a certain oracle; for barrenness had seized Egypt for nine years.

These traditions can be supplemented by a short passage of Manetho, preserved in Plutarch (*De Is. et Os.* 380D):

> For in the city of Eileithyia, as Manetho has recorded, they used to completely burn men alive, calling them Typhonians, and, by winnowing, removed and scattered their ashes. But this was done openly and at a particular time in the dog days.[68]

The similarity to the "human sacrifice" version in Apion is evident: the victim is a foreigner, certainly kidnapped; he symbolizes Typhon, the god of the foreigners, the hated enemy of the autochthonous Egyptians; the events take place annually

---

66. See te Velde (1977) 84.

67. Griffiths (1960) 5–6; (1966) 3–4; te Velde (1977) 83.

68. Cf. Plutarch *De Iside et Osiride* 362E-F, 363B-C, 364B. The information was taken from Manetho's *On Egyptian Customs and Piety.* See Hopfner (1940–41) 1: 72–73. The connection between the Jewish sacrifice of the red cow and the tradition described in Hecataeus-Diodorus has already been observed: see, e.g., Neher-Bernheim (1963) 112–13.

at a fixed date; the victim is sacrificed to a god; the sacrifice is burned alive; and finally, the ceremony is a kind of ancient vendetta and expresses hatred toward the victim and what he represents. Manetho may well have referred to his own time. The alleged contemporary sacrifice of foreigners in Egypt is mentioned by Greek authors even as late as the second century C.E.[69]

One apparent feature of Apion's "human sacrifice" version is missing from the Egyptian practice: the fattening of the victim for a year. For reasons connected with the logical sequence of this version, it was suggested above that the fattening of the victim should be regarded as an addition by the author of the framework story. The absence of this feature from the sacrifice of the "Typhonians" and its appearance in European traditions would tend to confirm this hypothesis.

There is yet another conspicuous absence: both Typhonian traditions, as we now have them, fail to mention an oath. It is possible that an omission occurred in the abridgment by Diodorus of Hecataeus's account (as happened with the wording of the oath in the direct account of the libel in Josephus). We may recall that a secret oath appears in the story about the scattering and burying of Osiris's dismembered body by Isis. She is said to have "summoned all the priests group by group and required them to swear to reveal to no one the trust (πίστιν) about to be given to them" (Diod. 1. 21. 5–6). Is this secret oath intended to counteract a possible oath of Typhon and his followers, which strengthened the bonds of fidelity between the conspirators? The tendency to reverse some of Typhon's actions and relate them in one way or another to his opponents is evident in the myths of Isis and Horus.[70]

Both the taking of an oath on such occasions and the contents of the alleged Jewish oath ("to show goodwill to no race") have their parallels in evidently Egyptian practice and tradition: an oath was mentioned in the above-quoted account of the Egyptian Buccoli who sacrificed and devoured two Roman soldiers (Dio Cass. 72. 4. 1). The misanthropic contents of the Jewish oath is reminiscent of an instruction ordained, according to Manetho, by Osarseph (Joseph-Moses): "to have contact with no one except the fellow conspirators" (συνάπτεσθαι δὲ μηδενὶ πλὴν τῶν συνομωμοσμένων, Joseph. Ap. 1. 239). The instruction is said to have been enhanced by an oath.[71] Moreover, the phrasing of the oath is actually identical to the principal precept imputed to Moses by Lysimachus (Joseph. Ap. 1. 309), whose account of the Jewish origo is evidently a collection of Egyptian ver-

69. See the sources in Frazer (1921) 1: 224 n. 1; Griffiths (1948a). They refer to Sextus Empiricus and Porphyry, and to Seleucus, an Alexandrian author active in Rome during the reign of Trajan, who wrote a work on human sacrifice in Egypt (Ath. 4. 172d).

70. See, e.g., Griffiths (1960a); (1960) 5, 15, 34, 99, 113; (1966) 7, 38, 147–49; (1970) 409, 551–55; te Velde (1977) 4, 53 ff., 94 and n. 6, 150–51. See also Plutarch De Iside et Osiride 358B, 363B, 373C.

71. The lepers and other polluted people in Egypt take an oath to abide by Osarseph's commands (Joseph. Ap. 1. 238). These comprise four basic instructions (para. 239): the first three are directed against Egyptian religious beliefs and practices (not to bow to the sculptures of the gods, nor to

sions of the Jews' residence in Egypt and their exodus-expulsion.[72] These parallels and the need to supplement it with the words "and especially not to the Greeks,"[73] indicate that the *Urtext* of the oath was a local, Egyptian invention.[74]

In the cannibalistic legend, Typhon is the murderer-conspirator, while in the story about his sacrifice, he (or rather the red-haired foreigner who represents him) is the subject of vengeance. This difference, however, should not affect the comparison with the two versions of the libel: what counts is the striking typological similarity between the stories, which indicates that the "human sacrifice" was inspired, like the "cannibalistic feast," by the plentiful mine of Typhon traditions, irrespective of the specific role of Typhon in each case. Furthermore, the inversion of the Exodus stories and of anti-Egyptian accounts is particularly noticeable in the series of anti-Jewish accusations in Hellenistic Egyptian literature.[75] The inversion technique may also explain the attribution of human sacrifice to the Jews.

THE COMPOSITE VERSION
AND THE STORY OF ANTIOCHUS IN THE TEMPLE

To close this discussion, we shall return to the question of authorship: who composed the story of Antiochus's visit to the Temple, and who invented the blood libel? As far as the first question is concerned, Heinrich Graetz and Elias Bicker-

---

worship animals but to sacrifice and consume them). The fourth instruction, prohibiting contacts with other people, cannot be—as might be suggested—an interpolation taken from the alleged Jewish oath in the ceremony of the blood libel. After all, that oath does not mention "the fellow conspirators." The instruction may well reflect a traditional Egyptian formulation of such an oath based on the oath in some version of the Osiris murder by the "conspirators." Given the context, the meaning of the fourth instruction is not universal, and the next paragraph (240) defines all the instructions as anti-Egyptian. On the question of the authenticity of the passages attributed to Manetho, see pp. 246–47 above.

72. The almost identical oath in Diodorus (34/35. 1. 2 fin.) was certainly inspired by the formulation of the oath in the blood libel and/or its sources. Cf. p. 327 below.

73. See p. 256 above, and cf. the addition of "Greek" in the text of the libel (para. 95).

74. *Pace* Bickerman (1976–80) 2: 226–27, who argues for a Greek origin of the oath, comparing it to an inscription of 220 B.C.E. from Crete (*Syll.*[3] I. 527, ll. 30 ff.). However, that oath is not universal but is applied against a neighboring city; its contents go into many minute details, situations, and possibilities, and the expression closest to the alleged Jewish oath is μήτε καλῶς φρονήσειν (= not to think "nobly"). Such an oath is not exactly equivalent to the "Jewish" vow "to show no goodwill to *any race*" (*Ap.* 2. 121). The late date and provenance of the Cretan inscription also diminish its weight as evidence for a Greek origin of the Jewish oath, and the parallels mentioned above tilt the balance in favor of an Egyptian source. After all, a variety of similar vows of animosity are known from Egypt and the ancient Near East, and they find their equivalents in plenty of negative advice, some of which is converted to positive advice (i.e., to show excessive goodwill toward an enemy), scattered throughout the Oriental (including biblical) wisdom literature.

75. See pp. 326–32 below.

man (following Josephus) have suggested that it was composed by a Seleucid court historian,[76] while Stern thinks that the story originated with "anti-Semitic Alexandrians, who regarded Antiochus as the prototype and a champion of Hellenic anti-Semitism against the enemies of mankind."[77] However, it still remains most probable that the story (as distinct from the libel) was composed by a Seleucid historian of the generation of Antiochus IV. The likely inclusion of the story in the work of Timochares, the Seleucid court historian, some time in the early twenties of the second century B.C.E., and its appearance in the original text of the advice of the Seleucid "friends" of Antiochus VII Sidetes,[78] can point only to an official Seleucid origin.

A story about ritual murders and cannibalistic acts would have justified the persecution of the Jewish religion and the imposition of restrictions in the eyes of the Hellenistic and Roman audience, whose positive opinion was highly prized by the Seleucids. The Druids were similarly persecuted and restricted by the Romans on the pretext that they indulged in human sacrifice and cannibalism.[79] Furthermore, the Jewish victims were of other races. Antiochus, therefore, is portrayed as a savior of the nations, avenging not only Greeks but also ridding the world of an oath of hatred and enmity against the whole of humanity.

There remains the question of the inventor of the blood libel. Who turned the two Typhon traditions into anti-Jewish libels, and when? And who combined them into one story? It is unlikely to have been the same author who composed the story about the visit of Antiochus IV to the Temple. The "cannibalistic feast" version is clumsily integrated into the Antiochus story. It is also unlikely that one and the same author invented both versions and then integrated them into one clumsy whole. This implies the prior existence of two independent anti-Jewish stories, both adaptations of the Typhon traditions. The origin of the two versions in the Typhon traditions and the parallels in Egyptian practices invite the conclusion that the two versions were invented by Egyptians, not Greeks, like the ass and leper libels. The conclusion is strengthened by the evident absence of the word "Greek" in the original versions. As far as the combined version is concerned, the parallel in the epitome of Dio Cassius (72. 41) of the cutting to pieces of a Roman soldier followed by the sacrifice of his comrade and culminating in a cannibalistic feast also suggests an Egyptian provenance.

The invention of the two versions of the libel, as well as the combined version, must be dated to the pre-Maccabaean period, most probably much earlier. If

76. Graetz (1872) 193–206; Bickerman (1976–80) 2: 251.

77. See Stern, *GLAJJ* 1: 412. Cf. Schäfer (1997a) 64–65.

78. See pp. 464–65 and 441–44 below.

79. Tcherikover (1961) 199, 478; see, e.g., Suetonius *Claudius* 35. 5; on Druid cult: Diodorus 5. 31; Tacitus *Annales* 14. 30; and many other sources.

Version A	Version B
Human Sacrifice	Cannibalistic "Tasting"
Egypt, Persian Period	Egypt, Persian Period

Combined Version (Sacrifice and Cannibalistic "Tasting")
Egypt, Pre-Maccabaean Period

The Seleucid Court Historians in the generation of the Revolt
(The Visit of Antiochus IV to the Temple and the combined version)

Timochares: Seleucid Court Historian, circ. 128 B.C.E.,
(The story of the Siege of Jerusalem by Antiochus VII Sidetes)
(see pp. 464–65)

Apollonius Molon: early first century B.C.E.,
(in his Anti-Jewish Treatise)
(see pp. 490–91)

Apion: first half of first century C.E.

Damocritus: second century C.E. (?)

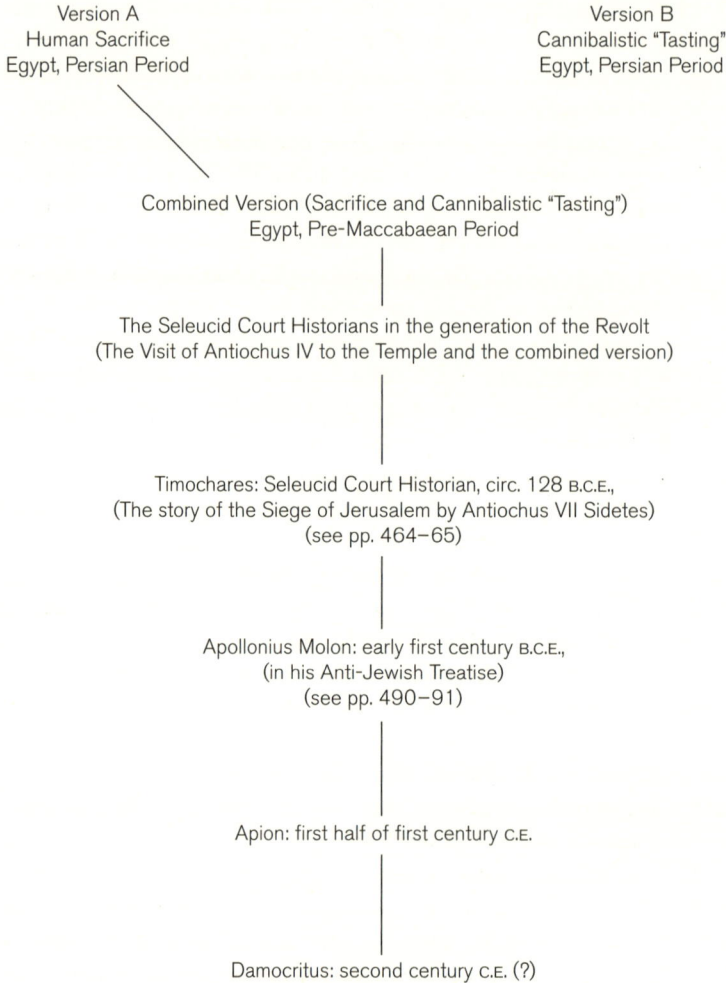

FIGURE 2. The Transmission of the Blood Libel

Theophrastus did draw on Egyptian sources of information in his description
of Jewish sacrificial practice (the complete burning of a live victim) and in his
statement that the Jews were the first to sacrifice humans,[80] this would indicate
that already by the beginning of the Hellenistic era Egyptians may well have
been attributing to the Jews the practice of human sacrifice involving burning the victim alive. In this case, the "human sacrifice" version, at least, would

80. See pp. 30–33 above.

have been invented in the Persian period, when hostility toward Typhon gained momentum, as manifested by the intensified anti-Typhonian cult in Egypt. The same may well apply to the cannibalistic version: symbolic daily execution and dismemberment of Seth was current in Egypt in the Persian period.[81]

Whatever the case may be, the combined version was already in circulation in the pre-Maccabaean period and would have reached the Seleucid court historian by some Egyptian-Greek source. The Seleucid author adapted it to serve his purposes, providing a historical background to the discovery of the "secret," and supplementing the episode with adequate literary coloring, especially "tragic" features. In this respect he is similar to the Idumaean settler in Egypt who provided a literary-historical context for one version of the ass libel by describing the "theft" of the ass from the Jewish Temple.[82] The Seleucid author also added to, and omitted from, the episode certain elements and details, as appropriate for internal and external consistency. In chapters 13–15 of this book, I shall elaborate on the question of how the story reached Apion.[83]

Did the blood libel influence the attitudes of Gentile intellectuals and leaders toward Jews and Judaism? One's impression is that the libel was not all that influential, perhaps because it lacked credibility for the majority of authors who wrote about the Jews. We shall see that Posidonius was quite familiar with the libel but omitted it all the same.[84] Even Tacitus fails to allude to it, although he amassed a great deal of anti-Jewish material, including the ass libel. Of all the references to the Jewish people, it survived only in Apion and the testimony for Damocritus and was repeated by Apollonius Molon and Apion.[85] However, Lysimachus of Alexandria, one of the most bitter anti-Jewish ethnographers, who almost certainly was acquainted with the blood libel,[86] did not record it, since his literary framework— an Egyptian ethnography[87]—allowed only an account of the Jewish *origo*. It is also difficult to assess the influence of the libel on the popular hostility toward the Jews. I would not, however, rule out the possibility that the rumors in Egypt attributing cannibalism to the Jews during the Diaspora revolt in the reign of Trajan were fueled to some extent by the early Egyptian anti-Jewish blood libel.[88]

---

81. See p. 273 above.

82. See pp. 217 and 223 above.

83. See pp. 455–57, 464–65, 490–91, and 515 below.

84. See pp. 443–44 and 455–57 below.

85. See p. 515 below.

86. This appears from the identity of the order imputed by Lysimachus to Moses and the Jewish oath; cf. pp. 275–76 above.

87. See p. 333 below.

88. *CPJ* no. 437; Dio Cassius 68. 32. 1–2. On Egyptian sources for the account of Dio Cassius, see Pucci (1983a) 132, 134. For cannibalism used to frighten the opponent, see Josephus *Antiquitates Judaicae* 13. 345–46; Frontinus *Stratēgemata* 3. 5 (or 4. 5).

8

Agatharchides of Cnidus on the Sabbath as a Superstition

In three of the previous chapters we have encountered the scholarship of Alexandria in the fields of ethnography, biography, and regional folklore. Agatharchides of Cnidus, the historian who flourished in Alexandria in the mid-second century B.C.E., gives us an insight into yet another field of Alexandrian scholarship. Agatharchides' talents, personality, and proximity to the Ptolemaic court facilitated his historiographical achievements. Some modern scholars regard him as the best and most eminent of the Alexandrian historians of the third and second centuries B.C.E., quite apart from his remarkable contribution to geographical and ethnographic literature.[1] This actually seems to have been the evaluation of Photius, the ninth-century patriarch of Constantinople, a polymath steeped in classical literature who preserved not a little of the geographical-ethnographical writings of Agatharchides: in Photius's estimation Agatharchides was on a par with Thucydides and even surpassing Thucydides in clarity.[2]

Agatharchides' references to the Jews are found in two fragments concerning

1. See the praise of Agatharchides as a historian in Fraser (1972) 1: 516–17, 543, 545; and as a geographer, 500–39; see also Peremans (1967); Gozzoli (1978); Verdin (1983); Burstein (1989) 1–21. For a less positive opinion of Agatharchides, see Murray (1970) 154–57, who rightly emphasizes how Agatharchides exaggerates various descriptions in *On the Red Sea*. Agatharchides himself was aware that certain passages would arouse disbelief (Diod. 5. 33. 7). Such exaggerations also appeared in his historical works (see pp. 300–301 below).

2. Jacoby, *FGrH*, II.A, no. 86, T2, para. 6 (pp. 205–6); on the sentence, see Leopoldi (1892) 63–64; Fraser (1972) 1: 546–47. For a detailed analysis of Agatharchides' style and vocabulary, see Palm (1955) 15–54; Fraser (1972) 1: 546–47, and bibliography there.

the occupation of Jerusalem by Ptolemy I in 302/1 B.C.E. at the time of the battle of Ipsus, the battle that decided the struggle between Antigonus Monophthalmus, the favorite of the Jews, and the other former commanders of Alexander's army who wished to divide up the Macedonian empire among themselves. The story of the occupation of Jerusalem is interesting in that it blames the fall of the city on the Sabbath prohibitions of the Jews. Agatharchides' description of the event and his comments on the Jews and their observance of the Sabbath were taken to have significant implications for research on developments both in the oral interpretation of the Torah, especially regarding Sabbath observance, and in the attitude of Greek literature toward the Jewish religion and its customs.

Agatharchides was not only exceptionally talented as an author and historian but had a multifaceted personality to match, with unexpected views on a range of political, social, and economic subjects, some of which may be regarded as liberal, even radical, considering the time, place, and particular context in which he worked. He speaks out, for example, against the despotism of the Ptolemies, against the oppression by superpowers of small nations aspiring to freedom, against the removal and transfer of populations on the grounds of economy or security, and against the cruel exploitation of prisoners of war and political detainees in enforced labor; he demanded the provision not only of proper nutrition and social conditions for imperial guards in remote places, but also of suitable rest and working conditions for slaves and prisoners. Agatharchides advocated a modest life free of greed and the pursuit of wealth and admiringly described the tribes and nomads of the far south. He was even concerned about preserving the environment. Some of these subjects, such as his views on war and peace, slavery and freedom, laziness and industriousness, parasitical life and responsibility, together with the special circumstances of Alexandria, where Jews, Greeks, and Egyptians lived side by side, necessarily would have influenced his perception of the Jewish Sabbath, the historical events in Jerusalem in 302/1 B.C.E., and other customs of the Jewish people.

AGATHARCHIDES—HIS POSITION, TIME, AND WORKS

Our information about Agatharchides has come mainly from his own introduction to his work *On the Red Sea* and the end of its fifth book,[3] and from Photius's introduction to the many extracts that he adduces from the same work.[4] This material is supplemented by random pieces of information from other sources and by expressions that may be traced back to Agatharchides' works. Significant

3. Photius *cod.* 250. 21, 445b–447b; *cod.* 250. 110, 460b (ed. Henry [1959–77] vol. 7).
4. Jacoby, *FGrH*, II.A, no. 86, T2, paras. 1–7 (pp. 205–6).

details about his life, especially his connection with the Ptolemaic court and the time of his expulsion from Egypt, were disputed in the past,[5] but today there is general agreement about the picture that has emerged of Agatharchides' life.[6] The only real disagreement that remains pertains to the relative chronology of his works and their exact compass. These impending questions have implications for Agatharchides' references to the Sabbath and the Jews.

For one reason or another, Agatharchides was not brought up by his own family but by Cineas,[7] who pulled the strings in the royal council of Ptolemy VI and even served as one of his two regents before the invasion by Antiochus Epiphanes in 169 B.C.E. It is not known when he began, but he was for a long time the secretary of Heraclides Lembus. The latter negotiated in 169 on behalf of the Ptolemaic court with Antiochus Epiphanes. This is the same Heraclides Lembus who wrote an epitome of the biographies of Hermippus of Smyrna, including the biography of Pythagoras.[8] Photius claims that it was the patronage of Heraclides Lembus that allowed Agatharchides to gain literary recognition. Agatharchides, therefore, was necessarily in close contact with the Ptolemaic court during the years 170–145/4, a period that saw great internal crisis, the Seleucid conquest of Egypt, the Roman intervention, and toward the end of the reign of Ptolemy VI a temporary rise in Ptolemaic fortunes as a result of a split in the house of Seleucus. Agatharchides' service in Egypt was terminated in 145/4, with the ascent of Ptolemy VIII Physcon (Potbelly) to the throne, the start of his reign of terror, and the outbreak of civil war, which was to last until 121 B.C.E. The Greek population supporting Physcon's sister-bride and rival, Cleopatra II, was persecuted by the king, and the Greek intellectuals fled for their lives, finding refuge mainly in Rhodes, western Asia Minor, and Athens. Agatharchides, already an exhausted old man, escaped to Athens, where he lived out the rest of his life.

Agatharchides wrote three great works: *On Europe, On Asia,* and *On the Red Sea.* He also produced some minor works about which we know nothing but their titles.[9] The first two great works were historical, and the third geographic-

---

5. See esp. Müller, *FHG* II, pp. liv–lviii; Susemihl (1892) 1: 688–90; Ed. Schwartz, *RE* s.v. "Agatharchides," col. 739; Brown (1973) 183. For refutations of these opinions, see esp. Jacoby, *FGrH,* II.a, no. 86, pp. 150–51; Fraser (1972) 1: 776 n. 172; Burstein (1989) 13–14, and esp. 16–17. Debates in the past touched mainly on the question of when Agatharchides left Egypt. He has even been mistakenly considered the tutor of one of the Ptolemaic kings.

6. See in the surveys of Fraser (1972) 1: 516–17, 539–52, 2: 744 n. 183; Burstein (1989) 12–21.

7. So the θρεπτός of Cineas (Jacoby, *FGrH,* II.A, no. 86, T2, para. 3 [p. 205]) must be understood, in light of the conditions of the time and place; and see Burstein (1989) 14, no. 5, who suggests that Agatharchides was of low birth; but there are also other possible explanations for his upbringing in the household of Cineas.

8. See above, p. 170.

9. For the list of works in Photius, see Jacoby, *FGrH,* II.A, no. 86, T2, paras. 2–3 (p. 205).

ethnographic. The lost works he is known to have written are a collection of *thaumasia* (wonder stories), an epitome of mythological poetry, and an ethical composition on friendship.

The two historical works are devoted to the history of the continents mentioned in their titles. *On Europe* was the larger and more detailed work, and it dealt with the history of the Hellenic peoples, apparently up until the time of Agatharchides himself.[10] It contained forty-nine books, of which we have fifteen short fragments, all found in Athenaeus except for one in Josephus.[11] *On Asia* was much shorter, containing only ten books, of which just five fragments have survived.[12] It dealt with the countries of Asia and Africa, including Egypt, Aethiopia, and Libya, reporting on the Assyrian, Babylonian, and Persian empires, the reign of Alexander, and the period of the Successors. This last period occupied the final two books of the work,[13] apparently extending to the death of the first generation of the Successors in the 280s.[14]

On the Red Sea comprised five books, of which the second and fifth book can be reconstructed to a great extent. Large parts of these two books have survived in Diodorus, Strabo, and Photius.[15] The work dealt with the geography and life of the inhabitants of southern Egypt, the great Aethiopia of that time, and the coasts on both sides of the Red Sea. It concentrates on the problems of existence, the daily struggle for survival, and the adaptations of the primitive-naive inhabitants to heat, winds, limited water, desert regions, and the changeable sea. By and large it is a sympathetic account of the Aethiopian tribesman as a humane variation of the so-called noble savage. Prominent in all this is the description of the gold mines in the southwestern desert of Egypt (Wadi 'Allaqi), notorious for the exploitation of political prisoners, prisoners of war, and their families.

In the epilogue to *On the Red Sea,* Agatharchides says that he has chosen not to write surveys on the islands in the Red Sea, their inhabitants, and the perfumes grown in the land of the Troglodites:

10. The fragments in Jacoby, *FGrH,* II.A, no. 86, frr. 14–17 (pp. 210–11), concern the reign of Philip V (end of third century B.C.E.). One of the fragments is explicitly said to be taken from the 39th book; the whole composition comprised forty-nine books; hence the work encompassed several more decades. There is therefore no justification for the doubts expressed by Jacoby, *FGrH,* II.a, no. 86, p. 153.

11. The number of books is given in Photius: Jacoby, *FGrH,* II.A, no. 86, fr. 2 (p. 207). The fragments were taken from *On Europe: FGrH,* II.A, no. 86, frr. 1–4, 20a (pp. 206–8, 220). All the following references are to the fragments in Jacoby.

12. Photius, fr. 2. The fragments from *On Asia:* frr. 5–17, 20b.

13. The eighth book deals with the reign of Alexander the Great: see frr. 2–3.

14. See further, pp. 284–85 below.

15. Diodorus 3. 12–48; Strabo 16. 4. 5–20; Photius *cod.* 250. On the work of reconstruction, see Burstein (1989) 21–29, and the reconstruction itself, 52–175.

> Having begged off, I abandoned the exposition entirely, because my age was unable to undertake the task, many things having been written by me about Europe and Asia, and since the *hypomnēmata* did not afford an accurate examination because of the disturbances in Egypt. (Phot. *cod.* 250. 110, 460b)

The word *hypomnēmata* here might appear to refer to notes that Agatharchides wrote for himself,[16] but another interpretation receives support from a quotation that Diodorus adduces from Agatharchides:

> I shall make a description of the remaining part, I mean the Arabian Gulf, having taken some [information] from the *hypomnēmata* in Alexandria, and having ascertained other [information] from eyewitnesses. (Diod. 3. 38. 1)

The term *hypomnēmata* here obviously refers to official material collected in the archive of the Ptolemies. The fragment preserved by Photius is thus referring to such official notes. We understand that Agatharchides ended *On the Red Sea* without including all the subjects he had undertaken to include, on account of old age and fatigue, and because he was deprived of the sources of information in Egypt. By the "disturbances in Egypt" he no doubt means the civil war that broke out in 145/4. It has been rightly conjectured that *On the Red Sea* was completed shortly after Agatharchides' arrival in Athens, when he was already an old man, and that his writing used to be supported by official notes and reports (*hypomnēmata*) kept in the royal archives in Alexandria.[17] These conclusions affect the answers to such questions as when Agatharchides finished writing all his works, what their chronological framework was, and what his sources were, and the answers in turn are relevant to the fragments on the Sabbath. For example, and above all, Agatharchides would have used the Ptolemaic archives for the history of the Diadochic period in his *On Asia,* and for subjects touching on the Ptolemaic kingdom in *On Europe.* This is not surprising considering his patrons' high status at court. It would seem that Agatharchides took his projects seriously, and that when he was no longer able to use official sources he preferred not to write at all.

Agatharchides' comments in his epilogue may help solve an important problem concerning the completion of *On Asia.* The contents of the fragments and their location in the work according to book number make it clear that Agatharchides reached only the end of the Diadochic period, while *On Europe* extended to his own time. It seems strange, then, that Agatharchides did not complete a Ptolemaic

---

16. One might understand Agatharchides to mean that he took with him in his flight to Athens notes that he had written for the continuation of his *On the Red Sea,* but that they were unsatisfactory because he had been unable to complete them in Egypt due to the disturbances there.

17. On the royal *hypomnēmata:* Peremans (1967) 437, 441–48; Fraser (1972) 1: 549, 2: 788, and n. 242; Burstein (1989) 30–31.

history of equivalent length to the middle of the second century B.C.E., especially considering that he had access to first-rate material unavailable to other Hellenistic historians. Felix Jacoby argued that post-Diadochic Seleucid and Ptolemaic histories were included in *On Europe,* since Agatharchides (so Jacoby) regarded the activity of the Seleucids and Ptolemies as part of the history of the Greek-Macedonian world. This suggestion is unacceptable on its own terms, has no parallel or evidence to support it, and would also raise a number of insoluble difficulties.[18] I suggest that Agatharchides interrupted his writing of *On Asia,* while still in Egypt, in order to finish *On the Red Sea* first, planning to return to *On Asia* afterward. He would have done so because he found himself continually having to provide the reader with background details about southern Egypt, Aethiopia, and the other countries neighboring the Red Sea. Such geographical descriptions were indeed given, sometimes at some length, in *On Asia,*[19] but Agatharchides must have realized that much more was required in order to properly describe the long reign of Ptolemy II (283–247 B.C.E.), which saw Ptolemaic military expeditions and civil missions to the Red Sea area, especially to Aethiopia (Diod. 1. 37. 5), the establishment of elephant supply depots,[20] intensive mining of gold in the southeastern Egyptian desert and of topaz gems from "Snaky" Island, and Ptolemaic control being asserted over the perfume supply regions.[21] All these were described in great detail in *On the Red Sea,* accompanied by extensive background surveys of the geography and population. It is therefore not a coincidence that *On Asia* extended only as far as the reign of Ptolemy I. Such a responsible approach is typical of Agatharchides. It is best demonstrated in his decision not to continue writing *On the Red Sea* once his access to the Ptolemaic archives had been cut off.

18. Jacoby, *FGrH,* II.a, no. 86, pp. 150–51. The reference to Magas, the king of Cyrene, in the fragment from *On Europe* (fr. 7), is one of a group of examples of gluttons adduced as a foil to the Spartans and their careful maintenance of physical fitness (frr. 10–11), thus not in the context of a history of Cyrene. It cannot, therefore, serve as evidence here. The same goes for the fragment from Agatharchides in Josephus *Contra Apionem,* adduced only as a parallel to the event that occurred in the Macedonian royal house (1. 205–8). Jacoby's proposal raises several problems. For example, there was no additional reference to the Jews in *On Europe;* otherwise Josephus in *Jewish Antiquities,* and all the more so in *Contra Apionem,* would have quoted it, referring the reader to Agatharchides; is it possible that an account of the history of the houses of Ptolemy and Seleucus in the third and second centuries, including the reigns of Antiochus III and IV, would have lacked such a reference?

19. See Diodorus 3. 11. 2 on Agatharchides' depiction of Aethiopia in the second book of *On Asia.* On identifying Agatharchides as the source for geographical reports of Arabia in Diodorus (2. 49–54), see Fraser (1972) 2: 773 n. 160. It is well established that the detailed description of the Nile in Diodorus (1. 32–41. 3) originated in Agatharchides (and see 41. 4). On other subjects concerning the Aethiopians discussed in *On Asia,* see Burstein (1989) 22–24.

20. On Ptolemaic elephant hunts, see Fraser (1972) 1: 172–80; Scullard (1975) 123–45; Huntingford (1980) 166–72; Burstein (1989) 6–12, 42 n. 2.

21. See Burstein (1983) 1–12, and there on other economic interests.

Agatharchides regarded the latter work as particularly important, since it filled a gap left by similar extensive works, each on a part of the known world.[22] Historical books, on the other hand, treating events also found in *On Asia* were two a penny, and the desire to write something more significant may also have influenced his decision to delay the completion of *On Asia* until he had finished his great geographical-ethnographical project. However, just as he was forced to end *On the Red Sea* without including everything he had planned to, for the same reason he was unable to resume writing *On Asia*. The proposed order of Agatharchides' writings is thus: *On Europe, On Asia,* and *On the Red Sea.*

The large quantity of material surviving from *On the Red Sea* and the introduction to Agatharchides by Photius provide us with a relatively broad picture of the man and his works, his outlook and writing methods. I shall now refer briefly only to those features that have some bearing on an understanding of the two "Jewish" fragments.

Photius made a detailed analysis of the style of Agatharchides.[23] Agatharchides himself also adduced examples of style that seemed to him praiseworthy from the writings of others (in his introduction to the fifth book of *On the Red Sea*).[24] It is worth mentioning again the evaluation of Photius that Agatharchides was superior in clarity even to Thucydides, whom Agatharchides greatly admired.[25] Agatharchides also had a tendency toward gnomology, the phrasing of sentences like proverbs with a moral point, especially the epigrammatic concluding sentences intended to be engraved on the mind of the reader.[26] In addition, Agatharchides played up the *tropē,* the dramatic turning point in a story.[27]

Agatharchides wrote no real philosophical work. Strabo calls him a Peripatetic (15. 2. 15). In Alexandria, this epithet was given not exclusively to a member of the Peripatetic school, but to any scholar specializing in a genre associated with the Peripatetics, such as biography.[28] Agatharchides was not in fact of this type, but he does seem to have accepted Peripatetic opinions on a range of subjects, although he was also influenced by the Epicureans.[29]

Most significant for understanding the "Jewish" fragments are his political and social views expressed explicitly or covertly in *On the Red Sea.* Agatharchides points to the inhumanity of the "kings of Alexandria," exemplified by the miserable life and isolation of the guards on Ophiodes (Snaky) Island, stationed on the

22. Photius *cod.* 250. 64, 454b.
23. T2, paras. 4–7.
24. Photius *cod.* 250. 21, 445–447b.
25. T2, para. 6, and see p. 290 below.
26. T2, para. 4. For an example from one of the Jewish fragments, see p. 230 and cf. p. 304 below.
27. T2, para. 5, and see p. 290 below.
28. See p. 169 above.
29. Leopoldi (1892) 50–65; Fraser (1972) 1: 540, 543–47; Burstein (1989) 15 n. 2, 53 n. 2.

island to secure safe procurement of the topaz gems found there, and especially by the shocking conditions of the forced workers and their families in the gold mines.[30] He also expresses opposition to the deification of Alexander the Great in an imaginary didactic speech presented before one of the Ptolemaic kings,[31] thereby indirectly criticizing Ptolemaic self-deification and the ruler cult established by Ptolemy II. Such positions are unexpected in the writing of an author so close to the seat of power, and so dependent for his livelihood on royal officials. Moreover, he explicitly calls the Ptolemies "tyrants,"[32] and Ptolemy I is called a *despotēs* in both the "Jewish" fragments.[33] It is also worth noting Agatharchides' empathy toward the inhabitants of the southern areas in their struggle for survival,[34] his transparent praise for the frugality of the Aethiopian tribes,[35] and his awareness of the need to preserve the countryside and the nature of Ophiodes Island.[36]

Some of Agatharchides' social and humanitarian positions are reflected also in the few fragments surviving from his historical works: his opposition to extravagance, waste, hedonism, and the pursuit of wealth;[37] his contempt for parasites and his criticism of idleness,[38] while at the same time emphasizing the need for a basic minimum daily rest for every worker.[39] To return to his political opinions, Agatharchides includes in his writings covert criticism of Rome, at the time effectively the patron of the house of Ptolemy.[40] Agatharchides was without doubt a historian with exceptional and unexpected views for his time, place, and personal circumstances.

There are scholars who believe that Agatharchides' anti-Ptolemaic stance and his reservations about Rome developed as a result of his personal experience at the beginning of the reign of terror of Ptolemy VIII Physcon, a longtime protégé of Rome.[41] Yet his political and social views seem well rooted in his

---

30. Ophiodes Island: Diodorus 3. 39. 5–9; Photius *cod.* 250. 82, 456b; the gold mines: Diodorus 3. 12–15 (Agatharchides' view in 12. 2 and 13. 1–3); Photius *cod.* 250. 24, 447b ff.; and see Davies (1955); Fraser (1972) 1: 543, 2: 779 n. 203.

31. Photius *cod.* 250. 18, 445b.

32. See Photius *cod.* 250. 24, 446b; Diodorus 3. 17. 3, 5; and see Fraser (1972) 1: 543–44, 550, 2: 779 n. 185; Burstein (1989) 28–29.

33. Josephus *Antiquitates Judaicae* 12. 6; *Contra Apionem* 1. 210.

34. See examples in Burstein (1989) 28–29.

35. See Photius *cod.* 250. 49, 451b.

36. Diodorus 3. 39; Photius *cod.* 250. 83, 456b–457a (changes in Ophiodes Island); Diodorus 3. 40. 2–7, esp. para. 2 (the changes in the seabed caused by the transportation of elephants); and see Fraser (1972) 1: 544, 2: 783 n. 203.

37. Frr. 2, 3, 6, 7, 11, 16, 17.

38. See pp. 298–300 below, and fr. 13.

39. See p. 300 below.

40. See Fraser (1972) 1: 545, 550, 552, 2: 785 n. 212.

41. So Fraser (1972) 1: 550; Burstein (1989) 34–35.

writing. Even if his work *On the Red Sea* may have considerable modifications from his time as a refugee in Athens,[42] it would not have been entirely reworked there; for example, the particularly detailed and dramatic description of working conditions in the gold mines (Diod. 3. 12–15), based on official reports and orders, would hardly have undergone revision or rewriting. The same applies to his historical works, and yet they already have references to the tyranny of the Ptolemies. It seems clear that his views were formed well before his exile, and could be explained as, among other things, those of an intellectual, possibly low-born,[43] experiencing at firsthand and for many years the decadent royal dynasty. His hostility to Rome is expressed in only one surviving comment (or perhaps two) in *On the Red Sea*. The Roman destruction of Corinth in 146 B.C.E. would have shocked a Greek such as Agatharchides arriving in Athens a year later, and the merciless destruction of Carthage in the same year may also have helped provoke him to add a few comments to his latest work prior to publication. This said, he may well have had reservations long before about the Romans' ruthless expansionist policy.

THE TWO FRAGMENTS ON THE JEWS

We have at our disposal two fragments of Agatharchides describing the capture of Jerusalem by Ptolemy I in the year 302/1 B.C.E. One fragment was included by Josephus in a consecutive account of the Diadochic period in *Jewish Antiquities* and adduced to support Josephus's own description of the event. Josephus begins with his own account (*AJ* 12. 4):

> [Ptolemy] captured Jerusalem using deceit and treachery. For he came on a Sabbath to the city as if to sacrifice without the Jews preventing him, for they did not suspect him to be hostile; and, they happening to be idle and at rest, because of the lack of suspicion and [because of] the day, he possessed the city without effort.[44]

Josephus now turns to the account of Agatharchides (5–6):

> (5) Agatharchides of Cnidus, who wrote a work on the deeds of the Successors, testifies to this account, imputing to us superstition, as if we lost our freedom because of it, saying thus: (6) "There is a nation called of the Jews (ἔθνος Ἰουδαίων λεγόμενον), who having a strong and great city, Jerusalem, overlooked (turned a

---

42. E.g., Photius *cod.* 250. 5, 442a-b.

43. See note 7 above.

44. κατέσχε δὲ οὗτος καὶ τὰ Ἱεροσόλυμα δόλῳ καὶ ἀπάτῃ χρησάμενος· ἐλθὼν γὰρ σαββάτοις εἰς τὴν πόλιν ὡς θύσων, μήτε τῶν Ἰουδαίων αὐτὸν ἀμυνομένων, οὐδὲν γὰρ ὑπενόουν πολέμιον, καὶ διὰ τὸ ἀνύποπτον καὶ τὴν ἡμέραν ἐν ἀργίᾳ καὶ ῥαθυμίᾳ τυγχανόντων, ἀπόνως ἐγκρατὴς γίγνεται τῆς πόλεως καὶ πικρῶς ἦρχεν αὐτῆς.

blind eye to) it coming under the control of Ptolemy, since they refused to take up arms;[45] but because of their untimely superstition (*deisidaimonia*) they endured having a difficult master (*despotēs*)."

The second fragment is adduced by Josephus in *Contra Apionem* while he is attempting to prove that the Jewish people was well known and mature at the beginning of the Hellenistic period (*Ap.* 1. 205–11):

> (205) I shall not hestitate from naming one who made mention of us in order, as he thought, to disparage us for foolishness, Agatharchides. (206) For during his narration of the affairs of Stratonice, how she came to Syria from Macedonia, having left her husband, Demetrius, but Seleucus did not wish to marry [her] as she had expected, and while [Seleucus] was making his expedition from Babylon, she caused a revolt in Antioch. (207) Then how the king turned back, Antioch was captured, and she fled. Being able to sail away quickly, she obeyed a dream preventing her, and was caught and killed. (208) Having said this beforehand, Agatharchides, making fun of Stratonice because of her superstition, uses as an example the account about us, and has written thus: (209) "The people called Jews, live in a city strongest of all, which the inhabitants happen to call Jerusalem. They are accustomed to be idle throughout the seventh day and not to bear arms in the said times nor touch farming nor be concerned with any other public work;[46] but having stretched out their arms in the temples [are accustomed] to pray until evening. (210) Ptolemy, the son of Lagus, entered the city with his force. The fellows instead of guarding the city observed the folly. The native land had taken a bitter master (*despotēs*) and the law was proved to hold a worthless custom. (211) The outcome taught all but those (the Jews) to flee to dreams and to the traditional interpretation concerning the law [only] whenever they are too weak in their human reasonings about problems."[47]

The fragment in *Contra Apionem* is longer and more detailed. It mentions several Shabbat prohibitions, dwells more on the circumstances that led to the city's capture, and provides, in detail, a moral to the tale. The short fragment in *Jewish Antiquities*, on the other hand, does not even mention that the city was taken on the Sabbath. It does, however, explicitly give superstition as the reason that led to the fall of the city, without explaining its nature. The longer fragment condemns the folly of the Jews without explicitly using the derogatory term "superstition."

---

45. ... ταύτην ὑπερεῖδον ὑπὸ Πτολεμαίῳ γενομένην ὅπλα λαβεῖν οὐ θελήσαντες....

46. Given the context, this is the only possible meaning of *leitourgiai*, not the more specific connotation of compulsory public offices and the like.

47. The concluding sentence: τὸ δὲ συμβὰν πλὴν ἐκείνων τοὺς ἄλλους πάντας δεδίδαχε τηνικαῦτα φυγεῖν εἰς ἐνύπνια καὶ τὴν περὶ τοῦ νόμου παραδεδομένην ὑπόνοιαν, ἡνίκα ἂν τοῖς ἀνθρωπίνοις λογισμοῖς περὶ τῶν διαπορουμένων ἐξασθενήσωσιν. To anticipate, the word τηνικαῦτα does not mean here "in this case" but responds to ἡνίκα ἄν ("then ... whenever ... "). That the sentence is general and not specific to one instance has important implications in an assessment of Agatharchides' attitude toward the Jews.

Josephus does not state which work of Agatharchides was his source for the fragment in *Contra Apionem,* but in *Jewish Antiquities* he refers to the work "on the deeds of the Successors" (para. 5). We do not know of a work of that name, and Photius does not mention such a work either.[48] It seems, then, that Josephus was referring to *On Asia,* a work that ended with two books on the Diadochic period.[49]

As for the connection between the two fragments, scholars have assumed that they are actually only one fragment, the original having been preserved in *Contra Apionem,* but abbreviated and modified by Josephus in *Jewish Antiquities.*[50] However, the quotation in *Jewish Antiquities* is adduced by Josephus as evidence for the truth of his story about Ptolemy's occupation of Jerusalem on the Sabbath. Why would Josephus quote Agatharchides in direct speech and yet abbreviate and modify his evidence almost out of recognition, even to omitting the Sabbath, when he already suffered from a serious shortage of sources on the history of the Jews in the Diadochic and Ptolemaic periods? He was obliged to use whatever he could find to fill the void, including irrelevant accounts such as the detailed and tiresome description of the Temple table in *pseudo-Aristeas* (*AJ* 12. 60–84). Furthermore, there are details essential for understanding the event that appear only in Josephus's preface to the shorter fragment ("using deceit and treachery," "as if to sacrifice," "they did not suspect him to be hostile"), thereby precluding this fragment being a mere paraphrase by Josephus of the longer one. The shorter fragment is also actually more characteristic of Agatharchides' style (according to the features outlined by Photius and Agatharchides himself),[51] while the longer one is somewhat convoluted. The short fragment is considerably clearer; its conclusion is memorably concise, similar to an aphorism, and comprehends the moral of the story ("because of their untimely superstition they endured having a difficult master"); it also conforms with Agatharchides' tendency to gnomology; and it effectively demonstrates the swift change in fortunes (*trope*) from greatness and strength to being a captured city ill treated by a cruel enemy.

We have then two fragments from two different works of Agatharchides. The short fragment in *Jewish Antiquities* is from *On Asia,* where its context was the continuous description of the events surrounding the battle of Ipsus in Syria and Coile Syria in 302/1 B.C.E. This narrative did not require Agatharchides to explain the nature of the superstition, and it was therefore also unnecessary

48. See T2, paras. 2–3.

49. *On Asia* itself is referred to variously as Ἀσιατικῶν (Ath. 4. 155c-d), περὶ Ἀσίας (Ath. 7. 539b-d); ἐν τῶν Περὶ τῆς Ἀσίας ἱστοριῶν (*FGrH,* IIA, no. 86, fr. 4); τὰ κατὰ τὴν Ἀσίαν (Phot. *Bibl.* 213).

50. See Reinach and Blum (1930) 39 n. 2; Stern, *GLAJJ* 1: 109; Troiani (1977) 121; Feldman (1993) 159; and apparently Kasher (1996) 210.

51. Jacoby, *FGrH,* II.a, no. 86, p. 154 correctly observes this but does not refer to the source of the fragment in *Jewish Antiquities.*

to explain that the event occurred on the Sabbath. Since this was the first (and only) mention of the Jews in the work, Agatharchides introduced them with the words "There is a nation called of the Jews." The longer fragment in *Contra Apionem* must have been taken from *On Europe,* since *On Asia* did not contain a history of Seleucus II, the background to the Stratonice affair,[52] and because the taking of Jerusalem is hardly likely to have been told twice in *On Asia.* It was adduced by Agatharchides as a parallel to the story of Princess Stratonice, the wife of Demetrius II, king of Macedonia, with whom she quarreled because of his connection with another woman, leading her to go to Syria in order to marry Seleucus II in c. 235 B.C.E.[53] The story, therefore, begins in Macedonia, and the context was the history of its rulers, the Antigonids. Since the Jewish parallel has to do with superstition, Agatharchides had to go into details, regarding both the superstition of Stratonice and that of the Jews. As already observed, Agatharchides completed this work before *On Asia.*[54] When he returned to the story in writing *On Asia,* there was no need for him to repeat word for word what he had written in *On Europe,* and he saw fit to abbreviate. It is not unusual for Agatharchides to write two versions of the same episode or subject in different works (as distinct from the same work). In *On the Red Sea,* he repeats, normally at greater length, things that he had written about the Aethiopians in *On Asia.*[55]

When Josephus and/or his assistants were looking for sources in preparation for the writing of a running history of the Jews in the period of the Diadochs for *Jewish Antiquities,* they naturally turned to the consecutive description of that period in Agatharchides' history of Asia. A decade later, in preparing the treatise *Contra Apionem,* information on the Jews was sought also in other works by Agatharchides, especially *On Europe,* from which we have the longer and more detailed fragment.

THE CAPTURE OF JERUSALEM IN 302/1 AND DEFENSIVE WARFARE ON THE SABBATH

The two fragments of Agatharchides adduced by Josephus are the oldest references to the Sabbath preserved in Greek literature. They have been the starting point for any discussion on the question of war on the Sabbath, and they have consequently also served as a milestone in the reconstruction of the developments in Pharisaic law in general.

From the mid-nineteenth century onward, the account of Agatharchides has

---

52. See pp. 284–85 above.
53. For the background to the episode, see Will (1979–82) 2: 299–300.
54. See pp. 283–86 above.
55. See note 19 above.

been quoted as proving that any type of warfare, including defensive warfare, was prohibited on the Sabbath. According to this assumption, the turning point came at the beginning of the religious persecutions and the Hasmonaean revolt (168/7 B.C.E.), following a particular event: a group of devotees, including women, children, and old people, fleeing to the desert caves, were attacked by the enemy on the Sabbath and, doing nothing to defend themselves, were cut down (1 Macc. 2.29–40; adapted in 2 Macc. 6.11). Mattathias the Hasmonaean reacted to this event by issuing an unambiguous order that defending oneself on the Sabbath was imperative in every situation, since there would otherwise be no chance to stand against the enemy. Many scholars, therefore, are agreed that it is from this point on that warfare on the Sabbath was permitted, albeit for defense only.[56]

This view was rejected by modern Orthodox rabbis, adhering to the old, traditional view that there were no principal changes and developments in Jewish oral law. They have been joined in the last generation, for other reasons, by secular Jewish scholars, including the present author,[57] who point out that a prohibition against self-defense on the Sabbath could never have been viable in any period and would not have been the norm in any case.[58] The latter reject the testimony of Agatharchides as evidence for a prohibition against any warfare on the Sabbath and regard Mattathias's pronouncement as doing nothing more than reinforcing a long-standing practice. Scholars who take this view have different opinions on a range of questions, such as the reconstruction of the occupation of Jerusalem in 302/1, the exact intent of Agatharchides, and the reason for his reporting such a prohibition; the motive of those who died in the cave for refraining from fighting on the Sabbath; the nature and significance of Mattathias's reaction to that event;[59] the position of the author of 2 Maccabees, and of later sources, regarding warfare on the Sabbath;[60] and the accepted position of Jews in Judaea and the Diaspora in the Second Temple period regarding offensive warfare on the Sabbath.[61] In general, all Jewish groups and sects seem to have forbidden offensive warfare, while defensive warfare in certain conditions was permitted by

56. For a detailed bibliography, see Bar-Kochva (1989) 474–75 and nn. 1, 3; supplemented by Rappaport (2004) 129–34.

57. See Bar-Kochva (1989) 474–93, and 474 n. 2 for bibliographical references.

58. The point had first been made by Radin (1915) 179–81; cf. Efron (1987) 21 n. 63; Bar-Kochva (1989) 475–77.

59. On this point, see Bar-Kochva (1989) 481–84. It seems to me upon reflection that, contrary to my interpretation twenty years ago, the group that died in the caves did in fact apply stricter rules, of the type also found in later books, such as the Book of Jubilees (50. 12), and the Damascus Scroll (12. 6).

60. See Bar-Kochva (1989) 484–92.

61. For an exceptional view that even offensive warfare was permitted on the Sabbath, see Ben-Shalom (1993) 89–93.

all but a few eccentric groups in Judaea and some Diaspora Jews by whom a strict interpretation of this and other Sabbath practices was adopted and adhered to throughout the whole period of the Second Temple. The present section will deal only with the event of 302/1, and the accounts by Josephus and Agatharchides.

The first task is to ascertain where Josephus found the information that he uses for his own account of the event, which precedes the fragment of Agatharchides in *Jewish Antiquities* (12. 4). Josephus's version provides many details that are not in the following short fragment: the Sabbath is explicitly mentioned; Ptolemy is said to have acted deceitfully, declaring that he was entering the city only in order to sacrifice (or rather initiate a sacrifice) in the Temple in honor of the Jewish God (as Hellenistic rulers occasionally did in Jerusalem and in other places). Consequently, the Jews did not suspect a plot to occupy the city, and it was for this reason that they did not defend themselves against him; and since there was no alert, and it was the Jewish day of rest, the Ptolemaic forces had no trouble occupying the city. Is all this an interpretation of Agatharchides by Josephus, or does it derive from another source?

It is not unusual for Josephus to adduce statements and accounts from internal sources and support them by quotations from Gentile authors on the same subject, even if the support is only partial.[62] However, he does occasionally also provide his own paraphrase of an account by a Gentile author, which he then supports by quoting the same source word for word, trying to create the impression that his own version is based on personal knowledge or a written source other than the one then adduced. In such a case, there is obviously close correspondence between the paraphrase and the following quotation.[63] There is no such correspondence in the present case. In fact, the fragment does not even hint that the "superstition" at issue is the observance of the seventh day. Why, then, would Josephus on his own initiative, and without assistance from any source, wish to show the reader in his own account that the Sabbath was very early on considered a superstition by the Greeks, although there is no mention of this in the fragment? Josephus, therefore, adduced Agatharchides to support information he drew from another source. This additional source was not the account by Agatharchides in *On Europe,* used by Josephus a decade later in *Contra Apionem*. Apart from the statement that the event occurred on the seventh day, when the Jews abstained from work, there is no mention there of the devious manner in which Ptolemy took the city. Josephus's version of the event is based on another source.

In order to identify Josephus's source, there are two more points worth considering. First, Josephus could not have invented the trick played by the king,

62. E.g., Josephus *Antiquitates Judaicae* 12. 132–35, as opposed to 135–36 (from Polybius).

63. E.g., Josephus *Antiquitates Judaicae* 13. 250 and 251 (from Nicolaus of Damascus); 318 and 319 (from Strabo-Timagenes).

implying as it does flexibility in Sabbath rules (see below). The story of the cave victims in 1 Maccabees had led Josephus to believe that there had been a sweeping prohibition on warfare on the Sabbath prior to Mattathias's proclamation (*AJ* 12. 272–77). Josephus, therefore, followed a source describing the trick. Second, in the sentence following the fragment, Josephus says: "Ptolemy took many captives from Mt. Judaea and places neighboring Jerusalem and Samaria and Mt. Garizim (Grizim) and led them all to Egypt and settled them [there]" (para. 7). This information certainly does not derive from *On Europe,* and had it come from *On Asia,* Josephus would have quoted this too in the name of Agatharchides. Significantly, *pseudo-Aristeas,* which elaborates on the expulsion of the Jews from Judaea to Egypt (paras. 12–27) and was copied almost word for word by Josephus (*AJ* 12. 28–33), makes no mention of the expulsion from Samaria or Mt. Garizim. Hence it must be concluded that Josephus used an internal source, one of those unknown internal sources that he frequently used in *Jewish Antiquities.*

The internal Jewish source indicates that the Jews were accustomed to defending themselves on the Sabbath. The reason given for the failure to stop the king from entering the city is the mistaken assumption of the residents that he had come just to offer sacrifice ("for they did not suspect him to be hostile"), and not that there was a prohibition against fighting on the Sabbath. The same thing could have happened on any other day of the week.[64] The next statement, however, refers to the second stage of the operation, that of getting control of the city: "and, they happening to be idle and at rest, because of the lack of suspicion and [because of] the day, he possessed the city without effort." It explains in brief how Ptolemy succeeded in holding the city even after his true purpose had been revealed: The king entered Jerusalem on the Sabbath peacefully, and then took advantage both of the Jews' lack of preparedness when acute danger was not considered imminent and of their custom of not bearing arms on their day of rest, a practice well known from the subsequent history of the Second Temple and Pharisaic rulings.[65] On the Sabbath, it was only when danger was manifest and immediate that arms could be taken up ready for battle. The story actually

---

64. See 1 Maccabees 29–30: Apollonius, captain of the Mysian mercenaries, occupied Jerusalem in 168 B.C.E. on the eve of the religious edicts and used the same trick, although not on the Sabbath. The Seleucid commander deceitfully made peace overtures to the Jews and won their trust; that is, the Jews took no precautionary measures. The Mysian-Seleucid force entered Jerusalem without hindrance, and the result was that "the city fell suddenly and a great blow struck it." According to the parallel in 2 Maccabees 5.25–26 (merely an invention of the author, based solely on 1 Macc.), the event occurred on the Sabbath. On the reasons why the author chose the Sabbath, see Bar-Kochva (1989) 485. Josephus was not acquainted with 2 Maccabees.

65. On the prohibition against carrying weapons on the Sabbath, see Herr (1961) 249, 354–56. The main sources: Tosefta Erubin 3. 5–6; PT Erubin 4. 3 (21d); BT Erubin 45a; cf. Mishnah, Sabbath 6. 3–4; Josephus *Vita Josephi* 161.

assumes that Ptolemy I was aware of, and fully exploited, this custom by playing his trick for entering the city, which he could have played on any day, intentionally on the Sabbath.

The event may now be constructed as follows. Ptolemy I entered the city under false pretenses. When he made his hostile intentions known (by a demonstration of force, occupying key positions, arresting influential people, and the like), the inhabitants had insufficient time to arm and organize themselves, and the city consequently fell to him like a ripe fruit. The difficulty in organizing quickly for defense is well illustrated by another event described in the Tosefta: "At the beginning they used to lay down their arms (on the eve of the Sabbath) in a house next to the wall; one time (the enemy) came back upon them, and [they] pushed on to take up their arms and killed each other" (Erubin 3 [4] 6).

Josephus used an internal source obviously knowledgeable of the Jewish rules. There is no reason to regard the description given as incorrect.[66] It has now to be seen whether this description squares with the reports in the two fragments of Agatharchides.

The fragment of Agatharchides in *Jewish Antiquities* is too short and vague to be used to conclude anything about the progress of the event. All that can be learned from it, by comparison with the fragment from *On Europe*, is that Agatharchides tended to omit details that did not serve his purpose in the given historical context. As for the longer fragment in *Contra Apionem*, all that is actually said is no more than that the Jews did not guard the city because of their observance of the Sabbath, that they allowed Ptolemy to enter with his army, and that as a result, the city fell into his hands. Although it is not stated explicitly, the reader might infer that the Jews from the outset had no intention of fighting on the Sabbath in any situation. The concluding sentences hint at a blind faith in divine assistance even when the inhabitants were not in desperate straits and could easily have defended their city, thanks to its topography and fortifications.[67]

At the same time, this version as well seems to contain traces of an earlier account reminiscent of the internal source used by Josephus: the author states that the Jews did not bear arms on the Sabbath, rather than saying simply that they did not fight;[68] that they did not guard the city; and that Ptolemy was allowed to enter the city. Since Agatharchides used Ptolemaic royal documents and first-class sources, he would have had access to reliable descriptions of the circumstances surrounding the capture of Jerusalem by Ptolemy I in 302/1. Strategic and tactical information such as this would certainly have been recorded accurately

---

66. See, e.g., Stern (1976) 1121; *pace* Radin (1915) 179–81.

67. See further, pp. 303–4 below.

68. τὰ ὅπλα βαστάζειν ("to bear arms"). The expression does not mean "to fight," for which the most similar expression is τὰ ὅπλα λαβεῖν ("to take up arms").

and in full detail to be kept in the archives for the planning of future military campaigns, in this case, together with the Jewish rules of military conduct on the Sabbath. Agatharchides must have abbreviated the original reports greatly and omitted many details. To understand why he did so requires a clarification of his position regarding the Sabbath in general.[69]

AGATHARCHIDES' ATTITUDE
TOWARD THE SABBATH AND THE JEWS

Josephus states twice that Agatharchides wanted to ridicule the Jews (*Ap.* 1. 205, 212). This was accepted by some scholars who have described Agatharchides as hostile toward the Jews, and even as an "anti-Semite."[70] Others have cleared him of any hostile intent, claiming that the disparaging word *deisidaimonia* (super-stition) was frequently used in Greek literature in connection with customs of foreign peoples (and, I would add, often also of Greeks).[71] This argument might seem to be corroborated by the fact that Plutarch, who did not show hostility toward the Jews,[72] called only the Sabbath a superstition.[73]

With regard to the use of the term "superstition" by Agatharchides, it is worth noting that in his fragments and testimonia (a considerable amount relative to that of his Alexandrian contemporaries), the term appears only once, and with regard to Stratonice in the episode preserved in *Contra Apionem* (1. 208). This is despite the presence in the (few) surviving passages from *On Europe* and *On Asia* of references to daily life and customs of cities and peoples, while the work *On the Red Sea* even describes in detail the lives of Aethiopians and other deeply superstitious African tribes. It should be observed, however, that the fragments from the historical works of Agatharchides have survived mainly in Athenaeus's *Deipnosophistai* (The Learned at Table) and therefore pertain to food and drink, where they express Agatharchides' negative opinion of *tryphē* (luxury).[74] As for

---

69. The analysis both of the account of Agatharchides (above) and of his aims (below) differs considerably from what I wrote in the past: Bar-Kochva (1989) 477–81.

70. Fraser (1972) 1: 517, 525; Schäfer (1997a) 84, 243 n. 15. In slightly softer tones: Efron (1962) 18; Sevenster (1975) 126–27; Gabba (1989) 642; Feldman (1993) 160; Kasher (1996) 211, 214.

71. Friedländer (1903) 363; Stern, *GLAJJ* 1: 105; id. (1976) 1124; Shatzman (1992) 18. On "superstition" by and large, see Martin (1997), (2004).

72. Feldman (1993) 160; (1996b) 529–52.

73. *De superstitione* 3, p. 166 A; 8, p. 169 C (= Stern, *GLAJJ* 1: 255–56). At *De Stoicorum repugnantibus* 38, 1051E (= Stern, *GLAJJ* 1: 257), Plutarch may seem to suggest that what the Jews, Syrians, and poets think about the gods is steeped in superstition, but it is not clear whether he is expressing his own opinion or someone else's, or whether the observation is meant to be taken seriously or is rhetorically sarcastic at the expense of the Stoics.

74. See Jacoby, *FGrH*, II.A, no. 86, frr. 2–3, 5–8, 10–11, 14–17 (pp. 207, 208–9, 209–10, 210–11).

On the Red Sea, the work concentrated on the daily struggle for existence of the local tribes, and their survival strategies, namely, adaptation to the difficult living conditions at the southern edge of the known world. Agatharchides repeatedly emphasized the power of necessity (*chreia*) in dictating the natives' lifestyle given the "nature" (*physis*) prevailing in those parts.[75] Consequently it would have been inappropriate to dwell on customs based on superstition, and those Agatharchides did mention could have been rationalized as stemming from the natives' struggle for survival.

At the same time, *deisidaimonia* appears in Diodorus (3. 6. 3) in a passage rightly considered to have been derived ultimately from Agatharchides.[76] It describes the irrational behavior of the Aethiopian kings before the time of Ptolemy II facing prophecies about the time of his death. However, this does not really detract from the positive portrayal of them in the account.

Be that as it may, the attitude of Agatharchides toward the Sabbath and the Jews should not be decided solely by his choice of the term *deisidaimonia*. The version of the story adduced in *Contra Apionem* provides additional data. Scorn for the behavior of the Jews on the Sabbath is prominent, and indeed Josephus rightly understood the story as deriding the Jews (paras. 205, 217). Thus they are said to pray in temples all the day with their hands outstretched (para. 209).[77] Agatharchides mocks the excessively long duration of the activity and the participation of "all the Jews" in the ceremony. Those features, being imaginary (let alone the fact that there was just one Temple in Jerusalem), were certainly not drawn from any official report on the 302/1 campaign but were added as a supplement by Agatharchides. Furthermore, Jerusalem is portrayed as the strongest of all cities (para. 209), a gross exaggeration for the time of Ptolemy I intended to emphasize the stupidity of the inhabitants, who apparently could easily have prevented the fall of the city had they been more sensible. The city fell because they paid attention to their foolish custom rather than to guarding the city ("The fellows instead of guarding the city observed the folly," para. 210). The very use of disparaging terms is a clear sign of Agatharchides' position: *anoia* (literally, "senselessness") and *phaulos* ("worthless").[78] Agatharchides' negative approach is expressed no less strongly in the conclusion: "The outcome taught all but those

75. See Diodorus 3. 15. 7, 18. 7, 19. 2, 23. 2, and many other places.

76. For Agatharchides as Diodorus's direct source, see, e.g., Dihle (1961) 223–24. For an intermediate source such as Artemidorus or Posidonius, see Fraser (1972) 2: 773 n. 159. In view of Diodorus's regular adherence to one source, and his evident direct dependence on Agatharchides in his account of the Aethiopian tribes, the suggestion of Dihle is more likely.

77. On extending the hands in prayer, see Alon (1977) 1: 181–84; and the summary in Kasher (1996) 214.

78. The subsequent *hyponoia* (interpretation) may also be colored by the earlier *anoia* (senselessness); on *hyponoia*, see p. 302 below.

(the Jews) to flee to dreams and to the traditional interpretation concerning the law (only) whenever they are too weak in their human reasonings about problems." Leaving aside "the traditional interpretation concerning the law," to be discussed later,[79] this means that when it is possible to make an efficient and successful defense, there is no justification for resorting to dreams and the like (i.e., omens and superstitions), which, however, is what the Jews did, and still do, and in this they differ from all other peoples.[80] In other words, they are the only people to rely on such methods in reaction to immediate dangers. This is a very strong statement. Its extreme formulation suggests that it refers not only to the situation described but to other developments as well; not only to the Sabbath customs but to a Jewish irrational way of thought in general.[81]

Whatever the case may be, the view Agatharchides expresses with regard to the Sabbath as a whole was evidently negative. This would explain the abbreviations he made in adapting the original Ptolemaic official report. Dwelling on the intricacies of Jewish law and the custom of warfare on the Sabbath and what exactly happened when Ptolemy's treacherous trick was discovered would have detracted from the clarity of the points Agatharchides was trying to make, namely, the absolute folly of the Sabbath custom, and the need to keep away from superstitions. Agatharchides, according to Photius, strove for clarity, and in any case he was not writing a military report for the benefit of the Ptolemaic army in future campaigns against the Jews in Judaea. He was critical of the house of Ptolemy, indeed of imperialism altogether, and had no motivation to see to the continuation of its despotic rule over small nations. The main point of his story about Stratonice, to which was appended the account of the capture of Jerusalem, was, as is explained in his conclusion, to condemn reliance on superstitions in situations that could be resolved rationally. The context was moral and universal rather than particular and military, and Agatharchides took the opportunity to condemn the Sabbath itself, and reliance on superstition in general.

Why was Agatharchides so negative toward the Sabbath? One strong possibility is that in principle he was against idleness, which was regarded as a vice by a few Greeks (and many Romans), as it tended to lead to undesirable developments both for the individual and for society at large. Roman authors accused the Jews of spending a seventh of their lives in idleness,[82] and the subject became a popular

79. See pp. 301–2 below.

80. Schäfer (1997a) 243 n. 15 rightly emphasizes the element of difference between the Jews and all the others.

81. See p. 304.

82. Cf. Tacitus on the Sabbath and the fallow year: "They say that they decided on rest on the seventh day because it (the seventh day) brought an end of labors; then, with inactivity leading them

laughingstock in Roman literature.[83] Agatharchides expresses his view against idleness in several places in *On Europe*. Thus he reports on a Lycian tribe that was enslaved to others because of its excessive idleness (Ath. 12. 527f); on the Dardani, who had too many slaves, and whose slaves fought for them when necessary (Ath. 10. 272d); and on the citizens of Zacynthus, who were militarily untrained because they lived in luxury (Ath. 12. 528a).[84] In *On the Red Sea*, Agatharchides reports during his account of Sabaean society that the king and his court become effeminate through idleness, and at the end of the passage he concludes: "Idleness is unable to preserve freedom for long."[85]

The examples show that Agatharchides' attitude toward idleness conforms with his expectation that a properly functioning society will take all measures to defend itself. In *On Europe*, he relates how Magas, the brother of Ptolemy II, completely neglected military matters and devoted himself to gluttony (Ath. 550c-d). In the introduction to the first book of *On the Red Sea*, Agatharchides inserted a didactic speech that is said to have been directed at an unnamed young Ptolemaic king, warning the latter of "softness" and neglect in defensive preparations against an imminent invasion of the Aethiopians, as well as alerting him to all sorts of other dangers. It is emphasized that the stronger always strives to wrest power from the weaker at the point of the sword. This is the way of the world.[86] In another place in *On the Red Sea*, Agatharchides elaborates on the behavior of the tribes of innocent, passionless fish-eaters of the Red Sea (whom he usually appreciates for their simple life), with undisguised criticism, in places verging on satire:

> For if someone drew his sword and was bearing it down they did not flee from under it, nor did they become angry when undergoing insult or blows, nor did the majority become irritated in sympathy with those receiving [such treatment]; rather, sometimes when their children or women were being slaughtered before their eyes they remained passionless in their dispositions, betraying no sign of anger or again of pity. All in all, falling in with the most shocking terrors they remained calm throughout, looking intently at the things being completed, nodding with their heads at each of the things. For this reason it is said that they do not use speech. (Diod. 3. 18. 3–6)

---

on, the seventh year was also given to idleness" (*Hist.* V. 4. 3). On Seneca's view of idleness on the Sabbath, see below, and cf. pp. 262–63 above.

83. Horace *Satires* 1. 9. 67–72; Juvenal *Satires* 2. 6. 159, 5. 14. 105–6; Martial *Epigrams* 4. 4; Persius *Satires* 5. 179–84.

84. The luxurious lifestyle of the citizens of Zacynthus is not the issue in this reference. Agatharchides states a little earlier that the Aetolians are eager to die in battle just as they are eager for luxury (Ath. 12. 527b-c).

85. Photius *cod.* 250. 102, 459a-b.

86. Photius *cod.* 250. 12–17, 445a-b.

Agatharchides, it may be presumed, did not intend this to be a realistic description of the way this people actually reacted to danger. He was perfectly capable of exaggerating beyond all proportion when he wished to, just as he did in describing the way the close followers of Alexander the Great and subsequently the Diadochi used golden luxury items (Ath. 4. 155c-d; 12. 539b-d), all for the sake of underlining a universal message.

The abstention from fighting on the Sabbath, like the other vices—idleness, apathy, luxuriousness—is thus responsible for hastening the end of a society at the hands of a stronger, more sensible opponent. Seneca's criticism of Jewish superstitions, among them the Sabbath, is instructive in this context:

> [Seneca] claims that they behave inexpediently, because for every seven-day period they lose around a seventh of their time in being idle, and by not doing on time many things that are pressing they are harmed. (August. *De civ. D.* 6. 11)

Notably, Agatharchides does accept that men need rest. In *On the Red Sea,* he bemoans the bitter fate of the mine workers in southern Egypt who he says toil ceaselessly day and night.[87] The Sabbath law in the Deuteronomy version of the Ten Commandments explains why the Sabbath should be observed: "that thy manservant and thy maidservant may rest as well as thou" (Deut. 5.14). Had Agatharchides been aware of this, he might have modified his attitude on the subject; but he was not acquainted with the Torah. The suggestion that he was familiar with the Septuagint is baseless.[88]

Apart from his opposition to the Sabbath on principle, Agatharchides may have had more immediate reasons. The relatively fiery tone of the argument, the scorn, and the dramatic formulation of the double conclusion to the fragment from *On Europe* all suggest that he was driven by more than mere ideals and theoretical reservations. Furthermore, there are indications to the effect that the account was influenced by everyday life in Hellenistic Egypt. The word "temples" appears in the plural, and they are described as places of prayer, namely,

---

87. Diodorus 3. 12. 3; Photius *cod.* 250. 18, 445b.

88. *Pace* Fraser (1972) 1: 517, 544, 2: 783 n. 204; and see also Stern, *GLAJJ* 1: 104 n. 1. Fraser compares the sentence in Diodorus 3. 40. 7, taken from Agatharchides ("For these in a moment returned to nature the spirit which it had given [to them]"), with the verse in Ecclesiastes 12.7 ("The spirit returned to God who had given it," in Hebrew and in the Septuagint). However, a Greek scholar such as Agatharchides, familiar with Greek tragedy and popular beliefs, would not have required Ecclesiastes for inspiration to write this sentence (see the collection of parallels from Euripides and Greek epitaphs in Hengel [1973] 228 n. 132: e.g., Eur. *Supp.* 1140, *El.* 59). Furthermore, Ecclesiastes was canonized only after the destruction of the Second Temple. Its Greek translation is evidently influenced by 'Aqilas and therefore must be dated no earlier than the second quarter of the second century C.E.

synagogues.[89] The concluding sentence actually says that the Jews continue to observe the Sabbath up to the present day. Agatharchides expresses dismay at the continuation of this custom, which is at odds with the opinion of "all." His negative attitude toward the Sabbath, therefore, may have been influenced by the tension this custom inevitably created between Jews and Greeks in Egypt. The observance of the Sabbath by the many Jewish soldiers in the royal service, and the official exemption they received from the Ptolemies (as from other rulers in the Hellenistic and Roman ages), inevitably posed internal problems and military difficulties for the Ptolemaic army, whether the Jews fought in their own units or were scattered in groups or individually in mixed, multiethnic, units.[90] If we are to rely on the direct and indirect references in the literature of Diaspora Jews and random information about them, Jewish soldiers in the Diaspora strictly observed the Sabbath and may have adopted more restrictions than was customary in the Holy Land.[91] Many (if not all) of them certainly refrained from offensive warfare, at least on the Sabbath, and from guarding and bearing arms when there was no immediate danger. It is easy to see that these restrictions would have created major difficulties in a multiethnic army. They would naturally have led to resentment on the part of Greek and Macedonian soldiers toward their Jewish brothers in arms, who relieved themselves of all routine and emergency duties not only on the Jewish holy days but one day a week as well, leaving the non-Jews to pick up the burden, increasing the military risks, and occasionally ruining the chances of a successful attack. The Jews, therefore, must have been perceived as enjoying an unfair exemption on the Sabbath at the expense of their neighbors.

Living in Egypt, Agatharchides could not have been unaware of the problem and remained indifferent, certainly not in the generation in which the Greco-Macedonian army was occupied in defending Egypt from the incursions of Antiochus Epiphanes, which would have aroused unrest among the Egyptian population. Agatharchides,in the tradition of Greek literature, did not favor parasites, as he makes clear elsewhere (Ath. 6. 251f).

Agatharchides may also have thought that keeping the Sabbath was not an original Jewish command ordained by Moses. In the Jewish excursus of Hecataeus of Abdera, the basic source of information about the Jews for Alexandrian

89. See the comprehensive discussion of the term "temples" in Kasher (1996) 214–15, proving that Agatharchides meant the synagogues in Egypt. See also Cohen (1987a) 161; Feldman (1993) 159. That "temples" in this case meant "synagogues" was first suggested by Büchler (1910/11) 139; cf. Joseph. BJ 4. 408, 7. 144.

90. On Jewish soldiers in the Ptolemaic army, see Tcherikover (1963) 30–44. For exemption of Jews from military service on the Sabbath, see, e.g., 1 Maccabees 10.34, 37; Josephus Antiquitates Judaicae 12. 150; 13. 52, 251; 14. 226, 228, 232.

91. See esp. 2 Maccabees 5.25–26, 8.25–28, 15.1–5; Josephus Antiquitates Judaicae 18. 322.

authors, there is no reference whatsoever to the Sabbath.[92] Agatharchides was very familiar with Hecataeus's *Aegyptiaca*.[93] He could have worked out that the Sabbath was no more than a later invention of the Jews designed mainly to shirk their duties, both military and civilian. Some support for this suggestion may be found in the concluding sentence of the fragment from *Contra Apionem*: Agatharchides calls the Sabbath prohibition *hyponoia* (para. 211), which literally means "under sense," a significance beyond the superficial meaning of something. It can mean even "folly" or "nonsense" but usually denotes interpretation (including metaphorical), and already in Plato's *Politeia* it applies to allegory. The Jewish "interpretation," namely, the regulations about the Sabbath, or at least about war on the Sabbath, had, according to Agatharchides, been handed down from generation to generation (a "traditional interpretation"; as an oral tradition?). Agatharchides could have learned something about the variety of methods applied by Jews in their interpretations of the ancient texts concerning the Sabbath from the Greek commentary on the Torah by his contemporary Aristobulus the Jew, who served in the Ptolemaic court.[94] Aristobulus invested considerable effort into proving that the earliest and greatest of the Greek authors endorsed and adopted the observation of the Sabbath and expressed this in their works. As evidence he adduced verses and fragments of verses that he attributed to Homer and Hesiod; among these are Jewish forgeries, verses taken out of context, and some that Aristobulus interpreted allegorically.[95]

The allegorical interpretations of Aristobulus raise yet another possible motive for Agatharchides' remarks against the Sabbath. In the third and second centuries B.C.E., when nearly anyone capable of holding a quill, with the exception of Agatharchides himself and a few others, felt compelled to write a commentary, usually allegorical, on Homer, the allegorical approach of Aristobulus was quite dangerous. This allegorical interpretation made it possible to distort everything written in the Greek tradition and Judaize it, as indeed Aristobulus had already done to Homer, Hesiod, Pythagoras, Socrates, and Plato.[96] Agatharchides' scorn for the Sabbath and his assertion that the folly in it was recognized by all may have been intended, among other things, to refute such "evidence" of the type provided by Aristobulus. The danger that Greeks would take these allegorical interpretations seriously would have spurred Agatharchides on to attack a cus-

92. See p. 123 above.

93. On the use of Hecataeus by Agatharchides, see Photius *cod.* 250. 64, 454b. For the influence of Hecataeus's account of the pharaonic kingdom on Agatharchides, see Murray (1970) 154–57.

94. On Aristobulus, see pp. 196–200 above.

95. Preserved in Clement *Stromateis* 6. 16 (137.4–138.4, 141.7b–142.1, 144.3), 5. 14 (107.1–4, 108.1); Eusebius *Praeparatio evangelica* 13. 12. 9–16, 13. 34–35a; and see Walter (1961) 75–78, 151–56; Holladay (1983–96) 3: 223, 234–38.

96. See p. 199 above.

tom that he regarded as encouraging idleness and endangering the freedom and the very existence of Greeks living among Oriental people.

As the secretary of Heraclides Lembus, who wrote a summary of the biographies by Hermippus of Smyrna, Agatharchides was certainly familiar with the writings of Hermippus. He may have been affected by the implied evaluation of Hermippus of one or more Jewish customs as virtually superstitions.[97] Yet Agatharchides did not actually need the influence of a predecessor to form his own opinion on such matters. We cannot know to what extent he was influenced in his attitude toward the Jews in general by the Egyptian anti-Jewish libels that in his time were being given Greek coloring and disseminated at the instigation of the court in Antioch.[98] At any rate, it is unlikely that he would have been negatively disposed toward the Jews because of their struggle against the Seleucids.[99] Agatharchides was outspoken in his criticism of Ptolemaic tyranny and was presumably just as opposed to the house of Seleucus. He criticized the dominance of empires over small peoples, and the deification of Hellenistic kings. He experienced the subjugation of Ptolemaic Egypt by Antiochus Epiphanes, and since his patron, Heraclides Lembus, conducted the negotiations that led to the surrender of Egypt, Agatharchides would certainly have been aware of the problematic personality of Antiochus IV Epiphanes.

. . .

Are the remarks and the overt and covert intentions of Agatharchides against the Sabbath sufficient to call him "anti-Semitic" or, rather, anti-Jewish? Given the present data and in light of what we know of his writings and views, it would require oversensitivity to make such a claim, which in any case cannot be proven. The criticism the Jews receive for their failure to defend themselves Agatharchides dishes out in like measure to the Aethiopians and others, including Greeks and Macedonians. The fish eaters in the Red Sea who are criticized for failing to defend themselves are appreciated, if not admired, by Hermippus for their simple and natural lifestyle. Nor do the implied charges of a certain tendency to idleness, to be parasites, to shirk military and civilian duties (a seventh of the time), necessarily indicate an overall hatred of Jews. These characteristics are far less degrading than some of the stereotypical negative features that Greeks attributed to many of the people and ethnic groups they encountered, and that even Agatharchides himself attributed to certain Greeks and Macedonians.

Agatharchides' concluding sentence states that the Jews, alone among nations, prefer to follow "dreams" even when a situation could be better dealt with by

---

97. See pp. 186–90 and 193 above.
98. See pp. 277–79 above.
99. *Pace* Efron (1962) 18 and others.

reason. The claim might at first sight indicate an underlying "anti-Semitism." A closer inspection reveals, however, that it is no more than a rhetorical-didactic exaggeration designed to drive home the universal lesson, namely, that over-reliance upon superstition brings disaster, as happened to the Jews. Were the sentence taken literally, it would mean that every nation on earth, save the Jews, behaves perfectly rationally in extreme situations as well as in everyday life, turning to superstition only when all other avenues have been explored. However, Agatharchides would not have regarded most, if any, humans as Stoic sages free of superstition, let alone entire nations. Most telling is that the story was adduced by Agatharchides in the context of the episode about a Macedonian princess who, two generations later, likewise relied upon "dreams" instead of taking the measures necessary to save her life. And was all humanity aware of the occurrences in remote Judaea in 302/1? This sort of exaggeration could have been applied to any other nation in the appropriate circumstances and context. That such a sentence concludes the story is not exceptional; Agatharchides often makes use of epigrammatic statements and aphorisms to express a moral or universal message regarding an episode or event.[100] Ultimately, the mention of the Jewish event alone as resembling the Stratonice episode does not by itself single out the Jews as a particularly superstitious people. In an account of European history that digresses to the ill-fated adventure of the former Antigonid queen in Syria, it is all but natural to draw a parallel to an event that also effected the interests of the House of Antigonus in Syria in the early Hellenistic period.

Agatharchides could hardly have been indifferent toward the Jews, but it is impossible to determine the tenor of his general attitude, and it is unclear how he would have reacted to their uniqueness in various spheres of life. His work *On the Red Sea* shows that Agatharchides was not a one-dimensional, opportunistic historian, but an opinionated personality with great, sometimes surprising social and political sensitivity. His temporary cessation of work on *On Asia*, which in the end proved to be permanent, prevented him from moving beyond the Diadochic period to times that would have provided him with good opportunities to refer to the Jews and given us greater insight into his positions on Jews and Judaism. Josephus, who bothered to quote at length two parallel passages

---

100. See note 26 above. Schäfer (1997a) 84 says: "Agatharcides' true subject is again Jewish separateness and self-isolation which he attributes to superstition and folly." Hence he concludes: "Agatharcides reveals himself here as a worthy spokesman of an Egyptian-Greek anti-Jewish tradition which articulates itself within different contexts and uses different motives." This interpretation is not supported by the text and does not pay attention to the specific historical and literary context of the reference to the Jews (including its stylistic features), nor to Agatharchides' extraordinary positions and unique worldview. As a matter of fact, there is not a single issue on which Agatharchides can be regarded as representing the common opinion of Alexandrian Greeks.

from Agatharchides on the same event, does not mention any other reference by Agatharchides to the Jews, which indicates that there was not any.

At the same time, the fragments of Agatharchides reveal a transitional stage between the relatively cool and unbiased writings of previous Greek authors and the openly hostile writing of later Greek and Roman authors. Agatharchides was the first Greek, so far as we know, to call a celebrated symbol of Jewish identification a superstition. From the next generation onward, Greek authors, and Romans in their wake, gradually began to portray an increasing number of Jewish customs as superstitions, including the Jewish religion altogether, applying the Greek term *deisidaimonia,* and its Latin equivalent, *superstitio.* The first of these authors known to us is Posidonius of Apamea, who enthusiastically described Mosaic Judaism but then went on to condemn the later Jewish priests and tyrants (the latter clearly the Hasmonaean rulers) for introducing customs stemming from superstitions such as circumcision and excision, the prohibition against eating certain types of meat, and so on (in Strabo 16. 2. 37).[101] Posidonius was very familiar with the writings of Agatharchides and was greatly influenced by them.[102] It is no coincidence that Cicero, who admired Posidonius, studied with him, and used his works as sources for his dialogues, is the first to have called the Jewish faith *barbara superstitio* (*Flac.* 28 [67]), thus paving the way for other Roman authors. It is true that authors such as Tacitus and Suetonius and their successors called not only Judaism but all barbarian religions superstitions,[103] yet there are later Latin authors who "grace" Judaism alone with this epithet. For example, Apuleius calls only the Jews *superstitiosi* in his geographical survey, which also lists the "learned" Egyptians, the Arsacides, Ityraei, and Arabs (*Flor.* 16).

101. See chapters 11–13 below. For an explanation of why Posidonius refrained from mentioning the Sabbath, see pp. 522–23 below.

102. So, e.g., the Posidonian description of labor in the silver mines in Hispania (preserved in Diod. 5. 36–38 = Jacoby, *FGrH,* II.A, no. 87, fr. 117 [pp. 308–9]) based on the model established for such descriptions by Agatharchides in his account of the forced labor in the gold mines in southeast Egypt. On the influence of Agatharchides on other passages of Posidonius, see Fraser (1972) 1: 517, 2: 773 n. 160, 744 n. 166; and see further Leopoldi (1893) 19 ff.; Schwartz (1887) 227; Jacoby, *FGrH,* II.a, no. 86, p. 151.

103. Such as Seneca, Tacitus, Quintilian, Suetonius, Horace, Fronto, and Apuleius. The same is expressed but in different formulations in Ovid, Tibullus, and Juvenal. See also Stern, *GLAJJ* 2: 60; Grodzynski (1974).

9

The Diachronic Libels
and Accusations (C)

Lysimachus of Alexandria and
the Hostile Accounts of the Exodus

The most detailed description of the Exodus from Egypt that has come down to us from the Hellenistic-Roman period was written by an author named Lysimachus. The account has been preserved in Josephus's *Contra Apionem* (1. 305–11). Independently of this passage, Josephus includes in the second book of *Contra Apionem*, in his own shortened formulation, a number of statements— mostly hostile—made by Lysimachus about the Jewish people and about Moses (2. 16, 20, 145, 236). Lysimachus's description of the Exodus is relatively detailed, and so of considerable value. Yet, despite its many implications for the history of hatred of the Jews, it has not received the attention it deserves.[1]

The value of Lysimachus' account lies not only in its detail, but also in its use both of Egyptian and Hellenistic-Egyptian versions and of most of the elements of the Exodus stories known to us from Hellenistic and Roman literature, not to mention elements unknown from other sources. Because of this surfeit of data, Josephus declared this account by Lysimachus to be the most hostile of all the versions on the Exodus (*Ap.* 1. 304).[2] Josephus even puts the hatred of Lysimachus toward the Jews and his unreliability on a par with those of Apollonius Molon,

---

1. Lysimachus's account of the Jews has attracted only brief surveys and commentaries: Müller (1877) 208–11; Reinach (1895) 117–20; Stählin (1905) 28–30; Schürer (1901–9) 3: 535–36; Böhl (1953) 101– 33; Gager (1972) 118–20; Stern, *GLAJJ* 1: 382–88; id. (1976) 1114–15; Troiani (1977) 135–37; Conzelmann (1981) 79–81; Whitaker (1984) 45–46; Goodman in Schürer et al., 3: 600–601; Aziza (1987) 55–58; Gabba (1989) 652–54; Feldman (1993) 143–44, 171–72, 192–94; Kasher (1996) 270–75; Schäfer (1997a) 27–28; Gruen (1998) 45–47; Labow (2005) 311–30.

2. For a similar estimation of Lysimachus as one of the most hostile pagan authors toward the Jews, see Stern, *GLAJJ* 1: 382; id. (1976) 1114; Aziza (1987) 56; Feldman (1993) 163, 171, 192; Gruen (1998) 46.

06

the celebrated orator of the first half of the first century B.C.E., whom Josephus regarded, along with Apion, as the greatest hater of the Jews. Josephus lumps them together in his derogatory reference to haters of Jews as the "Lysimachi and the Molons" (2. 236).[3] There is also special interest in the original additions made by Lysimachus himself; as we shall see, under cover of the Exodus stories, they reflect the contemporary confrontation between Jews and Hellenistic cities in the Holy Land at the end of the second century B.C.E. and were motivated by the deterioration in relations between Greeks and Jews in Egypt.

THE IDENTIFICATION OF LYSIMACHUS, HIS DESCENT, PERIOD, AND WORKS

The content of the testimonia in Josephus has allowed scholars to establish with a great degree of certainty that Lysimachus's account of the Jews appeared within an ethnography—an Egyptian history entitled, according to custom, *Aegyptiaca*,[4] or the like, and not in a monograph devoted to the Jews.[5] The main testimonium describes the expulsion of the Jews from Egypt in the reign of King Bokchoris, their ordeal in the desert, and their misdeeds in the inhabited land until they settled in Judaea and Jerusalem. One learns from this that the passage on the Jews appeared in the account of the times of Bokchoris (late eighth cent.) and was limited to those events that Lysimachus deemed to have happened during or close to the reign of that king (apart from the veiled hints to events contemporary with the author himself).

Josephus (or his assistants) used the work of Lysimachus directly. Josephus nowhere mentions using an intermediate source with regard to Lysimachus, as he does in some other instances in *Contra Apionem*,[6] and there is no indication that he used such a source. There is in principle no justification for inventing an intermediate source if there is no evidence or good reason for one. In the case of Josephus-Lysimachus, there is no reason even for suspicion.

---

3. Cf. the contemptuous expression "the Apions and the Molons" (*Ap.* 2. 295). On the attitude of Apollonius Molon toward the Jews, see below, pp. 469–516.

4. So, e.g., Fraser (1972) 2: 1092 n. 475; Stern, *GLAJJ* 1: 382; Conzelmann (1981) 79; Goodman in Schürer et al., 3: 601; Schäfer (1997a) 27. Yet the work could just as well have been called, like others of this type, περὶ Αἰγυπτίων (*On Native Egyptians*). In any case, one should not rely on Cosmas Indicopleutes, the sixth-century Byzantine merchant-monk, who counts Lysimachus among the authors who wrote *Aegyptiaca; pace* Susemihl (1891–92) 1: 479 n. 116; Conzelmann (1981) 79; Goodman, 601 n. 116. On the list in Cosmas, which is valueless, see in detail below, pp. 478–79.

5. Suggested by Gabba (1989) 652.

6. Mnaseas of Patara (*Ap.* 2. 112), as well as Posidonius of Apamea and Apollonius Molon (2. 79). On the question of Josephus's acquaintance with the writings of Apollonius Molon, see pp. 484–85 below.

Josephus provides no basic information about Lysimachus: nothing on his origin or period of activity, nor on the work referring to the Jews. He expresses his opinion only with regard to the degree of hostility Lysimachus manifested toward the Jews, and, as usual, adds his own words of censure against him and, in this instance, juxtaposed with Apollonius Molon (*Ap.* 2. 145: "ignorance and ill will"; 2. 236: "unimportant sophists," "misleading [corrupting?] the youth").

With Josephus silent on the matter, it was suggested that Lysimachus should be identified with the author of that name who was believed to have been active in Alexandria some time after 200 or 175 B.C.E.[7] Some rejected this suggestion, while others preferred to keep an open mind on the subject.[8] The question of Lysimachus's identity is not merely a *pro forma* inquiry. It has implications for the motives of the author, the reconstruction of the original content of the passage on the Jews, our understanding of its transmission by Josephus, and other issues. The examination of the question of the identity of our Lysimachus will therefore commence with a survey of the available information concerning the works and writing habits of Lysimachus of Alexandria and continue with an attempt to date him and establish his descent.

What we know of Lysimachus of Alexandria comes from a series of fragments and testimonia drawn mainly from scholia on poets such as Homer, Pindar, Sophocles, and Euripides, and from later authors and compilers such as Apollonius Rhodius, Athenaeus, Porphyry, and Photius, with additional, dubious references by other authors.[9] In two places, Lysimachus is called explicitly "Alexandrian."[10] The sprinkling of material in the scholiasts, who composed their works in the second and third centuries C.E., in Athenaeus and Porphyry in the same period, in Photius in the ninth century, and even in Eustathius, the twelfth-century Byzantine commentator on Homer indicates that Lysimachus was not unknown, and that his works were available in central libraries for most of the period during which the tradition of Greek literature was preserved.

The material that has survived from Lysimachus's works comes from only

7. See Müller (1877) 208; Radtke (1893) 101; Gudemann, *RE* s.v. "Lysimachos (20)," cols. 35–36; Fraser (1972) 2: 1093; Goodman in Schürer et al., 3: 601. For surveys and discussions of Lysimachus of Alexandria, see Müller, *FHG* III. 334–42 (text and short notes); Stiehle (1849) 99–110; (1850) 382–83; Susemihl (1891–92) 1: 463–64, 2: 674; Radtke (1893); Baumstark (1898) 691–703; Gudemann, *RE* s.v. "Lysimachos (20)," cols. 32–39; Jacoby, *FGrH* III. b, no. 382 (pp. 165–75); Fraser (1972) 2: 1092–93; Labow (2005) 312–15.

8. Without conclusive results: Jacoby, *FGrH* III. b, no. 382, p. 179; Stern, *GLAJJ* 1: 382; Conzelmann (1981) 2; Gruen (1998) 45; Kasher (1997) 270; *contra:* Müller, *FHG* III. 338 ff.; Gabba (1989) 652 n. 4; Gager (1972) 118–20; Troiani (1977) 135. In Jacoby's collection, the passage on the Jews is set apart from the passages of Lysimachus of Alexandria; See *FGrH* III. C, no. 621 (pp. 155–56).

9. See Jacoby, *FGrH* III. B, no. 382 (pp. 251–58).

10. Ἀλεξανδρεύς: *FGrH* III. B, no. 382, 2; 8 (pp. 251–52, 254).

two of his compositions: περὶ τῶν Θηβαίων παραδόξων (On the *Paradoxoi* of the Thebans), apparently in three books,[11] and *Nostoi* (Return Journeys [to the Homeland]). Another work is referred to by the name περὶ τῆς Ἐφόρου κλοπῆς (On the Plagiarism of Ephorus), but only the title remains.

The title of the first work presents some difficulty with regard to its genre and content. "Paradox" literature is well known to us; it deals with the unexpected, the surprising and marvelous, and is similar to the genre dealing with the wonderful (*thaumasia*).[12] Yet there is no hint of wonderful deeds in the passages surviving from Lysimachus's work.[13] It seems therefore that the title should be interpreted literally: "[views] against the common opinion." This meaning of the word is known from philosophical literature and is found in isolated arguments, in whole books, and in titles of works. It should suffice to mention the series of paradoxes of Zeno of Elea (famous for the paradox of Achilles and the tortoise);[14] the seventh book of Aristotle's *Physics;* and the works *On Stoic Paradoxes* by Cicero and Plutarch. There are many titles combining the word with the name of a place;[15] but their nature and content cannot be determined with confidence.

This suggested meaning of the title is corroborated by the content of a fragment in which Lysimachus describes the founding of Thebes through the legend of Cadmus and Europa, the son and daughter of Agenor, king of Tyre. Lysimachus thus regarded Cadmus and the first generation of Thebans as originating in Phoenicia—in conformity with the ancient classical tradition (e.g., Hdt. 2. 49, 5. 57–61)—and not in Egypt, as reported by Hecataeus of Abdera in his Egyptian ethnography (Diod. 1. 23. 4, 40. 3. 2) and was received in Alexandria as authoritative. The link between Cadmus and the Egyptians suited the way of thinking of people at the time, in view of the two settlements named Thebes, in Boeotia and in Egypt, and the Ptolemaic regime and its advocates must have been particularly motivated to adopt this version, which served both its external and its internal purposes. Although not invented by him, Lysimachus's version of the founding of Thebes, in this case, was aimed against the opinion once widely held in Alexandria on this subject.[16]

11. See *FGrH* III. B, no. 382, 2, l. 4 (p. 252 l. 2). The number written in the MS is ιγ´ (= 13); the Müllers raised the possibility of correcting to γ´ (= 3); see Müller, *FHG* III. 336. Jacoby (*FGrH* III. B, no. 382, p. 252) left the question open.

12. Susemihl (1891–92) 1: 464 regards the work as belonging to the genre of "wunderbare Ortslegenden."

13. Jacoby writes: "unerklärlich ist Παράδοξα im titel: was in den fragmenten steht ist absolut nicht das was dieser und ähnliche titel sonst decken." Jacoby offers no solution to the difficulty; see Jacoby, *FGrH* III. b, no. 382, p. 167.

14. See the commentary of Simplicius on the seventh book of Aristotle's *Physics* in *DG*, no. 947.

15. A partial collection of such titles can be found in Susemihl (1891–92) 1: 463–86.

16. On the background to the change in approach, see below, pp. 336–37.

From the second work by Lysimachus, *Nostoi,* we have a story about the settlement of the sons of Antenor in Cyrene and its vicinity, and their relations with
the earlier settlers from Troy, on the one hand, and with the Hellenes, on the
other; passages touching on the inhabitants of the island of Samos, on the place
where Heracles was conceived and born, and on the founding of cities by Acamas,
the son of Theseus; traditions concerning the children of Andromache and relating to genealogy, settlement, and government; and subjects connected with the
early history of Athens and Homeric heroes. Remarkably, though Lysimachus
lived in Alexandria, there is no hint in all of this of a connection with Egypt and
Egyptian figures, not even when he writes about Cyrene.

The third work by Lysimachus, *On the Plagiarism of Ephorus,*[17] is mentioned in a testimonium taken from Porphyry by Eusebius in the tenth book of
Praeparatio evangelica (3. 23), together with a work by the same title by Alcaeus,
the third-century B.C.E. poet from Messene (cf. *PE* 10. 1–2). In the same context, Eusebius-Porphyry list similarly named works against Ctesias, Herodotus,
Theopompus, and lesser-known authors. Since nothing has survived from
the work against Ephorus, and since no identifying detail apart from the title
appears, the identification of its author with Lysimachus of Alexandria has been
contested.[18] Yet Felix Jacoby had already noted the link between the particular
subjects of interest of Lysimachus of Alexandria and those of the Lysimachus
who accused Ephorus of plagiarism, making it likely that the two were the same
man.[19] Ephorus of Cymae in Aeolis (fourth cent. B.C.E.),[20] like Lysimachus of
Alexandria, emphasized foundation stories of settlements and cities, and genealogical connections between them,[21] and wrote a great deal about Thebes. Of the
thirty books that made up Ephorus's *Histories*—a sort of universal history with
special emphasis on Greece from the archaic period to near the end of the fourth
century—five books were devoted to the period of the hegemony of Thebes, a
number that seems somewhat disproportionate. This is not surprising in view
of Aeolians' origins in Boeotia. As appears from what remains of his works,
Ephorus was a compiler who did not mention the names of his sources but drew
from a great variety of historians, including Herodotus,[22] and that in spite of

17. Identifying the writer with Lysimachus of Alexandria: Susemihl (1891–92) 1: 464; Jacoby,
FGrH III. b, no. 382, p. 166.

18. Radtke (1893) 101; Gudemann, *RE* s.v. "Lysimachus (20)," col. 36.

19. See Jacoby, *FGrH,* III. b, no. 382, p. 173.

20. On Ephorus, see Schwartz, *RE* s.v. "Ephoros," cols. 1–16; Laqueur (1911) 161–206, 321–54;
Barber (1935); Momigliano (1935) 180–204; Andrews (1951) 39–45; Drews (1962) 383–92; (1963) 244–55;
Rubincam (1976) 357–66.

21. Polybius 9. 1. 4, 34. 1. 3–4; Strabo 10. 3. 5.

22. See Jacoby, *FGrH* II. A, no. 70 (pp. 37–109); II.C, no. 70 (pp. 23–103), and in various places in
the discussions mentioned in note 20 above.

Ephorus's own writing ability and originality, for which he was praised by as strict a critic as Polybius (12. 28. 10).[23]

The writing of a work on plagiarism, at the time generally regarded as a fairly acceptable practice,[24] suggests an author who keenly felt that original authorship should be acknowledged. We may assume that Lysimachus cited his sources in his own works. Can this be substantiated from the remains of his writings? Of eighteen testimonia and fragments from his works on Thebes and *Nostoi*, four are fragments between seven and fifteen lines long (in Jacoby's edition), and the rest are testimonia mostly containing just a few words. Because of their nature and length, the four fragments are of greater significance to the current question. In each long fragment, Lysimachus refers by name to more than one source; some of these sources are esoteric and otherwise unknown to us. There is no story or detail without its sources being named. If all of the sources agree on a point, Lysimachus notes it; if one source disagrees, even on the slightest detail, this too is mentioned for the reader's information.[25] Of the fourteen short testimonia, Lysimachus is seen in three to have named his sources,[26] and in another four, this may be inferred from the way the scholiast presents Lysimachus.[27] The lack of references in the remaining seven testimonia may be due to their extreme brevity or to the summarizing technique of the scholiasts. Thus the overall impression from these remains is that Lysimachus practiced what he preached.

The facts mentioned above concerning the titles and contents of works, and

23. Polybius criticized Ephorus only for his lack of understanding of land warfare (12. 5) and constitutional issues (6. 45. 1).

24. Indeed, it would be difficult to imagine the development, and especially the survival, of Greek and Latin literature without the extensive plagiarism of all kinds that went on. Legal sanctions and social ostracism were not adopted against these thieves of intellectual property, itself a notion barely recognized in a culture where pseudonyms were widely used and compilators were quite popular. Yet some voices of protest were heard against acts of plagiarism; see, e.g., Diogenes Laertius 8. 54; Porphyry *Vita Plotini* 17–18; and the extensive information Porphyry provides on acts of plagiarism by philosophers, historians, and poets, and on how they conceal their deeds (preserved in Eusebius *Praeparatio evangelica* 10. 3–4). Among the authors accused there of plagiarism we find Herodotus, Sophocles, Euripides, Plato, Demosthenes, Isocrates, Ctesias, Menander, Ephorus, and Theopompus. From the same source we also learn about the existence of a sort of genre dedicated to exposing literary thefts; a work of this type was usually called περὶ τῆς τινος κλοπῆς (On [Someone's] Plagiarism). Such works were written on Herodotus, Ctesias, Ephorus, and Theompompus, to name but a few.

25. See Jacoby, *FGrH* III. B, no. 382, frr. 2, 8, 9, 10a (pp. 251, 254). Jacoby presented the fragments in spaced lettering (see, e.g., no. 8—κατὰ λέξιν), but not separate from the testimonia, in order to allow the reader to see the context in which the scholiast adduced each fragment (see, e.g., no. 2, where the source is mentioned in the opening testimonium: someone by the name of Arizelos). This is Jacoby's practice in such cases.

26. Jacoby, *FGrH* III. B, no. 382, frr. 4, 11, 14 (pp, 252, 256).

27. Jacoby, *FGrH* III. B, no. 382, frr. 1b, 4, 12, 15 (pp. 251, 252, 256, 257).

Lysimachus's references to works of other authors, suffice for the conclusion that Lysimachus of Alexandria was a Greek, and not a Hellenized Egyptian as some scholars have suggested.[28] It is hard to believe that a Hellenized Egyptian would engage himself so fundamentally in distant subjects of archaic Greece, all the while referring consistently to esoteric Greek sources. The non-Egyptian origin of our author is manifest in the attribution by Lysimachus of a Phoenician rather than an Egyptian origin to Cadmus and the Thebans, and this in a work whose title indicates that it contradicts the common opinions. A Hellenistic-Egyptian author would not make such an effort to oppose a legend that could only increase the prestige of his pharaonic ancestors. Lysimachus of Alexandria's non-Egyptian origin can also be deduced from the absence of references to Egypt and Egyptian figures in his other genealogies. The work on Thebes may point to Lysimachus being a Boeotian immigrant or of Boeotian descent. We might have expected scholiasts to mention other such works by him on other cities had he written any.

As Lysimachus of Alexandria refers to Mnaseas of Patara (Ath. 4. 158c-d), a date after the year 200 or 175 B.C.E has been suggested for him.[29] A "ceiling" date can be suggested tentatively, before considering his identification with the Lysimachus cited by Josephus, in view of the choice of Ephorus as the subject for a work on plagiarism. As can be deduced from the list in the tenth book of Eusebius's *Praeparatio evangelica,* the authors chosen for attack in the genre of works on plagiarism were well known in their time, not esoteric or neglected. Ephorus was widely read in the last centuries B.C.E. but for various reasons fell into oblivion in the first century C.E.

This allows us chronologically to identify Lysimachus of Alexandria with the Lysimachus appearing in Josephus. Are the two to be identified, however? Was the author/compiler of the Exodus account a Greek? Or was he an Egyptian with a Greek education, like Manetho, Ptolemy of Mendes, or Chaeremon?

At first sight, there appear to be some obstacles to this identification. The detailed testimonium of Lysimachus on the Exodus is located after the testimonia of Manetho and Chaeremon, the Hellenistic-Egyptian authors, and in the introduction to Manetho's account we are told that it was the Egyptians who began the dissemination of hostile stories about the Jews. Furthermore, there is no sign

---

28. E.g., Schürer (1901–9) 3: 535; Goodman in Schürer et al., 3: 601 (indirectly); Kasher (1996) 270. It should, however, be made clear that the adjective "Alexandrian" alone is no evidence: it was restricted to those of Greek origin (Polybius in Strabo 17. 1. 2 [797]) only until the middle of the second century B.C.E., after which its application became more flexible. On the problems surrounding this term and on the literature written about it, see Kasher (1979) 249–53; Delia (1991) 23–28; Barclay (1996) 60–71.

29. See Jacoby, *FGrH* III. b, no. 382, p. 166; Goodman in Schürer et al., 3: 601. On the date of Mnaseas, see p. 210 above.

in the testimonium—as we now have it—of any explicit reference to the use of sources, although it is evident that the author relied on at least two sources, in contrast to what one should expect of Lysimachus of Alexandria.

These observations, however, fail to tilt the balance. The mention of a hostile Greek author after the mention of two hostile Egyptian authors does not contradict the way Josephus presents, at the beginning of his remarks, his quotations on the Exodus. The opening paragraph (*Ap.* 1. 223) goes on to state that the traditions about the Exodus were written by "several" authors in order to please the Egyptians. This formulation does not require all the authors to be Egyptian.[30] The blame for the absence of references to sources may rest with Josephus; it was his usual working habit to omit such references,[31] and in this case one may assume at the outset that he would not have wished to give more weight to the serious accusations made by Lysimachus.[32] Lysimachus could hardly be an Egyptian. First, the temples destroyed by the Jews are not Egyptian but are those of other people and their gods (paras. 209–10). This is not what one would expect of an Egyptian in such a story, and does not accord with the early Egyptian Exodus traditions preserved by Manetho (Joseph. *Ap.* 1. 238–40, 249). Second, Josephus says nothing about Lysimachus's origin. Josephus, who usually found a way to include some biographical details about the authors he mentioned or quoted,[33] should have been especially interested in the origin of the author-ethnographer who provided the most extensive and hostile account of the Exodus had he been of Egyptian descent, all the more so as he bears a Greek name. This would surely have been emphasized by Josephus in order to degrade him and detract from the value of his testimonium, as he did with both Manetho (1. 73) and Apion (2. 28–32).[34] It would not have taken too much trouble to discover the origin of Lysimachus. The arrangement of the *pinakes,* or catalogues, in the libraries

30. τῶν δὲ εἰς ἡμᾶς βλασφημιῶν ἤρξαντο μὲν Αἰγύπτιοι· βουλόμενοι δ' ἐκείνοις τινὲς χαρίζεσθαι παρατρέπειν ἐπεχείρησαν τὴν ἀλήθειαν, οὔτε τὴν εἰς Αἴγυπτον ἄφιξιν ὡς ἐγένετο τῶν ἡμετέρων προγόνων ὁμολογοῦντες, οὔτε τὴν ἔξοδον ἀληθεύοντες. The inclusion of Lysimachus in the list of Egyptian authors who wrote an *Aegyptiaca* according to Cosmas Indicopleutes, *Patrologia Graeca* 37, 342E–343A (Wolska-Conus [1973] 3: 456D–457A), is worthless. Apollonius Molon is also included in the same list. See in detail pp. 478–79.

31. Josephus treats the sources quoted by Apion differently because he also argues with Apion about the very reliability of those sources.

32. See further, pp. 324–25 below.

33. See *Ap.* 1. 16–18, 73, 112, 116, 129, 142, 162–63, 168, 172, 176, 183–84, 213, 228, 288; 2. 12, 28, 148, 223–25, 265–66, 270.

34. Josephus did not indicate the Egyptian origin of Chaeremon and felt no need to introduce him to his readers: Chaeremon, his younger contemporary, first an Egyptian priest and then a Stoic author, was quite famous for presenting Egyptian religion in Stoic terms. By and large, the degree of Chaeremon's hostility toward the Jews cannot be compared with that of Lysimachus. On Chaeremon, see van der Horst (1984).

of Rome and the Hellenistic world, followed the *pinakes* of Callimachus,[35] and therefore facilitated easy location of the various entries. Each major genre (in this case, "history") had a separate scroll or group of scrolls of the catalogue, and the internal arrangement was alphabetical according to the names of the authors. The entries themselves included detailed information, and the descent of the author could be found directly or indirectly.[36] Moreover, the *pinakes* took special care to distinguish between authors bearing the same name and to emphasize it.[37] Had the Lysimachus who wrote on Egypt not been a Greek, the *pinax* would have made this clear.

It is also worth noting that the three indisputably Egyptian authors who wrote an extensive Egyptian ethnography-history—Manetho, Ptolemy of Mendes, and Chaeremon—were priests. (Apion's alleged Egyptian descent is doubtful.)[38] This was observed in late testimonia, mainly from the Byzantine period, and was certainly based on information in the *pinakes*. The Egyptian authors who were particularly driven to exalt the Egyptian past, and who were best equipped with the capability and information to achieve this aim, belonged naturally to the priestly class.[39] Such authors also stressed their priestly status in their writings, as did Josephus with regard to himself (*Vita* 1–6). Had Lysimachus been an Egyptian priest, Josephus would have discovered his descent even more easily.

It must have been Lysimachus's Greek origin that encouraged Josephus to lump him together with Apollonius Molon, the celebrated Greek orator who was famous in Rome. It would sound rather strange to mention them in the same breath, especially in the form "the Lysimachi and the Molons" (*Ap.* 2. 236), if Lysimachus were an unknown Egyptian author,[40] and not a Greek writer. The

---

35. On the bibliographical work of Callimachus as a model for future *pinakes* and catalogues, see Blum (1991) 182, 202–6, 226, 238, and the references there to earlier research.

36. On the internal arrangement of the *pinakes* and the content of their entries, see Blum (1991) 161–63, 255–57, 280.

37. See Blum (1991) 234–36, 256–57, 282–83.

38. For testimonia on the descent of Manetho, see Jacoby, *FGrH* III. C, no. 608, T1–14 (pp. 5–10); on Ptolemy of Mendes, no. 611, T1–2 (p. 116); on Chaeremon, no. 618, T1–10 (pp. 145–46). On Apion, see note 40 below.

39. On the Egyptian priests as sources of information and preservers of ancient traditions, we have the testimony of, among others, Herodotus, Manetho, *pseudo-Aristeas,* Philo, and Tacitus. On this, see, e.g., Berthelot (2000) 204–6.

40. "Unknown" needs to be emphasized. In his efforts to defame Apion, Josephus attributes to him an Egyptian origin, bitterly arguing against Apion's presentation of himself as a Greek (*Ap.* 2. 28–29). At the same time, he joins Apion with Molon in the contemptuous expression "the Apions and the Molons" (*Ap.* 2. 295). Whatever his real descent, Apion was very famous in the Greek and Roman world, not least because of his lecture tours, and was considered Greek by his Greek and Roman readers and audience. On the question of his descent, which seems to have been half-Greek, see p. 241 and note 116 above.

veiled allusion to the Jewish attack on the centers of Greek worship in the Holy Land (1. 310) also sits much better with the aims and sentiments of a Greek author.[41]

The odds are that this Greek Lysimachus is indeed to be identified with Lysimachus of Alexandria. Although the name Lysimachus is not rare in the Greek *onomastikon,* we know of only two esoteric writers besides Lysimachus of Alexandria who had this name. Their time, provenance, and subject matter do not accord with the passages adduced by Josephus and the approximate period of their composition. Furthermore, a Greek who did not reside in Alexandria or at least in Egypt would hardly have been able to present such a detailed collection of old Egyptian traditions regarding the Exodus.

Some of the features of Lysimachus's account of the Jews are reminiscent of the writings of Lysimachus of Alexandria. For example, the relatively extensive treatment of the conquest and settlement in the new land within a story intended to report the stay in Egypt and the expulsion from there is reminiscent of the tendency of Lysimachus of Alexandria to dilate upon foundation stories. The original etymology for the Hellenistic name of Jerusalem is reminiscent of Lysimachus of Alexandria's predilection for etymological interpretations—both hostile and favorable—of names of people and places. These features are not peculiar to Lysimachus of Alexandria, but they are prominent in the few remains from his works.

A stylistic comparison leads to similar conclusions. Most of the remains are indeed testimonia in indirect speech, betraying the possible influence of intermediate sources (mainly, scholiasts), and they mainly contain genealogical material that is not really amenable to stylistic comparison. Yet one fragment contains a complete story: Lysimachus's account of the trials of the burial of Oedipus.[42] The account shows extensive use of participles, exemplifying the hypotactic style, whereby multiple participles are subordinated to each main verb. This style was widely used by authors in Alexandria and elsewhere both before and after the Roman conquest, when summing up the accounts of their predecessors, especially myths and other such stories. It is common in the summaries of tragedies and comedies (*hypotheseis*), mostly written by *grammatici.* It is also found in extensive works. To take just one example from a related genre: the *Bibliothēkē,* wrongly attributed to Apollodorus of Athens, summarizes earlier works (not oral traditions) concerning the Greek gods and heroes, often with similar constructions.[43] At the same time, it must be said that the transmission of the Lysimachus account by Josephus is in reported speech, which always at the outset raises the suspicion

---

41. See below, pp. 335–37.
42. Jacoby, *FGrH,* III. B, no. 382, 2 (6) VI, ll. 2–15 (p. 252).
43. See, e.g., the fourth chapter of the first book; there are many other examples.

of abbreviations, omissions, and paraphrases. Thus the examination of style can
only point to a similarity corroborating the proposed identity, while not proving it.

THE EXODUS:

TEXT, FORMULATION, AND ABBREVIATIONS

The proposed identification of the author with Lysimachus of Alexandria, together
with the information on the latter and his works, will help primarily in understanding the method of composition of the passage as we now have it, and in
solving some of its internal difficulties. I shall begin with a literal translation of
the passage (*Ap.* 1. 305–11):[44]

> (305) For (Lysimachus) says that in the reign of Bokchoris,[45] king of the Egyptians,
> the peoples of the Jews (ὁ λαὸς τῶν Ἰουδαίων),[46] being lepers[47] and afflicted with
> boils and having[48] certain other diseases, used to flee to the temples and beg for
> their livelihood; and when very many men succumbed to sicknesses[49] requiring

44. The translation is based on the version of MS S (Schleusingensis). In many cases, the readings of S and the *editio princeps,* which consistently adhered to S, are preferable to those of L
(Laurentianus), the manuscript upon which Niese based his text in his "canonical" edition of the
writings of Josephus (vol. 5 of the *editio maior* [Berlin, 1892]). S followed a textual tradition other
than that of L. On this, see further, pp. 480–81 below.

45. L: Βοχχόρεως. In the Latin version, *bochorem,* and so Niese. We should read Βοκχόρεως,
with S, and, indeed, also with L to para. 307. See also Jacoby, *FGrH* III. C, no. 621, p. 155, note to l. 5.

46. τὸν λαὸν τῶν Ἰουδαίων λεπροὺς ὄντας καὶ ψώρους. This clearly and unambiguously refers
to the whole of the Jewish people. The Latin version reads: *quosdam ex populo Iudaeorum, qui erant
leprosi et scabie pleni aliisque vexati languoribus* ("certain of the people of the Jews who were leprous
and full of boils and afflicted with other diseases"). The translators seem to have tried to solve the
obvious difficulty in the story: if all the Jews suffered from leprosy and boils and other diseases and
were drowned in the sea (para. 308), how did there remain any Jews to settle Judaea? The extant Greek
reading is the correct one, as may be seen by Josephus's repetition of it in his refutation (para. 313):
λέγει γὰρ ὁ λαὸς τῶν Ἰουδαίων. The definite article leaves no room for doubt. On the use of λαός
in Josephus to denote the Jewish people as a whole, see Meiser (1998) 61 n. 229; Gerber (2001) 135 ff.

47. λεπροὺς ὄντας κτλ. The description in Lysimachus has been turned by Josephus into
reported speech, beginning at para. 305 init., in the historic present, reflecting a continuous or
extended state. This was the background to the events, and only afterward (para. 306 ff.), when the
developments begin to unfold, does the narrator switch to the aorist to refer to actions not defined
by their duration. The aorist participle is freqently encountered in this passage. It indicates an action
that occurred prior to the action denoted by the finite verb of the sentence, or occasionally serves as
a substitute for the infinitive in reported speech. Here and there, when an action is to be stressed as
coextensive with another action, or simply extended, the author returns to the historic present. The
whole of the translation has been presented in the past tense.

48. L (Niese): ἐχόντων. Required here is ἔχοντας, which appears in S and the *editio princeps.*
This reading is preferred by Thackeray (1926) ad loc.

49. νοσηλίᾳ, emended by Bekker and Niese to νοσηλείᾳ. But according to the beginning of the
paragraph, the correct reading should be νοσηλείαις; see also the Latin: *in has aegritudines.*

treatment, there was crop failure (*akarpia*) in Egypt. (306) Bokchoris, king of the Egyptians, sent to [the oracle of] Ammon[50] to consult about the crop failure. The god told[51] [the king] to cleanse (*katharai*) the temples of impure (*anagnoi*)[52] and irreverent men (*dyssebeis*) by expelling[53] them from the temples into desolate places, and to sink [those] afflicted with boils, and lepers, since the sun was vexed at the existence of these, and to purify (*agnisai*) the temples,[54] and thus the earth would bring forth crops. (307) Bokchoris [continues Lysimachus] received the answers, and having called both the priests and the altar attendants, he ordered them to make a selection of the unclean (*akathartoi*)[55] and hand these over to the soldiers to lead them down to the wilderness;[56] and to bind[57] the lepers to rafts (?)[58] of lead

50. εἰς Ἄμμωνα, and in the Latin version, *ad ammonem*. Hudson (1728) 2: 1359 rightly reads εἰς ἄμμωνος, which is also the reading in para. 312. The emendation has been accepted by all editors: εἰς pertains to entry into the temple or the place of the oracle, to be understood in the sentence. Motion toward the god would require πρός or παρά.

51. L: ἐρεῖν ("to ask"), which is the opposite of the intent of the sentence. The Latin version has *respondisse* ("to have answered"). Hence probably Niese and Thackeray's emendations to ἀνελεῖν and ἀναιρεῖν respectively (both meaning "to answer," especially pertaining to the reply of an oracle). Niese's emendation suits the sequence of tenses in the passage, while that of Thackeray is palaeographically closer. Yet even closer palaeographically is the reading of S and the *editio princeps*, εἰπεῖν ("to say").

52. In accordance with the use of the verb ἁγνίσαι later in the same passage, the term ἄναγνοι should be interpreted to mean "impure."

53. L: ἐκβάλλοντα ("[by] expelling"). In S and the *editio princeps*, the participle appears in the aorist, ἐκβάλοντα ("having expelled"). So also Bekker, Naber, Thackeray, and Jacoby. The sequence of descriptions, however, would indicate that the reading of L is correct in this case.

54. καὶ τὰ ἱερὰ ἁγνίσαι (in the Latin version, <et> *templa purificari*). This denotes the ceremonial process of purification after the removal of the "impure."

55. The word ἀκάθαρτοι (literally, "unclean, unpurified"; cf. καθᾶραι, para. 306) refers back to the ἄναγνοι (para. 306).

56. κατάξειν αὐτοὺς εἰς τὴν ἔρημον. The Latin version does not translate these words. Niese thought that they should be omitted, perhaps because they repeated the description of this action in para. 308. Yet the words are required to clarify the instruction of the god.

57. ἐνδήσαντας ("having bound"). Thackeray hesitantly suggests ἐνδῆσαι ("to bind"), and this seems to be the correct reading. The structure of the sentence requires a command in reported speech (= the infinitive) pertaining to the second group, as for the first group.

58. The Greek manuscripts and the *editio princeps* read χάρτας, which usually means "papyrus sheets," or "a papyrus scroll." The entry in LSJ (s.v. χάρτης 2) suggests that this passage used the word in the borrowed sense of "leaf or thin plate." The word may refer to rafts or sheets of metal large enough to contain a good number of people. Naber's ([1896] p. xxxvii) proposed emendation λάρνακας ("boxes" or "chests") is unacceptable. This recalls the box into which Seth-Typhon tricked Osiris (Plut. *De Is. et Os.* 356C). In the story of Isis and Osiris, it is even said that the lid of the box was closed with lead (to prevent it being opened from inside). But a box with a closed lid (which is necessary in any responsible transportation) would not have required the captives to be bound to it, as is said to have happened in the account of Lysimachus, and such boxes could contain just a few people. And to avoid unnecessary speculation, it should be noted that the preposition εἰς does not need to mean "into." By the time of Lysimachus, it may have replaced ἐν + dative in the sense of "on."

so that they might sink[59] in the sea.[60] (308) After the lepers and those afflicted with boils had been sunk, the others were assembled in desolate places and exposed to destruction. But they gathered together to take counsel about themselves.[61] When night came on, they lit fire and lamps in order to protect themselves, and fasted the following night in order to beseech the gods about saving them. (309) On the following day, a certain Moses[62] advised them to take a risk[63] and cut one way (= strike out in one direction) until[64] they came to inhabited regions, and he called upon them not to show goodwill to anyone of men (= any man) or give the best[65] advice,[66] but the worst,[67] and to destroy any temples (*naoi*) and altars (*bōmoi*) of gods they might encounter. (310) When the others[68] agreed, doing what they had decided, they marched through the wilderness, and with a good deal of trouble they came to the inhabited country, and, both having been insolent to the people and having looted and burned the temples, they came to what is now called Judaea, and, having founded a city, are living there. (311) This town was called[69] Hierosyla

59. καθῶσιν, and the Latin version, *mergerentur* ("that they might sink"). Niese proposed emending to καθέθωσιν ("they will be cast down"), which is not appropriate in the context.

60. εἰς τὸ πέλαγος. On the use of εἰς as a substitute for ἐν + dative, see n. 58 above.

61. L: περὶ αὐτῶν ("about them"). Hudson (1728) 2: 1359, and all later editors, emend to περὶ αὑτῶν ("about themselves"). This is the reading of S and the *editio princeps*, and it is also apparent from the following sentence and the Latin translation.

62. L: μωσῆν. In the Latin version, *moysen*, and in S and the *editio princeps*, μωυσῆν. The latter is to be preferred, since Μωυσῆς, a transcription of the Egyptian, is used in references based on Egyptian and Hellenistic Egyptian sources; see p. 240 and note 109 above. MS S and the *editio princeps* again read this form (as against L) in the testimonium from Chaeremon (*Ap.* 1. 290). This is also the form in most instances in the manuscripts of other works by Josephus.

63. L: παραβαλλομένοις. In S and the *editio princeps*, παραβαλλομένους (so rightly Bekker, Naber, and Thackeray).

64. L: ἄχρι ἄν ὅτου. In S and the *editio princeps*, ὅτου is missing. Bekker and Naber omitted it, while Thackeray printed it in brackets. There is no justification for any change: ἄχρις οὗ ἄν is a normal expression, and in reported speech, οὗ becomes ὅτου. The reading ἄχρις of S and the *editio princeps* is obviously to be preferred to ἄχρι.

65. ἄριστα. Niese, in his *editio minor* ([1889] 46), rightly emended to τἄριστα.

66. εὐνοήσειν ... συμβουλεύσειν. Niese proposed emending to the aorist forms of the infinitive, εὐνοῆσαι ... συμβουλεῦσαι (probably because of the previous τινι, which might indicate a specific, one-time occurrence). Yet the intent is to denote a continuous future giving of advice. Thackeray has a present form, ἐννοεῖν, which is wrong.

67. μήτε ἄριστα συμβουλεύσειν ἀλλὰ τὰ χείρονα. In the Latin version, *neque bona suadentibus adquiescerent, sed pessima quaeque facerent* ("that they might not acquiesce to those giving them good advice, but do each thing very badly"). The translator may have been faced with συμβουλεύσαντι, but he could well have found it difficult to understand the nature of an instruction not to give good advice to anyone, when it was the Jews who appeared to need good advice at that moment. The reading as it stands is supported by the previous sentence, "<not> to show goodwill."

68. τῶν ἄλλων. In the Latin version, *cunctis*, apparently following a corrupt Greek reading or a misreading by the translator: τῶν ὅλων (all). There is no need to emend here. The current formulation is a summary: see below, pp. 319–20.

69. L: ὠνόμασται; S and the *editio princeps* rightly have ὠνομάσθαι.

(Ἱεροσῦλα = Temple Loot) after their disposition (*diathesis*).[70] Later, when they had become stronger, in time they changed the name in order <not> to be defamed;[71] the city was called Hierosolyma, and they were called Hierosolymites.[72]

The Greek text is fraught with difficulties, perhaps more than is usual in *Contra Apionem* (apart from the section preserved only in the Latin translation, 2. 52–113, which is particularly corrupt). The difficulties here arise partly from the transformation of the text into reported speech. The shift from direct to reported speech usually results in changes of grammatical forms and tenses, and even slight changes in the order of sentences or clauses, and accidental omissions may also occur. All this in turn causes copyists, who find the sequence of tenses and sentences hard to follow, to confuse the text still further with mistakes and even attempted corrections. The difficulties are aggravated by the abbreviation and compression of the Lysimachean text by Josephus.

That Josephus made certain omissions may be deduced from three references to Lysimachus in the second book of *Contra Apionem*. The first concerns the number of Jews expelled from Egypt in Apion's work (110,000), which, it is stated, is the same as in Lysimachus (2. 20). There is no reference to a number in the detailed account of Lysimachus. Later, Lysimachus is mentioned together with Apollonius Molon as calling Moses a wizard and deceiver (γόης καὶ ἀπατεών), and saying that "the laws [of the Jews] are teachers only of vice and not of virtue at all" (2. 145). Both these points are also absent from the detailed account. Although there Moses plays a central role and some of the negative laws attributed to him are elaborated upon, these insults to Moses' personality and teaching are missing. In the third reference to Lysimachus in book 2 of *Contra Apionem*, Lysimachus and Apollonius Molon again appear together, this time both are cited as saying that the Jews are "the lowest of men" (φαυλότατοι ἀνθρώπων, 2. 236). There is no parallel to this in the first book. How can the omissions be explained? The number of those expelled may have been accidentally omitted. The omission of the direct insults to Moses and his teaching seems to have been deliberate.

---

70. L:Ἱεροσόλυμα; S:Ἱερόσυλα, which is certainly the right reading. In the Latin version we find *quae urbs* ἀπὸ τῆς ἱεροσυλείας *id est a templorum expoliatione ex illorum qualitate denominata est* ("This city was named *apo tēs hierosyleias*, i.e., 'from the despoiling of temples,' after the character of those [people]"). The Greek expression was a gloss explaining the name of the city, found in the MS used by the Latin translator, who adduces and translates it (*id est a templorum expoliatione*), before continuing with his translation of the text proper. He translates διάθεσις somewhat freely as *qualitas* rather than *dispositio*.

71. πρὸς τὸ ὀνειδίζεσθαι. Hudson supplied the necessary μή.

72. ἱεροσολύμουσ; the Latin version, *hierosolymitae*. Niese and Naber emended toἹεροσολυμίτας, the usual form in Josephus. Yet it is not impossible that Josephus copied the formἹεροσολύμους from Lysimachus. This is a legitimate form for the adjective describing inhabitants of a place; cf. Σόλυμοι (but also Σολυμῖται).

Book 1 of *Contra Apionem* deals mainly with the antiquity of the Jewish people and the refutation of hostile accounts of the Exodus; the refutation of both the personal insults and the blasphemies against Jewish belief and law (excluding those directly pertaining to the residence in Egypt) was deferred to the second book. In that part of *Contra Apionem*, Josephus detailed and refuted the accusations, adding a general review of the theology and laws of Moses, without distracting the reader from the main argument.

Further abbreviations in the account may be discerned. For example, the statement that the diseased Jews "used to flee to the temples" (para. 305) suggests that the original account reported that they were attacked, insulted, or abused, and therefore required asylum. The observation "very many men succumbed to sicknesses requiring treatment" (para. 305) may suggest that no treatment was offered, and the sick were left to roam the streets. The clause "when very many men succumbed to sickness" would seem to indicate that, according to the original account, Egyptians contracted diseases from the Jews. A little later (para. 308) we are told that those who were expelled into the desert fasted on the second night after the expulsion, but there is no mention of the fast continuing into the next day, when, according to the passage, they prayed to the gods. Furthermore, as we have it, the people "were assembled in desolate places" (para. 308), that is, a number of places. This implies that the expelled were split into small groups and scattered in many places, the Egyptians' purpose being, presumably, to prevent the organization of an invasion force in the event that those expelled wished to return, and because smaller groups would have a greater risk of getting lost and of being "exposed to destruction" (para. 308). From the following sentence ("But they gathered together" etc.) we learn that this ploy failed: the expelled managed to group together, consider their position, and act in cooperation—not, however, in an attempt to return to Egypt, but to go in the opposite direction, toward Judaea. Finally, at the end of Moses' words of advice (para. 310), the text says "When the others agreed," not "When they all agreed"; this may indicate that the original account reported a difference of opinion between those who from the beginning supported the leadership and advice of the erstwhile unknown Moses and others, who hesitated or advocated other options.

THE TWO MAIN VERSIONS AND THEIR INTEGRATION

It appears from Josephus's report that Lysimachus's account is based on two main versions of the history of the Jews in Egypt and their expulsion.[73] The text also reveals traces of some stages in the development of each version.

---

73. Scholars did not pay attention to the existence of two different versions. Stern, while noting a "confusion," attributes it to the transmission (*GLAJJ* 1: 386). Kasher does not accept Stern's view:

At the beginning of the story, we are presented with "the nation of the Jews"—that is, all the Jews[74]—being diseased ("being lepers and afflicted with boils") and escaping to the temples (para. 305). According to the instructions of the god Ammon, they are drowned in the sea (paras. 306 fin., 307 fin.). The inevitable question arises: How there were Jews to be expelled if all the Jewish people was drowned in the sea? The god's instructions begin with reference to "impure and irreverent men" (para. 306). These in fact become the main subject of the story; they too are expelled from the temples, but they are not drowned along with the lepers and those afflicted with boils, being expelled instead into the desert (paras. 307–8), and they are the ones who under the leadership of Moses make their way to Judaea (paras. 308–11). That the story contains two versions may be seen from specific details as well, but this is especially obvious in the report of the instructions of the god Ammon, and the execution of these instructions, with the jumbled patchwork of sentences and actions concerning the lepers and the rest, on the one hand, and the impure and irreverent men, on the other hand (paras. 306–7).

However, it is not always easy to disentangle one version from the other. There are doublets, and compression and summarizing of details, quite apart from the omissions already mentioned, and the migration of elements from one version to the other creates a further complication. In order to reconstruct the independent development of the versions before they were joined together, we must not only follow the internal logic of the text as we now have it, but also avail ourselves of parallels in other Hellenistic sources concerning the Exodus.

Let us begin with a more detailed presentation of the two versions in their last stage of development, before being integrated into one story. According to the first version, all the Jews dwelling in Egypt in the reign of King Bokchoris were afflicted with leprosy, boils, and other diseases. They escaped to the temples and begged for their livelihood. They also infected "very many"—namely, many Egyptians. The resulting shortage of manpower in Egypt led to a crop failure. The king sent to the oracle of the god Ammon and was told to sink the diseased in the sea so as no longer to vex the sun. The instruction was executed. The afflicted were loaded onto rafts of lead (?), which were towed out to sea and sunk (paras. 305–8a).

The people at the center of the second version are "the impure and irreverent."

"The internal inconsistency was woven from the outset into the body of the plot, and can thus exemplify the rule, 'A lie has no legs'"; see Kasher (1997) 273. I am afraid there is no need nowadays to take an active part in Josephus's quarrel with Lysimachus. Schäfer (1997a) 223 n. 69 comments: "Lysimachus runs into contradiction when he distinguishes between the lepers and the impure persons and identifies the Jews with the lepers only, because the lepers are being drowned and only the unclean people are banished to the wilderness and thus 'saved'." See also Labow (2005) 318–19.

74. On the correctness of the reading of the Greek manuscripts here and its unambiguous reference to the Jewish people as a whole, see above, note 46.

From the instructions of the god Ammon, it appears that they caused the crop failure: the purification of the temples and their expulsion from Egypt was to ensure that "the earth would bring forth crops." Ammon ordered these people to be expelled into the wilderness. After a selection by the priests, they were led away by soldiers to desolate places, where they were left to their own devices. Those expelled managed to group together in one place, where they fasted and prayed to the gods. A man called Moses, appearing out of nowhere, told them to take their fate into their own hands and dare to walk in one direction away from Egypt until they should come across inhabited regions. He also told them to show hostility and cruelty to the local inhabitants and pillage and destroy their temples and altars. This policy they carried out until they reached the area later called Judaea, and here they founded the city of Hierosyla, called after their mistreatment of temples. Only later, out of concern for their reputation among the nations, did they change the name of the city to Hierosolyma (Holy Solyma).

The original formulation of the two versions underwent some stages of development, both adapting details that originated in the other version, or an independent variation of it. In the first version (sinking the lepers and those afflicted with boils), the reason for consulting the oracle of Ammon, expelling the diseased people from the temples, and drowning them in the sea was crop failure (*akarpia*), presented as the direct result of a shortage of agricultural manpower caused by very many workers—Jews, and Egyptians infected by them—falling sick. This reason does not suit what should have been the original formulation of the first version. First, the need to halt the epidemic is sufficient reason for consulting the oracle of Ammon and getting rid of the deceased. This, indeed, is what we find in several Hellenistic sources concerning the Exodus.[75] Second, crop failure does not result from a shortage of manpower for gathering the harvest. Indeed, according to the oracle of Ammon, the act of expulsion and drowning (a mixture of the two versions) would lead to the earth bringing forth crops (para. 306 fin.). This explanation—crop failure—would fit well in a story about a punishment imposed for disrespecting the gods (the second element in the second version). Thus lack of crops in an Egyptian context appears in Theophrastus as a punishment for disrespect in holy matters (Porph. *Abst.* 2. 27. 1).[76] Famine, like plague, is a widespread motif in Greek literature as a collective punishment for moral and cardinal sins and/or offenses against the gods.[77] We may conclude that at some

75. Explicitly: Diodorus 34/35. 1. 2; Pompeius Trogus in Justin 36. 1. 12; Chaeremon in Josephus *Contra Apionem* 1. 289; esp. Tacitus *Historiae* 5. 3. 1; and in a softer and inverse variation, Hecataeus in Diodorus 40. 3. 1.

76. See above, pp. 31–32.

77. The most famous example is the tale of woe that befell Thebes because of the crime of Oedipus. Warnings in this direction are constantly raised by Attic orators (e.g., in order to scare

stage in the development of the first version the original reason for the approach to Ammon, the infection of Egyptians as well by the plague, was replaced by crop failure, a component of the second version, and, as the infected Egyptians are said to have been "many," the new reasoning was supplemented by an inappropriate explanation that Egypt suffered from a shortage of agricultural workers. The first version may well have used the word *limos* (plague) originally, which was slightly corrupted later to *loimos* (famine). This would have encouraged the importation from the second version of the element of crop failure.

The second version itself is not free of contamination and suffers from additional elements imported from the first version or variations of it. The people expelled to the desert are portrayed as "impure and irreverent men" who populated the temples, as did the lepers and other diseased people in the first version. Seeking refuge in temples might be plausible for the "impure" (*anagnoi*), namely, the diseased,[78] but hardly for "irreverent" (*dyssebeis*) men. And indeed, later in the story (para. 307), the temple priests and altar attendants are told to make a selection of the "unclean" (*akatharoi = anagnoi*), and these are handed over to the soldiers to be led into the "desert," while the "irreverent" are not mentioned. The people in the temples are, accordingly, only the diseased. Parallel Egyptian traditions claim that the misfortunes came as a punishment for neglect of the gods.[79] I would therefore suggest that the original second version described only the expulsion of the irreverent. The "impure" were attached at some stage of its development, under the influence of the first version and its parallels.

Each version, then, had been contaminated by the other even prior to their conflation in one account. The original uncontaminated versions may be reconstructed in outline as follows:

> Version 1: All the Jews, being afflicted with leprosy, boils, and other diseases, spread epidemics throughout Egypt and sought refuge in temples. When many Egyptians were infected by the Jews, the Egyptian king sought advice from the oracle of Ammon. He was instructed to drown the diseased in the sea, and did so. Later additions: the misfortune—crop failure, shortage of agricultural workers.

> Version 2: Irreverent people (presumably Egyptians) annoyed the Egyptian gods, who reacted by causing a crop failure, which in turn brought about a famine in Egypt. The oracle of Ammon advised expelling the sinners to

---

jurors away from exonerating a murderer). The motif is also well known from literature both biblical and of other religions. See also on the Illyrians Appian *Illyriaca* 4–5.

78. Cf. in Manetho the synonym *miaroi; Contra Apionem* 1. 233, 236, 248, 251, and Josephus's refutation, 261, 296.

79. See p. 326 below.

desolate places, and it was done. This sets the scene for the ordeal in the desert, the appearance of Moses, the rallying together as one people, and their journey to Jerusalem. A later addition: The "impure" (= "unclean"; probably lepers and the like) join the "irreverent."

Who was responsible for patching together the two versions and their variants into one consecutive narrative? Lysimachus of Alexandria wrote a work against plagiarism. His testimonia reveal that he himself was consistent in presenting more than one version of each account and in acknowledging his sources.[80] There is no reason to suppose that he acted differently in his account of the Jews. He would have presented the two main accounts with acknowledgments, specific or vague (such as "There are those who say . . ."), as he had done in his other works. I would suggest, then, that Josephus himself is responsible for the unified account, the omission of the references to Lysimachus's sources, the resulting internal inconsistencies great and small, and the doublets.

Omission of names of sources and clumsy conflation of their accounts into one story is quite typical of Josephus. A well-known example is his continuous narrative on the Hasmonaean state (book 13 of *Jewish Antiquities*), where he draws upon Nicolaus of Damascus and Strabo (crediting them only occasionally), sometimes with the version of one appearing after the other's, and sometimes with the two versions ineptly mixed together, resulting in contradictions, inconsistencies, and doublets in the continuous narrative. Josephus himself contributes only occasional brief comments of his own for the sake of harmonization or as a bridge between one subject and another, and some banal concluding remarks.[81]

In the case of the account of the Hasmonaean state, Josephus usually deleted even the names of his direct sources; in the case of the Lysimachus extract, just names of the indirect ones, whose mention was considered to be far less compelling. And after all, listing Lysimachus's various sources would have given the anti-Jewish accusations some credit, and detracted from Lysimachus's image as an extreme hater of the Jews who related (or invented) vicious slanders against them.

As a result, the passage came out as one consecutive story. In fact, Josephus himself treated it as such, as appears from his rhetorical questions in the detailed refutation of the passage.[82] This is not surprising: Josephus's harmonizing notes in the history of the Hasmonaean state indicate that he wanted to present the account as one consecutive narrative. At least in the case of Lysimachus's account, one may guess that a long time had passed since the collection of the material up

---

80. See above, pp. 310–11.

81. See Hölscher (1904) 12 ff.; and below, pp. 402 ff.

82. See, e.g., *Ap.* 1. 314: how is it that the king drowned many Jews in the sea and expelled the rest into desolate places, and yet there remained alive so many Jews?

to the final stage of the writing and editing by Josephus, so that he could easily have forgotten that Lysimachus quoted or paraphrased two versions separately. In view of the refutation section that follows the passage (paras. 313–20), it is even more tempting to suspect Josephus of preferring at the outset to present the passage as one story in order to expose its absurdity more effectively.

THE EGYPTIAN SOURCES FOR THE ELEMENTS
OF THE TWO VERSIONS

We have now seen that Lysimachus's account of the Exodus contained two main versions, and that both were acknowledged in Lysimachus's original work. Tracing the various elements of the two versions in the literature both preceding and following Lysimachus would allow us to identify more clearly the elements peculiar to Lysimachus's account, and thereby recognize variations of the Exodus account that were popular before the time of Lysimachus but are now unknown to us from any other source.

The first version establishes the protagonists at the outset as "the nation of the Jews." Similarly, in Hecataeus's Jewish excursus, those who left Egypt were defined as one of the foreign peoples or tribes who left Egypt and settled in the regions of the Mediterranean and Mesopotamia, having acquired their national identity prior to the expulsion (Diod. 40. 3. 2). His argument with Egyptian traditions about the Egyptian descent of all nations indicates that Egyptian mainstream opinion in his time was that the Jews were basically autochthonous Egyptians.[83] This view also appears in one of the Egyptian traditions summarized by Manetho (Joseph. *Ap.* 1. 229, 233–40). Notwithstanding, the first version in Lysimachus, and another version in Manetho (*Ap.* 1. 82–91), suggest that Hecataeus also drew his counterview not only from his Jewish informer, but also from Egyptian ones, as he indeed does more than once in his account of the Jewish *origo* and *nomima*.[84]

Of the diseases listed—leprosy, boils, and "other diseases" (*Ap.* 1. 305)—leprosy is well attested in other sources,[85] one of which—Manetho—is Egyptian and earlier than Lysimachus. Boils are also mentioned in the version presented by the Augustan historian Pompeius Trogus (Justin 36. 12. 2). Manetho, like Lysimachus, also mentions in general terms other diseased people (*Ap.* 1. 229). Missing from Lysimachus's list is plague, to which Hecataeus may be understood to refer (Diod. 40. 3. 1: λοιμικὴ περιστάσις). It seems that the two main versions

---

83. See pp. 111–14 above.

84. See p. 116 above.

85. Manetho in Josephus *Contra Apionem* 2. 229, 233; cf. Timochares (via Posidonius) in Diodorus 34/35. 1. 2; Pompeius Trogus in Justin 36. 2. 12; and probably Tacitus *Historiae* 5. 3. 1 (*tabes*). On the ultimate source of Diodorus, see p. 412 below.

used by Lysimachus deliberately made no mention of pestilence. Then, as until recently, plague paralyzed the sufferer, and death occurred days after infection (see, e.g., the dramatic description of the plague—if this is what it is—in Thuc. 2. 47–54). Including plague would have made it difficult for any narrator to explain how the sufferers were able to congregate in public buildings such as temples and could continue to function when required.[86]

In the first version, there is no explanation of why the Jews were suffering from these diseases. From the account in Hecataeus of Abdera we can infer— despite the changes made by him in the Egyptian version—that the diseases were generally explained as a punishment for neglect of the gods (Diod. 40. 3. 1).[87] This link may also be discerned in the versions preserved by Diodorus (34/35. 1. 2) and Tacitus (*Hist.* 5. 3. 1). Manetho's account shows that there was a different view, according to which there was no particular reason for the diseases. They occurred naturally, as they do in any society, but all the more so in ancient Egypt. It was only after the lepers had been harmed by god and man that they partici- pated in sacrilegious acts (*Ap.* 1. 239–50).

The drowning of the Jews in the sea is unique to Lysimachus's account. In all other sources, the diseased are expelled, escape, or go into the desert of their own will.[88] This variation, it would seem, was invented as a reaction to the Jewish story about the drowning of the Egyptian army in the sea, in the way that plague and boils seem to reverse the biblical account of the Exodus.[89] The biblical account is prone to generalization; for example, the whole Egyptian army—infantry, chari- ots, cavalry, and all—are drowned in the sea (Exod. 14.23, 26, 28).[90] Similarly, the Egyptian counterstory talks of the "people of the Jews" altogether as having been drowned (*Ap.* 1. 305, 317). The counternarrative would have been self-contained and would therefore have exhibited no internal inconsistencies. Since it was a slander intended just to humiliate, the storyteller had no reason to bother with the subsequent existence of the Jewish people. At the most the original story may

86. Cf. the absence of plague affecting humans in the Pentateuch; plague afflicts only animals of all sorts (Exod. 9.1–7). Plague is not mentioned at all in the list in Psalms 105.30–32, but appears in Psalms 78.50, afflicting both man and beast. On the development of the tradition concerning the plague and the difficulty faced by the editor of the story in Exodus, see Löwenstamm (1987) 39–40. Lewy (1960) 120 thinks that plague is being referred to in Tacitus *Historiae* 5. 3. 1. Yet the description of the symptoms of the disease—*tabe, quae corpora foedaret*—together with the relatively energetic activity of the Jews, is better suited to leprosy and boils.

87. See p. 116 above.

88. See Hecataeus in Diodorus 40. 3. 1; Manetho in Josephus *Contra Apionem* 1. 251; Timochares (via Posidonius) in Diodorus 34/35. 1. 2; Pompeius Trogus in Justin 36. 1. 12; Apion in Josephus *Contra Apionem* 2. 8, 15; Tacitus *Historiae* 5. 3. 1.

89. On "counterliterature," see, in more detail, pp. 331–32 below.

90. Cf. *Sapientia Salmonis* 18. 6; Philo *De Vita Mosis* 1. 167, 179, where the destruction of the entire Egyptian army is emphasized.

have conceded that a few Jews had been saved, a survival motif known from the Oriental Flood stories, and that they were the ancestors of the Jews known to contemporary Egyptians. The first appearance of this counterstory is undatable.

Previous Egyptian elements were used for the basic second version as well. It has been suggested above that the original subjects of this version were "the irreverent," to whom were attached the "impure" during the development of the version. Each of these elements could be autochthonous Egyptians, foreign rabble, or a mixture of both, as the people expelled from Egypt are described in one way or another by Egyptian and Greco-Roman sources commencing with Manetho.[91] Accordingly, the Jewish people was formed only after leaving Egypt, and not in Egypt. These same sources report that those afflicted with diseases neglected the gods.[92] Theophrastus's Egyptian-inspired account about the great crises of early civilization in Egypt reports that neglect of the gods in Egypt was punished by famine (= crop failure).[93] This betrays the antiquity and origin of the second version. An early Egyptian parallel to the second version in its contaminated form can be inferred from the account of Hecataeus, who based his report on an Egyptian version. This report portrayed the Jews as a foreign nation dwelling in Egypt that neglected the gods and was punished with plague, causing an epidemic throughout the country, and was consequently expelled.[94]

One of the instructions imputed to Moses in the second version (para. 309)— "not to show goodwill to anyone of men (= any man)"—is actually identical to the oath attributed to the Jews in the blood libel (Joseph. Ap. 2. 121). This suggests that Lysimachus was acquainted with the blood libel, invented by the Egyptians.[95] The second one—"(not to) give the best advice"—recalls, in the positive form, maxims known from Greek and Roman literature,[96] but it may well have been inspired by ancient Egyptian wisdom. However, the instruction to destroy altars and temples seems to be rather an addition by Lysimachus in preparation for the

91. Manetho in Josephus Contra Apionem 1. 233–49; Strabo Geographica 16. 2. 35, and a passage from his Historica Hypomnemata, as quoted by Josephus, in Antiquitates Judaicae 14. 117; Chaeremon in Josephus Contra Apionem 1. 289–90; Apion in Josephus Contra Apionem II. 28; and this also seems to be the intent of Tacitus Historiae 5. 3. 1 ff. See also Celsus in Origen Contra Celsum 3. 5.

92. Manetho in Josephus Contra Apionem 1. 248–49; Timochares (via Posidonius) in Diodorus 34/35. 1. 1; hinted at in Tacitus Historiae 5. 3. 1; Clement in Origen Contra Celsum 3. 5.

93. In Porphyry De abstinentia 2. 27. 1; and see pp. 31–33 above.

94. See p. 116 above on the original version.

95. See the Lysimachus version μήτε ἀνθρώπων τινὶ εὐνοήσειν as against μηδενὶ εὐνοήσειν ἄλλῳ φύλῳ in the "Jewish" oath (Joseph. Ap. 2. 121). And see pp. 271–76 above on the Egyptian origin of the blood libel, and p. 279 on the absence of the blood libel in Lysimachus.

96. See, e.g., Hesiod Opera et Dies 266; Xenophon Anabasis 5. 6. 4; Cicero De officiis 1. 5, 52; Seneca De clementia 29. 1; Iamblichus De vita Pythagorica 30 [85]. Cf. the hostile variation on the Jews in Juvenal Satirae 14. 102–5: "to show the way and lead no one but the circumcised to a desired spring."

reference to the destruction of temples and altars close to the Jewish territory around Jerusalem (paras. 310–11).[97]

A more conspicuous novelty in the passage from Lysimachus, besides the drowning of the Jews in the sea, is the presentation of Moses. He appears in the desert out of the blue, with no prior notice and no apparent background or involvement in the events prior to the expulsion or in the expulsion itself (Ap. 1. 309; cf. the refutation by Josephus, 316). When the Lysimachean account is combined with a separate testimonium of his presenting Moses as a wizard and deceiver (Ap. 2. 145), it appears that Moses was said to have managed to convince the expelled people and impose upon them his authority through trickery and sleight of hand. The Moses portrayed here is quite unlike his namesake in other Hellenistic sources, where he is introduced (implicitly or explicitly)as an Egyptian priest or a governor, and his personal attributes and standing as a leader before the expulsion are presented favorably more than once.[98] I would guess that Moses was described in Lysimachus's second version as an unknown person in order to facilitate his portrayal as a wizard and deceiver. These negative features, unlike the wisdom and bravery usually attributed to him by other authors, provide an unflattering backdrop to Moses' authority and the negative heritage that he bequeathed to his people. Jewish stories about Moses performing miracles may have helped Egyptian storytellers arrive at this portrayal.

The Greco-Egyptian version of the Exodus closest to the Lysimachus passage was preserved in Diodorus, and was drawn, as has definitely been proved and is universally acknowledged, from Posidonius of Apamea. It shares a considerable number of elements with the Lysimachus passage, or rather with the second version in its contaminated form. In the Diodorus-Posidonius account about the advice of the friends of Antiochus VII to annihilate the Jews (Diod. 34/35. 1. 1–3), which derived ultimately from a contemporary Seleucid court historian, and therefore was prior to Lysimachus, it is said that the Jews were thrown out of Egypt because they were sinners hated by the gods, and because they suffered from leprosy. They took control of an area near Jerusalem, and their leader, Moses, gave them misanthropic laws. Moses advises the Jews, among others, "nor to show (other people) any goodwill at all" (para. 2), which is almost identical to the "advice" in Lysimachus. If the two accounts are not totally identical, it is probably because the Diodorus-Posidonius version telescoped its source to suit the context, so that unnecessary details were omitted. The great similarity

---

97. See further, pp. 334–36 below.

98. Manetho in Josephus Contra Apionem 1. 250; Posidonius in Strabo 16. 2. 35; Pompeius Trogus in Justin 36. 2. 11. Hecataeus praises Moses as φρονήσει τε καὶ ἀνδρείᾳ πολὺ διαφέρων ("greatly superior both in prudence and in courage," Diod. 40. 3. 3), which is the opposite of "wizard and deceiver." Cf. Tacitus's description of Moses as merely "one of the exiles" (Hist. 5. 3. 1).

enhances the distinction suggested above between the two versions transmitted in the original account of Lysimachus.

It must, however, be stressed that the version of Tacitus (*Hist.* 5. 3. 1), occasionally compared by scholars to the stories of Lysimachus,[99] is evidently different, despite a few similarities with other anti-Jewish Exodus stories, and it contains two major elements, unknown from any other account of the Exodus. Tacitus's story is set in the reign of Bokchoris; the epidemic (judging from the symptoms given, leprosy) afflicted only one group of people (we are not told whether they are Egyptian or not) who were disrespectful toward the gods; these people were expelled into the desert, and a man named Moses, presenting himself as sent from Heaven to lead the exiles, managed to save them from dying of thirst by following a herd of asses and finding a water source; after six days they reached inhabited land, took control of it, and built a capital city and a temple; at this time, Moses established the laws of the Jews, emphasizing the hatred of foreigners and customs designed to commemorate their trials and tribulations in the desert. The most prominent addition here is the story about the asses, hinting at the legendary link between the Jews and the god Seth-Typhon, a link that was emphasized in some of the Egyptian traditions of the Exodus, thus paving the way for the story about ass worship in the Temple (Tac. *Hist.* 5. 4. 2). Following the reference to the duration of the expedition, Tacitus repeats, with a slight variation, the circumvented aetiological explanation already given before him for the origin of the Sabbath (cf. Plut. *Quaest. conv.* 670D).

THE EGYPTIAN BACKGROUND TO THE HOSTILE TRADITIONS: SOURCES OF INSPIRATION AND TYPOLOGY

The hostile traditions about the Exodus, originating in literature, rumors, and Egyptian oral accounts, were motivated by the tension between the Egyptian and Jewish populations in Egypt. Not a few scholars have rightly claimed that the tension began in the Persian period,[100] and so too the hostile traditions.[101] It had already been claimed by Josephus that the hostile accounts of the Exodus had originated in Egypt itself (*Ap.* 1. 223), although the reasons he gives for the enmity of the Egyptians are not very convincing (224–26). The historical background and motives for the tensions between the Jews and the Egyptians have been the

---

99. See, e.g., Gager (1972) 127; Stern, *GLAJJ* 1: 386, 2: 35–36.

100. On the beginnings of the hostility in the Persian period, see esp. Yoyotte (1963) 133–43; see also, e.g., Radin (1915) 97–99; Lewy (1960) 10; Tcherikover (1961) 432 n. 79, 358–59, 361; Schäfer (1997a) 163–69; and others.

101. As observed in most of the references in the preceding note. For a different approach, attempting to trace the creation of these traditions to pharaonic Egypt, see Assmann (1997).

object of much interest in modern research.[102] In the present context it is worth surveying briefly some of the valid claims already made, and adding a few remarks and clarifications.

The specific causes of the development of the hostility between the two peoples were the cooperation between the Jews and the hated Persian government, the Jewish attitude toward Egyptian animal cults, and the Passover festival and all that that entailed. Jews found themselves between the hammer and the anvil, acting effectively as border guards for the Persian kings, and they may also have been carrying out internal security services, as happened later, in the Hellenistic period.[103] The Egyptian deification of animals was a cause of serious friction. For example, the Jewish sacrifice of animals in Elephantine led to the destruction of the local temple at the hands of an Egyptian mob in 410 B.C.E.[104] Other violent situations may be envisaged as occurring because of the Egyptian animal cult, such as pogroms in reaction to the Jewish slaughtering of certain animals for food, and even rioting following the accidental harming or killing of a sacred animal, like the lynching many years later of a Roman who had accidentally killed a cat (Diod. 1. 83. 6–9). Such outbreaks, similar to those that for centuries have dogged relations between Hindus and Muslims in India, would not have been uncommon events. Jewish households celebrated the Passover in words, music, and song commemorating the ten plagues and the destruction of the Egyptian army in the sea,[105] using the biblical text and embellishing it.[106] Such a widespread and annual celebration would naturally have raised the hackles of the Jews' Egyptian neighbors, leading not only to violent confrontations and attempts to prohibit Passover festivities,[107] but also to the creation of Egyptian

---

102. See in particular Reinach (1895) xvi; Radin (1915) 97–99; Heinemann (1939/40) 288–96; Baron (1952) 189–95; Tcherikover (1961) 361–77; Kasher (1974) 74, 80, 81–82; Stern (1976) 1111 ff.; Rappaport (1983) 38 ff.; Feldman (1993) 107–22; Schäfer (1997a) 121–69.

103. See the comprehensive survey of the material in Porten (1968) 28 ff.; (1984) 389 ff.

104. On the temple cult, which included sacrifices and burnt offerings, see Porten and Yardeni (1986) 1: 68–78.

105. On the Passover festivities of the Jews of Elephantine, see Porten (1984) 388–89; and in Egypt in general, Tabory (1996) 81–84. For the domestic and musical character of the Passover festivities in Egypt and Palestine, see the indirect references in *Sapientia Salmonis* 18.9–10, and Jubilees 49.10; and the direct account in Philo *De specialibus legibus* 2. 148.

106. Many detailed additions to biblical stories are prominent in a number of Jewish Hellenistic authors active in Egypt, such as Ezekiel the tragedian, Philo (*Vit. Mos.* 1. 94–180), and especially *Sapientia Salmonis;* they amplify both the alleged wickedness of the Egyptians and the seriousness of the plagues inflicted upon them. Such extreme additions are found even in Artapanus, whose attitude toward the Egyptians is relatively favorable. A basic survey of these additions may be found in Löwenstam (1987) 43–46, 120–22, and in various notes throughout. For more detailed discussions from the perspective of Greek culture, see Guttmann 2: 9–72; Winston (1979) 6–9, 292–329; Jacobson (1983); Holladay (1983–96) 1: 189–244, 2: 301–529; Cheon (1997).

107. For the document concerning Egyptian attempts to prevent the Passover festivities in

counterstories. In addition to these circumstances, tension was also greatly exacerbated by long-standing Egyptian xenophobia, repeated confrontations over living space and sources of income, the usual conflicts between neighbors, and the tendency to find scapegoats for national disasters such as foreign occupation, famine, and plague. Egyptian enmity in general, and the anti-Jewish slanders in particular, were but a natural reaction to the particular conditions prevailing in Egypt in the Persian period and later, and an inevitable result of the daily friction between two intolerant communities thrust closely together by circumstances, each fiercely loyal to its own religion and ancient traditions.

The sources of inspiration for the Egyptian stories were quite varied. Scholars have already observed, in various ways, that the hostile accounts of the Exodus were inspired by biblical stories.[108] The hostile accounts manifestly set out to invert the biblical account as much as possible. The plagues—especially the pestilence and the boils—and other trials that, according to the Bible, befell the Egyptians were turned on the Jews. Similarly, those characteristics commonly attributed to Egyptians by Greeks and other peoples—above all, their hatred of foreigners, their reclusiveness, and their outlandish cultic practices[109]—were foisted upon the Jews. The counterstories include many folkloristic motifs drawn from Egyptian reality, mythology, ways of life, and geography, such as leprosy, outbreaks of plagues, famines, consultations with the god Ammon, wars among the gods, and incursions of desert nomads and northern peoples, as well as their expulsion. The anti-Jewish oral and written literature also included tales inspired by the Seth-Typhon legends.[110]275The counterstories occasionally developed from

---

Elephantine, see Porten (1966) 125, no. 13B (Cauley [1923] no. 21); and more decisively and in more detail Porten (1984) 389; see also Schäfer (1997a) 124–28; Porten and Yardeni (1986) 54–55, no. 4.1.

108. On the development of the Egyptian accounts as a response to the Exodus stories, see Radin (1915) 96; Tcherikover (1961) 287 and n. 79; Stern (1976) 1111; Kasher (1975) 80; (1996) passim, and 273 on Lysimachus; Schäfer (1997a) 15 ff. For further bibliography pertaining directly to Manetho, see Gruen (1998) 58 n. 57. Terms commonly used are "counter history," "reply," and others of this sort. Not every response turns the original story on its head; see below on the Seth-Typhon stories. Gruen presents an exceptional approach according to which the Egyptian stories of the Exodus are based essentially on Jewish accounts glorifying their conquest of Egypt and making fun of the Egyptians and their gods, and should not be regarded as polemics aimed at the biblical accounts or as "counter history"; see Gruen (1998) 41–72. Some of Gruen's reservations are answered indirectly below, where a distinction is made between active-response and passive-response stories. Whatever the case may be, Lysimachus's account is certainly "counter history."

109. See, e.g., Sophocles Oedipus Coloneus 337–38; Plato Laws 953e; Strabo 17. 1. 6, 1. 19 (in the latter, Eratosthenes is named as a source); Juvenal Satire 15. 159 ff. (apparently an account of human sacrifice in Egypt); Diodorus 1. 88, 4–5; Cicero Respublica 3. 9. 15; and in Jewish Hellenistic literature: Sapientia Salmonis 19. 14–15; Philo De Abrahamo 107 and passim. On the absolute difference in customs: Herodotus 2. 35, 91. Cf. p. 275 above.

110. On which, see above, pp. 245–49, 271–76.

a combination of various associations and sources of inspiration. The leper libel, for example, was inspired by the prevalence of leprosy in Egypt, and the human tendency to blame aliens for its spread, together with the contempt for lepers. Some Egyptians who were more familiar with biblical stories could more easily make the connection between Jews and leprosy by noting that Moses is said to have received a sign from god when his hand was turned leprous (Exod. 4.6, 21; cf. Num. 12.10 on his sister). The leper libel was made more plausible by the common portrayal of the Jews as cut off from human society, the inevitable fate that also befalls lepers.[111]

In order to understand the perception of the anti-Jewish tales by the Egyptians, it is worth distinguishing between aggressive and "passive"-fatalistic stories. The aggressive ones contained violent attacks on the Jews, using primarily the method of inversion, so that it is the Jews who are humiliated and victimized. The "passive"-fatalistic stories retained the Jewish traditions in which the Egyptians are the victims, supplementing them with elements from Egyptian folklore and mythology, and especially in the context of the destructive character of Seth-Typhon, the bad god of Egyptian mythology, who was also considered the patron of foreigners, and specifically of desert nomads and Semitic peoples, and was consequently also identified with the god of the Hebrews. Manetho's account of the settlement of Moses and his followers in Avaris, the city of Typhon (*Ap.* 1. 87–90), and the cooperation and even identity between the Jews and the foreign occupiers of Egypt (81–90, 94, 241–250) are examples of the "passive"-fatalistic type;[112] to this type also belongs the aetiological legend describing Typhon, clearly through identification with Moses, as the founder of Judaea and Jerusalem, and implying a link between Typhon and the Sabbath commandment, by means of the story of Typhon's seven-day retreat through the desert (Plut. *De Is. et Os.* 363C-D). An extreme version identifying the god of the Jews with Seth-Typhon, without reference to the Exodus traditions, is expressed in the libel portraying the Jews as worshipping an ass in the Temple.[113] The "passive"-fatalistic stories culminate

---

111. Cf. the later aetiological explanation, transposing cause and effect, of Pompeius Trogus (Justin 36. 1. 15): the Jews refrain from contact with foreigners so as not to be hated by their neighbors, being mindful of their expulsion from Egypt because of the inhabitants' fear of infection (of leprosy and boils, 36. 2. 12). This self-isolation from other nations became, over the course of time, a religious practice.

112. The typology of Manetho's accounts and their influence on authors such as Lysimachus should not be affected by the much-discussed and complex "Manethonian problem": the question of authenticity; whether the present accounts derive from a summary; whether there are a number of layers, authors, or sources; and whether there are interpolations. Whatever the case may be, Manetho or putative later forgers did not invent the main elements.

113. See above, pp. 241–42, 244–46.

in the two versions of the blood libel, which also originate in the Typhon-Seth legends.[114]

This type of story, which is utilized nowadays mainly to rouse international public opinion, probably catered in particular to the lower Egyptian classes. The stories intensified the fear and hatred felt toward the neighboring Jews and accorded with the basic feelings of Oriental mobs, who were fatalistic in their approach to life and their perception of disasters. The aggressive stories served to give vent to Egyptian frustrations and boost the morale of the Egyptian national-ists. Some versions, such as that of Manetho, contained both types: on the one hand, the Jews are portrayed as lepers, while, on the other hand, they are identi-fied (or described as cooperating) with the aggressive occupiers who maltreat the Egyptians and all that they hold sacred.

THE WORK'S DATE,
HISTORICAL BACKGROUND, AND PURPOSE

The historical and thematic framework of the Lysimachus excerpt, which is lim-ited to the Jewish *origo,* the concentration on the behavior of the Jews in Egypt and their expulsion, and the overwhelming Egyptian features and motifs do not leave much doubt with regard to the subject and genre of the work it was taken from: The account of the Jews in Egypt was included in an Egyptian history and/ or ethnography written by Lysimachus. The *origo* of the Jews was actually an excursus, inserted into Lysimachus's work similarly to the Jewish excursus of Hecataeus of Abdera, which was attached to the latter's *Aegyptiaca.* The reasons of Hecataeus are quite clear to us, since we have the Diodorean paraphrase-epit-ome of this work. In the absence of his original work, Lysimachus's motives for abusing the Jews may become understandable after determining his exact date.

Lysimachus's work has been dated to various periods: between the times of Manetho and Apion (i.e., between the third century B.C.E. and the first half of the first century C.E.);[115] some time after Mnaseas of Patara (i.e., after c. 200 or 175 B.C.E.) and before Apion;[116] near the time of Mnaseas (at the turn of the second century B.C.E.);[117] in the first years of the internal struggle in Alexandria between Ptolemy Physcon and his wife, Cleopatra II (145–140 B.C.E.);[118] in the time of Apollonius Molon (the first half of the first century B.C.E.[119] or a little later, in the

---

114. See above, pp. 272–76.

115. Reinach (1895) 120; Gudemann, *RE* s.v. "Lysimachos (20)," col. 33; Gruen (1998) 45.

116. Susemihl (1891–92) 1: 479; Gager (1972) 118; Kasher (1997) 270.

117. Fraser (1972) 2: 1093.

118. Aziza (1982) 56; and see the response of Gruen (1998) 46 n. 17.

119. Gabba (1989) 652.

second half of the first century B.C.E.);[120] close to the time of Apion;[121] between 50
B.C.E. and 50 C.E.;[122] and generally, in the second or first centuries B.C.E.[123]

A clue to a more precise dating comes from the instruction attributed by the
author to Moses, that those expelled into the desert should destroy all the temples
and altars they encounter, and the assertion that this instruction was carried out
once they reached inhabited land (*Ap.* 1. 309–10). This is not mentioned just in
passing. It seems to be the climax of the account. Lysimachus goes so far as to offer
an innovative etymology for Jerusalem in this vein: "Temple Loot." The absurdity
of the explanation speaks for itself and exposes its central role in the story: the
name given to the city reflects the character and peculiarity of its inhabitants in
the future. Such veiled references to contemporary events are commonplace in
Hellenistic ethnographic literature, as in foundation stories (and likewise in literature of other peoples, including the Bible), where the deeds of contemporaries
are explained by the character and achievements of their ancestors. Attempts to
see in this instruction an echo of biblical commandments (e.g., Deut. 7.5)[124] fail to
convince.[125] Some scholars, indeed, have suggested that this reflects the deeds of
the Hasmonaeans against Greek sites of worship in the Holy Land.[126]

To be more accurate, Lysimachus does not say that the Jews destroyed the "temples and altars" in the area of Judaea around Jerusalem, but that they destroyed
sites that they came across in the inhabited land before they reached Judaea. The
second generation of Hasmonaean rulers did in fact mount an intensive effort
to destroy pagan "temples and altars" outside the territory of the Hellenistic-
Hasmonaean eparchy of "Judaea," the Jewish power base around Jerusalem. No

120. Susemihl (1891–92) 2: 674.

121. Gruen (1998) 45.

122. Jacoby, *FGrH* III. b, no. 382, p. 166; Troiani (1977) 135.

123. Stern, *GLAJJ* 1: 382; id. (1976) 1114; Wittaker (1984) 45; Schäfer (1997a) 27.

124. For various suggestions, see Gager (1972) 119; Conzelmann (1981) 80 n. 93; Kasher (1997)
274–75.

125. It would be going too far to attribute to Lysimachus a familiarity with the biblical commandment. The instruction was usually not mentioned in Jewish Hellenistic literature, where
instead violence against foreign worship was discouraged (see below, note 129). Lysimachus's statement is drawn from contemporary reality. It should be added that there is no connection between
Lysimachus's account and the stories of Manetho about the foreign occupiers—with whom the
"polluted Egyptians" cooperated—provoking the Egyptian gods and sacred animals (*Ap.* 1. 249).
Manetho does not mention burning and destroying temples, and Lysimachus is not talking about
the period before the expulsion from Egypt, but after the exiles had left the desert and were on their
way to Judaea. For the character of the description in Manetho, cf. the stories about the ill-treatment
by Cambyses of the bull Apis and his burning of the idols in the temple of the god Ptah in Herodotus
3. 28–29, 37, and 3. 16, 37, for the mutilation of dead bodies and mummies.

126. Müller (1877) 208; Stern, *GLAJJ* 1: 386; id. (1976) 1114; Conzelmann (1981) 80; Goodman in
Schürer et al., 3: 600; Kasher (1997) 274 (as a possibility).

"temples" (as opposed to "altars") were destroyed inside Judaea proper; they simply did not exist. In the days of the Hasmonaean brothers (Judas Maccabaeus, Jonathan, and Simon) the destruction of Hellenistic temples outside small Judaea was only sporadic. A systematic action against Hellenistic cult centers throughout Coile Syria and Phoenicia was taken by John Hyrcanus and Alexander Janaeus from 125 B.C.E. A *terminus post quem* can therefore be set in the last quarter of the second century B.C.E.[127]

This dating can be narrowed down a bit more: the instruction "to destroy any temples or altars" is practically identical to the words of praise for the Jews of the Holy Land who "destroyed . . . temples and altars" in pseudo-Hecataeus's *On the Jews* (*Ap.* 1. 193).[128] This praise for religious violence is unusual. Most Hellenistic Jewish authors of whatever sectarian affiliation would normally advocate religious tolerance, whether their target audience was Jewish or non-Jewish.[129] The unusual nature of the praise, its unprecedented provocative and aggressive tone, and the phrasing of the concluding comment of the author ("it is just to admire them for these [actions]")—all suggest that the similarity between the formulations of pseudo-Hecataeus and Lysimachus is not accidental, and that it was pseudo-Hecataeus who reacted to the statement of Lysimachus, and not vice versa. It is also rather doubtful that a book such as *On the Jews,* written by an orthodox Jew just for internal consumption, would have been known to an Alexandrian Greek. The observation that pseudo-Hecataeus reacted to Lysimachus's accusations may be supported by what looks to be a deliberate inversion: Lysimachus says that the Jews destroyed temples and altars in a foreign land they passed through on their way to Jerusalem; pseudo-Hecataeus stresses that the Jews destroyed all the temples and altars erected in their own land by

127. On the dating of the intensive destruction of foreign sites of worship in the Holy Land, see Bar-Kochva (1996d) 128–34.

128. Lysimachus: ναοὺς καὶ βωμοὺς . . . ἀνατρέπειν; pseudo-Hecataeus: νεὼς καὶ βωμοὺς . . . κατέσκαπτον. There were enough other words in Greek meaning "temples" and "altars." On the statement of pseudo-Hecataeus, see also Bar-Kochva (1996d) 128–34.

129. See Septuagint, Exodus 22.28 (prohibition against reviling the gods of nations); Philo *De specialibus legibus* 1. 53 (prohibition against insulting other gods); *De Vita Mosis* 2. 205–6 (not to mock the idols and icons of foreign gods); *Quaestiones et solutiones in Exodum* 2. 5 (not to scorn or rebuke other gods); *Hypothetica* in Eusebius *Praeparatio evangelica* 8. 6. 6–7 (the Jews did not conquer the Holy Land by force; it was freely handed over to them by the inhabitants); Artapanus in Eusebius *Praeparatio evangelica* 9. 27. 4, 6, 9, 12 (the positive and active part of Moses in founding the Egyptian religion); Josephus *Antiquitates Judaicae* 4. 207 (biblical prohibition against robbing the sacred sites of foreigners and cursing other gods); *Contra Apionem* 2. 237–49 (prohibition against mocking and rebuking gods of other peoples). There are exceptions to this rule in the Septuagint version of the commandments to destroy foreign sites of worship (e.g., Exod. 23.24 = Joseph. *AJ* 4. 192) and in the harsh words of the author of Wisdom of Solomon on the superstitions and false gods of the Egyptians (13–14). See also Philo *De vita contemplativa* 7–10.

newcomers.[130] Pseudo-Hecataeus wrote his treatise between 103 and 93 B.C.E.[131] The work by Lysimachus is, therefore, to be dated to the last decade of the second century, or a little earlier.

This conclusion draws attention to the special circumstance in Egypt that would have motivated the hostility of Lysimachus. He was writing in the reign of Cleopatra III (116–102 B.C.E.), a queen greatly influenced and sometimes even manipulated by the Jewish commanders of her army. All this was just a few years after about three decades of internal struggles in the reign of Ptolemy VIII Physcon (145/4–118), which had torn Egypt between the eccentric and monstrous king and his sister-wife, Cleopatra II. The queen was supported by the enlightened Greek population—mostly in exile—and especially by the Jewish soldiers who fought for her.[132] Her daughter, Cleopatra III, having suffered formerly from sexual abuse at the hands of her stepfather, needed strong and unreservedly loyal military support. This she found in the Jewish soldiers, their commanders, and the Jewish population as a whole, which had already demonstrated its loyalty to her mother during the many years of internal conflict and a reign of terror. That the Jews had the ear of the new queen caused the Greeks considerable anxiety. They must have felt themselves betrayed by the Greco-Macedonian regime, and many turned to support Ptolemy Lathyrus, Cleopatra III's rebel son, in his unflagging efforts at unseating his mother. The remarks concerning the hostile attitude of the Jews toward other peoples (not new observations in themselves) and the transparent reference to the Hasmonaean attacks on Hellenistic centers of worship expressed, among other things, the Greeks' apprehension regarding their future in Egypt, signaling to the new Ptolemaic government what could be expected from their intolerant Jewish allies.

The suggested dating toward the end of the second century B.C.E. helps explain why Lysimachus, contrary to Hecataeus of Abdera and others, returned to accepted classical Greek traditions concerning the origin of Cadmus and the founding of Thebes, thus removing any connection the pharaohs had with Greece, and avoided integrating Egyptian figures in his other stories and genealogies of classical Greece.[133] Greek intellectuals who were active in Egypt at the beginning of the Ptolemaic period grasped at trends existent already in the literature of Greece in its heyday,[134] striving to find at any price as close a connec-

---

130. Josephus *Contra Apionem* 1. 193: ἔτι γε μὴν τῶν εἰς τὴν χώραν, φησί, πρὸς αὐτοὺς ἀφικνουμένων νεὼς καὶ βωμοὺς κατασκευασάντων ἅπαντα ταῦτα κατέσκαπτον. . . .

131. On the dating of pseudo-Hecataeus, see Bar-Kochva (1996d) 122–42.

132. On the perverse personality of Ptolemy Physcon, the internal situation, and the status of the Jews, see, e.g., Bar-Kochva (1996d) 299–302; and Huss (2001) 596–625, and the references there.

133. See above, p. 309.

134. On this trend prior to the Hellenistic period, see Berthelot (2000) 192–96; Isaac (2004) 352–56.

tion as possible between the Egyptians and the Greeks, in order to accommodate themselves with the native population, especially the powerful priestly class, so as to reduce the level of alienation and tension in relations between the natives and the foreign occupying power. However, at the end of the second century there was no longer much sense in such flattery, and in the light of two centuries of close intimacy with the Egyptian population, and the ugly, recurring confrontations with it (especially in 217–180 and 145–116), a Greek author would regard such flattery as out of place, even offensive and ridiculous. Later Egyptian history provides an instructive parallel to this in the hostile and mocking attitude of second-century C.E. Roman literature toward Egypt; the fifteenth satire of Juvenal, which was widely read, is only one example of this. The oppression of the Greek intellectual class, including the most prominent figures who went into exile, at the hands of Ptolemy Physcon, who was supported by the native population and was deeply influenced by the Egyptian lifestyle,[135] necessarily led Greek authors to ignore legends concerning a common origin or the like between Greeks and Egyptians.[136] It stands to reason that the overall portrait of the Egyptians and their history in Lysimachus's work differed significantly from that in Hecataeus's *Aegyptiaca*.

135. On the suppression of the intellectuals and their exile, see especially Athenaeus 4. 184; Pompeius Trogus in Justin 38. 8. 6. For additional sources and a discussion of the background and the reliability of the sources, see the references in note 132 above.

136. For the same reason, the purpose for which hostile Egyptian traditions regarding the Exodus were adduced by a Greek author of that generation does not seem to have been a desire to gratify the Egyptians as Josephus explains to his readers (*Ap.* 1. 223).

10

Posidonius of Apamea (A)

The Man and His Writings

Posidonius deserves an introduction considerably more detailed than those devoted to other authors dealt with in this book, both because of the uniqueness of his approach to the Jews and Judaism, along with the number of surviving references, and because of the complexity of questions surrounding his life and writings. This survey concentrates on the question of his dates and origin, important landmarks in his biography, and the contents of some of his works. The celebrated "Posidonian question" will also be considered in general terms. Not all the major problems associated with Posidonius will be discussed here, but only those that have a bearing, direct or indirect, on the assessment of Posidonius's attitude and references to the Jews and related questions.

Posidonius of Apamea flourished in his adopted home of Rhodes at a time when it was one of the main centers of literary and intellectual activity in the Hellenistic world, alongside Alexandria and Athens. Leading contemporary figures, such as Cicero and Pompey, admired him and attended his lectures during their visits to Rhodes. Many of his writings in an unusually wide range of fields became standard works for generations to come and influenced later thinkers in a variety of ways. His younger contemporary, Cicero, was already in his philosophical dialogues providing characters presenting the Stoic view with Latin paraphrases of Posidonian positions. It is therefore strange at first sight that not even one of Posidonius's many works has survived. Moreover, given his popularity at the time, it is rather surprising that we have so little information about his personal life, considering the number of biographies we have of lesser philosophers, but this seems to be due less to design than to unfortunate accidents of transmission. He is not alone in this respect.

CHRONOLOGICAL FRAMEWORK

The canonic dates for Posidonius are 135–51 B.C.E. The dates appear to be clear cut, but they rest on two uncertain scraps of information. The first of these is a statement in the *Suda* entry for Posidonius that Posidonius went to Rome in the consulship of Marcus Marcellus.[1] This sentence is located at the end of a very brief biographical entry, where one would have expected a reference to Posidonius's death. The text is corrupt, and three plausible if speculative emendations to the sentence all change the report to read that Posidonius died in the consulship of M. Claudius Marcellus (51 B.C.E.).[2] The exact date of Posidonius's birth (135 B.C.E.) has been based on one or other of these emendations, with the aid of a dubious report in pseudo-Lucian's *Longaevi* of Posidonius's age at death as eighty-four.[3] Given that pseudo-Lucian occasionally exaggerates,[4] Posidonius is unlikely to have been older than eighty-four, but he may have been somewhat younger.

The only dates in Posidonius's biography that can be determined exactly are 87/6 B.C.E., when Posidonius (by the canonic reckoning, aged forty-nine) was sent by the Rhodians on an embassy to Rome,[5] and 60 B.C.E., when at home in Rhodes he (by the same reckoning, now aged seventy-five) sent Cicero a message.[6] It should also be noted that when his teacher, Panaetius of Rhodes, died in 110 B.C.E., Posidonius would have been, by this reckoning, twenty-five years old. The conventional dating, therefore, is serviceable but may be more than a few years off. The doubts just indicated justify a more rigorous investigation.

Posidonius could not have died before sending his letter to Cicero in 60 B.C.E., but assuming for the sake of argument that he died the next year (eight years

1. *Suda* s.v. Ποσειδώνιος (= Kidd 1: T1): ἦλθε δὲ καὶ εἰς ῥώμην ἐπὶ Μάρκου Μαρκέλλου. ἔγραψε πολλά.
2. The proposed emendations are as follows: Jacoby (*FGrH*, IIA, no. 87, T1 [p. 222]): Ῥώμην-ἐπὶ Μαρκέλλου-καὶ ἐτελεύτησεν ἐπὶ Μαρκέλλου-; Reinhardt (*RE* s.v. "Poseidonios," col. 564): ῥώμην-ἄμα τελευτήσας ἐπὶ Μάρκου; Theiler ([1982] T 1a): Μαρκέλλομ-καὶ ἐπανιὼν ἐτελεύτησε. Reinhardt and Theiler offer emendations that have Posidonius going to Rome in the year of his death. This is because 51 B.C.E. was the year in which Rhodes reaffirmed its treaty with Rome (Cic. *Fam.* 12. 15. 2), and Posidonius may have been in Rome in connection with this, although (as Kidd [1989] 4 points out) he would have been at least eighty by then. The advantage of Jacoby's emendation is that Posidonius is not said to have traveled to Rome at such an advanced age, and it explains the omission of the verb (by *homoeoarchton*—the scribe's eye would have jumped from the first ἐπὶ Μαρ... to the second ἐπὶ Μαρ...).
3. Pseudo-Lucian *Longaevi* 20 (= Kidd 1: T4).
4. Pseudo-Lucian puts Zeno's age at ninety-eight (only seventy-two according to Persaeus in Diog. Laert. 7. 28) and that of Chrysippus at eighty-one (only seventy-three according to Apollodorus in Diog. Laert. 7. 184).
5. Plutarch *Marius* 45 (= Kidd 1: F255). Laffranque (1964) 46 n. 1 refers erroneously to *Marius* 85.
6. Cicero *Ad Atticum* 2. 1 (= Kidd 1: T34).

earlier than the conventional date of death), and by adding the maximum of eighty-four years provided by pseudo-Lucian, we may fix the earliest possible year of birth for Posidonius at 143 B.C.E. The latest possible year of birth, on the other hand, may be set at 129 B.C.E., again based on the year of death. In his *Tusculanae disputationes*, written in 45 B.C.E., Cicero adduces a list of philosophers portrayed as self-imposed exiles, who, once they had left home, never returned.[7] All the philosophers named before Posidonius, who ends the list, were dead by the time of writing. Both the logic of the illustration and the general company of dead men suggest that Posidonius was also dead when Cicero wrote this passage. It has also been suggested that Posidonius was dead by 43 B.C.E., as he is not mentioned in Appian's account of the siege of Rhodes by Cassius (*BCiv.* 4. 65–81).[8] Even the year 45 B.C.E. would require us to accept the maximum life span of eighty-four years in order to establish a plausible year of birth (129 B.C.E.), and even this would hardly allow Posidonius time to study with his renowned teacher, Panaetius. Were Posidonius to have been born in 129 B.C.E., he would have been only nineteen years old when Panaetius died in 110 B.C.E. While this is still theoretically possible, an earlier date for Posidonius's birth would seem more reasonable. A later year than 129 B.C.E. is out of the question.

In conclusion, the maximum (eighty-four-year) life span for Posidonius may be set no earlier than 143–59 B.C.E., and no later than 129–45 B.C.E., giving a minimum possible span of seventy years (129–59), fourteen years less than the maximum span. The conventional dates for Posidonius assume the maximum span of eighty-four years but fall almost midway between the earliest and latest possible dates (135–51 B.C.E.). These may therefore be accepted, allowing for a margin of error of up to eight years, constrained by the maximum eighty-four-year span.[9]

This state of affairs might seem satisfactory by comparison with the information we have about many other intellectuals (as opposed to rulers) in the ancient world. Even so, such a large margin of error is problematic when dating some of the events in Posidonius' life, or assessing his age at the time of datable events.

ETHNIC DESCENT

Posidonius was born in Apamea, a Macedonian military colony on the Orontes in Syria.[10] It is not clear whether he was of Greco-Macedonian or Syrian-Semitic

7. Cicero *Tusculanae disputationes* 5. 107 (= Kidd 1: T3; and cf. Kidd 2: 7).

8. See Scheppig (1869) 12–13.

9. This is essentially the conclusion arrived at by Kidd 2: 8–9. Laffranque (1964) 47 allowed a wider margin of error for the year of death, 59–40 B.C.E., although a few lines earlier she too regards the year 43 as "une date extrême."

10. *Suda* s.v. Ποσειδώνιος 2107; Strabo 14. 2. 13; Athenaeus 6. 252e (= Kidd 1: T1–2); and see Kidd 2: 7–8; Laffranque (1964) 48–53. On the military colony, see Grainger (1990a) passim.

or mixed stock, nor how long he lived in his native city. In the context of his references to the Jews, answers to some biographical questions would not be without interest. Was Posidonius a son of those Macedonian military colonists who fought repeatedly—even in his time—against the Hasmonaeans, or was he born to Oriental parents? Was he familiar with the culture and traditions of Eastern nations? Could he speak and read Aramaic? Was Posidonius in Apamea long enough to form relationships with the local Jews and learn from them about Jewish history and customs?

Quite a few scholars in the past have described Posidonius as "Oriental" on the basis of passages attributed—arbitrarily—to him that appear to show Oriental influences.[11] I. J. Kidd, the coeditor of Posidonius's testimonia and fragments, argues that Posidonius was clearly Greek: "(Posidonius) had a Greek name, wrote in Greek, had his higher education in Greece, and lived the whole of his adult life in Athens and Rhodes, where he clearly felt at home."[12] The argument is not conclusive, as may be seen from another example: Zeno of Citium, the founder of Stoicism, had a Greek name, a Greek higher education, and lived all his adult life in Athens, where he may well have felt at home, but he is described as being of Phoenician stock, and proud of his Phoenician descent (Diog. Laert. 7. 1–3, 6, 12).

At the same time, it should be pointed out that the question of stock only partially affects the problem of early upbringing. The young Posidonius may have been brought up by native women speaking Aramaic;[13] but he may just as well have been a Syrian given a consciously Hellenic education from the outset. There is no evidence that he knew any language other than Greek, but we should bear in mind that there is no evidence that Zeno of Citium, for example, knew any language other than Greek either. Whatever the case may be, it would be difficult to prove that any perceived Oriental influences in Posidonius's philosophy derive from his early upbringing in Apamea.

It is tempting to try to fill in this major blank in Posidonius's life by examining the political and social conditions in Apamea and the Seleucid empire around 145–120 B.C.E., but we do not know at what age Posidonius left Apamea. The impressions of Posidonius the teenager would differ greatly from those of the boy or the infant Posidonius. Did his parents take him to Rhodes, or did he go there later and independently? If he went of his own accord, why did he go, and when? Although Rhodes in the latter half of the second century was past its heyday as a major commercial and maritime base, it was still prosperous and, furthermore, just then strategically placed at the crossroads between the Roman West, which now extended as

11. Pohlenz (1926) 257–65, and others; Reinhardt, *RE* s.v. "Poseidonios," cols. 628–36; Malitz (1983) 8.

12. Kidd 2: 7.

13. Laffranque (1964) 52.

far as the western coast of Asia Minor, and the Hellenistic East.[14] There were many material reasons why Posidonius's parents might be attracted to Rhodes.

Another factor, relating to Posidonius himself, suggests that he was quite young when he came to Rhodes. Posidonius's vast erudition and propensity for geometrical thinking[15]—for example, in the application of geometry and astronomy to geographical matters and even military tactics and deployment—indicates that he was exposed to a rigorous scientific education from an early age. This is indeed stated by one source.[16] In 145/4, the intellectuals of Alexandria had been expelled by the monstrous Ptolemy VIII Physcon or had sought refuge abroad, to the great benefit, we are told, of the islands and towns receiving them. Deprived of royal patronage, these intellectual refugees were obliged to teach what they knew for their living.[17] Some settled in Rhodes (Strabo 14. 2.13 [655]; Ath. 11. 489). It is usually argued or assumed that Posidonius went to Athens before moving to Rhodes,[18] but Posidonius may well have studied with these Alexandrian exiles or their pupils in Rhodes while still in his teens (around 125–115 B.C.E.). It should, of course, be taken into account that after 116, when Ptolemy VIII died, a good number of these intellectuals may well have returned to Alexandria, where they could expect much better facilities and financial rewards. Yet it is unlikely that all would have returned; the internal situation in Alexandria remained unstable.

STOIC EDUCATION: POSIDONIUS AND PANAETIUS

Panaetius of Rhodes is the only attested teacher of Posidonius, barring one exception.[19] As a matter of fact, the relationship between Panaetius and Posidonius is referred to explicitly only once, and this in a typical piece of Academic polemi-

---

14. For Rhodian geopolitical history, see Schmitt (1957) 173–92; Laffranque (1964) 68–70; Berthold (1984).

15. Posidonius's book defending Euclid against the Epicurean Zeno of Sidon was used as a source by later writers on the fundamentals of geometry (Procl. *In Euc. elem.* pp. 199.3–200.6 Friedlein [= Kidd 1: F46]; pp. 214.15–218.11 Friedlein [= Kidd 1: F47]).

16. Galen notes that Posidonius was the most scientific (ἐπιστημονικώτατος) of the Stoics because of his training in geometry (*De plac. Hipp. et Pl.* 8. 652, p. 653.14 f. M [= Kidd 1: T84]), and that having been brought up (τεθραμμένος) in geometry, he was more in the habit than other Stoics of following proofs (8. 390, p. 362.5–9 M [= Kidd 1: T 83]).

17. Athenaeus 4. 184c; cf. 4. 174d-e; Diodorus 33. 6–6a, 20; Justin 38. 8. 6.

18. E.g., Kidd 2: 7: "After an education in Athens with Panaetius, he settled in Rhodes ... and, according to Cicero, never returned to live in Apamea." Laffranque (1964) 60 suggests that while Posidonius was studying in Athens, he may have gone elsewhere now and then, including Rhodes, to acquire his scientific education, if no suitable teachers were to be found in Athens.

19. Pseudo-Galen *Historia philosophia* 3 (= Kidd 1: T11) gives a potted version of the Cynic-Stoic lineage, but Posidonius is presented—impossibly—as the student of Antipater of Tarsus. Panaetius of Rhodes, the student of Antipater and teacher of Posidonius, has been omitted, probably as the

cal rhetoric, where it is emphasized that while both Panaetius and his pupil Posidonius are Stoics, they do not agree on a particular Stoic doctrine (and it is Panaetius who is portrayed as unorthodox).[20] The testimonium should be treated not as evidence that Panaetius was the most important teacher of Posidonius, but that he was certainly one of his teachers. The argument of the Academic has force only if Panaetius was the teacher of Posidonius. The Academic is making the point that even a supposedly wise Stoic teacher and his outstanding pupil fail to agree (thus demonstrating the Academic thesis that no men, not even two supposedly like-minded Stoics, have the means to decide properly what is true and what is not). It is reasonable to suppose that Panaetius, a successful and popular Stoic teacher in his day, played some part in the molding of Posidonius as a Stoic.[21] As we shall see later, it may also be through Panaetius that Posidonius was introduced to Roman high society.

Panaetius is conventionally regarded as the seventh head of the Stoic school in Athens, from the death of his teacher, Antipater of Tarsus, in 129 B.C.E. to the time of his own death in 110.[22] Posidonius is usually assumed to have traveled first to Athens to study with Panaetius in his capacity as head of the Stoic school, remaining until the age of twenty-five or thereabouts (according to the conventional dating of Posidonius's birth in 135); and further, that after Panaetius's death Posidonius chose not to stay in the Stoic school in Athens but moved to Rhodes, where he opened his own school. This putative sequence of events is unsatisfactory. Beyond the questions of why Posidonius would abandon the Stoic school in Athens and why he would move to Rhodes at all, there is the far more difficult question of how he could have succeeded in mastering a different tradition of science in a variety of fields after a Stoic education in Athens.

These difficulties disappear if it is assumed that Posidonius began his scientific education prior to meeting Panaetius, and indeed there is no reason to assume otherwise.[23] Another question, however, the reverse of our previous difficulty,

---

result of a scribal error. The *Index Stoicorum Herculanensis* gives a much fuller account of the Stoic lineage, but the last *Life* in it is that of Panaetius. Posidonius is not mentioned among his pupils, but this is most probably due to the lacunose nature of the papyrus. See also Ludlam (2003) 50–52.

20. Cicero *De divinatione* 1. 6 (= Kidd 1: T10). The point at issue is fairly central to Posidonius's religious outlook and has a bearing on the question of the validity of divination. On Posidonius's references to Jewish divination techniques, see pp. 381–89 below.

21. See Kidd 2: 58 and references there to further discussion.

22. E.g., Kidd 2: 12 (on Posidonius being a pupil of Panaetius): "This must have been at Athens, where Panaetius was (if not at Rome) from at least 148/7 B.C. . . . until his death, *c.* 110 B.C., having succeeded Antipater as Head of the School in 129 B.C."; Steinmetz (1994) 647: "Nach dessen (des Antipatros) Tod wurde er (Panaitios), nun schon über 50 Jahre alt, dessen Nachfolger im Amt (129). Panaitios stand der stoischen Schule rund 20 Jahre bis zu seinem Tode (110 oder 109) vor."

23. On Posidonius's early training in geometry and his generally scientific mind-set, see note 16 above.

then presents itself. If Posidonius was already pursuing a scientific education in Rhodes, why would he have broken this off in order to study with a Stoic in Athens, where Panaetius is generally considered to have been head of the Stoic school?

It has been argued that there never was an organized Stoic school in Athens, and that all those Stoics who are portrayed as heads of the school are no more than artificial links in a chain of masters and pupils designed by heresiographers to lend some order to the scheme of philosophical development.[24] The reality was that each Stoic teacher could teach wherever he wished, usually in a public place, in the tradition of the sophists and the Cynics. A Stoic teacher would take pains to insist that his teaching reflected that of Zeno of Citium, the "father of Stoicism," in order to attract students who wished to study Stoicism, but the teacher's doctrines were invariably refined in response to interschool and intra-school controversies, and in order to suit his own personality and the needs of his pupils, while maintaining certain Stoic principles.[25] Panaetius was not the head of an organized Stoic school in Athens, but a famous teacher with his own brand of Stoicism. Posidonius may have made Panaetius's acquaintance not in Athens, but in Rhodes.

We know very little about the connections between Panaetius and his native land, the island of Rhodes. He was widely traveled. He had studied in Pergamum with the grammarian Crates of Mallos, and then at Athens with the Stoics Diogenes of Babylon (died 151 B.C.E.) and Antipater of Tarsus (died perhaps as early as 137). Panaetius appears to have been made a priest of Poseidon Hippios in the Rhodian city of Lindos around the middle of the second century, and that implies his return to Rhodes at that time. In 144 he followed in the footsteps of his teachers Crates of Mallos and Diogenes of Babylon by traveling to Rome, where he became a member of the intellectual circle patronized by P. Scipio Aemilianus (Africanus Minor). He accompanied Scipio on his mission to the East, traveling to Egypt, Syria, Pergamum, and Greece (140–138).[26] He thereupon divided his time between Athens and Rome, until his death in Athens in 110.

Panaetius never returned to settle in Rhodes, but he certainly visited there at least once, to become a priest of Poseidon Hippios at Lindos, and he may have visited more than once. It may be, then, that Posidonius, a budding student of science, first met Panaetius in Rhodes. Acquaintance with this distinguished Rhodian may have helped to promote Posidonius's position on the island.

Panaetius need not have spent much time in Athens during the period in which Posidonius was his pupil. He may have taken Posidonius with him to Rome

24. Ludlam (2003).
25. Ludlam (2003) 55.
26. On which, see, e.g., Férrary (1988) 595–602.

on one or other of his visits there. Acquaintance with Roman high society would also have raised the political standing of Posidonius in Rhodes. After Panaetius's death in 110 in Athens, Posidonius, now aged nineteen to thirty-two, would have returned to Rhodes, where he eventually began teaching his brand of Stoicism. This was not a rebellion against the orthodox Stoic establishment, there never having been one, but rather normal practice for a Stoic who chose teaching as a career. Opening a school meant no more than teaching students, wherever and whenever appropriate. Posidonius must also have begun at this stage to integrate his scientific theories with Stoic doctrines, modifying both in the process, and may from this time have continued his study of Stoicism and the various sciences through extensive reading, rather than personal acquaintance with teachers.

LANDMARKS IN POSIDONIUS'S LIFE AND CAREER

I shall now survey briefly what is known to us about some highlights in Posidonius's life after his training and when he had become a philosopher and teacher in his own right.

At the turn of the first century, Posidonius, now twenty-nine to forty-two years old, embarked upon his well-attested voyage around the rim of the western Mediterranean, probably by land through Marseilles to Cadiz, collecting stories about the hinterland without going too far inland to see for himself, and making scientific and cultural observations, before returning by sea to Rome.[27] His ethnography on the Celtic nations and tribes, for example, was based in part on his own visits to at least the southern fringes of Celtic territory, around Marseilles;[28] but most of it relied upon rumors and earlier sources. The whole account was planned by Posidonius for ulterior doctrinal purposes and designed accordingly.

One of the aims of the journey was clearly to test scientific theories that were of interest to Posidonius in his own theoretical construction of the world. We know that during his stay in Cadiz on the Atlantic seaboard, he measured the tides for at least one month. With his results he was able to refute a theory of his older contemporary Seleucus of Seleucia concerning the influence of the moon on tides.[29] The material Posidonius collected on this journey seems to have aided him in the writing of one of his greatest and most influential works, *On Ocean*—referring to the sea external to the Mediterranean, which was believed

27. Area of Marseilles: Strabo 4. 4. 5; 3. 4. 17 (= Kidd 1: T19, T23); Cadiz: Strabo 3. 5. 9, 1. 5; 2. 5. 14; 3. 5. 8; 13. 1. 67 (= Kidd 1: T14–18); the sea voyage from Cadiz to Italy: Strabo 17. 3. 4; 3. 2. 5 (= Kidd 1: T21–22).

28. Strabo 4. 4. 5 (= Kidd 1: T19).

29. Seleucus of Seleucia had written on this subject against Crates of Mallos, one of the teachers of Panaetius. See esp. Strabo 3. 5. 9 (= Kidd 2: F218, and 2: 777, comm. ad loc.).

to circumvent the entire landmass of the known world. In this work Posidonius displayed great erudition and skill in geography, astronomy, anthropology, and mathematics; the work was a major source for Strabo, who has preserved important pieces of it.[30]

We do not know whether there were any other motives for Posidonius's trip to the West. It has been suggested that Posidonius may also have served as a sort of political and trade ambassador for Rhodes.[31] This would certainly not have harmed his political career in Rhodes, and Rhodians may have helped to some extent in the preparations for the trip. Another possible source of help should not be overlooked: it seems more than likely that Posidonius began his trip in Rome,[32] and he may have obtained the assistance of Roman friends in the preparations for his journey. But what sort of support could he have been offered in any case? The most useful assistance would have been letters of recommendation to *xenoi* (guest-friends) in various ports of call, with whom he could stay during his visit. We know that he did stay with at least one host, in Marseilles (Strabo 3. 4. 17). His journey, therefore, may not have been as expensive as it first appears, certainly not requiring the huge investment that would have obliged Posidonius to serve his backers rather than concentrate on the advancement of his own scientific projects. At any rate, Posidonius may well have practiced what he preached so far as moderation is concerned, a subject dear to his heart (and one not unrelated to his Jewish ethnographical excursus).

The work *On Ocean* may have been published quite soon after Posidonius's return to Rhodes, perhaps in the late 90s. It was the sort of work that would have made a name for Posidonius if until now he was relatively unknown. At all events, he soon had enough of a reputation to be sent on an embassy to Rome in 87/6 to meet Marius during his last consulship. The purpose of the embassy may have been to promote relations between Rome and Rhodes after the Rhodians had successfully resisted a siege by Mithridates in 88. Rhodes had been the only island to hold out against Mithridates during his sweep through Asia Minor and the Aegean. The choice of Posidonius implies great confidence in him on the part of the ruling families in Rhodes.[33] Posidonius may already have had Rhodian citizenship at this time, but the embassy in itself does not give any indication either way. Nonnative philosophers had been sent, for example, by the Athenians to Rome over sixty years earlier.[34] It is interesting that Posidonius was chosen to

30. E.g., Strabo 1. 1. 8–9, 3.9; 2. 5. 43; 4. 1. 7; 6. 2. 11; 17. 1. 21 (= Kidd 1: T214, 221, 208, 229, 227, 207 respectively) and esp. 2. 2. 1–3. 8 (= Kidd 1: T49).

31. E.g., Laffranque (1964) 77–78.

32. The first part of his route seems to have been overland around the northern rim of the western Mediterranean, and the trip ended with a sea voyage back to Rome.

33. Kidd 2: 23 (T28 comm.).

34. Carneades, Diogenes of Babylon, and Critolaus, representatives of the Academic, Stoic, and

present Rhodes' case in Rome rather than Apollonius Molon, who was second to none in rhetorical ability. Apollonius Molon was sent to Rome on a similar mission only in 81 B.C.E., where he met with great success.[35]

Posidonius was certainly a citizen when he attained one of the highest political offices in Rhodes, the prytany.[36] There is no evidence that he passed through the customary course of office, but there is no evidence to the contrary either. It may be remarked that his fellow native citizen, the sculptor Plutarch of Apamea, having acquired Rhodian citizenship, did climb the political ladder up to the office of prytanis. It has, however, been questioned whether Posidonius "would have committed himself so fully to a political career,"[37] but there is no reason to suppose that a dedicated Stoic such as Posidonius—who had become a citizen of the polis in which he lived—would not have practiced what he preached, and become involved in the affairs of state at least to the extent of carrying out the offices expected of a good citizen. Stoic ethics required the wise man to fulfil all his duties, not only as a private man, husband and father, but also in the public sphere, as a citizen of his polis.

Posidonius was teaching in Rhodes in 78/7, when he was visited by Cicero, then aged twenty-eight or twenty-nine. In 79 Cicero had studied in Athens with Antiochus of Ascalon, who claimed to have returned to what he called the "Old Academy"; then toured Asia Minor with his brother Quintus; and finally reached Rhodes, where he studied Stoic philosophy with Posidonius and rhetoric with Apollonius Molon (Plut. *Cic.* 4.5). From Rhodes, Cicero returned to Rome in 77.

Posidonius was still teaching in 66, when he would have been about seventy years old. In that year, Pompey landed in Rhodes, presumably to boost his naval power against the pirates he was currently subduing (Strabo 11. 1. 6). While he was there he dropped in on a lecture given by Posidonius. Four years later, in 62, after his successful campaign against Mithridates and the conquest of Syria and Judaea, Pompey returned to Rhodes on his way back to Rome. He is said to have attended lectures by all the "sophists" (among them rhetoricians) of Rhodes, and paid them well. This may help to explain why Posidonius chose on that occasion to lecture on the superiority of philosophy to rhetoric (Plut. *Pomp.* 42. 5).[38] Anecdotes suggest that Pompey paid Posidonius great respect in his own hour of glory.[39]

Peripatetics respectively, comprised the Athenian delegation sent to Rome in 156 (Diogenes Babylonius, *SVF* 3: frr. 6–10).

35. See p. 472 below.

36. Kidd 1: T27. There is no indication as to when this was. It is usually assumed to have preceded the embassy, but Kidd 2: 22 (T27 comm.) is right to suspect that it came later.

37. Kidd 2: 22 (T27 comm.).

38. See further, p. 476 below.

39. Pliny *Naturalis historia* 7. 112; Solinus *Collectanea rerum memorabilium* 1. 121; Cicero *Tusculanae disputationes* 2. 61 (= Kidd 1: T36–38 respectively).

It has been argued that a vague and ambiguous remark in Strabo (11. 1. 6) indicates that Posidonius wrote an encomium on Pompey.[40] Among other things, this suggestion caused scholars to regard at least the Jewish excursus of Posidonius (preserved by Strabo) as originating in this hypothetical monography. There appears, however, to be a textual problem in this interpretation of the Strabonian reference, which led to other, more satisfactory readings.[41] Besides, one may doubt whether Posidonius would have been in a fit state to write an encomium of Pompey, after Pompey's successes in the Middle East and their meeting in 62. Two years later, Posidonius declined (by letter) Cicero's request to write a record in elaborate Greek of Cicero's consulship (Cic. *Att.* 2. 1. 2). Old age and gout—he is reported to have been suffering greatly (but Stoically) from gout in 62 (at least)—would have made Posidonius disinclined, if he had ever been inclined, to write encomia for self-seeking Romans. He may have ceased his writing activity altogether by this time. We know of no later activities. As already argued, the date of his death cannot be fixed with any certainty. One can say only that it falls between 59 and 46 B.C.E.

THE "POSIDONIAN PROBLEM"
AND POSIDONIUS'S WORKS

The main difficulty in Posidonian research is the relative paucity of this prolific author's literary remains. Only fragments and testimonia—albeit some three

---

40. καὶ τὴν ἱστορίαν συνέγραψε (sc. ὁ Ποσειδώνιος) τὴν περὶ αὐτόν (sc. τὸν Πομπήιον). See Reinhardt, *RE* s.v. "Poseidonios," cols. 638–40.

41. Reinhardt assumes that αὐτὸν refers back to Pompey, the nearest masculine singular noun. The sentence so understood, however, is problematic: in particular, τὴν ἱστορίαν suggests that Posidonius wrote the one and only work on Pompey, but there was already a well-known monograph on Pompey by Theophanes of Mytilene (Cic. *Arch.* 24). Aly (1957b) 4: 94 ff. argues that αὐτὸν could refer all the way back to τὸν Ὠκεανόν (Strabo 11. 1. 5). Schwartz (1931) 391 n. 22 emended περὶ αὐτόν to περὶ αὐτῶν to refer to the immediately preceding Iberians and Armenians, and this has been accepted by Theiler (1982) 2: 59 ff. Kidd 2: 331–33 remains undecided. See also Malitz (1983) 71–73. Franklin (2003) 103–4, and esp. 108, adheres to Reinhardt's hypothesis, arguing that Strabo 11. 1. 5–6 criticizes Posidonius for refraining from utilizing information with regard to the measurements of the "Caucasian Isthmus" provided to him by Pompey after the campaign against Mithridates VI. This indicates—so Franklin—that Pompey conveyed to Posidonius much information later used by Posidonius in his biography of Pompey. However, this is not exactly what Strabo says. He just notes ironically that Posidonius, as a friend of Pompey, who carried out an expedition in that region, should have been more accurate. This is no more than a small dig by a native of Pontus, who took advantage of his acquaintance with its neighboring regions and was adequately informed about the expedition of Pompey against the Armenian kingdom. The mistaken measurement could well have been found in one of Posidonius's geographical works, presumably in his celebrated "On Ocean," referred to by Strabo in the same paragraph.

hundred of them—have survived, scattered throughout Hellenistic and Latin literature, in philosophical works and doxographies of philosophers, histories and collections of anecdotes, works of professionals (such as the physician Galen), and even in the writings of Christian authors of later periods. The identification of additional passages has been the subject of controversy for the past century. Karl Reinhardt and Izak Heinemann, the leading authorities in Posidonian research in the first half of the twentieth century, presented a maximalist view, finding traces of Posidonius in a great number of surviving works of literature of late antiquity, including many passages from Philo Judaeus. The second half of the twentieth century saw a marked change.[42] The extreme "Pan-Posidonian" approach brought about an equally extreme reaction, with various scholars questioning whether Posidonius was an original thinker at all (while accepting that his influence was very great), and some going so far as to deny him many passages previously rightly attributed to him. This tendency is clearly seen in Edelstein and Kidd's edition of Posidonian fragments and testimonia (second edition, 1989), which includes only those passages explicitly attributed to Posidonius, although we have many other passages whose contents or other data leave us in no doubt as to their Posidonian origin.[43] A relatively moderate approach is taken in the edition of fragments and testimonia by the German scholar Willy Theiler; Theiler's edition, however, was published posthumously in 1982 in an incomplete and problematic state.

Posidonian fragments and testimonia have been preserved in scores of authors writing in various genres, but a list of his works, such as those provided by Diogenes Laertius in his biographies of several philosophers, has not come down to us. Attempts have been made in modern research to organize the hundreds of fragments and testimonia into some semblance of order. Lists have been made of works whose titles have survived, or whose titles may be surmised from the subject matter, particularly Stoic topics where we have the titles of similar works by other Stoics (such as *Politeia*).

The most up-to-date list of Posidonian works with attested titles includes twenty-four works of varying lengths—the longest, *Histories*, contained forty-nine or fifty-two books.[44] This might seem to be an impressive output, but when compared with bibliographies of other philosophers recorded in detail by Diogenes

42. The new trend actually started with an article by Dobson in the first half of the century: Dobson (1918) 179–95. See also Edelstein (1936) 286–325. The prevailing trend, however, remained that of Reinhardt and Heinemann. The turning point came only after the end of World War II, amid the general revision of many fundamental concepts of German philological research.

43. Kidd 1: xvii disagrees with "the more extreme form of Edelstein's position" but rightly regards the edition in the present circumstances as a much-needed tool clearly presenting the primary evidence (xviii).

44. Kidd 1: 39–92.

Laertius, sometimes containing hundreds of books,[45] it would be safe to say that the list garnered from the Posidonian remains represents only a fraction of his output. This only exacerbates the "Posidonian problem," making it more difficult to attribute even clearly Posidonian fragments to a particular work. For example, we have no clue as to the title or even the genre of the work in which Posidonius's celebrated account of the Golden Age was originally located (testimonia in Sen. *Ep.* 90). The testimonia reveal that Posidonius distinguished between two periods in human history, the ideal period and the period of decline. This conception is of vital importance for identifying Posidonius as the author of the Strabonian Jewish excursus,[46] and for other issues pertaining to Posidonian research by and large. Such, then, are the limitations within which we must operate.

To gain some impression of the wide range of interests of this versatile and prolific Stoic author, it will suffice to survey briefly some of those works for which we have titles and that are clearly attributable to Posidonius. The survey will be limited to include only those works that have some bearing on the Posidonian accounts of the Jews:

1. *Protrepticus* (Προτρεπτικοὶ λόγοι).[47] This type of work (in Latin called *exhortatio*) was intended to entice the reader by various means to take up the subject under discussion—in this case, Stoic philosophy, as may be deduced from its limited remains. Not a few philosophers tried their hand at this type of work, among them Aristotle, Cicero, Seneca, and others mentioned by Diogenes Laertius. It has been speculated that Posidonius tried to show in this work both the nature and the benefit of (Stoic) philosophy. He would have achieved the first objective by describing the mythological Golden Age as a society molded by philosophers, and the second objective by emphasizing the many contributions of those philosophers, including the invention of all the arts and crafts essential for civilization. It might appear, therefore, that those testimonia in Seneca concerning Posidonius's Golden Age derive from this work.[48] However, other reconstructions of this work's content are possible, while the account of the Golden Age may plausibly have found a place in any one of several other works of Posidonius, including, for instance, a work on the development of civilization.[49] The three testimonia that refer explicitly to the Posidonian *Protrepticus* are of no help in deciding this particular issue either way.

---

45. For example, Diogenes Laertius 2. 84–85 (Aristippus); 4. 4–5 (Speusippus); 5. 22–27 (Aristotle); 7. 4 (Zeno of Citium); 7. 189–202 (Chrysippus).

46. See p. 372 ff.

47. Kidd 1: F1–3.

48. See Hartlich (1898) 209 ff.; Summers (1910) 311–12; Reinhardt (1921) 392 ff.

49. Theiler (1982) 412 speaks of a composition such as Βίος Ἑλλάδος by Dicaearchus and a reaction to it. On the Golden Age, see p. 366 ff.

2. Works on the cosmos and the world order: (a) *Account of Nature* (Φυσικὸς λόγος);[50] (b) *On the Universe* (Περὶ κόσμου);[51] (c) Various works on meteorology;[52] (d) *On Gods* (Περὶ θεῶν).[53] This last work, referring to gods in the plural, would no doubt have attempted to square traditional cult and belief in the gods with Stoic physics, according to which one god is both the cause of all things and what governs the cosmos. The testimonia portray Posidonius as maintaining the general views of earlier Stoics, particularly Chrysippus with regard to the cosmic god. Worthy of note is the stress apparently laid by Posidonius on the Stoic distinction between two aspects of god, as pervading the whole of the cosmos and as having its seat in the outer sphere of the cosmos.[54] Posidonius differs slightly from Chrysippus in his view of *pneuma*, the material aspect of the cosmic god.[55]

3. *On Divination* (Περὶ μαντικῆς).[56] The testimonia note that Posidonius wrote this work in five books, more than earlier Stoic works on the same subject. The majority of Stoics believed in divination, but Posidonius's teacher, Panaetius, was the exception and seems not to have written a work devoted to this subject. Posidonius appears to have used as one of his sources the work on divination in two books by Antipater of Tarsus, the teacher of Panaetius. Cicero occasionally used Posidonius's work in his dialogue *De divinatione*.[57] The Posidonian view of divination will be discussed at length in chapter 11.[58]

4. *On General Inquiry* (Περὶ τῆς καθόλου ζητήσεως).[59] Posidonius delivered a lecture in 62 in the presence of Pompey, who—according to Plutarch's testimony—on his short tour of Rhodes "heard all the sophists." The lecture by Posidonius was published as a treatise. It attacked the rhetor Hermagoras of Temnos, who preceded Posidonius by a century, and who had gained a reputation for trespassing as a rhetor into the realm of philosophy. This is the only direct evidence for active Posidonian involvement in the long-running rift (*discidium*) between philosophers and rhetors on the standing of rhetoric as an independent discipline and the right of rhetors to express views on various

---

50. Diogenes Laertius 7. 134, 140, 143, 144, 145, 149, 153, 154 (= Kidd 1: F4–12).

51. Diogenes Laertius 7. 142 (= Kidd 1: F13).

52. Diogenes Laertius 7. 138, 152, 135, 144; Simplicius *In Aristotelis physica* 2. 2; Cleomedes *De motu circulari corporum caelestium* 1. 11. 65 (= Kidd 1: F14–19).

53. Diogenes Laertius 7. 148, 138–39; Cicero *De natura deorum* 1. 123; Lactantius *De ira Dei* 4. 7 (= Kidd 1: F20–23).

54. Kidd 2: 139 (F20 comm.).

55. See Ludlam, pp. 527–30 below.

56. Cicero *De divinatione* 1. 6; Diogenes Laertius 7. 149 (= Kidd 1: F26–27).

57. Kidd 2: 149 (F26 comm.).

58. See pp. 381–89 below.

59. Plutarch *Pompeius* 42. 5 (= Kidd 1: F43).

subjects, especially philosophical issues. The subject will occupy us in chapter 15, on the anti-Jewish ethnography of Apollonius Molon.[60]

5. *Introduction to Style* (Εἰσαγωγὴ περὶ λέξεως).[61] The writing of this work underscores Posidonius's keen interest in rhetoric. Posidonius himself had a highly rhetorical style,[62] which would accord with his view that only those with a decent philosophical education could apply rhetorical devices correctly in presenting their doctrines.

6. *Inquiries* or *Histories* (Ἱστορίαι).[63] This work contained forty-nine or fifty-two books, beginning where Polybius ended his account, namely, in the year 146,[64] when Corinth and Carthage were destroyed by the Romans, events symbolizing more than anything the arrival of Roman hegemony throughout the Mediterranean basin. The evidence suggests that Posidonius brought his work down to the First Mithridatic War (88–84 B.C.E.), but no later.[65] It would therefore have covered no more than fifty-eight to sixty-two years. Considering the size of the work, the accounts must have been fairly detailed. That this was the case may be seen from some of the fragments and can be discerned in the great number of stylistic features typical of an expansive work. Not a few marginal episodes also received detailed descriptions, clearly with an ulterior motive in view, namely, the veiled presentation of Posidonian moral doctrines.[66] As was typical of Hellenistic historiography, the work included many ethnographical excursuses (Ath. 4. 151e), some of which were quite elaborate. Not one of these excursuses has survived entire and in its original sequence. The ethnography on the Celts, for example, the most famous of all the excursuses, has reached us piecemeal, scattered throughout four or more later sources.[67] Of the remaining excursuses, it is worth noting the ethnographic surveys of the Parthians, the Cimbri, and the Thracians down to their tribal divisions.[68] The *Histories* of Posidonius would appear to have been a source of information for many subsequent authors, who summarized, reworked, paraphrased, or

---

60. See pp. 474–77, 491–92 below.

61. Diogenes Laertius 7. 60 (= Kidd 1: F44).

62. Kidd 2: 87–88; e.g., Strabo 3. 2. 9.

63. See Kidd 1: T1a, F51–78.

64. *Suda* s.v. Ποσειδώνιος 2108 (= Kidd 1: T1a).

65. Kidd 2: F51 comm., esp. pp. 277–80.

66. For example, the detailed account of the "philosopher" Athenion, who was tyrant of Athens for a short time in 88 B.C.E., during the Mithridatic War (Ath. 5. 211d–215b [= Kidd 1: F253]). On this episode, see pp. 177–78 above. For more examples, see pp. 424–31 below.

67. Athenaeus 4. 151e–152f, 154a-c; 6. 246c-d; Strabo 4. 4. 5, 4. 6 (= Kidd 1: F67–69, 274, 276).

68. Parthians: Athenaeus 4. 152f–153b (= Kidd 1: F 57 and 64); Cimbri: Strabo 2. 3. 6, 7. 2. 1–2 (= Kidd 1: F49. 303, and Kidd 2: comm. ad loc., pp. 259–62; F272); Thracians: Strabo 7. 3. 2–7 (= Kidd 1: F277a).

copied it (in direct or indirect speech). Identifying fragments of the *Histories* is part of the general "Posidonian problem." In the "Pan-Posidonian" period of scholarship, far too much historical information reported in surviving texts was attributed to Posidonius's *Histories*. However, there is no debate over some of the attributions. For example, books 33–37 of the vast historical *Library* by Diodorus Siculus, including affairs concerning Sicily itself, such as the slave revolt, are no more than an epitome, if rather detailed, of some books of the *Histories* of Posidonius.[69] Another large historical work that made extensive use of Posidonius was "the [events] after Polybius" (*Ta meta Polybion*) by Strabo. This work has not survived, but a number of passages from it that originate in Posidonius are found, for example, in the *Jewish Antiquities* of Josephus (books 13–14).

In chapter 12 I shall discuss in more detail the special way in which Posidonius worked his historical information. The historical value of the information and the methods Posidonius employed are totally, and deliberately, opposed to the factual and "pragmatic" history of Polybius, whose historical framework Posidonius claimed to continue. Posidonius regarded all his varied writings as falling within the province of philosophy, and remained above all a philosopher when he wrote the *Histories*. This applies not only to his *Histories*. Although Posidonius is often regarded as distinguishing between philosophy, on the one hand, and arts and sciences (*technai*), on the other,[70] it is a basic tenet of Stoic philosophy that the province of the wise man is *epistēmē* (knowledge = "science"); the three parts of philosophy—logic, physics, and ethics—together exhaust the fields of knowledge ("science") of the Stoic wise man; in other words, philosophy and science are not distinct entities, but are aspects of the same thing.[71] Indeed, Athenaeus explicitly notes that Posidonius's historical writing was subordinated to his philosophical doctrines (4. 151e). It was actually philosophy in the guise of history. Posidonius worked his historical material in a way that allows us—deprived as we are of the *Politeia* he may well have written—to learn about Posidonius's views on state and

---

69. See p. 412 note 38 below.

70. See, e.g., Kidd's organization of the fragments. Kidd's distinction between philosophy and science is based on Seneca *Epistles* 88 and 90 (F90 and F284 respectively), interpreted as if claiming that τέχναι are irrelevant to philosophy; but these letters show only that Posidonius considered τέχναι as not contributing to virtue itself, although preparing the soul for virtue (stated explicitly and concisely, 88. 20). The τέχναι remain firmly within the province of Stoic philosophy, since they are, after all, the inventions of wise men.

71. Posidonius may on occasion appear to distinguish between philosophy and another science but does not consider the two mutually exclusive. For example, rhetoric is portrayed as inferior to philosophy, but rhetoric is still an aspect of dialectic, itself an aspect of logic, which in turn is a part of philosophy.

society. He also adopted quite often a satirical style that in the nature of things distorted facts and created caricatures of the leading figures and their deeds. All this was done in order to underline the faults of the existing sociopolitical order, as a foil to the philosophical ideals Posidonius adhered to.

Among the outstanding Posidonian positions and conceptions expressed in the working of the historical and ethnographic material to be found in Posidonius's accounts of the Jews, it is worth mentioning in particular his sharp criticism of luxury, including greed, gluttony, extravagant displays of wealth, and various manifestations of riotous behavior, all characteristic of the period of decline; similarly, his reservations concerning luxurious temples and cult practices, as well as other religious extravagances; his criticism of peoples and tribes indulging in robbery, piracy, and human sacrifice; and his diagnosis that men, tribes, and nations are unequal, so that the more talented are worthy to rule and govern—by mutual agreement and even by contract—those less able to govern themselves.

11

Posidonius of Apamea (B)

The Jewish Ethnography in Strabo's
Geographica—Mosaic Judaism versus
Second Temple Judaism

In the context of the geographical description of the coast of Coile Syria and Phoenicia and of Judaea in Strabo's *Geographica* (16. 25–45), there is a mini-ethnography on the Jewish people (35–37). This excursus is the most enthusiastic account of the origin of the Jewish people to have been written by a non-Jewish ancient author. Strabo, a Greek from Asia Minor, flourished in Rome at the time of Augustus, when, in the wake of political and military developments, a number of accusations and libels concerning the origin of the Jews and the Mosaic legacy had already spread to the Roman world. Strabo's enthusiastic account of Mosaic Judaism is rather surprising, considering the hostile tendencies, and especially as the account goes on to criticize contemporary Judaism.

Thus Strabo's unique account is remarkable from every point of view and calls for a stringent examination, all the more so in light of a hypothesis raised in the past that this account derived from Posidonius of Apamea, the leading intellectual authority in the Hellenistic world at the time of the Hasmonaean state. This chapter will attempt to trace the source of the account, its meaning and purpose, and thereby clarify its philosophical and literary background.

THE CONTENT OF THE EXCURSUS
AND DEVELOPMENTS IN RESEARCH

According to Strabo's account, the forefathers of the Jews were Egyptian enlightened men led by Moses, an Egyptian priest who served as the governor of Lower Egypt. Moses and his followers could no longer put up with Egyptian animal cult worship but also rejected the Greek practice of anthropomorphizing their gods.

Instead, they believed in one divinity alone, the highest entity "enclosing" and "containing" the universe. They also developed new ideas concerning the correct way to serve their divinity and communicate with it. In order to practice their religion as they saw fit, without interference, they decided to leave Egypt of their own free will and build a new life for themselves in a new land. The emigrants chose to settle in Jerusalem and its environs, a rocky, arid wilderness that would normally be considered unappealing to settlers; their reasoning, however, was that precisely because of the nature of the land, their neighbors would not wish to occupy it, and hence there would be no threat of war. Following their pacifist principles, they even refrained from training the younger generation for war. This peaceful way of life was reflected in the internal running of the new settlement. There was no need for laws, official institutions, or law courts, since all accepted the moral authority of Moses. As for cult worship, the Jews worshipped their divinity modestly in a simple temple, refraining from high expenses and extravagant practices of the sort usually intended to appease the gods, such as possessions and extreme ecstasy. They communicated with their divinity by means of "incubation": suitable candidates, those pure in mind and body, would sleep in the temple and receive divine messages in their dreams. The religious and social harmony of the new society in Jerusalem became known to the neighboring peoples, some of whom accepted the authority of Moses and adopted the Jewish lifestyle. This idyllic atmosphere continued for a while with Moses' successors, but eventually a decline set in. First, there came to power "superstitious priests" who adopted strange customs such as circumcision of men and excision of women, and abstention from certain meats. Then came the "tyrant" priests, who used force to take command of their fellow Jews and of other peoples in Syria and Phoenicia and indulged in robbery and confiscation of property.

Even the most casual perusal of this account of the origin of Judaism is enough to show that it has no foundation in Jewish tradition and has little in common with historical Judaism or the tradition as formulated in the Second Temple period. Even the few general similarities differ greatly in their details. This account of Mosaic Judaism sounds utopian, and the philosophical design of various details, including the concept of the Jewish divinity, should not go unnoticed. It is quite clear that one of the main sources of information for the excursus, despite the great differences between them, is the Jewish ethnography of Hecataeus of Abdera.[1] Either Strabo or his intermediate source systematically

---

1. The connection between Strabo's account and the Jewish ethnography of Hecataeus has long been recognized; see Heinemann (1919) 120–21; Reinhardt (1928) 9; Aly (1957a) 197–207; Nock (1959) 7–8; Gager (1972) 41. These scholars refer mainly to the description of the Jewish faith. Cf. also Schlatter (1893) 341; Malitz (1983) 316. On the dependence of the excursus on Hecataeus, see also below, pp. 363–64 and 376, 379 and the appendix of Ludlam, pp. 534–35 below.

reworked the Hecataean ethnography, adapting it to his own ends, adding to it, and even inverting elements in accordance with his philosophical views and hopes for a better world.

Ever since the end of the nineteenth century, various scholars have claimed that Strabo took his Jewish excursus from Posidonius of Apamea.[2] This hypothesis became accepted as fact following the studies by the leading Posidonian scholars of the early twentieth century, Karl Reinhardt and Isaac Heinemann, who without hesitation regarded Posidonius as the source for Strabo's Jewish ethnography. They drew support from four or five details in the excursus that seemed to them to suit their reconstruction of Posidonian philosophy. They also noted that Strabo mentioned Posidonius as one of his three sources for the description of the Dead Sea (mistakenly called by Strabo "Lake Sirbonis") within his running geographical survey of Judaea (16. 2. 43). Scholars who in their wake also regarded Posidonius as the source for Strabo's Jewish excursus assumed that it was intended to serve as an ethnographic introduction to the story of the confrontation between Antiochus VII Sidetes and the Jews (132 B.C.E.) or of the conquest of Judaea by Pompey (63 B.C.E.).[3]

The change in research trends in the 1950s that saw scholars questioning the Posidonian origin of many passages attributed to him in the past[4] led to the gradual rejection by an increasing number of scholars of the attribution of Strabo's Jewish excursus to Posidonius.[5] They noted basic errors in the few proofs so far adduced in support of a Posidonian source (mainly regarding the concept of the divinity). They also claimed that earlier research was not sufficiently extensive and ignored the "appendix" to the excursus in Strabo (paras. 38–39), which do not sit well with a particular Posidonian position. They drew support from Josephus, who testifies that Apion used Posidonius and Apollonius Molon as his sources for the ass libel and the blood libel (Ap. 2. 79 ff.); a writer, it was argued, who

---

2. See Reinach (1895) 70, 89, 97, 99; Reitzenstein (1901) 77; Geffecken (1907) xi n. 5; Heinemann (1919) 113–21; Norden (1921) 276–82; Morr (1926) 269–71; Heinemann (1928) 72 ff.; Reinhardt (1928) 5–34; Munz (1929) 271–83; Bickermann (1937) 130–31; Jacoby, FGrH II. C, no. 87, fr. 70, pp. 196–99; Pohlenz (1948) 105; Lewy (1960) 13–14; Tcherikover (1961) 364–65; Strassburger (1965) 44; Hengel (1973) 469–71; Wacholder (1974) 92–94; Theiler (1982) 1: 112–14, 2: 96–99; Malitz (1983) 315–18; Bar-Kochva (1997a); Ludlam (1997); Berthelot (2003) 161–77; Bloch (2004). There are variations among the scholars mentioned above. For example, Norden argued that the ethnographic excursus of Polybius served as the primary source for Posidonius.

3. See below, pp. 448–51.

4. See above, pp. 348–49.

5. See Aly (1957a) 191–209; Nock (1959) 5–9; Gager (1972) 38–47; cf. also Stern, GLAJJ 1: 264–67, 305–6; Lebram (1974) 234–44; Gauger (1979) 211–24; Conzelmann (1981) 65–69; Attridge (1984) 171; Kidd 2: 951–52; Gabba (1989) 648; Shazman (1992) 24–25. The first to propose that Strabo used a Jewish source was Schürer (1901–9) 3: 156–57; cf. Stählin (1905) 23–24, 28.

could set down these libels as fact could not have written such an enthusiastic account of Mosaic Judaism, not to mention the praise for the Jewish rejection of anthropomorphism and particularly of animal deification.

It is worth making clear with regard to the last argument that the blood libel is nowhere to be found in the remains of the Posidonian corpus and seems to have been falsely attributed to him by Apion.[6] As for the ass libel, this and other charges against the Jews, including a hostile account of the emigration from Egypt, were indeed reported by Posidonius in the context of the advice of the "friends" of Antiochus VII Sidetes (preserved by Diod. 34/35. 1. 1–5). However, since the advice is said in that same account to have been rejected outright by the king, it is not immediately obvious what Posidonius himself thought about these accusations.[7] Any decision on this matter is dependent on a prior clarification of the source of Strabo's excursus and a number of related questions.

Three main hypotheses have been proposed to replace the earlier hypothesis that Posidonius was the source: (a) Strabo, who had a philosophical education, composed the excursus himself; (b) Strabo's source was a Stoic philosopher other than Posidonius; (c) Strabo's source was a Jew with a Stoic education. The third option seems to have been the most popular in the last generation.

THE TEXT OF THE EXCURSUS AND ITS COMPATIBILITY WITH THE "APPENDIX"

Before moving on to an examination of the content of the excursus, it is worth presenting the text in its entirety as it appears in Strabo:[8]

> (35) For a certain Moses, one of the Egyptian priests, holding a part of what is called the "<lower> land" (of Egypt),[9] departed thither (to Judaea) thence, disgusted at the state of affairs, and there set out with him many worshipping the divine entity (*to theion*). For he used to say and teach that the Egyptians did not behave rightly in likening the divine entity to wild beasts and cattle, nor the Lybians; and the

---

6. See below, pp. 455–57.

7. See below, pp. 444–48.

8. The translation here is based on the Greek text edited by Kramer (1844) 303–4; Meineke (1852) 3: 1061–62. Later editions differ very little (and insignificantly) from the text of Meineke and the apparatus of Kramer. See esp. *FGrH* II. B, no. 87, fr. 70 (pp. 264–65).

9. The MSS reading is ἔχων τι μέρος τῆς καλουμένης χώρας ("holding a part of the called land"). Corais proposed adding after τῆς the adverb κάτω ("lower"), which could easily have been omitted by later copyists, and this supplement has rightly been accepted by later editors. See Corais (1815) 4: 135. Cf., e.g., Strabo 1. 1. 23, 17. 1. 4. In light of the phrasing of the sentence, the word χώρα cannot be interpreted in the Hellenistic technical sense of a rural area in its entirety. This meaning would require too many (and implausible) changes in the sentence. The reservations of Gager (1972) 38 n. 41 are unjustified.

Greeks did not [behave] well in fashioning anthropomorphic [gods]. For [he said that] this one [thing] only was god, the [thing] encompassing us all and earth and sea, what we call heaven and cosmos and the nature of things-that-are. [He asked] who, having sense, would dare to form an image of this similar to one of the things around us? [And he said that] it was advisable to abandon the making of idols, and, having defined a sacred area (*temenos*) and a worthy precinct (*sēkos*), to honor [the divine entity] without an image. [He said that it was necessary for] good dreamers to incubate (i.e., sleep in the temple to receive divine messages in dreams), both for themselves and for the others.[10] [He said that] those living temperately and with justice should expect something good from the god, and at any time a gift and a sign, but [that] others should not expect [them].

(36) Well then, he (Moses) saying such things persuaded not a few prudent men and led [them] away to this place where there now is the founded settlement (*ktisma*) in Jerusalem. He easily possessed the place, it not being enviable, nor over which would anyone fight seriously; for it is rocky, and, while being well watered itself, has surrounding land that is barren, waterless, and rocky within [a radius of] sixty stades. At the same time, instead of arms [Moses] would use as protection sacrifices and the divine entity, thinking to seek a seat for it (the divine), promising to deliver such a worship and such a cult that would not disturb the users with expenses or spirit-possessions[11] or other strange affairs. Well then, he (Moses), being well reputed, established for them (the Jews) no accidental government, and from all [the neighbors] round about [people] joined [him] easily, because of the association [with him] and the [offers? prospects?] held out [for them].

(37) The successors remained for some periods in the same [ways], acting justly and being truly god-fearing; then when there were appointed to the priesthood people firstly superstitious and then tyrannical. From superstition were made customary the abstinences from the meats from which it is also now their custom to abstain, and the circumcisions and the excisions (of females) and other such things, and from the tyrannies [were made customary] the bands of robbers. For some, having rebelled from the country, harmed both it and the neighboring [country]; others, collaborating with the rulers, seized the [property] of others and over-turned much of Syria and Phoenicia. There was, nevertheless, some decency with regard to their acropolis. They did not cause it to be loathed as a tyrant's dwelling,[12] but exalted and respected it as a holy place. (16. 2. 35–37)

---

10. The MSS reading, generally accepted by editors, is αὐτοὺς ὑπὲρ ἑαυτῶν καὶ ὑπὲρ τῶν ἄλλων ἄλλους ("themselves for themselves and others for the others"). The word ἄλλους ("others") does not suit the context, which refers to the good dreamers as one whole group. Corais (ad loc.) suggested emending to read ἄλλως ("in another way"); but the whole point of this passage is that Mosaic society believed that divine messages were delivered only in dreams. It is more likely that ἄλλους is a mistaken addition, perhaps intended to restore a perceived verbal balance in the sentence, or it may be a misplaced marginal correction for the ἄλλους that occurs a little later at the end of para. 35.

11. θεοφορίαι literally means "god-carryings" and denotes demon possession and the like.

12. οὐχ ὡς τυραννεῖον βδελυττομένων. The genitive participle agrees with the pronoun αὐτῶν,

The excursus contains three elements customary in Greek and Hellenistic ethnographic literature: (a) *origo*—the origin and development of the people; (b) *nomima*—characteristic customs, including cult; (c) *historia*—later rulers. The geographic section, appearing in a considerable number of Greek and Roman ethnographies, is missing here because the excursus is located before the geographical description of Judaea. A long appendix was attached to the body of the excursus (paras. 38–39). Since various statements appearing in the appendix have been raised in support of the view that the excursus was not based on Posidonius, it will be worth clarifying already at this stage the relationship between the excursus and the appendix.

Strabo comments in the last sentence of the excursus that the later priests and the tyrants, despite the great differences between their behavior and that of Moses and his generation, continued to respect the Temple. Strabo then turns to the appendix, saying:

> For it is so by nature, and this is common both to Greeks and to barbarians; for being polis-dwellers they live under a common command (*prostagma*). For otherwise it would be impossible for the many to do one and the same [thing] in harmony with one other, which is what it is to live in a polis, and in any other way to live a common life. (16. 2. 38)

Strabo continues by explaining that the common command may be divine or human, and that the ancients honored the first sort more. This statement leads the author to adduce a list of various personalities, mythological and historical, Greek and barbarian, who "gave mankind divine commands"; the list includes, among others, Orpheus, Musaeus, Thraseas, Zamolxis, Minos, and Lycurgus. The first to be mentioned are those who were aided by oracles (para. 38); then comes a second group, of legislators who were prophets (para. 39). The detailed account of the second group ends with the comment that "Moses was one of them."

It is clear that the excursus and the appendix derive from different sources, and that Strabo was the one who combined them.[13] Although the appendix is detailed and is almost as long as the excursus, it has nothing to say about Jewish matters.

---

which naturally refers back to the main subject of the passage, the tyrants and not the Jewish people. The latter interpretation (e.g., Berthelot [2003] 164) has been influenced by reading the participle as "loathe," which of course a tyrant would not do with regard to his own seat of power. The verb, however, can have an active meaning in later texts (cf. LSJ s.v. βδελύσσομαι II), thus "cause to be loathsome," "cause to be an abomination," and this would seem to be the middle of that active sense, i.e., "cause *their own* acropolis to be loathsome [to the people] as a seat of tyranny." See also pp. 453–55 and note 47 below.

13. *Pace* Heinemann (1919) 116–18; Norden (1921) 282; Gager (1972) 30. Those who have seen the need to separate the appendix from the excursus include Jacoby, *FGrH* II. C, no. 87, pp. 196, 198; Aly (1957a) 201; Lebram (1974) 236; cf. Nock (1959) 6; Gabba (1989) 649. Their reasoning, however, has not been conclusive.

The two texts have been ineptly joined. The opening words "For it is so by nature" are intended to bridge the gap and present the appendix as an explanation for the last sentence of the excursus. The reader receives the impression that the following will explain why the Jewish tyrants continued to respect the Temple. The connection with the following sentence, however, and indeed the appendix as a whole, is forced and not at all obvious. One might understand that the Jewish tyrants respected the Temple because temples have served, among other things, as oracles, a source for divine commands. Yet there is no attempt in the appendix to explain this connection. Moreover, the second part of the appendix, concerning legislating prophets, is entirely redundant in this context. The final sentence identifying Moses with the second group is also artificial and forced. It suits neither the appendix, where he has failed to make an earlier appearance, nor the excursus, where Moses has not been presented as a legislator or a prophet. Last but not least, no attempt has been made to adapt the appendix to the excursus, not even by mentioning in the appendix the method of prophecy attributed to the Jews in the excursus. Not only is the particular technique of incubation not mentioned in the appendix, but there is no mention of dreams at all as a form of prophecy. If the first and last sentences of the appendix are omitted, the excursus and the appendix are seen to be entirely independent of each other.[14]

It may therefore be established that the appendix was originally a discussion concerning the source of divine commands (oracles and legislating prophets). Strabo took it from an unknown source and appended it to the excursus. He may have done this because he felt that the excursus lacked any reference to the activity of Moses as a legislator, something known to Strabo from Hellenistic ethnographies and other references to Jews in literature of the period. The passage on prophets and legislators might have filled this gap, and Strabo rounded it off with a short sentence on Moses the legislator. Yet Strabo did not make the appendix an integral part of the account in the excursus, nor did he transfer any details about Moses from the excursus to the appendix. He even refrained from adding a remark in the excursus to the effect that Moses gave laws to the

14. Linguistic-stylistic considerations do not by themselves decide the issue. The excursus is written paratactically and includes a speech containing factual statements, rhetorical questions, and sermonizing. The appendix, on the other hand, is written in the complex periodic style, with many quotations from classical literature, which are completely absent from the excursus where many an opportunity presented itself for their inclusion. Such stylistic considerations, however, are not compelling, since it might be argued that the differences are the result of Strabo's transition from one genre to another, from historical narrative concerning the Jews to a semiphilosophical survey resembling somewhat the Hellenistic sermon (*diatribē*). Likewise, the speeches of Thucydides differ from the style of his descriptions of battles, and Plato uses different genres in any one dialogue, with a consequent change in style. The phenomenon is most pronounced in authors who avail themselves of their literary heritage in all its genres.

Jews. His own contribution was limited to the initial and final sentences of the appendix. The careless combination of sources resulting in inconsistencies and anachronisms, the addition of misleading initial and final sentences, and failed attempts at harmonization are all characteristic of Strabo's geographical surveys and are also prominent in his geographical survey of the coastal plain of Judaea.[15]

It is therefore already apparent that the excursus is not an original piece of work by Strabo. Albeit based on previous sources, it is all of a piece, by one hand, with only a few minor changes by Strabo. Further evidence against Strabo as the original author of the excursus will be adduced later in the discussion. Another conclusion relevant to our discussion is that the intermediate source must be considered without reference to the content and sources of the appendix.[16] For various reasons, the appendix cannot be attributed to Posidonius.[17]

FEATURES OF THE EXCURSUS

Returning now to the excursus, we shall discuss in detail the prominent features in its presentation of Mosaic Judaism. I shall present their parallels in Greek, Hellenistic, and Latin literature and examine their connection both with the account of Hecataeus, the main ultimate source of the excursus, and with Posidonius, who should be reinstated as the intermediate source. Three features recalling the Posidonian "state of the wise" should be considered first: the background and characteristics of Moses and his sage followers; the absence of laws

---

15. See, e.g., the 90-degree turn of the coastline from Jaffa southward (para. 28); calling the Dead Sea Lake Sirbonis (paras. 42–44); mixing details pertaining to Lake Sirbonis with the description of the Dead Sea (paras. 42 init., 44 fin.); locating the Edomite settlement next to Lake Sirbonis (para. 34); the erroneous description of the dimensions of Lake Sirbonis and the location of Mt. Casius (paras. 32–33). This string of errors stems from Strabo's attempts to harmonize his three sources, Eratosthenes, Artemidorus, and Posidonius, the latter having wrongly called the Dead Sea Lake Sirbonis. The negligent combination of sources is particularly obvious in Strabo's extensive description of the Indian subcontinent and its inhabitants (15. 1. 1–73), which is chock-full of doublets and inconsistencies. The geographical survey of Judaea is generally outdated: e.g., the name "Strato's Tower" (para. 27) and the reference to Gaza as a city in ruins (para. 30). Among the few updates made by Strabo: the place of death of Pompey (para. 33) and the name Sebastia (para. 34). Other updates were made apparently by his sources (who had used even earlier sources). On serious anachronisms in other surveys, see Syme (1965) 365 (e.g., Strabo 17. 3. 15: "The Carthaginians rule even now over the most fertile part of Europe," meaning Hispania). On errors introduced by Strabo into the material copied from his sources, see also 16. 2. 26, together with Athenaeus 8. 333c (taken from Posidonius, explicitly mentioned as the passage's source).

16. *Pace* Gager (1972) 41.

17. The main reason is the difference between the list of legislators in the appendix and the parallel list in Seneca *Epistle* 90. 6, which derives from Posidonius. Some reservation with regard to prophecy and divination is also discernible in para. 39 ("whatever the degree of truth in them may be"), which is contrary to the strong conviction of Posidonius himself (see below, pp. 381–89).

and governmental institutions in the Jewish state; and the moral decline of the state into tyranny (subsections A–C). In order to facilitate matters, the remaining features will be discussed according to the order of their appearance in the excursus (subsections D–F) , apart from the account of the Jewish perception of the divine entity. Because of its complexity, the theological aspect will be discussed separately in an appendix to this book. The appendix has been written by my colleague Ivor Ludlam, whose expertise embraces Stoic physics, of which Stoic theology is a part.

A. The Origin of the Jews: Egyptian Theologians/Philosophers

The Exodus from Egypt is described not as a nationalistic uprising but as an internal Egyptian movement of theologians/philosophers lacking any nationalistic significance, with the departure being portrayed as voluntary and not as an expulsion. Furthermore, the leader was an Egyptian who served as a priest and was a senior official in the royal hierarchy. The movement became universal with the settlement in Judaea: the settlers were open to strangers who took an interest in their principles; as a result, members of neighboring nations accepted the leadership of Moses and adopted his religious and social way of life.

Such an account clearly rests on a few pieces of information from one or another source and is not entirely a figment of the imagination of the author of the excursus. It is enough to point to the statement that Moses was the governor of Lower Egypt. Where, then, did the author find these pieces of information? As has already been mentioned, and will become clearer in this discussion, Strabo's Jewish ethnography is essentially a sophisticated reworking of the Jewish excursus of Hecataeus of Abdera (Diod. 40. 3. 1–8). The descent of Moses and his followers and their emigration from Egypt, however, are exceptions to this. According to Hecataeus, the Jews were an alien people expelled from Egypt along with other foreign peoples. The Egyptian natives attributed a plague that had broken out in Egypt to the anger of the gods whose cult had been neglected. In order to appease them, the Egyptians decided to remove all the foreigners from the country (40. 3. 1–2). In this account there is no criticism of the Egyptian religion or praise for the Jewish faith. This is compatible with Hecataeus's positive opinion concerning Egyptian gods,[18] and with his impartial account of the Jewish religion.[19] Although we should be used to surprises in the Strabonian excursus on the Jews, it is still very much a surprise to find that the source of inspiration for the basic framework of the exceptionally favorable version of the Jewish *origo* is none other than Manetho, the Egyptian priest of the first half of the third century B.C.E. who had written a work in Greek on the Egyptian people in which

18. See Bar-Kochva (1996d) 98–99.
19. See above, p. 132 ff.

he had included a number of hostile accounts of the origin of the Jews—or if not Manetho, a similar source or one deriving ultimately from Manetho.[20]

Some basic elements seem to have been inspired—directly or indirectly— by Manetho's detailed account of the lepers who worked in the stone quarries (in Joseph. *Ap.* 1. 228–52): Manetho portrays Moses as an Egyptian priest from Heliopolis (238, 250, 265). Heliopolis was known in Greek literature as the seat of the wisest of the Egyptians, outstanding in wisdom and prudence;[21] Moses was placed at the head of the men who were allocated the city of Auaris (Αὔαρις) in Lower Egypt (238; whence it would have been a short step to portray Moses as the governor of Lower Egypt); Moses was openly hostile to Egyptian animal cult (244, 249); he was supported by "some learned priests" (235); and finally, Moses was not expelled from Egypt but left of his own accord (albeit in unflattering circumstances, and his companions were "unclean," 236, 248). The Strabonian excursus emphasizes six identical or similar points: (a) the Jews were Egyptian; (b) Moses was an Egyptian priest; (c) Moses served as governor of Lower Egypt; (d) Moses and his followers were sages;[22] (e) they were opposed to Egyptian animal cult; (f) they left Egypt of their own free will. The author of the excursus lifted these pieces of information out of their original context and transferred them to another one of his own making. After all, Hecataeus himself abandoned his Jewish informants and used a hostile Egyptian source for his account of the Jewish *origo,* transforming it into a new, unbiased version.[23]

A comparison of the two Jewish excursuses reveals why the author of the Strabonian excursus preferred in this instance to abandon the basic information of Hecataeus and draw from the account of Manetho or his like (omitting and/ or altering the hostile details and tone). While Manetho actually portrays Moses and his first followers as Egyptian priest-sages opposed to Egyptian cult, and even describes the "unclean" who joined Moses as Egyptian, Hecataeus portrays Moses as the leader of a foreign people in Egypt; having been expelled—so Hecataeus—Moses established for that same people an exclusive state whose very separatism was motivated from the outset by a grudge against other peoples and not by any admirable religious ideology. Hecataeus even goes so far as to describe Jewish practices as "somewhat [quite?] removed from [the society of] men and [somewhat?] hostile to strangers" (Diod. 40. 3. 4). The basic framework of this Hecataean version was unsuitable for the idealistic universal values the author of the excursus strove to illustrate.[24] At the same time, it was influenced

20. On the question of authenticity, cf. pp. 246–47 above.

21. Herodotus 2. 3; Hecataeus ap. Diodorus 1. 75. 2–3; Strabo 17. 1. 29; Plutarch *Solon* 26. 1.

22. See note 43 below.

23. See above, p. 116.

24. I had remarked on the inversion of Manetho's account in my article on Strabo (Bar-Kochva

by Hecataeus in its very portrayal of Mosaic society as exclusive, giving it a new, positive, and appealing shape.

More important than the identity of the ultimate sources is an understanding of the content and purpose of the excursus. This is manifestly a portrayal of the "state of the wise." Could Posidonius have been the source for this account?[25] In order to answer this question, we must first briefly consider the development of the utopian "state of the wise."[26]

The Stoic conception of the "state of the wise" is a development of the state described extensively in Plato's *Politeia*. The character called Socrates depicts a polis with three social strata: (1) the "guardians," later "philosophers," or wise men who govern the polis; (2) the military "aides"; and (3) the craftsmen and merchants (e.g., 434c7–8; 484a ff.). This polis is often regarded by scholars as Plato's only ideal state, but his Socrates actually began his depiction of types of states with a simple model that seemed to him "healthy" and "true": a society without

---

[1997a] 307, in Hebrew). Berthelot (2003) 169 takes issue with this point, although agreeing that Posidonius was the source for the excursus in Strabo. She seems to be arguing that Strabo's description of Moses in Egypt (namely, his status, deeds, followers, and departure) was the most common and widespread version of the Egyptian tradition, claiming that Strabo calls it ἡ κρατοῦσα μάλιστα φήμη ("the most prevalent report," para. 34 fin.). There is therefore no need to hypothesize a Posidonian familiarity with Manetho. However, this statement (ἡ κρατοῦσα κτλ.) in Strabo does not appear in the excursus (paras. 35–37) but in the previous fragment (para. 34 fin.). As clearly appears from the context, it does not refer to the story about Moses and his followers in Egypt and their exodus, but only to the actual Egyptian descent of the Jews. Strabo accepted this version, which he found in the excursus of Posidonius and elsewhere, and adopted it in other places as well (see, e.g., the testimonium in Joseph. *AJ* 14. 118). He presented it as a predominant rumor, just as other Greek and Roman authors did when they had to choose between various versions. Can anyone seriously entertain the notion that the "information" that Moses was an Egyptian priest and governor of Lower Egypt, that he opposed the Egyptian animal cult, that wise men followed him, and that they left Egypt willingly rather than by force derived from the most popular Egyptian tradition prevalent in the Greek world?

25. Suggested by Heinemann (1919) 116, in a brief note: "Dagegen paßt die Vorstellung von einer urspünglichen weisen und gerechten Herrschaft, der sich jeder willig unterordnet, trefflich zu der Geschichtsbetrachtung des P., nach welcher ursprünglich allenthalben 'bene imperanti bene pareretur nihilque rex maius minari male parentibus posset quam abire se regno' (Sen. *Ep.* 90. 5)." On the formulation of the Latin sentence quoted here, see below, note 36. Surprisingly enough, Heinemann's note seems to have been overlooked all these years, even though the similarity to the motif of the decline and fall (as opposed to the state of the wise) had already been underlined in the booklet of Reinhardt (1921).

26. It should be noted that expressions such as "state of the wise" and "city of sages" are not found in the ancient sources, although such a state or city is implied. The terms are used in modern scholarship with reference to Plato's "ideal state" in the *Politeia*, and to the Stoic ideal state. The leaders in Plato's *Politeia* are not actually described as *sophoi*, although they are portrayed as wise. The Stoics are more explicit and describe their ideal leaders as *sophoi* or *sapientes* (Zeno and Chrysippus in Diog. Laert. 7. 131, Posidonius in Sen. *Ep.* 90. 5), but not at every opportunity.

strata, from which the later three-tiered society derives (372e6–7). Apparently, in reaction to Plato's *Politeia,* Zeno of Citium, the founder of Stoicism, presented in his own *Politeia* a classless, but exclusive, society comprising only sages.[27] Their conduct is guided by the principles of reason, and there is consequently no need for the usual institutions and legal system. Zeno's book provoked a scandal in Athens, as it contained approval of incest and cannibalism, but even so we have little information about its content. Stoics of the late third century B.C.E., such as Chrysippus, attempted damage control by applying a decent interpretation to the more scandalous features of the book, while some even claimed that Zeno was not the author of those remarks, and, later still, that Zeno was not the author of the *Politeia* attributed to him.[28] Despite all this, the "state of the wise" remained a Stoic ideal.

We do not know in which work Posidonius wrote his version of the Stoic "state of the wise." There are several possibilities.[29] His account has been preserved only partially, among a number of testimonia adduced by Seneca in one of his letters to Lucilius (*Ep.* 90). Most of the testimonia, unfortunately, deal with the contribution of sages to the development of human material culture by the invention of crafts (*technai*). There is, however, one passage that allows a reconstruction of the basic outlines of the Posidonian state of the wise (paras. 5–6):

(5) Therefore, in that age that they regard as golden, Posidonius judges that the kingdom was in the hands of the wise. These restrained hands and protected the weaker from stronger; they persuaded and dissuaded;[30] and demonstrated useful and useless things;[31] their prudence[32] foresaw that nothing should be lacking for their people, their courage[33] warded off dangers, their beneficence[34] enriched and decorated their subjects. Ruling was a duty/service (*officium*), not [an attribute of]

27. On the echoes of Plato's *Politeia* in Zeno's *Politeia,* see Schofield (1991) 24 ff. Plutarch states explicitly that Zeno in his *Politeia* reacted to Plato's *Politeia* (*De Stoic. repugn.* 1034F).

28. Much has been written on Zeno's *Politeia.* See, e.g., Erskine (1990) 9–42; Schofield (1991) 3 ff., 104 ff. Of the earlier studies, it is worth mentioning Baldry (1959) 6–8 on the subject of Zeno's ideal state comprising only sages. On later Stoic attitudes toward Zeno's utopian state, see Plutarch *De Stoicorum repugnantibus* 1044–45; Clement *Stromateis* 5. 9; see also *SVF* 3: frr. 743–54.

29. See above, pp. 350–51.

30. As Kidd 1: 961 notes, "i.e., used argument, not force."

31. Kidd 1: 961: "i.e., the canon of conduct for the ordinary man." The Stoic wise men could understand their own conduct, but their subjects required some less philosophical criteria by which to live well.

32. *prudentia* = φρόνησις, for Zeno of Citium the general virtue of the Stoic sage (*SVF* 1: frr. 200–201), but later only one main virtue among several (e.g., *SVF* 3: frr. 262–66, 268, 274, 280).

33. *fortitudo* = ἀνδρεία, defined by Chrysippus as "the understanding of what should be chosen, what should be rejected, and what falls under neither of those two categories" (Diog. Laert. 7. 93).

34. *beneficentia*—a free translation of μεγαλοπρέπεια?

the kingdom. No one [of the kings],[35] as much as he had power, tried [his power] against those through whom he had begun to have power, nor did anyone have the inclination or cause for injury, since one who ruled well was obeyed well, and the king could threaten nothing greater against those obeying badly than that he leave[36] the kingdom.

(6) But with vices creeping in, the kingships turned into tyranny, and there began to be a need for laws; and these too, at first,[37] wise men brought forward.

Posidonius, then, set his "state of the wise" in the mythological and utopian Golden Age, so nostalgically described in many Greek and Latin versions ever since Hesiod (*Op.* 109–20). The combination of the two utopias in one presents a Posidonian account that is original with respect to both the "state of the wise" and the Golden Age. The uniqueness of the Posidonian account of the Golden Age will be considered in more detail below.[38] Here our concern is with the uniqueness of his version of the "state of the wise" in comparison with those of Plato and Zeno of Citium.

The Posidonian "state of the wise" has some prominent features:

a. It appears to have been a universal society encompassing all of mankind.[39] This is apparent from the contexts, the tone and content of Seneca's testimonia, and Seneca's own reactions. It also would have accorded with the Stoic conception of a return to a universal society of mankind. Hesiod's Golden Age society is also universal.

b. The state was headed by a sage king (para. 5). It is not surprising that the Posidonian sage is described as a king. Early (as distinct from mythological) society was conceived in Greek thought to have been ruled by kings.

c. The state comprised two classes: sages and commoners. The latter are referred to as people who needed to be restrained and so on. (para. 5 init.).

35. It appears in this account that originally the wise, who had the kingdom in their hands, regularly elected a king to rule over them.

36. *abiret* B, *abirent* later MSS. The correct reading need not be decided by considering whether their leaving the kingdom, or the king leaving the kingdom, would be the worst threat to urge against dissidents. The verb denotes voluntary departure and in the context could apply only to the king himself. His expulsion of the dissidents would have been forcible and would have required another verb, such as *eicio*.

37. *inter initia,* "among the beginnings," indicating that each city had a different beginning, and not all of them had a lawgiver.

38. See pp. 373–75. On the Posidonian Golden Age, see Rudberg (1918) 51 ff.; Reinhardt (1921) 392–408; Heinemann (1921) 88–107; Ganss (1952) 106–14; Cole (1967) 95; Theiler (1982) 2: 484–90; Kidd 2: 961–71.

39. Not all the accounts of the Golden Age offer a clear picture of the unity of mankind at that time. The general impression is of one society, but some accounts present various societies leading similar lives at some distance from each other (e.g., Pl. *Pol.* 271b; Ov. *Met.* 1. 100).

The sages are obviously the ones through whom "he (the king) had begun to have power" (para. 5 fin.). They are explicitly mentioned as the ones who prepared the laws after society became beset with vices and had sunk into tyranny (para. 6).[40] In what was not a hereditary monarchy, a sage class would have been required to allow the proper transfer of kingship from one king to another down the generations.

d. The state had no laws. There was no need for them, since all the subjects obeyed their wise leader. Legislation became necessary only later, in the period of decline (para. 6). The clear impression is that for the same reason there was no need for ordinary government institutions.[41]

e. The Golden Age "state of the wise" declined over time. It happened in two stages: at first, vices began to creep into it, and later, it was usurped by tyrants.[42]

This presentation of the "state of the wise" differs from both that of Plato and that of Zeno. As opposed to the "Platonic state," it is universal and not an individual polis; the Posidonian state is ruled by a wise monarch, and not a collective of wise "guardians"; it has no laws or government institutions, unlike the all-pervasive system described by Plato's Socrates in his *Politeia*. The Posidonian state is similar to that of Plato in that it has some social structuring, although of a different nature. As opposed to the Zenonian state, the Posidonian state is universal, socially structured, and ruled by a monarch; Zeno's state is exclusive, composed only of sages, and consequently has no leader. Neither state has laws or institutions; both are in fact cosmopolitan, albeit only of sages in the case of Zeno. The Posidonian account in general appears to be a mixture of the Platonic structured society where authority is in the hands of the sage class and the Zenonian universal society with Posidonian modifications and improvements.

The Posidonian utopian state is exemplified by Mosaic society. While the latter is in a historical setting, the similarities are manifest at almost every point, and they agree in their differences from the ideal states of Plato and Zeno. The leader, Moses, is wise and is accompanied by other sages.[43] From the statement that

40. The decline into tyranny could have been preceded by a breakup of society. Each individual polis would then have had a need for its own sage to produce laws, at which point the account would begin to conform with Greek tradition.

41. See further, pp. 370–72 below.

42. On these two stages of decline, see further, pp. 372–75.

43. Those who join Moses are called εὐγνώμονες ἄνδρες (para. 36), "prudent men," which is tantamount to calling them "wise." We may recall that Plato's Socrates in the *Politeia* attributes to the ruling class of the aristocratic state the similar characteristic of *euboulia*, "good counsel" (428b6), which he goes on to suggest is the only *epistēmē* that should be called *sophia* (428e–429a). This identification demonstrates the flexible use of various terms used to denote the wisdom of the leaders. See also note 26 above on the term "state of the wise."

the original followers of Moses ("not a few prudent men") were joined by their neighbors ("everyone round about easily joined"), it is quite clear that most of the citizens are not sages. Moses derives his authority from the assent of all the citizens to his right to govern because of his unique qualities. The state has no laws, law courts, or other governmental institutions (see subsection B). Jewish history is divided into two distinct periods: the ideal, Mosaic, period and the greatly diminished period when Judaism turned to "superstition" and subsequently to government by tyrants. In both his accounts, Posidonius refers explicitly to the rise of tyranny as symbolizing the decline (see subsection C).

Unlike the Posidonian mythological state of the wise, which is universal, the Posidonian Mosaic state is exclusive (although in a sense cosmopolitan). This change was necessary in the given context. In the Golden Age a state containing the whole of humanity was plausible. The Jewish state, however, was founded in the later historical age, when humanity was already in decline and divided along ethnic and religious lines. We may recall the censure of Egyptian and Greek religion in the Strabonian Jewish excursus. The Jewish state of the wise was established against the prevailing downward trend. It was only natural that contemporary sages aspiring to live in an ideal society would abandon the mainstream societies and establish their own state in which they could fulfill their vision. Posidonius, therefore, transferred his utopia from the mythological down to the historical period and adapted it to the new context. At the same time, the Jewish state of the wise is open to people from outside who are eager to accept its principles. This, then, is not an exclusive society in the usual sense of the term, but a society naturally inclined to cosmopolitan openness.

Significantly enough, there seems to be a close connection between the unique explanation of Jewish exclusivity in Strabo and explicit comments regarding the detachment of the Jews from other nations deriving from Posidonius. In the main report of Josephus on the siege of Jerusalem by Antiochus Sidetes in the year 132/1 (AJ 13. 236b–248), taken from Posidonius (via Strabo),[44] Jewish "non-mixing" (amixia) with other nations is explained as the result of their eusebeia (246). Stoic doxographies and other relevant sources explain eusebeia as "knowledge of serving god" (ἐπιστήμη θεῶν θεραπείας),[45] and knowledge is of course an essential quality of the Stoic wise man. The positive attitude toward Jewish exclusivity is contrary to the Hecataean approach (Diod. 40. 3. 4), and there is no parallel to it in Greek or Latin literature, where Jewish exclusivity is normally condemned and

44. See below, pp. 409–17. This is not some sort of circular argument: the identification of Posidonius as the source of the siege account in Josephus, based on source criticism, is valid without the identification of Posidonius as the source of the Jewish excursus in Strabo.

45. E.g., Diogenes Laertius 7. 119 = SVF 3: fr. 608; Stobaeus Eclogues 2. 60. 9 = SVF 3: fr. 264, ll. 40–41.

explained as the result of the hardships endured by the Jews after their expulsion from Egypt.[46] Only in Strabo's Jewish excursus is there a similar positive attitude toward the unique Jewish version of exclusiveness. It is presented there as conducive to the right belief and the proper worship of the divine entity. Its origins are in the voluntary emigration of the sages, who thereby obtained the means to practice and develop their philosophical religion without interference.

B. Jewish Society at the Time of Moses:
No Laws or Governmental Institutions

It was mentioned above how similar the lack of laws and governmental institutions in Mosaic society was to the Posidonian description of the state of the wise preserved in Seneca (*Ep.* 90. 5–6). This unusual feature needs to be more closely examined and compared with the Hecataean account of laws and governmental institutions in his description of the Jewish state. The literary and philosophical background to this characterization in Strabo also needs to be clarified.

Hecataeus goes into some detail in his account of the role of Moses in establishing the laws of the Jews. He accords Moses the prestigious title of *nomothetēs* ("legislator"; Diod. 40. 3. 6) and explicitly attributes to him a number of laws concerning, for example, military matters, the ownership of property, the raising of children, marriage. and burial (3. 7–8). Hecataeus even remarks that the Jewish book of laws closes with the statement "These are the words that Moses heard from God and gave to the Jews" (3. 6).

As for governmental institutions, Hecataeus states that "Moses laid down laws (ἐνομοθέτησε) concerning the constitution (*politeia*), and arranged (διέταξε) them" (3. 3). As part of his arrangements, he "picked out the men of most refinement and the most able to head the entire nation, and appointed them as priests" (3. 4). In addition to their cultic duties, he "appointed them to be the judges of the greatest disputes and entrusted to them the guardianship of the laws and customs" (3. 5). The priests were also authorized to choose the High Priest, to whom Moses bequeathed the position of leader of the nation (3. 5). One of his duties was to read the laws aloud in the people's assemblies (3. 6). Hecataeus thus lays great stress on the role of Moses as legislator and instigator of state functions.

The excursus in Strabo says nothing of all this. There is no mention of Moses as lawgiver or of governmental institutions. Indeed, all of that would have been redundant considering the style of leadership attributed to Moses there. Moses is said to have had the power of persuasion, to have been admired by all the inhabitants of Judaea and their neighbors, and to have instituted an unusual type of government. This glaring difference from the Jewish excursus of Hecataeus cannot

---

46. See esp. Manetho ap. Josephus *Contra Apionem* 1. 239; Diodorus 34/35. 1. 4; Pompeius Trogus ap. Justin 36. 1. 5; Lysimachus ap. Josephus *Contra Apionem* 1. 309; Tacitus *Historiae* 5. 5. 1.

be coincidental but is surely deliberate and must depend upon the sociopolitical outlook of Strabo's source for the excursus.

The account recalls the *Politeia* of Zeno of Citium, where governmental institutions are declared redundant, and the building of law courts is explicitly prohibited (Diog. Laert. 7. 33). We have already mentioned the attempt of Chrysippus to defend Zeno's *Politeia*, while later Stoics claimed that the *Politeia* had been falsely attributed to Zeno. Chrysippus adhered to the idea of a state without laws and institutions (*SVF* 3: Marcianus, fr. 314). Posidonius himself returned to a defense of the Zenonian *Politeia*, albeit indirectly. His respectable account of the Golden Age outlines a period in which there was no need for laws, thanks to the special qualities of the leaders . Only once the decline in morals had set in, which led to the transformation of kingships into tyrannies, did there arise any need for laws, and it was then that legislators appeared (para. 6). It may also be seen from Seneca's paraphrase of the Posidonian Golden Age that not only laws (mentioned explicitly in para. 6) but also ordinary governmental institutions were redundant before the period of decline. There is no reference to such institutions, but only to the authority of the kings, accepted and respected by all. The virtues and style of leadership of the leaders, the obedience of the subjects, and the general atmosphere all contributed to a society that had no need of governmental institutions of the usual type, just as it had no need of laws.

It is worth making clear that the lack of laws and governmental institutions in the Posidonian state is not to be attributed to its being set in the Golden Age. It is true that the accounts of the Golden Age by Plato and Ovid mention the lack of state organization and of laws, respectively (*Pol.* 271d-e; *Met.* 1. 89–93), and the redundancy of governmental institutions and laws follows from the perception that humans lived in harmony and perfect happiness, desiring little, with the little that they desired being provided for by nature.[47] Yet Posidonius seems to have regarded the Golden Age in a less rosy light; otherwise his kingly leaders would have been unnecessary, they would not have needed to protect the weak from the strong, nor would their wisdom (*prudentia*) have been required to care for the needs of humans (para. 5). Seneca's criticism of Posidonius in his *Epistle*

---

47. Cf. Plato *Laws* 677a–682: humans after the flood were primitive, and neither rich nor poor; consequently they had no need for a constitution or any legislation. Reference is also made there to *Odyssey* 9. 112–15, concerning the society of the Cyclopes, who lived in caves and on top of mountains. On the conception of the "Golden Age," see pp. 374–75 below. In this context, it is worth quoting the comment of Agatharchides of Cnidus on the Red Sea fish-eater tribes: "They are not governed by law, for why should a person who is able to act correctly without written law be a slave to decree?" (Phot. *cod.* 250. 49, 451b). These tribes live virtually in the innocence of a Golden Age, fearing no danger and without arms (Agatharchides in Diod. 3. 18. 3–6). Notably, Posidonius was acquainted with Agatharchides' work and was inspired by him in many respects; see p. 305 note 102 above.

shows that his own view of Golden Age society, a frugal pastoral society (paras. 30 ff.), differed from that of Posidonius. The reason for the absence of laws in Posidonian Golden Age society, therefore, is their redundancy because of the wisdom of the leaders, and not because of any pastoral conditions usually said to have prevailed in the Golden Age. The greater realism of the Posidonian account would have encouraged the reader to take the various sociophilosophical messages seriously, rather than dismiss the account as escapist myth.

The mere absence of laws and governmental institutions in Mosaic society in Strabo's account does not in itself prove that Posidonius was Strabo's source. The general idea was Stoic, passing from Zeno of Citium to Chrysippus and down to Posidonius.[48] This feature, however, should be considered along with the other peculiarly Posidonian details of the state of the wise discussed in the previous and subsequent sections. No wonder Moses is not referred to among the legislators in Seneca's *Epistle* (90. 6), which derives from Posidonius, although he does appear in the parallel, earlier list in Hecataeus (Diod. 1. 94. 2) and in other "canonical" lists, including the appendix Strabo attached to the excursus (para. 38).[49]

C. Moses and the Tyrants: The Golden Age and the Decline

The Jewish excursus of Hecataeus makes no distinction between Mosaic and later Judaism. The Jewish faith and customs are discussed *en bloc* and without any development from the time of their inauguration by Moses to contemporary Judaism. Authority passed from Moses to the High Priests, and they carefully preserved the traditional laws and customs. Hecataeus describes the Jewish people as exclusive, displaying here some critical reservation not to be found elsewhere in his fairly impartial account.[50]

Strabo's excursus makes no reservation concerning the exclusivity of Mosaic

48. On the Stoics and laws, see Erskine (1990) 16 and n. 13; Schofield (1991) 65–74 and elsewhere.

49. Berthelot (2003) 169–71 raises some reservations concerning the claim I made in my article on Strabo's excursus (Bar-Kochva [1997a] 323–25, in Hebrew) that the Posidonian Moses was not a legislator. The reservations are peculiar and not to the point. She further suggests that Posidonius played down the activity of Moses as a lawgiver because of the link between Moses and laws deemed misanthropic. However, Posidonius could have attributed any misanthropic laws to the superstitious priests who came after Moses, just as customs considered superstitious, such as circumcision and excision and abstinence from certain types of meat, were attributed to them and not to Moses. Posidonius would have achieved the central aim Berthelot imputes to him (to condemn the Hasmonaeans for using Moses as a foil; see below, note 119) far more efficiently and consistently had he written that the wise Moses legislated good laws, unlike the "tyrants" (the Hasmonaeans), who legislated misanthropic laws. Posidonius did not choose to portray Moses as a legislator, and this he did for philosophical reasons. He wished to present the figure of a (Stoic) wise leader in an ideal society, one who needed no laws in order to govern successfully, since all acknowledged his wisdom and moral authority.

50. See above, pp. 129–32 and 102 n. 31.

Judaism. Quite the contrary. Jewish exclusivity is presented as the best way for sages to serve the divine entity. Furthermore, unlike Hecataeus, Strabo distinguishes between Mosaic and contemporary Judaism. He states that after the period of Moses and his immediate successors, who remained faithful to his vision, there was a marked deterioration beginning with priestly rulers affected by superstitions, who initiated dietary laws, circumcision (of males), and excision (of females). These were followed by priestly tyrants who enslaved and robbed their own and neighboring peoples. Later Judaism, therefore, is the complete opposite of Mosaic Judaism: Mosaic worship was free of "strange practices" (para. 35), while later worship suffered from superstitious prohibitions and unacceptable acts. The subsequent decline into tyranny surely refers to the Hasmonaean state. Instead of leaders striving for internal and external peace and stability, there rose to power warmongering and rapacious tyrants who set about expanding the limits of their territory through military conquest. They oppressed their own people and are blamed, notably, for the existence of robber bands (λῃστήρια, para. 37). This recalls the description of the Hasmonaean conquests elsewhere in Strabo (16. 2. 28) and Pompeius Trogus (*Prol.* xxxix: *latrociniae;* cf. Justin 40. 2. 4). In another context, the Hasmonaean rulers are explicitly called "tyrants" (Strabo 16. 2. 40).

I have already noted that the distinction between periods in Strabo's excursus is similar to that appearing in the Posidonian account of the history of mankind adduced by Seneca.[51] This observation requires further elucidation. Posidonius distinguishes between two main periods: the Golden Age, the original and best period, in which wise kings ruled, and the subsequent period, which sank to the lowest depths with the rule of tyrants instead of kings. Seneca paraphrases the Posidonian reference to this bad period only in passing (*Ep.* 90. 6a), since his main concern at this point is to refute the Posidonian claim that the great inventions were made by sages. Even so, two stages may be discerned in the bad period: first, the spread of evils, and only after that, the onset of tyranny (*sed postquam subrepentibus vitiis in tyrannidem regna conversa*). The first is actually a transitional stage required by the subject matter: evils could not have spread during the period of the wise kings, who ruled with prudence and their principles of wisdom and justice, and the wise men themselves, being wise, could not have become tyrants; yet tyranny could not take root without evils to facilitate its appearance. An immediate change from kingship to tyranny might be possible in myths where the gods themselves can change anything at a stroke (as happens

---

51. The similarity between the Posidonian accounts of the ideal origin of mankind and the period of decline has already been remarked upon by Reinhardt (1928) 19, 76 ff. (cf. [1921] 392–401). He did not, however, consider the apparent differences between Seneca's and Strabo's accounts, which allowed the criticism of Gager (1972) 46–47.

in the Golden Age accounts of Hesiod, Ovid, and Virgil); but the Posidonian account gives the gods no role, and they are not even mentioned. A transitional stage could be envisaged, for example, as having rulers who appear wise because they continue the traditional customs instituted by their wise forebears, but due to incompetence or lack of ability fail to implement the customs correctly and gradually cause internal chaos that finally (as so often happened in Greek history) invites the rise of tyranny.

The Posidonian version of the Golden Age and subsequent developments is but one of the many variations in later literature on the Hesiodic myth of the ages of mankind.[52] Yet the Posidonian theory differs from all the others, both in the number of its periods and stages, and in their characteristics. This point may be illustrated by a few examples from other major versions in Greek and Latin literature.

The Hesiodic myth itself speaks of five ages (*Op.* 109–200). The ideal conditions of life in Hesiod's Golden Age, when human beings had all their needs supplied without any effort on their part, are completely different from the way of life in the Posidonian Golden Age.[53] Hesiod has no kings in his Golden Age, no tyrants in his Silver Age when unjust practices began to spread among mankind, nor in later ages when warfare predominates. In Plato's *Politicus* (272b) a distinction is made between the period of the rule of Cronus (identified with the Golden Age) and the subsequent period of the rule of Zeus. The period of Cronus is described as pastoral, and some Hesiodic ideal characteristics are there made extreme. It is emphasized that Cronus ruled exclusively, and for that reason there were no political constitutions (271e). In Plato's *Politeia* (544e ff.), aristocracy and four increasingly degenerate regimes are described, each with a different political constitution. Although the last of these regimes is tyranny, the process by which it is reached is completely different from that described by Posidonius. The version of Aristotle's pupil, Dicaearchus of Messenia, is particularly interesting. It serves, in the same way as the anthropological theory of his contemporary, Theophrastus, as a vehicle for preaching vegetarianism and abstention from animal sacrifice. Dicaearchus explicitly distances himself from the myths that preceded him, and divides the history of mankind into three periods: the Age of Cronus, the Nomadic Age, and the Agricultural Age. The Age of Cronus was a vegetarian period, when men did not work and had no cares. It was not, however, a period of boundless plenty. Men gathered their food from plants in moderation, enjoyed universal friendship, and warfare was unknown. In the Nomadic Age, men turned to shepherding and the eating of meat, and there began to be wars. Then came the Agricultural Age, lasting until the time of the author (in Porph.

---

52. See the survey of the various versions in Gatz (1967) 26–86.
53. See above, pp. 366–68.

Abst. 4. 2. 1–9). Also relevant to the present discussion is the version by Aratus of Soli, the third-century B.C.E. scholar-poet who managed among other things to study with Zeno of Citium. Aratus relates the myth of the goddess Dike and refers to three ages: the Golden, the Silver, and the Bronze (*Phaen.* 100–34). In the Golden Age there are no kings. The goddess Dike (Justice), living among people, supplies mankind with all their needs and urges them to preserve the principles of justice. The Silver Age sees the spread of evils among men, and Dike can no longer live among them. Yet she appears every evening, admonishes them, and calls them back to the path of righteousness. In the Bronze Age, men turn to warfare and murder, and Dike abandons them completely, returning to the heavens. Nothing is said of the type of regime in this period, nor are tyrants mentioned. I should add that the early Stoics did not exploit the notion of a Golden Age in their writings.[54]

Turning now from the pre-Posidonian Greek poets and thinkers to the Roman poets of the Augustan period: Virgil refers to only two periods, the Age of Saturn (= Cronus) and the Age of Jupiter (= Zeus). In both periods, government is in the hands of the gods. There are no kings in the first period, nor tyrants in the second. Yet laws exist from the very beginning (*Aen.* 8. 316–26). Finally, Ovid, in his celebrated version, presents four periods in great detail (*Met.* 1. 89 ff.). His Golden Age is pastoral to perfection. His Silver Age does not show moral decline in the behavior of men, but a certain degradation of the weather leads to a more difficult life for mankind. In neither period is the rule of men referred to, and there is no mention of kings or tyrants.

We may therefore establish—at least from those versions that have reached us—that the division of the evolution of human society adduced by Seneca in the name of Posidonius was unique to Posidonius. This account is very similar to the portrayal of Jewish history in the excursus of Strabo, both in its division into periods and in its characteristics. Both accounts distinguish between two main periods only, with the second being subdivided into two stages. Both call the stage of extreme degeneration "tyranny," and both refer to the rule of a wise man in the first period, an ideal reign that had no need of laws or governmental institutions.[55]

---

54. See Erskine (1990) 201; cf. Baldry (1959) 7, 12–13.

55. Stern, *GLAJJ* 1: 266, raises the possibility that the conception in Strabo's excursus concerning Jewish degeneration is influenced by the arguments of Theophrastus against animal sacrifice: according to Theophrastus, mankind originally refrained from eating animals, and only later, in the wake of a certain chain of events, did they begin to eat meat (Porph. *Abst.* 2. 5 ff., 27 ff.; and see pp. 19–20 above). However, the two stages in Strabo are quite the opposite: according to the formulation as it stands, abstention from certain meats is a superstition appearing only in the period of degeneration ("abstinences from meats from which it is also now their custom to abstain"). This would mean that the Jews formerly ate all types of meats. Posidonius respects general abstinence from meat on

D. The Settlement in Jerusalem and the Nature of the Area

According to Hecataeus, Moses led his people out of Egypt to an utterly desolate area nearby and founded there a city called Jerusalem (Diod. 40. 2. 2–3). Strabo's excursus repeats this claim but explains further that Moses chose Jerusalem because the surrounding area was parched and rocky (the settlement itself necessarily had a water supply on site), so that there was no concern about covetous neighbors or fear of conquest by foreigners. As a result, there was no need for military preparations of any kind. To illustrate this explanation, a short geographical survey of the city and its environs was integrated in the text. In addition, while Hecataeus states that Moses prepared the younger generation for war and "made military expeditions into the neighboring lands of the nations" (6–7), Strabo's excursus claims that "instead of arms [Moses] would use as protection sacrifices and the divine entity" (para. 36). The moral message is clear-cut: the wise avoid battles and conflicts well in advance, and at all cost, even at the expense of their basic comfort and standard of living.

The Hecataean version reflects the Greek tradition of foundations of *apoikiai* in unsettled areas, where military training was an essential feature.[56] Military training is spoken of with approval in Plato's *Laws* (941–44) and elsewhere, although pacifist sentiments were widespread in Greek literature and philosophy, including other Platonic writings. Wars were seen to be an inevitable part of human life and an important factor in its development (e.g., Pl. *Leg.* 625d5–7). This is in fact the prevailing attitude to war in Greek literature.[57]

The Stoics, perhaps under Cynic influence, envisaged a demilitarized ideal state. Zeno posited in his *Politeia* a classless state of wise people who, being wise, would all enjoy the same way of life and the same political system (Plut. *De Alex. virt.* 329A). He treats Eros as bestowing upon men "friendship" (*philia*), "consensus" (*homonoia*), and "freedom" (*eleutheria*) (Ath. 13. 561c). It goes without saying that such a political system *per se* would enjoy eternal peace. Chrysippus in his *Politeia*, probably using Zeno's *Politeia* as his source, quotes the Cynic Diogenes

---

the grounds of vegetarianism (Strabo 7. 3. 3), but he frowned upon abstinence from certain types of meat, explaining the custom as mere superstition. Similarly, for many generations, philosophers had been scathingly critical of the many prohibitions of this type among the Pythagoreans. Gager (1977) 46, who believes that the distinction between the two in the Jewish excursus is Strabo's own, draws attention to Strabo's account of the decline in Crete after the reign of Minos (10. 4. 8–9). Yet Minos is described in Strabo as a *nomothetēs* (legislator), while Moses in the excursus (as distinct from the actually independent appendix) is not. Furthermore, Minoan Crete is in no way portrayed as a state of the wise.

56. See above, pp. 120–22.

57. For surveys and discussion, see Nestle (1938); Dieckhoff (1962); Arnould (1981); Flower (1994) 215–17; Ostwald (1996) 102–18.

of Sinope on "the uselessness of arms" (Phld. *On the Stoics,* coll. 15. 31–16. 1).[58] Chrysippus clearly argued for a state without arms or army in his *Politeia* and wrote another work called *homonoia* (Ath. 6. 267b).

Posidonius's vision of a pacifist state was presented in his utopian account of the state of the wise in the Golden Age. Seneca's testimonium, which refers to the reign of the kings in the Posidonian state of the wise, makes no mention whatsoever of any military organization. The very description of the state of the wise as a universal society suggests a pacifist aspiration. Furthermore, this was a society that had no need of armed internal security. The reader is given to understand that the wise rulers, being wise, knew how to nip in the bud any internal friction.[59] It is not surprising that arms are not mentioned among the items whose invention Posidonius attributed to the wise. His detailed list of inventions is scattered throughout Seneca's *Epistle.*[60] It is not stated in the *Epistle* when these inventions were said by Posidonius to have been made, but the mention of Anacharsis and Democritus among the inventors (paras. 31–32) shows that at least some of the inventions were dated by Posidonius to the historical period and not to the Golden Age.[61] Arms that were developed in the historical period were therefore not invented, according to Posidonius, by the wise. Indeed, Posidonius would have been unable to accept such a claim.

This Posidonian position is reflected in his cosmopolitan vision appearing in the third book of Cicero's *De officiis,* part of which work is based almost entirely

58. See the edition of Crönert (1906) 61. On Zeno's *Politeia* as the intermediate source for Chrysippus's quote from Diogenes, see Baldry (1959) 10; Schofield (1991) 26 n. 10, and 50 ff.; cf. Nestle (1938) 39–40.

59. Plato (*Pol.* 271b) and Dicaearchus (Porph. *Abst.* 4. 2. 5, 7, 9) present the argument that there were no wars in the Golden Age because men led a pastoral life and had no ambitions for more than that (cf. Aratus *Phaen.* ll. 108–10). However, Posidonius did not regard the Golden Age in this way (see pp. 366–68 above). His reason for the absence of war would have been that the whole of mankind was one society and the leaders prevented internal strife (as is also indicated in the testimonium of Seneca, para. 5: "These [the wise leaders] restrained hands").

60. In para. 26, Seneca mentions "weapons and walls and instruments useful for war"; however, this is not said in the name of Posidonius but appears within the rhetorical arguments Seneca raises in order to refute the opinion of Posidonius that all inventions were the product of wise men. Seneca lists various inventions that he considers naturally of little value, and that consequently would not have been conceived by the wise philosophers (such as refined movements of the body and the breathing and blowing out of air to sound the trumpet, mentioned in this context). It is clear, therefore, that Posidonius did not mention these. The conclusion of the paragraph, which emphasizes the aspiration of the wise to achieve universal peace (as opposed to the development and invention of arms), only points out the rhetorical character of the argument.

61. Those inventions that benefited mankind were usually attributed to the period after the Golden Age, since the pastoral life had formerly supplied all the modest needs of mortals. Since Posidonius saw the Golden Age in a slightly different light, however, he may have attributed some of these inventions to the wise of the Golden Age.

on Posidonius.[62] I shall quote only two passages out of many that make the opinion of the author quite clear:

> Nature does not allow this: that we should increase our own means, supplies, and wealth at the expense of others. (*Off.* 3. 22)

> But those who say that citizens should be taken into account and that foreigners should not, they destroy the common society of humankind (*communem humani generis societatem*), and once this has been removed, beneficence, liberality, goodness, and justice will be completely removed, and those who remove them should be adjudged even impious against the immortal gods; for they are uprooting the society among humans (*inter homines societatem*) that was established by [the gods]. (*Off.* 3. 28)

The ideals of a "common society of humankind" and "beneficence, liberality, goodness, and justice" cannot go hand in hand with violent means for settling intercommunal conflicts, and certainly not with the desire to deprive other peoples of their freedom and property. At the same time it must be said that the peaceful cosmopolitan vision is common to all the Stoics and is not peculiar to Posidonius.

Examination of the brief geographical description of Jerusalem, however, suggests Posidonius as the most probable originator of the reference to the choice of Jerusalem by Moses. The description, although partly erroneous and exaggerated, is too similar for coincidence to the unique and tendentious geographical survey of the location, terrain, and water supply of Jerusalem by Timochares, a Seleucid court historian who wrote a monograph on Antiochus Sidetes (139–129 B.C.E.).[63] The version in Strabo is evidently a sophisticated adaptation of that survey, carefully adjusted to explain why Moses chose Jerusalem of all places for his settlement.[64] The survey of Timochares served as a preface to his account of the siege of Jerusalem by Antiochus VII Sidetes in 132/1 B.C.E.[65] The same siege is described in exceptionally great detail by Posidonius (preserved in Diod. 34/35. 1. 1–5; Joseph. *AJ* 12. 236–47).[66] Since identification of Strabo as the original author of the Jewish excursus has already been ruled out,[67] it does not require too much imagination to identify Posidonius as Strabo's (intermediate) source for the adapted geographical survey, and consequently for the excursus as a whole: Posidonius, born

---

62. See Kidd 2: 187 on the sources for the book. On Posidonius and imperial rule, see p. 427 below.

63. See the detailed discussion below, pp. 465–68.

64. See below, pp. 462–64.

65. See below, pp. 459–61.

66. See chap. 12, pp. 409–17. The argument is not circular; see note 44 above about Strabo's source for the excursus.

67. See pp. 360–62 above.

in Apamea, the nerve center of the Seleucid army, devoted special attention to the personality and achievements of Antiochus Sidetes, elaborating on his diplomatic and military campaigns.[68] Posidonius must have been familiar—certainly much more than any alternative candidate for the authorship of the Jewish excursus— with the survey of Jerusalem by Timochares, his elder contemporary, the court historian of Antiochus Sidetes.

E. Modest Temple and Cult

Hecataeus emphasizes that Jewish cultic customs differed completely from those of other peoples, and a note of reservation creeps in a little later: "He (Moses) established sacrifices and modes of conduct for everyday life differing from those of other nations; for as a result of their own (the Jews') expulsion from Egypt, he introduced a [way of] life that is somewhat (= quite?) removed from [the society of] men and [somewhat?] hostile to strangers" (Diod. 40. 3. 4).[69] Hecataeus would almost certainly have provided more explicit details about Jewish sacrifices, but Diodorus has omitted all of them (just as he omitted other details).[70] Strabo's intermediate source would have seen these, and it appears that he turned these details on their head. His account saw Jewish sacrificial practices differing in their frugality, refraining from lavish expenses and the sort of ecstatic activities engaged in by other peoples attempting to appease capricious gods. The author maintains this general tone by saying that "instead of arms [Moses] would use as protection sacrifices and the divine entity."

This essentially positive view of the foundation of a temple is not shared by the early Stoics. Zeno advocated a state without temples or cult, reasoning that there was no building worthy of god, and that no work of builders or artisans had much worth or holiness (Clem. *Strom.* 5. 12. 76).[71] Chrysippus, the second central figure in the development of Stoic thought, appears to have been ambivalent about holy places in his discussion of the question of whether one should be allowed to perform in temples socially unacceptable acts, such as urinating on the altar (Plut. *De Stoic. repugn.* 1044F). Later Stoics were by and large more moderate and seem to have adapted themselves to the mind-set of the average Greek, who observed tradition. Diogenes Laertius, the compiler-biographer of philosophers, states:

> [The Stoics claim that] good men are also god-fearers (*theosebeis*), for they are experienced in the customs concerning the gods; and *eusebeia* is knowledge of serving gods. Furthermore, [they say that] they will sacrifice to gods and are pure;

68. See pp. 424–31 below.

69. See further, pp. 130–32 above.

70. See above, pp. 103–4, 132, and note 121.

71. Cf. the testimonia in Plutarch *De Stoicorum repugnantibus* 1034B; Diogenes Laertius 7. 33; and Theodoretus and Epiphanius, *SVF* 1: 264, ll. 35 ff.

for they incline away from offenses concerning gods. And [they say that] the gods admire them; for they are both holy and just concerning the divine [entity]. And [they say that] only the wise are priests; for they have studied concerning sacrifices, the building of temples, purifications, and the other matters pertaining to gods. (7. 119)

A summary of cult requirements is given by Epictetus, the first-second century C.E. Stoic: "to anoint and to sacrifice victims, and to bring the first fruits, according to the custom of our forefathers, in purity, and not crassly or negligently, not in a miserly fashion nor yet beyond one's means, this is what all of us should do" (*Enchir.* 31).

The rejection of ostentatious and expensive sacrifice for social and moral reasons is not peculiar to the Stoics. Indeed, it was a commonplace in Greek literature.[72] It already appears in Hesiod (*Op.* 1. 336) and is well known, for example, from Plato's *Laws* (955e). In the time of Zeno of Citium, it was even picked out for emphasis by Aristotle's successor, Theophrastus, in his *Peri eusebeias,* arguing in particular against animal sacrifice.[73]

The positive attitude of Posidonius toward temples and sacrifices arises from the description of the siege of Jerusalem by Antiochus Sidetes, preserved, as has already been said, in Josephus *Jewish Antiquities.* He praises Antiochus for his *eusebeia,* which had induced him to respect the Jewish God (*AJ* 13. 242, 244). At the same time, the special circumstances of the event indicate that Posidonius is in fact critical of the wasteful and ostentatious nature of the victims and gifts sent by Antiochus to be sacrificed in the Jewish Temple.[74] This Posidonian position fits well with his praise for the simplicity of early Roman life, as expressed in their cult (in Ath. 6. 274b).[75] Posidonius also praises the laws of Zaleucus (Sen. *Ep.* 90. 6). These included the explicit instruction that "[the god] should not be served [by means of] great expenses" (Stob. *Ecl.* 4. 12. 7; cf. Diod. 12. 20. 2).

It may be stated in conclusion, therefore, that while the positive attitude toward temples and sacrifices, and the advocacy of modest cult practice, are not peculiarly Stoic, they certainly are features shared by Stoics. They do not reflect the early Stoa, however, which opposed temples and sacrifices altogether, or distanced themselves from such things; they are reflected, both explicitly and indirectly, in passages that derive from Posidonius.

---

72. A partial collection of sources touching upon this point is found in Wilhelm (1915) 219; Heinemann (1921) 114; Gager (1972) 42.

73. In Porphyry *On Abstention* 2. 14. 3, 19. 4, 20. 1, 60. 1, and in Stobaeus *Anthologia* 3. 3. 42. See also Theopompus, the younger contemporary of Theophrastus, in Porphyry *On Abstention* 2. 16.

74. See below, pp. 420, 426.

75. However, the account of Roman cult appearing in the same passage is not Posidonian.

F. Divination and Dreams

Hecataeus does not give details about the prophetic qualities of Moses. He describes him as a lawgiver who acted in accordance with the special circumstances of the migration and settlement, and only observes that the High Priest of the Jews functioned as "a messenger . . . of the commandments (προστάγματα) of the god" (Diod. 40. 3. 5), and that at the end of the Jewish book of laws it is written "Moses having heard these things from the god says [them] to the Jews" (3. 6).

Strabo's excursus actually hints that Moses received prophetic enlightenment in dreams during "incubation" in the Temple. Moses is said to have advised his followers on how to achieve divination in dreams. The passage (para. 35) allows us to list the following features of Jewish divination: (1) the dream is the recommended method of divination; (2) the dreamer himself interprets the dream; this means that there is no need for a separate class of dream interpreters; (3) the dreamer must be of a moderate temperament; (4) the dreamer must lead an upright life; (5) the dreamer must be strongly inclined to dream by nature; (6) the dream prophet will see the future not only of himself but of others; (7) "incubation" in the Temple is the best way of achieving dream divination.

This description of Jewish divination is far away from written or oral Jewish tradition, although individual elements may bear a passing resemblance to one or another verse or isolated deed of this or that biblical personality.[76] Despite the popularity of dreaming as a method of divination in the Near East and ancient Israel, Jews did not attribute it to Moses and the classical prophets (perhaps apart from Zechariah), nor was it a practice that these prophets recommended in their writings. It would suffice to mention the polemic of the prophet Jeremiah against dreamers (Jer. 23.27–28, 27.32, 29.8).

The popular belief in the prophetic power of dreams is well known in Greek culture from its early beginnings.[77] Greek philosophers accepted it (see, e.g., the summary in Cic. *Div.* 1. 5–6, 52–54).[78] Most of the prominent Stoics shared this belief in divination. Zeno of Citium argued for the divinatory power of dreams and oracles (e.g., Diog. Laert. 6. 149; Cic. *Div.* 1. 5–6). The next few generations

---

76. *Pace* Preuschen (1903) 34, 64, who claims that the source for the whole practice is biblical. On dreaming in the Bible, see recently Fidler (2005), and in the Near East, Oppenheim (1956).

77. See the surveys of Wachsmuth (1860); Bouché-Leclercq (1879–82) 1: 277–329; Dodds (1951) 102 ff.; (1973) 156–210; Pritchett (1979) 3: 92–101, 142–43.

78. Socrates is mentioned there presumably because of Plato's *Crito* 44a-b. As for Aristotle, the story appearing in *De divinatione* 1. 53 seems to have been taken from an early dialogue by Aristotle, *Eudemus, or On the Soul* (see Eudemus fr. 1 in Ross [1955] 16). In his later acroamatic work *On Dream Divination,* Aristotle rejected dream divination. It is highly doubtful whether Cicero knew Aristotle's acroamatic writings. Later Peripatetics, apparently apart from Theophrastus, rejected divination. On this last point, see Pease (1963) 57.

of Stoics proved, using Stoic principles, that the divine entity strives to reveal its intentions to mankind and has contrived special means of communication for this purpose (Cic. *Div.* 1. 82, 2. 101–2; cf. Cic. *Nat. d.* 2. 5 ff.). Stoics, including Chrysippus, Diogenes of Babylon, Antipater of Tarsus, and Posidonius himself, wrote various works on divination. Chrysippus devoted one of his two books on divination to dreams (the second concentrated on oracles). Antipater's two-book work on divination expanded on dreams, using Chrysippus as a source. Posidonius wrote a five-book treatise on divination with the aid of Antipater's work. Some material from Posidonius's treatise has reached us through the medium of Cicero's dialogue *De divinatione* (1. 6, 84, 123; 2. 33, 144). Antipater's pupil and Posidonius's teacher, Panaetius, seems to have been unusual for a Stoic in that he rejected the existence of divination (Diog. Laert. 7. 149; cf. Cic. *Div.* 1. 6; 2. 88, 97). Posidonius, on the other hand, regarded even astrology as a reliable means of divination (August. *De civ. D.* 5. 2. 5) and recommended dreams most highly. The most expressive and concise testimonium is in Cicero:

> But [Posidonius] thinks that men dream through the impulse of gods in three ways: first, that the soul itself foresees through itself, since it is held by a kinship with the gods; second, that the air is full of immortal souls, in which, as it were, stamped marks of truth are apparent; and third, that the gods themselves converse with sleepers. (*Div.* 1. 64)

Richard Reitzenstein, one of the first to suggest Posidonius as the source for Strabo's excursus, adduced this passage as proof that Posidonius saw dreaming as a legitimate form of divination.[79] Isaac Heinemann added that Posidonius was following the Pythagoreans in his belief that only a soul released from the bonds of sensation, for example by dreaming, was able to connect with the divine entity (Cic. *Div.* 1. 63).[80] Arthur Darby Nock, the great scholar of ancient religions, drew attention to another point: Cicero's summary of Posidonius makes no mention of the need to interpret dreams. The information is conveyed directly, and this is the case also in Strabo's excursus.[81] I would add that the Stoic speech opening Cicero's dialogue on divination even condemns dream interpreters explicitly, along with other suspect soothsayers (*Div.* 2. 12).

There are, therefore, two immediately discernible similarities between Cicero's summary of Posidonius's view of dream divination and Strabo's excursus: dreaming is the recommended form of divination; and there is no need for interpretation. A discussion of the other features requires some preliminary clarification of the structure and sources of Cicero's *De divinatione*, our main source of information for Stoic views on divination and dreams.

79. Reitzenstein (1901) 77.
80. Heinemann (1919) 115.
81. Nock (1959) 9.

Cicero wrote dialogues in the style of Aristotle, with speeches and counter-speeches, and himself appearing as one of the main speakers. In *De divinatione,* Cicero attacks dogmatic arguments for divination. The main speakers are Quintus, Cicero's brother, who is to defend all forms of divination, and Cicero, who is to argue against. The first book presents the various arguments for divination; the second book refutes them. In his introduction, Cicero declares that he will attempt to compare arguments and hints that the arguments in favor are Stoic, while the arguments against are based on the criticisms of the second-century B.C.E. Academic scholarch Carneades of Cyrene, the greatest representative of the Skeptical Academy (*Div.* 1. 6; cf. 2. 8–9, 100, 150).[82] The first book includes references to a number of philosophers—Plato, Aristotle, Dicaearchus, Zeno, Chrysippus, Diogenes of Babylon, Antipater of Tarsus, Cratippus of Pergamum, and Posidonius—in addition to Greek historians and events from Roman history. As happens in such cases, opinions sometimes diverge concerning Cicero's immediate sources for the various testimonia, and all the more so regarding the source of unattributed views appearing in the dialogue.[83] I shall be joining the many scholars who have followed in the footsteps of A. S. Pease, the Harvard philologist and author of a monumental commentary on Cicero's *De divinatione,* in claiming that Cicero's direct sources for the work were only two—Posidonius and the non-Stoic Cratippus—and that Posidonius was the main source for the first book. The references to other sources in the first book, according to this view, would also have been taken from Posidonius.[84] At the same time, I shall attempt to demonstrate that Posidonius was indeed the source of each passage discussed below.

It is now time to return to our comparison of the features in Strabo's excursus and the opinions about dream divination held by Posidonius. The third requisite feature of the dream diviner in Strabo's account is the virtue of temperance or moderation. We shall see below that this virtue is considered by Posidonius to be essential if the soul is to be separated from bodily sensation, that is, free from all thought, concern, and anger while in the sleep state, and is to be able to concentrate and be completely receptive to dream divination. A passage in Cicero, clearly summarizing Posidonius, dwells at some length on the subject of freeing the soul from its bodily chains in order to achieve the proper state for dream divination:

> From nature, however, there is a certain other argument that explains how great is the power of the soul when divorced from the sense of the body, which happens

82. On the structure of the dialogue and the position of Cicero himself, see Schofield (1986) 47–65.

83. See the bibliographical survey in Pease (1963) 19 n. 85; Pfeiffer (1976) 44–53.

84. See Pease (1963) 18–22 and esp. 21–22. Kidd 2: 149 is more circumspect. Pease's book comprises two long articles published in 1920 and 1923.

especially either to sleepers or to those in a frenzy (*mente permotis*). For just as the souls of the gods, without eyes, without ears, without tongue, perceive among themselves what each perceives (hence it is that men, even when they wish or vow anything in silence, have no doubt that the gods hear it), so the souls of men, when either released by sleep they leave the body, or frenzied (*mente permoti*) they are incited by themselves and move freely, they discern those things that souls thoroughly mixed (*permixti*) with the body cannot see. While it is perhaps difficult to apply this particular explanation of nature to that type of divination that we call artificial, nevertheless Posidonius investigates this too, as far as is possible. He thinks that there are in nature certain signs of future things. (*Div.* 1. 129–30; cf. 121: *ut igitur,* etc.)[85]

The Posidonian source of the passage is proved by the explicit reference to Posidonius at the end, and by the use of the term "nature" at the beginning. "Nature" is one of the trilogy "god," "fate," "nature," which Posidonius employs in order to demonstrate the principle of divination (*Div.* 1. 125, 129).[86]

The image of the release of the soul from the body appears in a similar form in another passage, indicating that this passage too is Posidonian, although only the example adduced at the end of it is attributed explicitly to Posidonius:

When therefore the soul has been called apart by sleep from the society and contact of the body, then does it remember past [things], discern present [things], and foresee future [things]; for the body of the sleeper lies as of a dead man, but the soul is strong and alive. How much more so will it do this after death, when it will have left the body completely. Therefore when death approaches it is much more divine (i.e., has greater powers of divination). . . . That the dying divine Posidonius establishes also with that example that he adduces, that a certain Rhodian who was dying named six people of the same age and said who would be the first of them, who the second, and so on, to die. (*Div.* 1. 63–64; cf. 81, 110, 113, 115, 116, 121)[87]

The need for moderation in food and drink in preparation for the proper release of the soul from the body with a view to dream divination is discussed elsewhere in *De divinatione*:

85. On the Posidonian source of the fragment as a whole, see Pease (1963) 21. So too Kidd 2: 428, 434; Long (1976) 72–75.

86. See Kidd 2: 434; cf. 426–28.

87. On Posidonius as the source for para. 63, see Pease (1963) 21. Kidd 2: 429, on the other hand, does not include this paragraph among his collection of Posidonian fragments. He remarks: "In 63, the power of divination of the soul in sleep, when withdrawn from the body, leads to the topic of such powers at the approach of death. Posidonius is merely cited for a famous instance of this." Even were we to overlook the arguments and evidence for Cicero's extensive reliance on Posidonius in *De diviniatione* 1, such reasoning would still appear overcautious.

And this indeed is the rationale of seers, and not dissimilar actually to [that] of dreamers. For things that occur to seers while awake [occur] to us while asleep. For the soul thrives in sleep, free from the senses and every burden of cares, while the body is lying and almost dead. Since it has lived from all eternity and has found itself with innumerable souls, it sees all things that are in nature, if only it has been so affected by temperate dishes and moderate drinks that it itself might keep watch while the body sleeps. This is the divination of the dreamer. (1. 115)

The explanation of the divinatory dream in terms of the separation of the soul from bodily sensation, and the comparison of the state of the dreamer with that of a dead man, both found in the two Posidonian passages quoted prior to this one, show that this last quotation is also Posidonian. The connection between eating and drinking and moderation is explained in an earlier long passage of Cicero (1. 61; cf. 2. 119) that quotes Plato (*Politeia* 9. 571d6–572b1). According to the text, trustworthy dreams are dreamt in a relaxed state achieved by retiring to sleep after a balanced meal that does not leave the person hungry or too full, nor angry, since all these states interfere with the ability of the soul in sleep to divine properly. It has already been rightly argued that the passage was not taken directly from Plato, but from Posidonius, acting here as an intermediate source.[88] This passage would have found a place in the Posidonian presentation of dream divination. "Quintus" himself explains that the personality and reputation of Plato suffice to tip the scales against the Epicurean denial of dreams: "Therefore will you put this man [i.e., Epicurus] before Plato and Socrates, who, even without giving an argument, would yet prevail over these petty philosophers by their authority?" (1. 62). It is worth noting that the quote from Plato stands in opposition to the Aristotelian claim that even hypochondriacs are capable of divination.[89]

The fourth feature required of the dream diviner is personal integrity, *dikaiosynē*, uprightness or (the usual translation) justice. There is nothing in the Posidonian fragments or testimonia—a small part of his actual output—that attributes this characteristic explicitly to the dream diviner, but his great work on divination would surely have required this cardinal virtue of a medium between god and man. There is indeed one expression in Cicero's *De divinatione* that indicates that this might have been the case. Since the passage is concerned with the preparations of the dream diviner before going to sleep, and specifically the need to achieve tranquillity, it certainly complements previous Posidonian passages examined above

88. Pease (1963) 21. Pease directs the reader's attention to the words *illo etiam exemplo*. The Platonic text shows that *sophrosynē* is "moderation," later one of the four cardinal virtues adopted by the Stoics. At 1. 115, quoted above, there are also Platonic echoes; cf. e.g., *Meno* 81c5–d1.
89. Cicero *De divinatione* 1. 81; cf. Aristotle *Problemata* 954a34 ff.; *Ethica Eudemia* 1248a39 ff.

and is very likely Posidonian itself. This conclusion is reinforced by the fact that the passage is in the first book of Cicero's *De divinatione*:[90]

> Therefore, just as one who gives himself to repose having prepared his soul with good thoughts and things conducive to tranquillity discerns certain and true things in sleep, so is the spotless and pure soul of one who is awake more prepared for the truth of birds, of the rest of the signs, and of entrails. (1. 121)

"Good thoughts" are essential for the reception of reliable dreams. The meaning of "good thoughts" may be elucidated by comparison with the characteristics required of a seer: he must have a spotless and pure soul (*castus animus purusque*). The double epithet *castus purusque* (i.e., ἁγνὸς καὶ καθαρός) pertains to sexual or religious purity rather than anything ethical in the philosophical sense, while *castus* alone may have had an ethical connotation. In this context, therefore, "good thoughts" would appear to be thoughts free of sexual or any other irreligious content. This is as near as Cicero comes to saying that the dream diviner is required to have a high degree of personal good conduct. His source, namely Posidonius, may have been a little more explicit.[91]

The fifth characteristic, the natural tendency to dream, is also to be found in Cicero's account, based on Posidonius:

> [This connection between cause and effect] is seen both by those to whom natural divination has been granted and by those to whom the course of things is made known by observation [of signs]. Although they do not discern the causes themselves, they do discern the signs and tokens of causes. . . . It is therefore not to be wondered at that those things are sensed in advance by diviners that nowhere are [= exist]. . . . And as in seeds there inheres the potential of those things that are produced by them, so in causes are stored future things whose being in the future either a frenzied soul or one released by sleep discerns, or reason or conjecture senses beforehand. (1. 127–28)

In this case, the argument cannot be described with certainty as Posidonian; all that may be stated with confidence is that Posidonius transmitted the argument. A clearer piece of evidence is to be found in one of the passages already quoted, where Posidonius presents three ways in which divine impulse affects dream divination (1. 64). One of these is the natural affinity of the soul to the gods,

---

90. *De divinatione* 1. 121 is similar to 1. 63, which is Posidonian (see note 85 above), and Posidonius is the source for 1. 123.

91. The words καθαρός and ἁγνός occasionally appear in one and the same sentence, albeit not always next to each other, in a socioethical sense: e.g., in Theophrastus *Peri eusebeias;* see Porphyry *On Abstention* 2. 19. 4–5. The ethical sense of the words in that context is indicated by τὸ ἔθος (19. 3) and καθαρὰν κακῶν τὴν ψυχήν (19. 4). However, each case should be examined in its own right, and no clear-cut decision can be reached in the present instance.

which allows it to foresee future events. In this context, it is worth noting the general Stoic opinion that only the souls of the wise are akin to the gods in that they are all rational entities; only the wise are loved by the gods; only the wise are true experts in any skill.[92] We have already seen that Posidonius required the dream diviners to have moderation, and possibly righteousness. These are two of the Stoic cardinal virtues, the virtues of the wise man. We may conclude from all this that the man best prepared to be a dream diviner is the Stoic sage. However, the emphasis on natural ability, the natural inclination to dream, is peculiar to Posidonius.

The sixth feature in the list, the ability of the dreamer to divine not only for himself but also for others what is to happen in the future, is reflected in examples of near-death divination adduced by Posidonius himself. We have already seen the example of the dying Rhodian (1. 64). It is immediately followed by another illustration:

> And this, as I said just now, happens more easily upon the approach of death, that souls prophesy future things. Hence also that [story] of Callanus, about whom I spoke before, and of the Homeric Hector, who while dying announces the approaching death of Achilles. (1. 64–65)

The first sentence is certainly Posidonian (cf. paras. 63–64). It is almost certain that the examples are also Posidonian. The story of Callanus, the Indian ascetic sage, appears a little earlier (1. 47). He prophesied the imminent death of Alexander just before he had himself burned to death. The examples Cicero adduces from Greek history and literature were taken from Posidonius, who himself used earlier sources.[93] Posidonius compares the ability of the dream diviner to that of a dying man and offers one explanation for both phenomena. The ability to divine for others, manifest in the "historical" accounts of dying men, would therefore be proven for the dream diviner as well.

The seventh characteristic touches upon the appropriate place for dream divination. Divinatory dreams received in temples are well known from Greek literature.[94] It has been observed that this is the meaning of the "third impulse" for divination according to Posidonius, the same impulse that leads humans to dream divination: "that the gods themselves converse with sleepers" (*Div.* 1. 64). Not a few classical

92. There are many such claims; see the index to mainly doxographical testimonia under the entry σοφός in *SVF* 4: 128.

93. Pease (1963) 22 n. 100. On the reference to Hector, see Kidd 2: 430 who refers to Sextus Empiricus *Adversus mathematicos* 9. 21, where the observation is attributed to Aristotle. Posidonius may have been Cicero's intermediate source for this as well.

94. See Bouché-Leclercq (1879–82) 1: 271 ff.; Dodds (1951) 161 ff. For a detailed description of the arrangement of temple incubation, see, e.g., the inscription in Dittenberger (1920) no. 1004.

sources mention "contacts" with gods in the context of temple incubation, and the custom was particularly well-established in the temples of Asclepius.[95]

Sleeping in temples is mentioned twice in Cicero's *De divinatione*. In the first book, "Quintus" quotes a few examples of the influence of various types of divination on the policies and decisions of Greek cities and says in connection with dreams:

> Indeed, Lycurgus, who moderated the state of the Spartans, reinforced his own laws with the authority of Delphic Apollo. . . . And also those who ruled over the Spartans, not content with their waking deliberations, used to sleep in a shrine of Pasiphae that is in a field near the city in order to dream, since they believed that oracles of repose were true. (1. 96)

The source for this reference to Lycurgus seems to be Chrysippus (see paras. 37, 39) or Antipater of Tarsus (para. 39). Both these Stoics wrote works on dreams, and Posidonius based his own work on their works. It is fairly certain, therefore, that Posidonius was Cicero's intermediate source for this information. The emphasis is on the Spartan rulers receiving oracles (i.e., dreams) in a state of repose (*quietis*). This idea is repeated in clearly Posidonian passages (1. 61, from Plato, *visa quietis*; cf. 63, 110, 113, 116, 121). The method adopted also suits the other requirements of Posidonius—the removal of the dreamer from earthly concerns (1. 110, 115, 121).

Another pertinent passage appears in the second book of *De divinatione*, where Cicero asks during his critique of the proponents of dream divination:

> Can Aesculapius or Serapis through sleep prescribe for us a health cure, [but] Neptune cannot for sea captains? And if Minerva gives [knowledge of] medicine without a doctor, will the Muses not give sleepers the knowledge of writing, reading, and the other arts? But if health treatment were given [in this way], these also, which I have mentioned, would be given [in the same way]; [but] since these are not given [that way], [knowledge of] medicine is not given [that way]; with this removed, the whole authority of dreams is removed. (2. 123)

Cicero, as he states in the introduction to the first book, here quotes, in the second book, popular beliefs accepted by the Stoics concerning the temples of the gods mentioned. It may therefore be inferred that Posidonius was favorably disposed toward a belief in therapeutic dreams through incubation in temples.[96]

---

95. See Pease (1963) 209 and n. 1; Kidd 2: 432. See, e.g., Virgil *Aeneid* 7. 88–91; Iamblichus *On the Mysteries* 3. 2. 3; Plutarch *De genio Socratis* 24; Origen *Contra Celsum* 7. 35.

96. Posidonius may have been the source for Strabo's account of sleep as a means of receiving divination on medical matters in the temple of Serapis (17. 1. 17). Strabo used Posidonius in his Egyptian geography (17. 1. 5, 21), borrowing perhaps from one of his geographical works. There is a striking resemblance between the attitude toward dreamers in the temple of Serapis and that toward dreamers in the Jewish Temple.

In conclusion, the discussion has identified seven characteristics in Strabo's excursus concerning the method of divination recommended by Moses. Six are to be found in one form or another in the small proportion of Posidonius's total output that reached us. The remaining characteristic (integrity) may be Posidonian. Not one of the features (apart, perhaps, from the demand for a prior natural inclination to dream) is peculiar to Posidonius, or even to Stoics in general, but they are not found in this combination in any other author. This in itself would suggest that Posidonius is the most likely candidate as Strabo's intermediate source.

G. Jewish Theology

The concept of the divine entity presented by Strabo is discused by Ivor Ludlam in the appendix to this book. The discussion shows that Strabo's detailed description of the Jewish faith derives ultimately from Hecataeus of Abdera and was almost completely taken from one intermediate source (apart from a few words of interpretation by Strabo himself). This intermediate source described the Jewish divine entity in peculiarly Posidonian terms. Thus the account as a whole is a Posidonian intensive reworking of Hecataeus concerning Jewish religion. Posidonius's concept of the divine indicates that he could not have accepted anthropomorphism and material representation of the divinity. This in fact applies also to other Stoics.[97]

STRABO'S DIRECT SOURCE

Now that the questions pertaining to all the features of the excursus have been clarified, we are in a position to evaluate the four or five possibilities so far offered regarding the identity of the intermediate source. One possibility to be rejected outright is that the author was a Stoicizing Hellenistic Jew:[98] a Jew would never attribute female excision to the Jews;[99] and a Jew, no matter what education he had received, and whatever might be the aims of his work, would hardly describe Moses and the Jews who left Egypt as Egyptians.[100] The same reasons for rejection are applicable to the possibility that the excursus received a Jewish reworking.

In the discussion above on the connection between the excursus and the "appendix" attached to it (paras. 38–39), it has already been shown that Strabo

97. For their careful treatment of popular beliefs and cults, refraining from public deploration and finding indirect and circuitous methods to express their disapproval, see pp. 395, 512–14 below.

98. See esp. Nock (1959) 8; Gager (1972) 47; Lebram (1974) 234; Gabba (1988) 647–48; cf. Schürer (1901–9) 1: 156.

99. Cf. Strabo 17. 2. 5 (in the Egyptian ethnography) and esp. 16. 4. 9, portraying female excision in certain parts of Ethiopia as an activity performed according to the Jewish manner (αἱ γυναῖκες Ἰουδαϊκῶς ἐκτετμημέναι).

100. Correctly observed by Norden (1921) 278; Stern, GLAJJ 1: 266; id. (1976) 1135–37.

himself could not have been the original author of the excursus. Moreover, given the way he wrote and adapted his sources, the ethnography we have is too sophisticated to be attributable to Strabo, despite the philosophical education he had received. It is hard to believe that an author of his type would have bothered (and was able) to turn the unbiased Jewish excursus of Hecataeus and the hostile Manethonian version on the origin of the Jews into such an elaborate and imaginative Stoic utopia, especially considering the anti-Jewish material being spread in his day. Strabo's adherence to Stoicism is in itself rather questionable.[101]

Posidonius is actually the only candidate remaining as the author of the excursus. Indeed, there is a great deal of specific evidence that Posidonius was Strabo's source: the unique features of his Jewish state of the wise;[102] the distinction between the Mosaic period and the two stages of decline and degeneration subsequent to it;[103] and the identification of the second stage of degeneration with tyranny.[104] Posidonius was also the direct source for the speech of Moses that describes the Jewish divine entity.[105] There are ample reasons to conclude that the restrained, moderate cult practices ordained by Moses,[106] and the implied praise of Jewish self-isolation originated in Posidonius.[107] He was almost certainly the intermediate source for the sophisticated geographical description of Jerusalem and its environs.[108]

In addition to all this, other statements and features of the excursus have parallels in fragments and testimonia surviving from the writings of Posidonius (albeit not always unique to Posidonius): the absence of laws and governmental institutions from the ideal state, and their appearance only in the period of decline and degeneration;[109] the nostalgic-utopian description of a society without wars and without arms and the reservation from the use of arms;[110] and six out of seven specific characteristics of the recommended way of prophesying (the seventh characteristic has no direct parallel, although it sits well with the Posidonian way of thinking).[111] The combination of all these features speaks for itself.

A number of general considerations arise from the sources relevant to the dis-

101. See Ludlam, pp. 535–36 below.
102. See above, pp. 365–70.
103. See above, pp. 372–75.
104. See above, pp. 373–74.
105. See below, p. 525 ff., 540–41.
106. See below, pp. 379–80.
107. See above, pp. 369–70.
108. See above, p. 378.
109. See above, pp. 370–72.
110. See above, pp. 376–79.
111. See above, pp. 381–89.

cussion: Posidonius is one of the three sources Strabo uses explicitly for his geography of Judaea (paras. 28, 43, 44), in which the excursus is placed. The other two have no connection with the Jewish excursus: Eratosthenes was not a Stoic, and he lived several generations before the Hasmonaeans; Artemidorus, who wrote at least one *Periplous,* was no philosopher. Furthermore, Strabo uses Posidonius a great deal throughout his *Geographica* and mentions him over seventy times. Posidonius was Strabo's main source for Seleucid affairs in his historical works,[112] as well as for the account of the siege of Jerusalem by Antiochus Sidetes.[113] An ethnographic excursus on the Jews by Posidonius must necessarily have preceded the last account.[114] Why then would Strabo have preferred the version of some anonymous Stoic author to the Posidonian excursus that was already at his disposal? Why would he have abandoned Posidonius, whom he regarded as one of the greatest historians and ethnographers (despite occasional disagreements on geographical matters), precisely here, having used him liberally for his account of the relations between the Seleucid kings and the Hasmonaean rulers in his historical work, and for Judaea and its environs in his *Geographica?*

In light of all the evidence, it would be superfluous to posit as Strabo's source for the Jewish excursus not Posidonius but an anonymous Stoic author, holding unique opinions identical to those of Posidonius (and acquainted with the inaccurate and tendentious survey of Jerusalem by Timochares etc.). There is no need to opt for an alternative when there are no cogent and decisive reasons for doing so (see also chapter 13 below).

POSIDONIUS AND MOSAIC JUDAISM: AIMS AND PERSONAL BACKGROUND

The idealization of the Mosaic period in the Posidonian account should puzzle historians for a number of reasons. Posidonius was born and educated in Apamea, a Seleucid military settlement that provided the Seleucid army with soldiers for the phalanx, the backbone of Hellenistic armies. His main literary-philosophical activity began during the Hasmonaean period, at a time when the Jews drove out of the Holy Land what remained of Seleucid control there, and in doing so contributed to the final collapse of the Seleucid empire. Furthermore, the Hasmonaeans forcibly converted ethnic elements in the vicinity, expelled the inhabitants of a good number of cities from their lands, and destroyed Hellenistic temples and centers of culture and cult. As a result, some contemporary and later Hellenistic and Roman authors circulated hostile descriptions of Mosaic

---

112. See below, p. 413.
113. See below, pp. 409–17.
114. See pp. 448–51 below.

Judaism as the source of all the evils, which they attributed to the Jews of their time. In doing so, they followed the Hellenistic practice of explaining national customs as having been established by a founder (and, with regard to the Jews, they also followed the example set by Hecataeus of Abdera). Posidonius instead took the unprecedented step of praising Mosaic Judaism, while at the same time condemning the deeds of the Hasmonaean leaders and their priestly predecessors and calling contemporary Jewish customs "superstitions," and the Hasmonaeans "robbers."[115] What, then, led Posidonius to write such an unusual and enthusiastic account of Mosaic Judaism? Since his account differs on all essentials from the Jewish tradition concerning Moses and Jewish settlement in the Promised Land, it is also worth asking whether Posidonius had any real information on historical Judaism (save what he found in the Hecataean Jewish excursus).

Posidonius can hardly be assumed to have been ignorant of Jewish religion and basic customs. He invested much effort in learning about distant cultures, even traveling to such places as Hispania, North Africa, and South Gallia in order to investigate local features, both of the land and of the inhabitants. In Apamea itself there was a Jewish community,[116] and Posidonius, even if he left Apamea at a young age,[117] would surely have taken a special interest in the religion and customs of such an important and curious element of his native city. Just like his younger contemporary, Alexander Polyhistor, he was able to avail himself of the writings of Hellenistic Jewish authors who presented Judaism to the Gentiles.[118] The dissimilarity between the Posidonian account and historical Judaism cannot, therefore, be ascribed to ignorance. It is intentional and designed to further a certain aim.[119]

115. This extreme reference to the Hasmonaeans, despite their position as rulers of an independent, recognized state, recalls the Greek description of highlanders who occupied lowland plains, which is actually what the Jews had gradually done since the Restoration. On this *topos* in Greek sources, see Isaac (2004) 406 ff. It need not, therefore, indicate exceptional naval aggressive activity by the Jews, as several scholars tend to think, although in the generation of Pompey the term "robbers" certainly acquired an additional connotation.

116. On the Jews in Apamea, see Millar in Schürer et al., 1: 13–15.

117. See above, p. 342.

118. On Alexander Polyhistor, see esp. Freudenthal (1875); and Stern, *GLAJJ* 1: 157–64; Schürer et al., 3: 2, 510–12.

119. Berthelot (2003) 174–76 believes that the enthusiastic description of Moses is merely a device to underscore the wickedness of the Hasmonaeans. Mosaic Judaism is in her words a "contremodèle exact" (176) of the Hasmonaeans. If this is the case, it is rather strange that Mosaic Judaism receives such extensive and elaborate treatment while the Hasmonaeans earn barely three sentences. A condemnation of the Hasmonaeans would surely have been much better served by a detailed description of their nefarious deeds than by prolonged enthusiastic praise of Moses. It would sound even stranger that Posidonius attempted to degrade the Hasmonaeans by attributing to the founder of their nation all possible virtues in his philosophical system, in the fields of religion, society, and

Posidonius, who condemned later Judaism and the Jewish leaders of his time, surely would not have intended to promote the Jewish religion and customs. His aim, as may be discerned from his historical writing in general, was to exemplify or underscore his philosophical or historiosophical principles. Moses' statement that "the Greeks did not [behave] well in fashioning anthropomorphic [gods]," a *lapsus calami* of a sort, not to mention the many disguised messages, is sufficient to establish the didactic nature of the account.[120] The narrative medium was more attractive to readers, and they were often more likely to absorb philosophical ideas while immersed in a fascinating story or historical account. Educators have always been well aware of the advantages of this method over straightforward lecturing or preaching. Posidonius would certainly have been aware of it, being not only a great thinker, but also an excellent lecturer and teacher, and well versed in rhetoric.[121] It was already noted in the ancient world that Posidonius deviated quite openly from historical truth and adapted his material to his own philosophical end. In so doing, he did not refrain, in his description of societies, from embroidering beliefs and customs in order to make them more worthy of praise or blame (Ath. 4. 151e). We have already seen reflected in the Jewish excursus the religious, social, and political ideals of Posidonius. The degree of exaggeration and deliberate deviation from historical truth may be seen not only in the idealization of Mosaic Judaism, but also in the condemnation of contemporary Jews, where the Hasmonaeans leaders and their accomplishments receive harsh

---

state, and bothering to enlist for this purpose even his unique version of the Golden Age. Furthermore, there are more than a few elements in the description of Mosaic Judaism that are hardly the opposite of the deeds and convictions of the Hasmonaeans: the conception of the divinity; refraining from anthropomorphism and material representations of the divinity; the almost exhausting detail regarding many elements of dream divination; and reverence toward the Temple (maintained even by the tyrants, as explicitly stated at the end of para. 37). Had Posidonius truly wished to blacken the name of the Hasmonaeans at any price, even going to the lengths of attributing to their forefathers all the ideals cherished and preached by him as a foil, why did he not attribute to them the institution of the "superstitions," such as circumcision and excision and abstinence from types of meats? Why did he go out of his way to miss his mark by attributing these practices to "superstitious priests" who preceded the "tyrants"? In the same vein, why did he not attribute to the Hasmonaeans real misanthropic and misoxenic laws and customs? The actual terms *apanthrōpia*, *misanthrōpia*, and *misoxenia* are not mentioned (despite the evident use made of Hecataeus's excursus), and the customs inherited by "tyrants," namely, the Hasmonaeans, from the "priests" are merely "superstitions." The deploration of the Hasmonaeans is actually only a by-product of the excursus, exemplifying the Posidonian conception of the universal stages of deterioration. Finally, does not the negative reference to Greek anthropomorphic religion clearly reveal the real universal purpose and message of the account? See also note 24 above and note 124 below.

120. The contempt for Egyptian animal cult recurs in Greek literature; see Bar-Kochva (1996d) 98 and n. 137; Isaac (2004) 357.

121. See, in more detail, p. 347 above and pp. 474–77, 491–92 below.

descriptions such as " bands of robbers," and the Ethiopian-Egyptian custom of female excision is attributed to Jews of his time (para. 37).

Why was the genre of the ethnographic excursus chosen for this exposition? It was the most appropriate genre for the delivery of a detailed survey of an ideal society and its customs. In choosing to use it, Posidonius followed an established literary tradition. Already in the time of Hecataeus of Abdera, Hellenistic ethnography had developed a utopian or semi-utopian direction, with the idealizing of certain Eastern peoples and distant races beyond the known world often in an attempt to present role models for the developing Hellenistic society. The discovery of new cultures and societies in a period of general change and instability politically and socially motivated Hellenistic intellectuals to look for new models. Methodically similar responses to current developments can be found in later Hellenistic and even Roman ethnography as well (e.g., the *Germania* of Tacitus).

In literature of the time, two types of utopian ethnographies were common: one dealt with imaginary, mostly mythological peoples; the second with existing peoples. Good examples of the first sort are Hecataeus's work on the Hyperboreans of the far north and the utopia of Euhemerus on the Panchaeans, a tribe located on an island in the Indian Ocean. The remoteness of these imaginary peoples allowed the authors full freedom of imagination. At the same time, portraying social and political ideas through the agency of merely legendary peoples could have the drawback of arousing incredulity, and the ideas presented therein might appear unrealistic or impracticable. No such drawback afflicted the second type of ethnography, which dealt with well-known, existing, and successful peoples. Information on a certain people would be collated, fashioned, and interpreted in a manner that would convey the ideals and vision that the author wished to present. The best-known examples of this type are the monumental *Aegyptiaca* of Hecataeus of Abdera and the *Indica* of Megasthenes. Both served as models for later ethnographies in many respects, and not least the central didactic aspect.

Posidonius wrote at least one utopia. This was not in the form of an ethnography, but rather his presentation of the myth of the Golden Age. The ideal Golden Age society has acquired clearly Posidonian lines. Just like ethnographies of the first type, this account would have suffered from its mythological background. The heroes were legendary, its location was unknown, and its time was set vaguely in the first generations of mankind. The myth could be no more than an illustration, and hardly proof that the social model presented was practicable. Only the description of a well-known and existing society in the historical period, cast in Posidonian fashion, could demonstrate that the Posidonian vision was no mere pipe dream but had indeed already existed, thus providing proof of the model's practicability. The period of Mosaic Judaism was indeed set well after the end of the mythological Golden Age. It began in a period when there was already a well-developed Egyptian culture boasting many previous dynasties of kings—a period, according to Posidonian conceptions, entirely degenerate in religious and cultic terms. From this unpromising beginning sprang Mosaic society, a real, historical society—and if it happened once, it could happen again.

The similarity between the Judaism presented by Posidonius and his account of the Golden Age is the best evidence for the explanation presented above for the unusual description of Mosaic Judaism given by Posidonius. His description of Jewish society reduces the geographical extent of the Golden Age society but brings it much nearer, and makes it more relevant, to his own time. The exclusivity of the Jews, condemned by many authors, and the transition to a new country, are favorably reinterpreted by Posidonius to his own didactic advantage. He exploits these elements to fashion a practicable, credible model otherwise similar to that presented in his account of the Golden Age. Thus Posidonius could not only repeat what he had said about the Golden Age and the decline into tyranny but also underscore two additional messages. First, The way of life described in the account of the Golden Age is not lost for ever and only to be recalled with nostalgia, but is a socio-politico-religious plan worth realizing and realizable. Second, Posidonius could incorporate in his Jewish ethnography, by means of the speech he attributes to Moses, criticism of contemporary cultic practices, explicitly referring to the Greeks. The account of the Golden Age did not allow this, since no character at that time had experienced the period of degeneration and could not have referred to it in such a speech. By the very nature of that account, Posidonius had had to be content with a more restrained criticism of various contemporary corruptions and distortions, especially regarding religious subjects. The purportedly historical Moses could be more outspoken than Posidonius in his criticism of the religions popular in the time of Posidonius.

When Posidonius attributed to Moses criticism of anthropomorphism, which was common among many peoples, including the Greeks, he had an additional consideration in mind: the Stoics were not explicit in their condemnation of idol worship, at least not in public. The character Lucius Balbus, representing the Stoic view in Cicero's dialogue *On the Nature of the Gods,* is made to say that the ignorant many believe that gods have the form of a man (2. 45; cf. the criticism in paras. 59, 70). Yet we find him claiming that cult practice is important (2. 71, 79), and nowhere does he demand the scrapping of cult practice. Balbus consistently refrains from touching the heart of the problem. While he claims that the gods exist, he describes them, by means of etymologies, as forces of nature, noble qualities (such as faith and prudence), and things beneficial to man (such as corn and wine, 2. 59 ff.).[122] Balbus's speech well illustrates the dilemma of the Stoics: on

122. The speech of Balbus most clearly exemplifies the Stoic double standard. It must be noted, however, that Cicero's *De natura deorum* is a fictitious dialogue written by a Roman non-Stoic. While Cicero, as usual in his philosophical writings, bases his arguments on Greek philosophical

the one hand, their physical-theological system requires the denial of anthropo-morphism, but, on the other hand, their acceptance in society requires a degree of adaptation. The Stoics recognized the importance of cult practice in maintain-ing social order and understood that the ordinary man (a fool, in Stoic terms), being unable to grasp the true world-order and its governance, would accept no type of cult practice other than what he was used to. The tension between what the Stoic knew to be true and what could safely be said in a society of fools led Posidonius to a compromise typical of the Stoics. He has Moses, a historical model, an Egyptian wise man (but wise in the Posidonian Stoic sense), voice what are after all Stoic sentiments as if they are Mosaic. It is Moses, not Posidonius, who criticizes idol worship and anthropomorphism in general. Posidonius, like other philosophers, adopted a similar indirect strategy, and other methods of subterfuge and camouflage, whenever he wished to criticize contemporary prac-tices and leaders.[123]

Posidonius chose Judaism as the vehicle for his own ideas because of the accepted image of Jewish belief and cult. The Hellenistic world was aware that the Jews believed in one god and refrained from any representations of the divine. This view of the Jews had already led authors at the beginning of the Hellenistic period to describe the Jews as a community of philosophers. It would have cre-ated a favorable climate for a philosophical description of Mosaic Judaism that readers might have found credible. Posidonius took into account his readers' possible negative attitude toward contemporary Jews in distinguishing Mosaic Judaism from the later Judaism of the tyrants. The tyrants do not represent original Judaism, which had once been guided by enlightened principles. This form of presentation also suited Posidonius's conception of the degeneration in the lifestyle of mankind and individual peoples.[124]

texts, he adapts the arguments to his Roman audience, according to his own aims. With regard to the point concerning us here, however, parallels may be found, for example, in two testimonia of Diogenes of Babylon, an important third-second B.C.E. Stoic who taught Antipater of Tarsus who taught Panaetius, the teacher of Posidonius; see Diogenes, *SVF* 3: frr. 32–33 (pp. 216–17). Cf. also Diogenes Laertius 7. 147, where "Stoics" explain popular gods as various aspects of the one God.

123. See below, pp. 422–32; cf. pp. 512–14 on the Stoics and the Epicureans.

124. The main points in this section were discussed in my article (Bar-Kochva [1997a] 331–37, in Hebrew). Berthelot (2003) 173 responds that were the aim of Posidonius to prove that such a society as was described in the excursus had existed historically, in support of its practicability in the present, he would have taken Rome as his model. Posidonius, so the argument goes, did present various Roman individuals in a positive light, while contemporary Jews were as repugnant to him as to others. For this reason, the portrayal of Judaism as a role model would have been regarded as inconsistent by his readers. A society that had degenerated to such an extent could not be regarded as ideal. However, by the same token, human society of the Golden Age would not have been regarded as an ideal to strive for because of the subsequent decline. As for the possibility of portraying Rome as an ideal society, would Posidonius have been able to present the Rome of the kings (to Roman

Despite all that has been said so far, it may be supposed that Posidonius would not have chosen the Jews to illustrate the practicability of his Stoic ideal state if his own attitude toward Judaism and the Jews had not been basically favorable. In light of his theological views, it is only to be expected that Posidonius would have sympathized with Jewish insistence on monotheism as well as their resistance to anthropomorphism and any material representation of the divine. Posidonius may also have had contacts with Jews while still a youth in Apamea that had left upon him positive impressions and memories. At any rate, there seem to have been good relations between Jews and Gentiles in that mixed Syrian city. Posidonius would have been able to distinguish between them and the "tyrants" in Judaea. The late Menachem Stern drew attention to the fact that Apamea was one of only three mixed cities in Syria and the Holy Land in which the Gentile inhabitants did not harm their Jewish neighbors during the time of the great Jewish revolt against the Romans (Joseph. *BJ* 2. 479).[125] Posidonius was not the only Apamean author to express enthusiasm for Mosaic Judaism: Numenius, the second-century C.E. Pythagorean philosopher, called Plato "Moses speaking Attic."[126]

· · ·

Posidonius's positive view of Mosaic Judaism has not been transmitted by those Romans who were his students or who used him as a source in their own writing, such as Cicero and Seneca; they refer only to contemporary Jews, in contexts where their comments on Judaism had no need to encompass Mosaic Judaism, and where any positive reference would only have detracted from their purpose. Positive remarks on the forefathers of the Jewish people are hardly to be expected in Cicero's law-court speech in defense of Flaccus, a Roman noble charged with extorting from Jews money donated for the Temple in Jerusalem while serving as propraetor and governor of Asia Minor.[127] For all these reasons, one cannot

---

readers) or of the early Republic (to the general reader) as a society conforming with his religious, social, and political ideals? Did Romans believe in a divinity that in any way reflected his conception? Did they refrain from anthropomorphism or from the construction of many temples? Did they believe that one god was in all things? Was dream divination the only technique they employed to foretell the future? Could they, by any stretch of the imagination, be presented as pacifists? Much detailed work on Roman history and religion was already common knowledge in Posidonius's time, leaving him little leeway for adaptation to his Stoic principles. The Jews were still far more obscure, and the rumors about their origin and customs were highly inconsistent, to say the least. Posidonius could allow himself to do what he wished with the material at his disposal and knead the data into the shape required for his ends. Besides, Posidonius considered Roman history after 146 as a deterioration (p. 422 below).

125. Stern, *GLAJJ* 1: 143; id. (1976) 1124–25.

126. See in Stern, *GLAJJ* 2: 63a–e.

127. See esp. Lewy (1960) 79–114, and cf. Cicero's own observation that a defense lawyer does not express his own opinions in a court of law but adapts his speech to the needs of the case (*Clu.* 139).

tell what these Romans really thought—if they had any opinion at all—about "Mosaic" Judaism. Cicero, however, seems to have adopted the description of contemporary Judaism as a *deisidaimonia*, being the first Roman author on record to call the Jewish religion *barbara superstitio* (*Flac.* 28 [67]), thus inspiring quite a few later authors.[128] Conservative Roman authors rejected Judaism because of the threat it posed, along with other Oriental religions and cults, to Roman tradition and social stability. At the same time, traces of the Posidonian version, positive but marginal, may be detected in the Jewish ethnography of Tacitus, despite his overall great hostility.[129] Only Varro seems to have been decisively influenced by the positive account of Posidonius.[130] Posidonius may well have inspired his compatriot Numenius of Apamea. Despite Posidonius's apparently limited influence on Roman authors with regard to Mosaic Judaism, his great fame in Rome may have contributed somewhat to the fashion of contemporary Roman society to convert to Judaism or at least to take a positive interest in it; but this hypothesis still lacks textual evidence.

128. See p. 305 above.

129. Norden (1921) 297; Jacoby, *FGrH* II. C, no. 87, pp. 197–98; Bickermann (1937) 173; cf. Lewy (1960) 123 n. 37; Malitz (1983) 314–15; Bloch (2002) 17–26; (2004) 286–90. The link between the Jewish excursus of Tacitus and that of Posidonius is clearly seen in the description of the Dead Sea; see *Historiae* 5. 7 together with Strabo 15. 2. 42–44.

130. See esp. Varro in Augustine *On the City of God* 4. 31. On this passage, see Norden (1921) 298–301; Stern, *GLAJJ* 1: 207 ff., against Heinemann (1919) 121 n. 1.

12

Posidonius of Apamea (C)

Josephus on the Siege of Jerusalem
by Antiochus VII Sidetes (132/1 B.C.E.)—
Antiochus the Pious and Hyrcanus the Tyrant

In book 13 of his *Jewish Antiquities,* Josephus describes in relatively great detail the siege of Jerusalem by Antiochus VII Sidetes (paras. 236–47). The account contains unique features not to be found elsewhere in Josephus's works. A few scholars have already assumed that Josephus's version is based, directly or indirectly, on Posidonius.[1] Some consider Nicolaus or both Nicolaus and Strabo to be Josephus's immediate sources.[2] Others have suggested that Josephus drew on a Jewish source, alone or in addition to Gentile sources.[3] The account expresses definite views on the religion and customs of the Jews, and on their ruler as well. Establishing its source, or sources, and tracing its veiled messages may add to our understanding of Posidonius's attitude toward Jews and Judaism.

THE STORY OF THE SIEGE AND ITS RESULTS

Josephus's account (*AJ* 13. 236–52) runs as follows:

> (236) Antiochus, being angry on account of the things he had been made to suffer by Simon, invaded Judaea in the fourth year of his reign and the first of Hyrcanus's

---

1. See Scheppig (1869) 33–36; Nussbaum (1875) 35; Albert (1902) 30; Schürer (1901–9) 42; Marcus (1943) 350 note c; Adriani (1965) 88; and implied by Schürer et al. 1: 22; Malitz (1983) 310–11; Stern, *GLAJJ* 1: 184 has his doubts; cf. Friedländer (1903) 347–48; Böhl (1953) 124.

2. Nicolaus: Albert (1902) 30; Schürer (1901–9) 42; Marcus (1943) 350 note c; Stern, *GLAJJ* 1: 184; id. (1991) 460 n. 81 (based on Posidonius). Nicolaus or Strabo: Rajak (1981) 67–68; and, in effect, Hölscher (1904) 12.

3. Beloch (1879) 91; Hölscher (1904) 12; cf. Thoma (1994) 131–32. *Contra:* Rajak (1981) 67, 69, 70.

400 THE HASMONAEAN PERIOD

rule, in the 162nd Olympiad. (237) Having ravaged the countryside (*chōra*), he shut Hyrcanus in the city itself, and, surrounding it with seven camps, he at first accomplished nothing at all, both because of the strength of the walls and because of the excellence of those besieged and moreover because of the lack of water, from which a great rainstorm relieved them, when it poured down with the setting of the Pleiads. (238) But opposite the north part of the wall, where it happened also to be level, having set up one hundred towers three storeys high, he put up in them military units. (239) By making attacks every day and cutting a ditch, deep, and great and wide and double, he blockaded the inhabitants. They for their part contriving many sallies, if ever they fell upon the enemy unawares, did many things to them, but when the enemy perceived them,[4] they withdrew with agility. (240) When Hyrcanus observed that his great numbers were harmful, both because the supplies were being consumed more quickly by them and because no work was done such as would be reasonable from so many hands, he separated and drove out the useless (among the city's population), and as much as was in the prime of life and fighting fit, this [part] he kept. (241) Antiochus, however, prevented those rejected from going out, and they, [trapped] between the walls, suffering torments, began to die pitifully. Just then, however, the festival of Tabernacles came round, and those inside, taking pity, received them back in. (242) When Hyrcanus sent to Antiochus and requested a truce for seven days on account of the festival, Antiochus, deferring to piety (*eusebeia*)[5] toward the Deity, held a truce and moreover sent in a magnificent sacrifice: golden-horned bulls and gold and silver cups full of all sorts of spice. (243) Those at the gates, having received the sacrifice from those supplying it, led it to the sanctuary, while Antiochus feasted his army, differing very much from Antiochus Epiphanes, who, having captured the city, had sacrificed pigs on the altar and besprinkled the Temple with their fat, violating the customs of the Jews and their ancestral piety, for which things the nation was made hostile and irreconcilable. (244) All called this Antiochus, however, because of an excess of religious observance (δι᾽ ὑπερβολὴν τῆς θρησκείας), "pious" (*eusebēs*).

(245) Hyrcanus, having acknowledged his (Antiochus's) reasonableness, and having learned his seriousness toward the Deity (τὴν περὶ τὸ θεῖον σπουδήν), sent an embassy to him, requesting [that he] restore to them their ancestral constitution. He (Antiochus), although he had thrust aside[6] the plot[7] of those urging to

---

4. The reading of Niese followed by Marcus, αἰσθομένων, is surely wrong. Hudson's emendation αἰσθομένοις is closer to the MSS reading, parallels the dative in the earlier clause, and is intelligible.

5. Given the Stoic features of the account, *eusebeia* might have its Stoic sense of "knowledge of serving the gods" (ἐπιστήμη θεῶν θεραπείας—Diog. Laert. 7. 119; Sext. Emp. *Math.* 9. 123; Stob. *Ecl.* 2. 60. 9, 67. 20). However, Antiochus Sidetes, despite his positive—even "Stoic"—qualities, could hardly be described in terms specific for the Stoic wise man. Philosophers in their nontechnical writings would often take into account the concepts of laymen, and the term here should therefore be understood in its popular sense of "piety."

6. Reading the aorist participle ἀπωσάμενος as concessive.

7. The MSS read ἐπιβουλήν (plot). Marcus emends to ἐπιστολήν (letter), adopting also an earlier emendation, οὐκ ἀπωσάμενος, so that Antiochus is portrayed as not rejecting a letter from

root out the nation because of the nonmixing (*amixia*) of their way of life with regard to others, did not consider it;[8] (246) but believing that they (the Jews) were doing all according to piety (*eusebeia*), he replied to the envoys, that the besieged hand over their weapons and pay tribute (*dasmos*) to him for Jaffa and the other cities alongside Judaea and, having received a garrison, be freed of war on these conditions. (247) But they, while (they agreed) to endure the other things, they did not agree [to endure] the garrison, not coming into contact with others because of the nonmixing (*amixia*). Instead of the garrison, however, they would give hostages and five hundred talents of silver, of which they immediately gave three hundred and the hostages when the king consented; among whom was also a brother of Hyrcanus; but he pulled down the crown (i.e., battlement) of the city [wall]. (248) On these conditions, then, Antiochus raised the siege and withdrew.

(249) Hyrcanus opened the tomb of David, who surpassed [all] kings ever in wealth, and conveyed out three thousand talents of silver and, starting off from[9] these, became the first of the Jews to maintain mercenaries. (250) He also had friendship and an alliance with Antiochus and, receiving him into the city, supplied the army unsparingly and liberally in all things. And Hyrcanus set out with him when he was making an expedition against the Parthians. A witness for us of these things is also Nicolaus of Damascus relating thus: "Having set up a trophy by the river Lycus, having defeated Indates the general of the Parthians, Antiochus remained there for two days, Hyrcanus the Jew having requested [this] because of some ancestral festival in which it was not customary for the Jews to march out." (252) And in saying this he does not lie: for the festival of Pentecost had come round after the Sabbath, and it is not possible for us to march either on Sabbaths or on a festival. (253) But having engaged Arsaces the Parthian, Antiochus lost a great part of the army and was himself killed.

SOURCES OF THE STORY

A. Josephus's Direct Sources

Josephus's main source was certainly not Jewish, nor was it an oral tradition passed down through the generations. The Gentile touch is discernible, first and foremost in the statement that "the setting of the Pleiads" rescued the besiegers from a shortage of water (para. 237), in the dating of the event according to the Olympiads (para. 236), in the phrase "the customs of the Jews" (para. 243), and in the consistent use of the third person whenever reference is made to the Jewish people. An examination of the enthusiastic episode concerning the generous

---

Hyrcanus. Neither emendation is entirely necessary. The awkward structure of the sentence may be ascribed to the summarizing of the advice of the king's counselors reported in the original account (see pp. 410–12 below).

8. I.e., the immediate, unconditional restoration of the Jews' ancestral constitution.

9. Following the emendation of ὑπό to ἀπό: see Niese ad loc.

ceremonial sacrifice that Antiochus sent to the Temple (paras. 242–44) shows that even this is drawn from a Gentile author.[10] We may also note the request of Hyrcanus to restore to the Jews "their ancestral constitution" (para. 245). The source of this information seems to have been unaware of the annulment of restrictions on the Jewish religion by the Seleucid authorities, officially declared over thirty years before. Finally, it is highly unlikely that the words of praise heaped on Antiochus would have been taken from a Jewish source or added by Josephus. They are at odds with the description of Antiochus Sidetes in 1 Maccabees (15.25–31, 36–41) and in *Jewish Antiquities* itself in an earlier account (12. 225–26). Likewise, the negative portrayal of Hyrcanus stands in marked contrast to the spirit of Josephus's report in the following accounts (e.g., paras. 273, 282, 288–89, 299–300) and to the favorable image of "Johanan the High Priest" in Jewish tradition.

In a 1904 booklet on the sources of Josephus, Gustav Hölscher established that two lost works—Nicolaus's *Histories* and Strabo's historical work—were the main sources for Josephus's account of the Hasmonaean state in his *Jewish Antiquities*.[11] The evidence on the whole was convincing, although Hölscher was not always accurate. Much more evidence has since accumulated, and one may still disagree with the analysis and attribution of certain passages, paragraphs, and sentences.[12] The most telling proof is that Strabo and Nicolaus are explicitly mentioned by Josephus as his sources for several statements and events.[13] Josephus did, of course, occasionally use internal Jewish oral or written sources and official documents as well. In the same booklet, Hölscher established another rule that has been universally accepted: Josephus, for his earlier account of the Hasmonaean state in the *Jewish War*, condensed Nicolaus of Damascus and consulted no other source.[14] It should be noted here that Strabo's accounts of Hasmonaean rulers were included in his *Ta meta Polybion* ([Events] Subsequent to Polybius), and not in his *Historica hypomnēmata* (Historical Records), a work that seems to have recorded only select events of an earlier period.[15]

An analysis of the account in *Jewish Antiquities* concerning the development

10. See pp. 413–15 below.

11. Hölscher (1904) 11–17, 36–43; id., *RE* s.v. "Josephus" (2), col. 1994 ff.; cf. Schürer (1901–9) 1: 82–84; Schürer et al. 1: 50–51.

12. See, e.g., Bar-Kochva (1989) 187 n. 111, and note 27 below. As far as the siege by Antiochus VII is concerned, Hölscher failed to notice the basic contradiction between para. 250 and paras. 237–48, and he suggested a Jewish source for paras. 140–44.

13. *Antiquitates Judaicae* 13. 251, 287, 319, 347; 14. 35, 68, 104.

14. Hölscher (1904) 17–19; cf. Schürer (1901–9) 1: 83–84.

15. On Strabo's historical works, see Strabo 1. 1. 23, 2. 1. 9, 11. 9. 3; cf. *Suda* s.v. Πολύβιος. For a survey of the various views regarding Strabo's works—their number, titles, and structure—see Dueck (2000) 69–71. It appears from Strabo himself that he wrote three historical works: one on the

of the relationship between Hyrcanus and Antiochus Sidetes shows that Josephus used two sources that did not coincide. The main body of the account (paras. 237–47; henceforward, the "long siege story") elaborates on the great scarcity of basic foodstuffs in the city and the stubborn refusal of the Jews in the negotiations to allow foreign troops into the city. This objection was finally acknowledged by Antiochus, who thereupon waived this condition, recognizing the pious character of the Jewish separateness from foreigners (13. 245, 247). The "long siege story" ends with the lifting of the siege and Antiochus's withdrawal from Judaea. Afterward, Josephus relates that Hyrcanus had opened King David's tomb and removed from it three thousand silver talents, which enabled him to hire mercenaries (249). Then comes the following story (250; henceforward, the "reception story"):

> He also had friendship and an alliance with Antiochus and, receiving him into the city, supplied the army unsparingly and liberally in all things.

This is puzzling, to put it mildly. Where could the supplies have come from in a starved, exhausted, and besieged city? And in quantities sufficient to provide Antiochus's large army with everything they needed "unsparingly and liberally"?[16] Furthermore, does this happy atmosphere tally with the end of the "long siege story," where we are told that, contrary to the agreement (δὲ καὶ), the battlements were demolished (para. 247), indicative of lingering mutual bitterness and mistrust? Above all, the "long siege story" reports that Antiochus and his troops were not allowed into Jerusalem because of the principle of Jewish separateness, while in the "reception story" they are warmly accepted into the city. This last discrepancy invalidates a possible response that the "reception story" refers to a later diplomatic-ceremonial courtesy visit of Antiochus and his troops to Jerusalem or to a separate military expedition. On the strict principle of separateness, as presented and stressed in the report of the "long siege story," Antiochus and his army would not have been welcomed in Jerusalem, whether as conquerors or as guests. Furthermore, were this a new episode in a single source being followed by Josephus, one might have expected an introductory sentence to

---

period after 146, the closing date for Polybius's *Histories* (*Ta meta Polybion*); the second a selection of historical events preceding 146 (*Historica hypomnēmata*); the third a treatise on Alexander the Great (*Hai Alexandrou praxeis*). There is no justification for the tendency of many scholars to deviate from Strabo's explicit statement about his own works.

16. It might be suggested that the text implies that the supplies for Antiochus were paid for by the silver taken from David's tomb. From the parallel in the *Jewish War* (1. 61), however, it is clear that according to Josephus's source, the money from the grave was used only for convincing the king to raise the siege and for recruiting mercenaries. In any case, talents of silver would hardly have enabled the inhabitants of a besieged, starved city in a devastated land to immediately produce food and provide the enemy troops in the city with all things, "unsparingly and liberally" (para. 249). The reliability of the tomb episode is itself rather dubious (see below, note 22).

the "reception story" explaining that this is a later visit or a later expedition; but there is no such remark.

We are therefore obliged to assume that Josephus used two sources that recorded two different versions of the same event. Josephus himself did not preface any introduction to the "reception story," because he realized from the context of the original accounts that the two sources referred to the same event. He disregarded the contradictions, in line with his habit of mixing parallel sources—even when contradictory—without attempting to harmonize them. This is particularly noticeable in his account of the Hasmonaean state in *Jewish Antiquities,* which is a patchwork of parallel and sometimes contradictory accounts from different sources. In most cases there is no attempt at harmonization.[17]

The use of two contradictory sources may immediately be detected at the beginning of the account, when Josephus dates the invasion as follows: "in the fourth year of his (Antiochus VII's) reign and the first of Hyrcanus's rule, in the 162nd Olympiad." (236). The two sets of dates do not coincide: the dating according to the regnal years brings us to 135/4 B.C.E., while the 162nd Olympiad covers the years 132–128. There is no way of reconciling the two datings.[18]

The two sources need to be identified and distinguished. As Nicolaus and Strabo are the two main sources used by Josephus for the account of the Hasmonaean state, and there are no real traces of an internal Jewish source here, we may assume that Nicolaus and Strabo were Josephus's sources in this case as well. The chronological contradiction can now be explained. Hölscher proved convincingly that the regnal years in Josephus's account of the Hasmonaean state and Herod's reign were taken from Nicolaus, while the Olympiad reckoning derived from Strabo.[19] Our main interest, however, is the colorful and lively account referred to as the "long siege story."

The key to distinguishing between the two sources, as already established by Hölscher, is the parallel account in the *Jewish War* (1. 61), which derives solely from Nicolaus. Details in *Jewish Antiquities* that are identical to those in the *Jewish War* may be traced back to Nicolaus. Components of the other account should, therefore, be traced back to Strabo. The version in the *Jewish War* (1. 61) reads as follows:

---

17. See, e.g., *Antiquitates Judaicae* 13. 276–77 vs. 278–79; 301–16 vs. 318–19; 348–50 vs. 351; 352 vs. 353; 356 vs. 358; 14. 34 vs. 38–41.

18. For attempts to harmonize the dating in Josephus, and on the dates in Porphyry and Eusebius, see Thackeray (1943) 347 n. a; Vermes in Schürer et al. 1: 202 n. 5; cf. Graetz (1888) 652–54.

19. Hölscher (1904) 40–41; cf. 11–12. It is supported, in this case, by the context as well; see next note. On the reference to the Olympiad year at *Bellum Judaicum* 1. 415 (= *AJ* 16. 136), based on Nicolaus, see the explanation of Hölscher, 40–41: it was mentioned by Nicolaus in that exceptional case because of the special context, the establishment of the five-year cycle of games in Caesarea. Incidentally, Posidonius (like Polybius and Strabo) also used the Olympiad system; see Malitz (1983) 64 and n. 30.

Antiochus, being angered by [what] he had suffered [at the hands of] Simon, marched to Judaea and besieged Hyrcanus, sitting down against the Jerusalemites. And he (Hyrcanus) opened the tomb of King David, who was the wealthiest of the kings, and taking away more than three thousand talents, both persuaded Antiochus to raise the siege by [payment of] three hundred talents, and, using the surplus, was the first [of the Jews] to maintain mercenary troops.

This account begins by stating that Antiochus's expedition was an angry reaction to what he had suffered at the hands of Simon, Hyrcanus's father.[20] Antiochus is said to have invaded Judaea and besieged Jerusalem (cf. *AJ* 13. 236–37). So far the two versions run parallel (except for the mixed dating, which does not appear in the *Jewish War*). From here on, however, they differ: the version in the *War* says not a single word about the dramatic and complex events that took place in Jerusalem according to the "long siege story." Might this silence be attributed to the omission of material by Josephus in keeping with the epitome that the first two books of the *War* constituted? Probably not. Josephus tended to preserve even in the most abbreviated accounts of the *Jewish War* something of the piquant (e.g., 1. 57–60, 72–84). Indeed, he pays attention to the scandalous looting of King David's tomb in this very account, and it is unlikely that Josephus would have passed over other extraordinary pieces of information had they been reported in the sole source for his earlier book. This itself would suffice to indicate that the source for the "long siege story" is not Nicolaus but Strabo. It is worth noting that in the *Jewish War* it is said that Hyrcanus "persuaded" (πείσας) Antiochus with money to lift the siege. There is no hint of a payment following an ultimatum from the king, as asserted in the "long siege story," nor of the other conditions for lifting the siege.

The conclusion is corroborated by a comparison of the episode of the opening of the tomb of David in both of Josephus's works. The *Jewish War* tells us that Hyrcanus removed from David's tomb three thousand silver talents and with three hundred of them persuaded the king to lift the siege. The rest were used to hire mercenaries. *Jewish Antiquities* also reports—in the "long siege story"—the payment of the three hundred talents (out of a debt of five hundred), before the blockade is lifted (para. 247).[21] There is, however, no indication in *Jewish*

20. The parallel sentence in *Jewish Antiquities* is followed by the dating by regnal years, according to which the expedition took place in the first year of Hyrcanus. The date of the expedition is thus properly explained by the former sentence. The second part of the dating, that of the Olympiad, bringing us at the earliest to the fourth year of Hyrcanus, is obviously less connected with the opening sentence. For the background to Antiochus VII's hostility to Simon, see *Antiquitates Judaicae* 13. 226–27, and on its source in Nicolaus, p. 407 below. This further suggests that the regnal years were taken from Nicolaus, and the Olympiads from Strabo.

21. The sum of three hundred talents seems to have been the *phoros*, the annual tax, which implied recognition of the supremacy of the Seleucid king, and the outstanding two hundred talents

Antiquities of the source of this money. The tomb episode appears there only after the king has departed (para. 249), and precedes the "reception story." The treasure is not used there for paying the tribute, but only for maintaining mercenaries. Yet the tomb episode in both accounts of Josephus clearly derives from the same source, namely, Nicolaus. The reason why Josephus in *Jewish Antiquities* omitted a reference to the payment to the king during his report of the tomb episode is because he had already mentioned that payment earlier in the "long siege story" (para. 247). The question then arises why the tomb episode was not recounted on that occasion, in its appropriate context. The most plausible answer would be that the tomb episode was not taken from the same source as the "long siege story." We may note, indeed, that the "reception story" follows the Nicolaean tomb episode. Since the tomb episode derived from Nicolaus, the "long siege story" would have been taken from Strabo.

The payment of three hundred talents, then, was reported in both sources used by Josephus, but with two differences: Strabo (= the "long siege story") did not explain the source of the money and mentioned an obligation to pay five hundred talents, of which three hundred were immediately remitted (*AJ* 13. 247), while Nicolaus recorded the tomb episode in his story of the siege to explain the source of the money, adding a note about future mercenaries and referring to three hundred talents only (*BJ* 1. 61).

Nicolaus's fingerprints may be detected in another reference in the tomb episode. Josephus reports in the sequence of Herod's reign that the Idumaean-Jewish ruler tried to follow Hyrcanus's example and find treasures in David's tomb. Herod himself took part in the attempt to enter the tomb but was deterred by an epiphany. In order to atone for the sacrilege, Herod erected a monument on David's tomb (*AJ* 16. 179–82). Josephus goes on to criticize Nicolaus for not having mentioned that Herod personally descended to the tomb (183–87). Here again Nicolaus is Josephus's main source for the Herodian era; the reference to Hyrcanus's attempted theft as an earlier Jewish precedent is designed to make Herod's attempt appear less pernicious. Such an intention could hardly be attributed to Josephus. The reference to Hyrcanus was certainly included in the report about Herod by Nicolaus, Herod's court historian. Even if the story about Hyrcanus was not invented by

---

were a special tribute for the recently occupied "corridor" to the sea (Jaffa-Gazara-Pegai). It might appear from the previous paragraph (246) in the version of the *Jewish Antiquities* that the whole sum (five hundred talents) was a tribute imposed on the "corridor" to the sea; but if this were so, it would be an excessive amount. The sum of three hundred talents was equal to that of the annual *phoros* of the whole of Judaea (see 1 Macc. 11.28, 13.15; and see Bar-Kochva [1977] 172–73; Stern [1995] 51 n. 5, 78 n. 22). Indeed, in his abbreviated account of the siege, taken from Posidonius of Apamea (pp. 412–13 below), Diodorus states explicitly that Antiochus obtained from Hyrcanus the *phoroi* owed to him (34/35. 1.5). The two hundred outstanding talents were therefore an additional payment for the "corridor."

Nicolaus—and when it comes to this most creative court historian one can never know[22]—Nicolaus certainly knew about the story and recorded it in the sequence of his report on the Hasmonaean rulers.

And there is another point. The "long siege story" praises Antiochus Sidetes' personality and his attitude toward the Jews. But in a previous chapter in *Jewish Antiquities,* Josephus accuses Antiochus of "covetousness and dishonesty" and even of "lawless conduct" (*paranomia*) and "unjust treatment" of Simon (13. 225–26).[23] It has already been established that Josephus's account of Simon's rule (143–135 B.C.E.) in *Jewish Antiquities* (13. 213 ff.) derives solely from Nicolaus,[24] who in turn drew from 1 Maccabees for a large part of his section on Simon, including the statement quoted above (cf. 1 Macc. 15.27). Nicolaus sharpened the meaning of the biblical phrases deploring the Seleucid king in 1 Maccabees. He was certainly not an ardent admirer of Antiochus VII.

There is also another piece of evidence: in his account of the relations between Simon and Antiochus Sidetes, deriving from Nicolaus, Josephus says: "And he (Antiochus) sent envoys to Simon, the High Priest of the Jews, concerning friend-

22. See Bar-Kochva (1977) 182–85 for doubts about the historicity of the episode involving Hyrcanus. I have suggested that the story was invented by Nicolaus. However, I tend now to think that the story is a defamatory rumor spread through the years by the opponents of the Hasmonaean family to explain the source of money for the compensation to Antiochus Sidetes and for hiring mercenaries. The rumor may have inspired Herod or just been used by Nicolaus, his court historian, for his obvious purposes. Fischer (1975a, 1983) tries to give credence to the story by a rather bold numismatic conjecture. His theory fails for a number of reasons. First, the tetradrachm bearing the portrait of Antiochus Sidetes, which Fischer attributes to John Hyrcanus, is based on the Attic standard (17.5 g). However, following the special relations between Ptolemy VI and Alexander Balas, the Seleucid coins from Coile Syria and Phoenicia were minted according to the Ptolemaic standard (14.2 g for a tetradrachm) as from the reign of Alexander Balas. This applies also to the coins of Antiochus VII Sidetes; they even show the Ptolemaic eagle on the reverse. The tetradrachm discussed by Fischer must have been minted elsewhere, probably in north Syria. Second, the identification of the monogram on that coin with the first Greek letters of the name of Hyrcanus seems rather fanciful. Third, in view of the style of Hasmonaean minting and the strict religious convictions of John Hyrcanus, a human portrait (and of foreign king at that), which even Herod did not allow himself, would be inconceivable on a coin of Hyrcanus. Fourth, the floral ornament on a bronze coin of Antiochus Sidetes, compared by Fischer to the above-mentioned tetradrachm, is not the lily of the Jewish High Priest but is more likely to be the pomegranate flower, symbol of Antiochus Sidetes (*sidē* = pomegranate). Fifth, the monogram BA on another bronze coin, discussed by Fischer and used to support his proposal, has nothing to do with Alexander Jannaeus. The coin probably belongs to Antiochus VIII Gryphus (see Meshorer [1982] 1: p. 56, nos. 5–7), and the monogram, which is very convoluted, seems to indicate the name of the minter, and not BA[ΣΙΛΕΥΣ], as suggested by Fischer. Finally, the silver tetradrachm that is the basis of Fischer's hypothesis has been attributed by Newell to the mint of Damascus (Newell [1939] 45 nn. 62–63; 103; and pl. 8), and there is no reason why this should not be accepted.

23. Cf. Friedländer (1903) 347–48.

24. Hölscher (1904) 9, 11; cf. Bar-Kochva (1989) 452–53.

ship and a military alliance (*symmachia*). And he (Simon) readily accepted his offer and provided the soldiers besieging Dora with much money and supplies" (*AJ* 13. 223–24). The similarity between the two passages is too striking to be purely coincidental.

Nicolaus's account (the "reception story") may thus be reconstructed according to the *Jewish War* and its surviving fragment in *Jewish Antiquities:* after a short siege, Hyrcanus decided to appease the king in every possible way and went so far as to open David's tomb in order to pay the annual tax, contract a military alliance with the king, admit him to the city, and lavishly provide the troops with supplies. Strabo's version (the "long siege story"), on the other hand, recorded a protracted and difficult siege, Sidetes' enormous military efforts, the hunger and shortages in the city, the truce during the "festival of Tabernacles," the presents of the king to the Temple, the negotiations, the terms of surrender, the refusal to admit a garrison, and finally the demolition of the battlements and the king's departure.

The identification of Nicolaus as the source of the "reception story" may be further supported by the paragraphs subsequent to the "reception story." They recount that Hyrcanus accompanied Antiochus on his expedition against the Parthians. To enhance this report, Josephus quotes Nicolaus in direct speech, mentioning him explicitly (para. 251). The connection between the reference to the military alliance and the participation of Hyrcanus in the Eastern expedition is obvious.[25]

It should be stressed that the absence of any reference in the *Jewish War* to the participation of Hyrcanus in the Eastern expedition of Antiochus Sidetes does not pose any difficulty. The "reception story" and the report about the expedition were not located side by side in Nicolaus's *Histories,* since two years separated them.[26] This is also apparent from the introduction of Hyrcanus in the later event as "Hyrcanus the Jew," in the quotation from Nicolaus (para. 251).[27] It would appear that Strabo's account did not record the Jewish participation in

25. The introductory statement, "A witness to these [things] is *also* Nicolaus of Damascus," does not indicate that Josephus used another source for his narrative, as has been suggested by Pucci (1983b) 120. If not merely a literary convention, this is simply a device used by Josephus to give the (false) impression that he is using more than one source; see, e.g., *Antiquitates Judaicum* 13. 287, 319, 347; and cf. his phrasing in 12. 135; 14. 104.

26. On the chronology and duration of this expedition, see Schwartz (1995), and references there to earlier views.

27. And a similar absentee: in the subsequent paragraph in the *Jewish War* (para. 62), Josephus says that Antiochus Sidetes' expedition against the Medes provided an opportunity for Hyrcanus to launch a campaign against his neighbors. In *Jewish Antiquities,* Josephus explains that Hyrcanus began his campaign with the arrival of the news of Sidetes' death on his Eastern expedition. Neither reference notes that Hyrcanus himself participated in the same expedition. The dating of Hyrcanus's campaign against his neighbors immediately after the expedition (129/8 B.C.E.) is unacceptable

the expedition. It was not consistent with Jewish "nonmixing" with other people stressed so much (and justified) in his version of the siege, the "long siege story" (paras. 245, 247).

To conclude this section, then, the narrative of the siege in *Jewish Antiquities* runs as follows: after some consecutive paragraphs, which derive from Nicolaus, describing the reign of Simon (paras. 213–35), the story opens with Nicolaus's note on the motive for the invasion of Judaea (para. 236); Josephus mixes the datings from Nicolaus (regnal years) and Strabo (Olympiads); the opening sentence is followed by a detailed account of the siege up to the king's departure (the "long siege story"), which derives exclusively from Strabo (paras. 237–48); Nicolaus returns to tell about the looting of David's tomb (para. 249); then comes the second version—the reception of the king and the troops in the city and the alliance treaty (the "reception story," para. 250a); Josephus goes on to use Nicolaus again for the report on Hyrcanus's participation in the expedition against the Parthians and the halting of the entire army for two days because of a Jewish holiday (paras. 250b–253). All this means that apart from the opening "mixed" sentence, Josephus placed side by side in his account in *Jewish Antiquities* two different versions: first, the "long siege story" from Strabo (paras. 236–48), and then, without a break, the version of Nicolaus: the episodes of the tomb, the king's reception, his troops, and the participation of Hyrcanus in the Eastern campaign (paras. 249–53). Josephus omitted from Nicolaus's account the opening description of the start of the siege, which was rendered redundant by the preceding "long siege story" from Strabo. Josephus failed, as usual, to blend the two accounts into one convincing whole. The tomb episode and the reception story from Nicolaus are incongruous, the former entirely out of place in every way following Strabo's "long siege story."

B. Sources Used by Strabo, Diodorus, and Plutarch

The actual subject of our investigation is the "long siege story" (paras. 237–48). It has just been concluded that this detailed version derives from Strabo. Strabo, however, was not a contemporary of the events; nor was he really an original historian, but mainly a compiler. It is evident from the incompatibility of the two versions of the siege that Strabo did not use Nicolaus for this event,[28] and one must look elsewhere for his sources of information regarding the siege.

---

on historical counts (see Stern [1965] 149; Bar-Kochva [1989] 560–62), and the excavations in Mt. Garizim and Marisa in the last decade of the last century indeed proved that it took place sixteen years later (see Barag [1992/93]; Bar-Kochva [1996d] 131 and nn. 28–29); Shatzman (2005) 237–40. Hyrcanus's campaign was probably recorded in a much later context in the *Histories* of Nicolaus. The mistaken chronological sequence may well be Josephan.

28. In his *Geographica* Strabo used one reference from either the *Histories* or the biography of Augustus written by Nicolaus (15. 1. 72–73); hence the hypothesis of some that Strabo used Nicolaus intensively as a source for his historical work. However, Strabo's work on the period after Polybius's

The "long siege story" in Josephus's account of the siege has a strikingly similar parallel in Diodorus (34/35. 1. 1–5), preserved by Photius, the ninth-century
patriarch of Constantinople (*cod.* 244, 379a–380a).[29] Both Josephus and Diodorus
say that when the city ran out of supplies, Hyrcanus tried to negotiate; however,
the king was advised to annihilate the Jewish people; the counselors accused the
Jews, in Josephus, of "the nonmixing (*amixia*) of their way of life with regard
to others" (para. 245), and, in Diodorus, "[the Jews] alone of all nations did not
take part in dealing with any other people" (para. 1; cf. para. 3: "not to share table
with any other nation"). Both authors go on to say that Antiochus rejected the
accusations and disregarded the advice; he took hostages, imposed an annual
tribute, and destroyed the city walls or battlements.[30] In addition, the Josephus
version praises Antiochus Sidetes for his piety (*eusebeia*) toward the Jewish God,
as against Antiochus Epiphanes, who "sacrificed pigs on the altar and besprinkled the Temple with their fat" (para. 243), while according to Diodorus, the
king's advisers recounted as a historical precedent that Antiochus had sacrificed
a pig and smeared the holy books with its broth (para. 4). The disagreements are
marginal and originate in a slight paraphrase made by Josephus, Diodorus, or
Strabo.[31] The real difference is in the elaboration and emphasis of the two versions: while Josephus describes the siege in great detail and refers only briefly to
the practical advice of the anti-Jewish counselors and to one of their accusations,

---

Histories was written much earlier than his *Geographica,* probably even before Nicolaus's *Histories.*
One would also doubt whether a respectable person would have actually copied detailed accounts
from a work written in the same language by an author living at the same time in the same city.

29. For the full quotation of the text, see pp. 441–42 below.

30. There is a difference between Josephus and Diodorus with regard to the treatment of the
walls. Josephus speaks of the destruction of the battlements (*stephanē*), while Diodorus (cf. Porph..
ap. Eus. *Chron.* 1. 255) refers to the demolition of the walls (noted by Schürer [1901–9] 260 n. 6).
Josephus's version seems to be correct in view of the general atmosphere of reconciliation in the
detailed account preserved by him. Diodorus was thus inaccurate in his paraphrase, and Porphyry
drew on his version. Rajak (1981) 71 n. 9 prefers Josephus's version because it is more "precise" as
against the "general" statement by Diodorus. She rightly compares the former to the token demol-
ishing of a small part of the Giscala wall in Josephus *Bellum Judaicum* 4. 117.

31. In addition to the discussion in the previous note, another marginal difference deserves
attention. Diodorus has ὗν ("pig," acc. sing.), while Josephus has ὗς ("pigs," acc. pl.), which may be
influenced by his former reference in *Antiquitates Judaicum* 12. 252, based on 1 Maccabees 1.47. The
reference to fat is rather similar in both accounts. Diodorus has τῷ ἀπὸ τούτων ζωμῷ; Josephus, τῷ
ζωμῷ τούτων, except that Diodorus is referring back to τὰ κρέα ("pieces of meat"), which are not
mentioned by Josephus. If Diodorus preserves the original phrasing, it is also possible that Josephus,
having mistakenly omitted τὰ κρέα, made one pig many in order to account for τούτων ("of these").
Finally, the original account may well have described holy books and the area "around the Temple"
being smearing with pig fat. It may be suggested that Josephus omitted the reference to the defilement of the books because his source explicitly stated that this was Antiochus IV's reaction to the
"misanthropic laws" contained in those books (see Diod. 34/35. 1. 3–4).

Diodorus condenses the military events into a few sentences but fully records the advice of the king's "friends," including a detailed account of the anti-Jewish accusations and libels said to have been raised by them.

Either Diodorus himself or Photius omitted most of the details about the siege. By and large, Diodorus did not show much interest in military details;[32] analysis of his accounts of siege campaigns and field battles indicates substantial abbreviations of his sources, including the omission of even essential passages and data.[33] The absence of the siege account can be attributed to Diodorus's concern not to exceed the length he had set for his work. He may have considered yet another siege account to be redundant in a work that already contained a good number of siege campaigns. But this is still only a guess. One can never be quite certain with a dull and unoriginal author such as Diodorus why he decided to shorten such a narrative. At the same time, the abbreviation could be the work of Photius, who is known to have omitted details detracting from his main theme.[34] Photius would not have found the detailed military and diplomatic information useful for his overt, specific purpose in quoting the passage, to prove that "Diodorus is lying" with regard to the Jews (379a).

The reason for the omission of most of the accusations and the libels in Josephus's account is quite obvious: Josephus could not be expected to have incorporated in his consecutive historical narrative extreme accusations and defamatory stories about the Jews, even were they to be flatly denied in the exposition. It would have been impossible to refute point by point all the charges and libels with reference to their appropriate historical and literary contexts in what was designed as a coherent and consecutive history. Josephus later gave a full and detailed refutation of such stories in his *Contra Apionem*, written precisely for the sake of argument. Notwithstanding, as shown above, explicit references to the counselors' advice are clearly discernible in Josephus's version of the reaction of the king to the anti-

32. See even the comment of Sacks (1990) 99, probably Diodorus's most ardent advocate, and n. 67 there for more references.

33. A good parallel can be provided by Diodorus's account of Demetrius Poliorcetes' siege of Rhodes in 305–304 B.C.E. (20. 81 ff., esp. 93–94). A comparison with a literary papyrus found in Egypt in 1918 shows that both derive from a common source, certainly Hieronymus of Cardia. Each contains information not found in the other, with Diodorus omitting episodes and detailed portions of the narrative; see Hornblower (1981) 29–31. For Diodorus's negligence in cutting military accounts in his sources, sometimes in the most important sections, see, for example his version of the battle of Gaza, based on the accurate and detailed account by Hieronymus of Cardia (19. 81–84). Diodorus skips over the developments in the center of the battlefield as well as those on Demetrius's right wing. On the lacunae in Diodorus's version, see Kromayer and Kahnes in Kromayer and Veith (1903–32) 4: 434–46, esp. 441–45; Delbrück (1920) 1: 243. It is difficult to accept the interpretation of Seibert (1969) 173–74.

34. On the method of Photius, see Palm (1955) 16–26, 29 ff., 48 ff.; Hägg (1975) 9 ff., 193–203, esp. 211–12; Treadgold (1980) passim.

Jewish accusations and his rejection of the practical advice, as well as in the brief (and actually out of context) mention of the extreme acts of defilement performed by Antiochus IV in the Jerusalem Temple. These do not significantly disturb the fluency of the historical narrative.

Despite their different emphases, the two accounts are so similar that they clearly derive from a common source. Posidonius of Apamea was recognized as Diodorus's source for the events surrounding the siege.[35] The strongest argument appears from the analysis of Diodorus's sources and method of compilation. A comparison with certain surviving Posidonian fragments proves that Diodorus drew on Posidonius's *Histories* from book 33 of his *Historical Library* to book 37, covering the period from 146 to 86 B.C.E., and it has long been established that Diodorus was in the habit of adhering to just one source, in one or more books or on one subject (the "Einzelquelleprinzip"). Thus in the first book of the *Historical Library*, which is devoted to Egyptian ethnography and history, he drew mainly on Hecataeus of Abdera,[36] whereas Hieronymus of Cardia was his sole source for early Hellenistic history in books 18–20 (excluding accounts on Sicily, his native country).[37] In books 33–37 Diodorus drew on Posidonius even with regard to Sicilian history.[38] The contentions of two or three scholars, who relate Diodorus's account of the siege of Jerusalem to another source, do not stand up to criticism.[39]

35. Müller, *FHG* II, p. XV; III, p. 251 and fr. 15; Susemihl (1891–92) 2: 142–43; Reinach (1895) 56–59; Schürer (1901–9) 1: 42; Stählin (1905) 24; Radin (1915) 170; Heinemann (1919) 119–20; Norden (1921) 281–82; Meyer (1921–23) 2: 268 n. 3; Reinhardt (1928) 28–29; Bickermann (1927) 251, 260; Jacoby, *FGrH*, II. A, no. 87, fr. 109, pp. 294-95; II. C, pp. 196, 208–9; Schürer et al. 1: 21–22; Rajak (1981) 68; Theiler (1982) 1: 111 (fr. 131a), 2: 95–96; Malitz (1983) 309–12. With hesitation: Gager (1972) 126; Stern, *GLAJJ* 1: 142–43, 168; id. (1991) 706; Kidd 2: 949–50; Bar-Kochva (1996b) 22–24; Berthelot (2003) 177 ff. Kidd does not include the excerpt, since the collection is restricted in principle to fragments and testimonia that were explicitly attributed to Posidonius (see pp. XV-XVII).

36. See the detailed bibliography and some new arguments in Bar-Kochva (1996d) 14–15, 289–90.

37. See the latest discussion by Hornblower (1981) 18–75, esp. 32–62, and references to earlier literature there.

38. On Posidonius as the source for these books of Diodorus, see Toepelmann (1867) 44; Schep-pig (1869) 36–37; Busolt (1890) 321 ff., 405 ff.; Schwartz, *RE* s.v. "Diodoros," col. 690 ff.; Norden (1923b) 144; Reinhardt, *RE* s.v. "Poseidonios," col. 630 ff.; Jacoby, *FGrH* III. C, no. 87, p. 157; Rosenberg (1921) 199 ff.; Strassburger (1965) 42; Momigliano (1975) 33–34; Malitz (1983) 34–41. For Posidonius as the source of Diodorus's Sicilian history in these books, see Athenaeus 12. 542b = Diodorus 34. 34 (noted by Momigliano, 33–34).

39. Willrich (1895) suggests Polybius as Diodorus's source, which is impossible in view of the chronological framework of Polybius's *Histories* (but see Willrich [1900] 87, 89, 147). Aly (1957a) 199–200 points out that Strabo's Jewish excursus, which, as he says, is believed by a number of schol-ars to draw on Posidonius, uses the form *Mōsēs* (Μωσῆς, 16. 2. 35 ff.) while Diodorus uses *Mōysēs* (Μωυσῆς). However, Diodorus used these two different forms in two places in his work adhering to the sources he used; see p. 240 above. Gager (1972) 126 notes that Josephus (*Ap.* 2. 79) does not mention Posidonius among the Greek authors who referred to Antiochus IV's "motives for raiding

The account of the siege of Jerusalem seems to have been taken from somewhere in books 12–14 of Posidonius's *Histories*.[40]

All this leads to the inevitable conclusion that the "long siege story" in Josephus is also based on Posidonius. As is almost universally acknowledged, Josephus himself was not acquainted with Posidonius's works,[41] but Strabo, his intermediate source, did have direct access to the Posidonian corpus. Strabo evidently utilized much of it extensively in the *Geographica,* explicitly mentioning Posidonius more than seventy times. The Jewish excursus is just one example. As for Strabo's historical work, as its title—*Ta meta Polybion*—shows, it was a consecutive history of the years subsequent to those covered by Polybius (Strabo *Geogr.* 11. 9. 3; *Suda,* Codex A, s.v. Polybios), that is, from 146 B.C.E. onward. This matches the starting point of Posidonius's historical work (*Suda,* Codex A, s.v. Polybios).[42] In view of the identical historical framework and the extensive use made of Posidonius in the *Geographica,* it is inconceivable that Strabo did not use Posidonius's *Histories* as one of the main sources for his own work. As we shall see below, Posidonius's fingerprints are all over Josephus's "long siege story."

Attention should also be paid to another, shorter version of the siege. The sacrifice sent by Antiochus VII to the Temple is recorded in somewhat more detail in a work attributed to Plutarch (*Apophthegmata* 184F):

When the Jews, while he (Antiochus) was besieging Jerusalem, asked for a respite of seven days for the greatest festival, he not only granted this, but, having prepared

---

the Temple." However, Josephus was not directly acquainted with Posidonius's *Histories* (see note 41 below). See also Böhl (1953) 124 (followed by Schäfer [1997a] 59) and Rajak (1981) 68 n. 5 for arguments and counterarguments.

40. Malitz (1983) 66, 309, suggests the fifteenth book; Kidd 2: 299 suggests "books 14–16." Müller, *FHG* III. 256, Norden (1921) 297 n. 11, and Theiler (1982) 2: 95 advocate the seventh book, which is impossible. According to Jacoby's reconstruction, it was somewhere in the twelfth–sixteenth books (*FGrH* II. A, no. 87, p. 155). The *oikonomia* of Posidonius's *Histories* has not yet been established; see Jacoby, *FGrH* II. A, no. 87, p. 155; and Malitz (1983) 64. Hence the different suggestions. As an episode from the time of Antiochus VII's Eastern expedition is said by Athenaeus to have been taken from the fourteenth book (see below, pp. 424–25), the siege of Jerusalem could not have been included later than book 14.

41. The absence of any mention of Posidonius by Josephus in the recurring references to his sources for the Hasmonaean period in the *Jewish Antiquities* is sufficient evidence. I would add that had Josephus been acquainted with the *Histories* of Posidonius, he would surely have adduced the main part of the Posidonian excursus (Strabo 16. 2. 35–36) in his *Contra Apionem* as the best proof that the greatest Greek authors were aware of the Jews and admired them. For the same reason it is clear that Josephus did not consult Strabo's *Geographica.* The efforts of Shahar (2004) to show that Josephus was deeply influenced in his geographical account of Judaea by Strabo's *Geographica* do not hold water; cf. Dueck (2005) 319–20, who also refers to Diller (1975) 7–19, 25–165, on authors before the second century C.E. being unfamiliar with Strabo's *Geographica.* See also p. 451 below.

42. See Malitz (1983) 63; Kidd 2: 5.

golden-horned bulls and a mass of incense and spices, he led a procession up to the gates; and, having handed over the sacrifice to their priests, he returned to the camp. The Jews, amazed, placed themselves in his hands immediately after the festival.

There is a basic similarity between this version and that in Josephus. Both versions portray the Seleucid king as overgenerous and extravagant, and as manifesting piety for the Jewish God. At the same time, Plutarch mentions incense, a procession, and Antiochus's personal participation in it, all elements that are absent from Josephus's version, and omits the Josephan reference to " gold and silver cups." That there are details peculiar to each version indicates that neither is the source of the other; rather, both versions derive from a common source containing the features common to both,[43] and most probably the details peculiar to each. The abrupt end in Plutarch ("The Jews, amazed," etc.) well suits the literary genre of apophthegms and does not detract from this conclusion: Plutarch had no need to tell us more for his didactic lesson in the given context, and the omission of the reference to the protracted siege and breach of the agreement just contributes to bringing home his message more effectively.

Is it possible that this episode alone was based on a Jewish source?[44] The event is well integrated into the "long siege story" taken from Strabo-Posidonius, and it presents the background to the opening of negotiations, as a confidence-building measure leading to the first contacts between the two sides. As to the possible source(s) of the *Apophthegmata*, the answer depends on the identification of the author of that book.[45] If the collection was indeed made by Plutarch—and there are some weighty arguments in favor of authenticity—it is worth bearing in mind that the references to Jews and certain other topics in Plutarch clearly demonstrate that he was not acquainted with Jewish-Hellenistic sources, not even the writings of Josephus, his contemporary. Despite his wide reading, he had access to only minimal and fairly confused information on Jewish subjects.[46] Plutarch's influence (if not his hand) is indeed discernible in the passage under discussion: the description of the "seven days" (the festival of Tabernacles in the "long siege story") as "the greatest festival (ἑορτή)" may be compared with a statement made by Plutarch elsewhere concerning the importance of that holiday (*Quaest. conv.*

43. So Stern, *GLAJJ* 1: 564; Malitz (1983) 320 n. 66. Contrary to Büchler (1898) 197.

44. Büchler (1898) 197 suggested that Plutarch drew on Josephus's *Antiquitates Judaicum*. This is rightly rejected by Stern (1991) 460 n. 81.

45. For the arguments of the supporters of authenticity, see Babbitt (1931) 3–7; for a summary of the views of the opponents, see Ziegler, *RE* s.v. "Plutarchos," cols. 863–66.

46. Too much effort has been spent on the attempt to trace specific halachic rulings in Plutarch's references to the Jews; thus Alon (1977) 135; Feldman (1996b) 533 ff.; and others. See Bar-Kochva (1997a) 406 n. 62.

6. 2: "the greatest and holiest of their festivals"). Acceptance of the claim of inauthenticity would make a Jewish source for the information even more remote:
this is the only episode in the *Apophthegmata* that deals with Jews. In short, given
that the episode in Josephus is well integrated in the story, and in view of the
possible sources of information for the *Apophthegmata* (whether it is authentic or
not), it seems highly unlikely that this episode was drawn from a Jewish source.

To sum up, the story of the siege of Jerusalem by Antiochus Sidetes contains two conflicting accounts that have been compiled side by side into a single
continuous narrative. The first—the "long siege story"—derives from Strabo,
who took it from Posidonius.[47] The second—the "reception story"—which is very

47. The suggestion that Posidonius served as the direct or indirect source for Josephus's account
of the siege in *Jewish Antiquities* has already been voiced in the past by several scholars (although
they failed to discern two different versions in the Josephan account), but it has not gained universal
acceptance (see note 1 above). A recent discussion of the issue can be found in Berthelot (2003) 188–
95, esp. 192–95, reacting to a preliminary version of this chapter that was published in Hebrew (Bar-
Kochva [1996b]). She argues that although Posidonius was indeed the source for Diodorus's account
of the siege and for Strabo's Jewish excursus, he was neither the indirect source for Josephus nor the
direct source for Strabo and Plutarch; according to Berthelot that source was, rather, Timochares, a
court historian of Antiochus VII, whom I had suggested as a source for Posidonius's version of the
siege (Bar-Kochva [1996b] 39, and see chapter 14 below). Here are her arguments, and my responses:
(a) The victim bulls and the other presents sent to the Temple during the Jewish holiday (Joseph. *AJ*;
Plut. *Apopht.*) are not mentioned by Diodorus. However, the Diodorean account concentrates on the
advice of the "friends," and the rest, especially the dramatic account of the siege (in which the reference to the special presents was included), is either omitted or extremely abbreviated, as can well
be expected of Diodorus, and even more of Photius (see further, pp. 411–12 above). (b) Posidonius,
who condemned the practices of contemporary Jews in his Jewish excursus (Strabo 16. 2. 37), would
not have praised Jewish *amixia* (nonmixing [with other people]) as *eusebeia* (*AJ* 13. 246). The praise
was invented by Josephus for his rebuttal of the anti-Jewish arguments of the "friends." However,
even if it were true, this cannot be used as an argument for rejecting the identification of Posidonius
as the indirect source for the "long siege story" in its essentials. As for the specific argument concerning Posidonius's attitude toward Jewish *amixia*, in his Jewish excursus he introduces Jewish
self-isolation most favorably as the escape found by Moses that allowed his followers to adhere
undisturbed to the right faith and proper religious rights (identical with Posidonius's personal
convictions). This is exactly what is said in Josephus: the reason for Jewish *amixia* is their *eusebeia*.
Posidonius's condemnation of later Judaism is irrelevant: the explanation of Jewish *amixia* obviously reacts to the accusation by the king's counselors recorded by Diodorus-Posidonius that Moses
shaped the Jewish exclusivity, instructing them to avoid interaction with other people. Incidentally,
even (the Hasmonaean) tyrants and their predecessors get away in the excursus with the charge of
introducing or adopting superstitious customs, but are not blamed for hatred of strangers or misanthropy (cf. p. 453 note 46 below). There is thus no reason not to accept that the response in Josephus
is basically Posidonian, even if one may argue that the precise phrasing of the sentence is Josephan.
The last possibility by itself is dubious: the third person is used in the passage consistently to refer to
the Jews, which in Josephus's writings indicates adherence to the phrasing of a non-Jewish source,
and *amixia* is not a Josephan or Jewish-Hellenistic term (see note 85 below). (c) In a passage of
Plutarch's biography of Pompey (*Pomp.* 28. 4), deriving, according to Hermann Strassburger, from

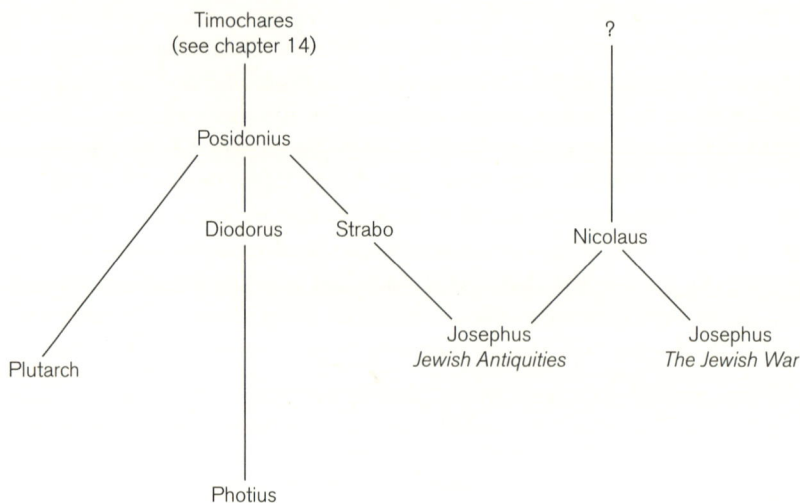

FIGURE 3. The Transmission of the Jerusalem Siege Account

short, derives directly from Nicolaus of Damascus. Partial parallels for the first, long account are to be found in Diodorus and Plutarch, and they, too, derive from Posidonius.

A comparison of the parallel accounts shows that Josephus reported the essence of the "long siege story" as he found it in Strabo, making a few unimportant omissions and alterations here and there, for example, omitting the procession of bearers of gifts for the Temple up to the gates of the city, in which Antiochus himself is said to have participated (recorded by Plutarch). It is possible that some of the modifications of Posidonius's text had already been made by Strabo. Of more significance is Josephus's omission of the slanders and accusations against the Jews detailed by the king's counselors, leaving only the accusation of exclusive-

---

Posidonius, it is noted that man is not ἀνήμερον ζῷον οὐδ' ἄμικτον ("a wild creature nor unsocial"). Hence (so Berthelot) Posidonius could not have praised Jewish *amixia*. But the sentence refers to the isolationism of pirates, who must favor remote cliffs as facilitating their nefarious business, and it serves to explain Pompey's policy of settling them in cities. What is the connection between this somewhat Aristotelian observation and the Jewish self-isolation, which was motivated, as implied by Posidonius in his Jewish excursus (preserved by Strabo even per Berthelot), by the most noble religious aims? As to the attribution of the passage from Plutarch's biography of Pompey to Posidonius, it is extremely doubtful. Posidonius's *Histories* closed with the year 84 at the very latest (see p. 352 above), and the hypothesis that he wrote a biography of Pompey rests on a problematic sentence that does not bear the weight of such speculation (see p. 348 note 40 above). Finally, Timochares was no philosopher and therefore was unable to invent such a sophisticated "philosophical" account.

ness (paras. 245–46). Josephus may be responsible for the explanation that the seven-day ceasefire took place at the Feast of Tabernacles. He also integrated into the story, in a fairly artificial way, his own comparison of Antiochus Sidetes and Antiochus Epiphanes: "Antiochus [Sidetes] . . . differing very much from Antiochus Epiphanes, who, having captured the city, had sacrificed pigs on the altar and besprinkled the Temple with their fat" (para. 243). If this note was not indeed in his source, the very comparison and its content were inspired by the words of the counselors that he found in the original story and omitted from his own account. In the original, it was reported that "the friends" advised Antiochus Sidetes to learn from the deeds of his predecessor and destroy the Jews. Among other things, "the friends" reported (favorably) his predecessor's desecration of the Temple with pigs' fat (Diod. 34/35. 1. 4).[48]

THE PECULIARITIES OF THE "LONG SIEGE STORY"

The Josephus-Strabo-Posidonius account of the siege contains a number of peculiarities and absurdities. An analysis of the account reveals features typical of the historiographical approach and aims of Posidonius, and an attitude toward the Jews that is paralleled in his Jewish excursus. First, then, let us briefly survey the main peculiarities in the account:

1. The siege towers: Antiochus drew up one hundred siege towers, each three storeys high, on the northern side of the wall, where the ground "happened also to be level" and placed in them military units (para. 238). Hellenistic siege towers were designed to facilitate artillery fire into a city from close range with good protection, and to carry to the wall the battering rams used to pierce the city's fortifications. The heavy towers moved on gigantic wheels and were dragged by large numbers of soldiers and service personnel up to the wall. Because of their great bulk, the towers used to be assembled on site, and they could be moved only on a flat surface. The number of towers reported here seems wildly exaggerated, and I have been unable to find another instance even approaching it. The exaggeration is manifest also from the possibilities of the deployment of the towers in the given terrain. Greek and Hellenistic siege towers measured 8–22 meters in width,[49] with intervals between them. A hundred towers, therefore, would have extended 1,600–4,200 meters. The larger figure is more probable, since Hellenistic siege towers tended to be consider-

48. Cf. note 31 above.
49. See Droysen (1889) 219–26; Kromayer and Veith (1928) 236–37; Marsden (1969–71) 2: 84–88; Garlan (1974) 226–34.

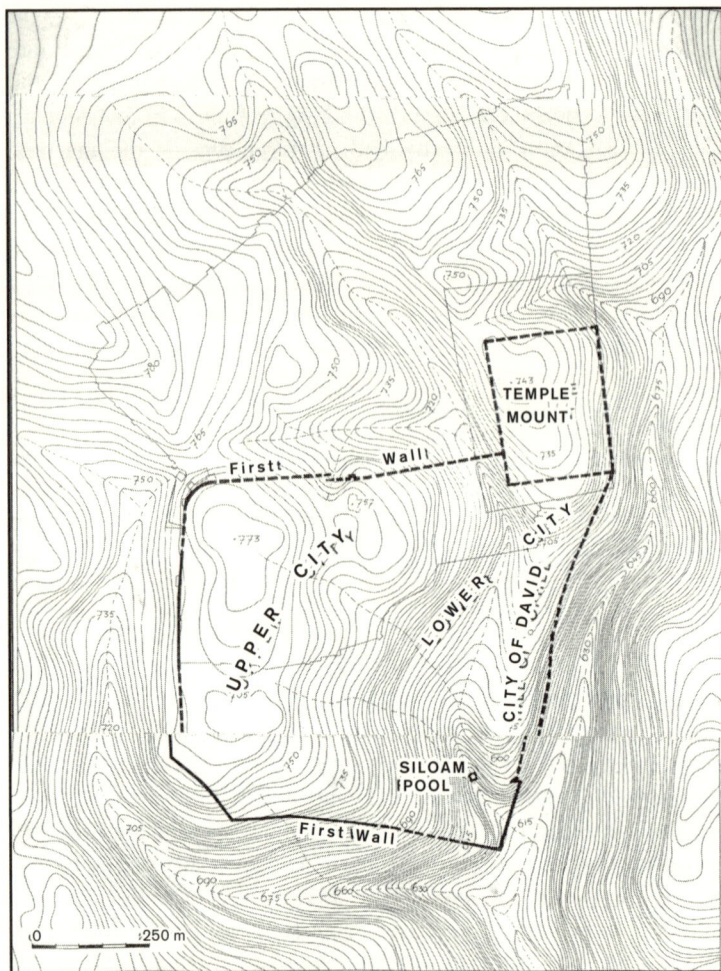

Jerusalem in the Early Hasmonaean Period

ably larger than the earlier versions used by the Successors. At the beginning of the reign of John Hyrcanus, the two sections of the wall facing north extended to about 900 meters, of which less than half faced flat ground.[50] Even toward the end of the Second Temple period, when the city expanded considerably to

50. See Avi-Yonah (1956) 306–7, 310–11; (1966) no. 25; Avigad (1980) 66; Sivan and Soler (1985); Bahat (1989) 38–39. Since the 1970s, it has become increasingly apparent that, at the time of the siege, the Upper City of Jerusalem was already inhabited and fortified. The wall to the northwest of the Temple

the north and west, the northern part of the then so-called third wall was just about 1.3 kilometers long.[51]

2. The camps and the ditch: The Seleucid army surrounded the city with seven camps and dug a ditch of double width and depth in order to contain the inhabitants within the walls (para. 239). This was definitely unnecessary: the city was surrounded by deep and wide ravines on the west, south, and east. The story itself states that only the terrain on the north was level. The towers positioned in that section would certainly have prevented any exit in that direction. Because of the terrain, the majority of the Seleucid force must have been concentrated to the north. Given that this section extended about 400 meters, a ditch would have been redundant, whatever the actual number of towers. Moreover, judging from the single ditch that surrounded the Seleucid camp at the battle of Magnesia (Livy 37. 37. 10–11), a double ditch would have measured around 24 cubits in width and at least 3 cubits in depth. It would have required a great deal of time and enormous effort to dig such a ditch in the hard, rocky surface of the Judaean hills. A ditch to protect the wall was later dug by one of the Hasmonaean rulers, and this was achieved only with much toil (Strabo 16. 2. 41; Joseph. *AJ* 14. 61; *BJ* 5. 149). Last, but not least, in view of all the installations described, one may wonder how those expelled from the city by Hyrcanus were still able to cross to the area "between the walls" (para. 241).

3. The noncombatant population: John Hyrcanus expelled the "useless" population from the city (paras. 240–41). Hyrcanus is thus portrayed as a ruthless tyrant, or worse, since even the most vicious Greek tyrants are not reported as having done this. It was customary in the Greek world—even in cities ruled by a ruthless tyrant—for women, children, and the aged to be removed to safety when a siege was impending, and, if this was impossible, for them to be protected properly.[52] The forced expulsion of all noncombatants would have seriously harmed the morale of the soldiers. "Useless" people in this sense were to be found in every family and household. Public opinion would not have stood for the brutal expulsion of all noncombatants, and the perpetrator would certainly not have remained as popular as Hyrcanus did. Josephus and the Hebrew sources are unanimous in stressing that John

Mount ran south from its western edge for a distance of about 350 meters, where it met the northern section of the first wall at its eastern end. The accessible flat ground faced the site of the two later towers, the Antonia and Hippikos on the northeastern corner of the Temple and the northwestern corner of the first wall respectively, and the first wall between the Tyropoion Valley and the small valley to the west.

51. See Avi-Yonah (1956) 313–15; (1966) map no. 114.

52. See, e.g., Schaps (1982) 194–95, 198–99. For active female involvement, see Schaps passim; and Kearns (1990) 335 ff.

Hyrcanus was admired by all sections of the nation, including the Pharisaic sages, even after he allied himself with the Sadducees in his final years.[53] There is no trace of indignation, let alone outrage, against Hyrcanus in Jewish internal sources, and not even a reference to it.

4. Antiochus's donation and the feast: Antiochus sent to the Temple a magnificent sacrifice in the midst of the armistice declared on the holiday of Tabernacles (para. 242). Putting the two versions of Josephus and Plutarch together reveals that the sacrifice consisted of bulls with golden horns and cups of gold and silver filled with a mass of incense and spices. In Plutarch, these luxurious offerings were brought to the city gates in a procession led by the king himself. According to Josephus, Antiochus arranged a feast for his soldiers on that occasion (para. 243). The proximity of the feast to the procession, and the accompanying explanation ("differing very much from Antiochus Epiphanes," etc.), indicate that the feast was dedicated to the Jewish God.

Formal suspension of hostilities during enemy festivals was common practice in ancient Greek tradition (though not always strictly observed).[54] The procession and offerings recall the procession of the First Fruits described in the Mishnah (Bikkurim 3.3), which itself recalls an Eleusinian procession.[55] However, it is quite difficult to understand how, in the midst of a protracted siege in a waterless, rocky, and infertile region, which must have exhausted the besieging force and consumed its supplies, the king could still afford to donate golden-horned bulls and gold and silver cups full of incense and spices. Moreover, he transfers all these to the enemy, whom he was trying so hard to starve into submission. That Antiochus feasted his army in honor of the Jewish God, and that he personally participated in the procession, appears even more imaginary, no matter what his motive, or how positive his attitude to the Jewish faith and cult might have been.[56]

53. AJ 13. 292, 299–300. On the favorable image of John Hyrcanus in rabbinic literature, see Yadayim 4. 6; Ma'aser Sheni 5. 15; Sota 9. 10; Tosefta Soṭa 13. 9–10, and the subsequent discussion in the Palestinian and Babylonian Talmud (cf. Bar-Kochva [1977] 187–90); BT Berakhot 29a. See also Targum Ps. Jonathan, Deut. 33.11, later prayers (Masekhet Sofrim 20. 7), and medieval midrashim, which confuse Mattathias with "Johanan the High Priest," or present Johanan as the father of Mattathias. For a (incomplete) discussion of Hyrcanus's image in Josephus and early Jewish sources, see Thoma (1994).

54. See the survey of Pritchett (1974–91) 1: 121–26.

55. Noted by Lieberman (1962) 144–46; Baer (1985) 1: 324, and the sources there (esp. Il. 10. 294, 437; Od. 3. 384; Syll.³ I. 83; IG I. 76). For the sacrifice of animals with gilded horns as a common practice, see, e.g., Odyssey 3. 437 ff.; Theophrastus in Porphyry De Abstinentia 2. 15. 1, 60. 2.

56. Rajak (1981) 66 notes: "Contributions to the sacrifices at subject temples are characteristic acts of Hellenistic monarchs. But what could have brought Antiochus to send a sacrifice to an enemy

5. Antiochus as a ruler showing piety: The sacrifice to the Jewish God is explained (para. 242) by the king's piety toward the divine entity. The author reiterates the king's piety several times in the course of the story, once even describing it as "an excess of religious observance" (ὑπερβολὴ τῆς θρησκείας), and calling the king "*eusebēs*" (para. 244). The term *eusebeia*, whatever its precise meaning in the given context may have been,[57] expresses special respect toward the religion of the Jewish ancestors (paras. 243–45).

Hellenistic kings occasionally described their attitude toward local cults as *eusebeia* (including Antiochus III toward the Jews: Joseph. *AJ* 12. 140), but neither this nor the statement in the story, nor indeed the sacrifice itself, conforms with the image of a king who had been struggling against the Jews ever since his ascent to the throne (1 Macc. 15.27 ff.), and sits even less well in the wider context of a royal house that had conducted a thirty-year war against the Jews. The terms of surrender imposed on the Jews, and the demolition of the battlements, contrary to the agreement, are more in line with Seleucid policy. Significantly enough, the author of 1 Maccabees, who may well have witnessed the siege,[58] has nothing favorable to say about Antiochus Sidetes (as opposed to some other Seleucid kings), accusing him instead of dishonesty and treachery (15.25–31, esp. 27), and of pouring his wrath on the Jews (15.36, 40).[59] Antiochus VII did not even use the epithet Eusebes, adopted by several Seleucid kings, which might have inspired such a story, but Sidetes, Soter, Euergetes, Kallinikos, and "the Great."[60]

The peculiarities listed above highlight four conspicuous traits of the "long siege story" as a whole:

1. The story exhibits extreme exaggeration with regard to military installations and constructions, food and utensils, feasts and luxuries. The impression

---

temple before the cessation of hostilities?" At the end of her discussion, Rajak accepts the account as historical, altering only the sequence, and proposing to date the episodes after the raising of the siege. For Rajak's interesting interpretation as a whole, see pp. 435–39 below.

57. See note 5 above.

58. On the date of composition of 1 Maccabees and the closing verses of the book, see Bar-Kochva (1989) 157 ff. The author of 1 Maccabees does not describe the siege, since it was beyond the chronological framework of his work.

59. Rajak (1981) 81 notes in this context that "expression of public esteem for the Jewish cult was not the outcome of religious sentiment, or learned investigation, but simply of the contemporary state of international relations." This still does not explain the emphasis on the special attitude of Antiochus VII to the Jewish deity (which is not Josephan, as it appears also in Plutarch), and its exaggerated expressions. The question of whether *eusebēs* was in fact one of Antiochus VII's titles (see Rajak [1981] 70) does not make much difference (see below).

60. See, e.g., the inscription from Acre; Landau (1961); and Pompeius Trogus (Justin 38. 10. 6). *Pace* Rajak (1981) 81.

given is of an affluent Seleucid society conducting a life of wasteful luxury, even in circumstances where a different pattern of conduct would normally be expected.

2. The personality of Antiochus VII Sidetes is described rather positively. He is called *eusebēs* and is portrayed as displaying tolerance and magnanimity toward his enemy.

3. The Gentile source regards the Jewish faith and cult with great admiration. The Jewish God is introduced as the "divine entity." Antiochus, who sends donations to his cult, is said to have done this out of *eusebeia*. Furthermore, the author deplores, at least by implication, the harsh treatment of the Temple at the hands of Antiochus Epiphanes and explains Jewish "nonmixing" with other nations as a manifestation of their piety (para. 246).

4. In contrast to the favorable account of the Jewish religion, one can detect a definite condemnation of John Hyrcanus, the Jewish ruler. He is described as a ruthless tyrant who disregards public feelings: the author attributes to him the unprecedented expulsion of the noncombatant population of the city. Indeed, the wretches are admitted back inside the walls by the combatants, not by the tyrant. The military achievements of Hyrcanus are quite poor; he depends only on the natural, topographical strength of his city and the individual bravery of the defenders (paras. 237–38).

HISTORIOSOPHY, ETHICS, AND NOSTALGIA

The first two characteristics of the account—the exaggerated affluence of the Seleucid army and the inordinately favorable description of Antiochus Sidetes—both find parallels in Posidonian fragments and testimonia. The first characteristic may be explained by Posidonius's ethical doctrine, historiosophic conception, and literary approach; the second by his biography and personal background.

The contrast between the luxurious life of the Hellenistic world and the decent, ascetic norms of conduct in ancient Roman society (up to the destruction of Carthage) is used by Posidonius to explain the downfall of the Hellenistic monarchies—especially of the Seleucids—and the rise of Rome to its dominant position in the ancient world. According to Posidonius, after 146 B.C.E., when the morals of republican Rome started to deteriorate (Diod. 34/35. 33. 4 ff.),[61] the Seleucid empire had already reached its nadir with little chance of recovery. There was actually nothing new in this conception. Polybius had long before identified the life of comfort and ease as the main reason for the deterioration of Hellenistic civilization, contrasted with the healthy and demanding Roman way of life (with

61. On the Roman decay after 146 B.C.E. according to Posidonius, see esp. Steidle (1958) 16 ff.; Strasburger (1965) 46 ff.

Rome also benefiting from its "mixed" constitution).[62] Posidonius thus continued the *Histories* of Polybius not only in its chronological sequence, but also in its historiosophic conception. However, while Polybius adhered to his "pragmatic" historiographic method, which demanded absolute loyalty to historical truth, Posidonius would consistently pick and choose from the historical material and reshape it to illustrate his philosophical and historiosophic concepts and tendencies.[63] Posidonius's didactic approach to history was recognized already in antiquity. Athenaeus, for example, who preserves a relatively large number of fragments of Posidonius's *Histories* in his *Deipnosophistai*, comments on the principle of the selection of material as follows:

> Posidonius, the one from the Stoa, in the Histories that he compiled, writing up, in a way not alien to the philosophy that he preferred, many usages and customs among many [people] (4. 151e)[64]

Athenaeus knew what he was talking about. He also wrote a work on the Seleucid kings (5. 211a). This has not been preserved, but if it was anything like his *Deipnosophistai*, it would have been a compilation of a good number of sources, including Posidonius. Athenaeus would have been in a good position, therefore, to compare the characteristics of Posidonian narrative with those of other authors on parallel subjects. To help demonstrate the degeneration of the Hellenistic world, Posidonius exaggerated his descriptions of the waste of quantities of food and the extravagant use of luxury items such as perfumes, spices, incense, and gold and silver plates. Some of his accounts are extremely grotesque and must be considered caricatures of life in the Hellenistic kingdoms.[65]

62. This feature of Polybian history is well known and does not require detailed documentation. For a discussion of explanations for the rise and fall of states in Greek literature from Herodotus to Polybius, see de Romilly (1977); and in Polybius: Walbank (2002) 193–211. On the presentation in Greek literature of degeneration into a life of luxury as the reason for the decline of states, see pp. 62–69 above.

63. Reinhardt (1954) 83, 84, 90, expressed it thus: "Posidonius . . . continues Polybius, though on philosophical principles"; "Whatever he shows is a philosophical view of the world of action speaking to the senses"; "With regard to the final aim of both of them, the task of history and the task of philosophy, in the view of Posidonius they coincide: both ought to be medicinal."

64. See also the evaluation of Nock: "History is defined by a rhetorician as 'philosophy by examples' (Dion. Hal. *Ars. rhet.* XI. 2) and philosophers turn freely to history as to poetry for examples of virtue and vice, their reward and punishment or neglect. Peripatetics wrote biographies and a cultural history. Strabo, whose Stoicism has been mentioned earlier, expressed the belief (I. 1. 23 [13]) that his own historical work was of service to moral and political philosophy. But if Strabo was a professed Stoic, Posidonius was a professional Stoic: and he is the only notable professional philosopher of antiquity known to have written a monumental account of recent history" (Nock [1959] 4); cf. Bringmann (1986) 54; Sacks (1990) 150; Marcovich (1991) 736.

65. On the satirical element in Posidonius in general, cf. Reinhardt, *RE s.v.* "Poseidonios" (3), col. 632; Rudberg (1918) 11–15; Reinhardt (1954); Strasburger (1961) 31, 40–42; Bar-Kochva (1976) 99

The best illustration of the unrealistic shaping of historical material by Posidonius may be found in two fragments preserved by Athenaeus.[66] The first describes a local skirmish between the Syrian cities of Apamea and Larissa,[67] both famous Seleucid military settlements. Apamea traditionally supplied the best phalanx soldiers of the army, and Larissa the elite cavalry.[68] The reader would, therefore, be anticipating an interesting direct confrontation between the two leading tactical contingents of the Seleucid army, affording the opportunity to compare and contrast the advantages and disadvantages of both combat units (cf. Polyb. 18. 28–32, where the phalanx and the Roman legion are contrasted). It was all the more provocative, then, to find instead a caricature of military preparations. The combatants wore not the usual helmet, but the *petasos,* the wide-brimmed hat of the young ephebes, with a visor to keep off the sun. That comfort was of more concern than defense is emphasized by the observation that the visors not only produced shade but also allowed a breeze to keep the neck cool. The daggers and pikes were covered with rust and dirt (Hellenistic armies actually overindulged in polishing and brandishing their weapons: e.g., Polyb. 11. 9. 1–2). Furthermore, "they brought along with them donkeys loaded with wine and dishes of every variety, alongside which lay small flutes and single pipes." The scene recalled, as stated explicitly by Posidonius, an assembly of comedians rather than military troops (Ath. 4. 176b). We might compare them to a group of sated middle-aged citizens on a picnic or a hunting party.

The second passage refers to the subject of our discussion—Antiochus VII Sidetes. The historical background is not made explicit, but it can be deduced from Athenaeus's introductory sentences:

> In the fourteenth book [of the *Histories*], talking about his (Antiochus Grypus's) namesake, Antiochus (VII Sidetes), the one who campaigned into Media against Arsaces, (Posidonius) says that he (Antiochus) would hold crowded receptions every day, in which, apart from what was consumed and heaped as scraps, each of the banqueters would take away whole-limbed meat of land, winged, and sea animals, prepared undivided, capable of filling a cart; and after this, masses of honey-cakes and wreaths of myrrh and frankincense with man-sized felt cloths of golden fillets. (12. 540b-c; cf. 5. 210c-d)

On the irony in Posidonius, which departs from the historical truth, see Reinhardt, *RE,* col. 637; id. (1954) 85–87; Desideri (1973) 249–51; Kidd 2: 866, on Athenaeus 5. 211d–215b ("This is hardly historical objectivity, but clearly is not meant to be"); cf. Sacks (1990) 152 n. 139. For other aspects of Posidonius's historiography, see Gigon (1967); von Fritz (1977); Malitz (1983) 409 ff.

66. On the verbal accuracy of the fragments quoted by Athenaeus, see Brunt (1980) 30–32.
67. On the historical background, see Kidd 2: 285.
68. See Bar-Kochva (1979) 28–29; Grainger (1990a) 39–40, 59, 126–27.

The account is sheer fantasy. It might seem at first sight that Posidonius is describing a festival in Antioch,[69] although even in such a case the description would still be grotesque. The situation is actually far more absurd than that. Athenaeus's identification of Antiochus Sidetes in this context as the Antiochus "who campaigned into Media against Arsaces" (Arsaces VI = Phraates II) suggests that the episode occurs during the Eastern expedition. After all, Antiochus Sidetes was not the only Seleucid king who embarked upon an expedition against Arsaces (and against the Parthians), and it would have been much more natural to identify him by one of his four or five nicknames, especially Sidetes, or by his patronymic (cf. Ath. 5. 210e: "Antiochus . . . the son of Demetrius"). Furthermore, the identification of the same Antiochus as the man who "went to war against Arsaces" appears once again in Athenaeus (10. 439c), this time as an introduction to a Posidonian testimonium that explicitly records the aftermath of that expedition; and this is the only other reference to Arsaces in Athenaeus's fifteen books. Both references would, therefore, appear to derive from a Posidonian account of the Eastern expedition.[70]

Corroborative evidence comes from the account of Antiochus VII's expedition by Justin, in his epitome of Pompeius Trogus. It has long been suggested that Pompeius Trogus's account of Selucid history in the second century B.C.E., derived directly or indirectly from Posidonius.[71] Here is one paragraph from that account:

> But he was prepared no less for luxury than for military service, since eighty thousand armed men followed three hundred thousand camp attendants, the greater number of whom were cooks, bakers, and actors. Certainly, there was so much silver and gold that even the common soldiers fastened their boots with gold and trampled on the material, for the love of which peoples contend with the sword. Also, the kitchen utensils were made of silver, just as if they were advancing to a feast, not a war. (Justin 38. 10. 1–4)

69. Suggested by Kidd 2: 299: "These lavish popularizing public feastings were probably held after Tryphon's collapse, or possibly after the taking of Jerusalem." Cf. Malitz (1983) 287.

70. The original location of the fragment, book 14 of the *Histories,* does not help to date the event, since the order of composition of the work by Posidonius is open to debate; see note 40 above.

71. The question of Pompeius Trogus's direct and indirect sources for his books on the second half of the second century B.C.E. is indeed still debatable. While some argue that Trogus merely adapted Timagenes to Latin (e.g., von Gutschmid [1882] 548–55; [1891] 465–79; Schanz-Hosius [1935] 322–25), others considered that he made an original contribution (e.g., Wachsmuth [1891]) and that he also used other sources directly, such as Posidonius (Wachsmuth [1895] 108–16) or Strabo (Rizzo [1963] 75), or used these two indirectly (Amantini [1972] 107–9; Salomone [1973] 136). One scholar denied that Trogus made any use of Timagenes (Momigliano [1934] 56; cf. Seel [1955] 18–23). The variety of views reveals some agreement with regard to Posidonius's influence on Pompeius Trogus. The general atmosphere of the passage under consideration points to Posidonius as the source.

Note especially the references to manifestations of military decadence, such as recurring feasts and great quantities of cooks, bakers, silver, and gold; and the sarcastic remark that it was the soldiers who "followed" their attendants. The feasts described in the earlier quoted Posidonian fragment in Athenaeus (12. 540b-c) are therefore not set in Antioch but in the midst of a dangerous military campaign, a thousand miles or so from home, deep in hostile country and rugged terrain. The similarity with the events at the Jerusalem siege is remarkable. The great exaggeration of military installations, the extravagant presents to the Jewish deity in the time of the Jerusalem siege, and especially the curious feast the king is said to have conducted for his soldiers all find their literary parallels in the passages quoted above. They are all links in the chain of consistently highly exaggerated descriptions of the degenerate affluent lifestyle of Hellenistic civilization, the identified reason for its downfall.

These are not the only Posidonian fragments in this vein (cf., e.g., Ath. 5. 210e, 12. 540a-b, 15. 692c-d). To end this discussion, here are two more of them. The first contains Posidonius's grotesque account of everyday life in the Seleucid cities in general:[72]

> At any rate, with the people in the cities, (relieved) from distress with regard to necessities because of the abundance of the land, bestowing many gatherings in which they feast continuously, using the gymnasia as if baths, anointing themselves with expensive oil and perfumes, and inhabiting "ledgers" (γραμματεῖοι)—for thus they call the commons of the dining companions—as if private houses, and in these filling their stomachs for most of the day with wines and dishes so as to carry many away besides while also being serenaded by the sound of a much rattling tortoise-shell, so that the cities altogether echo with such noises. (Ath. 12. 527e-f)

Contrast this with Posidonius's praise for the modest way of life of the ancient Romans:

> For hereditary among them, as Posidonius says, used to be endurance; a frugal way of life; a plain and simple use of the other things pertaining to possession; moreover, a wonderful piety (*eusebeia*) toward the divine; righteousness and great care not to offend in relations with all men; together with the practice of agriculture. [...] Formerly, so frugal were the inhabitants of Italy that even [still today], says Posidonius, those who were very well off for a livelihood, trained their sons in drinking water mostly and in eating whatever they happened to have. And often, he says, a father or mother would ask a son whether he wanted to dine on pears or walnuts, and after eating some of these he was satisfied and went to bed. (Ath. 6. 274a, 275a)[73]

72. On the background, in the late 130s or early 120s B.C.E., see Kidd 2: 300–301.

73. Cf. Polybius 6. 57. 5; 31. 25; 36. 9. See also Posidonius's comment on the deterioration of the Etruscans in Diodorus 5. 40. 4–5. On the Posidonian conception of early Roman history, see, e.g., Harmatta (1971).

In an essentially similar manner, Posidonius explains how Mithridates I (Arsaces V), the founder of the Parthian empire, reached his great territorial achievements and managed to hold the kingdom together despite its vast dimensions and national heterogeneity. In book 33 of Diodorus's books evidently based on Posidonius, the empire founded by Arsaces V is described up to the borders of India. The passage (para. 18) emphasizes the abstinence of the king from luxury (*tryphē*) and arrogance, unlike the custom of other rulers. The passage is worth quoting, since it also demonstrates the Posidonian ideals regarding the proper way to rule an imperial power—enlightened and fair treatment of subject populations:

> Arsaces the king, having aspired to fairness and *philanthrōpia,* had a natural out-pouring of good things and increased the kingdom all the more; for extending it to the territory of India, as it was under Porus, he reigned without danger. Although he had advanced to such a size of kingdom, he did not aspire to luxury or arrogance, which things tended to follow most dynasties, but to fairness toward those ranged under him, and courage toward those ranged against him. In general, having acquired control of many peoples, he showed the Parthians the best customs of each.

This approach accords well with Posidonius's attitude toward Roman imperialism and imperial rule by and large.[74] He is prepared to consent to imperial rule, and is even favorably disposed to its arrangements, so long as they do not turn to despotism, but remain fair and beneficial to both sides. This model of constructive imperialism was a typical Stoic compromise with the existing world order, apparently a temporary substitute for the Posidonian universal vision.

Now to the second characteristic of the siege account, the admiration of the personality of Antiochus Sidetes. Despite the grotesque descriptions of the affluent atmosphere in his camp, the king is regarded with affection by Posidonius of Apamea, and with good reason. The reign of Antiochus Sidetes was the swan song of the Seleucid empire. He was the last sovereign of that house who tried to stop the political decline, investing great effort in reinvigorating and expanding the empire. He did manage to pull it together and, among other successes, even managed to forge an alliance with John Hyrcanus, and attach him to his great expedition to the Eastern satrapies against the Parthians. Had the anabasis been successful, and had Antiochus lived on to carry out his plans, the Parthian advance might have been halted for some generations. Driving the Parthians out of Babylonia, his victories inspired great enthusiasm and earned him the epithet "the Great." However, he was then taken by surprise and challenged to battle by

---

74. On Posidonius and Roman imperialism, see Cappelle (1932) 99–103; Strassburger (1965) 34–37. For a striking example of Posidonius's treatment of "local imperialism," see Athenaeus 6. 263d-e (tribes in the Black Sea region).

Phraates on unfavorable ground while most of his troops were still stranded in their winter quarters all over the country. The king insisted on taking a stand in the great tradition of Macedonian bravery and paid a heavy price: the Seleucid army was broken, and many troops captured; he himself committed suicide on the battlefield.[75] His death accelerated the downfall of the empire. His heirs displayed a lack of ability and exhausted themselves in an internal struggle for the throne.[76]

Despite the eventual failure of Antiochus Sidetes, his accomplishments and efforts were favorably recalled by the Hellenistic world. Posidonius of Apamea, himself a native of the Seleucid empire, shared this appreciation. As an adherent to the Stoic cosmopolitan ideal, he may well have favored from the outset any effort toward unification and the renewal of a multinational empire. Whether such an empire would have stood up to the humane principles of the cosmopolitan vision—especially with regard to the fair treatment of subjects—is another question. Posidonius endeavored to indicate, in his semifictitious account of the treatment of the Jews by Antiochus Sidetes, that there were indeed grounds for optimism.[77]

The favorable attitude of Posidonius toward various aspects of Antiochus Sidetes' personality can be traced not only in Josephus's account of the siege and its parallels. We have already seen how Posidonius's account was compressed in Justin's version of Sidetes' preparations for his Parthian expedition (38. 10. 1–4). Posidonius's approach and ideas appear in Pompeius Trogus-Justin in a number of other passages referring to Sidetes' Parthian expedition. First, the general outline:

> Therefore Antiochus, mindful that both his father had been hated because of pride and his brother had been despised because of sluggishness, [fearing] lest

75. The main literary sources are Justin 36. 1. 10, 38. 9. 4 ff.; Diodorus 34/35. 15–19; Josephus *Antiquitates Judaicum* 13. 251; Appian *Syriaca* 68; Eusebius *Chronica* 1. 255 ff. See Schwartz (1996); cf. Will (1979–82) 2: 341–49.

76. The comment of E. R. Bevan, the historian of the house of Seleucus, in the opening of his survey of the reign of Antiochus Sidetes, guided historians in the last century: "But the new claimant was not a man like the other ineffectual personalities who flit across the stage in that time of ruin and confusion. One more man capable of rule and of great action, one more luminous figure, the house which had borne the Empire of Asia had to show the world before it went into darkness" (Bevan [1902] 2: 236). Bevan closes the survey with a comment on Antiochus Sidetes' death: "It was the death-blow of the Seleucid dynasty. The last great king of that house was gone; for the last time it had stood before the world as the imperial house of the East. It had no more revivals. And the last real king whom it produced embodied in a striking way the typical qualities of his once-impulsive energy, a high and generous courage, the old Macedonian delight in wassailing and war. Like his predecessors, Antiochus VII drank freely in his convivial hours" (246).

77. Cf. the passage quoted below from Justin 38. 10. 5–6, based indirectly on Posidonius. This recalls the complex attitude of Posidonius toward the Roman Republic and its rule over other nations. On Posidonius and Rome, see Strassburger (1965); Arskine (1990) 200–202.

he fall into the same vices, having married Cleopatra, his brother's wife, he took vengeance with the utmost energy against cities that had defected at the beginning of his brother's rule and, having conquered them, added them again to the borders of the kingdom; he subdued the Jews as well, who had liberated themselves by arms in the Macedonian (i.e., Seleucid) empire under Demetrius his father. (Justin 36. 1. 9–10)

Underlying the summary of Justin appears to be an account of mistreatment of subject peoples by Demetrius I and II, and redress by Antiochus VII, although the latter did not refrain from retaliatory measures against his enemies before he managed to get them under control. The concern for the treatment of subject peoples by a ruler echoes the Posidonian passage on Arsaces V already quoted, where the character of the king is unambiguously positive. A further positive example is described in another passage of Justin reporting the campaign of Antiochus Sidetes against the Parthians, and this—preceded by the highly exaggerated account of Antiochus's camp quoted above (38. 10. 1–4)—must also derive from Posidonius. In this passage, Antiochus is the enlightened ruler defending his newly acquired subjects in the East, and they in turn come to his aid. The new Parthian king, Arsaces VI (Phraates II), deviated according to Posidonius from the fair policy of his predecessor, and is a foil to Antiochus's character. After having reached their peak, it would seem that the Parthians started to deteriorate; at any rate, here, their new king has become arrogant and inimicable to his subjects, while Antiochus is heaped with praise:

Many Oriental kings hastened to meet Antiochus in his advance, surrendering themselves and their kingdoms with contempt [expressed] for Parthian arrogance. Nor was the conflict long in coming. Antiochus, when, as the victor in three battles, he had occupied Babylon, began to be considered great. Therefore, with all the peoples defecting to him, nothing remained to the Parthians except the ancestral territories. (38. 10. 5–6)

On Antiochus's death, Pompeius Trogus-Justin also has to say:

On the march he was met by the king of the Parthians, against whom he fought more bravely than his army did [...] Phraates made funeral rites for him (Antiochus) in a regal manner. (38. 10. 9–10)

Finally, concerning Antiochus's burial in Syria:

Meanwhile, the body of Antiochus, who had been killed by the king of the Parthians, having been sent back in a silver coffin for burial in Syria, arrived, and it was received with great assiduity on the part of cities and King Alexander. (39. 1. 5–6)[78]

---

78. On the dating of the burial to the reign of Alexander II (Zabinas), see Bellinger (1949) 62.

The references in the last two passages to the courage of the king and the grief of the Syrian citizens after his death find parallels in the remains of the Diodorus-Posidonius account of the expedition (34/35. 16–17; see further, below).

There is, however, another fragment explicitly ascribed to Posidonius that attributes to the Parthian king the following words at the (temporary) burial:

> Your (Antiochus VII's) recklessness and drunkenness have caused your overthrow; for you expected to drain the kingdom of Arsaces in great cups. (Ath. 10. 439e)

Athenaeus introduced this quotation with the following:

> Another drink lover was the like-named Antiochus, the one who went to war against Arsaces in Media.

This indicates that the "drunkenness" in question is not a metaphor to express Sidetes' imperial aspirations, but quite literally his love of drinking, based on former reports, including, presumably, those exaggerated ones concerning frequently recurring banquets in the camps carried out during the expedition. Posidonius therefore seems to have summarized his ambivalent attitude toward Antiochus Sidetes through the mouthpiece of the Parthian king: on the one hand, he possessed the admirable qualities of courage and far-sighted initiative; on the other hand, there was his drunkenness and dissolute lifestyle.

There is a further example of ambivalence in an anecdote of Plutarch from the Parthian expedition (*Apoph.* 184D-E). It precedes the passage, based on Posidonius, about the sending of expensive gifts to the Jewish Temple:[79]

> Antiochus, who campaigned a second time against the Parthians, having wandered away from his friends and servants in some hunt and pursuit, entered, unrecognized, a farmhouse of poor people; and at the meal, having brought in a discussion about the king, he heard that in other things he was worthy, but by entrusting most things to wretched friends, he overlooked and often neglected necessary things through being too hunt-loving. Then he was quiet, but with the [coming of the] day, when some of his bodyguards arrived at the farmhouse, and when he became manifest after the purple and the diadem were brought to him, he said: "Ever since the day I put you on, for the first time yesterday I heard true words about myself."

The episode relating how Antiochus Sidetes set off on a hunt during the campaign and lost his way is doubtless critical of the king's irresponsibility, with more than a hint at his pursuit of pleasure and entertainment no matter what the situation. It is even stated explicitly that the king's love of hunting led him to neglect his duties and to delegate authority to counselors (*philoi*, "friends") who were not worthy of the role. At the same time, however, the anecdote actually praises

---

79. *Apophthegmata* 184F. See the passage above, pp. 413–15, and the discussion there on its source.

Antiochus for his fairness toward his subjects, who indeed showed him great approval. The ambivalence and general content of this anecdote, and its proximity to a similar anecdote in Plutarch drawn from Posidonius, all suggest that Posidonius is the source for this anecdote, too.

Another factor contributing to Posidonius's perception of Antiochus would have been his own personal biography. The great Stoic philosopher was born in Apamea between 143 and 129 B.C.E., at a time when the city had regained its central position in the briefly rejuvenated empire. Posidonius would still have been quite young, perhaps just an infant, when the bitter news of the king's death and the collapse of the expedition reached the city.[80] The overwhelming shock and grief in the capital, Antioch, was recorded by Diodorus-Posidonius (34/35. 17–18). Nearly every household had lost at least one of its members, and the end of an epoch must have been keenly felt. The Parthian enemy would soon be approaching the gates, and the Seleucid kingdom was now in terminal decline. Similar scenes of mourning and panic undoubtedly occurred in Apamea, the city of the heavy infantry. The emotional reactions he witnessed as a child, or the stories he heard about the events in his infancy, may well have deeply affected Posidonius, who in his maturity would naturally recall them in exaggerated form. The personality and character of the dead king, the last of the great Seleucid emperors, was therefore nostalgically described. At the same time, Posidonius was obliged to explain the final disaster. This he did, as was his wont, according to his ethical and historiosophical conception: affluence and luxury caused the military misfortune. Yet even here, it is continually stressed that the king remained brave and honorable to the last (Diod. 34/35. 16).

The third and fourth features of the account of the Jerusalem siege, the contrast between the praise of basic Judaism and the condemnation of the contemporary Jewish ruler, are to be explained by the Jewish ethnographic excursus of Posidonius, preserved by Strabo in the *Geographica*. Antiochus shows particular respect to the divine entity, the Jewish God, since he is suitably *eusebēs*. The Jewish God is indeed perceived in the ethnographic excursus according to the principal lines of the Posidonian theology (para. 35a).[81] On the other hand, Posidonius expresses his indignation at the attitude of John Hyrcanus toward the Jews, his own people. This may be compared with his portrayal in the excursus of the tyrannical leaders, destructive to their own people as much as to their neighbors (para. 37b).

The Jewish excursus sheds further light on the aims of the episode concerning the victim and the presents sent by Antiochus VII to the Temple. The story is told not only to praise Antiochus as a model of the *eusebēs*, but also to offer a veiled criticism of the appalling waste of resources, which is especially inappropriate

80. On his age, see pp. 339–40 above.
81. See the appendix, pp. 535–41 below.

in the context of a siege and the prevailing conditions. Standing in counterpoint to the criticism, which is implied by the exaggerated tones of the account, are Posidonius's remarks in the excursus regarding the simple cult maintained by Moses and his followers and their restrained expenses on the Temple (para. 36b).[82] Posidonius thus also uses the episode of the victim as another vehicle for criticism of the degenerate and luxurious lifestyle of the Seleucid rulers, a lifestyle already satirized in the unrealistic description of wasteful employment of military installations and constructions during the siege. We should see in the same light the feast in honor of the Jewish God that the king is said to have arranged for his soldiers during the Jewish holidays. The feast is only briefly mentioned in the text we now have. It may well have been presented in greater detail in the original, paralleling as it does other Posidonian stories about extravagant drinking parties and feasts the king arranged for his soldiers on his fateful expedition against the Parthians. The victim and feast episode exemplifies once again Posidonius's ambivalent attitude toward Antiochus VII.

The connection between the excursus and the "long siege story" is revealed, above all, in the explanation found in the story for Jewish obstinate detachment from other peoples. The passage relates that the king rejected the advice of his "friends"-counselors to destroy the Jews because of their *amixia* (nonmixing), "believing that they were doing all according to piety" (*eusebeia*, para. 246). The anti-Jewish accusations of the "friends" that survived in the version of Diodorus-Posidonius are aimed explicitly against the deeds and laws of Moses, which are described as isolationist to the extent of "misanthropy" (Diod. 34/35. 1. 1b–3). The context indicates that, according to the "friends," the Jews adopted their deplorable practices as a reaction to their traumatic expulsion from Egypt as lepers, and the connection is explicit in the expulsion accounts of a number of Hellenistic and Roman authors.[83] Now in the Jewish excursus, Posidonius explains the departure from Egypt of Moses and the Egyptian sages who accompanied him as motivated by a desire to establish a new society in which they could adhere to their beliefs and practice their cult unmolested, free from idols of men and animals, thus serving in the correct manner the divine entity (which is identical to the Posidonian deity). They established their new location in a rocky, dry, and consequently isolated region (Strabo 16. 2. 36a). The community founded by Moses is therefore exclusive by its very nature.[84] The self-isolation instituted by Moses was thus intended to allow the Judaean community to practice proper worship of the divine entity.[85]

82. See pp. 379–80 above.

83. See p. 131 note 116 above.

84. Cf. pp. 369–70 above.

85. Cf. note 47 above in response to Berthelot (2003) 193–94. To support her arguments that the

THE KERNEL OF HISTORICAL TRUTH

With all that has been said above, what historical-factual information can be retrieved from Posidonius's highly exaggerated and partisan account of the Jerusalem siege? The preliminary question is whether to prefer Nicolaus's version to the Strabo-Posidonius account. In other words, we need to decide whether the siege was short, ending when the city gates were opened wide to receive the king and his troops; or a protracted blockade, terminated only after long negotiations and the acceptance of harsh conditions. To judge from a comparisons of details with those of independent sources and with geographical and physical features, the detailed Strabo-Posidonius account, despite its imaginary and tendentious features, seems closer to the actual events. The demolition of the city's battlements, for example, is also hinted at in the closing verses of 1 Maccabees (16.23). This detail does not seem to coincide with the cordial spirit of the "reception story."

Which details of Posidonius's account may be considered reliable? The chronological statement that the siege took place in the 128th Olympiad (132–128 B.C.E.) can be accepted. As the expedition of Antioches Sidetes against the Parthians, in which Hyrcanus participated, commenced in the spring of 130,[86] the siege should be dated to 132/1, rather than 131/30. A series of coins struck in Jerusalem in 132/1 and 131/30, bearing the name of Antiochus VII alongside Jewish symbols, seems to corroborate this.[87] We can further accept that the main military effort of the Seleucid army was concentrated, as might be expected in view of the terrain, on the northern sector of the wall, or rather on two of its sections, where the ground was relatively even.[88] Remains of ammunition apparently belonging to the early

---

reference to Jewish *amixia* (nonmixing) is Josephan and not Posidonian (by itself insufficient to prove a non-Posidonian source for Josephus's account), she adds: "La justification de l'amixia juive par la piété des Juifs n'est autre que le discours caractéristique des apologètes juifs, tel que nous le connaissons par la Lettre d'Aristée (cf. paras. 128–171), et plus tard par l'oeuvre de Philon." However, the word *amixia* appears in Josephus only in the "long siege story," and neither it nor its cognate adjective *amiktos* appears at all in *pseudo-Aristeas*, even when one might have expected it (e.g., *ps.-Aristeas* 130, 139, 142, 150). In addition, the reason for Jewish exclusivity offered by *pseudo-Aristeas* (called by various names such as *diastolē*; see 153) is not Jewish *eusebeia* or any other equivalent term, but serious flaws among the Gentiles (*ps.-Aristeas* 129–69): bodily pollution (dietary and sexual) or spiritual pollution (animal worship, cruelty). Philo, who tries on more than one occasion to justify Jewish exclusivity, uses the adjective *amiktos* about eight times, usually together with *akoinōnētos* (ἄμικτος καὶ ἀκοινώνητος), to denote abhorrent individuals or groups, such as Caligula and cannibals. Only once does this combined expression appear in Philo in a Gentile argument against the Jews. Is then the use of *amixia* "characteristic of Jewish apologists"?

86. On the chronology of the Eastern expedition and its phases, see the detailed study of Schwartz (1996).

87. See Meshorer (1982) 160–61 and pl. 56; Houghton (1983) 83–84; Meshorer (1995) 203–4.

88. See p. 418 above and note 50.

Hasmonaean period (scattered arrows and artillery stones) found in the area of the so-called David's Tower may be related to Antiochus's siege around the northwestern corner of the wall.[89] At the beginning of the siege, the king's troops suffered from a lack of water. The northern sector was indeed waterless, and the natural exit of the Gihon well (about 1 kilometer to the south) was then concealed.[90] The plight is said to have been relieved by heavy, autumnal rain filling up the hollows, pits, and provisional cisterns in the area. The story does not refer to a water supply inside the city, but one would imagine that the Jews could rely on Shiloh, the city pools, and other reservoirs. As the siege dragged on, the Jews suffered from a great shortage of food and other provisions. A seven-day truce for the religious holiday of Tabernacles (sometime in October) is not impossible, as this is rooted in Greek tradition. The ceasefire helped in restoring mutual trust. Negotiations between the two sides commenced soon after the holiday. A testimonium in the Scroll of Fasting dates the withdrawal of "King Antiochus" from Jerusalem to 28 Shvat (= end of winter),[91] probably referring to the removal of the siege by Antiochus VII.[92] It appears, then, that the negotiations dragged on for a few months until the early spring of 131. Finally, the Jews accepted the terms imposed on them: they undertook to surrender their weapons and to recognize Seleucid supremacy by paying the *phoros* and a special tribute for the "corridor" to the sea,[93] and gave hostages; they succeeded only in rejecting the king's demand to reintroduce the Seleucid garrison into the holy city. The king, however, was not content with this and destroyed the battlements as well,[94] which, presumably, had not been agreed upon. Beyond that, however, it is difficult to tease out real facts from tendentious imagination.[95]

89. See Sivan and Soler (1985), (1994); Shatzman (1995) 54.

90. Haker (1956) 198–99; Ussishkin (1994) 18. See also Josephus *Bellum Judaicum* 5. 140, 410, 505. On the blocking of the 'Ain Rogel well (Bir Aiyub), see Josephus *Antiquitates Judaicum* 9. 255; Haker (1957) 199–200.

91. For the calculation of the dates, see Parker and Dubberstein (1956) 42. However, allowance must be made for an accidental difference in the cycle of intercalation between the Babylonian fixed astronomical calendar (on which this equation is based) and the Jewish "flexible" calendar, based on ad hoc observations.

92. For a rejection of the proposal that the reference is to the withdrawal of Antiochus V Eupator in 162 B.C.E. (1 Macc. 6.62–63), see Bar-Kochva (1989) 550. For a survey of the interpretations, see Noam (2003) 291–92.

93. See note 21 above.

94. See note 30 above.

95. The short chronological note in Eusebius *Chronica* I. 255 (ed. Schoene = Stern, *GLAJJ* no. 457b) may reflect a corruption in his source, Porphyry, or else Eusebius himself may be responsible for the corruption. The siege is dated there to the third year of the 162nd Olympiad, i.e., 129 B.C.E., which is certainly wrong and contradicts other data mentioned above. The corruption is most obvious in the main sentence: *per obsidionem muros urbis evertebat, atque electissimos ipsorum tru-*

Whence did Posidonius take the basic historical information and the accusations and libels? The answer to this question requires a separate investigation (see chapter 14).

EXCURSUS: WAS THE JERUSALEM SIEGE BY ANTIOCHUS SIDETES STOPPED BECAUSE OF A ROMAN DIPLOMATIC INTERVENTION?

The only concerted analysis so far attempted of the story of the siege of Jerusalem by Antiochus Sidetes as related by Josephus is that of the learned British scholar Tessa Rajak in an interesting article extensive both in breadth and in depth.[96] The article draws attention to seemingly three major difficulties in the story: (1) there appears to be no real military reason obliging Antiochus to stop the siege and come to terms with the Jews;[97] (2) the episode concerning the sacrifice sent by Antiochus to the Temple does not make sense if dated to the time before the cessation of hostilities;[98] (3) the compliments to the Jewish religion and Jewish customs, taken from a Gentile author, sound strange in the given context.[99]

On the basis of these considerations, Rajak conjectures that Antiochus was forced to stop the siege because of an external reason that was deliberately left unrecorded. The pious sacrifice occurred only after the blockade was raised, and the Jewish religion was praised as never before in order to disguise in a way the real background for Antiochus's retreat.[100] Rajak hypothesizes that it was a stern Roman warning that convinced the king to stop the siege. She tries to support her view by dating the *senatus consultum,* quoted in *Jewish Antiquities* 13. 259–66, to the time of the siege.[101] The document given to Jewish delegates had been dated

---

cidabat ("by means of the siege he began to tear down the walls of the city and slaughter their elite"). As already mentioned, only the battlements were destroyed, and hostages were taken, but there is no reference to a slaughter of the leading citizens. Such a drastic punishment would hardly have contributed to the reconciliation and cooperation so evident after the siege. If this is not entirely the product of Porphyry's or Eusebius's imagination, it may be due to a misunderstanding (by Porphyry or Eusebius) or a mistranslation of the text (by Eusebius—slaughtering the elite may conceal a more mundane phrase, such as destroying the topmost parts of the wall). In any case, Porphyry did not obtain his mistaken information from a Seleucid source, and it has no value in a reconstruction of the events of the siege.

96. Rajak (1981). See also Rajak (2001) 81–98 (unchanged).
97. Rajak (1981) 66, 71–72.
98. Rajak (1981) 66–67.
99. Rajak (1981) 70–71.
100. Rajak (1981) 72, 79: "The king would wish at all costs to expunge his humiliation from the record. Weakness was explained as piety and magnanimity; and for this to be possible, the Jews had to be held up as worthy recipients. . . . Thus, to save face, Antiochus eulogized the Jews and Judaism, and the king's propaganda entered the Greek historical tradition."
101. Rajak (1981) 72 ff.

by a good number of scholars (following the sequence in Josephus) to some time after the siege, during the years 128–125 B.C.E.[102] Rajak argues against this dating that the decree mentions the request of the Jews that "Jaffa, and ports, and Gazara and Pegai and whatever other cities and places Antiochus took from them in war, contrary to the decree of the senate, will be restored (to them)" (para. 261); she contends that there was no point in raising this demand after the agreement between Antiochus and Hyrcanus, and if Antiochus had defied it, Hyrcanus would not have accompanied him on his expedition against the Parthians.

The first (and basic) point raised by Rajak does not pose a real difficulty. The reason for stopping the siege is quite obvious: Antiochus VII had achieved his main aims in the surrender agreement. The siege was terminated in early spring 131, just a year before the king set out on his great expedition against the Parthians (spring 130).[103] He prepared himself for the expedition well in advance by settling his relations with the various ethnic elements of his realm so as to secure his domestic front, as well as guaranteeing a supply of auxiliaries for his future crucial undertaking (cf. Justin 36. 1. 9–10; 38. 10. 5–6). The subjugation of the Jews was just one of these preparatory steps, as appears from Josephus-Nicolaus (*AJ* 13. 250). Once this aim had been achieved, there was no point in prolonging the siege, even less so since it was hard on the besiegers as well. The Seleucid army was vulnerable because of the scarcity of food in the neighborhood, the long lines of supply through the mountainous region, and its deployment in the field in winter. The relatively relaxed Seleucid military life (especially in the time of Antiochus VII)[104] would not have encouraged the king to press for a spectacular military victory at any price in the Roman manner.

Turning to the two versions of the siege story, according to Josephus-Strabo-Posidonius, Hyrcanus agreed to surrender Jewish weapons and give hostages, recognized formal Seleucid supremacy (symbolized by the payment of the *phoros*),[105] and undertook to pay special tributes (δασμὸν ... τελεῖν) for the cities of the "corridor" to the sea (Jaffa-Gazara-Pegai), occupied and settled by his father Simon (*AJ* 13. 246–47). According to Josephus-Nicolaus, Hyrcanus paid the *phoros* and a tribute and supplied auxiliaries for the king's Eastern expedition (*AJ* 13. 250–52; *BJ* 1. 62). These must have been satisfactory terms from the king's point of view, certainly in the given circumstances. On balance, he had achieved even more than he could have expected from Simon in 139,

102. See Stern (1965) 148–51; (1991) 83–87, and references there to other scholars.

103. On the chronology, see pp. 433–34 above.

104. See some of the sources, p. 424ff. above. The tendentious portrait provided by Posidonius, although highly exaggerated, reflects a deterioration in the standards of the Seleucid army, which never matched up to the austerity of Roman armies.

105. Diodorus 34/35. 1. 5; and see p. 405 note 21 above.

upon whom he tried—unsuccessfully—to impose tough conditions (1 Macc. 15.28–36).[106]

As for the other two difficulties pointed out by Rajak, and the solution she suggests, they are based on the assumption that the story is real history in its details and would therefore be presented correctly if the sequence of the sacrifice episode were to be altered. The account, however, would still remain highly unrealistic and imaginary.[107] Considering that its source, Posidonius of Apamea, wrote philosophy in the guise of history,[108] the details of the episode as they stand need to be regarded and evaluated not only in the light of historical logic, but also, and especially, in the light of Posidonius's views and didactic purposes. In his ingenious version of the siege story, Posidonius used only a kernel of historical data as a framework for illustrating through a creative narrative his historiosophic and philosophical ideas, as well as his personal and subjective feelings. The description of the luxurious sacrifice and the praise of the king for the Jewish faith are, like other episodes and details in the account, fictions that serve Posidonius's purposes perfectly well.[109]

The dating of the Roman document (AJ 13. 259–66) to the time of the siege, as suggested by Rajak, is not compelling and itself raises great difficulties. Rajak's argument against the accepted dating fails to take into account that Hyrcanus agreed to Seleucid supremacy over the corridor to the sea by complying with the king's demand to pay tribute for "Jaffa and the other cities alongside Judaea" (AJ 13. 246). This payment was in addition to the annual *phoros*,[110] which means that the region had a different status from Judaea proper. Having naturally anticipated Hyrcanus by occupying the "corridor" before the siege of Jerusalem, Antiochus must have taken the necessary measures to control it, mainly by the posting of garrisons (as he had intended to do in Jerusalem, 246). He did not have any reason to withdraw them, certainly not to evacuate "the ports," after the termination of the Jerusalem siege. If the stationing of garrisons in the "corridor" does not appear among the peace terms, it is only because it was already a fait accompli; the peace agreement includes only new Jewish undertakings forced on them as a condition for raising the siege. In the first years after the death of Antiochus VII, Hyrcanus was hesitant in applying force to restore former Jewish territorial

---

106. The total sum of five hundred talents, which was agreed upon, is admittedly only half of what he demanded of Simon (1 Macc. 15.31). However, Simon was ready to pay just one hundred, and only for Jaffa and Gazara (15.35), and by the standards of Oriental bargaining, getting half of his original financial demand was quite an achievement for the Seleucid king. To this should be added the other conditions of surrender, which were not requested in the year 139.

107. See pp. 417–22, 433–35 above.

108. See pp. 422–31 above.

109. See pp. 417–32 above.

110. See p. 405 note 21 above.

gains. He did after all turn to his aggressive expansionist policy only sixteen years later.[111] Beginning in 128, a request by the Jewish delegation to the Senate to help restore Jewish rights in the coastal region was thus only natural. There is, therefore, at the outset, no justification for rejecting the accepted dating of the document to after Sidetes' death.

Apart from this, there is a major obstacle to attributing the Senate's decree to the time of the siege. The document does not mention a Jewish request to raise the siege (which would have been much more acute to the Jewish delegates than the question of the "corridor"), nor does it even mention the siege. Would the Jews only ask, for example, to bar Seleucid troops from passing through the country of the Jews or "that of their subjects" (para. 262), or to be compensated for the devastation of their lands (para. 263), without mentioning that Jerusalem was under heavy siege? In fact, the Senate only renewed the old—indeed, obsolete—treaty with the Jews but deferred deliberations about the Jews' practical requests to support their territorial claims until the Senate "should have leisure from its own affairs" (para. 265).[112] The Romans thus agreed only to renew the meaningless treaty. This had never stopped the Seleucids in their struggle against the Jews in Judaea. Besides, the Jews were hardly able to send a delegation to Rome at the height of a "hermetic" siege of Jerusalem, with the approaches to the sea occupied and actually blocked. The logistics would have been troublesome enough in time of peace.

The delegation was sent, therefore, as usually assumed, and as appears from the sequence in Josephus, sometime after the death of Antiochus Sidetes, that is, around 128 B.C.E., with a request to exert influence on his successors in Antioch and persuade them to withdraw the garrisons from the "corridor," to recognize

111. The sequence of events in *Antiquitates Judaicae* 13. 254–58 and *Bellum Judaicum* 1. 62–63 is mistaken. As has been established by the archaeological excavations and surveys of the last fifteen years, the occupation of Idumaea-Mt. Hebron and the region of Samaria took place only in 112–107 B.C.E. See p. 408 note 27 above for references.

112. Rajak is aware of the absence of any reference to the siege and responds: "We should expect the Jews to have made a naked request that Rome arrange for the siege to be lifted; the senatorial record gives a list of some of their formal demands, and these are such as are relevant to a future settlement of the area. The envoys would, however, first have apprised the senate of the current situation, in a 'briefing' which would not have entered the record" ([1981] 77 n. 20). All this is hardly credible in the midst of a hard siege of the Jewish capital; and why would Antiochus Sidetes have stopped the siege without an explicit official demand embodied in a *senatus consultum*? Rajak responds: "For Rome to weaken her support of the Seleucid King, and to hint disapproval for his enemy, was enough to step him back" (78). However, the Roman document in *Antiquitates Judaicae* 14. 145–48, dated to the first year of the reign of Hyrcanus (so, rightly, Stern [1965] 146–48, 157–58; [1991] 79–82) explicitly certified the right of the Jews to security within the borders of Judaea, and in the newly occupied areas, but did not deter Antiochus from occupying Judaea and besieging Jerusalem. The document under discussion is much softer in its support for the Jews.

the rights of Jews in the region, to pay compensation for the damage caused by the Seleucid occupations, and to warn the new Seleucid rulers against further attempts at conquering Judaea, and even at trespassing in the "corridor" during any future incursions against the Ptolemies and cities in the southern coastal plain. One would suspect that the postponement of deliberations by the Senate to a time of "leisure from its own affairs" is a diplomatic evasive maneuver. It meant in fact a rejection of the request, since the *senatus consultum* is dated to the second week of February (para. 260), the only month devoted by the Senate to hearing foreign delegations,[113] and the Jewish emissaries are at the same time seen back home (paras. 263, 265). The Senate may well have been reluctant to intervene effectively in Seleucid-Jewish affairs after the death of Antiochus Sidetes, so as not to further weaken the Seleucids in face of the advancing Parthians.[114]

In conclusion, there is no real evidence or compelling reason for believing that Roman political pressure forced Antiochus Sidetes to stop the siege of Jerusalem and come to terms with the Jews.[115] The decisive considerations, after all, are that there is not only no demand in the Roman resolution to raise the siege, but no siege at all is mentioned there, and that the Selucid court should have been well satisfied with the king's achievement and have had no reason to invent unreasonable excuses for his decisions.

113. See Talbert (1984) 208–9, 412.

114. It should be added that the emendments to the text of the document in Josephus *Antiquitates Judaicae* 13. 262 suggested by Rajak (1981) 75–76 are philologically and historically unnecessary. The text as it stands sounds correct. It refers to Antiochus VII's defiance of the Roman call for the security of Judaea and its annexed parts mentioned in the resolution from the year 135/4 (*AJ* 14. 147; see note 112 above).

115. Cf. the short comment by Gruen (1984) 2: 670 n. 265. The attempt of Berthelot (2003) 192, 195, to support Rajak's hypothesis fails to produce new arguments.

13

Posidonius of Apamea (D)

The Anti-Jewish Libels and Accusations in Diodorus and Apion

We have seen in chapters 11–12 that Posidonius used Moses and Mosaic Judaism to portray his own religious, social, and political ideals. We have also observed that in accordance with his theory of two main periods in the development of civilization he went on to describe the period of decline of Judaism, where first, under the rule of priests, customs crept into Judaism that were based on superstition, leading to a later phase where greedy tyrants gained power and maltreated not only their own people, but also their neighbors. On the other hand, we are in possession of two extremely anti-Jewish passages associated, rightly or wrongly, with the name of Posidonius. Both severely criticize Moses and the laws he instituted for the Jewish people. These passages also record the three most damning and humiliating libels launched against the Jewish people in the ancient world: the leper libel, the ass libel, and the blood libel.

In light of these passages, not a few scholars have described Posidonius as "anti-Semitic" and the like.[1] Others have rejected this view,[2] and some have had difficulty appraising his position.[3] The discussion below will consider the attribution of these passages to Posidonius, what was and was not included in Posidonius' account, and, above all, Posidonius's attitude toward the accusations and the libels adduced by him.

---

1. E.g., Stählin (1905) 23–24; Schürer (1901–9) 3: 21; Bentwich (1914) 207–8; Radin (1915) 169–70, 231; Baron (1952) 156; Isaac (1956) 76; Tcherikover (1961) 384–85; Efron (1962) 27; Sevenster (1975) 9, 51–52, 90–91; Kasher (1996) 376–78.

2. See the references in note 13 below.

3. Stern, *GLAJJ* 1: 143; Gager (1983) 41; Gabba (1989) 46–48; Berthelot (2003) 195–97.

THE ANTI-JEWISH TESTIMONIA
ATTRIBUTED TO POSIDONIUS

The first passage is a testimonium in the second book of *Contra Apionem* in which Josephus relates the ass libel and the blood libel. The libels have been adduced above in chapters 6 and 7, where the question of the primary sources and the transmission of the two libels were discussed. I shall here once again summarize the content of the libels as reported by Josephus: when Antiochus Epiphanes entered the Temple in Jerusalem he found the golden head of an ass worshipped by Jews. Worse still, he also found a Greek being fattened by the Jews with a variety of luxurious dishes prior to his sacrifice on the altar in the Temple and a cannibalistic feast to be made from his body in the groves.

Josephus declares that he is citing Apion. He announces in his introduction to the ass libel that Posidonius and Apollonius Molon were those who "furnished him (Apion) with kindling wood of that sort" (para. 79), and repeats this claim in more detail in his introduction to the blood libel, where he states: "The same authors (i.e., Posidonius and Apollonius) also invented the story in order to excuse the sacrilege committed by Antiochus Epiphanes against the Temple and the Jewish people" (para. 90). It appears that Apion stated that he had taken the story from Posidonius and Apollonius Molon.

The previous chapter has given us an opportunity to become acquainted with the historical framework of the content of the second passage, the extremely abbreviated account of Diodorus Siculus of the siege of Jerusalem by Antiochus Sidetes.[4] There is now no doubt that this version, which has reached us through Photius, the ninth-century patriarch of Constantinople, ultimately derives from Posidonius.[5] Before proceeding with a discussion of this passage, it will be necessary to quote it in full:

> When King Antiochus (VII Sidetes), he (= Diodorus) says, was besieging Jerusalem, the Jews held out for a time, but when all their supplies were exhausted they were compelled to conduct negotations concerning a cessation of hostilities. The majority of his friends (*philoi*) advised him (= the king) to take the city by force and to destroy utterly the race (*genos*) of the Jews: for [the friends said that] they (= the Jews) alone of all nations did not take part in mingling with any other nation and considered all [people to be] their enemies. They (= the friends) pointed to the ancestors of them (= the Jews) also, [who] as impious (*asebeis*) and hated by the gods, [had been] driven out of all Egypt. (2) For[, they said,] those being white [with leprosy] or having leprous marks on their bodies had been assembled and driven across the border for the sake of purification; the outcast had occupied

4. See pp. 410–13 above.
5. See above, p. 412 and note 38.

the territory round about Jerusalem and, having organized the nation of the Jews, made traditional the hatred against men (τὸ μῖσος τὸ πρὸς τοὺς ἀνθρώπους); and because of this they even introduced wholly unusual customs (νόμιμα παντελῶς ἐξηλλαγμένα): not to share table with any other people (*ethnos*), nor to show [them] any goodwill at all. (3) [His friends] reminded him (= the king) also of the former hatred that his predecessors had felt against this nation. For Antiochus, the one called Epiphanes, having defeated the Jews, entered the innermost sanctuary of the god's temple, where it was lawful for the priest alone to enter. Finding there a stone statue of a heavily bearded man seated on an ass, with a book in his hands, he supposed it to be an image of Moses, the one who had founded Jerusalem and had put together the nation, and in addition to these [deeds] had ordained for the Jews the misanthropic and lawless customs (τὰ μισάνθρωπα καὶ παράνομα ἔθη). And having abhorred (στυγήσας)[6] the [Jews'] misanthropy of all nations, he (Antiochus Epiphanes) desired to rescind the[ir] laws. (4) Wherefore, having sacrificed before the image of the founder and the open-air altar of the god a big sow, and both poured its blood over them and, having prepared its flesh, ordered, with the broth of the [flesh], their holy books, containing the xenophobic laws (*misoxena nomima*), to be sprinkled; while the lamp, called by them undying and burning continually in the temple, [he ordered] to be extinguished; and [he also ordered] to compel the High Priest and the rest of the Jews to partake of the flesh. Going through these [events], the friends were strongly urging Antiochus to destroy utterly the [Jewish] nation (*ethnos*), or, if not that, to abolish the laws and force them to change their ways. (5) But the king, being "greathearted" (*megalopsychos*) and civilized ("humane," *hēmeros*) in [his] manners, having taken hostages, acquitted the Jews of the charges (ἀπέλυσε τῶν ἐγκλημάτων τοὺς Ἰουδαίους), having both exacted the tribute that was due and dismantled the walls of Jerusalem. (Diod. 34/35. 1–5; in Phot. *Bibl. cod.* 244, 379)

This full text of Diodorus-Posidonius allows us to examine the reliability of Apion's claim that the story of the entrance of Antiochus into the Temple and his discovery of a golden ass head and a fattened Greek destined for sacrifice had been found in Posidonius. Supposing for a moment that Apion's account has derived from Posidonius, where, and in what context, would Posidonius have used such a story?

An account of Antiochus IV's forced entry into the Temple and of the anti-Jewish accusations and libels could obviously have been included only in Posidonius' *Histories,* and—as it seems, inevitably—only in the context of the report about Antiochus Sidetes' siege of Jerusalem, as they appear in Diodorus:[7] the historical

6. The translation of Walton (1967) 35, "shocked" for στυγήσας, is mistaken. The usual sense of the verb is "to abhor," "to detest"; and so, as an active aorist, στυγήσας would be translated "having abhorred." στυγήσας by itself is an emendation suggested by Wetstein for σύσησας of the MSS. Reiske suggested συννοήσας, which is out of place (see Walton, 35).

7. Cf. Heinemann (1919) 119–20; Bickerman (1976–80) 2: 251; Stern, *GLAJJ* 1: 142; id. (1976) 1124.

narrative of the *Histories* commenced in 146 B.C.E., namely, more than two decades after the intrusion into the Temple. A comparison of the testimonium of Apion with the Diodorus-Posidonius version, however, reveals two major differences. First, the ass story: according to Apion, Antiochus IV saw in the Temple the golden head of an ass; according to Diodorus, a stone statue of Moses seated on a whole ass and holding a book.[8] The second version, although it contradicts the Jewish claim of abstention from sculpture of humans and animals, is far less hostile, and certainly not mocking. Greek readers could also have regarded the sculpture as an expression of the "founder cult" common in the Greco-Roman world.[9] It could also have been understood merely as a votive offering, as is explicitly presented in Tacitus's Jewish excursus (*Hist.* 5. 4. 2).

The conclusion is that Apion falsely named Posidonius as his reference for the ass-head story.[10] It makes no difference in this context whether Apion used Posidonius's work directly or indirectly. Josephus did not challenge Apion on this count, although he piled on any available argument in order to refute the libels, since he did not have at hand the *Histories* of Posidonius and did not bother to consult it.[11]

The second major difference between Apion and Diodorus relates to the blood libel, which is missing from the latter version. There are traces in Diodorus, however, indicating that it had been omitted at some stage in the transmission: the story relates how Antiochus Epiphanes entered the Jewish sacred place and saw a statue of a "heavily bearded man seated on an ass with a book in his hands." Antiochus understood that this was the sculpture of Moses "who ordained for the Jews their misanthropic and lawless customs." This means that he was already well acquainted with the Jews' "misanthropic and lawless customs." Then comes the concluding sentence: "Having abhorred such hatred directed against all nations, he desired to rescind the(ir) laws." Yet the cause for the king's sudden abhorrence of Jewish customs and the consequent drastic steps taken against the laws of the Jews certainly could not have been the sight of Moses riding an ass, or of the book Moses was holding. The (alleged) character of the Jewish laws was already known to Antiochus IV, whose dynasty had already been ruling Judaea continuously for a generation, as may also be understood from the wording of the story itself. The sight of the book is not what first revealed to Antiochus its contents. What, then, was the shocking discovery that

---

8. Noted, e.g., by Heinemann, Bickerman, and Stern; see note 7 for references.

9. See pp. 238–39 above.

10. So, rightly, Heinemann (1919) 119; Bickermann (1927) 251; Stern, *GLAJJ* 1: 184; Schäfer (1997a) 60. Kidd 2: 949 offers the unlikely suggestion that Josephus is the one who identified Posidonius as the source of the account.

11. On this question, see pp. 450–51 below.

led Antiochus to take unprecedented steps against the Jews? Whoever invented the story certainly wished (as suggested by Josephus) to justify the religious persecutions of Antiochus Epiphanes and would have needed to convince the reader. It seems, therefore, that the original version of the advice of the "friends" did contain the blood libel.[12]

Who omitted the blood libel? Was it Diodorus, Posidonius, or perhaps Photius? An evaluation of Posidonius's attitude toward the accusations, and the libels as a whole, will facilitate an answer to this question.

THE REACTION OF ANTIOCHUS VII SIDETES

The only surviving direct indication regarding Posidonius's attitude toward the accusations and libels is found in Diodorus's version, in the reference to Antiochus Sidetes' reaction to the advice of the "friends" (para. 4):

> And the king, being "greathearted" (*megalopsychos*) and civilized ("humane," *hēmeros*) in [his] manners (*ēthos*) ... acquitted the Jews of the charges (ἀπέλυσε τῶν ἐγκλημάτων τοὺς Ἰουδαίους).

We might appear to be able to conclude from this that Posidonius dismissed out of hand all the accusations and libels, as indeed a number of scholars have assumed from this sentence.[13] Others have argued that the formulation is Diodorean, and that the position of Posidonius cannot be inferred from it.[14] It has also been suggested that Posidonius accepted the accusations with reference to the Jews of his own time.[15] Matters, however, are much more complicated than they at first appear. The statement that the king acquitted the Jews is not in itself sufficient evidence that Posidonius shared this positive opinion, especially since the author explains the acquittal as the result of the king's characteristics, namely, that he was *megalopsychos* and *hēmeros*. It is necessary therefore to attempt a clarification of the meaning and intent of these two terms.

It should be made clear at the outset that the sentence retains the form it had in Diodorus, and is not a summary by Photius. Comparison of some long excerpts in Photius's *Bibliotheca* from *codex* 238 onward, which are also preserved in other sources, proves that in these excerpts Photius adhered to his sources, apart from slight and insignificant linguistic improvements. Abbreviations were made

---

12. Thus Heinemann (1919) 119; Malitz (1913) 311 n. 69; Stern (1976) 1124; Rajak (1983) 68; Kidd 2: 950.

13. Wendland (1912) 109 n. 3; Heinemann (1919) 120; Bickerman (1976–80) 2: 251; Jacoby, *FGrH* II. C, no. 87, p. 197; Stern, *GLAJJ* 1: 142–43; id. (1976) 1124; id. (1991) 607; Conzelmann (1981) 60; Malitz (1983) 311; Kidd 2: 950

14. Rajak (1981) 69.

15. Berthelot (2003) 186–87 (but otherwise in 195–97).

only in order to avoid duplications and stylistic awkwardness, or with regard to redundant details that detract from the main issue or the kernel of the story.[16] These things apart, it is unlikely that Photius made changes to the deliberations in the royal council, which he quoted precisely in order to show that Diodorus wrote lies about the Jews. He would not have abbreviated the king's reaction to the libels and accusations, and the phrasing is certainly not his own.[17]

To return to the meaning of the two terms, *hēmeros* is simply "humane," "civilized," with no philosophical overtones. It contrasts with the behavior of Antiochus Epiphanes and the advice of his "friends," and its attribution to Antiochus Sidetes may have originated with Posidonius to express opposition to excessive violence and senseless bloodshed, or with Diodorus, who uses the term dozens of times in his work. Whatever the case may be, the term *hēmeros* has little bearing on our inquiry. By contrast, the other term, *megalopsychos,* has many meanings, some popular, and some more philosophical.[18] The use of a philosophical term by a philosopher in a nonphilosophical sense is not exceptional.[19] If we understand the term in one of its popular senses—"greatheartedness," the characteristic of one who acts leniently—the sentence could be taken to mean that although Antiochus VII knew that the words of the "friends" were true, he decided to be lenient with the Jews and acquit them, rather than destroy them, and be content with the taking of hostages and the partial destruction of the walls of Jerusalem. If, however, we adopt another popular sense of *megalopsychos—* "fair," "aspiring to truth and justice"—Posidonius could be seen as portraying the king as deciding justly to acquit the Jews, which suggests that Posidonius himself regarded the libels and accusations in a completely negative light.

The picture becomes no clearer in light of the use of the words *megalopsychos* and *megalopsychia* in Diodorus. They appear more than thirty times, most frequently in the sense of "greatheartedness" in matters of money and pride, a meaning that does not suit the present context. The terms have several other senses in Diodorus, however, most of which may be more suitable: fairness and the pursuit of justice (1. 70. 6); nobility (15. 63. 2, 20. 25. 2, 31. 27. 7); courage (1. 67. 7);

16. See p. 103 note 34 above.

17. This does not detract from the possibility that Photius, and not Diodorus, is the one who omitted the detailed description of the siege itself (see pp. 410–12 above). Photius was accurate in the extracts he copied, but at the same time he copied only what was required for his needs.

18. For the colloquial usage, see, e.g., Xenophon *Cyropaedia* 4. 2. 14; Agesilaus 8. 3–4; Isocrates 9. 3. 59; Polybius 1. 8. 4, 64. 5; 22. 21. 3; 29. 24. 13; 31. 28. 9. For Diodorus, see below.

19. Thus, for instance, Aristotle does not always use common words in the technical sense he has given them. At *Rhetorica* 1419b8–9, for example, he uses ἐλευθερώτερον (freer) in a nontechnical sense, having defined and used ἐλευθεριότης earlier (1366b7–9, 15–16) in the same technical sense as in *Nicomachean Ethics* 1107b8–10 and elsewhere in his technical works. Cf. also the flexible use of *kosmos* in some of his works.

leniency instead of expected tough measures (2. 28. 5); refraining from vengeance for injustice done (1. 92. 4; 17. 69. 5, 84. 1); and broad-mindedness (30. 21. 3). The first two senses would have the king believing that the accusations and libels are untrue, while the latter senses would portray him believing the opposite.[20] Those appearances of *megalopsychia* in Diodorus where the source is Posidonius are of particular interest. In one case the word appears in opposition to financial greed and perhaps to arrogant pride (5. 29. 5); in another case it appears as generosity in financial matters (33. 22. 1); in a third case it denotes a fair attitude toward those deserving of it (34/35. 23).

Let us turn now to philosophical usage. The pre-Socratics had already given the adjective *megalopsychos* and the noun *megalopsychia* some philosophical connotations.[21] Neither term appears in Plato,[22] but the *megalopsychos* person is described in detail by Aristotle, and *megalopsychia* has a special meaning in Stoic doxographies and testimonia of Panaetius. The philosophical meanings may have influenced popular usage as well.

In his *Nicomachean Ethics* (1123a34–1125a16) Aristotle exalts *megalopsychia* as an ornament (*kosmos*) of all the virtues (*EN* 1124a1–2).[23] For the sentence under discussion, some features of the term may be relevant. The *megalopsychos* is characterized as a sincere man who does not disguise his feelings and speaks frankly about his loves and hatreds. In addition, he is not vindictive and tends to write off evils done to him personally. Is the Aristotelian meaning applicable to Posidonius? While scholars used to see Aristotle as a major source of inspiration for Stoic thought,[24] since F. H. Sandbach's landmark study of the whole issue, it has become widely accepted that Aristotle's works were little read by the Stoics. Reference used to be made frequently to the following statement by Strabo:

20. Berthelot (2003) 183–84, esp. n. 8, takes for granted that *hēmeros kai megalopsychos* is identical to *philanthrōpos/philanthrōpia*, which appear several times in Diodorus in books where Posidonius served as a source (33. 15. 1, 18. 1; 34/35. 3. 1, 20. 1; 36. 4. 8; 37. 26. 1). From this she concludes that the text intends to say that the king decided to treat the Jews leniently. The equation, however, is quite arbitrary, nor is it reasonable, considering that the word *philanthrōpia* itself, not to mention the common Hellenistic expression *philanathrōpos kai epieikēs*, appears in Diodorus innumerable times, while *hēmeros kai megalopsychos* appears only in our passage.

21. E.g., Democritus, D-K 68 B 46: μεγαλοψυχίη τὸ φέρειν πραέως πλημμέλειαν ("magnanimity is bearing transgression with mildness").

22. It appears three times in *spuria*, in a colloquial usage: *Alcibiades* 140c, 150c; *Definitiones* 412d.

23. Cf. *Eudemian Ethics* 1232a19–1233a30; for argument, 1232a32–38.

24. Most notably, in this context, Gauthier (1951), whose monograph on the history of the concept of *megalopsychia* may still be read with profit; his treatment of the Stoics, however, suffers from the assumption that they reacted to Aristotle (e.g., "La morale stoïcienne va reprendre le problème des rapports de l'homme et du monde au point exact où l'avait laissé Aristote," 121–22). For Gauthier's description of Posidonius's view of *megalopsychia*, see 143–44.

"There is in him (i.e., in Posidonius) much inquiry into causes, that is much in the manner of Aristotle (*to aristotelizon*), from which men of our philosophy abstain because causes are hidden from us" (2. 3.8). While this was once interpreted to mean that Posidonius used much Aristotelian material and was consequently well acquainted with his corpus, it is more likely to mean that he, like Aristotle, indulged too much in "inquiry into causes," and it has been cogently argued that there is positive evidence only for Posidonius's acquaintance with Aristotle's *Meteorologica*.[25] This still does not prove that Posidonius did not use other works by Aristotle, given the little we now have of Posidonius's writings. Be that as it may, caution must be exercised when using Aristotle to understand Posidonius.

There is no reference to the term under discussion in the philosophical sense that can be decisively proved to be Posidonian. It appears twice in Latin translation (*magnitudo animi*) in Seneca in passages said to have been drawn from Posidonius (*Ep.* 87. 32, 35),[26] but in view of the context, it would appear to be Senecan rather than Posidonian,[27] and in any case, the references do not provide much help toward a definition of the term (cf. Cic. *Off.* 3. 24).

In Stoic doxographies *megalopsychia,* instead of being a *kosmos* to all the virtues, as in Aristotle, is subordinated to "courage" (*andreia*), one of the four cardinal virtues. It is defined once as "the knowledge [that] causes [one] to be above the things that may happen to good (*spoudaioi*) and bad (*phauloi*) [persons alike]."[28] The Stoic often use the terms *spoudaioi* and *phauloi* as equivalent to the "wise" and "foolish" (people).[29] All this means that the *megalopsychos* is unaffected spiritually by chance events and does not occupy his mind with them.

Megalopsychia has an elevated position in the thinking of Panaetius,[30] traditionally regarded as Posidonius's mentor. It replaces "courage" (*andreia*) as one of the four cardinal virtues, alongside "wisdom," "justice," and "moderation," and includes, among other things, the readiness to take risks (Cic. *Off.* 1. 65) and contempt for external things (66). The adherence of the *megalopsychos* to the truth may be especially relevant for our discussion:

25. Sandbach (1985) 59–62, with references there to former views. He raises only as a possibility the suggestion that the passage in Strabo imputes to Posidonius conscious imitation of Aristotle, not a knowledge of the corpus. But see the remarks of Ludlam in the appendix, pp. 535–36 below, suggesting that it is Strabo himself who links Posidonius with Aristotle.

26. Regarded as evidence by Heinemann (1919) 120.

27. See Kidd 2: 630, 632–33.

28. *SVF* 3: 264, p. 64, ll. 23–24, 37–38; 265, p. 65, ll. 10–11; 269, p. 66, ll. 17–18; 274, p. 67, ll. 28–29; 275, p. 67, ll. 40–42.

29. See Adler's index, *SVF* 4: s.v. φαῦλος, where many references are given equating φαῦλος with ἄφρων and κακός, and s.v. σόφος, which includes many references equating σοφός with σπουδαῖος.

30. On the *megalopsychia* in Panaetius, see esp. Dyck (1981).

> Therefore we wish men brave and "greathearted" (*viros fortes et magnanimos*) to be good and simple, friends of truth, and not at all deceitful; these [qualities] are at the heart of the praise (literally "from the central praise") of justice. (Cic. *Off.* 1. 63)

This said, however, we do not have evidence proving that Posidonius shared Panaetius's definitions. In another field we know that he did not.[31]

This survey of the popular and philosophical usages of the terms *megalopsychos* and *megalopsychia* reveals that the wording of the king's reaction cannot determine the attitude of Posidonius toward the charges and libels. And we are still faced with the question of whether the wording in Diodorus is Posidonian and faithfully reflects the intentions of Posidonius. A conclusion may be reached only by examining the compatibility of the image of Moses and the Jews in the advice of the "friends" with that in Posidonius's Jewish excursus.

THE ORIGINAL LOCATION OF POSIDONIUS'S JEWISH EXCURSUS

Before beginning the examination proper, the context for the Jewish excursus in the Posidonian corpus should be established. It may prove essential for evaluating the perception of the reader of the advice of the "friends." In the tradition of Hellenistic historiography, the excursus would have served as an introduction to the significant political and/or military developments in the relations between the ruling kingdom in the area and the Jews.[32] Since 146 B.C.E., the starting point for Posidonius's *Histories,* no event of such significance to the regional power had occurred between the Seleucids and the Jews as the invasion of Judaea and the siege of Jerusalem by Antiochus VII Sidetes in 132/1. The Jews were practically independent already before 146 and had been recognized *de jure* by the Seleucids as such in 142/1. The campaign of Antiochus Sidetes against Judaea, and his siege of Jerusalem in 132/1, effectively returned the situation to where it had been before the declaration of independence. Posidonius regarded the siege as of extreme significance, and this may be appreciated by looking at the length of the account of the siege. The abbreviated version of Diodorus, emphasizing the advice of the "friends," taken together with the "long siege story" in Josephus, elaborating on the events of the siege itself, together with Plutarch's account of the sacrifice sent by the king to the Temple,[33] indicates that Posidonius's account of the siege was particularly detailed. No other affair, whether political or military, between the

---

31. See pp. 343, 382 above.

32. Cf. Diodorus 40. 3 (introduction to the conquest of Judaea and Jerusalem by Pompey); Tacitus *Histories* 5. 2 (introduction to the siege of Jerusalem by Titus).

33. See pp. 409–17 above.

Seleucids and the Jews prior to 132 has been related in such detail, not even in the contemporary Jewish source, 1 Maccabees.[34]

The siege story was therefore the first suitable opportunity for Posidonius to inform the readers about the Jews, their origins, their customs, their leaders, and the geography of their land. It was also the best opportunity, since no other development between the Jews and the Seleucids in the period from the siege through 84 B.C.E., the last year of his *Histories*, was as significant. Some of the events in the first years of Alexander Jannaeus (103–101) had similar significance for the relations between the Jews and the Ptolemies. However, they did not lead to the reoccupation of Judaea by the Ptolemies, and Posidonius, born in Apamea, naturally concentrated on "northern" history, using Seleucid sources. It is no accident that most of the fragments and testimonia of Posidonius have to do with Seleucid history.[35]

A parallel to the location of the Jewish excursus precisely in the context of the war conducted by Antiochus Sidetes against the Jews is to be found in the summary by Justin of the *Philippic Histories* by Pompeius Trogus (36. 2. 1–16). The excursus appears *in extenso* after a particularly condensed account of Seleucid history from Demetrius I to the defeat of the Jews by Antiochus Sidetes (35. 1–36. 1). Can the location of the excursus in Pompeius Trogus-Justin tell us whether the Jewish excursus in Posidonius immediately preceded or followed the siege story? Considering that the aim of an ethnographic excursus is to explain the described events, as seen from many parallel ethnographic excursuses of other nations in Greek and Hellenistic literature and from the location of ethnographic excursuses concerning Jews in other authors, such as Diodorus and Tacitus, it would appear that the position of the excursus in Pompeius Trogus after the siege story is exceptional, perhaps because in that case it does not contribute much to the historical narrative. The parallel in Pompeius Trogus-Justin is thus important for the matter of the general location: the defeat of the Jews by Antiochus VII Sidetes served as a suitable opportunity.[36]

A different opinion concerning the location of Posidonius's Jewish excursus was voiced by Karl Reinhardt. He argued that the excursus did not appear in the *Histories* but in a book by Posidonius on the exploits of Pompey, where it served as an introduction to the conquest of Judaea and Jerusalem by Pompey (similar to the location of Hecataeus's Jewish excursus in Diodorus). Reinhardt draws support from the reference to Pompey in Strabo toward the end of the account

---

34. On the dating of 1 Maccabees to some time after the death of Antiochus Sidetes in his campaign against the Parthians, see Bar-Kochva (1989) 152 ff.

35. Norden (1921) 281–82 and Malitz (1983) 312–13 also consider the excursus to have been connected to the siege story, but their reasoning is insufficient. Cf. Stern *GLAJJ* 1: 265.

36. This is also the opinion of Jacoby, *FGrH* II. C, no. 87, p. 196 (without explanation). Cf. Pompeius Trogus *Prol.* 36.

of the geography and history of Judaea (para. 46; the Jewish excursus appears in paras. 35–37).[37] This is, however, no evidence, since the reference to Pompey is intended to explain who governed Judaea in the time of Strabo. Immediately following it there are reported events and developments subsequent to the time of Pompey: the rise of Herod the High Priest (meaning Hyrcanus II), and in more detail Herod the king, presented as his son, followed by his own sons, and it is even stated that while one was exiled to Gaul, the others remained in some of the regions controlled by their father.

Jörgen Malitz, in his well-balanced monograph on the *Histories* of Posidonius, rightly rejects Reinhardt's proposal on the grounds that Posidonius, who used his ethnographic excursuses of the Iberians and Gauls as introductions to their great struggles with the Romans, would hardly have dispensed with an ethnographic excursus on the Jews in his *Histories*.[38] It should be added that in 84 B.C.E., when Posidonius finished writing his *Histories,* he had no reason to believe that he would be writing a later work in which he might be able to insert an ethnography on the Jews. Furthermore, the very assumption, originating with Reinhardt, that Posidonius of Apamea wrote an encomium of Pompey, is extremely doubtful.[39]

It is worth noting here that unlike Posidonius's *Histories,* Strabo's historical work contained no Jewish excursus; one appears in his later *Geographica*. The same is true of a number of other ethnographic excursuses of peoples that were included in the *Geographica*. It is difficult to believe that all these also appeared in an earlier work by the same author. When Strabo was writing his historical work, he may already have decided to embark upon an exhaustive geographical work, and had chosen to include the ethnographies there. Strabo's geography was quite different in its subject matter from standard Hellenistic geography, which was concerned mainly with physical geography and cosmological matters. He emphasized sites and settlements, in the tradition of the Greek *periplous* and *periegesis* genres, drawing on material from such works. The ethnographic excursus was necessary for this subgenre of geographical writing. The excursus is what gave the information about settlements significance beyond a mere list of names and their locations.

The conclusion that the Jewish excursus did not appear in Strabo's historical work is also supported by the fact that Josephus, who often cites that work in *Jewish Antiquities* (books 13–14), did not refer to the Jewish excursus of the *Geographica* in his final treatise, *Contra Apionem,* published nine years later. The first book of this work was written to refute Apion's claim that the Jewish people was young, lacking tradition and roots, and unknown in the history of

37. Reinhardt (1921) 26 ff.
38. Malitz (1983) 313–14.
39. See p. 348 above.

civilized nations. Yet Josephus could manage to find in Greek literature only vague hints of the activity of Jews in the fifth century, and more explicit accounts on the Jews in the fourth (not all of them genuine). Had he been acquainted with Strabo's Jewish excursus, he would not have missed the opportunity to include the conclusive evidence of a highly reputable and admired Greek author regarding both the antiquity of the Jews, originating in the remote time of Moses, and the special admiration of Greeks toward those Jews. For the same reason (but this is not the only one), it is clear that Josephus did not know Strabo's *Geographica* or Posidonius's *Histories*.[40]

THE LIBELS AND ACCUSATIONS
IN LIGHT OF THE POSIDONIAN MATERIAL

The structure and contents of the advice of the "friends" in Diodorus now needs to be considered in more detail. It consists of two parts: the first part (paras. 1–2) concentrates on the origins of the Jewish people in Egypt, their departure from there, and the special laws of Moses; the second (paras. 3–4) tells of the visit of Antiochus Epiphanes to the Temple in Jerusalem, his discovery in the Temple of the statue of Moses riding an ass, the king's decision to root out the laws of the Jews, and his desecration of the Temple.

The first part portrays the ancestors of the Jews as lepers and impious people who were exiled from Egypt. According to the "friends," the Jews' misanthropy— hatred of strangers, to go by its external features—developed with the settling of the Jewish people in Jerusalem and its environs into a tradition passed from generation to generation of Jews. Laws were adapted to accommodate it, such as the prohibition against eating in the company of strangers and against showing them goodwill. It is not stated explicitly but may be understood by the reader that the hostility of Jews toward strangers is the result of their expulsion from Egypt, just as it had been explained in Greek literature ever since the Jewish excursus of Hecataeus of Abdera.[41] The second part of the advice complements the first: it relates, among other things, that Moses settled the Jewish people in Jerusalem and established the "misanthropic and lawless customs." The statue discovered in the Temple is of Moses riding an ass, holding in his hand the Jewish book of laws. The account of the advice of the "friends," which Posidonius used as a source, also contained the blood libel, the harshest expression of Jewish misanthropy.[42] As the first step in the new war against the customs of the Jews, Antiochus Epiphanes ordered a pig to be sacrificed in the Temple, and the Jewish holy books to be

40. Cf. p. 413 note 41 above.
41. See p. 131 above.
42. See above, pp. 443–44.

defiled with the fat of the pig—all this before turning to stamping out the Jewish laws and customs.

The contents of the two parts, taken separately or together, are in marked contrast to the spirit and intent of the Posidonian Jewish excursus, where the author evidently enthuses about Moses by embodying Posidonian religious, social, and political ideals in his thoughts and deeds. As the excursus served as an introduction to the story of the siege of Jerusalem by Antiochus Sidetes, Posidonius would certainly not have accepted such a contrasting, negative description of Moses. The differences between the excursus and the advice of the "friends," as we shall see, can be discerned not only in the characterization of Moses and Mosaic Judaism, but also of contemporary Jews.

Various details reveal differences between the Jewish excursus and the advice of the "friends." The most outstanding of these are the following, beginning with the period identified by Posidonius as the ideal, namely, the period of Mosaic Judaism:

1. In the excursus, Moses was a senior Egyptian official with noble views concerning divinity and society, and his followers were enlightened men who aspired to worship the divine entity in a suitable manner; they were not a rabble of lepers hated by the gods, nor were they impious, but quite the opposite.
2. In the excursus, Moses and his followers were not expelled from Egypt but rather left of their own accord in order to preserve their religious mode of conduct without interference.
3. In the excursus, there is no trace of legislation by Moses, nor of a book of laws bequeathed by him. There was no need for laws in that ideal society.[43]
4. In the excursus, there is no hint of misanthropy. The Jews were not expelled from Egypt, the usual reason given for Jewish misanthropy, nor was there any other reason in the excursus for the hatred of strangers to develop. Indeed, far from hating strangers, the Jews received into their midst the peoples of neighboring Judaea who of their own free will wished to join them.[44]

Now a comparison of the advice of the "friends" with the account in the excursus of the subsequent period of decline. This account, it may be recalled, is divided into two stages: the rule of the priests with their inclination to superstition, and then the self-seeking rule of tyrants:[45]

43. See pp. 370–72 above.
44. See p. 369 above.
45. On the division, see pp. 372–73 above.

1. The "friends" introduce the libels and accusations in the context of the reign of Antiochus Epiphanes, a time that would necessarily have preceded the Posidonian stage of Jewish tyrants, while succeeding the Posidonian Mosaic ideal state, placing it in what Posidonius portrayed as the period of priestly rule. The priests were inclined to superstition, leading them to instigate customs such as the circumcision of men and women and abstention from types of meat. These customs, in Posidonius, stem from "superstition"; they do not even hint at the hatred of strangers, nor did they lead to the hatred of strangers. Were Posidonius to have thought so, he would not have refrained from making this explicit. The paragraph on the period of decline in which the Jewish customs are referred to (37) is quite detailed and not abbreviated.[46]

2. In the excursus, it is said that Moses established a cult free of anthropomorphism, images, and animal worship. There is no change in this aspect of worship in the period of decline, in contrast to the report of the "friends" concerning the presence of a statue in the Temple of Moses riding an ass.

3. The excursus ends with the statement that, despite their negative behavior in other respects, the tyrants respected the sanctity of the Temple (para. 37 fin.). It is even noted that they refrained from turning it into the seat of tyranny. Since tyrants did not turn temples into government buildings, this would imply that the Jewish tyrants did not place in the Temple statues of themselves, at a time when other Hellenistic rulers were encouraging self-deification and personality cults.[47]

Support for the conclusion that Posidonius necessarily rejected the account of the "friends" comes from the "long siege story" of Josephus-Strabo-Posidonius. It provides the basic answer to the claim of the "friends" that the Jews are misanthropic. The answer virtually reflects the content of the Jewish excursus. In the story it is said that Antiochus Sidetes rejected the advice of the "friends" to

46. Berthelot (2003) 185, aware that Posidonius says nothing whatsoever in the excursus about the hatred of strangers, has him hint about it anyway: "On peut donc reconstituer le raisonnement suivant: dans le cas Juifs, les lois imposées par les prêtes superstitieux, qui avaient pour but d'ériger une barrière entre les Juifs et les autres peuples, ont conféré au peuple Juif un caractère misanthrope et hostile aux étranger, qui se reflète dans une attitude aggressive vis-à-vis de leurs voisins." This chain of reasoning has little to do with Posidonian Judaism. The suggested chain, superstition-laws-character-behavior, finds no parallel even in Posidonian accounts of other peoples (Berthelot's reference to Hahm [1989] 1339, 1344, is irrelevant and misleading), nor in those accounts of contemporary pagan authors who condemn the Jewish hatred of strangers. Variations on this so-called anthropological theory are to be found in the writings of critics of Judaism beginning with the rationalism of the eighteenth century up to "scientific" anti-Semitism of the nineteenth and twentieth centuries, which is where they should remain.

47. All the above further refutes the interpretation of Berthelot (2003) 164, 184–87. See also p. 359 note 12 above.

destroy the Jewish people, since he believed that Jewish *amixia* stemmed from their *eusebeia* (para. 245). The same reasoning appears again in order to justify the stubborn opposition of the Jews during the negotiations with the king regarding his demand to install a garrison in Jerusalem (para. 247). This, then, is the reply of Posidonius to the charge of the "friends" against Jewish misanthropy: it is not a form of misanthropy developed as a reaction to bad experiences in a remote past, but self-isolation originating with aspiration toward *eusebeia*.[48] The Posidonius excursus holds Moses responsible both for the cause and for the effect, portraying him as leading his followers voluntarily out of Egypt and into Judaea in order to realize their ambition to practice their worship in the proper surroundings.

In light of all of the above, the term *megalopsychos,* discussed above, needs to be understood in the following popular senses, nontechnical senses also being used by philosophers such as Aristotle and Panaetius: "fair," "pursuing justice and truth," "rising above personal feelings," and so on. Thus Posidonius told his reader that although Antiochus VII Sidetes was personally offended by the Jewish revolt (cf. Joseph. *AJ* 13. 236), as any imperial ruler would be by any revolt, and although the atrocities on both sides naturally led to mutual ill will, the king ignored all that and was able to examine the accusations and libels brought before him objectively, in an attempt only to arrive at the truth. For this reason, he acquitted the Jews on every charge. The second term, *hēmeros,* means "civilized," in the context. The behavior of Antiochus Sidetes is contrasted with that of his predecessor, Antiochus Epiphanes, who took uncivilized steps against the Jews, steps considered unacceptable in relations between ruler and subjects. Posidonius, who had a very clear opinion regarding correct relations between ruler and subjects,[49] regarded Antiochus Epiphanes' behavior as uncivilized.

Would the average reader have necessarily understood correctly the expression *megalopsychos kai hēmeros,* and especially that flexible word *megalopsychos,* in this context? As we have just seen, Posidonius explained a little later in the same passage (Joseph. *AJ* 13. 246) that the charges of the "friends" (explicitly referred to) were rejected by the king on the grounds that Jewish self-isolation was a result of an aspiration to *eusebeia*. This effectively demolishes the charge of *misanthropia* that is at the heart of the accusations, and would have sufficed to give the reader the proper orientation regarding the position of the king (and the author) toward the accusations and libels, if it was not explicitly stated.

What clinches the argument is the context in which the account appears. The reader reached the advice of the "friends" almost immediately after the detailed

---

48. On *amixia,* cf. p. 415 n. 47 and p. 432 n. 85.

49. On the opinion of Posidonius regarding the proper relations between peoples, see above, pp. 377–79, 427.

excursus on Jews and Judaism. It would have been obvious to anyone just having read the excursus that the charges of the "friends" portraying Moses as the source of Jewish misanthropic practices were groundless. Thus the statement that Antiochus Sidetes acquitted the Jews of all the accusations because he was *megalopsychos* actually required neither explanation nor detailed refutation of the accusations. Even if the Jewish excursus had been located after the siege story (which is not the case), it would still have served as sufficient refutation of the charges and libels, making further explanation of the king's rejection of his counselors' advice entirely superfluous.

WHO OMITTED THE BLOOD LIBEL?

Having settled the question of the attitude of Posidonius toward the advice of the "friends," we are now in a position to return to the question, who omitted the blood libel from the account of the advice of the "friends"? Diodorus does not usually pass over such stories. He must have been quite happy to demonstrate Jewish *misoxenia*, an expression that he found already in the ethnographic excursus of Hecataeus (40. 3. 4).

Was the omission made in the transmission of Diodorus? Photius quotes Diodorus in order to criticize him for his attitude to the Jews as reflected in the advice of the "friends." He states that "Diodorus is lying with regard to the institutions and laws of Moses, the Exodus, and the foundation of Jerusalem," and that "in order not to be caught in the disgrace of lying, while contradicting himself, he (Diodorus) attributed the tale of lies to other people (i.e., the "friends"), whom he connects in friendship with Antiochus" (*Bibl. cod.* 244, 380a). Photius even blames Diodorus for lying in the unbiased excursus on the Jews in book 40, which was taken from Hecataeus of Abdera (381a). For Photius's Byzantine readers, the blood libel would have proved more than anything else the unreliable character of Diodorus's account. Despite recurring persecutions of Jews, the Greek Orthodox Church adopted the medieval anti-Semitic blood libel only in the sixteenth century.[50]

This brings us to Posidonius as the remaining candidate for omitting the blood libel. If there is indeed any need to prove the negative opinion of Posidonius with regard to human sacrifice, in light of Stoic ethics, we have his position spelled out in his ethnographic excursus on the Celts, preserved in Strabo (4. 4. 2–6). The excursus is negative from beginning to end and does not distinguish between an ideal period and a later period of decline. The Celtic people is described, among other things, as senseless (ἀνόητος, 5), warlike (ἀρειμάνιος, 4), and foppish

---

50. See, e.g., Ankori (1984) 191 ff.

(φιλόκοσμος, "ornamentation-lover," 4—the opposite of Posidonian simplicity). Prominent in the excursus are the relatively detailed descriptions of various types of human sacrifice allegedly practiced by the Celts (5–6). Posidonius emphasizes that they were stopped by the Roman conquerors, since they were "opposed to our customs" (ὑπεναντίων τοῖς παρ' ἡμῖν νομίμοις)—that is, they were inhuman.

Why did Posidonius omit the anti-Jewish blood libel of all things? Inclusion of the blood libel would have required refuting it, since it was presented by the "friends" as the criminal manifestation of Jewish misanthropy attributed by them to Moses. Just a brief reference to it by the king, similar to his reaction to the self-isolation, relying only on what appeared from the preceding ethnographical excursus, would not have sufficed against such an abhorrent and shocking story. Refuting it would have required elaboration, and this would have been rather difficult to integrate into the sequence of a historical narrative. For similar reasons, Josephus chose to omit from his version of the siege of Antiochus VII in *Jewish Antiquities* the accusation and the ass and leper libels altogether but discussed the same set of anti-Jewish charges in detail in his later polemic *Contra Apionem*. The excessive cruelty imputed to the Jews by the blood libel would, in any case, have overshadowed the serene, ideal humane picture of Mosaic Judaism, and raised doubts about its reliability.

Apion, therefore, twice misled the reader when he attributed to Posidonius the two libels. His version of the ass libel was quite different from that in Posidonius (apart from the word "ass," which appeared in both), and the blood libel did not appear in Posidonius at all. Apion the "Stoic" used the name of Posidonius, who recorded other anti-Jewish accusations, to lend his version of the libel respectable authority. This is not surprising for a notorious grammarian-orator characterized by his contemporaries (one of them his former student) and later authors (none of them Jewish) as unreliable, and even as an imposter and charlatan, and that is not to mention other deplorable features of his pompous personality described by others (e.g., "the cymbal of the world," Tiberius; "the drum [*tympanum*] of his own fame," Pliny the Elder).[51] For a man with a reputation for fabricating "sources," who went so far as to write that he had obtained autobiographical information from the shadow of Homer in the underworld (as well as describing

51. See Seneca *Epistula* 88. 40–41; Pliny *Naturalis Historia*, pref. 25; 30. 6, 18; Gellius *Noctes Atticae* 5. 14, 6. 4, 8; Athenaeus 1.16f–17b; Aelianus *De natura animalium* 10.29; there a number of detailed examples. Given the quality of some of these sources and the personal acquaintance of their writers with Apion, there is no reason to doubt the information. This also appears from an inscription that almost certainly belongs to Apion of Alexandria (*OGIS* no. 662). See also the comprehensive survey of van der Horst (2002) 207–27, who traces similar features in the remains of Apion's main work, *Glossai Homeri*. However, the many attacks of Josephus against the personality of Apion and his unreliability should be used only as supportive evidence (e.g., *Ap.* 2. 3, 13–16, 135–36).

himself as an eyewitness of a number of famous and fabulous stories)[52], attaching the name of Posidonius to Apollonius Molon as his source for the blood libel was all the same thing. Josephus, who was not familiar with the *Histories* of Posidonius, took Apion's claims at face value and assumed that Apion's account did indeed reflect that of Posidonius.[53]

52. Noteworthy among them are the tales about Androcles and the lion, the boy and the dolphin, and a personal "interview" with Penelope about her suitors.

53. On the version of Apollonius Molon, mentioned as a further authority for the libels, see below, p. 469 ff.

14

The Geographical Description
of Jerusalem by Timochares,
the Siege, and the Libels

Posidonius of Apamea was not an eyewitness to the events of 132/1 B.C.E. and may not even have been born when the siege took place. Yet his version, however imaginary and tendentious it may have been, abounds in detail. When Posidonius wrote his *Histories* in Rhodes, forty to fifty years after the siege, he is unlikely to have held personal interviews with eyewitnesses, or based his account on notes from earlier interviews, and he obviously required a written source for his version of the siege. It is now time to attempt to trace his source both for the siege of Jerusalem and for the anti-Jewish accusations and libels.

THE TESTIMONIUM:
CHRONOLOGY AND FRAMEWORK

We have at our disposal one testimonium from an author called Timochares, preserved by Eusebius (*PE* 9. 35), who found it in Alexander Polyhistor's Jewish anthology (first century B.C.E.). The testimonium provides the first known topographical description of Jerusalem by a Greek author:

> Timochares says in his *On Antiochus* that Jerusalem has a circumference of 40 stades, and that it is hard to take, being shut in on all sides by precipitous ravines, and that the whole city flows with water so that the gardens too are irrigated by the waters flowing away out of the city. [He also says that] the middle [zone] up to 40 stades from the city is waterless (ἄνυδρον), but from the 40 stades [zone outward] is again waterlogged (κάθυδρον).[1]

---

1. Τιμοχάρης δέ φησιν ἐν τοῖς Περὶ Ἀντιόχου τὰ Ἱεροσόλυμα τὴν μὲν περίμετρον ἔχειν σταδίους μ'· εἶναι δ' αὐτὴν δυσάλωτον, πάντοθεν ἀπορρῶξι περικλειομένην φάραγξιν. ὅλην δὲ τὴν πόλιν

The passage refers to those unique features of Jerusalem that are of essential interest to the besiegers of a city. It is large and "hard to take." The author lists the reasons: precipitous ravines protecting the city on all sides, an overabundant water supply within the city, and the lack of water and agriculture outside the city. The wall is not mentioned, since the existence of a wall around every ancient city was taken for granted. It has rightly been noted that the only Antiochus who besieged the city of Jerusalem was Antiochus VII Sidetes.[2] Antiochus III, supported by the Jews, besieged only the citadel, held by the Ptolemaic garrison (Joseph. AJ 12. 133), while Antiochus IV did not carry out any siege operations in Jerusalem.[3] His son, Antiochus V Eupater, besieged only the Temple (1 Macc. 6.48–54), but there is no reference in the passage to the citadel or to the Temple. Moreover, the passage under consideration is quoted by Eusebius from Alexander Polyhistor, following a detailed account of Solomon's Temple (9. 34, also taken from Alexander Polyhistor but originating in Eupolmus, the Jewish Hellenistic author sent by Judas Maccabaeus to Rome); had there been a reference in Timochares to the Temple, its defense, and water supply, Alexander Polyhistor (and Eusebius) would not have failed to quote it. By a process of elimination, therefore, it appears that the geographical survey has formed the whole or part of the prelude to the account of the siege of Jerusalem by Antiochus VII Sidetes in the year 132/1.

TIMOCHARES' SURVEY AND
THE SIEGE BY ANTIOCHUS SIDETES

Does Timochares' geographical survey in fact accord with the geographical data in Posidonius's version of the siege of 132/1 B.C.E. as preserved in Josephus and Diodorus? There were just two geographical references in this version. First, the water supply: Josephus tells us that the besiegers suffered from severe "lack of water" and were relieved only by a "downpour of rain" (AJ 13. 237), but does not mention any shortage of water inside the city, only scarcity of "provisions" (para. 240). Similarly, Diodorus refers only to a shortage of supplies among the besieged (34/35. 1. 1). Timochares asserts that the region surrounding the city was "waterless," while the city itself had plenty of water, which even irrigated

ὕδασι καταρρεῖσθαι, ὥστε καὶ τοὺς κήπους ἐκ τῶν ἀπορρεόντων ὑδάτων ἐκ τῆς πόλεως ἄρδεσθαι· τὴν δὲ μεταξὺ ἀπὸ τῆς πόλεως ἄχρι τεσσαράκοντα σταδίων ἄνυδρον εἶναι, ἀπὸ δὲ τῶν μ' σταδίων πάλιν κάθυδρον ὑπάρχειν.

2. See Stern, GLAJJ 1: 134; cf. Shatzman (1990) 21.

3. See 1 Maccabees 1.20–1, 29; 2 Maccabees 5.11. Antiochus Epiphanes is the choice of Laqueur, RE s.v. "Timochares," col. 1258, as well as of Pédech (1964) 562 and Gabba (1989) 642. Jacoby, FGrH II. B, no. 730, p. 595, is undecided, as is Momigliano (1993) 83.

gardens outside the city. This indeed accords with the conditions of water supply in the immediate vicinity of the city (as distinct from the surrounding neighborhoods) at that period. The Gihon spring, which was outside the wall, was covered (and so camouflaged) by deep rubble. Its water flowed into the city through the old Hezekiah canal to the Shiloh pool. The water of the Shiloh pool was used in time of peace to irrigate gardens in the Kedron Valley (as it is today). Jerusalem also benefited from a few small wells and many pools and cisterns quarried out of the rock.[4] There was no visible source of flowing water close outside the walls,[5] certainly not in the northern sections outside the city where the Seleucid military efforts were concentrated (Joseph. AJ 13. 238), or anywhere nearby, and reservoirs would have been emptied by the citizens of Jerusalem before the enemy arrived.

The second geographical point referred to in the siege account appears at first sight not to conform with Timochares' geographical survey. While Timochares states that the city is "shut in on all sides by precipitous ravines," Josephus says that the wall was accessible on the north side (AJ 13. 238),[6] which indeed was the case (cf. the map on p. 418 above). The difference, however, is not significant. As a matter of fact, only three sectors of the so-called First Wall and the Temple Wall, then the outer walls facing north, were readily accessible, and together they occupied no more than 400 meters out of about 4,000 meters of the walls.[7] Be that as it may, considering that Timochares' survey, as appears from the division of the region into three concentric areas, was short, schematic, and general, his omission of three weak points in the city's defenses, all in all 400 meters in length out of a 4-kilometer wall, cannot be seen as a mistake contradicting the account of the siege. The best parallel for this is provided by Josephus, who was personally well acquainted with the topographical conditions of the city at the time of the Roman siege of 70 C.E. In his general topographical survey, which precedes his exceptionally detailed account of the Roman siege, Josephus uses terms similar to those of Timochares ("surrounded by deep ravines," BJ 5. 141) to describe just the outer flanks of the Lower and Upper City, which together correspond to the territory of the Hasmonaean city (apart from the Temple Mount). He even goes on to say that "the most ancient wall" (the First Wall, namely, the Hasmonaean) was "hard to conquer (δυσάλωτον) because of the ravines and

4. See Hecker (1956) 198–99; Ussishkin (1994) 18, on the Shiloh; and Josephus Bellum Judaicum 5. 140, 410, 505. On other sources of water in the city, see Hecker, passim.

5. On the distant 'Ain Rogel (Bir Aiyub), which seems to have been covered by the earthquake in the reign of King Uzziah (Joseph. AJ IX. 225), see Hecker (1956) 199–200.

6. κατὰ δὲ τὸ βόρειον μέρος τοῦ τείχους, καθ' ὃ συνέβαινεν αὐτὸ καὶ ἐπίπεδον εἶναι....

7. See pp. 417–19 above for this point and for the topographical data discussed below.

the hill above them on which it was built" (para. 142). The precipitous nature of the area is described even more dramatically by Tacitus (*Hist.* 5. 11. 3).[8] Neither Josephus nor Tacitus in his general survey refers to the flat sections in the north, although Titus broke into the city through these weak points.

Timochares, as a biographer of Antiochus VII, can well be expected to stress the inaccessibility of the city, in preparation for an account of what was to be a protracted and difficult siege that ended without the city falling or being occupied by the king's troops. The length of the siege would thereby be mitigated, while the king's success in persuading the inhabitants to come to terms would be exalted. A similar reasoning would account for the somewhat exaggerated account of the water supply inside the city and the false information about a 40-stade radius of barren area outside, two factors providing a clear preliminary advantage to the besieged over the besiegers.[9] The circumference of the city is also exaggerated. Forty stades (7.6 km) is almost double the real circumference of the city at that period. Even in the time of the Great Roman War, when the city's northern limits were considerably extended, its circumference stood at just 35 stades (Joseph. *BJ* 5. 159). Exaggeration of the circumference of Jerusalem is found for various reasons in the writings of Jewish Hellenistic authors of the Hasmonaean period.[10] Timochares' purpose is also evident in the wild exaggeration of the statement that the area to a radius of 40 stades from the city was arid. This can apply only to the desert region to the east of the city. The statement that the area beyond this radius was fertile and well watered rests upon a superficial knowledge about agriculture in the region to the north and west, and the distance is inaccurate with regard to the fertile region in the east (the Jericho Valley is about 20 kilometers—100 stades—from Jerusalem). But after all we do not expect familiarity or accuracy from one who had no need to personally traverse these regions. The mention of gardens outside the city watered from within the city underlines the statement that the city itself was well watered, while at the same time not contradicting the statement that the area outside the city was arid: the reader would understand that during the siege the water was cut off and the Seleucid army would not have enjoyed the produce of the gardens.

8. "But they had strengthened the city (already) steep in location with works and fortifications that would have been sufficient to protect even things on the level; for two skillfully built walls closed two hills. . . . The ends of the rock were broken away, and towers, where the mountain had helped, were raised up to a height of 60 feet, and in the valley up to 120, with a wonderful view, and [of] equal [height] to any people looking from afar."

9. See also Shatzman (1990) 21.

10. Pseudo-Hecataeus in Josephus *Contra Apionem* 1. 197 (50 stades); *pseudo-Aristeas* 105 (40 stades). See Bar-Kochva (1996d) 110–11; and cf. 27 stades in *Schoinometresis Syria* quoted by Eusebius *Praeparatio evangelica* 9. 36. 1.

JERUSALEM IN THE JEWISH EXCURSUS OF STRABO-POSIDONIUS AND THE ACCOUNT OF TIMOCHARES

The passage of Timochares is manifestly similar to the short description of Jerusalem set within the account of Mosaic Judaism in the Strabo-Posidonius Jewish excursus. It should be recalled that the excursus as a whole was originally located in Posdionius's *Histories,* as an ethnographic introduction to the story of the siege.[11] The topography is described in Strabo as follows:

> For it is rocky, itself well watered (εὔυδρον) but having distressing and waterless (ἄνυδρον) encircling land, within 60 stades also rocky. (Strabo 16. 2. 36)[12]

The similarity of the two passages can hardly be accidental.[13] The subjects in both descriptions appear in the same sequence: (a) the topography of the city (rock; ravines); (b) internal water supply; (c) division of the area outside according to agricultural factors (water; soil). There is also an evident correspondence in the use of the compounds *euhydron* and *anhydron* in Strabo, and *kathydron* and *anhydron* in Timochares. Above all, the peculiar concentric division of the area outside Jerusalem present in both descriptions finds no parallel in the many other accounts of Jerusalem. Indeed, I have been unable to trace in Greek and Latin literature a similar division of a real city and its surroundings into concentric circles.[14] This is not to say that Timochares invented the division of a city's area into concentric zones, but the fact that there is no surviving parallel suggests that such a division was uncommon.

It has been argued that Strabo (i.e., Posidonius) could have relied on any realistic description of Jerusalem, since his account is geographically accurate.[15] However, the statement that the area in a radius of 40 or 60 stades from Jerusalem was desolate is generally true only with regard to the region east of the city (the Judaean desert). The argument further ignores the similarity not only in details but also in the structure and subject order of the passages, linguistic usage, and especially the peculiar geographical division into concentric circles, all of which can hardly be considered the only way to describe

---

11. See pp. 448–51 above.

12. ἔστι γὰρ πετρῶδες αὐτὸ μὲν εὔυδρον, τὴν δὲ κύκλῳ χώραν ἔχον λυπηρὰν καὶ ἄνυδρον, τὴν δ' ἐντὸς ἑξήκοντα σταδίων καὶ ὑπόπετρον.

13. The similarity was noted in passing by Jacoby, *FGrH* II. C, no. 87, p. 198; Stern, *GLAJJ* 1: 135, 306. Stern is mistaken in stating that the viewpoint of Strabo's survey is that of the besieged.

14. Deborah Gera drew attention to the description of the imaginary city of Atlantis as surrounded by concentric bands of sea and earth (Plato *Critias* 113d). This account may have inspired Timochares or an earlier writer to describe a real city as surrounded by concentric bands of some quality or another.

15. Gager (1972) 42 n. 54.

Jerusalem.[16] It should be added that neither Posidonius nor Strabo ever visited Judaea, not to mention Jerusalem.[17]

Posidonius adapted and abbreviated Timochares' survey, adding contributions of his own, to serve the needs of his ethnographic excursus in the same systematic and sophisticated way that he had adapted the account by Hecataeus (and Manetho or a source drawing on him) to his didactic purposes, including turning details on their head.[18] In accordance with the political ideals of Posidonius, it is reported that Moses aspired to establish a model, peace-loving, community, of the sort that had no need to defend itself. The absence in Strabo-Posidonius of any reference to the ravines surrounding the city is therefore to be expected. The geographical description was integrated by Posidonius into the ethnographical excursus just to explain why Moses chose to settle in Jerusalem.[19] It is preceded by the statement that the place was unattractive to other people, allowing easy possession of it, and affording hope that Moses' followers would not have to face wars in the future. In the sentence subsequent to the short geographical survey, it is also indicated that Moses refrained from military training. Any reference to the defensive advantages of Jerusalem would have been incongruous and even misleading with regard to the real reason why the Jews provided no military training.

There are also other well-calculated additions, omissions, and alterations. The soil of the surrounding land, described by Timochares as infertile because of the lack of water, is now also "rocky," an "improvement" by Posidonius, who was

---

16. Strabo himself in the *Geographica* provides an additional geographical survey of Jerusalem as a short introduction to his brief report of Pompey's conquest (16. 2. 40). Its beginning is influenced, even verbally, by the first three statements he found in Posidonius: ἦν γὰρ πετρῶδες ... ἐντὸς μὲν εὔυδρον, ἐκτὸς δὲ παντελῶς διψηρόν ("For it was rocky ..., within well watered, without entirely parched"). But from then on, there is no similarity, as the survey is adapted to the events surrounding Pompey's siege of the Temple (as opposed to the city, which Pompey had occupied without a struggle). Strabo details the depth and width of the trench and notes that the rocks removed from it during its digging were used to build the Temple and its towers. These were the elements that played a part in the later storming of the Temple by Pompey (see Strabo 16. 2. 40 and esp. Joseph. *AJ* 14. 57–68, deriving from Strabo and Nicolaus). Strabo seems to have attached to the Posidonian survey of Jerusalem geographical details concerning the Temple from a description of Pompey's siege of the Jerusalem Temple in his *Hypomnemata*, Strabo's earlier historical work. The account of Pompey's siege in his *Geographica* is delivered in a few short sentences in which the sequence of events is disturbed: exploiting the day of fasting for the attack, filling in the trench, and destroying the walls.

17. This is evident from, among other things, the mistakes made in Strabo's account of the geography of the country. Posidonius was one of his three sources and is responsible for some of his major mistakes (see p. 362 note 15 above).

18. See pp. 363–67, 370, 379 above and 534–35 below.

19. See pp. 378–79 above.

eager to stress the point that the Jerusalem region was unattractive to potential invaders. He thereby hints that the area outside the city was also unsuitable for irrigation. Just to drive the point home, Posidonius described the view as "distressing" and chose not to mention the gardens irrigated by water from the city. The reference to the third zone described by Timochares as "again water-logged" was redundant for the purposes of Posidonius, and it was therefore omitted. Mention of the area might even have caused the reader to think that, despite everything, economic considerations may actually have driven settlement in Jerusalem. A distance of 40 stades (so Timochares) from agricultural land is not all that unreasonable, even considering ancient transportation conditions. Perhaps for this reason, Posidonius increased Timochares' 40 stades to 60 (11.4 km). This having been said, the difference may be due to a scribal error.[20] At the same time, Posdionius did not pass over the reference to the availability of water within the city, since this explained how it was possible at all for Moses to establish a settlement in such a barren and rocky area. However, he described the site as "rocky" so as to include the city itself in the area that could not be cultivated.

TIMOCHARES, THE SIEGE STORY, AND THE LIBELS

We have seen that Posidonius took Timochares' geographical prelude to the siege account and adapted it to his purposes in the framework of an ethnographical excursus also preceding an account of the siege; we have further seen that there is no real discrepancy between Timochares' survey and the account of the siege based on Posidonius in Josephus and Diodorus. Posidonius used only one source for the siege story, as appears from the consistency of his account (reconstructed by combining the versions in Diodorus and Josephus). It therefore stands to reason that Posidonius, who completed his historical work in about 84 B.C.E., drew from Timochares the basic historical details for his didactic-tendentious version of the siege, as well as the advice of the king's "friends," including their detailed reference to Antiochus IV's visit to the Temple and the presentation of the anti-Jewish libels and accusations, which was inserted by Posidonius into his account of the counsel of war of Antiochus Sidetes during the siege of Jerusalem (in Posidonius, without mentioning the blood libel[21]).

Timochares, however, did not invent the story about the entry of Antiochus

---

20. Timochares' account was related by Eusebius in reported speech, a mode that naturally led to errors, and appeared in two versions (Posidonius and Strabo). In addition to possible scribal errors in the MSS, it is particularly suspicious that the circumference of Jerusalem is the same length as the radius of the internal zone in Timochares.

21. See pp. 455–57 above.

IV into the Temple. There was no reason why he should invent such a story, being a historian of Antiochus VII Sidetes who came to an accommodation with the Jews, and even had Jewish auxiliaries accompany him on his Parthian campaign. Moreover, most of the kings subsequent to Antiochus IV (including Antiochus VII Sidetes himself) belonged, or presented themselves as belonging, to the rival branch of the royal house descended from Seleucus IV, the elder brother of Antiochus Epiphanes. They naturally regarded Antiochus IV as a usurper, and at least the first of his successors, Demetrius I, loved to defame him, as can be deduced from the scandalous stories preserved by Polybius, his close friend. We can assume that Timochares (or rather the king's counselors) drew on some royal source from the time of Antiochus Epiphanes or Antiochus Eupator, his son-successor, that strove to justify (or apologize for) both the sacrilege committed by the king in the Jewish Temple and the unprecedented persecution of the Jewish religion (as was actually indicated by Josephus, *Ap.* 2. 90, 97).[22] However, it would not be the ultimate source for the accusations and libels themselves. Their origin must be looked for in the Egypt of the Persian or early Hellenistic period.[23]

TIMOCHARES' WORK:
PURPOSE, GENRE, AND CHARACTERISTICS

The Eusebian testimonium contains the only information we have on Timochares and his work. Yet some clues to Timochares' date, place, and position do exist. The relatively detailed survey of Jerusalem in the framework of such a monograph indicates that the work on Antiochus VII was quite long. Despite his enormous efforts to restore the strength and unity of the Seleucid empire, Antiochus Sidetes was not a glorious military commander or a celebrated builder of monumental enterprises, either of which might justify an extensive monograph on his achievements by a later historian. An ancient author would hardly have chosen Antiochus VII of all rulers of antiquity (even of the Seleucid kings) as the subject of a monograph (as compared to a short biography) unless he had a special personal motivation to do so. Taken together, these considerations, the apologetic purpose reflected in the shaping of the geographic survey, and the likelihood that Timochares reported the elaborate advice of the king's counselors, all suggest that Timochares was no ordinary author but a court historian of Antiochus VII, or at least a person close to the court. Detailed accounts of the deliberations of rulers, commanders, and counsels of war are naturally to be found in the works of court scribes or hangers-on, and the reports tended to be apologetic when necessary. If Timochares was indeed a court historian or the like, he had access to first-hand

22. See pp. 276–77 above on the blood libel.
23. See above, pp. 271–76.

information and was also an eyewitness to many of the events he described. The work was probably composed not long after Antiochus Sidetes died in his attempt to thwart the expansion of Parthian influence westward (129 B.C.E.).

More may be said about the extent and characteristics of this information if we first consider the genre Timochares chose to write in and its features. The name of the work, which might have helped considerably in determining the genre, has not reached us. Eusebius does write at the beginning of the testimonium "Timochares says in his work on Antiochus (ἐν τοῖς περὶ Ἀντιόχου)," but this is not the title, or at least, not as it would have been originally formulated. A title would at least have specified which Antiochus was the subject of the work. At the same time, the way the work is presented does reveal something about its contents: the account was about a certain Antiochus, and since the testimonium deals with the siege of Jerusalem, it follows that the work as a whole included the deeds or life of Antiochus Sidetes.

The genre may be identified by the usual practice in the time of Timochares of describing the life and deeds of prominent political personalities. Biographies as we conceive of them today, rather than the collections of anecdotes, were not yet being written in the second century B.C.E. about political figures, but only about outstanding intellectuals, especially philosophers or poets.[24] The historical monograph was completely different from the biography familiar to the general reader from the biographies of Suetonius and Plutarch. The difference is immediately obvious in a comparison, for example, of Arrian's *Anabasis of Alexander* with any of these biographies. For our purposes, it will suffice to note that the historical monograph usually did not open with a detailed story concerning the formative years and experiences of the hero, his place of birth, and his upbringing and education; at most it would devote to them a brief survey. Nor was the choice of material guided by moral or didactic aims or by a desire to emphasize the character of the hero, and it was not arranged according to features of character or themes (as often in Plutarch and Suetonius, respectively). The monography began practically with his first significant political or military deeds. The account henceforth, however, was much more extensive than that to be found in a biography. As a result, while the biography would be only one book-scroll in length at the utmost, the historical monograph could run to several "books."

The account contained dates, and it was arranged chronologically; the impres-

---

24. For the beginnings of political biography with the writing of Cornelius Nepos in the second half of the first century B.C.E., see Geiger (1985) 9–115, and see 46–51 on the historical monograph. For a somewhat differing opinion on the character of biographies on authors and philosophers, see Momigliano (1993) 65–89. Whatever the case may be, the term *bios* was applied to works on the lifestyle of cities and peoples, to collections of anecdotes about politicians, and to full-fledged biographies on intellectual figures.   ·

sion one obtains is that the authors reported almost all the events and details at their disposal indiscriminately, unless they encountered data obviously opposed to their own basic attitude toward the hero, or sources drastically contradicting the "vulgate" (if they happened to be using one). Historical monographs, therefore, unlike ordinary historical works, contained a wealth of information not only about matters affecting the fate of the ruler and his country, such as great battles, international relations, and internal struggles for power, but also about less significant events and the everyday activities and spectacles accompanying them, such as audiences, ceremonies, festivals, symposia, unusual and curious phenomena, soothsaying, visits to temples, relations with the gods, illnesses, injuries, recoveries, military preparations, exercises, river crossings, loyalty, disobedience, fatigue of commanders, soldiers, and subjects, marriages of the commander (and occasionally even of his companions), and so on. However, despite the great detail, the historical monograph did not devote special attention to marginal court anecdotes and petty gossip (although some instances do appear now and then), such material being grist for the mill of biographies, where these stories would throw much light on the subject's character and motives.

The author's approach toward the hero was dictated by the degree of his personal affinity to, or dependence upon, him, causing many monographs to be encomia to a larger or lesser extent. Even Polybius, who so rebuked contemporary historians for their "pathetic" writing and their remoteness from historical truth, ignored his own principles when he wrote his panegyric monograph on his fellow citizen Philopoemen. In the nature of things, the further removed the author was from dependence upon the subject, his descendants, or followers (which could happen only with regard to figures of a far higher caliber than Antiochus VII), the more the monograph tended to be objective. Time and lack of personal commitment, however, were not always decisive factors in distancing the author from his subject, since many historical monographs are distinctly nostalgic.

The title of this work, if it followed, for instance, the example of titles of works on Alexander the Great, would have been something like τὰ κατὰ τὸν Ἀντιόχου τὸν Δημητρίου (Matters Concerning Antiochus Son of Demetrius) or περὶ τὰς τοῦ Ἀντιόχου τοῦ Δημητρίου πράξεις (On the Deeds of Antiochus Son of Demetrius") or the like. It would appear, then, that the work of Timochares contained an account of the deeds of Antiochus VII Sidetes from his ascent to the throne in 139 down to his death in the Parthian campaign in 129. The work included a great deal of material in extreme detail, concerning events great and small, developments during his reign, and daily life at court and in the camp during his military expeditions. It was clearly extensive and may have comprised a number of books. Timochares, a court historian or the like, would naturally have portrayed his hero panegyrically.

In view of the genre and the chronological framework of the monograph written by Timochares, it may further be suggested that this work was the source used by Posidonius not only for the account of the siege of 132/1 but also for the reign of Antiochus VII Sidetes as a whole. Posidonius's unique version of various events and episodes concerning Antiochus Sidetes and his reign, mainly stories about, and references to, banquets held during the military expeditions, have reached us by way of Athenaeus and Justin-Pompeius Trogus. The identification of Timochares as Posidonius's source for all these may throw into greater relief the Posidonian features and design in the Jerusalem siege account, and in the other testimonia relating to the reign of Antiochus Sidetes. The exaggeration of the military installations deployed by Antiochus Sidetes during the siege of Jerusalem, for example, reaches enormous dimensions that do not compliment the king, and could not have been the work of a court historian, but must be seen as a reworking by Posidonius. Another example would be the grotesque description of luxury and wastefulness in the banquets and receptions held in the Seleucid camp during the Parthian campaign.[25] At the same time, the identification of Timochares as the source for Posidonius also tells us that Posidonius used a well-informed source, one who may well have witnessed many of the events at firsthand. This would explain the great quantity of data in Posidonius, and the degree to which not a few of these pieces of information match the conditions of time and place, even after the panegyric coloring by Timochares and the peculiarly Posidonian reworking of the material.

25. See, e.g., the passages from Athenaeus and Justin-Pompeius Trogus adduced above, pp. 423–31, and there on the Posidonian reworking.

15

The Anti-Jewish Ethnographic
Treatise by Apollonius Molon

Apollonius Molon, the celebrated rhetor who was active in Rhodes in the first half of the first century B.C.E., was considered by Josephus to be, along with Apion, the most venomous of Jew haters. In the concluding sentence of *Contra Apionem*, Josephus expresses his hope that his discussion about the Jewish precepts will suffice to refute the libels of "the Apions and the Molons" (2. 295). What Josephus seems to regard as a refutation of Apollonius Molon would appear to be his detailed description of Jewish customs and faith, including the famous passage on Jewish "theocracy" (2. 165 ff.).[1] The polemics take up about half of the second book of *Contra Apionem* (2. 151–286),[2] while Apion is explicitly attended to in the first half of the book.

That such a large part of Josephus's counterspeech (*antirrēsis*, 2. 1) should be devoted to a refutation of Molon's anti-Jewish accusations made more than 150 years earlier indicates how damaging Josephus regarded Molon's work, and how influential he believed it still was on the opinion of intellectuals in Rome and throughout the Hellenistic world of his time. This is hardly surprising:

1. To be more precise, as appears from Josephus (2. 149–54, 182–84, 295), the combination of a detailed description of the laws with the Jewish "theocracy" is intended to show that the laws of the Jews guide the individual and the public toward *aretai* rather than bad, corrupt deeds—as Apollonius Molon, Lysimachus, and others claim (2. 145)—while also answering the charge of Molon that the Jews have contributed nothing to civilization, whether in the arts or in practical inventions (2. 148; on the last matter, see below, pp. 497–504).

2. Gerber (1997) in a comprehensive monograph on this part of *Contra Apionem* establishes that this part, like the section prior to it, is essentially apologetic, contra those who regard it as essentially an encomium. See, e.g., Balch (1982) 102–22; cf. Feldman (1996b) 177–236, esp. 233.

Apollonius Molon occupied a central position in the rhetorical profession of his own day, both as a practicing speaker and as a teacher and author. He won great respect throughout cultured society, so much so that Roman statesmen and generals flocked to his door, and their references ensured him an outstanding reputation among future generations.

Yet very little of Molon's work has survived, and his work on the Jews is no exception. The references in Josephus usually comprise short testimonia, followed by sharp and long replies by Josephus, including harsh personal abuse. Apollonius Molon is occasionally mentioned alone, sometimes together with Posidonius of Apamea, and sometimes juxtaposed (in the singular or the plural) with Lysimachus of Alexandria.[3] In various testimonia, Molon rebukes Moses for being a wizard and a deceiver whose laws contain only bad and nothing good; he lists a string of negative qualities he finds in the Jews, such as atheism, misanthropy, cowardice, recklessness, primitiveness, and a lack of inventiveness; he even calls the Jews "the most inferior of humans" (2. 236). The more detailed testimonia include the ass and blood libels; Josephus tells us that Apion claims to have drawn the two libels from Posidonius of Apamea and Apollonius Molon (2. 79).

We appear to be presented with a different appraisal of the Jews, however, in a relatively detailed fragment of Apollonius Molon preserved in Eusebius's *Praeparatio evangelica* (9. 19. 1–3). The fragment contains an unbiased account of the Jewish patriarchs from the end of the Flood to the birth of Moses, and Abraham is even presented there as "wise." At first sight this account would appear to be at odds with the testimonia in *Contra Apionem*. The very detailing of the beginnings of Jewish history and its links with the mythological Flood testifies to the primacy of the Jews, and this itself is a form of positive appreciation when the general tendency of anti-Jewish authors was to present the Jews as a young people, lacking historical roots and a cultural tradition, and consequently legal rights enshrined in the heritage of ruling nations. It was against this tendency that Josephus devoted the first half of the first book of *Contra Apionem*.

Not much research has been carried out on Apollonius Molon and his attitude toward the Jews, although the content of the testimonia would indicate that he was the most extreme anti-Jewish author of all the first-rank Hellenistic and Roman intellectuals.[4] A close examination of the testimonia raises a series of questions still to be answered. Did Apollonius Molon write a monograph on the Jews, or were his comments included in one or more works concerning other

3. 2. 16, 79, 145, 148, 236, 255, 258, 262, 270, 295.
4. On Molon's attitude toward the Jews, see Müller (1877) 230–31, 285–88, and passim; Reinach (1895) 60–64; Schürer (1901–9) 3: 532–36; Radin (1915) 198–99; Gager (1972) 95, 119; Stern *GLAJJ* 1: 148–49; Heinemann, *RE* s.v. "Antisemitismus," suppl. 5 (1931) col. 34; Sevenster (1975) 8, 96–98; Conzelmann (1981) 72–74; Goodman in Schürer et al. 3: 1, 598–600; Philhofer (1990) 204, 217; Schäfer (1997a) 21–22 and passim; Yavetz (1997) 98; Kasher (1996) 521–23, 532–36, and passim.

topics? If he did write a monograph on the Jews, what was its literary genre, and what was the the work's title? Was Josephus directly acquainted with Molon's comments? Is there any basis for the accusations and personal insults hurled at Molon by Josephus? How does the unbiased account of the Jewish patriarchs square with serious accusations in the testimonia of *Contra Apionem*? What were Apollonius Molon's sources of information on the Jews? What was the context from which the testimonia were taken? What is the literary and cultural background to the accusations, some of which are unique to Molon? How did Molon regard the positive, even enthusiastic, Jewish excursus of Posidonius of Apamea, his contemporary and the greatest philosopher of that generation, who was also active in Rhodes? Last but not least, why was Molon so hostile toward the Jews?

THE LIFE AND WORKS OF APOLLONIUS MOLON

Despite his importance and impact, there are just a few testimonia on the life and works of Apollonius Molon and on his career as a teacher of rhetoric and an orator, and not much has been written on them.[5] The most important of the testimonia are scattered throughout the books of Cicero, a great admirer of Molon (especially in his *Brutus*). Since the testimonia are so scanty, it is worth attempting to squeeze out of them as much information as possible on the personal and cultural background of Apollonius Molon, on his personality, and on his work as a whole. This information may have some bearing on our understanding of his work on the Jews.

Apollonius Molon was a native of Alabanda in Caria in southwest Asia Minor. He received his education in rhetoric from Menecles, a fellow citizen of Alabanda, one of the important figures associated with the "epigrammatic" branch of the "Asian" school (Cic. *Brut.* 325). Apollonius Molon was so called in order to distinguish him from another contemporary Apollonius, nicknamed Malakos, who was also a pupil of Menecles. Molon may have been his father's name, or it may have been a nickname (= "the Walker"; Strabo 14. 2. 13). At some stage in his early life, perhaps in the twenties of the second century B.C.E., Apollonius Molon moved to neighboring Rhodes, already a center of rhetoric, philosophy, and grammar, and there he established his reputation as a pleader in the law courts, a teacher of rhetoric, and a writer. By the end of the nineties of the first century at the very latest, Apollonius Molon was well known in Rome, thanks to his rhetorical writings and successes as an orator and teacher in Rhodes.

Molon may already have visited Rome in 87 B.C.E., in either a private or a public

---

5. A collection of the fragments and testimonia for the life and works of Apollonius Molon is to be found in Jacoby, *FGrH* III. C, no. 728 (pp. 687–89). For a brief discussion of various aspects of the available information, see Susemihl (1891–92) 2: 489–94; Brzoska, *RE* s.v. "Apollonios (85)," II. 1: cols. 141–44; Schürer (1901–9) 3: 531–34.

capacity; Cicero records that he devoted himself to study with Apollonius Molon in Rome in that year (*Brut.* 307). This piece of information has been held suspect for various reasons, and there is no need to discuss the problem here.[6] It is clear that in 81, during the dictatorship of Sulla, and after the end of the Second Mithridatic War, Apollonius Molon was sent by the citizens of Rhodes to plead before the Roman senate and present their request for compensation for the damage caused by the First Mithridatic War (*Brut.* 312; and see App. *Mith.* 24–27). He took the opportunity to raise the Rhodians' request for the rebellious city of Caunus to be returned to their control (Strabo 14. 2. 3). In the performance of this public duty, Apollonius Molon received an unusually favorable welcome: he was allowed to address the Senate in Greek without the aid of an interpreter, something previously unheard of in dealings with foreign envoys (Plut. *Cic.* 4. 6). His arguments before the Senate accomplished the desired results, and the Rhodians achieved their objectives. Apollonius Molon even remained in Rome for a while in order to teach rhetoric. One of his pupils was Cicero, then at the beginning of his career as a law-court advocate. Cicero recognized the great contribution of Molon to his performance in his first speeches and set his gratitude down in writing (*Brut.* 312).[7]

Molon's early fame and visit (or visits) to Rome, and the activity of Posidonius of Apamea, attracted Roman statesmen and men of letters to Rhodes to study at the feet of these two masters. Those wishing to improve their rhetorical ability prior to future tests in Rome would go to consult and train with Apollonius Molon. The most prominent of the pilgrims were Cicero in 78 B.C.E. (Cic. *Brut.* 316, *De or.* 1. 75, and elsewhere) and Julius Caesar in 76 (Plut. *Caes.* 3. 1). Suetonius adds that after the civil war, Caesar wished to retire to Rhodes and dedicate himself to the study of rhetoric under the supervision of Apollonius Molon (*Jul.* 4).

We do not know how long Apollonius Molon continued his varied activity. The last piece of information we have on him relates to 75 B.C.E. (Plut. *Caes.* 3. 1; Suet. *Jul.* 4). He is not mentioned among the "sophists" whose lectures were heard and generously remunerated by Pompey, who stopped in Rhodes on his way back to Rome in 62 B.C.E. (Plut. *Pomp.* 42D-E), a year after the Jews of Judaea lost their independence; the silence is all the more telling as Posidonius delivered on that occasion a lecture aimed against the rhetors. It seems that Molon was no longer alive by then.

In addition to this information, there survive in the sources several superlative words of praise that confirm the impression that Apollonius Molon did enjoy a unique standing among the intellectuals of his and later generations. Plutarch, for example, calls him σοφιστεύοντος ἐπιφανῶς καὶ τὸν τρόπον ἐπιεικοῦς εἶναι δοκοῦντος ("a brilliant technician ["sophist"] and considered of gentlemanly

6. See Susemihl (1891–92) 2: 491 n. 128, and bibliography there for earlier comments on the same subject.

7. On the influence of Molon's unique method on Cicero, see Davies (1968) 303–15.

character"; *Caes.* 3. 1). In another context, Suetonius calls him *clarissimus dicendi magister* ("the most famous master of rhetoric"; *Caes.* 4). Cicero's words of praise show that these assessments are not merely late and unfounded. He ranks Molon, for example, as *actori summo causarum et magistro* ("the top pleader of cases and teacher"; *Brut.* 307). In another place he calls him *summo illo doctore istius disciplinae* ("the top expert of that discipline of yours"; *De or.* 1. 75), and again, *summum illum doctorem* ("that top expert"; 1. 126). Apart from the attacks and abuse launched against him by Josephus in *Contra Apionem,* ancient sources have nothing but praise for Apollonius Molon, both for his character and for his professional standing. Apollonius Molon's image in ancient literature was definitely very different from that of Apion.

Josephus accuses Molon of bringing disgrace upon married women and of castrating youths (*Ap.* 2. 270). The context for his attack on Molon is a description of Jewish "theocracy," and more specifically, a survey of the intolerance of various cities and peoples toward foreigners and anyone offending their religion, in contrast to the favorable treatment of foreigners by Jews. Josephus mentions, among others, the Persians, noting ironically that Apollonius Molon admired the Persians presumably because Greece had tasted their bravery and sacrilegious conduct during the Persian Wars. It is immediately after this that Josephus adds parenthetically that Apollonius Molon used to imitate two Persian customs—disgracing women and castrating youngsters. He is hinting at the Hellenic traditions concerning the brutal treatment meted out by the Persians to the Ionian cities (Hdt. 6. 32), which became over generations an outstanding example of a despicable and outrageous crime (e.g., Quint. *Inst.* 3. 7. 21). Josephus seizes upon the opportunity to remind the reader of the Torah prohibition against castration (271 ff.).

Are Josephus's remarks based on real information about the life of Molon? In view of the artificial compilation of charges in the passage, the absurd statement that the Greek Apollonius Molon admired the Persians for harming temples in Greece and the parallels between the activities imputed to Molon and those attributed to the Persians in Asia Minor (Molon's native land!), which do not coincide with Molon's good reputation and record as a Rhodian patriot,we may suspect that Josephus is merely mudslinging at any price, as he does elsewhere with his frequent denigration of Molon,[8] and in accordance with the tactics of historians and orators in the classical period, including Josephus himself.[9] Yet

8. Ignorance and ill will, para. 145; an insignificant sophist soliciting youths, para. 232; one of the senseless and foolish, para. 255; a man who found satisfaction in lies and libels, para. 295. On the wide use of personal invective in *Contra Apionem,* see Kasher (1996) 20–22.

9. There is no need to dwell on the invention of libels by historians in the ancient world. Since *Contra Apionem* is close to the rhetorical genre of the counterspeech (*antirhēsis*), it is worth recalling briefly the defamation methods of the orators. The classic example is Cicero's speech against

Josephus may have arrived at these charges because of Molon's positive attitude to one or another Persian custom (not a rare trait in Greek literature).

The fragments and testimonia on Apollonius Molon's works are also few and quite short. The information we have concerning his works is also often doubtful or essentially mistaken. One piece of information that must be taken seriously is that Apollonius Molon wrote many works on the art of rhetoric (Quint. *Inst.* 3. 1. 16). One of his works is said to have been devoted to rhetorical ornamentation (Phoibammon *On Rhetorical Forms* 1. 44).[10] Since the anti-Jewish testimonia are too short to allow identification of typical rhetorical techniques, it would be redundant to discuss in detail here stylistic features and trends of the "Asian" school of rhetoric, to which he appears to have belonged. I shall say only that he paved his own way, and he clearly did not adopt the symmetrical and ornate "epigrammatic" style of his teacher, Menecles; nor did he adopt the rapid speech rich with synonymous words, phrases, and sentences that characterized the other stream of the "Asian" style.[11] Among the many speeches he delivered (and probably published), for himself and for others, only the two addressed in Rome are known to us by name: *Against the Citizens of Caunus* (κατὰ Καυνίων, Strabo 14. 2. 3) and *On Compensation for the Rhodians* (*De Rhodiorum praemiis*, Cic. *Brut.* 312).

Apollonius Molon, like other contemporary rhetors and philosophers, tried his hand at other literary genres. According to Porphyry, Molon solved a problem in the text of Homer.[12] Hence it can be inferred that he was a practicing gram-

---

Piso, where every detail of Piso's life and deeds is systematically misconstrued in order to blacken his name. The theoreticians of rhetoric (as distinct from its critics, such as Sextus Empiricus) were usually careful not to recommend mudslinging, describing the ideal orator as a moral agent and a speaker of truth (*auctor veritatis*). At the same time, they included among rhetorical techniques certain methods that could be abused, such as arousing anger, hate, condemnation, and ridicule against the opponent; accusing witnesses of being motivated by bribery, fear, hate, friendship, etc.; hiding the truth when the good of the people demands it; expressing an opinion on things about which the speaker has no inkling, and so on. Among sources worth noting are Plato *Phaedrus* 260 ff.; Aristotle *Ars rhetorica* 1419b (3. 19. 3); Cicero *De oratore* 2. 30, 185–90, 207, 240–41, 349; id. *De inventione*, 1. 22; Quintilian 2. 17. 36, 4. 1. 14, 5. 23. 33; Sextus Empiricus *Adversus rhetoricos* 2. 10–12 ("mislead the judge," 11); *Rhetorica ad Herrenium* 1. 5. 8 (falsely attributed to Cicero).

10. See the edition of Spendel (1856) 44, ll. 11 ff.

11. On the "Asian" style, see Wilamowitz-Moellendorff (1900) 1–52; Norden (1923a) 1: 126–52.

12. See the passage in the edition of Schräder (1880–82) 1: 126–27. Porphyry raises the question of why Homer, in *Iliad* 9. 5, refers in his description of the storm only to Boreas and Zephyrus, the north and the west winds respectively, and not to all four winds, as happens in the storm scene at *Odyssey* 5. 295–96. According to Porphyry, Apollonius Molon solved the problem by saying that Homer in the *Iliad* passage was alluding to two emotions that possessed the Achaeans: one wind represented fear and apprehension of the future, and the other, sorrow. The Achaeans feared the will of the gods and were sorry about what had happened. Porphyry appears still to be following Molon when he states that Thespesia (a divine wind mentioned at *Il.* 9. 2) is none other than the will of the god.

marian, a profession current among rhetors in Rhodes, and that he wrote a commentary on Homer.[13] This book may have contained a rhetorical and linguistic commentary, as was usual in grammatical works of rhetors; they claimed that their art began already with Homer. The testimonium in Porphyry also shows that the book had included an allegorical commentary, a method of interpretation that engaged the attention of orators. This may throw some light on an otherwise unintelligible connection between Josephus's statement that Molon was "one of the mindless and foolish" and the following highly critical remark against allegorical commentaries (*Ap.* 2. 255).

Another of Molon's works for which we have testimonia was called *Against the Philosophers*. A scholion on Aristophanes (*Nub.* 144) reports that in this work Apollonius Molon claimed among other things that the Pythian oracle praising Socrates is fake, since it is not in hexameter; and indeed, the oracle quoted in the testimonium is in iambics. Diogenes Laertius refers to Apollonius Molon's hostile attitude toward Plato, exemplified by a sharp comment (3. 34); the comment most probably derives from *Against the Philosophers*. Apollonius Molon's hostile attitude toward philosophers also appears in a remark Cicero puts into the mouth of Mucius Scaevola, an admirer of Stoicism who served in many capacities in Rome, including that of consul. The speaker claims that when he reached Rhodes, he discussed with Apollonius Molon things he had heard from Panaetius, the mentor of Posidonius of Apamea, and the most prominent Stoic in the last third of the second century B.C.E. Apollonius Molon reacted by mocking philosophy and expressing his scorn for its leading lights (*De or.* 1. 75). Notably, it has recently been argued that Apollonius Molon published a *bios* of Pythagoras. If this is to be accepted, it must have been a hostile monograph.

The perpetual rivalry between philosophers and rhetors explains the writing of *Against the Philosophers* and the mockery expressed in it.[14] The question of whether rhetoric was an art based on knowledge, and who was qualified to engage in it, provoked a controversy already among the pre-Socratics and became full blown by the fourth century with the likes of Plato and Isocrates taking sides. Cicero called the controversy between the two disciplines a rift (*discidium, De or.*

13. See Susemihl (1891–92) 2: 184 n. 199b and references there.

14. A great deal of material on the relations between orators and philosophers is to be found scattered throughout the following books: Sudhaus and Radermacher (1895) v–xlii; Gomperz (1912) 1–48; Jebb (1962) 2: 36 ff.; Kennedy (1963) 26–124, 264–334, esp. 321–30; (1994) 51–63, 84–90. Much research had been done on the rift (*discidium*) between philosophers and orators already in the nineteenth century; see the sources in Sudhaus and Radermacher (1895). Among the relevant works that have come down to us entire: Plato *Gorgias* and *Phaedrus;* Isocrates *Adversus sophistas;* Aristotle *Ars rhetorica;* Cicero *De oratore;* Quintilian *Institutio oratoria* (see esp. the prooemium, para. 11 ff.); Sextus Empiricus *Adversus rhetoricos.* The subject is dealt with sporadically in these works. For the suggestion that Apollonius Molon wrote a *bios* of Pythagoras, see Staab (2007).

3. 60 ff.), and, relying on Plato's *Gorgias,* he attributed its beginning to Socrates. The controversy continued with variations for some centuries and was still going strong in the generation of Cicero and Apollonius Molon. Philosophers, apart from the Peripatetics, who had a more favorable attitude,[15] condemned the various kinds of orators and teachers of rhetoric, arguing that only philosophers had the knowledge required to govern the state, teach pupils, or deliver speeches of substance, while rhetoric in the hands of the rhetors was not a proper *technē,* since it lacked any real knowledge, subject matter, or benefit. The philosophers' claim naturally provoked sharp reactions from the rhetors.

We have no explicit evidence for Posidonius's position with regard to this issue, but there is no reason to think that he deviated from the traditional Stoic view that only the Stoic wise man was the true orator.[16] One testimonium offers much support. In the description of Pompey's journey from the East back to Rome in the year 62, Plutarch (*Pomp.* 42D-E) reports that during his stay in Rhodes "all the sophists" lectured in his presence, among them Posidonius, who later published his lecture with the title περὶ τῆς καθόλου ζητήσεως (*On General Inquiry*). The lecture was aimed against Hermogenes of Temnos, who was active one hundred years earlier. Posidonius chose this subject, and this target, presumably because Hermogenes was one of the most influential rhetors of the ancient world, thanks to his theory of "stasis,"[17] and, as appears from name of the treatise of Posidonius, because Hermogenes expressed his opinion on inquiry, a philosophical occupation. The term appears in the titles of a number of works, both by Stoics and by other philosophers. Posidonius thus chose to attack a famous rhetor of the not too distant past whose theory was often applied by his contemporaries (including Cicero in *De inventione* and *Partitiones oratoriae,* where he teaches his son the elements of rhetoric). He launched his attack, however, on home ground, a philosophical issue, by means of which he could more easily prove the inability of any rhetor to express an opinion of any worth in various fields.

Posidonius would have regarded himself as the opposite of the rhetors in that while they could not engage in philosophy, he was qualified and worthy to discuss

---

15. The Peripatetics were not at loggerheads with the rhetors. Aristotle and the early Peripatetics regarded rhetoric as a useful tool and wrote works on the subject. As may be seen from the list in Diogenes Laertius (5. 42 ff.), Theophrastus even went so far as to write twenty works on various aspects of rhetoric. On the positions of Aristotle and his successors, see Kennedy (1963) 290–99, 322–23; (1994) 90–93.

16. On the unique position of the Stoics, see Kennedy(1963) 290–99, 322–23; (1994) 90–93; and see, e.g., Cicero *De oratore* 2. 157–59; 3. 65–66; Sextus Empiricus *Adversus rhetoricos* 6–7. For a different kind of criticism of rhetoric, that of the Stoics, see Cicero *De oratore* 2. 157–59.

17. On Hermogenes and "stasis," see Matthes (1958); Barwick (1961); Kennedy (1963) 303 ff. Posidonius seems to have reacted to the theory of "stasis" in another place as well: see Quintilian *Institutio oratoria* 3. 6. 31–38 (= Kidd 1: F189).

matters of rhetoric. Among other things, he wrote a work entitled Εἰσαγωγὴ περὶ λέξεως (*Introduction to Style*),[18] and he practiced what he preached: Cicero, Strabo, and Seneca testify to his distinctive and praiseworthy rhetorical style,[19] which even, according to Strabo (3. 2. 9), rouses the reader on mundane subjects, such as the number and wealth of mines in Spain. The rhetoric in some of the Posidonian fragments at our disposal bears this appraisal out.[20] Posidonius, therefore, could promote by personal example the philosophers' claim that only they had the knowledge necessary for the appropriate delivery of speeches on any subject.

Time and place conspired to make the paths of Apollonius Molon and Posidonius of Apamea cross. They were of the same generation; both moved to Rhodes and early on achieved fame and success in their respective fields; both were admired by prominent figures in Roman culture and politics and taught distinguished visitors. Posidonius was in the main a philosopher, and Molon a rhetor; but, in keeping with the times, both tried their hand at other forms of writing. There is no explicit statement in the relatively tiny number surviving testimonia that the two men ever met or ever commented on each other (which they certainly did). Yet after all that has been said about the tension between philosophers and rhetors, and considering the mocking tone adopted by Apollonius Molon toward philosophers, specifically Plato, Panaetius, and the Stoics in general, together with the negative attitude of Posidonius toward rhetors, and his disdain for anyone non-Stoic,[21] we may suspect that there was more than a little rivalry between them. This rivalry would have been fueled by the fame and popularity that they both enjoyed, by the fact that they were active at the same time in a relatively confined area, each in his own field, but attempting to attract fee-paying students from the same pool of ambitious young men.[22] It may not be coincidental that Cicero, who admired both, and visited Rhodes in order to learn from each of them in the same year (78 B.C.E.; Plut. *Cic.* 4), never mentioned them together and wrote about his time of study in Rhodes with each of them separately, as if he had made two separate trips to Rhodes or had visited two separate places. This may be contrasted with a six-month stay in Athens in 79 B.C.E. after which Cicero was not averse to reporting that he studied simultaneously with the philosopher Antiochus of Ascalon and the teacher of rhetoric Demetrius the Syrian (*Brut.* 316). No wonder Molon did not participate in the Rhodian delegation to the Senate, headed by Posidinius (87 B.C.E.), although he was then probably staying in Rome.

18. Diogenes Laertius 7. 60 (= Kidd 1: F44).

19. See Kidd 1: T33, 103, 106.

20. See Kidd 2: T103 comm. (p. 88).

21. See, e.g., *nos autem, qui sapientes non sumus, fugitivos, exules, hostes, insanos denique esse dicunt* ("But they say that we who are not wise are runaway slaves, exiles, enemies, and, to top it all, insane" (Cic. *Mur.* 61).

22. The importance of the material aspect as a factor in the tension between philosophers and rhetors receives thorough treatment in the doctoral dissertation of Liebersohn (2002).

APOLLONIUS MOLON'S WORK ON THE JEWS
AND ITS LITERARY GENRE

Some scholars have supposed that Molon wrote a monograph or polemical work entitled *Against the Jews*. Others believe that his hostile remarks on the Jews were found throughout one or more works on other themes. A history of Egypt has been suggested as a possible candidate.[23]

A late Christian source has been quoted as evidence in support of the last suggestion. Cosmas Indicopleutes, the sixth-century C.E. Alexandrian merchant who became a monk, refers in the twelfth book of his *Topographia Christiana* to a number of authors who wrote works called *Aegyptiaca* (Egyptian Affairs). One of these authors is Apollonius Molon. According to Cosmas, these works included accounts about Moses and the Exodus.

Let us take a look at the context. As Cosmas writes in his preface, the twelfth book of his *Topographia Christiana* is intended to prove mainly that many classical authors testified to the antiquity and authenticity of the teaching of Moses and the teachings of the prophets. For this purpose, in two consecutive paragraphs, he mentions authors who wrote about Babylonian affairs (*Chaldaika*) and those who wrote about Egyptian affairs (*Aigyptiaka*). Apollonius Molon is mentioned in the second paragraph. The first paragraph is a conflation of two sources used by the author-compiler, to which he has added from his own imagination: Cosmas reports that those authors who wrote about Babylon, being "the most ancient," mentioned the Flood and the Tower of Babel and saw with their own eyes the building of the tower, which was made "presumably because at the time of the Flood, humans wished to find refuge and salvation."[24] All this, according to Cosmas, fits with what is written in the Torah. Cosmas further claims to adduce from these authors a list of kings who ruled until the Flood, and finds a parallel for each one in the Genesis list of the generations from Adam to Noah (Aloros = Adam, Alaapros = Seth, etc.).[25] A closer look, however, shows that Cosmas did not draw directly on Babylonian sources but on quotations from Berossus found in Josephus's *Contra Apionem* and in the first book of Eusebius's *Chronika*.[26] To all

23. See Susemihl (1891–92) 1: 491 and nn. 134–36 (a work on Egyptian history); Schürer (1901–9) 3: 534 (a polemical work); Lewy (1960) 79 n. 3 and 95 n. 94 (a speech); Stern, *GLAJJ* 1: 148; Malitz (1983) 306 (monograph); Gabba (1989) 640–67 (monograph); Goodman in Schürer et al. 3: 1, 599 (a polemical work); Kasher (1996) 435 (points scattered throughout several works).

24. Cosmas is probably referring to Abydenus, whose version of the Babel myth in his history of Assyria is adduced by Eusebius (*PE* 9. 14).

25. See *Patrologia Graeca*, 37, col. 453, 341 B–C. In the latest edition, Wolska-Conus (1968–73) vol. 3, this passage is 453 B–C.

26. See *Contra Apionem* 1. 129–30; Eusebius *Chronica* (ed. Schoene), 1: p. 7, l. 10; p. 25, l. 9 = Jacoby, *FGrH* III. C, 1, no. 680, frr. 3, 4. The verbal influence of Josephus on Cosmas is evident: Josephus writes

this Cosmas added his own contribution that Babylonian authors saw with their own eyes the building of the tower.

The paragraph on the authors who wrote about Egyptian affairs is composed in the same vein:

> Those who wrote about Egyptian affairs (or "who wrote works entitled *Aigyptiaka*")— namely, Manetho, Chaeremon, Apollonius Molon, Lysimachus, and Apion the grammarian—mention Moses and the Exodus of the children of Israel from Egypt. Being Egyptian and writing about Egyptian affairs (or "writing works entitled *Aigyptiaka*"), they lead [us] altogether in the occurrences according to places (the scenes of the events), and some even speak disrespectfully of Moses as a rebel who incited a mob of beggars and deformed people and went to Mt. Sinai and Jerusalem, and [say] that they were called Jews.[27]

This passage, like the earlier passage on the Babylonian authors, is based on *Contra Apionem*. First, Cosmas lists only authors mentioned in *Contra Apionem*. Second, *Contra Apionem* contains references made by all these authors to the Exodus (Molon: *Ap.* 2. 10). Third, Josephus states explicitly that Chaeremon and Apion wrote books entitled *Aigyptiaka* (*Ap.* 1. 288; 2. 9), and Cosmas could easily have inferred (as modern scholars have) from the quotation from Lysimachus adduced by Josephus (*Ap.* 1. 305–11) that Lysimachus also wrote a book of that name. Fourth, Cosmas portrays Apollonius Molon as an Egyptian author, like all the others.[28] This is obviously a generalization based on Josephus's statement that the anti-Jewish accusations and libels originated with, and were spread by, Egyptians (*Ap.* 1. 223–26; 2. 28). Fifth, similarly to his treatment of Apollonius Molon, Cosmas identifies Lysimachus, Chaeremon, and Manetho only by name, apart from grouping them together as Egyptian authors who wrote on Egyptian affairs. Josephus supplied no basic information on these three. Cosmas does not even point out that Manetho was an Egyptian priest, and only Apion is singled out as a grammarian, a detail Cosmas could have found in *Contra Apionem* (2. 2, 12, 15). Finally, later on, Cosmas reacts to the passage adduced above by quoting word for word two statements from *Contra Apionem*. Though in Josephus these statements are located at some distance from each other, Cosmas combines them into one continuous statement without noting that they are taken from Josephus.[29] In *Contra Apionem*, the two statements are both very close to a passage in which Josephus responds to

---

ὁ Βηρῶσος, ταῖς ἀρχαιοτάταις ἐπακολουθῶν ἀναγραφαῖς περί τε τοῦ γενομένου καταλυσμοῦ...καθάπερ Μωϋσῆς; and Cosmas writes οἱ τὰ Χαλδαϊκὰ γὰρ συγγραψάμενοι, ὡς ἀρχαιότεροι...ἐμνήσθησαν ἐν τοῖς ἑαυτῶν συγγράμμασι τοῦ τε κατακλυσμοῦ...κατὰ τὸν Μωϋρανγλέσέα.

27. The text: *Patrologia Graeca*, 37, col. 453, 341D (Wolska-Conus [1968–73] 3: 453D).

28. On the Greek descent of Lysimachus, see pp. 312–16 above.

29. Cosmas, *Patrologia Graeca*, 37, 342E–343A (Wolska-Conus [1968–73] 3: 456D–457A) = *Contra Apionem* 2. 154–55; Cosmas, 343A (W-C 457A) = *Contra Apionem* 2. 172.

comments made by "Apollonius Molon, Lysimachus, and others" about Moses and his teaching, and the statements are part of Josephus's response to these comments (2. 145–50). Thus Cosmas's total dependence on Josephus cannot be disputed.[30]

That Apollonius Molon wrote a work on Egyptian affairs is therefore the invention of Cosmas.[31] Were Apollonius Molon's comments on the Jews, then, taken from a work or some works dedicated to other subjects? The testimonia of Eusebius and Josephus, taken together, decide the issue.

Eusebius introduces an account of the Jewish patriarchs by Apollonius Molon as follows: "Molon, who wrote an abusive work (*syskeuē*) against the Jews says that after the Flood . . .". Eusebius is clear and unambiguous, and the account does not appear in *Contra Apionem*. While it is true that he did not take the account directly from Apollonius Molon but—as stated later in his report—from the Jewish anthology of Alexander Polyhistor, the latter source must be regarded as credible. Other passages taken from this anthology, quoted mostly by Eusebius, show that Alexander Polyhistor took care to indicate from which author, which work, and often, which book of that work, each extract derived.

The relevant sentence in Josephus requires some philological examination. The eleventh-century manuscript L (Laurentianus), the earliest manuscript, regarded for many years as the most trustworthy and the *Vorlage* of all the manuscripts of *Contra Apionem*, is clearly corrupt in its version of the passage (2. 148):

ἄλλως τε καὶ τὴν κατηγορίαν ὁ Ἀπολλώνιος οὐκ ἀθρόαν ὥσπερ ὁ Ἀπίων ἔταξεν, ἀλλὰ σποράδην, **καὶ δὴ εἴπας** ποτὲ μὲν ὡς ἀθέους καὶ μισανθρώπους λοιδορεῖ, ποτὲ δ' αὖ δειλίαν ἡμῖν ὀνειδίζει καὶ τοὔμπαλιν ἔστι ὅπου τόλμαν κατηγορεῖ καὶ ἀπόνοιαν. λέγει δὲ καὶ ἀφυεστάτους εἶναι τῶν βαρβάρων καὶ . . . κτλ.

(and [because] Apollonius arranged his condemnation [of us] in another way, not concentrated as Apion did, but scattered, **and indeed having said,** now scorns [us] as atheists and haters of men, and now again reproaches us for cowardice, and there is a place where he blames us for recklessness and madness. And he also says that [the Jews] are the most primitive of barbarian [peoples] and . . . etc.)

30. The passage continues after what has been quoted here with Cosmas stating that the authors mentioned by him wrote about the Jews going to Mt. Sinai. The extracts from Lysimachus and Chaeremon quoted by Josephus, however, which provide a continuous narrative on the events following the Exodus and preceding the entry into "Judaea," clearly show that neither mentioned Mt. Sinai. Apion, on the other hand, is quoted by Josephus as referring to the ascent of Moses on Mt. Sinai and his stay there for forty days (*Ap.* 2. 25). Cosmas attributed such an account of the events at Mt. Sinai to Lysimachus and Chaeremon as well. This is but another example of negligent generalizing on the part of Kosmas.

31. So also Schürer (1901–9) 3: 536; Goodman in Schürer et al. 3: 601 n. 116, but without presenting specific evidence.

32. The Greek reading used for the Latin translation in the sixth century c.e. was already corrupt. In the translation we find *quippe cum aliquando nos sine deo et hominibus odiosos appellet*

The reading καὶ δὴ εἴπας ("and indeed having said") is in itself problematic, and the location of δή after καί ("and indeed") is strange in the context, since Josephus has already mentioned more than once how hostile Molon is toward the Jews. Even stranger is the aorist participle εἴπας ("having said") whose connection to the verb λοιδορεῖ ("scorns") is incomprehensible.[32] The solution is to be found in the fifteenth-/sixteenth-century manuscript S (Schleusingensis). The MS was not inspected at the time Benedict Niese prepared his canonical edition of *Contra Apionem* and has actually remained neglected in the research of the twentieth century. The neglect of S has recently been redressed by Volker Siegert in his forthcoming Münster edition of *Contra Apionem*. Siegert's thorough examination proves definitely that S is independent of L and represents another chain of transmission.[33] It is now also quite clear that the first printed edition, the *editio princeps* of 1544,[34] was not based on L,[35] but on S.[36] Siegert's findings are invaluable for many important issues in the research on *Contra Apionem*. I would add from my own observations that in most cases the different readings of S and the *editio princeps* are preferable to those of L.[37]

("when indeed sometimes someone calls us without god and hateful to men"). *appellet* (in Greek προσαγορεῖ) seems to be a compromise between εἴπας and λοιδορεῖ. Niese offered a supplement, *exempli gratia:* καὶ δὴ εἴπας ποτὲ μὲν <δεισιδαιμονεστάτους πάντων ἄλλοτε> ὡς ἀθέους καὶ μισαν-θρώπους λοιδορεῖ ("and although saying once <that they are the most superstitious of all> elsewhere he derides them as atheists and misanthropes"). See Niese 5: 73. A putative omission at a stage prior to L could not be satisfactorily explained on philological grounds.

33. See Anhang I in F. Siegert, *Flavius Josephus, über die Ursprünglichkeit des Judentums, Contra Apionem*, vol. 2 (Göttingen, forthcoming). I am obliged to Professor Siegert for sending me this appendix as well as the readings of S relevant to some chapters of this book.

34. Edited by the Flemish scholar A. P. Arlenius and published by Froben in Basel.

35. Cf. Thackeray (1926) xix (a variation); Schreckenberg (1972) 52–53; id. (1996) 63–64; Bar-Kochva (2000a) 18–19, relying on the *editio princeps*. It is worth noting that *syngraphē* in this context cannot mean "writing" (i.e., writings), which in any case is far less common. Given the reputation of Molon's written work, it is hard to believe that Josephus would have claimed that Molon's defamation of the Jews was scattered throughout all his compositions.

36. Such as result must have long been anticipated. In his introduction to his edition of the writings of Josephus, Arlenius says that he did his work in the private library of Diego Hurtado de Mendoza, the ambassador of Charles V in Venice, and was helped by his assistant, Sigismund Galenus. Arlenius emphasizes that after the many corruptions that he found in the manuscripts of *Antiquitates judaicae*, the editing of *Bellum Judaicum* and "other books" was less troublesome, since the manuscripts of these works that were available in the library of Mendoza were more exact, and he received additional manuscripts from Johannes Crotus and Petrus Gellius (*Praefatio*, p. 4 *verso*). As MS L of *Contra Apionem* is extremely corrupt, one could surmise that a considerable number of the many differences from L and its descendants in the *editio princeps* reflect the readings of at least another manuscript available at the time. Cf. Bar-Kochva (2000) 17 n. 34. On the library: Hobson (1999).

37. See notes on pp. 45–46, 165, 208–9, 316–19 above.

In the case under discussion, instead of καὶ δὴ εἴπας, S and the *editio princeps* read διὰ πάσης τῆς συγγραφῆς ("throughout the whole composition"). This version gives sense to the passage ("because Apollonius arranged his condemnation [of us] in another way, not concentrated ... as Apion did, but scattered throughout the whole composition, (he) now scorns [us] as atheists ... and now again reproaches us for cowardice").[38] The reasons for the distortion in L are understandable, and its stages can be reconstructed.[39] At the same time, the reading of S could hardly be an amendment by a copyist or an editor.[40]

Josephus thus says that the accusations against the Jews are scattered "throughout the whole composition" of Apollonius Molon, and not "concentrated" in one chapter. An excursus is naturally compact, and were it to have existed, the condemnations would have been concentrated and not scattered. This corroborates the statement of Eusebius-Alexander Polyhistor that Apollonius Molon wrote a work devoted solely to the Jews.

According to an alternative hypothesis that has been voiced, the comments were scattered in an anthology by Molon devoted to a number of peoples and arranged according to subjects. However, there is no example for such an arrangement of ethnographic material, despite the abundant information about a variety of subgenres or literary frameworks: individual monographs; excursuses; "mini-excursuses"; a number of excursuses on various peoples incorporated in one work, scattered or in one sequence; collections of ethnographies on different nations forming an independent work; and anthologies devoted to just a single ethnographic topic (such as *origo*). An anthology of the last type must also be excluded, since Molon's comments refer to a variety of topics. In any case, such a suggestion would ignore the explicit statement of Eusebius-Alexander Polyhistor.

The conclusion is that Apollonius Molon wrote a monograph on the Jews,

---

38. Cf. Schürer (1901–9) 3: 355; Thackeray (1926) 350, referring to the reading of the *editio princeps*.

39. There may have been two or three stages to the corruption: homoeoteleuton in the first stage, where the eye of the copyist jumped from the ending of πάσης to the similar ending of συγγραφῆς, and thereby omitted the words τῆς συγγραφῆς; in the second stage, the words διὰ πάσης were misheard by a later copyist, who wrote them down as δὴ εἰπάσης, which sounds very similar in the Byzantine accent; in the third stage, someone attempted to bring at least some sense to the sentence by emending to δὴ εἴπας.

40. A typical editor of the fifteenth/sixteenth century would not have made an emendation that assumed a corruption in two or three stages. Only such luminaries as Politian and Victorinus were able to make such sophisticated assumptions and emend accordingly, but even they did so only rarely. This level of sophistication became more widespread only in the last quarter of the nineteenth century, with the publication in 1871 of *Adversaria Critica* by the great Danish philologist (and politician) J. N. Madvig. In this landmark work, Madvig first categorized the commonest mistakes of the copyists (pp. 8–95) and then established the means to correct them (pp. 95–184). The rules and methods that he determined allowed even average editors to discover errors and correct them, and one no longer needed to be a Bekker or a Bernays, working with a "sixth sense."

titled *On the Jews* or the like.[41] It was not a polemical oration. The style and the unbiased character of the fragment on the Jewish patriarchs do not fit such a speech. Moreover, an oration would have comprised a running sequence of negative arguments and abuse, not "scattered" charges. The passage quoted by Eusebius suggests that the work was an ethnography. In such a work there was room for, among other things, remarks about the origin of the Arab tribes and their leadership, which appear in the fragment. As shown above, Molon's fields of literary work extended beyond the professional interests of orators.

Applying as a criterion the usual structure of a Hellenistic ethnography,[42] the passage about the patriarchs would naturally have been found in the *origo*, the section usually opening an ethnographic monograph. Following this passage would have come the story of the stay of the children of Israel in Egypt and their expulsion from there. That Molon described the Exodus is corroborated by an explicit testimony in the discussion by Josephus on the various datings of the Exodus in Hellenistic literature (*Ap.* 2. 16), with further circumstantial evidence coming from testimonia on Molon's negative remarks concerning the activity of Moses as a legislator, and his calling Moses a wizard and a deceiver (2. 145).[43] The second section on the *nomima* would have given an account of Jewish institutions, customs, and laws, all attributed to Moses, and the third section on "history" would have told of the deeds and exploits of the Jewish leaders, particularly those contemporary with the author. It stands to reason that the ethnography also included a section on the geography of Judaea.

Apollonius Molon planned his work to appear to be "scientific" and objective, along the lines of Hellenistic ethnographies since Hecataeus of Abdera: that is to say, a work in which the customs and character of the people under discussion are explained as the result of the special conditions of their origin (and often, in addition, of their land's geographical features).[44] The explicit criticism and judgmental comments against the Jews were scattered throughout the descriptions of their beginnings, their customs, and their history, in order for them to appear credible, as if based on real information concerning the history of this people. Not every phase in Jewish *origo* and history was blemished. Thus the personality and deeds of Abraham were portrayed favorably, which must have contributed to the seemingly unbiased and "scientific" appearance of the ethnography.

Does the conclusion that Molon wrote a Jewish ethnography accord with our evidence for the title of the work? Eusebius presents Apollonius Molon at the

41. On the generic title, see Bar-Kochva (1996d) 187–91.

42. On the structure of the Hellenistic ethnography, see Bar-Kochva (1996d) 10–13, 192–219.

43. The connection of these details to the Exodus already appears in the account of Lysimachus, *Contra Apionem* 1. 309.

44. See on this Bar-Kochva (1996d) 12, 23–24, 217–19. Cf. pp. 96–97 above.

beginning of the passage on the patriarch as follows: "Molon, who wrote an abusive work (*syskeuē*) against the Jews (*kata Ioudaiōn*)". This description is to be understood as referring to the title and/or aim of the work. Since the other passages adduced by Eusebius from Alexander Polyhistor are in most cases accompanied or introduced by the titles of the works from which they come, one may argue that in the present case Eusebius hints at the title of the work and not its objective. However, the title *Against the Jews* does not suit an ethnography, and it belongs to the genre of rhetorical polemics (which Molon's monograph could not have).[45]

It seems that in this case Eusebius preferred to present the work of Molon according to its main aim, known to him from Josephus's recurring notes in *Contra Apionem*. That the presentation of Molon's work was formulated by Eusebius, and not taken from Alexander Polyhistor,[46] is supported by the use of the word *syskeuē*. It is a late word, appearing relatively frequently from the beginning of the second century C.E., and it means in this context an abusive work.[47] One of Eusebius's main claims in the ninth book of *Praeparatio evangelica* was that the books of the Bible relating the beginnings of the Jewish people are corroborated by the accounts of Greek authors (9. 1. 1–2). Presenting Molon's book as essentially hostile would actually strengthen the value of its favorable testimony regarding Abraham; Eusebius introduces Molon's account as the correct version, rather than the accounts of "anonymous authors" who said that Abraham came from the stock of Belus, the only giant to have survived destruction at the hands of the gods as punishment for *asebeia* (18. 2–3).

After all, titles of books that have reached us from antiquity quite often differ from the names given by the authors. The original title—usually relating to the contents—could well have been altered in the process of transmission to reflect the purpose of the book. If this was the case with Molon's anti-Jewish work, it was a wise decision.

Was Josephus acquainted directly with Molon's work or only with quotations

---

45. A title containing the word *kata* (against) with a noun in the genitive case is usual in speeches for the prosecution. To take one example, more than half the speeches of Demosthenes that we have are of this type. Two works of Apollonius Molon were entitled *Against the Citizens of Caunus* and *Against the Philosophers*.

46. This is also the opinion of Goodman in Schürer et al. 3: 1, 599.

47. Conzelmann (1981) 72 suggested translating the word as "Gaukelei" (a "conjuring trick"); Goodman in Schürer 3: 599, following Schürer (1901–9) 3: 534, proposed "polemic." The noun is cognate with the verb *syskeuadzō* which means "to compose," "to pack up," "to contrive" (in a negative sense), and has various meanings: "equipment," "intrigue," "false accusation." In the present case, the term would seem to have the meaning "libelous composition," "collection of libels," or the like. This is the sense in which Eusebius uses it a number of times in *Praeparatio evangelica* (5. 5. 5, 36. 5; 10. 9. 11, 20). The noun and verb appear in his *Ecclesiastica historia* in the sense of "intrigue" and similar meanings (1. 3. 6; 3. 33. 2; 4. 16. 7, 18. 7; 6. 9. 4; 10. 8. 5, 7).

from it adduced by Apion?[48] His comment that Molon's negative remarks about the Jews (unlike those of Apion) were scattered throughout his work would indicate that Josephus was directly acquainted with it.[49] Molon's book was certainly available in Rome, and Josephus must have been sufficiently motivated to look at this monograph on the Jews, before devoting a considerable proportion of the second book of *Contra Apionem* to a response. It is also unlikely that Molon's praise for the Persians (2. 270), which Josephus singles out for particular reproach (distorting its original meaning), was adduced by Apion in Molon's name. There would have been room for such praise in an extensive monograph of Molon on the Jews, which, besides discussing the Jews, their customs, and religion, presented some comparison with, and references to, other peoples.

It may be asked why Josephus did not use Molon's account of the Jewish patriarchs in the first book of *Contra Apionem*, where he presented evidence for his claim that Greek authors also testify to the primacy of the Jews (paras. 161–218), if he was indeed directly acquainted with Molon's work. The fact is that Josephus also failed to adduce Molon's dating of the Exodus as evidence for this same argument, although he mentions the dating in another context in the second book (para. 16). I would guess that Josephus was reluctant to name Molon in support of his arguments in the first book of *Contra Apionem* because in the second book he does everything to undermine his credibility. Similarly, Josephus chose not to rely on Apion for evidence of Jewish antiquity because he wished to accuse him of extreme unreliability. Apion's account of the Exodus, touching also on the event at Mt. Sinai, appears only in the second book (2. 6, 9, 15, 21, 25), in Josephus's concentrated attack on Apion's accusations against the Jews.[50]

APOLLONIUS MOLON'S SOURCES OF INFORMATION

Molon's account of the beginning of Jewish history, as it has been preserved in Eusebius, runs as follows:

> (1) Molon, who wrote an abusive work against the Jews, says that after the Flood the man who was saved came down with his sons from Armenia, since he was expelled by the locals. After crossing the land between them, he came to the hilly region of

48. On the use of an intermediate source by Josephus in this case, see Heinemann, *RE* s.v. "Antisemitismus," suppl. 5 (1931), col. 34.

49. Why would Apion say this about a work that was entirely devoted to the subject of the Jews? This would have produced an impression quite the opposite of the one he wished to produce. It is worth adding that the reference to Apollonius Molon, *Contra Apionem* 2. 79, in the framework of Josephus's argument with Apion, cannot be used as evidence that Josephus's acquaintance with Molon's account was only secondhand.

50. Of the Egyptian authors, the only one who is adduced as testimony for the primacy of the Jews is Manetho. The first two quoted passages (1. 75–90, 94–101) do not contain anti-Jewish

Syria, which was desolate. (2) Three generations later, Abraham, meaning "father-loving," was born. Since he was a wise man, he pursued the desert. After taking two wives, one a local and a relative, the other an Egyptian, a servant, twelve sons were born to him from the Egyptian. These departed to Arabia, divided the land, and were the first to reign over the inhabitants. Since then until this day there have been twelve Arab kings bearing names identical to them. (3) From his wife was born one son, called in Greek Gelos (Laugh, Laughingstock). Abraham died at a good old age, and Gelos and his local wife had eleven sons, and the twelfth, Joseph; and the third [generation] from him, Moses. (*PE* 9. 19. 1–3, taken from Alexander Polyhistor)

Molon's account is clearly based ultimately on the story in Genesis. It is also clear, however, that the information reached him through an intermediate source. The most obvious indication of this is that the name of Abraham is not interpreted as it is in the Bible (Genesis 17.5), but etymologically ("father-loving"), indicating a knowledge of Hebrew, and apparently Aramaic.[51] Furthermore, the passage frequently diverges from the Genesis accounts of Noah and Abraham: the man saved from the Flood (not mentioned by name) was expelled with his sons from the mountains of Armenia by the locals; Abraham is portrayed as of the third generation after the Flood (and not the tenth as in Genesis); his birth and early activity appear to have taken place in the hilly region of Syria (not in Ur of the Chaldees in Mesopotamia); his lawful wife and the wife of his son Isaac are locals (not Mesopotamian); the passage ascribes the twelve sons to Isaac and completely overlooks Jacob; Ishmael is not mentioned, and his twelve sons, the kings of the

accusations. In the third part of the first book of *Contra Apionem* (paras. 223–320), where Josephus struggles against the anti-Jewish libels, commencing with the hostile Egyptian traditions concerning the Exodus (including the collection of the Greek Lysimachus, 1. 305–11), there appear hostile accounts—quoted and paraphrased—from Manetho, describing the stay of the Jews in Egypt (paras. 227–51); it would seem that Josephus adduced the first two passages in support of the primacy of the Jews because they were based, according to Manetho, upon ancient Egyptian writings, which would sup-port Josephus's claim for Jewish primacy (paras. 73, 104). As a matter of fact, Josephus did not attack Manetho personally, nor did he accuse him of malicious intentions in the response to the hostile versions. He even pointed out that some of Manetho's account was faithful to the ancient sources (paras. 228, 287), although in the rest of the account he had erred in his editing and arrangement of the material and in following the haters of the Jews (para. 287). On this last point, cf. Gruen (1998) 59–60.

51. For the source of this explanation of the name Abraham (Avraham), see the suggestion of Isidore Lévy, appearing in Reinach (1895) 60, that the name was misread as Abraham (raham = loving). Ginzberg (1925–38) 5: 207 n. 4 draws attention to Isaiah 41.8, "the seed of Abraham my lover," and 2 Chronicles 20.7, "to the seed of Abraham thy lover" (adduced in Stern *GLAJJ* 1: 151). The first suggestion is plausible as far as the composition of the name is concerned, while the biblical verses do not seem to be based on some etymological interpretation but rather on the relationship between Abraham and God. This is how, for example, the medieval author of Yalkut understood the verses: see Yalkut Shimʿoni, Isaiah 40, no. 444. Cf. ʾAvot de-Rabbi Nathan, 2nd version, ch. 43. Hence also the Arabic name of Abraham, *el-ḥalil* (= the beloved).

Arab tribes ("presidents" in Gen. 25.16), are portrayed as the sons of Abraham; and finally, Moses is treated as the grandson of Joseph.[52]

The etymological interpretation of the name of Abraham suggests that a Hellenistic Jewish source was used, directly or indirectly.[53] This source was familiar with the original biblical accounts and had a good command of Hebrew, and probably Aramaic. He allowed himself to deviate from biblical interpretation and turn to etymology, as often happened in Hellenistic Jewish literature, which added homilitic interpretations to the scriptures—in this case, if for no other reason than that the biblical interpretation of "Abraham" (Gen. 17.5) was itself a sort of "midrash." The Jewish intermediate source also added an original geographical-historical background to the connection of the patriarchs with Syria (namely, the Holy Land). After the Flood the sole survivor came down from the mountains of Armenia, because he "was expelled by the locals," and moved through the lowland in between to the hilly region of Syria (preferring the hills upon flat, fertile Mesopotamia, probably in anticipation of a new flood). The reader is not told how there were suddenly other people in Armenia. This obviously indicates an abbreviation of the text. Molon may have confused a reference (or a story) in his source to tensions and conflicts between Noah and his neighbors before the Flood. Such stories are known from the midrashic literature. The next sentence is even more interesting and once more exposes an abbreviation by Molon: "Since he (Abraham) was a wise man, he went for the desert." The statement is an explanation for Abraham's wandering in the Beer Sheva Desert and the Negev. Abraham's wisdom thus convinced him that wandering in the desert was the right thing to do. At first sight one may think that Abraham was trying to find a safer haven from floods, but three generations are said to have passed since the Flood, and a Jewish author would hardly have linked Abraham's movements to it. Molon cannot be considered the inventor of an explanation that introduced as a wise man the patriarch of a race he elsewhere describes unequivocally as "the most inferior of humans" (Joseph. *Ap.* 2. 236). Why then was it wise for Abraham to depart to the desert? It does not seem to be related to the episode of the separation between Abraham and Lot, his nephew, since Abraham did not turn then to the desert but remained in the "hilly region" and even strengthened his hold there, establishing himself in Hebron (Gen. 13.5–18). The answer may be found in the Oriental image of the desert as a source of inspiration for the founders of religions, from Moses through Zoroaster to Mohammad. Hence also the motif

52. For a partial list of the differences, see Reinach (1895) 60–61; Stern, *GLAJJ* 1: 151–52; Conzelmann (1981) 72.

53. Stern, *GLAJJ* 1: 148–49, speaks about "Jewish Hellenistic circles." He further suggests that Molon may well have received information from Jews in Caria, his native region. The features of the text taken as a whole indicate that the source used was not an oral, but a written one.

of "the longing for the desert" recurring in literature of the biblical prophets and the period of the Second Temple, which culminated in the retreat of Jewish sects to the Judaean desert. Abraham accordingly aspired to find a "pure" place, clean of the sins and evils of civilization, where he could feel close to God and contemplate divine matters. The romanticizing of the desert was alien to Greek literature, and therefore the sentence could be a remnant only of a midrashic interpretation by a Jew.

Other divergences from the biblical account may be regarded as an attempt to simplify the genealogical-ethnographic-geographical background, whether by the same source or by Apollonius Molon himself. If the report in his source was particularly detailed, Molon may have had difficulty following the genealogical and geographical intricacies, and this might explain an attempt on his part to simplify. There are also indications that Alexander Polyhistor, Eusebius's intermediate source, shortened the account here and there, as was his wont.[54] This too may have had some effect on the divergences from the biblical account noted above. Notwithstanding, they are no more than one might expect in an account by a Hellenistic Jew.

The hypothesis, therefore, that Molon's version is based directly on the biblical account must be rejected,[55] as must the suggestion that Molon's account was influenced by the tradition later received by Nicolaus of Damascus (adduced by Josephus, *AJ* 1. 160), according to which Abraham, heading an army out of the "land of the Chaldaeans beyond Babylon," occupied and ruled Damascus,[56] and only later settled in Canaan, which is Judaea.[57] At the same time, the notion of some indirect, remote link between Molon's account and the "northern" version of the beginning of the Jewish people, known from Pompeius Trogus (Justin, 36. 2. 1–6), should not be discounted altogether, despite the great difference in

54. Abridgment is evident from the way in which some of the events and personalities are presented, taken together with the number of participial forms used in the passage under discussion. On Alexander Polyhistor's habit of abbreviating the passages he cites in reported speech, see Freudenthal (1875) 33.

55. Reinach (1895) 61 believes that the source for Molon's version is the Pentateuch, with divergences being the result of a superficial reading.

56. The correct reading in Josephus is ἐβασίλευσε Δαμασκοῦ ("was king of Damascus"), and not just ἐβασίλευσεν ("was king"), preferred by Niese. This appears from the MSS tradition (including Eus. *PE* 9. 16. 3), as well as from the geographical sequence and the reference to "Abraham's house."

57. Suggested by Feldman (1996b) 183. The tradition reported by Nicolaus seems to be a Jewish legend, based on an early exegesis on the name Eliezer of Damascus, Abraham's steward-slave (Genesis 15.2). Such an interpretation may have sounded more plausible than the familiar ones: "Eliezer of Damascus for whom I pursued kings to Damascus" or "by whom I pursued kings to Damascus" (Genesis Rabba 44, 14 [ed. Theodor-Albeck, p. 431]). The tradition may also have come about as an aetiological explanation for the name of the place called "Abraham's house" or the like, which was still in existence, according to Nicolaus, in his time in Damascus (Joseph. *AJ* 1. 160).

detail.[58] The analysis of the Molon passage suggests that there was a Jewish-Hellenistic story about the emigration of Noah to "the hills of Syria," and of the Jewish patriarch from there to the desert, and afterward to Egypt.

For some of the testimonia hostile to the Jews, Molon's direct source seems to have been Lysimachus's work on the history of Egypt, from which Josephus adduced a compilation of Egyptian versions of the Exodus (*Ap.* 1. 304–11). In two places in the second book of *Contra Apionem,* Josephus indicates a similarity between claims made by Molon and Lysimachus about Moses and the Jews. In one place he says that "Apollonius Molon, Lysimachus, and others" portrayed Moses as "a wizard and a deceiver (γόης καὶ ἀπατεών)," and that his laws "indicate ... [only] evil and nothing containing virtues" (2. 145). In another place, Josephus says that "the Lysimachi and the Molons and other authors like them"[59] portray the Jews as "the lowest of humans" (φαυλότατοι ἀνθρώπων, 2. 236). As Lysimachus's work should be dated to the last quarter of the second century B.C.E.,[60] he may well have inspired the accusations in Molon.

Josephus formulated these accusations briefly and summarized things that both authors had written about in detail. In Lysimachus, the accusations were included in his account of the Exodus,[61] and the description of Moses at least was also included in Molon's parallel account. In addition to points of contact

58. Stern, *GLAJJ* 1: 149, appears to be more definite about the link. Source criticism of Trogus's account indicates that the process was rather complicated. The version of Pompeius Trogus differed substantially from the fragment of Apollonius Molon: Abraham in Pompeius Trogus-Justin is not of the third generation after the Flood, but the fourth in the line of kings whose seat is in the celebrated city of Damascus (described also as the origin of the Assyrian kings); Abraham (the king) in this version does not leave "the hilly region of Syria" and departs to the desert; Isaac is not mentioned, and the central figure in the Jewish genealogy is Israel (not Abraham; and the name Jacob is missing), described as the most important of the kings of Damascus; Israel has ten sons (not twelve); each son is allocated a separate kingdom, with the kingdom of Judas, following his sudden death, being annexed to the remaining sons, who were then called after him Iudaioi (none of this is to be found in Apollonius Molon). Pompeius Trogus's divergences from the biblical account are too great to be attributed to a Jewish-Hellenistic source (see also Trogus's statement that the Jews observe Egyptian cults, 36. 1. 13, 16). The treatment of Judaea and the Jews also makes it less likely that we are facing a distorted account of the origin of the kingdom of the "ten tribes" or a version by a Samaritan Hellenistic author. Adding to these considerations the positive remarks concerning the cult in Damascus and the statement that the Jews were subjected to a foreign rule only from the reign of Xerxes, we are obliged to surmise that the account is based on a combination of pieces of information that have reached Pompeius Trogus, a Gaul residing in Rome, directly or indirectly from Jews (via a pagan Hellenistic author used by him [Timagenes?]), and snippets about two of the most famous kings of Damascus (Azelus and Adores = Hazael and Ben Hadad) and the local cult. These were blended together, and the abbreviation by Justin probably contributed to the clumsy result. At the same time, it could be just a translation of a Jewish excursus by Timagenes.

59. On the use of the plural as a form of mockery, see Kasher (1996) 521, following Müller (1877) 290 and parallels there.

60. See above, pp. 333–36.

61. See above, p. 316 ff.

between the two authors, it is worth recalling that the first version in Lysimachus presented the diseased in Egypt as Jews from the beginning (*Ap.* 1. 305), while other Hellenistic authors (excluding Hecataeus) presented them as Egyptians who only after the expulsion became a separate entity.[62] In this respect, Molon's account fits that in Lysimachus, describing as it does the beginning of the history of the Jewish people from the time of the patriarchs, which meant that the Jews were a definite ethnic group before the time of their stay in Egypt. Molon differs from Lysimachus, however, in portraying Moses as the grandson of Joseph, and this is not accidental: it serves to hint at the origins of Moses' wizardry. In Molon's account, Moses was not an unknown wizard who suddenly appeared out of the blue, as Lysimachus had described,[63] but presumably a well-known magician who had inherited his art from Joseph, and who had ancestral rights because of his direct descent from Abraham. Pompeius Trogus, in similar fashion, described Joseph as a magician and Moses as his son and heir (Justin 36. 2. 7–11). Molon may have diverged from Lysimachus in other respects, too. The term "deceiver," "charlatan" (ἀπατεών), while explaining the epithet "wizard," could have been intended to counter the Jewish claim of a divine source for the laws given by Moses to the Jews.

Now to the blood and ass libels. According to Josephus, Apion named Apollonius Molon along with Posidonius of Apamea as his source for these libels (*Ap.* 2. 79). In the previous chapter I suggested identifying Timochares, the Seleucid court historian, as the source of both Posidonius and Molon.[64] I also showed that Posidonius omitted the blood libel, while his version of the ass libel differed from that of Apion.[65]

Apollonius Molon may well have used the same source as Posidonius. There are similarities of formulation and content between some of the anti-Jewish accusations embedded in Josephus's testimonia on Molon and the "advice" of the counselors of Antiochus Sidetes as reported by Posidonius (preserved in Diod. 34/35. 1. 7–5). The most outstanding similarity is the reference to misanthropy, which appeared for the first time in both to denote the hostile attitude of the Jews toward all humanity,[66] and the use of the verb (μὴ) κοινωνεῖν in connection with their detachment from, or aversion to, other nations;[67] the forceful condemna-

---

62. See above, p. 325.
63. See above, p. 328.
64. See above, pp. 464–65.
65. See above, pp. 241, 445–47.
66. Timochares (via Posidonius) in Diodorus 34/35. 1. 2–3; Molon in *Contra Apionem* 2. 148.
67. Timochares in Diodorus 34/35. 1. 2; cf. para. 1: ἀκοινωνήτους εἶναι; Molon in *Contra Apionem* 2. 258.

tion of Moses' laws also appears to be similar, although the exact formulation of Apollonius Molon has not survived.[68]

Molon's treatise had included the blood libel. Apion mentions him together with Posidonius as his sources for the libel, while Posidonius had in fact omitted it from his version of the anti-Jewish accusations and libels.[69] This leaves Apollonius Molon as the real direct source for Apion's account of the blood libel.

The ass libel seems to have appeared in Molon in its "soft" version, as it did in Posidonius, namely, a sculpture of Moses seated on an ass.[70] Elsewhere, Molon accused the Jews of atheism (*Ap.* 2. 148) because they declared their faith in a god with no size or shape.[71] This would not be consistent with the hard version that they deified the head of an ass. In the "soft" version, the statue does not symbolize any divinity but reflects a "founder" cult: Moses and his laws stand at the center of Molon's account of the character of the Jewish people, and the portrayal of the statue in the Temple of Moses with his book of laws would have emphasized the Jews' blind obedience to, and admiration for, Moses the wizard and charlatan. Molon, contrary to Posidonius,[72] obviously presented the ass libel as a historical fact. Josephus, for his part, felt no reason to mention, much less attack, Molon's "soft" version of Moses riding on an ass, because he answered Apion's "hard" version with three clear refutations (2. 81–88). The historical and historiographical refutation, which is the most compelling, is applicable to both versions: none of those foreigners who had entered the Temple, including Pompey and Titus, had ever found a trace of an ass or the head of an ass, but only the purest of cults; all those historians and choniclers who had written about the intrusion of Antiochus Epiphanes into the Temple regarded his act as sacrilegious but said nothing about him finding the statue of an ass or the head of an ass or anything even remotely similar (2. 82–84).

From the little of Molon's Jewish ethnography that has survived, therefore, several sources for it may be detected: a Jewish Hellenistic source, Timochares, and Lysimachus. It is most probable that Apollonius Molon had at his disposal more sources. Whatever the case may be, unlike most contemporary Hellenistic-Roman authors, he was exposed to pro-Jewish and Jewish works, but his treatment of the Jewish people is hostile and cannot be ascribed to slavish copying of his sources. His hostility, therefore, must be accounted for by some other, more particular reasons.

---

68. Timochares (via Posidonius) in Diodorus 34/35. 1. 2; Molon in *Contra Apionem* 2. 145. The similarity is not in formulation but in content and intent, and this is emphasized by Josephus's reply in para. 146.

69. See pp. 445–47 above.

70. See pp. 238–41 above.

71. See pp. 506–14 below.

72. See pp. 451–55 above.

MOLON'S ETHNOGRAPHY AND
POSIDONIUS'S ETHNOGRAPHICAL EXCURSUS

The island of Rhodes was home to two literary giants of the age: Apollonius Molon, a leading orator and rhetor; and Posidonius of Apamea, the celebrated Stoic philosopher. We have seen that there were good reasons and some indirect indications for the development of bitter, inevitable rivalry between the two (as a matter of fact, it was inevitable).[73] Posidonius wrote an ethnographical excursus exalting Moses and early Judaism, presenting it as a model, ideal society along Stoic lines. By contrast, Molon wrote a particularly negative ethnography of the Jews, treating the activity of Moses as the cause of all the evils he, Molon, attributes to the Jewish character. The Posidonian excursus was part not of some esoteric work, but was included in his monumental *Histories,* published in 84 B.C.E., and therefore would not have been overlooked by Molon. Would then a disputative rhetor like Apollonius Molon have failed to react in his own hostile treatise to such an extremely curious and highly favorable description of the Jews in a major work by his compatriot, and his professional, if not personal, rival?

The second book of *Contra Apionem* contains a scattering of testimonia on Apollonius Molon that together sound like echoes and responses to Posidonius's account. I shall survey some of the testimonia, examining them *per se*, ascertaining whether there are parallels to them in Greek or Latin literature, and noting what is peculiar to them. We shall then be in a position to decide whether they are a reaction to Posidonius's portrait of Mosaic Judaism or merely either a recycling of earlier claims made against the Jews, or original claims made by Molon.

A. Jewish Cowardice

According to Josephus, Apollonius Molon blamed the Jews for cowardice: ποτὲ δ' αὖ δειλίαν ἡμῖν ὀνειδίζει ("He then rebukes us for cowardice," 2. 148). There is no parallel to this rebuke in any of the many surviving accusations and libels against the Jews. Quite the opposite. The impression one gets from Greek and Roman authors, including the most hostile of them, is that the Jews are intensively occupied with military matters, display courage in battle, and despise death.[74] The participation of Jewish soldiers in Hellenistic armies was well known, as were

---

73. See pp. 475–77 above.

74. This may be seen already in the account by Hecataeus of Abdera (Diod. 40. 3. 3, 6–7), which became a sort of vulgate for later authors. Jewish courage in battle and their contempt for death are particularly emphasized by Tacitus: "They regard the souls of the fallen in battle as eternal ... hence ... their contempt for death" (*Hist.* 5. 5. 3). See also the edict of Julius Caesar in *Antiquitates Judaicae* 14. 193 and the remarks of Dio Cassius (touching on the two great revolts against Rome, 66. 6. 1–3; 69. 13. 3). These are but select examples.

the military successes of the Hasmonaean brothers against the Seleucid armies, and the wide territorial expansion and occupations by the Hasmonaean rulers took place in the generation of Molon. The Jews were nearly always considered a belligerent people. This is clearly discernible from the writings of Josephus, their ardent defender. Tacitus imputes cowardice to peoples that remained oppressed for a long time (*Agr.* 11, 15), but not to the Jews. In any case, Molon wrote his comment when the Jews were independent and were oppressing others. The charge of cowardice, therefore, appears strange on all counts.[75]

Faintheartedness in battle (as opposed to other fears) leading to a failure to act properly and respectfully was considered by the Greeks to be particularly despicable. It would surely be redundant in this survey to adduce Greek poets, historians, and thinkers who praise courage in battle.[76] Yet in order to understand the terms and philosophical background both to Molon's claim and to Josephus's reaction, it may be worth turning briefly to Aristotle's definitions concerning the status of courage among the virtues, the circumstances in which it is displayed, and its most exalted expressions, as against the Stoic approach, as well as to Aristotle's reservations concerning bold acts that are not part of courage at all (*EN* 1114b5 ff.; *EE* 1228b2 ff.): courage (*andreia*) is one of the virtues and is the first virtue discussed by Aristotle. Cowardice (*deilia*) is the opposite of it. The fullest expression of courage is risking the danger of battle, meaning being prepared to die. Another way to define courage is as the middle way (*mesotēs*) between two negative extremes: cowardice and thoughtless bravado or recklessness (*thrasytēs*), lacking all awareness of danger until the moment of action, at which point fear and hesitation set in. The truly courageous man knows what dangers he is getting involved in, and is afraid in due measure, but knows how to overcome his fear in order to do what is necessary (*EN* 1115a15 ff.; *EE* 1228a27 ff.). Aristotle concludes by observing that all democratic states and all types of rulers honor those who fall in battle (*EN* 1115a30), while retreat from the battlefield is considered a disgrace (1116b20). Aristotle's remarks essentially reflect Greek popular traditional conceptions. Apollonius Molon's conception of *andreia* would not have differed on principle from the conventional view, where courage in battle was the supreme expression of this virtue, while its opposite,

75. Troiani (1977) suggests that Jewish reluctance to fight on the Sabbath was interpreted as stemming from cowardice. However, it was explicitly explained by Agatharchides as a superstition (Joseph. *AJ* 12. 6), and the observance of the Sabbath as a whole was presented as such by later Greek and Roman authors, along with other explanations, but never in the context of cowardice; so Joseph. *Antiquitates Judaicae* 12. 5–6; *Contra Apionem* 1. 208–10; and cf. Seneca's remarks preserved in Augustine *De civitate Dei* 6. 11; Plutarch *De superstitione* 169C; Persius *Satirae* 5. 179 ff. (hinted at).

76. For two celebrated passages from the beginning of Greek literature in praise of death on the battlefield: Homer *Iliad* 15. 494–95; Tyrmaeus, ed. Gentili-Prato (1988) I, fr. F, ll. 1–2, with the opposite sentiment later in the fragment.

cowardice, was also primarily thought of in the context of the battlefield. And rhetors, including Molon, had nothing personal against the Peripatetics, unlike their tense relations with the Stoics. Notably, the Stoic conception of *andreia* was somewhat different, being concerned not with a readiness for self-sacrifice in battle but with awareness, or rather (theoretical) knowledge of dangers.[77]

One possible source of inspiration that springs to mind for Molon's accusation of Jewish cowardice is the Jewish ethnography of Posidonius where the pacifist approach of Moses plays a central role in Mosaic Judaism. Posidonius explains that Moses, an Egyptian priest, led his supporters out of Egypt in order to be able to observe his faith and perform his cult undisturbed by the Egyptians. This might be negatively construed to mean that he declined to face dangers in defending his convictions. Furthermore, Moses is said to have led his supporters to Jerusalem of all places because he assumed that the dry and rocky nature of the area would repel other peoples, and wars would consequently not arise (Strabo 16. 2. 36). Posidonius is even more explicit when he goes on to say: "Instead of arms, [Moses] would use as a protection sacrifices and the divine entity." All of this is the exact opposite of what Hecataeus wrote in his Jewish excursus, according to which Moses trained the youth for war in the face of expected dangers (Diod. 40. 3. 6–7). It is also contrary to the usual practice of Greek colonization, with a new settlement investing much of its resources in military training.[78]

This extreme pacifistic policy of avoiding confrontation at all cost would have come in for criticism from Greek authors, even those who expressed a hope in the possibility of an end to wars and eternal peace. It could easily be explained—by a biased rhetor such as Molon—as the result of cowardice.

We do not know exactly how Apollonius Molon described Jewish cowardice. Josephus does not quote him but sums up the matter in one word, as he does with regard to the other charges referred to in the same paragraph. A good rhetor would certainly not have spared words in explaining exactly what he had in mind. If Molon wished to exploit Greek values to his advantage, he would have said explicitly that the Jews were afraid to die on the battlefield.

This last point is indirectly supported by the reaction of Josephus. Immediately before the testimonium of Molon we are discussing, when responding in general to Molon's accusations against the Jews, Josephus gives a condensed list of Jewish characteristics, among which he mentions *karteria*, the ability to withstand external pressures, and θανάτου περιφρόνησινς, contempt toward death

---

77. The common Stoic definition of courage is ἐπιστήμη δεινῶν καὶ οὐ δεινῶν καὶ οὐδετέρων ("knowledge of things terrible and not terrible, and neither of these"); see *SVF* 3: frr. 262, 266, 274, 275; cf. the definition of Zeno of Citium: ὁριζόμενος τὴν φρόνησιν . . . ἐν δ' ὑπομενετέοις ἀνδρείαν ("defining practical wisdom with regard to things that should be suffered, as courage"), *SVF* 1: fr. 201.

78. See pp. 376–79 above.

(2. 146). Josephus is more forthcoming after presenting Molon's accusations: he expands on the preparedness of Jews to suffer torture and death for their adherence to their ancestral laws,[79] and he adds that death on the battlefield is the easiest death of all, since it is not accompanied by torture, the fate of those who die for their religious beliefs; and those who go into battle are not hampered by everyday prohibitions, as opposed to those who are obliged to follow the religious commandments, including dietary laws and those having to do with sexual matters (2. 232–35). All this is said ostensibly to emphasize the loyalty of the Jews to their laws, and their dependence on them, the main subject of the last section of *Contra Apionem*. This section of the work is a reply to the work by Apollonius Molon. Would Josephus's comparison between death on the battlefield (which he praises at 2. 294) and the more courageous death in passive defense of one's faith not also be a reaction to Apollonius Molon's remarks on Jewish cowardice and fear of death on the battlefield?

Apollonius Molon, accordingly, treated the "information" that he found in Posidonius as any rhetor would: he gave it a new look, interpretation, or treatment that suited his general purpose. This is what was taught in rhetorical exercises in schools: a student chose a *topos* on which to deliver two opposing speeches, paying special attention to the invention of new ideas or interpretations. This in fact is also what Posidonius did with the basic material on the Jews that he found in the Jewish excursus of Hecataeus of Abdera. If a philosopher could do it, how much more so might it be expected of a professional rhetor of the standing of Apollonius Molon?

The hypothesis that Apollonius Molon reacted to the account by Posidonius may solve an apparent contradiction that Josephus found in Molon's work. Josephus notes in the same context (2. 148) that on the one hand Molon accuses the Jews of cowardice (*deilia*), and on the other hand, of recklessness (*tolma*) and madness (*aponoia*). According to the context, the reference is obviously to eagerness for battle and to fighting style. Wishing to expose a contradiction, Josephus did not have any interest in recording Molon's explanation for these conflicting terms, all the more so as every accusation in the same paragraph had been introduced by just a single word. I would suggest that, playing on the Posidonian distinction between Mosaic and contemporary Judaism, Molon leveled the charge of cowardice at Mosaic Judaism, the Judaism of the past, while the charge of unrestrained recklessness and madness was leveled at his contemporary Jews, namely, the Hasmonaean rulers.[80] Regarding this latter issue there was no reason for Molon to disagree with

79. The formulation by Josephus is a paraphrase of a description of the Jewish martyrology in the testimonium adduced from pseudo-Hecataeus in *Contra Apionem* 1. 191.

80. The assumption that this has to do with the Hasmonaeans appears already in Troiani (1977) 179–80.

Posidonius, who described the Jewish leaders of his time as "robbers" harassing both their own and neighboring peoples (Strabo 16. 2. 37). Recklessness, certainly when coupled with madness, is hardly a synonym for bravery in Greek, and Apollonius Molon uses it only disparagingly.[81]

At the same time, there is another possibility, somewhat different from the former one. One scholar has drawn attention to a parallel combination of cowardice and recklessness in war found in a late author's comment on the Egyptians, rightly defining it as an ethnographic stereotype.[82] In his love-romance *Leucippe and Clitophon,* Achilles Tatius (mid-second century C.E.) states:

> For an Egyptian man when afraid is slave to cowardice, and when confident is eager for a fight; both not in moderation, but rather he bears misfortune too weakly, superiority too rashly. (14.9)

The exact meaning appears from the episode preceding this comment: the Egyptians are eager to fight so long as they are confident of an easy victory and keep the upper hand, but if they face a superior force or when the tide of battle turns against them, they decline to engage or take to their heels, respectively. By and large this is no more than a shameful expression of cowardice.

The terms "cowardice" and "recklessness" appear together in the Aristotelian treatment of *andreia.* The combination is not only a well-known individual behavioral phenomenon but has been imputed to races as well, as in Tacitus's description of the Gauls and the Britons (*Agr.* 11: *audacia* and *formido*). Judging from the parallels, it appears that Molon attributed to the Jews not only cowardice by nature, inherited from Moses, but also, in a contemptuous way, eagerness for battle, to the extent of "madness," namely, ferocity and/or excessive cruelty on the battlefield when faced with a considerably inferior opponent. Could this stereotype have been applied by Molon to the Jews out of the blue, and contrary to their accepted image—even in the writings of their extreme opponents—as people who are ready to risk their lives and who despise death? I doubt very much that Molon would have gone so far without being acquainted with the unique Posidonian account, and having a strong personal motive to reject it. In doing so, Molon did not disregard the popular image of the Jews as warlike people but gave it a scornful interpretation.

---

81. *Pace* Feldman (1996b) 220–21, who gives the word *tolma* a positive significance in this context. While it is true that the word may in some contexts have a positive significance (examples in Feldman), it also has a negative one (e.g., Pl. *Ap.* 38d; *Leg.* 193d, 197b; Arist. *EE* 1220b39, 1228a29, where the parallel to *thrasos* is *thrasytēs,* the extreme whose opposite extreme is cowardice, and the "middle way" between these two is courage; and cf. what was said above about Aristotle's observations). Its appearance with *aponoia* indicates the negative intent of the expression. So too in Josephus, *Bellum Judaicum* 3. 479; 4. 558; 5. 274; *Antiquitates Judaicae* 6. 264; 19. 304.

82. Bohak (2003) 42. The interpretation below, however, differs from that of Bohak.

B. The Jews as the Most Primitive and Uninventive of Peoples

Josephus briefly summarizes a number of times claims that he found in Apollonius Molon concerning the primitiveness and uninventiveness of the Jews: "He (Molon) says that [the Jews] are the most primitive (*aphyestatoi*) of barbarian (peoples), and because of this they are the only ones to have contributed no invention (*eurēma*) to [human] life" (2. 148). Josephus offers some elaboration at the end of the specific reply to this accusation: "Hence arises the charge some launch against us, that we have not provided any inventors of new deeds (*erga*) or words (*logoi*)" (2. 182). Earlier he refers to Apion, and it appears that Apion based his arguments on Apollonius Molon: "But (says Apion) we have not provided amazing men (*thaumastoi*), such as those who were outstanding in inventing certain arts (*technai*), or wisdom (*sophia*)" (2. 135).[83] Thus Apollonius Molon mentioned the lack of any contribution by the Jews to human culture, whether in the practical or the theoretical arts.

Apart from the above testimonia, charges concerning the uninventiveness of the Jews in practical matters are unknown in Greek and Latin literature, while nothing is written on the lack of any contribution to *logoi* until the beginning of the dispute between Christians and pagans.[84] The Jews were even described at the beginning of the Hellenistic period as a nation of philosophers who have ideas similar to those of the Greeks.[85] Even the most outspoken of the Jews' enemies did not condemn them as primitives.[86] At various times they were accused of having

---

83. In connection with Greek wisdom, Apion, paraphrasing Molon's accusation (*Ap.* 2. 135), names Socrates, Zeno, Cleanthes, and himself. The reference to the philosophers was not taken from Apollonius Molon but was an addition made by Apion. It may be that Molon adduced a number of personalities as an example, but not philosophers, and certainly not Socrates and the early Stoics. He deplored Socrates and Plato in his treatise "Against the philosophers" and the Stoics despised the professional rhetors. Apion, on the other hand, presented himself as a Stoic.

84. The only known ancient parallel—and this only partial—appears in Celsus, the anti-Christian philosopher contemporary with Marcus Aurelius. See Origen *Contra Celsum* 4. 31. 4, where Celsus is quoted as follows: μηδὲν πώποτε ἀξιόλογον πράξαντας, οὔτ' ἐν λόγῳ οὔτ' ἐν ἀριθμῷ αὐτούς ποτε γεγενημένους ("They never did anything worthy of note and never created anything to do with language or number"). Celsus does not go into detail, but mentions arithmetic; this may be because in a previous sentence he had emphasized the origin of the Jews in Egypt, and the Egyptians were believed to have invented arithmetic. The first in the modern age to accuse the Jews of failing to contribute inventions to science and works to the arts was Voltaire, who was deeply impressed by the views of Greco-Roman authors known to him mainly from *Contra Apionem*; see Katz (1980) 40, and 38.

85. Clearchus in Josephus *Contra Apionem* 1. 179; Megasthenes in Clement *Stromateis* 1. 15 (72. 5); cf. Theophrastus in Porphyry *De Abstinentia* 2. 26. 3.

86. This has nothing to do with insults voiced by Roman authors against Jewish beggars in Rome, their behavior, and their halting language (e.g., Cleom. 2. 1; Juv. 6. 524; Artem. *Onirocr.* 3. 53). On the background, see Lewy (1960) 197–203.

certain superstitions, but superstitions in the ancient world were not associated particularly with primitiveness: they were common to all peoples, including
those who contributed significantly to material and spiritual culture. Moses is
portrayed as a wise man even by those Hellenistic authors (apart from Apion, of
course) who condemned the customs and laws he established.[87]

Josephus was clearly embarrassed and had trouble dealing with these unprecedented accusations. The basic problem was that he was unable to point to any
practical Jewish invention recognized by the Greeks as advancing civilization,[88]
or to any significant contribution made by the Jews to Greek literature or thought,
the only contribution his Greco-Roman readers would regard as being of value.
Concerning practical inventions, Josephus failed to find any answer,[89] and chose

87. Hecataeus of Abdera in Diodorus 40. 3. 3; Manetho in Josephus *Contra Apionem* 1. 238,
250; Posidonius in Strabo 16. 2. 34; Diodorus 1. 94. 2; Pompeius Trogus in Justin 36. 2; in effect,
Chaeremon in Josephus *Contra Apionem* 1. 290; pseudo-Longinus *De sublimitate* 9; even Tacitus
Historiae 5. 3. 1–4. 1; Numenius of Apamea in Clement *Stromateis* 1. 22 (150. 4) and the parallels.
Moses is absent from the list of sages in Celsus because he is portrayed as a wizard (Origen *C. Celsum*
1. 16). See also Gager (1972) 25–79; and see esp. Josephus *Contra Apionem* 1. 279, from which it appears
that anti-Jewish Egyptian authors also regarded Moses as "a wonderful figure . . . and even divine."

88. While Josephus does say that Abraham taught the Egyptians arithmetic and astrology (*AJ*
1. 167), it may be inferred from the sentence that follows that Abraham did not invent these crafts
but only transmitted them to the Egyptians from the Chaldaeans. Josephus merely interpreted a
vague piece of information he found in Berossus (para. 158). Josephus was not acquainted with the
account of Artaphanus, according to which Abraham taught Pharaoh astrology (Eus. *PE* 9. 18. 1; cf.
pseudo-Eupolemus, in Eus. *PE* 9. 18. 2); this is apparent from the fact that he attributes to Moses
and Joseph none of the many inventions mentioned by Artaphanus. Similarly, there is no trace in
Josephus of the accounts of pseudo-Eupolemus concerning the inventions attributed to the patriarchs and Moses (see the references in note 92 below), and this suffices to answer in the negative
the much-debated question—whether Josephus was acquainted with the compilation of Alexander
Polyhistor on the Jews, in which these accounts were adduced. The absence of any reference to
Alexander Polyhistor in the pretentious *Contra Apionem* speaks for itself. It should be added that
the description of Abraham as a stargazer in the Book of Jubilees 12. 15 and in rabbinic literature
(Tosefta Qiddushin V. 17 [ed. Zuckermandel, p. 343]; Bavli, Baba Bathra 16B; Bavli, Yomah 27B) is not
necessarily influenced by Hellenistic or Jewish Hellenistic literature, as some have argued; it is much
simpler to assume that the description rests on Genesis 15.5 ("Look now toward heaven, and tell the
stars, if thou be able to number them") and on Abraham's origin in Ur of the Chaldees, a place where
astronomy was extensively practiced (the connection is made in Philo *Abr.* 77).

89. Despite all that has been said in the scholarly literature, there is no real evidence that Josephus
was acquainted with the philosophical works of Philo. If he did know some of them, he would most
probably have rejected the allegorical interpretation, as he did that concerning Homer (*Ap.* 2. 256).
It would seem that allegorical interpretation was not widespread in Judaea at that time, and the few
examples of it in the Judaean desert scrolls are exceptions that prove the rule (on these, see Kister
[1998] 109–11, and 111 n. 36 on the meaning of Philo's remarks concerning allegorical interpretation
by the Essenes [*Quod omnis probus liber* 82]). The reference to Philo in Josephus *Antiquitates Judaicae*
18. 259–60 is quite vague and can only suggest that Josephus did not rate Philo highly in the history of
Greek thought. It is difficult to assess whether and how many of Philo's writings were known at that

to overlook the charge. The case of the *logoi* was only slightly easier. In the absence of real evidence, Josephus tried more than once to respond, but without much success. Recording the charge (*Ap.* 2. 135–36), he notes that his account of certain Jewish figures in the *Jewish Antiquities* provides an answer. Josephus probably had in mind biblical personalities like King Solomon and other wise men and poets. However, this argument remains brief, without quoting examples, in contrast to the usual verbosity of *Contra Apionem*. Being aware that only evidence from the Greek corpus counts in such exchanges (*Ap.* 1.2, 4), Josephus chooses to use general terms, indicating that his *Jewish Antiquities* contains much relevant evidence, as if this is obvious and requires no further elaboration, in preference to mentioning particular biblical figures—unknown to the non-Jewish reader—which would have only detracted from his argument. Josephus, however, aware of the weakness of this response, provides another one: the Jews observe the old laws of the Torah and do not depart from them to the left or to the right; there is no need to emend them, improve them, or add to them; this leaves other peoples with the mistaken impression that the Jews are uncreative; the Jews are in fact potentially creative but do not need to realize this potential, since everything has been handed down to them from previous generations in their Torah (2. 182–84); philosophers with revolutionary ideas concerning religion and morality appear among other peoples, whose faith and customs are unstable and lacking unity (2. 180, 187).[90] Josephus resorted to this convoluted explanation because of the difficulty in presenting the Torah as an invention of human beings. Sensing that this response would still not satisfy an outside audience, Josephus offers toward the end of the treatise yet a third answer, this time referring to the Torah from another angle, that of its reception (2. 295): The Jews were the first to "find" the Torah, and to adhere to its precepts, and this suffices to refute Molon's charges. Josephus thus overrides the difficulty by giving "inventiveness" a new meaning. This is the most he could do in view of the terms of reference of the classical world on the one hand, and the Jewish conviction regarding the divine origin of the Torah on the other.

It is unlikely that Apollonius Molon directed his remarks against the early Hellenistic authors who had described the Jews as a community of philosophers. Those references to the Jews had been few and far between, in short passages within a wider context on other subjects entirely, and not in monographs on the Jews or ethnographic excursuses; it is further doubtful whether all of them were available

---

time in Rome. Philo owes his reputation and fame to the church patriarchs, who wrote after the time of Josephus, and primarily to Clement of Alexandria, who was active in the last quarter of the second century C.E.; Philo was still unknown to Justin the Martyr, who was a contemporary of Josephus in Rome. On the circulation of Philo's writings, see Runia (1993); (1995) 54–55, 228–39.

90. Cf. the criticism of Sextus Empiricus regarding the continual changing of the laws in Athens as opposed to the conservatism of "barbarian" people: *Adversus rhetoricos* 34–35.

to Molon in Rhodes.[91] Molon certainly had no reason to invest effort in searching for scraps of material on the Jews in the many thousands of book-scrolls written at the end of the classical period and the beginning of the Hellenistic period. At any rate, earlier thinkers and authors had not portrayed the philosophers as the inventors of the practical arts. It is also unlikely that Molon was familiar with, and reacted to, the compositions of pseudo-Eupolemus or Artaphanus, who portrayed Moses as an inventor.[92] These are esoteric Hellenistic Jewish authors who were unknown even to Josephus,[93] Clement,[94] or Pliny the Elder, although the latter tried to collect all the available material on inventors and their inventions.[95]

What, then, led Apollonius Molon to accuse the Jews of being primitive? Molon's evidence for the primitiveness of the Jews is their lack of any original contribution to inventions, practical or spiritual. At the heart of this evidence is the assumption that practical inventions, like the *logoi,* are the work of wise men. The link between wise men and practical inventions first appears pointedly only in the writings of Posidonius of Apamea, and it is unique to him. Earlier Stoics had attributed to wise men only the invention of language; after the first stage of language, in which basic words originated naturally—these are the onomato-poeic words—the wise men invented more complex words, such as the names of the world, the elements, the gods, and so on.[96] It was also customary to attribute to wise men the writing of laws.[97] These inventions, however, are all in the area

91. On the disappearance and gradual reappearance of the writings of Theophrastus in the first century B.C.E., see p. 38 and note 78 above.

92. Pseudo-Eupolemus on Moses as inventor of the alphabet: Clement *Stromateis* 1. 23 (153. 4) = Eusebius *Praeparatio evangelica* 9. 26. 1. Artaphanus on Joseph as an inventor (of land division, determination of borders, land fertilization, and measurement) and on Moses as an inventor (of boats, construction cranes, Egyptian weapons, more complex war-engines [apparently artillery], pumping equipment, and even philosophy): Eusebius *Praeparatio evangelica* 9. 27. 4, 12. See also Guttmann 2: 81–82; Wacholder (1974) 77–83; Holladay (1983–96) 1: 137–38 nn. 3, 6, and 232 n. 46.

93. See note 88 above.

94. See the list of inventions and inventors in *Stromateis* 1. 16, and there also for the sources of information Clement had at his disposal, and for the literature that concerned itself with inventions and inventors.

95. For Pliny's list of inventors, see below. Philo, who was preoccupied with the figure of Moses, states explicitly that Moses received practical inventions or crafts (such as arithmetic and geometry, music, philosophy, astrology and the other sciences) from the Egyptians, Greeks, Assyrians, and Chaldaeans (*De vita Mos.* 1. 23–24). Philo, like Josephus after him, regards Moses' sole original con-tribution to be his laws and considers him to be "the best of legislators anywhere" (*De vita Mos.* 2. 12).

96. On this subject, see Barwick (1957) 29–33, 80–87, and sources there. All this is in contrast to the position of the Epicureans; see, e.g., Lucretius *De rerum natura* 5. 1028–90 (esp. 1041–43, 1050–51).

97. For explicit statements on this made by Dicaearchus, a first-generation Peripatetic and pupil of Aristotle, see Diogenes Laertius 1. 40. Dicaearchus, unlike others, attributes only legislation to the sages. Lists of legislators were scattered throughout Greek and Hellenistic literature; see, e.g., Strabo 16. 2. 38–39; Diodorus 1. 94; Seneca *Epistulae* 90. 6; Josephus *Contra Apionem* 2. 154.

of language and thought, not in the area of practical tools and action. We even have indirect expressions of disdain for inventions such as building and sculpture in Zeno, the father of Stoicism. In a famous passage that has survived from his *Politeia*,[98] Zeno says that in the ideal state of wise men, there would be no temples or statues, since the gods are to be honored with what is worthy of them, and not with the products of artisans. Zeno thus hints that sages do not indulge in such activities. A detailed and direct criticism of Posidonius is to be found on this matter in a letter of Seneca to Lucilius (*Ep.* 90), which has often been referred to in the discussion on the Jewish excursus of Strabo-Posidonius (chapter 11). Seneca, himself a Stoic, expresses his own opinion regarding the origin of these inventions and the talents of the various inventors. The passage speaks for itself:

> All these things were invented by the sharp wits (*sagacitas*) of humans, not their wisdom. . . . These two (the hammer and tongs) were invented by someone alert and smart, not great and elevated. . . . All these things may have been invented by reason, but not right reason (the Stoic expression *recta ratio* = ὀρθὸς λόγος). The inventions are of an ordinary man, not a sage. . . . "All of these things," he (Posidonius) says, "were invented by a sage; but matters too small for him to bother with he left to lesser assistants." On the contrary, these things were invented by none other than those who are concerned with these things even today . . . , they are the inventions of the lowest slaves. Wisdom dwells higher up and does not teach the hands [anything]. It is the great teacher of souls. . . . Even if a sage invented [certain tools, devices, etc.], he did not invent them in his capacity as a sage; for he did many things that are done, as we see, as successfully by fools and even with more experience and expertise. (paras. 11, 13, 24, 25, 26, 33)

The fact that this was a common view, not peculiar to the Stoics (apart from Posidonius), is confirmed by the very detailed list of inventors that has come down to us from the ancient world. It is concentrated in the last part of the seventh book of *Naturalis historia* (191–215) by Pliny the Elder, who flourished about a century after Apollonius Molon. Pliny, as was his wont, uses numerous earlier sources. Noteworthy among those explicitly mentioned are Hesiod, Ctesias, Aristotle, Theophrastus (who wrote two books on inventions: Diog. Laert. 5. 47), Hegesias, Brossus, and particularly Gellius, that is, Gnaeus Gellius.[99] Other,

---

98. *SVF* 1: frr. 264–67. The quotation from Zeno appears almost word for word in seven sources and is consequently to be considered accurate.

99. This is Gnaeus Gellius, the author of the *Annales*, who flourished a generation before Molon and Posidonius. His identity can be inferred from a reference in Marius Catorinus, the fourth-century Latin orator and grammarian who became a Christian. Catorinus details the part played by Cadmus in bringing writing from Phoenicia to Greece (cf. Pliny *NH* 7. 192) and mentions as sources Demetrius of Phaleron, Hermocrates, and Roman authors: Cincius, Fabius, and Gellius. These latter are three of the earliest historians of Rome (Cincius and Fabius were active at the end of the third century B.C.E.). The account of Catorinus: Keil (1874) 4: 23.

lesser-known authors and poets are also named, while many other sources are referred to merely as "others" (*alii*) or as national traditions ("the Egyptians say" and the like). It is also worth mentioning that Aulus Gellius (second century C.E.) reports in the introduction to his *Attic Nights* that there are authors who call their books εὑρήματα (Inventions; the Greek appears in his Latin text).[100] The names of some of these authors have come down to us in other sources, some esoteric and some famous, such as Theophrastus and Ephorus. From the beginning of the decline of classical Greece, therefore, and certainly at the time of Apollonius Molon and Posidonius, there was a widespread literature about, or at least a fashion for titles having to do with, inventors and inventions (in addition to references to such matters in works on other subjects),[101] and the condensed summary of this literature in Pliny the Elder is quite instructive for our inquiry.

The inventors mentioned by name in Pliny are nowhere considered sages or philosophers, with the exception of Anacharsis the Scythian, who, according to one source not named by Pliny, invented the potter's wheel, while "others" attributed this invention to a certain Hyperaubius of Corinth (*HN* 7. 198). The remaining inventors are gods, sons of gods, mythological and eponymous heroes, city founders, and military leaders, but a greater number than these are men known only by name, apparently men of technical skills, but not of high social status or intellectual abilities. There are also inventions attributed generally to peoples or cities (many to the Egyptians and the Athenians). The talents required for the inventions mentioned are not features of philosophers and sages, and Seneca pointed out the absurdity of any such claim: "He (Posidonius) was not far from saying that even shoemaking was invented by the sages" (para. 23).

Posidonius was the first, and as far as we can tell, the only author to attribute practical inventions to "sages," his terminology for philosophers. Seneca in the letter to Lucilius argues with Posidonius's account on practical inventions and summarizes it, listing the most basic of occupations: grinding and baking, building, the invention of iron tools (such as hammers and tongs), locating veins of iron and copper, weaving and spinning, and even the most basic of agricultural tasks such as plowing, sowing and weeding. All of these, according to Posidonius, were invented by sages. Seneca does not quote Posidonius but only reacts to the account, and it is most likely that the original list was more detailed.

100. These were works named περὶ εὑρημάτων (or *De inventis*) and dealing with practical inventions, as opposed to rhetorical works called περὶ εὑρέσεως (or *De inventione*) whose purpose was to teach how to devise arguments appropriate to the occasion without relying too much on improvisation (see, e.g., Cicero's *De inventione*). A discussion of rhetorical inventions is also to be found in general rhetorical works such as the first two books of Aristotle's *Ars rhetorica*.

101. On the genre, see Thraede (1962a) 1191–1278; (1962b) 158–86. For a concentration of the scattered information on inventors and inventions in the mainstream Greek classical tradition, see Kleingünther (1933); Tiede (1972) 146–77.

In two cases, Seneca argues with Posidonius over the specific identity of the inventors. We learn from Seneca that Posidonius had mentioned Anacharsis, the sixth-century Scythian prince-sage, as the inventor of the potter's wheel for making ceramic artifacts and even attempted to prove his point by establishing that verses referring to the production of ceramics in Homer were inauthentic.[102] We have already seen that Anacharsis is also mentioned in Pliny's list, where the source is unnamed. Seneca does not dispute the identity of the inventor but argues that Anacharsis arrived at this invention by chance, and not because of his wisdom, and the invention could have been made as easily by anyone else (para. 31). Posidonius further attributes the invention of dome building to the pre-Socratic philosopher Democritus, and here Seneca does dispute the attribution, asserting that the method was known before then (paras. 32–33). From the argument over Anacharsis and Democritus it follows that the "sages" meant by Posidonius are not only figures associated with the mythological Golden Age—which might have been inferred from the appearance of the argument in Seneca's discussion of the Posidonian state of the wise in the Golden Age—but also figures from historical periods.[103]

. . .

Posidonius presents Moses and those who followed him out of Egypt as Egyptian philosopher-sages, and the state they established in Jerusalem and its environs as the realization of the later Posidonian state of the wise. Posidonius dwells only on the religious, social, and political aspects of this state, since these are the aspects that emphasize the ideals he wished to promote. It is only natural that in this framework he did not touch on marginal issues, such as the Jews' inventive skills. After all, the ethnographic excursus could not, and was not meant to, provide a comprehensive account of Jews and Judaism, and its message, in any case, had very little to do with the Jews themselves.

Apollonius Molon reacts to Posidonius's description of the Jewish state of the wise with arguments based on Posidonius's own conceptions, supported by information gleaned from invention literature. Whichever work of Posidonius included his conception of the inventor sages, whether one in praise of philosophy or describing the origins of culture,[104] it could not have been esoteric and had to

---

102. On doubts concerning the attribution of this statement to Posidonius, see Kidd 2: 969; but there is no real reason to doubt the reference to Democritus.

103. Cf. the remarks of Dicaearchus in his work Βίος Ἑλλάδος (The Lifestyle of Greece), dating the practical inventions after the period of peace that had prevailed among men (Porph. Abst. 4. 2); and cf. the opinions of Roman thinkers who transplanted the Golden Age to the period of the first kings of Rome (e.g., Cic. Rep. 2. 21–22; Off. 2. 41–42; Lucr. 5. 1105–44); see Kidd 2: 962–63.

104. On this question, see p. 350 above.

be familiar to Apollonius Molon; in any event, a work extolling the virtues of philosophy, its primacy, and its benefits for the human race would not have escaped the attention of the great rhetor who wrote a work against the philosophers.

Molon's reply was actually as follows: not only were the Jews not a select community of wise men (as Posidonius claims), but quite the contrary: they were, and still are, the most primitive and lowly of men. One has only to observe that unlike most peoples known to us the Jews have contributed nothing to the advancement of humanity, neither in the field of practical inventions, as one would have expected from sages, according to Posidonius's own argument, nor in the field of *logoi*. Beat the enemy at his own game.

It is not impossible that Molon also expanded and supported his argument with references to the invention literature. In any case, he could have concluded from works available to him that no practical invention had been attributed to the Jews.

C. The Refusal to Accept People
with Different Beliefs into Jewish Society

> Apollonius did not consider all these (Greek examples mentioned by Josephus) in his accusation that we do not welcome into our midst those with other convictions about the divinity. (*Ap.* 2. 258)[105]

This accusation provides a clearly different, additional reason for the Jewish aversion to foreigners. It is unknown in the literature prior to Molon. It appears only when conversions to Judaism became an issue in Rome.[106] The common accusations concerning the Jewish attitude toward other peoples were "hatred of foreigners" (*misoxenia*) or "hatred of humans" (*misanthrōpia*), and the alleged commandment "not to show a positive attitude toward humans" (with or without the addition "especially not Greeks") and its variations. "Softer" expressions are "not to have contact with some [foreigner]," "not to dine in the company of foreigners," and *apanthrōpia*, detachment from human society.[107] The very use of such expressions, as well as their accompanying explanations, indicates unconditional enmity toward foreigners and the surrounding world. Some authors of the time explained this characteristic as a reaction to the harsh experiences suffered by the leper Jews doing hard labor in the quarries of Egypt, while others emphasized

---

105. ὧν οὐδὲν λογισάμενος ὁ Μόλων Ἀπολλώνιος ἡμῶν κατηγόρησεν, ὅτι μὴ παραδεχόμεθα τοὺς ἄλλαις προκατειλημμένους δόξαις περὶ θεοῦ . . .

106. See, e.g., Juvenal 14. 102–4.

107. See Hecataeus in Diodorus 40. 3. 4; Manetho in Josephus *Contra Apionem* 1. 239; Lysimachus in Josephus *Contra Apionem* 1. 309; the blood libel, Josephus *Contra Apionem* 2. 122; Pompeius Trogus in Justin 36. 1. 15; Tacitus *Historiae* 5. 5. 1; Philostratus *Against Apollonius of Tyana* 5. 33; and in effect also Celsus in Origen *Contra Celsum* 3. 5.

the ordeal of the Jews during their expulsion from Egypt and their wandering in the desert.[108] What seemed clear was that the Jews were not prepared to welcome foreigners. Ethnic origin and/or a share in the traumatic past alone determined whether one was a member of the Jewish people or not.

Yet in the present testimonium the aversion to foreigners does not stem from a difference in ethnicity or common experience. The Jews refuse to embrace people who are unwilling to adopt their religious views. It might appear at first sight that Apollonius Molon was reacting merely to the expulsions of locals and the compulsory conversions to Judaism performed by the Hasmonaean rulers. Yet Hellenistic authors, both contemporary with Molon and later, mentioned only the imposition of the laws of the Jews, particularly concerning circumcision,[109] without referring to beliefs and convictions. Moreover, the formulation of the testimonium indicates a voluntary willingness on the part of foreigners to be accepted into Jewish society. They are rejected on the grounds of differences of view concerning divine matters. This was not the case with the pagan population in the new Jewish territories.

This is how Josephus, too, understood Apollonius Molon, as may be seen from the passage prior to this testimonium, and from the reply following it. That the testimonium and the preceding passage are linked may be understood from the beginning of the testimonium: "Apollonius did not consider all these in his accusation" (2. 258). In the former passage, Josephus states, among other things, that Plato, while praising Homer as a poet, would still banish him from his state "so that he would not cause the correct opinion about god to disappear by means of stories" (2. 256).[110] In his direct reply following the testimonium, Josephus compares the Jews with the Athenians, who punished and expelled people for holding a different religious belief (2. 263–66).[111] The refusal of the Jews to accept people of different religious beliefs thus appears consistent with the behavior of the most enlightened and best of Greeks.

108. Hecataeus in Diodorus 40. 3. 4; Manetho in Josephus *Contra Apionem* 1. 237–38; Lysimachus in Josephus *Contra Apionem* 1. 309; Timochares (via Posidonius) in Diodorus 34/35. 1. 2; Pompeius Trogus in Justin 36. 1. 15; and in effect also Tacitus *Historiae* 5. 3. 1.

109. See Josephus (who drew on Nicolaus and via Strabo on Timagenes of Alexandria) in *Antiquitates Judaicae* 13. 257–58, 319, 397; 15. 254; Ptolemaeus the historian in Ammonius *De adfinium vocabulorum differentia*, no. 243 (Stern, *GLAJJ* no. 146).

110. Cf. Plato *Respublica* 2. 383a–c, 386–387b, 398a.

111. Josephus is exaggerating. There were in Athens foreigners who were allowed to worship their gods so long as they did it alone or in public in centers where foreigners were concentrated, such as Piraeus (see, e.g., the opening of Plato's *Respublica* concerning the procession there in honor of the Thracian goddess Bendis). In the previous paragraph (251), when he tries to find faults with polytheism, Josephus says that the Athenians passed laws "naturalizing" foreign gods. Josephus, like Molon, conceals facts when convenient and ends up contradicting himself.

The way in which Apollonius Molon presented his charge seems to have been a reaction to Posidonius's description of the formation of Jewish society under the leadership of Moses. It appears from the testimonium that Apollonius Molon claimed—with disapproval—that people who do not accept the principles of the Jewish faith are not accepted into Jewish society. In the Jewish excursus of Posidonius, the society established by Moses is principally non-national. At first, by force of circumstances and the place itself, Moses—an Egyptian himself—was joined by the enlightened Egyptian sages who shared his view of the essence of the divinity. They left Egypt of their own volition and removed themselves from others by settling in the isolated region of Jerusalem, in order to keep to their religion without interruption. Posidonius hints at the religious fanaticism of the Egyptian population, which would have prevented the proper observance of the new cult. In the same vein, he says in another place preserved by Josephus that the separateness (*amixia*) of the Jews stems from their piety (*eusebeia*, AJ 13. 247).[112]

It follows that those who were eager to accept the Jewish religion with all that that entailed would have been allowed to become members of Jewish society. Sure enough, once Moses had established this extra-ordinary, ideal society, neighboring people joined them of their own free will and "easily" (Strabo 16. 2. 36).[113] The reader is given to understand that the neighbors who joined Moses and his community accepted his religious point of view, and that Moses admitted them without imposing difficulties. What Posidonius had presented in a positive light, therefore, Apollonius Molon presented negatively.

D. The Jews as Atheists

Apollonius . . . now scorns us as *atheoi*. (*Ap.* 2. 148)[114]

Before considering the reasons for such an attack, the meaning of the plural adjective ἄθεοι in this context needs to be clarified. The word *atheos* was originally used in Greek literature to describe a man who did not fear the gods, who dared to commit wrong without regard for the possible retribution of the gods, and who, as a consequence of his deeds, was forsaken by the gods. The meaning of the word was extended to denote also a villain, a man without conscience or goodwill, and so on. This use of the word does not touch upon the man's belief or lack of belief in the gods or his dedication in fulfilling the requirements of cult worship. Such a man could even manifest excessive zeal in cult practice.

---

112. On this reference see p. 432 above.

113. . . . ἁπάντων προσχωρησάντων ῥᾳδίως τῶν κύκλῳ διὰ τὴν ὁμιλίαν καὶ τὰ προτεινόμενα (" . . . and from all [the neighbors] round about [people] joined [him] easily because of the association [with him] and [offers? prospects?] held out [to them]").

114. ὁ Ἀπολλώνιος . . . ποτὲ μὲν ὡς ἀθέους μισανθρώπους λοιδορεῖ.

Atheos was, therefore, never a synonym for *asebēs* ("impious," describing one who does not respect the gods and/or does not perform his cult duties). This meaning appears in tragedy and comedy of the fifth and early fourth centuries B.C.E.[115] It might be thought, then, that Apollonius Molon is criticizing the moral behavior of the Jews, especially since they are also called misanthropes in the same sentence.[116]

This usage, however, was the only one for as long as all Greeks continued to believe in the existence of the gods, and there were no real heretics as such. The change began with the appearance of Diagoras of Athens, in the second half of the fifth century B.C.E. Diagoras, a poet who had begun his career by praising gods, stopped believing in their existence and received the epithet *atheos*, which henceforward could be used to describe men of his sort, disbelievers, and not merely villains and their like. At the end of the fifth century, Theodorus of Cyrene also earned the epithet *atheos* for this reason.[117] The most famous example of the new meaning is found in Plato's *Apology*, written in the first years of the fourth century. Socrates, at one point in his trial, attempts to discover what lies behind the official charge against him, and raises the possibility that he is considered "a complete disbeliever" (τὸ παράπαν ἄθεος), and his refutation clearly shows that he means by this someone who does not believe that there are gods at all (26c).

The plural form *atheoi* appears in Plato in this same sense in the twelfth book of *Laws*: those people carried away by the philosophers who interpret the world as some sort of mechanism become disbelievers (*atheoi*, 967a). The appearance of such men and the spread of disbelief in the existence of the gods were what first led to the need to prove the existence of the gods (*Leg.* 886b–888a), proofs that the "Athenian" supplies in the tenth book of *Laws*. The term *atheos* thus gradually changed to mean a man lacking a belief in the existence of gods, and this became its accepted meaning. With a few exceptions,[118] the moral, weaker sense of the term was no longer employed, certainly not in the time of Apollonius Molon, centuries after the first appearance of the new usage.

The unequivocal meaning of the term *atheos* in the time of Molon also removes the possibility that by applying the plural form *atheoi* he is criticizing the Jewish belief in only one god (hence lacking belief in the existence of many gods). Furthermore, there are numerous examples one could add to Plato's use of

115. See, e.g., Aeschylus *Persae* 809; Aristophanes *Plutus* 49, 496; *Thesmophoriazousae*, 672–73, 721.

116. So Radin (1915) 194, who translates "wicked."

117. On the atheism of Diogenes and Theodorus, see the edition of fragments by Winiarczyk (1981), and references in the key, p. 52. On both, and other so-called atheists, see Winiarczyk (1984) 96–98.

118. See, e.g., Lysias 6. 32 (ἀθεωτέρους γίγνεσθαι). Such formulae can last a long time in rhetoric, but not centuries down to the time of Molon.

the plural *atheoi*. A good illustration would be Porphyry's mention of *atheoi*, who are blamed for *atheia* ("disbelief in the existence of the divinity").[119] The *atheoi* are those who do not believe in the existence of the divinity (*to theion*). Were Molon to condemn the Jews for their lack of belief in the existence of a plurality of gods, he would have written, for example, that the Jews do not believe in "our" gods, the gods of the Greeks, but only in one god (just as Socrates was said to believe not in the gods of the city, but in new, daemonic things; *Ap.* 26b5)[120]

So far as we can tell from the sources at our disposal, Apollonius Molon was the first to accuse the Jews of atheism.[121] This charge was later brought against the Jews only rarely; later, it seems, it was used mainly against Christians.[122] The popular religious charges against the Jews were that they did not believe in the gods of the Greco-Roman world, or the Egyptian gods, that they lacked respect or even despised the gods,[123] and that they were therefore guilty of *asebeia*, all according to the inclinations of the accuser.[124] In nearly every case, the Greco-Roman sources say that the Jews believe in a divinity of some sort,[125] even those who accused the Jews of religious wrongdoing.

What caused Apollonius Molon to accuse the Jews of atheism? Josephus has given only an extremely concise summary of Molon's accusation, but from Josephus's response we are able to learn in this case somewhat more about the content of the original charge. The passage of interest to us is where Josephus gives an extensive analysis of the nature of the Jewish divinity:

119. In Eusebius *Praeparatio evangelica* 1. 2. 1, l. 7 (*atheoi*) which parallels l. 15 (*atheia*).

120. A similar formulation, albeit with a different intent, may be found elsewhere in Josephus, with regard to Apollonius Molon. In his introduction to the account of the blood libel (based on Apion), he says that Apollonius Molon "accused us that we do not worship the same gods as others" (*Ap.* 2. 79). As also appears from the context, this refers not to the belief in gods itself but to cult worship. We shall see below that Molon, although well aware of the existence of the Jewish Temple and even mentioning it and the cult practiced in it, was of the opinion that it was all a deception, and that in fact the Jews did not believe in any divinity.

121. Already remarked upon by Sevenster (1975) 96–98, but his interpretation of "atheism" is mistaken, and he confuses it with *asebeia*.

122. Ptolemaeus the geographer in *GLAJJ* no. 336a, para. 31; Aristides, *GLAJJ* no. 371, l. 6; Julian the Apostate, *GLAJJ* no. 481a, l. 11; no. 486a, l. 12; and Dio Cassius 77. 14. 2.

123. Hecataeus in Diodorus 40. 3. 1, 4; Manetho in Josephus *Contra Apionem* 1. 239, 249; Timochares-Posidonius in Diodorus 34/35. 1. 1; Lysimachus in Josephus *Contra Apionem* 1. 301, 309; in effect, also Cicero *Pro Flacco* 28, 69; Apollonius Molon himself, *Contra Apionem* 2. 79; Pliny *Naturalis historia* 13. 46; Tacitus *Historiae* 5. 3. 1; 4. 2, 4; 5. 2; Aristides, *GLAJJ* no. 371, l. 7; Celsus in Origen *Contra Celsum* 3. 5.

124. Hecataeus in Diodorus 40. 3. 1; Manetho in Josephus *Contra Apionem* 1. 248; Lysimachus in Josephus *Contra Apionem* 1. 306; Cicero *Pro Flacco* 28, 69; Apion in Josephus *Contra Apionem* 2. 125; Florus *Epitome* 1. 40. 30. Müller (1877) 210, Gager (1972) 119, Sevenster (1975) 98–99, and Kasher (1996) 272 are mistaken in their interpretation of the terms *asebeia* and *dyssebeia*; atheism is not the issue.

125. Theophrastus in Porphyry *De Abstinentia* 2. 26; Hecataeus in Diodorus 40. 3. 4–6; Hermippus in Josephus *Contra Apionem* 1. 164–65; Mnaseas in Josephus *Contra Apionem* 2. 114; Agatharchides in

Well then, what are the commands and the injunctions? They are both simple and well known. The first and leading [of them] says of the god that the god contains everything together, is perfect and blessed, master of himself and everything, and is the beginning, the middle, and end of all things; while he is known because of his gracious deeds and actions, clearer than all else, we still cannot say anything about his form or size. No material, even the most perfect, is worthy for making a statue of him, nor is any art designed to imitate him an art; we know nothing like him, we have no concept, nor is it permissible to speculate. We see his deeds: light, heaven, earth, sun, the birth of animals, the fruit of the trees. These the god made not with hands, not with effort, not with any cooperation, but when he wished, the things came to be so immediately. (*Ap.* 2. 190–91)

That the passage is an answer to specific arguments of Molon's accusation appears from the effort invested in the explanation, and the somewhat defensive tone. The main point is that the god is indeed indescribable so far as form and size are concerned, but he is recognized by his providential deeds.[126] It may be deduced that Apollonius Molon called the Jews atheists, and he made an assertion to the effect that the Jews claim that their god cannot be visualized or compared to anything existing. This claim would have been incomprehensible to the average Greek (if not to certain philosophers): if the god has no form and is invisible and is unlike anything else, in what way can he be said to have any existence? Someone describing the divinity in such terms is inviting the suspicion that he does not believe in the divinity at all but hides his disbelief behind a smoke screen of words. As we shall see, such charges were also leveled, *mutatis mutandis,* against the Epicureans and the Stoics, whose views on the divinity were unconventional, to say the least.

Josephus *Contra Apionem* 1. 210; Polybius in Josephus *Contra Apionem* 2. 84; Josephus *Antiquitates Judaicae* 12. 136; Alexander Polyhistor in Eusebius *Praeparatio evangelica* 9. 19; Diodorus 1. 94. 2; Cicero *Pro Flacco* 28. 69; Varro in Augustine *De civitate Dei* 4. 31; Timagenes in Josephus *Contra Apionem* 2. 83–84; Pompeius Trogus in Justin 31. 1. 13; Strabo in Josephus *Antiquitates Judaicae* 14. 66–67; pseudo-Longinus *De sublimitate* 9. 9; Apion in Josephus *Contra Apionem* 2. 11, 121; Tacitus *Historiae* 5. 4. 2, 5. 3; nor are these all of the sources; cf. also the reference to Jews in the work on the system of Epicurus by one of his admirers, Diogenes of Oenoanda in Asia Minor, apparently a short time after the Diaspora revolt or the Bar Kokhba revolt. The work is entirely engraved on the walls of a temple that Diogenes set up in honor of Epicurus and that has been gradually excavated since its discovery in 1884. On a shard of facing stone discovered within the last decade, Diogenes calls the Jews, in reaction to the events of the time, πάντων . . . δεισιδαιμονέστατοι ("the most superstitious of all," meaning the most entrenched in their own religion), and πάντων . . . μιαρώτατοι (in this context, "the most brutal of all"—perhaps referring to the revolt of the Jews at the time of the Trojan or the Bar Kokhba revolt); see Smith (1998) 118–22.

126. 2. 191: ἔργοις μὲν καὶ χάρισιν ἐναργὴς καὶ παντὸς οὑτινοσοῦν (S; L: οὕτινος) φανερώτερος, μορφὴν δὲ καὶ μέγεθος ἡμῖν ἄφατος. Cf. 2. 167: καὶ δυνάμει μὲν ἡμῖν γνώριμον, ὁποῖος δὲ κατ' οὐσίαν ἐστὶν ἄγνωστον.

Where did Apollonius Molon find that the Jewish divinity could not be visualized or compared with any existent thing? It was common knowledge that the Jews did not believe that God had a human shape and that they did not worship idols or images.[127] Yet this would hardly have been given the interpretations mentioned and would not have led (indeed, did not lead) other authors to charge the Jews with atheism. Abstention from, and even prohibition of, idol worship and/or anthropomorphism *per se* were not interpreted as atheism. To give just a few illustrations: Xenophanes' sharp attack against anthropomorphism was never described as atheism, nor was the abstention from idol worship attributed rightly or wrongly to the Persians and to the Magi, the Median priests of the Persian kings (e.g., Hdt. 1. 131; Diog. Laert. 1. 6); Plato describes in *Cratylus*—in the guise of etymology—the beginnings of religion as a direct worship of the visible forces of nature, the sun, the moon, and the stars, and not of images. According to this interpretation, the word *theos* (god) derives from *thein* (to run), since the heavenly bodies are in continual motion (397c-d); similarly, Hecataeus of Abdera reports on the origins of Egyptian religion (Diod. 1. 11 ff.): there was first the natural and direct worship of the heavenly bodies, to which were later added as gods the five elements of nature (fire, water, etc.), and humans who had contributed to mankind, including the kings of Egypt. Only much later were temples established, and after that, when copper and gold mines were discovered, were the gods represented by statues (Diod. 1. 15. 3–5).

An interesting parallel may be adduced from the development of Roman religion. It matters not for our purposes whether Apollonius Molon was familiar with its details; what concerns us is that his contemporaries did not identify the absence of idol worship with atheism. Sources from the time of Varro onward— parallel with the final stage of Molon's literary career—describe the original Roman cult as being "pure," without any images whatsoever. Varro, perhaps the most learned, prolific, and extensive Roman author, writing in the first century B.C.E., stated that the Romans worshipped their gods for 170 years without an idol. This statement has survived in Augustine, who quotes it in the context of a comparison Varro made with the Jewish custom (*De Civ. D.* 4. 31).[128] Varro's

---

127. Hecataeus in Diodorus 40. 3. 4; Varro in Augustine *De civitate Dei* 4. 31; Josephus *Contra Apionem* 2. 82; indeed also Polybius, Strabo, Nicolaus, Timagenes, Nestor, and Apollodorus, as reported in Josephus *Contra Apionem* 2. 84; Strabo 16. 2. 35; Livy, preserved in a scholion to Lucan 2. 593 (*GLAJJ* no. 133); Tacitus *Historiae* 5. 5. 4; 9. 1.

128. Varro's remarks, including a comparison of the Jewish god with Jupiter, did not go unnoticed. The second-century C.E. Herennius Philo of Byblos writes that "Varro" in Phoenician means "Jew." See Lydus *De magistratibus* 1. 12 (Stern, *GLAJJ* no. 328). The familiarity of Philo of Byblos with Varro's comments on the Jews is known to us also from another work of Lydus, *De mensibus* 4. 53 (= *GLAJJ* no. 324). There is no reason to suppose that this was the only reaction in the ancient world to Varro's remarks.

statement, which may well have been based on pontifical traditions, is supplemented by similar remarks made by Plutarch in his biography of Numa (*Num.* 8): Plutarch repeats the number 170 years and says that these are the first years of the existence of Rome. He adds that the Romans built temples, but that they were empty of idols. Numa even forbade the worshipping of idols of men or animals. Plutarch's account clearly conflates several stages of evolution, but the basic information concerning the absence of idols is indirectly confirmed by additional literary sources. In Ovid's *Fasti*, for example, Numa sets out to establish the cult in forests, fields, and springs without a temple and without idols (3. 285 ff.; 4. 649 ff). It is also worth noting that Tacitus says that Vespasian on his campaign in Judaea sacrificed to the god Carmel on Mt. Carmel, a god without form or temple (*Hist.* 2. 78. 3). No less instructive is the account by Tacitus in his German ethnography, according to which the Germans do not anthropomorphize their gods or build temples for them but worship them in the forests (*Germ.* 9; cf. on the Nahanrvali, 43. 3). This picture does not conform with what we know of the German religion from archaeological remains and from other literary sources,[129] and it seems to contradict Tacitus himself in an earlier passage (*Germ.* 7). Tacitus made a hasty generalization according to the custom of certain tribes or specific ceremonies held in forests.[130] It has already been demonstrated that Tacitus sorted and selected his material, and to a large extent shaped it, for practical purposes of the moment, according to philosophical conceptions or according to his understanding of the custom of the early Romans.[131] Relying on an examination of the features of the world of Roman gods and cults, Georg Wissowa, the celebrated authority on Roman religion, stated that the early Roman religion was a cult without idols in open sacred places; the second stage saw the establishment of sacred buildings; and at the same time or only later, under Etruscan and Greek influence, the representation of gods in the form of idols.[132]

Where, then, did Apollonius Molon find the idea that the Jewish divinity could not be visualized or compared to any existent thing? I would suggest that his source of information was Posidonius's Jewish excursus. Strabo reported Posidonius's account of the Jewish religion with a certain amount of reworking:

> For this one thing only is a god: that which surrounds all of us and earth and sea, that which we call both heaven and cosmos and the nature of all things that are. Now [he asked] who, having sense, would dare to make an image of this, similar to one of the things around us? (16. 2. 35)

129. See on this subject Perl (1990) 160–61.
130. On the possibility of a generalization by Tacitus, see Grönbech (1977) 2: 139.
131. See on this subject esp. Wolff (1934) 121–66, and there, 134–36 on religion in German tribes.
132. See Wissowa (1912) 32 ff. On archaeological evidence for the transition, see Latte (1960) 149 ff.

Whatever the original Posidonian formulation of the definition of the Jewish divinity in the first sentence may have been,[133] the rhetorical question of the second sentence shows that the Jews not only do not worship an idol and a mask—already illustrated in detail by Strabo-Posidonius in the sentence prior to this extract—but also claims that it is impossible to compare their god with any existent thing. This also means that it cannot be described with respect to form or size.

How does Molon's charge of Jewish atheism fit in with the information he had on the existence of a Jewish temple and of sacrifices to the Jewish god? The Jewish temple and the sacrifices performed in it occupy an important part in most descriptions of the Jews in Greek and Hellenistic literature.[134] The special function of the Jewish temple in the Mosaic state is also given prominence in the Jewish excursus of Posidonius (Strabo 16. 2. 36), and both the latter and Apollonius Molon himself recorded Antiochus IV's intrusion into the Jerusalem Temple (*Ap.* 2. 79). The position held by Apollonius Molon may be compared to some extent with the common attitude adopted with regard to the Epicureans. Although Epicurean epistemology could prove the existence of the gods, and despite Epicurean insistence that the gods should be respected and worshipped (including prayers and sacrifices), many argued that the Epicureans' denial of divine providence proved that they did not believe in the gods and that they merely put up a pretense in order not to offend public opinion—so, for example, the Skeptic Cotta, in Cicero's *De natura deorum,* who in his capacity as the *pontifex maximus* conforms strictly to the ancient Roman religion. Cotta states that Epicurus is toying with his readers when he says that he believes in the gods:

> No gods seem to Epicurus to exist, and what he said about the immortal gods he said to avert ill will. For he could not have been so witless as to make up a god similar to a manikin, and only in outline at that, not in solid condition, furnished with all the limbs of a man but totally lacking the use of the limbs, *something insub-*

133. See Ludlam's provisional reconstruction, p. 538 below: "For this one thing only is god: that which surrounds all of us and earth and sea, [(namely), heaven, the commanding principle, intelligent and firelike pneuma, the cosmos]. And what sane man . . . ". Pneuma, an element both firelike and airlike, pervades the whole of the cosmos, is the uniting force of the cosmos, governs the cosmos, and in one aspect may be identified with the cosmos. Although it pervades the whole of the cosmos, its seat is in that part of the cosmos where it is most firelike and airlike, the outer sphere, which is here called heaven (οὐρανός). God, identified in various aspects with all those, is consequently indescribable in terms of form or size and is similar to nothing known to man.

134. See, e.g., Theophrastus in Porphyry *De Abstinentia* 2. 26; Hecataeus in Diodorus 40. 3. 4; Mnaseas in Josephus *Contra Apionem* 2. 112–14; Polybius and others in Josephus *Contra Apionem* 2. 84; Timochares-Posidonius in Diodorus 34/35. 1. 1–5; Posidonius in Strabo 16. 2. 36–37; Apion in Josephus *Contra Apionem* passim; Antonius Iulianus in Minucius Felix *Octavius* 33. 2; Plutarch *Moralia* 184E-F; Tacitus *Historiae* 5. 3. 2; 4. 2; 5. 1, 4.

stantial and transparent, conferring nothing to anybody and granting nothing, caring nothing at all and doing nothing. In the first place, a being of this nature cannot exist, and, seeing this, Epicurus in fact does away with the gods, in speech retains them. (1. 123; cf. 3. 3) [135]

Even closer to Molon's position is Cotta's criticism of the Stoics, although coming from the opposite direction. The Stoics, believing in a governing power in nature, mock the unenlightened many who believe that gods are anthropomorphic. At the same time, they consider the cult of the gods to be obligatory, and, with the aid of etymological interpretation, regard the gods as symbols of natural forces, human attributes, and so on.[136] Cotta reacts to this as follows:

Zeno first of all, then Cleanthes and later Chrysippus, took the great and hardly necessary trouble of explaining the rationale of imaginary stories and explicating the reasons why each of the names is so called. When you [Stoics] do this, you are actually admitting that the state of affairs is different by far from the opinion of men; for those who are called gods are the essences of things, not the figures of gods. . . . Therefore let all of such a great error be driven from philosophy, [namely,] saying things unworthy of the immortal gods when we are discussing the immortal gods. (3. 63)

Similar criticisms of the Stoics were voiced by many,[137] and it is interesting that Cicero wrote Cotta's speech in the years 78–75 B.C.E.,[138] a short time after his return from Greece, where he also had visited Apollonius Molon in Rhodes.

135. Before this quotation "Cotta" names his source: "That is therefore truer, no doubt, which the friend of all of us, Posidonius, said in the fifth book of his work on the nature of the gods, that it seems to Epicurus . . . ". Cicero-Cotta summarizes properly the essence of Posidonius's account, while not necessarily translating it accurately. This is Cicero's normal practice when dealing with Greek philosophical arguments. Posidonius's criticism itself appears in this passage out of its original context, and therefore does not contain all the original arguments. Yet it is clear that it was not originally directed only against the notion of helpless anthropomorphic gods, but against the very anthropomorphizing of the gods. The formulation is intended to portray the Epicurean gods in a ridiculous light, such that even the Epicureans could not believe in them.

136. For Zeno's firm stand against statues and images, see *SVF* 1: fr. 264. On the Stoic god, see below, pp. 526–31; cf. Balbus's speech in Cicero *De natura deorum* and his presentation of the Stoic position regarding cult worship and etymological interpretation (paras. 45, 59, 70–71, 79); and cf. Seneca in Augustine *De civitate Dei* 6. 10.

137. See, e.g., Augustine *De civitate Dei* 4. 27. 3–4; Augustine cites Mucius Scaevola—who was himself a *pontifex maximus,* but also a Stoic—on the religion of philosophers. Scaevola says that this is a doctrine that cannot be divulged to the many for fear of the harm it might do to the life of the city (cf. Joseph. *Ap.* 2. 169–70). Among the statements that he attributes to philosophers is at least one from a Stoic source: "Real gods have neither sex nor age nor distinct body parts." On Augustine's sources for this passage, see Glucker (1993) 82–83. Cf. also Cotta's remarks on Democritus in Cicero *De natura deorum* 1. 120–21.

138. See Pease (1955) 25.

It is in this spirit that we should regard Molon's attitude toward the existence of the Jewish temple and the sacrifices performed in it. The Jewish god, lacking form and size and comparable to nothing in existence, is no god at all. The Jews declare their belief in a god only to protect themselves from the serious charge of atheism. To this end, they invented an ineffable god. In order to fool mankind into thinking that their belief is real, they established a temple for this fictitious god and perform sacrifices inside it.[139] In this criticism, Molon actually expressed his opinion on the religious conception of Posidonius of Apamea as well.

It might be speculated that Apollonius Molon could have found an abstract conception of the Jewish divine entity in a Hellenistic Jewish source with philosophical tendencies, or in some Greek source. Yet the fact that it was found in a work by Posidonius, his contemporary and neighbor, suggests that Molon reacted in this case rather to Posidonius's version, and that it was because of what he found in Posidonius that he called the Jews atheists.

MOLON'S ANTI-JEWISH WORK: ITS CONTENTS, STRUCTURE, AND MOTIVATION

In the previous section I adduced four major anti-Jewish accusations peculiar to Apollonius Molon that could be explained as being Molon's response to the portrait of the Mosaic state in the Jewish excursus by Posidonius. There would have been additional reactions in Molon's ethnographic treatise to the Posidonian excursus, and the desire to react to it may have led Molon not only to invent claims, but also to select certain details from the literature available, in preference to other versions. Thus, for example, he chose to open the *origo,* the story of the origin of the Jews, with the patriarchs, Abraham, Isaac, and Israel, according to the account he found—directly or indirectly—in a Jewish Hellenistic source, and not with the story of the Jews' origin or stay in Egypt and their expulsion from that country, which was the story all previous Hellenistic authors used to begin their account of the Jews. In this way, Molon could prove that the Jews were not "Egyptians" or "Egyptian sages," as Posidonius presented them, but a separate entity having nothing to do with the Egyptians and their celebrated wisdom. For the same reason, Molon followed Lysimachus in his presentation of Moses as "a wizard and a deceiver" who influences the rabble, in stark contrast to other earlier Hellenistic and Egyptian presentations of him as an Egyptian priest and even a sage.[140] This was also (but not only) in reaction to Posidonius, according to whom Moses prevailed upon his community of sages with the aid of reason, the

---

139. Molon's version of the ass libel does not imply that the Jews regard the ass as a divinity; see above, pp. 221–22, 240–41.

140. See note 87 above.

complete opposite of wizardry and deceit. I have already noted the differences in Molon's and Posidonius's reporting of the libels, for which they presumably had a common source: Molon reported and Posidonius omitted the blood libel; Molon reported the story of the statue of Moses riding on an ass as nothing but the truth, while Posidonius rejected it. Last but not least: the choice of the ethnographic genre by Molon, the professional rhetor, if it was not merely an imitation, could well have been motivated by an ambition—which not infrequently drives rival authors—to replace Posidonius's Jewish ethnography as the authoritative and ultimate account on the subject. A simple refutation, like a book review in our time, would not have accomplished this goal.

This is not to say that the work of Apollonius Molon was written as a systematic and consistent reaction to the Jewish excursus of Posidonius, in which every argument and every detail responded to one of his rival's assertions. For that purpose Molon would have written a speech or a refutation, in which he would have mentioned Posidonius explicitly as his target. It seems that Molon's work did not mention Posidonius even once.[141] The ethnography would have been written according to the rules and tradition of the genre and would have had its own independent dynamic, the anti-Jewish accusations being scattered throughout the treatise (as stated by Josephus), thus bestowing upon the work a veneer of credibility. It could have included not a little information bearing no relation to the excursus of Posidonius. At the same time, at least some of the anti-Jewish accusations were fashioned as clear ripostes to statements made by Posidonius, and the selection of at least some of the material was influenced by the same desire to reply to the excursus of Posidonius. Beyond this, nothing can really be established concerning the extent of Molon's reaction to the Posidonian excursus.

It is indeed to be expected of a polemical orator such as Apollonius Molon that even in an ethnography he would include (disguised) polemical responses. This practice was not unusual in Hellenistic ethnographic literature. Posidonius, for example, reacted to the assertions made by Hecataeus of Abdera in his Jewish excursus.[142] Hecataeus himself reacted (sometimes explicitly) in his Egyptian ethnography to the Egyptian *logos* of Herodotus. Manetho may have reacted both to Hecataeus and to Herodotus in his account of Egypt,[143] and the curious version by Artaphanus of the activity of Joseph and Moses in Egypt was aimed to a large extent against Manetho and his like. The customs and history of the Jewish people, like those of other peoples, were subject to an overt and covert ethnographic discourse throughout the Hellenistic-Roman period. Other authors of

141. As Josephus was directly acquainted with Molon's ethnography, had there been an explicit reference there to Posidonius's enthusiastic report on the Jews, Josephus would not have ignored it.

142. On this, see above p. 356 and references there, note 1.

143. On Manetho and Herodotus, see Josephus *Contra Apionem* 1. 73; and Mendels (1990) 93–95. Cf. on "counter biographies," p. 183 above.

the time, excepting compilers such as Diodorus, were not content with copying or summarizing their predecessors but chose to add something substantial of their own, or react and argue with them or even mold the old material anew. The Jewish excursus of Tacitus is just one example. This discourse becomes explicit and dominant a little later in the descriptions of the Jewish people written in the context of the bitter exchanges between Christians and pagans.

Were the fierce anti-Jewish accusations of Apollonius Molon influenced also by personal animosity and motives? Did he know Jews in Caria, where he was born, or in Rhodes, and did such an acquaintance have any formative influence on his position?[144] Did someone commission from him the anti-Jewish work? We can say only that the conclusion that Apollonius Molon chose the "scientific," seemingly unbiased ethnographic genre rather than an invective, polemical speech may at the very least suggest that his work was not commissioned by an anti-Jewish lobby, nor was it an immediate response to a specific dramatic event or the deterioration in the relationship between the Jews and the Hellenistic world. The treatise would not have been written after the conquest of Judaea and Jerusalem in 63 B.C.E. (if Apollonius Molon was still alive and active at that date, which is rather doubtful): Molon would hardly have blamed the Jews for being cowards or have described the presence of a sculpture of Moses riding an ass in the Jewish Temple, which could have easily been refuted by the eyewitness testimony of Pompey and his followers (cf. Joseph. *Ap.* 2. 82).

144. So Schürer (1901–9) 3: 534; Goodman in Schürer et al. 3: 1, 599. Stern (*GLAJJ* 1: 149) raised the possibility that Molon's information was based on an acquaintance with Jews of Caria.

Conclusion

The detailed analysis of Greek authors and their accounts of the Jews obliges us to reject the accepted notion of a consistently linear development in the attitude of Greek authors toward Judaism. That reconstruction assumes a logical, coherent line from admiration at the time of first contacts between Greeks and Jews through a cooling-off period as Greeks learned more about the Jews to extreme hostility with the rupture between Jews and the Greek world following the religious persecutions by Antiochus Epiphanes. The split is said to have exacerbated by the aggressive policy of the Hasmonaean rulers against the centers of Hellenistic culture. Proposed variations on that reconstruction are also rather questionable.

The actual state of affairs was far more complex and tangled. Many variables, such as the origin of each author, his places of residence, his sources of information, his personal contacts with Jews, his views concerning religion, society, and state, his professional discipline, his philosophical affiliation, the various aims that motivated and guided his writing in general, and the literary features, including the genre, of the specific work in which the Jews were mentioned by him, all these have a bearing on what he wrote about the Jews, indeed often more of a bearing than the contemporary state of relations between Greeks and Jews. A diagram outlining the attitude of Greek intellectuals toward the Jews and Judaism during the period encompassed by the present book would present not so much a straight diagonal line from admiration to hostility but an erratic series of peaks and valleys. For example, negative accounts of some of the customs of the Jews (and of their ancestors) appeared already at the beginning of the Hellenistic period (Theophrastus and Hecataeus of Abdera), while an enthusiastic description of Mosaic Judaism, or positive comments on the Hasmonaean leaders, were expressed more than two centuries later (by Posidonius of Apamea and Timagenes of Alexandria, respectively).

Elaborating a bit on the pre-Hasmonaean period, it should be stressed that the opinion of Josephus and the many scholars who have followed him (with their own variations) that Greek authors active before the reign of Antiochus IV admired the Jews and portrayed them as role models cannot be accepted at face value. This evaluation is too sanguine even in the case of Greek authors of the period of the first generation of the Diadochs. That three of these authors (Theophrastus, Clearchus, and Megasthenes) presented or described the Jews as "philosophers" is no indication that all of them were enthusiastic about the practices of the Jews, if for no other reason than that Greek philosophers generally did not automatically appreciate the morality of rival philosophers. And indeed, one author of the Diadochic period (Theophrastus) attributed to the Jews customs that were considered by respectable, normative Greeks to be abhorrent: manifestations of extreme cruelty to men and animals; and another one (Hecataeus) at least some tendency to seclusion from human society, as well as some hatred of strangers (if not much worse than that), leading to eccentric practices in many fields of human activity. Nor did Greek authors of the period (such as Clearchus) attribute to the Jews wisdom greater than that of the Greeks, as usually thought, or claim that the Jews attained their physical-theological conceptions prior to the Greeks (Megasthenes), and there is no evidence to support the hypothesis that the myth about the Greek "theft" of Jewish wisdom originated with these Greeks (Clearchus, Megasthenes, and Hermippus, who lived a century later). The myth was in fact invented by Hellenistic Jews in the mid-second century B.C.E. As for the few elements of Jewish behavior adduced by two of these authors (Clearchus, Hecataeus) as worthy of emulation, in one case (Hecataeus) they are not central features of the Jewish character and way of life, nor are they described as such (and are attributed by the same author also to the Egyptians), while in the other case (Clearchus) they were in fact Indian features, alien to the Jews. In the latter case, they had been mistakenly attributed to the Jews primarily because of the linguistic similarity between *Ioudaioi* and *Indoi,* without actually knowing anything about the Jews (save for their location in Syria), and were mentioned at the outset not in order to praise the Jews, but to serve the author's polemic debate with a rival philosophical group (the Cynics), and at the same time to advocate a restrained lifestyle. The imaginary, actually unknown Jews were used just as a veiled instrument to bring home Clearchus's messages. This could likewise be done with other peoples. At the end of the third century B.C.E., one Greek author (Hermippus), usually regarded as praising the Jews with his claim that some of their prohibitions were emulated by Pythagoras, was in fact ridiculing the Greek philosopher as a charlatan who drew some of his senseless prohibitions from barbarians.

At the same time, Josephus and a good number of modern scholars were right in arguing that the extreme negative expressions by Greek authors against the Jews, consciously intended to single them out for abuse and censure, first appeared only in the aftermath of the persecutions of Antiochus Epiphanes. This statement requires some clarification and modification. The hostile expressions were voiced by Greeks just in the Seleucid realm (the Seleucid court scribe[s] and Timochares), and as a reaction to the events in Judaea. The extreme negative trend percolated in one or two generations into Alexandrian Greek literature (Lysimachus of Alexandria), around the end of the second century B.C.E., where old Egyptian anti-Jewish material was recycled and utilized in reaction both to growing Jewish influence in the Ptolemaic court and to the conquests of the Hasmonaeans. Circulation increased in the northern parts of the Mediterranean basin (Apollonius Molon and one of the Greek sources of Pompeius Trogus), apparently in response to the foreign policy of the Hasmonaean state. In addition, the persecutions by Antiochus Epiphanes did not receive unanimous support and justification from Greek intellectuals. Far from it. Of course there were the Seleucid court scribes serving their masters, and some who followed them for one reason or another, but still others (including the great Polybius) placed the blame on Antiochus and his greed and would not justify the harsh steps he had taken against the Jews (these authors are listed in *Ap.* 2. 83–84). Moreover, there was at least one prominent and highly influential Greek philosopher and scholar born in the Seleucid power center (Posidonius of Apamea) who presented all the libels and accusations used to justify the deeds of Antiochus (omitting the blood libel) only to reject them out of hand.

Even the aggressive policy of the Hasmonaean state toward the Hellenistic population did not lead to one type of reaction by Greek authors. While some (Lysimachus, Apollonius Molon, and the Greek sources of Pompeius Trogus) explained the deeds of the Hasmonaeans as manifestations of negative features developed by the Jews after their expulsion from Egypt, and accordingly described the Jews' stay in Egypt and the Exodus in a hostile manner (in line with the Egyptian traditions at their disposal), Posidonius of Apamea heaped praise upon Mosaic Judaism, distinguishing it from the degenerate "superstitious" Jewish rulers of his time. Posidonius of Apamea, the leading figure in the culture and literature of his time, wrote an enthusiastic account of the origin of the Jewish people and the noble characteristics of Moses and those who followed him to Judaea, a description that is the most favorable to have come down to us from the ancient pagan world. There were even Greek authors (Timagenes and Strabo, who drew on him) who, far from condemning the policies and violent deeds of the Hasmonaeans, described their conversion of foreigners as a step that the neighboring peoples, annexed to the Hasmonaean state, underwent voluntarily. The hostile direction was to become prominent in literature only in the Roman period and for reasons connected with tensions and dramatic developments in the relations between Jews and the Gentiles in Judaea, Alexandria, and Asia Minor, as well as in the wake of religious and social trends in Rome itself.

The anti-Jewish material by itself was basically Egyptian, not Greek. The libels and accusations utilized by Greek authors against the Jews were invented by autochthonous Egyptians, as has been claimed by Josephus and modern scholars. These anti-Jewish stories appeared as a reaction to the special circumstance of the Jewish diaspora in Egypt in the Persian period. However, from here on, one has to depart from the accepted historical reconstruction. Though the anti-Jewish accusations were transmitted to Greeks via native-Egyptian Hellenistic authors, they were not adopted and spread by Greeks before some Seleucid court scribe(s) applied them as a response to the turbulent events occurring in Judaea under the rule of Antiochus IV. At first these Egyptian traditions were utilized for defending the unprecedented religious persecutions by Antiochus Epiphanes, and later for condemning the aggression of the Hasmonaean rulers. As for Greek authors living in Egypt, only the growing tension between Jews and Greeks in Egypt in the reign of Cleopatra III (116–101), after the despotic reign of Ptolemy VIII Physcon, and particularly the increase in Greek apprehension due to Jewish dominance in the Egyptian military high command, motivated Alexandrian Greek authors (beginning with Lysimachus) to adopt the old Egyptian traditions and elaborate on them. These fears were exacerbated by the expansion of the Hasmonaean state and its close ties with the Jews in Egypt. The reconstruction suggested above is at least what can be deduced from the available sources. And to avoid mistakes: Mnaseas of Patara and Agatharchides of Cnidus, who flourished in Alexandria in the first half of the second century, were not anti-Semites, as some scholars tend to think.

Thus it appears from the perspective of Greek literature of the Hellenistic period that events in the Holy Land share responsibility with developments in the Jewish diaspora for the the emergence and spread of anti-Jewish feelings. This conclusion obviously invites modern parallels, which in turn have influenced trends in contemporary research. Recent attempts to claim that pagan anti-Semitism grew and spread in Greek society only because of the presence of Jews in the Diaspora and that Greek authors never condemned the Hasmonaean expansion, or the other extreme, that only the policies and actions of the Jewish state bear the blame, do not hold water. The Egyptian origin of the major accusations and libels, and the later anti-Jewish Alexandrian literature, culminating in Apion, do not leave room for doubt as to the part of the Diaspora. With regard to the role of Jews in Judaea, almost all Greek authors known to us (save Timagenes) sharply criticized the Hasmonaean conquests and harsh treatment of the Gentile population. Besides, the background and dating of the first hostile Greek accounts indicate that events in the Jewish homeland had a decisive effect on the adoption of Egyptian traditional anti-Semitism by Greek authors, and a not insignificant influence on its growth down the years.

. . .

Aside from the question of the basic attitude of the Greek authors toward the Jews, what did these Greeks really know about the Jews, and how were Jewish life and history seen through Greek literary eyes of the Hellenistic age? The many variables that affected the general character and tone of references to the Jews (personal background, aims, genre, and context) also shaped the selection and content of the information. It is, therefore, quite difficult to produce a uniform and systematic picture of Jews and Judaism in light of the writings of the authors discussed in this book. The difficulty is aggravated by the fact that some authors certainly were well aware that they attributed to the Jews fictitious customs and characteristics (and not only vicious ones).

If we try to define the components of Jewish identity—a subject that nowadays preoccupies Jewish intellectuals—no feature common to all Greek authors can be found, even in authors who explicitly declare that they intend to introduce the Jewish people to the reader. Probably the best-known feature of the Jewish lifestyle in late antiquity, the Jewish seclusion, though mentioned by five authors (Hecataeus, the Seleucid court scribe[s], Lysimachus, Posidonius, and Apollonius Molon), is absent in an equal number of sources (Theophrastus, Megasthenes, Hermippus, Mnaseas, and Agatharcides), while one (Clearchus) describes a Jew whose conduct is the exact opposite of self-isolation. The strict avoidance of material representation of the divinity, another prominent feature of Jewish identity, is mentioned by only three authors (Hecataeus, Posidonius, and Apollonius Molon). Yet it is hardly credible that these two features escaped the notice of some authors who referred to the Jews. This certainly applies to those who invented or adapted the ass libel (the sources of Mnaseas, the Seleucid court scribe[s], and Apollonius Molon), and all the more so to post-Hecataean writers (end of the fourth century B.C.E.).

The Jewish excursus of Hecataeus of Abdera marks a turning point in the quality and quantity of knowledge on the Jews at the disposal of Greek authors. Based on interviews with Egyptian Jews, it provided plenty of useful material, despite the evident intensive Greek coloring and mistakes. It not only served as a basic source of information for later Greeks but also shaped their conceptions of early Jewish history. Hecataeus formed the Jewish *origo* in line with the traditional scheme of Greek foundation legends, crediting the legendary founder (in this case, Moses) with all later customs, institutions, laws, and the religion of the "colony." Adhering to his method to provide causal reasoning for every custom and institution based on events from the time of the "foundation," Hecataeus explains the Jews' exclusivity as a reaction to their experiences at the time of the expulsion from Egypt. This explanation was adopted by both anti-Jewish authors (the Seleucid scribe[s], Lysimachus, and Apollonius Molon; cf. Tacitus) and the most favorable author (Posidonius) alike, who introduced adaptations and alterations of the original Hecataean explanation. As a result of their dependence on Hecataeus's account, later authors (except for Apollonius Molon) do not refer to the period of the patriarchs or the kings of the First Temple, who were forgotten or ignored by Hecataeus in accordance with his preconceived scheme.

However, the main absentees in Hecataeus's version are three major features of Jewish life: the Sabbath, kosher food, and circumcision. Thus Hecataeus refrains from using Jewish dietary laws as an explanation for Jewish seclusion, a line of reasoning that must have occurred to such an intelligent man and was later popular in Jewish Hellenistic literature. The omission is not accidental: Hecataeus had important reasons connected with the main purpose and context of his Jewish excursus to pass over in silence the practices of circumcision and abstention from certain foods. The Sabbath, however, was missing for what one may call technical reasons.

The absence of these three predominant Jewish practices in the Hecataean excursus is mainly (but not only) to blame for their absence from most later references to the Jews. Each is mentioned just once in subsequent Greek literature of the Hellenistic period. However, they must have been well known in intellectual circles. Efforts to force the Jews to violate these practices were central to the religious persecutions of Antiochus Epiphanes. The three practices were discussed at length in the writings of Hellenistic Jews (not all of which were written for insiders) as basic features of Jewish identity, and an important Jewish court personality (Aristoboulus; apparently not the only one) attempted to trace the Sabbath in the writings of canonical Greek poets and philosophers. The food restrictions and observations of the Sabbath actually formed the bottom line of privileges granted to Jewish communities and soldiers in royal service. By 301 B.C.E. at least, the Sabbath was targeted by Hellenistic rulers as an Achilles heel of Jewish troops in Judaea and Jewish mercenaries/military settlers in the Diaspora. Despite Jewish seclusion, the three customs could not have been overlooked in the public discourse and practice of mixed cities and villages, nor inside the "Ivory Tower" of Alexandrian scholars.

Hecataeus's list of Jewish *nomina* is supplemented by only a few other sources on Jewish practices. Agatharchides elaborates on the Sabbath prohibitions and customs (with forgivable exaggerations and accusations) in the context of a story designed to deliver a universal practical message about disasters caused by relying on superstitions. Posidonius, who probably knows much more about real Judaism than what can be extracted from his account, cites circumcision and abstinence from certain meats as examples of the deterioration of the Jewish lifestyle into superstitious customs after the age of Mosaic Judaism. Despite his own knowledge and acquaintance with Agatharchides' works, Posidonius does not mention the Sabbath among the superstitions of late Judaism, nor is it included in his favorable account of Mosaic Judaism, possibly because he was ambivalent about the overall advantage of the Sabbath: it had positive social aspects, on the one hand, but, on the other, its effects on Greek-Jewish relations in mixed cities and in the Hellenistic armies were negative. Posidonius's reference to the introduction of excision of females by the Jewish priests in the age of deterioration is just another example of his tendency to exaggerate—wildly, from the Jewish point of view—in the service of his didactic goals. Other less important practices are mentioned here and there in accordance with the author's purpose and context: avoidance of *blasphēmia* (Hermippus) and the modest character of Jewish cult and the Jerusalem (pre-Herodian) Temple (Posidonius). In addition, we find interesting variations of the Hecataean interpretation of Jewish theology and cosmology (Posidonius and probably also Apollonius Molon) and departures from the Hecataean tradition on Jewish descent (the Seleucid court scribe[s], Lysimachus, Posidonius, and Apollonius Molon). Ancient authors were often tempted to take the liberty of inventing or reintroducing imaginary *origo* legends (in the case of the Jews, not just hostile stories). If there is any unexpected, useful information in this literature it is that provided on the marginal custom of the parade to the Jerusalem Temple headed by golden-horned bulls on one of the Jewish holidays (Posidonius), a ceremony that recalls the account in Mishnah, tractate Bikkurim.

At the same time, features that have nothing to do with Jews and Judaism are attributed or imputed to them, including cruel sacrifice practices and possibly even human sacrifice (Theophrastus), on one hand, and, on the other, such flattering traits and practices as Indian-style *karteria* and *sōphrosynē* (Clearchus), the lifestyle and daily schedule of philosopher-astrologists (Theophrastus), and the incubation of prophetic dreams in the Jerusalem Temple and an extreme pacifistic policy in the age of Mosaic Judaism (Posidonius). And there is no need to list the diverse anti-Jewish accusations and libels (the Seleucid court scribe[s], Lysimachus, and Apollonius Molon), their obvious aim being to point out Jewish *misanthrōpia* and *misoxenia*.

In view of the characteristics and shortcomings of the writings at our disposal, it is no wonder that little reliable information about Jewish daily life has survived. Thus we do not get any idea about the physique and color of the Jews, in contrast to accounts of "barbarian" people in Greek and Roman literature. The Hebrew language is only hinted at in one cursory reference to the name Jerusalem (Clearchus), while in a sarcastic note by another author (Lysimachus) it appears as if Jews at the time of the Exodus from Egypt were speaking Greek.

One can assume that in addition to including the accusations surviving in the *testimonia*, the lost Jewish ethnography of Apollonius Molon elaborated on a good number of Jewish characteristics and practices, and that Josephus reacted to their presentation in one way or another (without mentioning Molon) in the second book of *Contra Apionem*. Regrettably, it would be speculative to try to extract these observations from the Josephan text. It is fairly certain that the six-book Jewish monograph by Teucer of Cyzicus (first century B.C.E.) contained even more information on a variety of issues, but, unfortunately, it was totally lost, most probably not long after publication.

· · ·

The introduction to this book called for a detached approach free of emotional involvement, and for comprehensive individual examinations of each Greek author, embracing all relevant details. These analyses have shown repeatedly that a number of expressions and references that at first sight appear positive, even enthusiastic, or have been so interpreted by scholars are either negative or, in the best case, impartial. Other references and stories that have been described as hostile are not hostile at all or appear in a source that itself had no malicious intent. Some references—be they apparently vitriolic or, to the contrary, full of admiration—turn out after examination to be far less dramatic, often written by authors with no real interest in the Jews, their purpose being to act as a vehicle for the conveyance of messages that have nothing to do with the Jews. Quite a few instances of notorious expressions are actually no different—or even less malicious—than the accusations and libels launched by Greeks and Romans against barbarian peoples and tribes, and even Greek groups, especially close neighbors and foreign minorities, and should be treated accordingly. After all, in the Hellenistic age, when vicious rumors and pejorative names were invented and spread by the Greeks against other people, and even the inhabitants of Crete were consistently blemished as "ever liars, evil beasts, idle bellies" (best known from Paul's epistle to Titus, 1.12), occasional defamation of the Jews was just one of these things. The common tendency to categorize these sources as pro-Jewish or anti-Jewish is therefore erroneous and misses the point. These reservations are expressed without attempting to mitigate the degree of hostility and hatred manifested toward Jews in accounts whose nature, motives, and aims are in all respects clearly anti-Jewish, such accounts becoming more and more virulent in the Roman age. In sum, great caution should be exercised before labeling Greek authors as "anti-Semitic" or "Judaeophiles," both charged terms that bear strong modern connotations. Similar caution must be exercised before utilizing the writings of these authors as evidence or support for general or particular theories with regard to various fields of research on Jews and Judaism.

Appendix

The God of Moses in Strabo

By Ivor Ludlam

Strabo ascribes to Moses the following description of the Jewish divinity:

> For only this one [thing] is god: that which surrounds all of us and earth and sea,
> [the thing] that we call both heaven and cosmos and the nature of the things-
> which-are. (16. 2. 35)[1]

This quotation has been used by some scholars to support their claim that Strabo's Jewish excursus must surely have derived from Posidonius, while others have used it to prove the exact opposite.[2] Since the arguments on both sides depend upon a comparison of the views expressed in the passage with those of Posidonius, it seems reasonable to begin our discussion with a short review of Stoic physics, of which Stoic theology is one part. I shall attempt to reconstruct and demarcate some of the views of Posidonius that seem to have differed from those of other Stoics, and that have a bearing on the opposing arguments concerning Strabo's source of information for Jewish belief.

---

1. εἴη γὰρ ἓν τοῦτο μόνον θεὸς τὸ περιέχον ἡμᾶς ἅπαντας καὶ γῆν καὶ θάλατταν, ὃ καλοῦμεν οὐρανὸν καὶ κόσμον καὶ τὴν τῶν ὄντων φύσιν.

2. The passage serves as proof for a Posidonian source esp. in Reinhardt (1928) 6–15. Other scholars who attribute this passage to Posidonius include Reinach (1895) 99 n. 2; Norden (1921) 296 ff.; Heinemann (1919) 111 ff.; id. *RE* s.v. "Antisemitismos," suppl. 5 (1931) col. 34 f. This same passage, however, is used to refute the claim of a Posidonian source in Aly (1957a) 191 ff., esp. 196. We shall return to the arguments of Reinhardt and Aly later.

POSIDONIAN STOIC PHYSICS

I have argued elsewhere that there was never one organized Stoic school that imposed orthodoxy upon its members.[3] Each Stoic was at liberty to develop, within limits, Stoic theory as he saw fit, and Posidonius appears to have been no exception. My reconstruction of the aspects of Posidonian Stoic physics (including theology) relevant to the Strabo passage is based upon a consideration of the development of these aspects in Stoic physics from Zeno onward.

A basic tenet of Stoic physics is that there is only one thing which is—that is, one thing which does not come to be and pass away—and this is the *ousia* (substance). The many things we see in the universe are not constant but come to be and pass away, and their existence is by virtue of the *ousia,* of which they are no more than ever-changing aspects. According to the Stoics, therefore, the many things of this universe cannot be called "things-which-are" (*onta*), and instead they are called bodies (*sōmata*). It may be observed at once that the Strabo passage as it stands is not Stoic, since it refers to things-which-are.

Bodies in Stoic terminology are not merely discrete masses of matter. The Stoics defined body as that which could affect or be affected, and, conversely, anything that could affect or be affected was regarded as a body. Examples of body would be a table, a soul, and bravery. More than one body could occupy the same place simultaneously. Some bodies would be aspects of other bodies, and all bodies, as has already been mentioned, were aspects of the *ousia.*

Stoics claimed that the *ousia,* although in practice indivisible, may be conceived by the intellect to consist of an active and a passive aspect. The active acts on the passive and thereby causes the variations in the *ousia* that are perceived as bodies.[4] The passive aspect was identified with unqualifed matter (*hylē*), and the active aspect with god (*theos*) or the Logos, which is best left untranslated. Since the two aspects were considered inseparable in reality (for there is no unqualified matter in the cosmos, and no unqualifying god), it was quite common to regard the *ousia* as either (passive) matter or (active) god as occasion demanded. The Stoics tended to identify the *ousia* in its material aspect with what medical practitioners considered to be the material life force. For the early Stoics, therefore, the *ousia* was "creative fire," but medical advances led later Stoics to identify the *ousia* with warm breath (*pneuma*).[5] Since Posidonius was one of these later Stoics, we shall concentrate on the concept of *pneuma.*

3. See Ludlam (2003) 33–55.

4. On all this, see *SVF* 1: fr. 85 ff., and 2: fr. 463 ff. The notional analysis of the *ousia* into two aspects and their recombination into a complex whole is referred to in the Stoic doxography in Diogenes Laertius (7. 137–38).

5. See Solmsen (1961) passim. Zeno and Cleanthes advocated "creative fire" (πῦρ τεχνικόν), while Chrysippus and later Stoics adopted *pneuma.*

Doctors had used "breath" to explain certain functions of the soul (*psychē*), the driving force of a living body. The early Stoics, among them Zeno and Cleanthes, while regarding the *ousia* as "creative fire" (the heat that provides life to living things), resorted to the concept of *pneuma* to explain certain phenomena of the *psychē*. In accordance with contemporary medical theory, these Stoics assumed that the seat of the soul was situated in the warmest part of the living body (in most cases, this was the area around the heart), and that from this seat the soul sent commands to the rest of the body. The orders were transmitted by the *pneuma,* warm breath pervading the whole body. Its very presence throughout the body was what allowed it to serve as a transmitter. The Stoics regarded the whole cosmos as a living creature and therefore attributed to it a soul. By analogy with other living bodies, the cosmic soul needed to have its seat in the warmest part of the cosmos. Cleanthes located the commanding principle of the soul and the source of the creative heat in the *aithēr*—the pure, white hot air surrounding the cosmos.[6] The *aithēr* differed from the air surrounding the earth; part of it constituted and the rest nourished the sun and the other heavenly bodies located in it in the outer sphere of the cosmos.

This scheme of things already required the *pneuma* to be everywhere, in order to transmit the commands of the commanding principle. Chrysippus, the "second founder of the Stoa," adopted a more recent medical theory, according to which the life principle was no longer the creative fire but *pneuma* itself. For this reason, he regarded the *ousia* not as creative fire but as *pneuma*. The *pneuma* continued to have as one of its functions the role of transmitting the commands of the commanding principle to the rest of the body (in this case, the cosmos), but now that *pneuma* was identified with the *ousia* itself, it replaced the creative fire as the commanding principle. In practical terms there was not much difference, since Chrysippus also located the commanding principle of the cosmos in the *aithēr*. Now, however, the *aithēr* was identified with the *pneuma* in its purest and hottest form.

As has already been mentioned, bodies are to be regarded as no more than various aspects of the *ousia*. Chrysippus provided a physical explanation for the existence of bodies, and this may be summarized as follows: currents of air and *pneuma* (warm breath, as distinct from air) pervade the body and preserve its internal unity by means of "tension" (*tonos*), while also constituting the permanent state (*hexis*) of the body, and other characteristics such as hardness and brightness.[7] As we shall soon see, the explanation of bodies and their characteristics by means not only of *pneuma* but also of air in general was problematic; but Chrysippus's very conception of *pneuma* itself was in need of correction.

---

6. The "commanding principle" is a rough translation of the Greek τὸ ἡγεμονικόν.

7. Plutarch *De Stoicorum repugnantibus* 1053F = *SVF* 2: fr. 449; cf. Long and Sedley (1987) 1: 287–89.

If the *ousia* is the only thing that actually is (as all Stoics claim), it follows that it cannot be a compound of elements. Either the elements are things which are, in which case the *ousia* would not be the only thing which is, or the elements are things which are not, and that would produce an absurdity where the thing which is would be composed of things which are not. Yet the medical and Chrysippean *pneuma* (warm air) is essentially a compound of air and fire. Furthermore, if, as Chrysippus claimed, the *pneuma* (along with air) bestowed upon bodies their characteristics, their unity, and their very existence, the *pneuma* would need to be prior to fire and air, both bodies with characteristics, unity, and existence; yet fire and air, as components of the composite *pneuma*, need to be prior to the *pneuma*.[8] It seems that Posidonius, active some four or five generations after Chrysippus, produced an elegant solution to the problem of priority. While continuing to regard the *ousia* in its material aspect as the *pneuma*, he reinterpreted this *pneuma* as a simple material,[9] whose purest form is prior to the four elements—fire, air, water, and earth—all of which are condensed forms of *pneuma*.[10] It might be objected that any one of the four usual elements could just as well be considered prior to all the others, which are all rarified or condensed forms of it.

8. Cf., e.g, *SVF* 2: fr. 442.

9. There is no direct evidence that Posidonius's concept of *pneuma* was his own innovation, or that it was designed to meet certain difficulties that had arisen in Stoic physics; but this may be deduced in part from the attested fact that (at least) two Stoics intermediate between Chyrysippus and Posidonius—Panaetius and Boethus—denied the notion of *ekpyrōsis*, the cosmic conflagration that marked the end of one cosmic cycle and the beginning of another (Kidd 2: F13, F99a comm.), although this had been one of the hallmarks of Stoic physics from Zeno down to at least Chrysippus. Conflagration was the point in the cosmic cycle at which god (the active aspect of the *ousia*) and matter (the passive aspect of the *ousia*) were uniformly mixed in their purest forms, without god qualifying matter in any way to form other bodies. This was the stage before god sowed his seeds and thereby began the formation of the next cosmos. If such an outstanding Stoic as Panaetius objected to this theory, we must ask ourselves what could have constituted a reasonable Stoic objection. The most obvious answer appears to me to be that the *pneuma* adopted by Chrysippus in preference to the creative fire as the primary matter of the *ousia* came to be perceived as incompatible with the theory of cosmic conflagration. The medically approved *pneuma* was a compound of air and fire, while the primary matter present at the conflagration had to be a simple element. The perceived inconsistency could be solved either by rejecting the notion of conflagration or by insisting on the simple nature of the primary matter. It would seem that Panaetius and Boethus, and most probably others of that time, too, chose the first alternative. Posidonius, however, returned to the notion of conflagration (Kidd 2: F13 comm.), which may itself suggest that he was the first to regard *pneuma* as a simple element and not a compound.

10. The description of generation and destruction in Diogenes Laertius 7. 142 may derive from a book by Posidonius called *On the Cosmos* by way of a summarizing doxographer who left out many details. The elements are formed from each other by a process of condensation and rarifaction (Kidd 2: F13 comm.), which is reminiscent of the theory Anaximenes of Miletus offered to explain the origin of the other elements out of his primary element, air. The *pneuma* would need to have been even more rarified than fire, the first element to originate from it by condensation. Diogenes Laertius

Pure *pneuma*, however, unlike the four elements, also has a crucial role to play in the running of the cosmos, and this would have been the main reason for it being considered prior. How crucial rarified *pneuma* was for the running of the cosmos may be appreciated from its identification by Posidonius with god, who, according to Posidonius, is "intelligent and firelike" *pneuma*.[11]

We may now turn to the further inconsistency in the theory of Chrysippus noted above, namely, the claim that both *pneuma* and air were responsible for the existence and the characteristics of bodies. Since *pneuma* was no more than hot air, it was not strictly accurate to talk about *pneuma* and air as if they were two distinct entities.[12] We have already seen that regarding *pneuma* as prior to all four elements solved the problem of *pneuma* itself. The same reassessment of *pneuma* also removed the need for air as a cause of the existence and characteristics of bodies, since *pneuma* alone now became responsible for the existence and characteristics of all bodies, including all four elements with their opposing characteristics.

Posidonius, then, seems to have been the first Stoic to have regarded *pneuma* as simple rather than compound, and to have made this *pneuma* the sole cause of all bodies and their characteristics, both animate and inanimate, hot and cold, hard and soft. We might say that he was more generous in his conception of *pneuma* than previous Stoics, who required the services of air as well to do much of the work. Posidonius's *pneuma* was versatile in the extreme, the cause of all things in the cosmos, including bodies of opposing characteristics. We may

does record that other bodies are created out of a mixture of the four elements. He does not mention that still more *pneuma* is required to unify both the elements themselves as elements and the bodies formed by them as bodies. The rarified nature of *pneuma* may also have explained this material's ability to pervade elements and bodies in order to unify them and give them characteristics.

11. Posidonius describes god as πνεῦμα νοερὸν καὶ πυρῶδες—"intelligent and firelike *pneuma*" (*SVF* 2: fr. 1009). Kidd 2: F101 comm. notes that later testimonia attribute this theory to Stoics indiscriminately, but this seems to have happened under the influence of Posidonius. God is *pneuma* at its most rarified, when it is not condensed into one or other of the elements, and it is this rarified *pneuma* that pervades the rest. For objections to this theory, see Alexander of Aphrodisias *De mixtione* 224, 32 (ed. Bruns) = *SVF* 2: fr. 310. The most rarified *pneuma* is firelike, and not fire. Posidonius seems to have associated intelligence with extreme heat (cf. the theory outlined below), and rarified *pneuma* may have been considered hotter than fire.

12. Furthermore, by writing that the very characteristics of bodies, such as hardness and brightness, were "airs and *pneumata*" (Plut. *De Stoic. repugn.* 1053F, 1054A = *SVF* 2: fr. 449), Chrysippus could not consistently explain how air and fire, in his view the two compounds of *pneuma*, could themselves have distinguishing characteristics. Alexander of Aphrodisias provides more objections to this theory of Chrysippus (*SVF* 2: fr. 442). Chrysippus clearly felt the need to regard both air and *pneuma* as jointly responsible for the existence and characteristics of bodies, and it may be worth speculating what his reasons were. *Pneuma* would have had to be regarded as one of the causes, since this was what (medical) scientists of the time regarded as the life principle; but being warm air, *pneuma* may not have explained to Chrysippus's satisfaction (or that of his critics) the existence of cold or inanimate bodies, while (cold) air may have done so.

now appreciate that his identification of god with intelligent and firelike *pneuma* actually specifies which aspect of *pneuma* is god: *pneuma* when it is intelligent and firelike—that is, in its most rarified form.[13]

There are traces in our sources of a theory in which this view of *pneuma* would make sense, and this theory could only be advanced by someone with the conception of *pneuma* that we have attributed to Posidonius. This theory, as I reconstruct it, explains how different variations of *pneuma* unify bodies in different ways.[14] Every variation of *pneuma* provides a body with its characteristics (such as hardness and brightness), but beyond this, it also organizes a complex body in a certain overall way—and here, too, Posidonius advances on the theory of Chrysippus. Cold *pneuma*,[15] for example, unifies parts into an inanimate whole body (this *pneuma* is identified with the basic permanent state, *hexis*); warm *pneuma* unifies inanimate parts into a whole animate body with basic biological functions (this *pneuma* is identified with *physis*, nature); additional, warmer *pneuma*, provides certain animate bodies with sensation and appetition and unifies the whole body as an animal (this *pneuma* is identified with *psychē*, the soul); somewhat hotter *pneuma* can suffuse certain animals and unify the whole body as a "logical animal," such as a human (this *pneuma* is identified with *logos* or *nous*). It would seem that the place of god in this scheme is as the hottest *pneuma*, unifying the whole cosmos as the most intelligent animal of all.[16]

No Stoic before Posidonius could have invented a theory that presupposes that simple (not compound) *pneuma* is the *ousia*. On the other hand, our sources indicate that Posidonius was the last of the great innovators in Stoic physics;

---

13. And not that because all *pneuma* is intelligent and firelike, it is to be identified with god. In any case, the claim that all *pneuma* is intelligent and firelike would necessarily entail that all things are intelligent and firelike, since *pneuma* is the material aspect of the *ousia*, substance. The only time that the *ousia* is completely firelike and intelligent is precisely in the cosmic conflagration, when god and all matter are one and the same.

14. The following reconstruction is based on *SVF* 1: fr. 158, 2: frr. 458–60, together with Kidd 2: F100, 101, 139 comm.

15. I make this assumption. Posidonius seems to have seen a correlation between activity and heat, at least in the case of god: by extension, the hotter a body, the more active, and vice versa; thus intelligence is very hot, and a living body is warm, while inanimate bodies *per se* may be very cold.

16. According to the fourth-century C.E. orator and Peripatetic philosopher Themistius (*SVF* 1: fr. 158), it is god that is now *nous*, now *psychē*, now *physis*, and now *hexis*. It is possible that in one way all the other types of unifying *pneuma* could be seen as aspects of the main type of unifying *pneuma*, god; but god was explicitly identified by Posidonius with firelike and intelligent *pneuma*. By analogy with the other unifying types of *pneuma*, Posidonius may well have regarded god as that which unifies the whole cosmos as the most intelligent animal. All Stoics agreed that god needed to pervade the whole cosmos in order to govern it; but, in this very capacity as that which pervaded the whole of the cosmos, god could be the only type of *pneuma* able to organize the cosmos as a whole body. This cosmic-unifying function would differentiate god (often identified by Stoics with *nous* and *logos*) from the *nous*

indeed, he seems to have been considered by later excerptors and doxographers to be the repository of Stoic physics, since many of our testimonia on Stoic physics earlier than Posidonius can be traced back to his writings. All the evidence points to this pneumatic theory being Posidonian.

To conclude this discussion of Stoic physics: according to my reconstruction, the Posidonian god was identified with firelike and intelligent *pneuma,* the hottest of all the types of unifying *pneuma.* It pervaded the cosmos, unifying the cosmos as the most rational animal, and in this aspect could itself be identified with the cosmos. It also governed the cosmos, as a soul governs a body, with its seat in the hottest part of the body, whence commands issued forth, conveyed by the *pneuma* itself, to all parts of the body. While the hottest part of an animal is usually around the heart, in the case of the cosmos, the hottest part was the outer sphere. Thus god pervaded the cosmos, but its ruling principle (*hēgemonikon*) had its seat in heaven (*ouranos*).

REINHARDT, ALY, AND
THE DEBATE OVER STRABO'S SOURCE

We return now to the passage in Strabo with which we began, which describes the god of the Jews. Karl Reinhardt, the leading Posidonius scholar of the first half of the twentieth century, used this passage to support his claim that Posidonius was Strabo's source. His arguments dwelled mainly on the conception of god as the heavens surrounding us.[17] He considered Posidonius to be the source for this part of Strabo's account, although, as Reinhardt himself showed with an abundance of examples, the concept was hardly new and was not even peculiar to the Stoics. Reinhardt also faced another difficulty arising from the expression "the nature of the things-which-are." The concept of "things-which-are" (*onta*) is familiar to us from the writings of philosophers such as Plato and Aristotle, but the Stoics did not use it. They always talked about bodies (*sōmata*). As we have seen, the Stoics acknowledged only one thing as having being, and this was the *ousia,* substance, of which all bodies (such as tables, souls, virtues) were aspects. Reinhardt seems to have believed that he could escape the difficulty by adducing parallels from Aristotle and elsewhere in which the cosmos or *ouranos* is identified with nature or the nature of everything.[18] He did not, however, adduce a single Stoic parallel.

---

or *logos* of a rational animal within the cosmos; in material respects there would seem to be little difference, both types of *pneuma* being very hot and rarified, with god, presumably, being a little more so.

17. Reinhardt (1928) 9–14.

18. Reinhardt (1928) 10. We shall return shortly to consider the term *physis* in Aristotle, and more generally, the formula "the nature of the things-which-are." 19. Aly (1957a) 196–98. We shall be comparing later the Strabonian passage with Hecataeus's account preserved in Diodorus.

The difficulty remains, and we shall see that Strabo also uses the term *physis,* "nature," in the sense of "essence," of the "things-which-are," and not in the Posidonian sense of the warm *pneuma* that unifies bodies as living organisms. It would seem from all the reasons given here that Posidonius, the Stoic philosopher, could not be Strabo's source.

It was later observed by W. Aly, in his monograph on Strabo, that the concept of god as the heavens surrounding us was not peculiar to Posidonius.[19] He rejected the possibility of Posidonius being Strabo's source after comparing the passage with a Posidonian fragment that says: "God is intelligent *pneuma* pervading the whole *ousia.*"[20] Aly claimed that Posidonius saw the spirit of god pervading everything, while Strabo's source regarded the divinity as encompassing everything, which is something else entirely.[21] There is, however, no substance to this argument. The Posidonian god does indeed pervade everything, as described in the testimonium Aly adduces in support of his claim. This has also been touched upon in my reconstruction of Posidonius's pneumatic theory, where *pneuma* unifies what it pervades as a body of a certain type: the hottest *pneuma* pervades in its entirety the whole of the *ousia* and unifies it as the most intelligent animal (the cosmos). Yet this same *pneuma* in its hottest (most intelligent) and purest form is concentrated in the hottest part of the cosmos, in the *aithēr,* the outermost sphere of the cosmos, where it is the commanding principle, the *hēgemonikon,* of the world.[22] As already mentioned, doctors, and Stoics in their train, hypothesized that the commanding principle of an animal had its

19. Aly (1957a) 196–98. We shall be comparing later the Strabonian passage with Hecataeus's account preserved in Diodorus.

20. θεός ἐστι πνεῦμα νοερὸν διῆκον δι' ἁπάσης οὐσίας, Kidd 1: F100.

21. Cf. Stern, *GLAJJ* 1: 306; Conzelmann (1981) 67.

22. Diogenes Laertius 7. 148 (= Kidd 1: F20) reports the views of Zeno (= *SVF* 1: fr. 163), Chrysippus (= *SVF* 2: fr. 1022), and Posidonius on this point. As so often in Diogenes Laertius, it seems that the views attributed to Zeno and Chrysippus derive from an interpretation by Posidonius, who has a vested interest in showing that his position reflects those of his Stoic forebears. For this reason, Posidonius wrote in his *On Gods* that he, Chrysippus, and Zeno claimed that the essence (*ousia*—the non-Stoic usage of Diogenes Laertius possibly following his source) of god was the whole of the cosmos and *ouranos.* Kidd notes the difficulty in the identification of *ouranos* with the whole cosmos (Kidd [1988] 2: 139). My own view is that Posidonius, by virtue of his pneumatic theory, was the only philosopher who could claim that god could pervade the cosmos and thereby be the cosmos, not just part of it. At the same time, in the same work, *On Gods,* Posidonius calls *ouranos* "the governing principle of the cosmos" (Diog. Laert. 7. 139 = Kidd 1: F23). It is standard Stoic physical theory that the governing principle governs by pervading the body over which it has control. To sum up, in Posidonian physics, the *ouranos,* the governing outer sphere of the cosmos where the *pneuma* is at its hottest, is one aspect of god, while the cosmos itself, unified as a rational animal by the *pneuma* pervading it, is another aspect of the same god.

seat in the warmest part of the body, whence it pervaded and thereby controlled the entire body. By extension, the Stoics regarded the cosmos as a living body and located the commanding principle in its hottest part. Consequently, Posidonius, too, located the commanding principle of the firelike and intelligent *pneuma*— pervading the cosmos and unifying it as a rational body—in the outer sphere of the cosmos, the *ouranos* (heaven). Since *ouranos* encompasses the cosmos, god as the commanding principle encompasses the cosmos. It is god as the unifying principle of the cosmos that pervades the cosmos.

Reinhardt, then, attempted to prove that Posidonius was Strabo's source but actually showed that the terms used by Strabo were far from peculiar to Posidonius, while Aly's argument against Posidonius as the source fails to take into account the complexity of Stoic, especially Posidonian, physics. The debate would seem to have reached an impasse.

FROM NARRATIVE IN HECATAEUS
TO A SPEECH IN STRABO

At this stage, we have presented no arguments proving conclusively that Posidonius is the source, and indeed, the phrase "the nature of the things-which-are" would seem to preclude any Stoic as the source, let alone Posidonius specifically. A closer examination of the internal structure of the passage, however, leads to some surprising conclusions concerning the source. Here is the passage in context:

> For he [= Moses] said and taught that the Egyptians were not behaving rightly in likening the divinity to wild animals and beasts, nor the Lybians; nor were the Greeks [behaving] well,[23] in sculpting anthropomorphic [statues]. For this one thing[24] only is god: that which surrounds all of us and earth and sea, [the thing] that we call both heaven and cosmos and the nature of the things-which-are. Of this [thing], who in his right mind would dare[25] to form an image similar to anything around us? (Strabo 16. 2. 35)[26]

23. Two negatives appear for emphasis and may hint at the hidden intentions of the original author.

24. τοῦτο (this) is neuter.

25. θαρρήσειε. The verb is in the optative, indicating remoteness (a "potential optative"), but it also continues the indirect speech in which most of the passage is cast.

26. ἔφη γὰρ ἐκεῖνος καὶ ἐδίδασκεν, ὡς οὐκ ὀρθῶς φρονοῖεν οἱ Αἰγύπτιοι θηρίοις εἰκάζοντες καὶ βοσκήμασι τὸ θεῖον, οὐδ᾽ οἱ Λίβυες· οὐκ εὖ δὲ οὐδ᾽ οἱ Ἕλληνες, ἀνθρωπομόρφους τυποῦντες· εἴη γὰρ ἓν τοῦτο μόνον θεὸς τὸ περιέχον ἡμᾶς ἅπαντας καὶ γῆν καὶ θάλατταν, ὃ καλοῦμεν οὐρανὸν καὶ κόσμον καὶ τὴν τῶν ὄντων φύσιν. τούτου δὴ τίς ἂν εἰκόνα πλάττειν θαρρήσειε νοῦν ἔχων ὁμοίαν τινὶ τῶν παρ᾽ ἡμῖν ... On the speech from which this passage derives, see below. I suspect that further traces of the speech are to be found in paras. 35–36, but they do not concern us here.

Here, as elsewhere in Strabo's Jewish ethnography, the influence of Hecataeus of Abdera is clearly discernible.[27] In his survey of Judaism and the Jews, Hecataeus has this to say about Moses:

> He did not set up at all any statue of gods through not believing the god to be anthropomorphic, [believing] rather that only the heaven surrounding the earth is god and lord of all. (Diod. 40. 3. 4)[28]

Two stages are easily discernible in the writing of Strabo's presentation: the main account and a short sentence in which a writer (at some stage in the transmission) adds an explanation in his own words: "[the thing] that we call both heaven and cosmos and the nature of the things-which-are." The main account is in reported speech, following "he said and taught," and all the verbs in it are consequently in the optative. The short sentence in direct speech breaks the flow of the reported speech attributed to Moses, and its verb ("we call") is in the indicative. The verbs of the account return to the optative after this sentence, reflecting the return to reported speech. For convenience, we shall henceforth call the main part of the account "the speech," and the short sentence "the interpolation."

Hecataeus's account was part of a narrative survey. In Strabo this has the form of a speech by Moses, given in reported speech with verbs in the optative. The speech writer was certainly not Hecataeus. Nor was he the interpolator, since, as the writer of the speech, he would not have needed to break the continuity of the speech he was composing, but could blend anything he wished to say into the speech itself, as part of the speech. We may see that the speech writer did add his own comments, for example, in the case of his criticism of the Greeks, which now appears as a criticism made by Moses. The interpolation, therefore, was added to the text after Hecataeus's original account had been cast into the form of a speech. The speech itself (in reported speech) was the work of an intermediate source, and the interpolation may have been either the work of an intermediate source or the work of Strabo himself. That Strabo was the interpolator is not only a more economical hypothesis, but there is also strong circumstantial evidence to support it, as we shall soon see. We shall therefore consider the speech writer to be the only intermediate source.

How did the speech writer utilize the account by Hecataeus? Beyond his basing a speech by Moses on it, we find several differences in detail. Moses no longer finds fault only with the worship of anthropomorphic gods, but also with the representation of gods in the form of animals; the targets of his criticism are made explicit (the Greeks, and the Egyptians and Lybians, respectively); god no longer

27. See p. 356 note 1 above.

28. ἄγαλμα δὲ θεῶν τὸ σύνολον οὐ κατεσκεύασε διὰ τὸ μὴ νομίζειν ἀνθρωπόμορφον εἶναι τὸν θεόν, ἀλλὰ τὸν περιέχοντα τὴν γῆν οὐρανὸν μόνον εἶναι θεὸν καὶ τῶν ὅλων κύριον.

encompasses only the earth, but "all of us and earth and sea." Furthermore, while Hecataeus identifies god with the surrounding heaven (both masculine), Strabo's account identifies both god and heaven separately with "that which surrounds" (neuter). This expresses a change of emphasis, from god as a masculine concrete individual (albeit not in the shape of a man) to god as something more impersonal if not less of a concrete individual *per se*.[29] We should note that in Strabo's account the word "heaven" does not appear in the speech itself, but in the interpolation. We shall return to this point later in the discussion.

THE IDENTITY AND MOTIVES OF THE INTERPOLATOR AND THE INTERMEDIATE SOURCE

A. *The Identity of the Interpolator*

It is now time to ask a number of mutually dependent questions. Who added the interpolation? What do the terms comprising it signify? If we can show that the argument of the speech cannot stand without the interpolation, it would appear that the interpolation has replaced part of the speech. If this is so, what did the interpolation replace?

As already mentioned, there seems to me no sufficient reason to assume the existence of two intermediate sources between Hecataeus and Strabo to explain the existence both of the speech and of the interpolation. That is, an intermediate author recast Hecataeus in the form of a speech, and Strabo added the interpolation.[30] It might be objected that the interpolation includes terms that are not Stoic, such as the expression "the nature of the things-which-are," and since Strabo was a Stoic, the interpolation could not be by him. While it is true that Strabo portrayed himself as a Stoic,[31] it is also true that he could regard himself as a Stoic and yet not bother too much with the details of Stoic doctrine. In his time it was already customary for a man wishing to appear cultivated to finish his

29. In ancient Greek, the neuter form of an adjective with the definite article was often used to express an abstract entity (e.g., "the just" = "justice"; "the beautiful" = "beauty"). The expression could still be taken to denote a concrete particular (e.g., "the just thing," "the beautiful thing"), and this would be the case especially if the adjective were a participle (e.g., "the commanding thing" rather than "commanding"). Thus we should not regard "the surrounding thing" as entirely abstract, but rather as a depersonalizing concrete particular. The addition of other epithets in the intermediate account may have had the effect of abstracting by making god less localized.

30. Gager (1972) 4 suggests another interpretation, but he too regards Strabo as the author of the sentence that I have called here the "interpolation."

31. Strabo clearly wished to be considered a Stoic. See, e.g., 1. 34. 2, "our Zeno"—i.e., "my Zeno": Strabo always talks about himself in the plural; the Zeno in question is the founder of Stoicism; 1. 3. 2, "our [= my] people even said that only the wise man is a poet"—a purely Stoic notion, but note the use of the past tense. Cf. *SVF* 3: frr. 654–55.

education by doing the rounds of the philosophical schools. He would attend the courses of teachers from the various schools and finally choose which school best suited his purposes.[32] Standard Stoic doctrine is in fact alien to some of Strabo's concerns—for example, his desire to include in his "colossal" work not only the beneficial and the noteworthy, but also the pleasurable (1. 1. 23). There is no doubt that Strabo had had a taste of Stoic education, but he mentions none of his Stoic teachers by name. This may not strike anyone as unusual until it is pointed out that Strabo does mention, and more than once or twice, his Peripatetic studies, and names at least one of his Peripatetic teachers. We learn by the way that he studied the writings of Aristotle (16. 2. 24), perhaps with his Peripatetic teacher, Xenarchus, and most probably in Rome (14. 5. 4).

Could it be, then, as a result of his Peripatetic education, that Strabo himself wrote "[the thing] that we call both heaven and cosmos and the nature of the things-which-are"? This is no doubt possible; but the general education of his day would have sufficed. Aristotle himself observes that people—not necessarily philosophers—use the words "heaven," "cosmos," and "nature" in various senses according to the context, but all three are identical only in one sense. In his work *On Heaven,* Aristotle notes that "heaven" and "cosmos" are identical when they mean "the general composition of everything" (where "everything" has the sense of "the universe").[33] In his discussion of the definitions of the term "nature" in the *Metaphysics,* Aristotle says that one of the meanings people attribute to it is "the elements of those things-which-are by nature" (pertaining to one or more of the four elements); another meaning is "the being (*ousia*) of those things-which-are by nature" (1014b31 ff.).[34] So the three terms "heaven," "cosmos," and "the nature of the things-which-are" can all denote in popular

32. Strabo himself describes this round of philosophical studies as a regular activity required of any person with a claim to culture (1. 1. 22). He regards a man's higher education as an indication of his social status: indeed, honor, reputation, and social status appear to be the factors motivating Strabo to write and "philosophize" (see, e.g., 1. 1. 22–23; 1. 2. 1 fin.). Strabo describes his "colossal" work as befitting a philosopher (1. 1. 13). He means here by "philosopher" no more than "man of culture" and is certainly not thinking of a man who takes philosophy too seriously and spends more time on studying it than is socially acceptable.

33. Aristotle *De caelo* 280a21: ἡ δὲ τοῦ ὅλου σύστασίς ἐστι κόσμος καὶ οὐρανός. It seems to have been quite usual already before Aristotle to treat the two terms "heaven" and "cosmos" as interchangeable; cf. Plato *Timaeus* 28b2: ὁ δὴ πᾶς οὐρανὸς ἢ κόσμος ἢ καὶ ἄλλο ὅτι ποτὲ ὀνομαζόμενος μάλιστ᾽ ἂν δέχοιτο, τοῦθ᾽ ἡμῖν ὠνομάσθω ("The whole heaven—or cosmos, or whatever else he would most accept being called—let him be called this by us").

34. The common use of the term "nature" in the sense of "elements" justifies one of Aristotle's definitions of "nature," namely, "matter" (*hylē*). The term "things-which-are" (*onta*), which appears in our interpolation, is indeed frequent in Aristotle, but it is widespread throughout Greek literature, with the significant exception of Stoic philosophical writings.

parlance the sum of all things (i.e., the universe), and it is only as the universe that they all share a particular meaning. Interestingly, none of these terms is identified by Aristotle with his notion of god; but this has no bearing on the argument that appears in Strabo's account. First, it is said there that Moses identified god with "that which surrounds," and it is "that which surrounds" (not god) that is identified with the following three terms in the interpolation. Second, Aristotle himself testifies to the identification made in common language between "heaven," "cosmos," and "the nature of the things-which-are." Strabo, then, is not using these terms in a manifestly Peripatetic sense and is certainly not thinking of Aristotle's unmoved mover; it is most likely that he chose to use these terms according to common, nontechnical, usage. We must now examine Strabo's motives for doing so.

We have already seen that the intermediate source formulated the theological opinions of Moses in the form of a speech, in reported speech, with main verbs appearing in the optative and later in the infinitive. We have also seen that the interpolation, appearing in the indicative, breaks this structure and appears to be adding an explanation or an elucidation: "[the thing] that we call both heaven and cosmos and the nature of the things-which-are." Yet the interpolation is not a simple addition to the speech. The interpolation has replaced something in the speech. One of the terms originally appearing in the speech would have been *ouranos*, "heaven," since this appears in Hecataeus (the source upon which the speech is based), and in the interpolation. Strabo saw this in his source and used it in his interpolation. Hecataeus described heaven as surrounding the earth, and it is clear that the original speech included an identification between "that which surrounds" and heaven. Strabo's interpolation identifies heaven on the one hand with "that which surrounds" and on the other hand with the nature of the things-which-are, the sum of everything in common parlance. The Hecataean account is sufficient to explain the identification with "that which surrounds." Was there something else in the original speech of the intermediate source that induced Strabo to understand heaven also in the sense of "the general composition of everything"? If there was, why would Strabo have bothered to replace it with his interpolation, which effectively creates a contradiction between "that which surrounds" and "the nature of things-which-are"?

B. What the Interpolation Replaced in the Intermediate Source

The intermediate source must have made some sort of connection between "that which surrounds" and "the sum of everything." The only philosophical system in which heaven could be simultaneously (but in different aspects) "that which surrounds," the whole cosmos, and everything in it would have been the system of Posidonius.[35] According to my reconstruction presented earlier, Posidonius regarded the purest, hottest, and most active *pneuma* as the factor unifying the cosmos as a rational animal, and doing so by pervading every part of the cosmos. He also regarded this same pure *pneuma* pervading the cosmos as controlling the cosmos from its natural seat in the cosmos, the hottest part of the cosmos, the outer sphere, namely, *ouranos* (heaven). We should note that in Hecataeus "heaven" appears before "god," while in Strabo it appears afterward, at the head of a list of terms describing god. The transposition would have been made by the intermediate source. It seems reasonable to suppose that the Stoic author of the speech wished to identify the god of Moses (as portrayed by Hecataeus) with the Stoic (Posidonian) god, and it was this that led to the change in places: "heaven," common to the Stoic and the Mosaic god, could head the list of Stoic terms describing god (now also attributed to the Mosaic god). It seems that the original speech would have contained a list of terms and expressions describing this god, since the aim was to indicate the folly of belief in anthropomorphic gods. An argument proving the nonanthropomorphic nature of god would have achieved this aim as well but would have been too long and technical in any speech, and incongruous in this one, where such arguments are notably absent. I present a partial reconstruction *exempli gratia* of this part of the original speech, with the words in square brackets representing that part of the original text that has been replaced by the interpolation. The terms I propose show how the Mosaic god of the outer sphere could gradually come to be identified with the cosmos altogether. We can only speculate on the number and nature of the terms that have been replaced by the interpolation. I present the bare terms, with no attempt at reconstructing the actual formulation.

εἴη γὰρ ἓν τοῦτο μόνον θεὸς τὸ περιέχον ἡμᾶς ἅπαντας καὶ γῆν καὶ θάλατταν, [ὁ οὐρανός, τὸ ἡγεμονικόν, πνεῦμα νοερὸν καὶ πυρῶδες, ὁ κόσμος.] τούτου δὴ τίς ἂν εἰκόνα πλάττειν θαρρήσειε νοῦν ἔχων ὁμοίαν τινὶ τῶν παρ' ἡμῖν . . .

For this one thing only is god: that which surrounds all of us and earth and sea, [(namely) heaven, the commanding principle, intelligent and firelike pneuma, the cosmos.] Of this [thing], who in his right mind would dare to form an image similar to anything around us?

C. The Motives of the Interpolator

Strabo appears to have replaced the list he saw in his source (not necessarily identical to the one I have proposed here) with another list free of philosophical

---

35. The popular identification of "heaven" with "cosmos"—as we have seen noted by Aristotle (note 33 above)—is only in the sense of "the general composition of everything," and not in the sense of "that which surrounds."

jargon. We have already seen that the terms he uses are not even peculiar to Peripatetic philosophy. When Strabo, in his interpolation, says "what we call," he does not mean "we, the Stoics," but "we, speakers of everyday Greek," and he is making a direct appeal to his readers. The speech at this point was clearly too technical for Strabo's taste, but some sort of list was necessary—even Strabo could see that—to show the folly of worshipping anthropomorphic gods. Terms such as "heaven," "cosmos," and *pneuma,* which I suggest may have appeared in the original speech, allowed Strabo to conclude that the subject was the all-pervading god—despite the previous sentence in which the god was explicitly all-encompassing—and Strabo duly wrote in nontechnical language "what we call heaven and cosmos and the nature of the things-which-are," terms that are all identical only in the sense of "the sum of everything," as we have seen above. The very attempt to substitute non-Stoic terms for Stoic ones, or to use terms in a non-Stoic sense, demonstrates that Strabo was unaware of the dynamic nature of the list and its intended aim to portray god as both all-encompassing and all-pervading. Such a portrayal was impossible in anything but Stoic terms, and in non-Stoic terms necessarily led to contradiction. Perhaps Strabo assumed that such a contradiction already existed in his source (imperfectly understanding Stoic physics), and made the best of a bad job by at least demystifying the technical jargon.

What did Strabo have against Stoic terminology, especially considering that he fancied himself to be a Stoic? Why did he not understand Stoic theology? Strabo seems to have been no different from many intellectuals of his time in his distaste for physical speculations. His criticisms on this subject are directed in particular against Posidonius (2. 3. 8):

> So much against Posidonius as well [for now; for] many [of his opinions], as many as are on geography, receive the treatment appropriate to particular [discussions]. As many [of his opinions] as are more to do with physics, they are to be examined elsewhere, or not even considered; for there is much study of causes (*to aitiologikon*) in [his work], and Aristotelizing, from which our people [i.e., the Stoics!] lean away, because of the concealment of causes.[36]

Some have interpreted this passage of Strabo as an attack on Posidonius for turning toward the philosophy of Aristotle. This is unlikely, since Posidonius did not in fact adopt Peripatetic physics, or anything like it. After praising Posidonius for his contributions to the study of geography, Strabo criticizes his physics,

---

36. τοσαῦτα καὶ πρὸς Ποσειδώνιον· πολλὰ γὰρ καὶ τοῖς καθ' ἕκαστα τυγχάνει τῆς προσηκούσης διαίτης, ὅσα γεωγραφικά· ὅσα δὲ φυσικώτερα, ἐπισκεπτέον ἐν ἄλλοις, ἢ οὐδὲ φροντιστέον· πολὺ γάρ ἐστι τὸ αἰτιολογικὸν παρ' αὐτῷ καὶ τὸ Ἀριστοτελίζον, ὅπερ ἐκκλίνουσιν οἱ ἡμέτεροι διὰ τὴν ἐπίκρυψιν τῶν αἰτιῶν.

and particularly his tendency to seek out causes and philosophize in the style of Aristotle. Now, to seek out causes and to philosophize in the style of Aristotle are not two separate criticisms, but one and the same. Strabo is here using the common rhetorical figure of *hendiadys,* the presentation of one idea through the medium of two expressions. In other words, Strabo is protesting against the attempts of Posidonius to look for causes in the way that Aristotle does.[37] The criticism, therefore, is not against the opinions of Posidonius, but against his method of enquiry in this field. This is not the place to consider whether this criticism has any foundation, but it is worth spending a few moments to survey the contents of this field of Stoic physics. In a passage that is generally accepted to derive from Posidonius, Diogenes Laertius tells us that one of the divisions of Stoic physics was into three parts: (1) On the cosmos (e.g., observation of the heavens); (2) on elements (e.g., speculation concerning the composition of the cosmos and its parts; (3) on causes (*aitiologikos topos*—e.g., biological questions such as the nature of the ruling principle—*to hēgemonikon*—in the soul; events in the soul; seeds; the sources of phenomena in nature; sight).[38]

If Strabo opposed the studies of Posidonius in the field of causes of things, he may well have opposed some of the causes peculiar to Posidonius, such as the central Stoic concept of the ruling principle in its Posidonian form—or at least its use in the context of the cosmos. This concept must have featured in the Posidonian list of terms describing god, since it is a necessary bridge between the Hecataean all-encompassing god of Moses and the all-pervading god that is another aspect of the same thing in the Posidonian account. Strabo was clearly not at home in Stoic physics. He failed to appreciate the importance of physics as the basis for Stoic ethics and seems to have had little interest in it. This attitude reflects the general atmosphere of his time. As he himself says, "our people" refrain from such speculations (2. 3. 8).

D. The Identity of the Intermediate Source

It remains only to determine the identity of the Stoic author of the speech of Moses in the intermediate source. Only one candidate has made his presence felt throughout this discussion, and that is Posidonius.

The author identifies god with the all-encompassing heaven and the whole cosmos at one and the same time. This suggests a Stoic author who not only established heaven—the outer sphere of *aithēr*—as the seat of the ruling principle

---

37. See Sandbach (1985) 59: his "own guess" is that "Strabo wished to represent [Posidonius] as consciously following Aristotle's lead in trying to find the causes of things."

38. Diogenes Laertius 7. 132–33. It is generally regarded as a Posidonian testimonium; see Kidd 1: F98; Long and Sedley (1987) 43B. Diogenes seems here to have used a handbook written shortly after the time of Posidonius.

of the cosmos, but also regarded the material of the ruling principle as the highest form of unifier, providing the cosmos with its being, in the form of the most rational animal. This material, therefore, may be regarded not only as the ruling principle of the cosmos, but as the cosmos itself. Later testimonia that attribute such a view to Chrysippus and even Zeno must be regarded as suspect; only Posidonius had a system in which such a position could be maintained. Thus Posidonius must be regarded as the source for these testimonia.[39]

In addition, Posidonius discussed the concept of the ruling principle in that part of Stoic physics that dealt with causes, a part of Stoic physics that was peculiar to Posidonius. We have seen that Strabo was not happy with Posidonius's inquiry into causes. Therefore, when Strabo encountered the ruling principle in the speech supposedly delivered by Moses—and we have seen that the concept had to appear there—he had at least one good reason to replace the term with something less technical.

E. The Motives of the Intermediate Source

To conclude this discussion, we may ask what purpose Posidonius may have had in attributing such a speech to Moses. The additions made by Posidonius to the description of the Jewish god in Hecataeus suggest that he used the character of the Jewish leader as a mouthpiece through which he could express his Stoic views and attack positions widely held in the Greek world on the sensitive issue of the nature of religion.[40]

The speech of Moses, therefore, teaches us nothing about the way Posidonius understood the Jewish divinity, but only about his own religious conception and his struggles with his Greek contemporaries. His Greek contemporary reader, however, may well have treated the work as a true account of the god of the Jews.

---

39. Teachers of philosophy routinely attributed their own opinions to their philosophical predecessors (especially the founder of the school), thereby presenting themselves as the true representatives of the philosopher with whose doctrines students wished to become acquainted.

40. The Stoics posited one god. At the same time, they did not reject outright the gods of Greek religion. Instead, they explained the gods as aspects of the one god. It is not clear whether they took this notion seriously or maintained it only to prevent the multitude or the city authorities from taking measures against them. Whether because of their belief in the one god, or their belief in the usual gods as aspects of the one god (as various forces of nature), the Stoics were forced to conclude that anthropomorphic statues of gods were somewhat mistaken. Such a conclusion, however, would not have been popular, though it may have been tolerated if expressed by a non-Greek.

Adriani, M. 1965. "Note sull' antisemitismo antico." *Religione e Civiltà: Studi e Materiali di Storia della Religioni* 36: 663–98.

Albeck, H. 1959. *A Commentary on the Mishnah: Seder Zerayim.* Jerusalem. [In Hebrew]

Albert, K. 1902. *Strabo als Quelle des Flavius Josephus.* Aschaffenburg.

Alon, G. 1977. *Jews, Judaism, and the Classical World.* Jerusalem.

Altheim, F., and A. Stiehl. 1970. *Geschichte Mittelasiens im Altertum.* Berlin.

Aly, W. 1957a. *Strabonis Geographica* IV. Leipzig.

———. 1957b. *Strabon von Amaseia.* Bonn.

Amantini, L. S. 1972. *Fonti e valore storico di Pompeo Trogo (Iustin XXXV et XXXVI).* Genoa.

'Amir, J. 1996. "Die εὐσέβεια des Theophrast." In J. Glucker and A. Laks, eds., *Jacob Bernays: Un philologue juif,* 105–22. Lille.

Amit, M. 1996. "Worlds Which Did Not Meet." In I. M. Gafni et al., eds., *The Jews in the Hellenistic-Roman World: Studies in Memory of Menahem Stern,* 251–72. Jerusalem. [In Hebrew]

Andrewes, A. 1951. "Ephoros Book I and the Kings of Argos." *Classical Quarterly* 45: 39–45.

Ankori, Z. 1984. *Encounter in History: Jews and Christian Greeks in Their Relation through the Ages.* Tel Aviv. [In Hebrew]

Antonetti, C. 1990. *Les Étoliens: Image et religion.* Paris.

Applebaum, S. 1986. "Hasmonean Internal Colonization: Problems and Motives." In A. Kasher et al., eds., *Man and Land in Eretz Israel in Antiquity,* 75–79. Jerusalem. [In Hebrew]

———. 1989. *Judaea in Hellenistic and Roman Times.* Leiden.

Arafat, K. W. 1996. *Pausanias' Greece*. Cambridge.

Arbesmann, R. 1929. *Das Fasten bei den Griechen und Römern*. Giessen.

———. 1969. "Fasten." *Reallexicon für Antike und Christentum*, vol. 7: cols. 447–73. Stuttgart.

Arens, W. 1979. *The Man-Eating Myth: Anthropology and Anthropophagy*. New York.

Arlenius, A. P. 1544. *Flavii Josephi Opera*. Basel.

Arnim, H. von. 1898. *Leben und Werke des Dio von Prusa*. Berlin.

Arnould, D. 1981. *Guerre et paix dans la poésie grecque de Callinos à Pindare*. New York.

Asheri, D. 1966. *Distribuzioni di terre nell' antica Grecia*. Turin.

Assmann, J. 1997. *Moses der Ägypter: Entzifferung einer Gedächtnisspur*. Darmstadt.

Attridge, H. W. 1984. "Historiography." In M. Stone, ed., *Jewish Writings of the Second Temple Period*, 157–84. Compendia Rerum Iudaicarum ad Novum Testamentum, Section II, Vol. II. Assen.

Aujac, G. 1983. "Strabon et le Stoïcisme." *Diotima* 11: 17–29.

Avigad, N. 1980. *Discovering Jerusalem*. London.

Avi-Yonah, M. 1956. "Archeology and Topography of Jerusalem in the Time of the Second Temple." In M. Avi-Yonah, ed., *The Book of Jerusalem*, 1: 305–19. Jerusalem. [In Hebrew]

———. 1966. *Carta Atlas of the Second Temple, the Mishna, and the Talmud*. Jerusalem. [In Hebrew]

Aziza, C. 1987. "L'utilisation polémique du récrit de l'Exode chez les écrivains alexandrins (IV-ème siècle av. J.-C.—Ier siècle ap. J.-C.)." In W. Haase, ed., *Aufstieg und Niedergang der römischen Welt*, II, vol. 20. 1: 41–65. Berlin.

Babbitt, F. C., ed. 1931. *Plutarch's Moralia*. Vol. 3. Loeb Classical Library. London and Cambridge, Mass.

Baer, Y. F. 1985. *Studies in the History of the Jewish People*. 2 vols. Jerusalem. [In Hebrew]

Bahat, D. 1989. *Carta's Great Historical Atlas of Jerusalem*. Jerusalem. [In Hebrew]

Balch, D. L. 1982. "Two Apologetic Encomia: Dionysius on Rome and Josephus on the Jews." *Journal for the Study of Judaism in the Persian, Hellenistic, and Roman Period* 13: 102–22.

Baldry, H. C. 1959. "Zenon's Ideal State." *Journal of Hellenic Studies* 79: 3–15.

———. 1965. *The Unity of Mankind in Greek Thought*. Cambridge.

Balfour, H. 1897. "Life History of an Aghori Fakir." *Journal of the Anthropological Institute* 26: 240–57. London.

Barag, D. 1992/93. "New Evidence on the Foreign Policy of John Hyrcanus." *The Israel Numismatic Journal* 12: 1–12. [In Hebrew]

Barber, G. L. 1935. *The Historian Ephorus*. Cambridge.

Barclay, J. M. G. 1996. *Jews in the Mediterranean Diaspora: From Alexander to Trajan (323 B.C.E.–117 C.E.)*. Edinburgh.

———. 2000. "Judaism in Roman Dress: Josephus' Tactics in the *Contra Apionem*." In J. U. Kalms, ed., *Internationales Josephus-Kolloquium, Aarhus 1999*, 231–45. Münster.

Bar-Ilan, M. 1993. "The Hand of God: A Chapter in Rabbinic Anthropomorphism." In G. Sed-Rajna, ed., *Rashi 1040–1990: Hommage à Ephraim E. Urbach, Congrès européen des études juives*, 321–35. Paris.

———. 2000. "India and the Land of Israel: Between Jews and Indians in Ancient Times." *Journal of Indo-Judaic Studies* 4: 39–77.

Bar-Kochva, B. 1976. *The Seleucid Army.* Cambridge.

———. 1977. "Manpower, Economics, and Internal Strife in the Hasmonaean State." In H. van Effenterre, ed., *Armées et fiscalité dans le monde antique,* 167–96. Colloques Nationaux du Centre National de la Recherche Scientifique, no. 936. Paris.

———. 1989. *Judas Maccabaeus.* Cambridge.

———. 1994. "Judaism and Hellenism: Between Scholarship and Journalism." *Tarbiz* 63: 451–80. [In Hebrew]

———. 1996a. "An Ass in the Jerusalem Temple: The Origins and Development of the Slander." In H. Feldman and J. Levison, eds., *Josephus' Contra Apionem: Studies in Its Character and Context with a Latin Concordance to the Portion Missing in Greek,* 310–26. Leiden.

———. 1996b. "Antiochus the Pious and Hyrcanus the Tyrant: A Chapter in the Historiography of the Hasmonaean State." *Zion* 61: 7–44. [In Hebrew]

———. 1996c. "The Hellenistic 'Blood Libel': Its Contents, Sources, and Transmission." *Tarbiz* 65: 347–74. [In Hebrew]

———. 1996d. *Pseudo Hecataeus, "On the Jews": Legitimizing the Jewish Diaspora.* Berkeley and Los Angeles.

———. 1997a. "Mosaic Judaism and Judaism of the Second Temple—Strabo's Jewish Ethnography." *Tarbiz* 67: 296–336. [In Hebrew]

———. 1997b. "On the Festival of Purim and Some Practices of Sukkot in the Period of the Second Temple." *Zion* 62: 387–407. [In Hebrew]

———. 1998. "Aristotle, the Learned Jew and the Indian 'Kalanoi'." *Tarbiz* 67: 435–81. [In Hebrew]

———. 1999. "The Battle between Ptolemy Lathyrus and Alexander Jannaeus in the Jordan Valley and the Dating of the Scroll of the War of the Sons of Light." *Cathedra* 93: 7–56. [In Hebrew]

———. 2000a. "The Anti-Jewish Ethnography of Apollonius Molon." *Tarbiz* 69: 5–59. [In Hebrew]

———. 2000b. "The First Greek Account Concerning the Jews: Theophrastus' Anthropological Theory and Jewish Sacrificial Practices." In J. Schwartz et al., eds., *Jerusalem and Eretz Israel; Arie Kindler Festschrift* 1: 43–69. Tel Aviv and Ramat Gan. [In Hebrew]

———. 2000c. "Lysimachus of Alexandria and the Hostile Traditions on the Exodus." *Tarbiz* 69: 471–506. [In Hebrew]

———. 2000/1. "Greek Wisdom—Half, Third, and Quarter." *Sinai* 125: 119–35. [In Hebrew]

———. 2001a. "Megasthenes on the 'Physics' of the Greeks, the Jews, and the Brahmans." *Tarbiz* 70: 143–70. [In Hebrew]

———. 2001b. "On Abraham and the Egyptians: A Hellenistic-Greek or a Hellenistic-Jewish Composition." *Tarbiz* 70: 318–26. [In Hebrew]

———. 2002. "The Conquest of Samaria by John Hyrcanus: The Pretext for the Siege, Jewish Settlement in the 'Akraba District, and the Destruction of the City of Samaria." *Cathedra* 106: 7–34. [In Hebrew]

———. 2003. "Doris—Herod's First Wife." *Cathedra* 110: 5–18. [In Hebrew]

———. 2004. "The Settlement Lexicon of Mnaseas of Patara: On the Idumaean City Adorayim and the Theft of the Ass Head from the Jerusalem Temple." *Tarbiẓ* 73: 517–54. [In Hebrew]

———. 2006. "The Jewish Ethnography by Hecataeus of Abdera." *Tarbiẓ* 75: 51–94. [In Hebrew]

Baron, S. W. 1952. *A Social and Religious History of the Jews: Ancient Times*, vol. 1, *To the Beginnngs of the Christian Era*². New York.

Barrow, H. W. 1892–94. "On Aghoris and Aghorapanthis." *Journal of the Anthropological Society of Bombay* 3: 197–251.

Barwick, K. 1957. *Studien zur Sprachlehre und Grammatik der Stoiker*. Berlin.

———. 1961. "Augustus Schrift *De rhetorica* und Hermagoras von Temnos." *Philologus* 105: 97–110.

———. 1964. "Zur Erklärung und Geschichte der Staseislehre des Hermagoras von Temnos." *Philologus* 108: 80–101.

Bauckham, R. 1996. "Josephus' Account of the Temple in *Contra Apionem* 2.102–109." In L. H. Feldman and J. R. Levison, eds., *Josephus' Contra Apionem: Studies in Its Character and Context with a Latin Concordance to the Portion Missing in Greek*, 327–47. Leiden.

Baumstark, K. 1898. "Lysimachos von Alexandrien." *Philologus* 53: 691–703.

Beard, M. 1986. "Cicero and Divination: The Formation of a Latin Discourse." *Journal of Roman Studies* 76: 33–46.

Beckerath, J. von. 1997. *Chronologie des Pharaonischen Ägypten: Die Zeitbestimmung der ägyptischen Geschichte von der Vorzeit bis 332 v. Chr.* Mainz.

Bekker, I. 1855–56. *Flavii Josephi Opera omnia*. Leipzig.

Bella, B. M. 1938. ΦΛΑΒΙΟΥ ΙΩΣΗΠΟΥ ΚΑΤ' ΑΠΙΩΝΟΣ· ΕΙΣΑΓΩΓΗ, ΜΕΤΑΦΡΑΣΙΣ, ΣΗΜΕΙΩΣΕΙΣ. Athens.

Bellinger, A. R. 1949. "The End of the Seleucids." *Transactions of the Connecticut Academy of Arts and Sciences* 38: 51–102.

Beloch, H. 1879. *Die Quellen des Flavius Josephus in seiner Archäologie*. Leipzig.

Beloch, K. J. 1927. *Griechische Geschichte*². Vol. 4.I. Berlin and Leipzig.

Ben-Shalom, I. 1993. *The School of Shammai and the Zealots' Struggle against Rome*. Jerusalem. [In Hebrew]

Bentwich, N. 1914. *Josephus*. Philadelphia.

van Berg, P. L. 1972. *Corpus cultus Deae Syriae: Études critiques des sources mythographiques grecques et latins*. Leiden.

Bernays, J. 1857. *Grundzüge der verlorenen Abhandlung des Aristoteles über die Wirkung der Tragödie*. Breslau.

———. 1866. *Theophrastos' Schrift über Frömmigkeit*. Berlin.

Berthelot, K. 1999. "Κοινωνία et φιλανθρωπία dans le *Contre Apion* de Flavius Josèphe." In J. U. Kalms and F. Siegert, eds., *Internationales Josephus-Kolloquium, Brüssel 1998*, 94–123. Münster.

———. 2000. "The Use of Greek and Roman Stereotypes of the Egyptians by Hellenistic Jewish Apologists, with Special Reference to Josephus' *Against Apion*." In J. U. Kalms, ed., *Internationales Josephus-Kolloquium, Aarhus 1999*: 185–221. Münster.

———. 2003. "Poseidonios d'Apamée et les juifs." *Journal for the Study of Judaism* 34: 160–98.

Berthold, R. M. 1984. *Rhodes in the Hellenistic Age.* Ithaca.

Berve, H. 1926. *Das Alexanderreich auf prosopographischer Grundlage.* 2 vols. Munich.

Bevan, E. R. 1902. *The House of Seleucus.* 2 vols. London.

———. 1913. *Stoics and Sceptics.* Oxford.

Bickerman[n], E. 1927. "Ritualmord und Eselskult." *Monatschrift für Geschichte und Wissenschaft des Judentums* 71: 171–87 (= id., *Studies in Jewish and Christian History* [Leiden, 1976–80] 2: 225–55).

———. 1937. *Der Gott der Makkabäer.* Berlin.

———. 1938. *Institutions des Séleucides.* Paris.

———. 1976–80. *Studies in Jewish and Christian History.* 3 vols. Leiden.

———. 1988. *The Jews in the Greek Age.* Cambridge, Mass.

Bickerman, E., and H. Tadmor. 1978. "Darius I, Pseudo-Smerdis, and the Magi." *Athenaeum* n.s. 56: 239–61.

Bidez, J., and F. Cumont. 1938. *Les mages hellénisés: Zoroastre, Ostanès et Hystaspe d'après la traditio grecque.* Paris.

Bing, P. 1988. *The Well-Read Muse: Past and Present in Callimachus and the Hellenistic Poets.* Göttingen.

Blankert, A. 1940. "Seneca (Epist. 90) over natuur en cultuur en Posidonius als zijn bron." PhD diss., University of Amsterdam.

Bloch, H. 1879. *Die Quellen des Flavius Josephus in seiner Archäologie.* Leipzig.

Bloch, R. 1999. "Mose und die Scharlatane." In J. U. Kalms and F. Siegert, eds., *Internationales Josephus-Kolloquium, Brüssel 1998*, 142–57. Münster.

———. 2002. *Antike Vorstellungen vom Judentums: Der Judenexkurs des Tacitus im Rahmen der griechisch-römischen Ethnographie.* Stuttgart.

———. 2004. "Posidonian Thoughts—Ancient and Modern." *Journal for the Study of Judaism in the Persian, Hellenistic, and Roman Period* 30: 284–94.

Bludau, A. 1906. *Juden und Juderverfolgung in alten Alexandria.* Münster.

Blum, R. 1991. *Kallimachos: The Alexandrian Library and the Origins of Bibliography.* Madison, Wis.

Blundell, S. 1986. *The Origins of Civilization in Greek and Roman Thought.* London.

Bochart, S. 1663. *Hierozoicon, sive bipertitum opus de animalibus Sacrae Scripturae.* 2 vols. London.

Bohak, G. 2003. "The Ibis and the Jewish Question." In M. Mor et al., eds., *Jews and Gentiles in the Holy Land in the Days of the Second Temple, the Misnah, and the Talmud*, 27–43. Jerusalem.

Böhl, M. T. de Liagre. 1953. *Opera minora.* Groningen.

Bollansée, J. 1999a. "Hermippus of Smyrna." In G. Schepens, ed., *Felix Jacoby, Die Fragmente der griechischen Historiker Continued.* Pt. 4: *Biography and Antiquarian Literature,* 4.A: *Biography.* Leiden, Boston, and Cologne.

———. 1999b. *Hermippus of Smyrna and His Biographical Writings: A Reappraisal.* Leuven.

Bottin, C. 1928. "Les sources de Diodore de Sicile pour l'histoire de Pyrrhus, des successeurs d'Alexandre le Grand et d'Agathocle." *Revue Belge de Philologie et d'Histoire* 7: 1307–27.

Bouché-Leclercq, A. 1879–82. *Histoire de la divination dans l'Antiquité*. 4 vols. Paris.

———. 1907. *Histoire des Lagides*. 3 vols. Paris.

Bouffartigue, J., and M. Patillon. 1979. *Porphyre, De l'abstinence*. Vol. 2. Paris.

Bousset, W. 1901. "Die Himmelsreise der Seele." *Archiv für Religionswissenschaft* 4: 136–69, 229–73.

Bousset, W., and H. Gressmann. 1926. *Die Religion des Judentums im späthellenistischen Zeitalter.*[3] Tübingen.

Boyce, M., and F. Grenit. 1975. *A History of Zoroastrianism*. Vol. 3. Leiden.

Boysen, C. 1898. *Flavii Josephi Opera ex versione Latina antiqua*. Pt. 6: *De Iudaeorum vetustate sive contra Apionem*. Corpus Scriptorum Ecclesiasticorum Latinorum, vol. 37. Vienna and Leipzig.

Bracht Branham, A., and M. O. Goulet-Cazé, eds., 1996. *The Cynic Movement in Antiquity and Its Legacy*. Berkeley and Los Angeles.

Braun, M. 1938. *History and Romance in Graeco-Oriental Literature*. Oxford.

Breasted, J. H. 1912. *Development of Religion and Thought in Ancient Egypt*. London.

Bréhier, É. 1914. "Posidonius d'Apamée, théoricien de la géometrie." *Revue des Études Grecques* 27: 44–58.

Breloer, B. 1933. "Megasthenes (etwa 300 v. Chr.) über die indische Gesellschaft." *Zeitschrift für Semitistik und verwandte Gebiete* 88: 130–64.

Bretzl, H. 1903. *Botanische Forschungen des Alexanderzuges*. Leipzig.

Bringmann, K. 1986. "Geschichte und Psychologie bei Poseidonios." In O. Reverdin, ed., *Aspects de la philosophie hellénistique*, 29–66. Fondation Hardt, Entretiens 32. Geneva.

Brink, K. O. 1946. "Callimachus and Aristotle: An Inquiry into Callimachus' ΠΡΟΣ ΠΡΑΞΙΦΑΝΗΝ." *Classical Quarterly* 40: 11–46.

———. 1956. "Οἰκείωσις and οἰκειότης: Theophrastus and Zeno on Nature and Moral Theory." *Phronesis* 1: 123–45.

Broschmann, M. 1882. *De γάρ particuli usu Herodoteo*. Leipzig.

Brown, T. S. 1949. *Onesicritus: A Study in Hellenistic Historiography*. Berkeley and Los Angeles.

———. 1955. "The Reliability of Megasthenes." *American Journal of Philology* 76: 18–33.

———. 1957. "The Merits and Weaknesses of Megasthenes." *Phoenix* 11: 11–24.

———. 1958. *Timaeus of Tauromenium*. Berkeley and Los Angeles.

———. 1960. "A Megasthenes Fragment on Alexander and Mandamis." *Journal of the American Oriental Society* 80: 133–35.

———. 1973. *The Greek Historians*. Lexington, Mass.

Brumbaugh, R. S., and J. Schwartz. 1979/80. "Pythagoras and Beans: A Medical Explanation." *Classical World* 73: 421–22.

Brunt, P. A. 1980. "On Historical Fragments and Epitomes." *Classical Quarterly* 31: 477–94.

———, ed. 1983. *Arrian*. Vol. 2. Loeb Classical Library. London and Cambridge, Mass.

Büchler, A. 1898. "Le fète des Cabanes chez Plutarque et Tacite." *Revue des Études Juives* 37:181–202.

———. 1902. "Theophrastos' Bericht über die Opfer der Judea." *Zeitschrift des Altestamentische Wissenschaft* 22: 202–28.

———. 1910/11. "Graeco-Roman Criticism of Some Jewish Observances and Beliefs." *The Jewish Review* 1: 17–29, 131–45.

van Buitenen, J. A. B. 1978. *The Mahabharata*. Vol. 1. Chicago.

Bunbury, E. A. 1959. *History of Ancient Geography²*. New York. (1st ed., 1879)

Burkert, W. 1961. "Hellenistiche Pseudopythagorica." *Philosophia* 105: 233–34.

———. 1966. "Greek Tragedy and Sacrificial Ritual." *Greek, Roman, and Byzantine Studies* 7: 87–123.

———. 1972. *Lore and Science in Ancient Pythagoreanism*. Cambridge, Mass.

———. 1983. *Homo Necans: The Anthropology of Ancient Greek Sacrificial Ritual and Myth*. Berkeley and Los Angeles.

———. 1985. *Greek Religion: Archaic and Classical*. Oxford and Cambridge, Mass.

———. 1993. *Platon in Nahaufnahme: Ein Buch aus Herculaneum*. Stuttgart and Leipzig.

Burstein, S. 1989. *Agatharchides of Cnidus on the Erythraean Sea*. London.

Burton, A. 1972. *Diodorus Siculus, Book I*. Leiden.

Busolt, G. 1890. "Quellenkritische Beiträge zur Geschichte der römischen Revolutionszeit." *Jahrbücher für klassische Philologie* 141: 321–49.

Cappelle, W. 1925. "Griechische Ethik und römischer Imperialismus." *Klio* 25: 86–113, 413–31.

———. 1956. "Theophrast in Ägypten." *Wiener Studien* 69 (*Festschrift Albin Lesky*): 173–80.

Cardini, M. T. 1969. *Pitagorici testimonianze e frammenti²*. 3 vols. Florence.

Casson, L. 1989. *The Periplus Maris Erythraei: Text with Introduction, Translation, and Commentary*. Princeton.

Cauley, A. E. 1923. *Aramaic Papyri of the Fifth Century B.C.* Oxford.

Chadwick, J. 1996. *Lexicographia graeca*. Oxford.

Chambry, E. 1925–26. *Aesopi Fabulae*. Paris.

Cheon, S. 1997. *The Exodus Story in the Wisdom of Solomon*. Sheffield.

Cherniss, H. 1964. *Aristotle's Criticism of Presocratic Philosophy*. New York.

Chroust, A.H. 1962. "The Problem of the Mysterious Disappearance and Rediscovery of the Corpus Aristotelicum." *Classica et Mediaevalia* 23: 50–67.

———. 1972. "Aristotle's Sojourn in Assos." *Historia* 21: 170–76.

———. 1973. *Aristotle: New Light on His Life and on His Lost Works*. 2 vols. London.

Clemen, C. 1920. *Griechische und lateinische Nachrichten über die persische Religion*. Giessen.

de Cleva Caizzi, F. D. 1966. *Antisthenis Fragmenta*. Milan.

Cohen, G. M. 2006. *The Hellenistic Settlements in Syria, the Red Sea Basin, and North Africa*. Berkeley.

Cohen, S. 1986. "Anti-Semitism in Antiquity: The Problem of Definition." In D. Berger, ed., *History of Hate: The Dimension of Anti-Semitism*, 43–47. Philadelphia.

———. 1987a. "Pagan and Christian Evidence of the Ancient Synagogue." In L. I. Levine, ed., *The Synagogue in Late Antiquity*, 159–81. Philadelphia.

———. 1987b. "Respect for Judaism by Gentiles according to Josephus." *Harvard Theological Review* 80: 409–30.

Cole, T. 1967. *Democritus and the Sources of Greek Anthropology.* Hartford.

Conzelmann, H. 1981. *Heiden-Juden-Christen: Auseinandersetzungen in der Literatur der hellenistich-römischen Zeit.* Tübingen.

Corais, A. 1815. Στράβωνος Γεωγραφικῶν Βιβλία Ἑπτακαίδεκα. 4 vols. Paris.

Coutant, V., and V. L. Eichenlaub. 1975. *Theophrastus, De ventis.* Notre Dame.

Cowley, A. E. 1923. *Aramaic Papyri of the Fifth Century B.C.* Oxford.

Creuzer, F. 1806. *Historicorum graecorum antiquissimorum fragmenta.* Heidelburg.

Crönert, W. 1906. *Kolotes und Menedemos.* Munich.

Crosby, H. L. 1951. *Dio Chrysostom.* Vol 5. Loeb Classical Library. London and Cambridge, Mass.

Cross, R. L. 1979. *A Study of Sadhus in North India.* Berkeley.

———. 1992. *The Sadhus of India: A Study of Indian Asceticism.* New Delhi.

Cumont, F. 1929. *Les religions orientales dans le paganisme romain*[4]. Paris.

van't Dack, E. 1982. "Politique dans l'historiographie grecque." In E. Van't Dack et al., eds., *Egypt and the Hellenistic World: Proceedings of the International Colloquium, Leuven 24–26 May, 1982,* 407–20. Leuven.

Dahlquist, A. 1962. *Megasthenes and Indian Religion.* Stockholm.

Dandamaev, M. A., and V. G. Lukonin. 1989. *The Cultures and Social Institutions of Ancient Iran.* Cambridge.

Daniel, J. L. 1979. "Anti-Semitism in the Hellenistic-Roman Period." *Journal of Biblical Literature* 98: 45–65.

Davies, J. C. 1955. "Diodorus III. 12–4 v. 36–8." *Journal of Hellenic Studies* 75: 153.

———. 1968. "Molon's Influence on Cicero." *Classical Quarterly* 18: 303–15.

Delatte, A. 1915. *Études sur la littérature pythagoricienne.* Paris.

———. 1922. *Essai sur la politique pythagoricienne.* Liège and Paris.

Delbrück, H. 1920. *Geschichte der Kriegskunst*[3]. Berlin.

Delia, D. 1991. *Alexandrian Citizenship during the Roman Principate.* Atlanta.

Dimitrakos, D. 1964. Μέγα λεξικὸν ὅλης τῆς γλώσσης. Athens.

Denis, A. M. 1970. *Introduction aux pseudépigraphes grecs d'Ancien Testament.* Leiden.

Dennis, H. G. 1988. *Human Sacrifice in Ancient Greece.* Ann Arbor.

Denniston, J. D. 1950. *The Greek Particles*[2]. Oxford.

Derret, J. D. M. 1960. "The History of Palladius on the Races of India and the Brahmans." *Classica et Mediaevalia* 21: 64–135.

———. 1975. "Megasthenes." *Der Kleine Pauly,* vol. 3: 1150–54. Munich.

Desideri, P. 1973. "Posidonio e la guerra mitridatica." *Athenaeum* 51: 3–29, 237–54.

Destinon, J. von, 1882. *Die Quellen des Flavius Josephus in der Jüd. Arch. Buch XII-XVII = Jüd. Krieg Buch I.* Kiel.

Diamond, F. H. 1974. "Hecataeus of Abdera: A New Historical Approach." PhD diss., University of Southern California.

———. 1980. "Hecataeus of Abdera and the Mosaic Constitution." In S. M. Burstein and L. A. Okin, eds., *Essays in Ancient History and Historiography in Honor of Truesdell S. Brown,* 77–95. Lawrence.

Dieckhoff, M. 1962. *Krieg und Frieden im griechisch-römischen Altertum.* Berlin.

Diels, H. 1875. *Simplicii in Aristotelis Physicorum: Libros quattuor posteriores commentaria (commentaria in Aristotelem graeca*, IX–X). Berlin.

Diels, H., and W. Schubart. 1904. *Didymos, Kommentar zu Demosthenes*. Berlin.

Dierauer, U. 1977. *Tier und Mensch im Denken der Antike*. Amsterdam.

Dietrich, M., and O. Loretz. 1992. *Jahwe und seine Ashera: Anthropomorphes Kultbild in Mesopotamien, Ugarit und Israel*. Münster.

Dihle, A. 1961. "Zur hellenistischen Ethnographie." In *Grecs et Barbares*, 205–39. Fondation Hardt, Entretiens 8. Geneva.

———. 1973. "Posidonius' System of Moral Philosophy." *Journal of Hellenic Studies* 93: 50–57.

Diller, A. 1934. "Geographical Latitudes in Eratosthenes, Hipparchus, and Posidonius." *Klio* 27: 258–69.

———. 1952. *The Tradition of Minor Greek Geographers*. Lancaster, Pa.

———. 1975. *The Textual Tradition of Strabo's Geography*. Amsterdam.

Dillon, J., and J. Hershbell. *Iamblichus: On the Pythagorean Way of Life*. Atlanta.

Dimock, E. D. 1978. *The Literature of India*. Chicago.

Dindorff, G. 1845–46. Ἰωσήπου τὰ εὑρισκόμενα. 2 vols. Paris.

Dobson, J. F. 1918. "The Posidonius Myth." *Classical Quarterly* 12: 179–95.

Dodds, E. R. 1951. *The Greeks and the Irrational*. Berkeley and Los Angeles.

———. 1973. *The Ancient Concept of Progress*. Oxford.

Dölger, F. J. 1922. ΙΧΘΥΣ: *Der heilige Fisch in den antiken Religionen und im Christentum*. Vol. 2. Münster.

Doran, R. 1985. "Pseudo-Hecataeus." In J. H. Charlesworth, ed., *The Old Testament Pseudepigrapha*, 2: 905–19. New York.

Dornseiff, F. 1938. *Echtheitsfragen antik-griechischen Literatur: Rettungen des Theognis, Phokylides, Hekataios, Choirilos*. Berlin.

Dörrie, H., and M. Baltes. 1993. *Der Platonismus in der Antike*. Vol. 3. Stuttgart and Bad Cannstatt.

Dougherty, C. 1993. *The Poetics of Colonization*. New York.

Dover, K. J. 1960. *Greek Word Order*. Cambridge.

Dragona-Monachou, M. 1974. "Posidonius' 'Hierarchy' between God, Fate, and Nature and Cicero's *De divinatione*." *Philosophia* (Athens) 4: 286–305.

Drerup, E. 1923. *Demosthenes im Urteil des Altertums*. Würzburg.

Drews, R. 1962. "Diodorus and His Sources." *American Journal of Philology* 83: 383–92.

———. 1963. "Ephorus and History." *American Journal of Philology* 84: 244–55.

———. 1973. *The Greek Accounts of Eastern History*. Washington, D.C.

Drioton, E. 1957. *Pages d'Égyptologie*. Cairo.

Drodge, A. J. 1989. *Homer or Moses: Early Christian Interpretation of the History of Culture*. Tübingen.

Droysen, H. 1889. *Heerwesen und Kriegführung der Griechen*. Freiburg.

Droysen, J. G. 1887–88. *Geschichte des Hellenismus*. 3 vols. Gotha.

Dudley, E. R. 1937. *A History of Cynicism*. London.

Dueck, D. 2000. *Strabo of Amasia: A Greek Man of Letters in Augustan Rome*. London.

———. 2005. "Yuval Shahar, Josephus Geographica." *Scripta Classica Israelica* 24: 318–20. (Review)

Dunbabin, T. J. 1948. *The Western Greeks.* Oxford.

Duncan, J., and M. Derrett. 1960. "The History of Palladius on the Races of India and the Brahmans." *Classica et Mediaevalia* 21: 64–99.

Dürhauer, U. 1977. *Tier und Mensch im Denken der Antike.* Amsterdam.

Düring, I. 1957. *Aristotle in Ancient Biographical Tradition.* Göteborg.

———. 1966. *Aristoteles: Darstellung und Interpretation seines Denkens.* Heidelberg.

Dyck, A. 1881. "On Panaetius' Conception of μεγαλοψυχία." *Museum Helveticum* 38: 153–61.

Edelstein, L. 1936. "The Philosophical System of Posidonius." *American Journal of Philology* 57: 286–325.

———. 1966. *The Meaning of Stoicism.* Cambridge, Mass.

Efron, J. 1962. "The Hasmonean Kingdom and Simeon ben Shatah." PhD diss., The Hebrew University, Jerusalem. [In Hebrew]

———. 1987. *Studies on the Hasmonean Period.* Leiden.

Eichholz, D. E. 1965. *Theophrastus, De lapidis.* Oxford.

Eitrem, S. 1991. "Dreams and Divination in Magical Ritual." In C. A. Faraone and D. Obbink, eds., *Magika Hiera: Ancient Greek Magic and Religion,* 175–87. Oxford.

Ekroth, G. 2002. *The Sacrificial Rituals of Greek Hero-Cults.* Liège.

Eliade, M. 1954. *The Myth of Eternal Return.* New York.

Engers, M. 1923. "De Hecataei abderitae fragmentis." *Mnemosyne* 51: 229–41.

Eph'al, I., and J. Naveh. 1996. *The Aramaic Ostraca of the Fourth Century B.C. from Idumaea.* Jerusalem.

Erbse, H. 1977. *Scholia graeca in Homeri Iliadem.* Vol. 5. Berlin.

Erskine, A. 1990. *The Hellenistic Stoa: Political Thought and Action.* London.

Falconer, W. A., ed. 1923. *Cicero, De senectute, De amicitia, De divinatione.* Loeb Classical Library. London and Cambridge, Mass.

Faraone, C. A., and D. Obbink, eds. 1991. *Magika Hiera: Ancient Greek Magic and Religion.* Oxford.

Farnell, L. R. 1909. *The Cults of the Greek States.* 5 vols. London.

———. 1928. *Greek Hero Cults and Ideas of Immortality.* Oxford.

Farquharson, A. S. L. 1944. ΜΑΡΚΟΥ ΑΝΤΩΝΙΝΟΥ ΑΥΤΟΚΡΑΤΟΡΟΣ ΤΑ ΕΙΣ ΕΑΥΤΟΝ. Oxford.

Feldman, L. H. 1968a. "Abraham the Greek Philosopher in Josephus." *Transactions and Proceedings of the American Philological Association* 99: 143–56.

———. 1968b. "Josephus' Portrayal of Man's Decline." In J. Neusner, ed., *Religions in Antiquity: Essays in Memory of E. R. Goodenough,* 336–53. Leiden.

———. 1983. "The Jews in Greek and Roman Literature." In M. Stern, ed., *The Diaspora in the Hellenistic-Roman World,* 265–85. Jerusalem. [In Hebrew]

———. 1984. *Josephus and Modern Scholarship (1937–1980).* Berlin.

———. 1985. "Josephus as a Biblical Interpreter: The 'Aqedah." *Jewish Quarterly Review* 75: 212–52.

———. 1987. "Hellenization in Josephus' *Jewish Antiquities: The Portrait of Abraham.*" In L. H. Feldman and G. Hata, *Josephus, Judaism, and Christianity,* 133–53. Detroit.

———. 1988. "Pro-Jewish Intimations in Anti-Jewish Remarks Cited in Josephus 'Against Apion'." *Jewish Quarterly Review* 78: 187–251.

———. 1990. "Origen's *Contra Celsum* and Josephus' *Contra Apionem:* The Issue of Jewish Origins." *Vigiliae Christianae* 44: 105–35.

———. 1993. *Jew and Gentile in the Ancient World.* Princeton.

———. 1996a. "Josephus' Portrait of Aaron." In R. Katzoff et al., eds., *Classical Studies in Honor of David Sohlberg,* 162–92. Ramat Gan.

———. 1996b. *Studies in Hellenistic Judaism.* Leiden.

———. 1998a. *Josephus' Rewritten Bible.* Leiden.

———. 1998b. *Josephus's Interpretation of the Bible.* Berkeley.

Ferguson, J. 1975. *Utopias of the Classical World.* Ithaca.

Férrary, J.-L. 1988. *Philhellénisme et impérialism: Aspects idéologiques de la conquête romaine du monde hellénistique, de la seconde guerre de Macédoine à la guerre contre Mithridate.* Rome.

Festugière, A. J. 1937. "Sur une nouvelle édition du 'De Vita Pythagorica' de Jamblique." *Revue des Études Grecques* 50: 470–94.

———. 1945. "Grecs et sages orientaux." *Revue de l'Histoire des Religions* 130: 29–41.

Fidler, R. 2005. *Dreams Speak Falsely.* Jerusalem. [In Hebrew]

Filhofer, P. 1990. *Presbyteron Kreitton: Der Alterbeweis der jüdischen und christlichen Apologeten und seine Vorgeschichte.* Tübingen.

Finkelberg, A. 1998. "On the History of the Greek Cosmos." *Harvard Studies in Classical Philosophy* 98: 103–36.

Finkelstein, L. 1942–43. "Pre-Maccabean Documents in the Passover Haggadah." *Harvard Theological Review* 35: 293–332; 36:1–38.

Fisch, M. H. 1937. "Alexander and the Stoics." *American Journal of Philology* 58: 59–82, 129–51.

Fischer, T. 1975a. "Johannes Hyrkan I auf Tetradrachmen Antiochos' VII?" *Zeitschrift des Deutschen Palästina-Vereins* 91: 191–97.

———. 1975b. "Zu Diodor 40.2: Der jüdische Verfassungsstreit vor Pompejus." In *Festgabe des Althistorischen Seminars Tübingen, Prof. Dr. K. F. Stroheker zum 60 Geburtstag,* 50–54. Tübingen.

———. 1983. *Silber aus dem Grab Davids?* Bochum.

Floratos, C. S. 1972. *Strabon über Literatur und Posidonius.* Athens.

Flower, M. A. 1994. *Theopompus of Chios.* Oxford.

Flusser, D. 1949. "The 'Blood Libel' against the Jews in Light of the Views of the Hellenistic Period." In M. Schwabe and J. Gutman, eds, *Commentationes iudaico-hellenisticae in memoriam Iohannis Lewy,* 104–24. Jerusalem. [In Hebrew]

———. 1988. *Judaism and the Origins of Christianity.* Jerusalem.

Fornara, C. W. 1983. *The Nature of History in Ancient Greece and Rome.* Berkeley.

Fortenbaugh, W. W. 1984. *Quellen zur Ethik Theophrasts.* Amsterdam.

Fortenbaugh, W. W., and P. Steinmetz. 1989. *Cicero's Knowledge of the Peripatos.* New Brunswick, N.J.

Fortenbaugh, W. W., et al., eds. 1992. *Theophrastus of Eresos: Sources for His Life, Writings, Thought, and Influence*. Pt. 1. Leiden.

Fraechter, K., ed. 1926. *Friedrich Ueberwegs Grundriss der Geschichte der Philosophie*. Vol. 1: *Die Philosophie des Altertums*. Basel.

Franklin, C. 2003. "To What Extent Did Posidonius and Theophanes Record Pompeian Ideology?" *Digressus Supplement*: 99–116.

Fraser, P. M. 1972. *Ptolemaic Alexandria*. 3 vols. Oxford.

———. 1994. "The World of Theophrastus." In S. Hornblower, ed., *Greek Historiography*, 167–91. Oxford.

Frazer, J. G. 1900. *Pausanias and Other Greek Sketches*. London.

———. 1913. *The Golden Bough: A Study in Magic and Religion*³. 12 vols. London.

———. 1921. *Apollodorus*. 2 vols. Loeb Classical Library. London and Cambridge, Mass.

Freeman, K. 1946. *The Pre-Socratic Philosophers: A Companion to Diels, Fragmente der Vorsokratiker*. Oxford.

Freudenthal, J. 1875. *Hellenistische Studien: Alexander Polyhistor und die von ihm erhaltenen Reste jüdäischer und samaritanischer Geschichtswerke*. Breslau.

Friedländer, M. 1903. *Geschichte der jüdischen Apologetik als Vorgeschichte des Christenthums*. Zurich.

Fritz, K. von. 1926. *Quellenuntersuchungen zur Leben und Philosophie des Diogenes von Sinope*. Leipzig.

———. 1940. *Pythagorean Politics in Southern Italy*. New York.

———. 1977. "Posidonius als Historiker." *Historiographia antiqua: Commentationes Lovanienses in honorem W. Permans septuagenarii editae*, 163–93. Leuven.

Fuchs, H. 1926. *Augustin und der antike Friedensgedanke*. Berlin.

Fuks, G. 2001. *A City of Many Seas: Askelon during the Hellenistic and Roman Periods*. Jerusalem. [In Hebrew]

Furley, D. 1987. *The Greek Cosmologies*. Cambridge.

Gabba, E. 1989. "The Growth of Anti-Judaism or the Greek Attitude towards the Jews." In W. D. Davies and L. Finkelstein, eds., *The Cambridge History of Judaism*, 2: 614–56. Cambridge.

Gager, J. G. 1972. *Moses in Greco-Roman Paganism*. Nashville.

———. 1983. *The Origins of Anti-Semitism: Attitudes toward Judaism in Pagan and Christian Antiquity*. New York.

Ganss, W. 1952. "Das Bild des Weisen bei Seneca." PhD diss., Freiburg, Switzerland.

Garlan, Y. 1974. *Recherches de poliorcétique grecque*. Paris.

Gatz, B. 1967. *Weltalter, goldene Zeit und sinnverwandte Vorstellungen*. Hildesheim.

Gauger, J. 1979. "Eine missverstandene Strabonstelle (zum Judenbericht XVI.2.37)." *Historia* 28: 211–24.

———. 1982. "Zitate in der jüdischen Apologetik und die Authentizität der Hekataios Passagen bei Flavius Josephus und im Ps. Aristeas Brief." *Journal of the Study of Judaism in the Persian, Hellenistic, and Roman Period* 13: 6–46.

Gauthier, H., and H. Sottas. 1925. *Un décret trilingue e l'honneur de Ptolémée IV*. Cairo.

Gauthier, R. A. 1951. *Magnanimité*. Paris.

Geffcken, J. 1907. *Zwei griechische Apologeten*. Leipzig and Berlin.

Geiger, A. 1857. *Urschrift und Übersetzung der Bibel*. Breslau.

Geiger, J. 1985. *Cornelius Nepos and Ancient Political Biography*. Stuttgart.

Gentili, B., and C. Prato. 1988. *Poetarum elegiacorum testimonia et fragmenta*[2]. Vol. 1. Leipzig.

Gerber, C. 1997. *Ein Bild des Judentums für Nichtjuden von Flavius Josephus: Untersuchungen zu seiner Schrift 'Contra Apionem'*. Leiden.

———. 1999. "Des Josephus Apologie für des Judentum: Prolegomena zu einer Interpretation von *Contra Apionem* 2. 145 ff." In J. U. Kalms and F. Siegert, eds., *Internationales Josephus-Kolloquium, Brüssel 1998*, 251–69. Münster.

———. 2001. "Die Bezeichnungen des Josephus für das jüdische Volk, inbesondere in *Contra Apionem*." In J. U. Kalms, ed., *Internationales Josephus-Kolloquium, Amsterdam 2000*, 135–43. Münster.

Gerlitz, P. 1954. *Das Fasten im Religions geschichtlichen Vergleich*. Erlangen.

Giannantoni, G. 1983–90. *Socratis et Socraticorum reliquiae*. 4 vols. Naples and Rome.

Giannini, A. 1966. *Paradoxographorum graecorum reliquiae*. Milan.

Gigon, O. 1935. *Untersuchungen zu Heraklit*. Leipzig.

———. 1959. "Cicero und Aristoteles." *Hermes* 87: 143–62.

———. 1962. *Vita Aristotelis Marciana*. Berlin.

———. 1967. "Der Historiker Poseidonios." In *Festgabe Hans von Greyarz*, 83–99. Bern.

———. 1972. *Studien zur antiken Philosophie*. New York.

———. 1980. "Poseidonios und die Geschichte der stoischen Philosophie." *Arkhaiognosia* 1: 261–99.

Ginsburg, M. S. 1934. "Sparta and Judaea." *Classical Philology* 29: 117–22.

Ginzberg, L. 1925–38. *The Legends of the Jews*. 7 vols. Philadelphia.

Giovannini, A. 1995. "Les origines de l'antijüdaïsme dans le monde grec." *Cahiers du Centre G. Glotz* 6: 41–60.

Glucker, J. 1993. "Augustiora." *Grazer Beiträge* 19: 51–101.

———. 1998. "Arieh Kasher's Translation and Commentary of Josephus' *Against Apion*." *Zion* 63: 89–123. [In Hebrew]

Glucker, J., and A. Laks. 1996. *Jacob Bernays: Un philologue juif*. Lille.

Goldschmidt, E. 1935–36. "Die Israel-Quellen bei Tacitus." *Der Morgen* 11: 175–78.

Goldstein, J. 1976. *I Maccabees: A New Translation with Introduction and Commentary*. New York.

Goldstein, N. W. 1935. "Cultivated Pagans and Ancient Anti-Semitics." *Journal of Religion* 19: 346–64.

Gomperz, H. 1912. *Sophistik und Rhetorik*. Leipzig and Berlin.

Gonda, J. 1970. *Visnuism and Sivaism: A Comparison*. London.

Goranson, S. 1994. "Posidonius: Strabo and Marcus Vipsanius Agrippa as Sources on Essenes." *Journal of Jewish Studies* 45: 294–98.

Gorman, P. 1983. "Pythagoras Palaestinus." *Philologus* 127: 30–42.

Gottschalk, H. B. 1980. *Heraclides of Pontus*. Oxford.

Gould, J. B. 1970. *The Philosophy of Chrysippus*. Leiden.

Gozzoli, S. 1978. "Ethnographia e politica in Agatharcide." *Athenaeum* 56: 54–79.

Graeser, A. 1975. *Zenon von Kition: Positionen und Probleme*. Berlin.

Graetz, H. 1872. "Ursprung der zwei Verläumdungen gegen das Judentum vom Eselskul-
     tus und von der Lieblosigkeit gegen Andersglaübige." *Monatschrift für Geschichte und
     Wissenschaft des Judentums* 21: 193–206.

———. 1888. *Geschichte der Judäer von dem Tode Juda Makhabis bis zum Untergange des
     jüdaischen Staates.*⁴ *Geschichte der Juden, III.2.* Leipzig.

Graham, A. J. 1962. *Colony and Mother City in Ancient Greece.* Manchester.

———. 1982. "The Colonial Expansion of Greece." *The Cambridge Ancient History*², 3:
     83–162. Cambridge.

———. 2001. *Collected Papers on Greek Colonization.* Leiden.

Grainger, J. D. 1990a. *The Cities of Seleucid Syria.* Oxford.

———. 1990b. *Seleucus Nikator: Constructing a Hellenistic Kingdom.* London.

Grant, R. M. 1980. "Dietary Laws among Pythagoreans, Jews, and Christians." *Harvard
     Theological Review* 73: 299–310.

Green, P. 1990. *Alexander to Actium: An Essay on the Historical Evolution of the Hellenistic
     Age.* Berkeley.

Griffin, M. T. 1976. *Seneca: A Philosopher in Politics.* Oxford.

Griffiths, J. G. 1948a. "Diodorus Siculus and the Myth of Osiris." *Man* 40: 83–84.

———. 1948b. "Human Sacrifice in Egypt: The Classical Evidence." *Annales du Service des
     Antiquités de l'Egypte (Le Caire)* 48: 409–23.

———. 1960a. *The Conflict of Horus and Seth.* Liverpool.

———. 1960b. "The Flight of the Gods before Typhon: An Unrecognized Myth." *Hermes*
     88: 374–76.

———. 1966. *The Origins of Osiris.* Berlin.

———. 1970. *Plutarch, De Iside et Osiride.* Swansea.

———. 1976. Review of *Diodorus Siculus,* Book I, by A. Burton. *Classical Review* 26:
     122–23.

Grodzynski, D. 1974. "Superstitio." *Revue des Études Anciennes* 76: 36–60.

Grönbech, W. 1977. *Kultur und Religion der Germanen.* Darmstadt.

Gross, R. L. 1992. *The Sadhus of India: A Study of Hindu Asceticism.* Jaipur and New Delhi.

Gruen, E. 1984. *The Hellenistic World and the Coming of Rome.* 2 vols. Berkeley.

———. 1998. *Heritage and Hellenism: The Reinvention of Jewish Tradition.* Berkeley and
     Los Angeles.

———. 2002. *Diaspora: Jews amidst Greeks and Romans.* Cambridge, Mass.

———. 2005. "Greeks and Jews: Mutual Misconceptions in Josephus' 'Contra Apionem.'"
     In C. Bakhus, ed., *Ancient Judaism in Its Hellenistic Context,* 32–51. Leiden.

Güngerich, R. 1927. *Dionysii Byzantii Anaplus Bospori.* Berlin.

———. 1950. *Die Küstenbeschreibung in der griechische Literatur.* Münster.

Gutas, D. 1985. "The Life, Works, and Sayings of Theophrastus in the Arabic Tradition." In
     W. W. Fortenbaugh et al., eds., *Theophrastus of Eresus: On His Life and Work,* 2: 63–102.
     New Brunswick, N.J.

Guthrie, W. K. C. 1952. *Orpheus and Greek Religion*². London.

———. 1965–81. *A History of Greek Philosophy.* 6 vols. Cambridge.

Gutschmid, A., von. 1882. "Trogus und Timagenes." *Rheinisches Museum* 37: 548–55.

———. 1891. "Timagenes und Trogus." *Rheinisches Museum* 46: 465–79.

———. 1893. *Kleine Schriften*. Vol. 4. Leipzig.

Guttmann, Y. 1929. "An Antisemitic Slander from the End of the Second Temple Period." In *Memorial Book for Y. N. Simhoni*, 181–85. Berlin. [In Hebrew]

———. 1946. "Theophrastus on the Sacrifices in Israel." *Tarbiẓ* 17: 155–65. [In Hebrew]

Habicht, C. 1975. "Hellenismus und Judentum in der Zeit des Judas Maccabäus." *Heidelberger Akademie der Wissenschaften für das Jahr 1974*: 97–110.

———. 1985. *Pausanias' Guide to Ancient Greece*. Berkeley.

Hägg, T. 1975. *Photios als Vermittler antiker Literatur*. Stockholm.

Hahm, E. D. 1989. "Posidonius's Theory of Historical Causation." In *Aufstieg und Niedergang der römischen Welt*, II, vol. 36. 3: 1324–36. Berlin.

Halévy, J. 1903. "Le culte d'une tàte d'âne." *Revue Semitique* 11: 154–64.

Hamilton, R. H. 1961. "Cleitarchus and Aristobulus." *Historia* 10: 448–58.

Hansen, G. C. 1965. "Alexander und die Brahmanen." *Klio* 43/45: 351–80.

———. 2000. "Der Judenexkurs des Hekataios und die Folgen." In J. V. Kalms, ed., *Internationales Josephus-Kolloquium, Aarhus 1999*, 11–21. Münster.

Harmatta, J. 1971. "Poseidonios über die römische Urgeschichte." *Acta Classica Universitatis Scientiarum Debreceniensis* 7: 21–25.

Harris, M. 1977. *Cannibals and Kings: The Origins of Cultures*. New York.

———. 1985. *The Sacred Cow and the Abominable Pig*. New York.

Harrison, J. E. 1922. *Prolegomena to the Study of Greek Religion*³. Cambridge.

Hartlich, P. 1898. "De exhortationum a Graecis Romanisque scriptorum historia." *Leipzige Studien* 9: 209–30.

Hartsuiker, D. 1993. *Sadhus: India's Mystic Holy Men*. Rochester.

Haussleiter, J. 1935. *Der Vegetarismus in der Antike*. Berlin.

Havet, E. 1873. *Mémoire sur la date des écrits qui portent les noms de Bérose et de Manéthon*. Paris.

Hecker, M. 1956. "Water Supply of Jerusalem in Ancient Times." In M. Avi-Yonah, ed., *The Book of Jerusalem*, 191–220. Jerusalem. [In Hebrew]

Heinemann, I. 1919. "Poseidonios über die Entwicklung der jüdischen Religion." *Monatschrift für Geschichte und Wissenschaft des Judentums* 63: 113–21.

———. 1921–28. *Poseidonios' metaphysische Schriften*. 2 vols. Breslau.

———. 1939. "Judaism in the Eyes of the Ancient World." *Zion* 4: 269–93. [In Hebrew]

———. 1939/40. "The Attitude of the Ancient World toward Judaism." *Review of Religion* 4: 385–400.

———. 1954. "Anthropomorphism." *Biblical Encyclopaedia*, 2: cols. 785–87. Jerusalem. [In Hebrew]

Heinze, R. 1910. "Tertullians Apologeticum." *Bericht über die Verhandlungen d. Kön. Sächs. Ges. d. Wiss. zu Leipzig, Phil.-hist. Kl.* 62: 281–310.

Hengel, M. 1973. *Judentum und Hellenismus*². Tübingen.

———. 1976. *Juden, Griechen und Barbaren*. Stuttgart.

Henry, R. 1959–77. *Photius, Bibliothèque*. 8 vols. Paris.

Henten, J. W. van, and R. Abush. 1996. "The Jews as Typhonians and Josephus' Strategy of Refutation in *Contra Apionem*." In L. H. Feldman and J. R. Levison, eds., *Josephus'*

Contra Apionem: Studies in Its Character and Context with a Latin Concordance to the Portion Missing in Greek, 271–309. Leiden.

Hermann, C. F. 1902. *Platonis Dialogi secundum Thrasylli Tetralogias dispositi*. Vol. 6. Leipzig.

Herr, M. D. 1961. "The Problem of War on the Sabbath in the Second Temple and the Talmudic Period." *Tarbiẓ* 30: 242–56, 341–56. [In Hebrew]

Herschensteiner, J. 1962. *Kosmos, quellenkritische Untersuchungen zu der Vorsokratiker*. Munich.

Hobson, A. 1999. *Renaissance Book Collecting: Jean Gralier and Diego Hurtado de Mendoza, their Books and their Bindings*. Cambridge.

Hogg, G. 1958. *Cannibalism and Human Sacrifice*. London.

Höistad, R. 1948. *Cynic Hero and Cynic King*. Uppsala.

Holladay, C. R. 1977. *Theios Aner in Hellenistic Judaism*. Missoula.

———. 1983–96. *Fragments from Hellenistic Jewish Authors*. 4 vols. Atlanta.

Hölscher, G. 1904. *Die Quellen des Josephus für die Zeit von Exil bis zum jüdischen Kriege*. Leipzig.

Hopfner, T. 1940–41. *Plutarch, Über Isis und Osiris*. 2 vols. Prague.

Hornblower, J. 1981. *Hieronymus of Cardia*. Oxford.

Horowitz, M. C. 1974. "The Stoic Synthesis of the Idea of Natural Law in Man: Four Themes." *Journal of the History of Ideas* 35: 3–16.

Horsley, R. A. 1978. "The Law of Nature in Philo and Cicero." *Harvard Theological Review* 71: 35–59.

Horst, P. W. van der. 1984. *Chaeremon: Egyptian Priest and Stoic Philosopher*. Leiden.

———. 2002. *Japeth in the Tents of Shem*. Leuven.

Houghton, A. 1983. *Coins of the Seleucid Empire from the Collection of Arthur Houghton*. New York.

How, W. W. 1970. "Cicero's Ideal in his De Republica." *Journal of Roman Studies* 20: 24–42.

Hudson, J. 1720. ΦΛΑΒΙΟΥ ΙΩΣΗΠΟΥ ΕΥΡΙΣΚΟΜΕΝΑ. 2 vols. London.

Hughes, D. D. 1991. *Human Sacrifice in Ancient Greece*. London.

Huntingford, G. W. B. 1980. *The Periplus of the Erythraean Sea*. London.

Huss, W. 2001. *Ägypten in hellenisticher Zeit, 332–30 v. Chr.* Munich.

Ionsius, H. 1781. *De scriptoribus historiae philosophicae*. Jena.

Isaac, B. 2004. *The Invention of Racism in Classical Antiquity*. Princeton.

Isaac, J. 1956. *Genèse de l'antisémitisme: Essai historique*. Paris.

Jacobson, H. 1976. "Hermippus, Pythagoras, and the Jews." *Revue des Études Juives* 135: 145–49.

———. 2006 "Artapanus Judaeus." *Journal of Jewish Studies* 57: 210–21.

Jacoby, A. 1926. "Der angebliche Eselskult der Juden und Christen." *Archiv für Religionswissenschaft* 24: 265–82.

Jacoby, F. 1909. "Über die Entwicklung der griechischen Historiographie und den Plan einer neuen Sammlung der griechischen Historiker-Fragmente." *Klio* 9: 80–123.

Jaeger, W. 1934. *Aristotle: Fundamentals of the History of His Development*. Oxford.

———. 1938a. *Diokles von Karystos*. Berlin.

———. 1938b. "Greeks and Jews: The First Greek Records of Jewish Religion and Civilization." *Journal of Religion* 18: 127–43.

———. 1947. *Theology of the Early Greek Philosophers.* Oxford.

Japhet, S. 1977. *The Ideology of the Book of Chronicles and Its Place in Biblical Thought.* Jerusalem. [In Hebrew]

Jebb, R. C. 1962. *The Attic Orators from Antiphon to Isaeus.* 2 vols. New York.

Jellicoe, S. 1968. *The Septuagint and Modern Study.* Oxford.

Jesi, F. 1958. "Rapport sur les recherches relatives à quelques figurations du sacrifice humain dans l'Égypte pharaonique." *Journal of Near Eastern Studies* 17: 194–203.

Johnson, S. R. 2004. *Historical Fiction and Hellenistic Jewish Identity: Third Maccabees in Its Cultural Context.* Berkeley and Los Angeles.

Jones, H. L. 1917–32. *The Geography of Strabo.* 7 vols. Loeb Classical Library. Cambridge, Mass.

Jones, R. M. 1926. "Posidonius and the Flight of the Mind through the Universe." *Classical Philology* 18: 202–28.

———. 1932. "Posidonius and Solar Eschatology." *Classical Philology* 28: 113–35.

de Jonge, A. 1997. *Traditions of the Magi.* Leiden.

Juster, J. 1913. *Les juifs dans l'empire romain, leur condition juridique, économique et sociale.* 2 vols. Paris.

Kalota, R. S. 1978. *India as Described by Megasthenes.* Delhi.

Kaplony-Heckel, U. 1983. "Das Dekret des spätern Königs Ptolemaios I Soter zugunsten der Götter von Butto (Satrapenstele) 311 v. Chr." In O. Kaiser, ed., *Texte aus der Umwelt des Alten Testaments,* 1: 613–19. Gütersloh.

Karttunen, K. 1986. "Graeco-Indica: A Survey of Recent Work." *Arctos* 20: 73–86.

———. 1989. *India in Early Greek Literature.* Helsinki.

———. 1997. *India in the Hellenistic World.* Helsinki.

Kasher, A. 1974. "The Propaganda Purposes of Manetho's Libellous Story about the Base Origin of the Jews." In B. Oded, U. Rappaport, et al., eds., *Studies in the History of the Jewish People and the Land of Israel,* 3: 69–84. Haifa. [In Hebrew]

———. 1985. *The Jews in Hellenistic and Roman Egypt: The Struggle for Equal Rights.* Tübingen.

———. 1986. *Jews, Idumaeans, and Ancient Arabs.* Tübingen.

———. 1996. *Against Apion: A New Hebrew Translation with Introduction and Commentary.* Jerusalem. [In Hebrew]

———. 2003. "The Footsteps of 'Counter History' in Manetho's Version of the Exodus." In A. Oppenheimer and M. Mor, eds., *Jews and Gentiles in the Holy Land in the Days of the Second Temple, the Mishnah, and the Talmud,* 1: 52–82. Jerusalem. [In Hebrew]

Katz, J. 1980. *From Prejudice to Destruction: Anti-Semitism, 1700–1933.* Cambridge, Mass.

Kaufmann, I. 1937–60. *History of the Israelite Religion.* 4 vols. Jerusalem. [In Hebrew]

Kearns, E. 1990. "Saving the City." In O. Murray and S. Price, eds., *The Greek City from Homer to Alexander,* 323–44. Oxford.

Keil, H. 1874. *Grammatici latini.* Vol. 4. Leipzig.

Keller, G. A. 1946. "Eratosthenes von Kyrene und die Sterndichtung." PhD diss., Zurich University.

Kennedy, G. 1963. *The Art of Persuasion in Greece*. Princeton.

———. 1994. *A New History of Classical Rhetoric*. Princeton.

Kern, O. 1922. *Orphicarum fragmenta*. Berlin.

Kessels, A. H. M. 1969. "Ancient Classification of Dreams." *Mnemosyne* 22: 389–424.

Keuls, E. 1970. "The Ass in the Cult of Dionysus as a Symbol of Toil and Suffering." *Anthropological Journal of Canada* 8.1: 26–46.

Keydell, R. 1956. "Martin, Arati Phaenomena." *Gnomon* 30: 575–81. (Review)

Kidd, I. G. 1997. *Aratus, Phaenomena: Translation and Commentary*. Cambridge.

Kienitz, F. K. 1953. *Die politische Geschichte Ägyptens vor 7. bis zum 4. Jahrhundert von der Zeitwende*. Berlin.

Kirfel, W. 1920. *Die Kosmographie der Inder nach Quellen dargestellt*. Bonn and Leipzig.

Kirk, G. S., J. E. Raven, and M. Schofield. 1983. *The Presocratic Philosophers*². Cambridge.

Kister, M. 1998. "A Common Heritage: Biblical Interpretation at Qumran and Its Implications." In M. E. Stone and E. G. Chazon, eds., *Proceedings of the First International Symposium of the Orion Center for the Study of the Dead Sea Scrolls*, 101–11. Leiden.

Kleingüntler, A. 1933. ΠΡΩΤΟΣ ΕΥΡΕΤΗΣ, *Untersuchungen zur Geschichte einer Fragestellung*. Leipzig.

Kochman, M. 1981. "Status and Extent of Judah in the Persian Period." PhD diss., The Hebrew University, Jerusalem.

Koets, P. J. 1924. Δεισιδαιμονία: *A Contribution to the Knowledge of the Religious Terminology in Greek*. Utrecht.

Koster, W. J. W. 1951. *Le mythe de Platon, de Zarathoustra et des Chaldéens: Étude critique sur les relations intellectuels entre Platon et l'Orient*. Leiden.

Kraemaer, R. S. 1993. "Jewish Mothers and Daughters in the Greco-Roman World." In S. J. D. Cohen, ed., *The Jewish Family in Antiquity*, 89–112. Atlanta.

Kramer, G. 1844. *Strabonis Geographica*. Berlin.

Krappe, A. H. 1947. "Ἀπόλλων Ὄνος. *Classical Philology* 42: 223–34.

Kromayer, J., and G. Veith. 1903–32. *Antike Schlachtfelder*. 5 vols. Berlin.

———. 1928. *Heerwesen und Kriegführung der Griechen und Römer*. Munich.

Labhardt, T. 1881. "Quae de Iudaeorum origine iudicaverint veteres." PhD diss., Augsburg University.

Labow, D. 2005. *Flavius Josephus Contra Apionem, Buch I*. Stuttgart.

Lafargue, M. 1985. "Orphica (Second Century B.C.–First Century A.D.)." In J. H. Charlesworth, ed., *The Old Testament Pseudepigrapha*, 2: 795–80. New York.

Laffranque, M. 1964. *Poseidonios d'Apamée*. Paris.

Landau, Y. H. 1961. "A Greek Inscription from Acre." *Israel Exploration Journal* 11: 118–26.

de Lange, W. 1976. *Origen and the Jews: Studies in Jewish-Christian Relations in Third-Century Palestine*. Cambridge.

———. 1991. "The Origins of Anti-Semitism: Ancient Evidence and Modern Interpretations." In S. L. Gilman and S. T. Katz, eds., *Anti-Semitism in Times of Crisis*, 21–37. New York.

Laqueur, R. 1911. "Ephoros." *Hermes* 46: 161–206, 321–54.

Lasserre, F. 1966. *Die Fragmente des Eudoxos von Knidos*. Berlin.

Latte, K. 1960. *Römische Religionsgeschichte*. Munich.

Launey, M. 1949–50. *Recherches sur les armées hellenistiques*. 2 vols. Paris.

Lebhardt, T. 1881. *Quae de Iudaeorum origine iudicaverint veteres*. Augsburg.

Lebram, J. C. H. 1974. "Der Idealstaat der Juden." In O. Betz et al., eds., *Josephus Studien: Untersuchungen zu Josephus, dem antiken Judentum und dem Neuen Testamentum, O. Michel zum 70. Gebrutstag gewidmet*, 233–53. Göttingen.

Leipoldt, J. 1933. *Antisemitismus in der alten Welt*. Leipzig.

Leo, F. 1901. *Die griechisch-römische Biographie nach ihrer literarischen Form*. Leipzig.

Leopoldi, H. 1892. *De Agatharcide Cnidio*. Rostock.

Leschhorn, W. 1984. *Gründer der Staat: Studien zu einen politisch-religiosen Phenomen der griechischen Geschichte*. Stuttgart.

Lévy, I. 1927. *Recherches sur les sources de la légende de Pythagore*. Paris.

Lewis, D. M. 1957. "The First Greek Jew." *Journal of Semitic Studies* 2: 264–66.

Lewy, H. (= J.). 1938. "Aristotle and the Jewish Sage according to Clearchus of Soli." *Harvard Theological Review* 31: 205–35.

Lewy, J. 1960. *Studies in Jewish Hellenism*. Jerusalem. [In Hebrew]

Licht, J. 1957. *The Thanksgiving Scroll*. Jerusalem. [In Hebrew]

Lieberman, S. 1934. *Hayerusalmi Kiphshuto*. Vol. 1. Jerusalem. [In Hebrew]

———. 1962. *Hellenism in Jewish Palestine²*. New York.

———. 1965. *Greek in Jewish Palestine²*. New York.

Liebersohn, Y. Z. 2001. "The Dispute Concerning Rhetoric in Hellenistic Thought and Its Background." PhD diss., Bar-Ilan University,, Ramat Gan. [In Hebrew]

Liebes, Y. 2000. *Ars poetica of Sefer Jetsira*. Jerusalem.

———. 2001/2. "'A Greek Contribution to the Faith of Abraham': A Response to B. Bar-Kochva (*Tarbiẓ* 70 [2001] pp. 327–352)." *Tarbiẓ* 71: 249–64. [In Hebrew]

Lilla, S. R. C. 1971. *Clement of Alexandria: A Study in Christian Platonism and Gnosticism*. Oxford.

Lippold, H. 1950. *Die griechische Plastik*. Munich.

Liver, J. 1959. "King, Kingship." *Encyclopaedia Biblica* 4: 1085–1112. Jerusalem. [In Hebrew]

Lloyd, A. B. 1974. Review of *Diodorus Siculus, Book I*, by A. Burton. *Journal of Egyptian Archeology* 60: 287–88.

———. 1976. *Herodotus, Book II*. 3 vols. Leiden.

Loeb, E. M. 1927. *The Blood Sacrifice Complex*. New York.

Loewenstamm, S. A. 1987. *The Tradition of the Exodus and Its Development*. Jerusalem. [In Hebrew]

Long, A. A. 1976. "L. Edelstein, I. G. Kidd: Posidonius." *Classical Review* 26: 72–75. (Review)

Long, A. A., and D. N. Sedley. 1987. *The Hellenistic Philosophers*. 2 vols. Cambridge.

Lorberbaum, Y. 2000. "'The Doctrine of Corporeality of God Did Not Occur Even for a Single Day to the Sages, May Their Memory Be Blessed' (*The Guide of the Perplexed* I. 46): Anthropomorphism in Early Rabbinic Literature—A Critical Review of Scholarly Research." *Jewish Studies, Journal of the World Union of Jewish Studies* 40: 3–54. [In Hebrew]

———. 2004. *Image of God: Halakhah and Agada*. Jerusalem. [In Hebrew]

Lovejoy, A. O., and G. Boas. 1935. *Primitivism and Related Ideas in Antiquity*. Baltimore.

Ludlam, I. 1997. "Antipater of Tarsus: A Critical Edition of the Fragments and Testimonia with a Commentary." PhD diss., Tel Aviv University.

———. 2003. "Two Long-Running Stoic Myths: A Centralized Orthodox Stoic School and Stoic Scholarchs." *Elenchos* 24: 33–55.

Luria, S. 1923. *Antisemitismus in der alten Welt.* Berlin.

———. 1926. "Die ägyptische Bibel (Joseph -und Mosesage)." *Zeitschrift für die Altestamentliche Wissenschaft* 33: 94–135.

Luz, M. 1980. "The Spurious Platonic Dialogues: A Study of Their Historical and Philosophical Background." PhD diss., The Hebrew University, Jerusalem. [In Hebrew]

———. 1982. "Clearchus of Soli as a Source of Eleazar's Deuterosis." In U. Rappaport, ed., *Josephus Flavius, Historian of Eretz-Israel in the Hellenistic-Roman Period,* 79–90. Jerusalem.

Lynch, J. P. 1972. *Aristotle's School: A Study of Greek Educational Institutions.* Berkeley.

Madvig, J. N. 1871. *Adversaria critica.* Copenhagen.

Malitz, J. 1983. *Die Historien des Poseidonios.* Munich.

Mansfeld, J. 1986. "Aristotle, Plato, and the Preplatonic Doxography and Chronology." In G. Cambiano, ed., *Storiografia e dossografia nella filosofia antica,* 1–59. Turin.

———. 1990. "Doxography and Dialectics: The *Sitz im Leben* of the 'Placita'." In H. Temporini and W. Haase, eds., *Aufstieg und Niedergang der römischen Welt,* II, vol. 36. 4: 3056–229. Berlin.

———. 1992. "*Physikai doxai* and *Problemata physika* from Aristotle to Aëtius (and Beyond)." In W. W. Fortenbaugh and D. Gutas, eds., *Theophrastus: His Psychological, Doxographical, and Scientific Writings,* 63–111. New Brunswick, N.J.

Marcovich, M. 1964. "Pythagorica." *Philologus* 108: 29–44.

———. 1978. *Eraclito frammenti.* Florence.

———. 1990. *Pseudo-Iustinus, Cohortatio ad graecos.* Berlin.

———. 1991. "Posidonius. Vol. I: The Fragments. Ed. by L. Edelstein and I. G. Kidd." *Gnomon* 63: 736–37. (Review)

———. 2001. *Origenes, Contra Celsum, Libri viii.* Leiden.

Marcus, R. 1943. *Josephus, Jewish Antiquities, Books XII–XIV.* Loeb Classical Library. Cambridge, Mass.

———. 1946. "Antisemitism in the Hellenistic Roman World." In K. S. Pinson, *Essays on Antisemitism*², 61–78. New York.

Marmorstein, A. 1927. *The Old Rabbinic Doctrine of God.* New York.

Marsden, E. W. 1969–71. *Greek and Roman Artillery.* 2 vols. Oxford.

Martin, D. 1997. "Hellenistic Superstition: The Problems of Defining a Vice." In Per Bilde et al., eds., *Conventional Views of the Hellenistic Greeks,* 136–61. Aarhus.

———. 2004. *Inventing Superstition: From the Hippocratics to the Christians.* Cambridge, Mass.

Martin, J. 1956. *Histoire du texte des Phénomènes Aratos.* Paris.

Martin, V. 1959. "Un recueil de diatribes cyniques: Pap. Genev. inv. 271." *Museum Helveticum* 16: 77–115.

Matthes, D. 1958. "Hermagoras of Temnos." *Lustrum* 3: 58–214.

Maurach, G. 1975. *Seneca als Philosoph.* Darmstadt.

McDougall, J. I. 1983. *Lexicon in Diodorus Siculus*. Hildesheim.

Meek, C. K. 1931. *Tribal Studies in Northern Nigeria*. Vol. 2. London.

Mehl, A. 1986. *Seleukos Nikator und sein Reich*. Leuven.

Mehler, A. 1846. *Mnaseae Patarensis Fragmenta*. Leiden.

Meineke, A. 1852. *Strabonis Geographica*. Leipzig.

Meiners, C. 1716. *Geschichte des Ursprungs, Fortgangs und Verfalls der Wissenschaften in Griechenland und Rom*. Lemgo.

Meiser, M. 1998. *Die Reaktion des Volkes auf Jesus*. Berlin.

Mélèze-Modrzejewski, J. 1981. "Sur l'antisémitisme païen." In M. Olender, ed., *Le racisme, mythes et sciences, pour Léon Poliakov*, 411–39. Brussels.

———. 1989. "The Image of the Jew in the Greek Thinkings." In A. Kasher, G. Fuks, and U. Rappaport, eds., *Greece and Rome in Eretz Israel*, 3–14. Jerusalem. [In Hebrew]

Menching, G. 1926. *Das heilige Schweigen*. Berlin.

Mendels, D. 1983. "Hecataeus of Abdera and a Jewish 'patrios politeia' of the Persian Period (Diodorus Siculus XL, 3)." *Zeitschrift für die Alttestamentliche Wissenschaft* 95: 94–110.

———. 1986. "Greek and Roman History in the Bibliotheca of Photius—A Note." *Byzantion* 56: 196–206.

———. 1990. "The Polemical Character of Manetho's *Aegyptiaca*." *Studia Hellenistica* 30: 91–110.

———. 1992. *The Rise and Fall of Jewish Nationalism*. New York.

———. 1998. *Identity, Religion, and Historiography: Studies in Hellenistic History*. Sheffield.

Mengis, K. 1920. *Die schriftstellerische Technik im Sophistenmahl des Athenaios*. Paderborn.

Meshorer, Y. 1982. *Ancient Jewish Coins*. Vol. 1. New York.

———. 1995. "The Coins of the Hasmoneans." In D. Amit and H. Eshel, eds., *The Times of the Hasmonean House*, 197–209. Jerusalem. [In Hebrew]

———. 1997. *The Treasury of Jewish Coins*. Jerusalem.

Meuli, K. 1946. "Griechische Opferbräuche." In *Phyllobolia für Peter von der Mühll zum 60 Geburtstag*, 185–288. Basel.

Meyer, E. 1904. *Aegyptische Chronologie*. Berlin.

———. 1921–23. *Ursprung und Anfänge des Christentums*. 3 vols. Stuttgartand Berlin.

———. 1928. "Gottesstaat, Militärherrschaft und Ständewesen in Ägypten." *Sitzungsberichte der preussischen Akademie der Wissenschaften, Phil.-hist. Kl.* 28: 495–532.

Meyer, R. 1963. "Elia und Ahab." In M. Hengel et al., eds., *Abraham unser Vater: Festschrift O. Michel*, 356–68. Tübingen.

Miller, W. 1913. *Cicero, De officiis*. Loeb Classical Library. London and Cambridge, Mass.

Milne, J. S. 1907. *Surgical Instruments in Greek and Roman Times*. Oxford.

Minar, E. L. 1942. *Early Pythagorean Politics in Practice and Theory*. Baltimore.

Mithardy, D. C. 2000. "Dicaearchus of Messana: The Sources, Text, and Translation." In W. W. Fortenbaugh and E. Schütrampf, eds., *Dicaearchus of Messana*, 3–123. New Brunswick, N.J., and London.

Mizugaki, W. 1987. "Origen in Josephus." In L. H. Feldman and G. Hata, eds., *Josephus, Judaism, and Christianity*, 325–37. Detroit.

Molland, E. 1936. "Clement of Alexandria on the Origins of Greek Philosophy." *Symbolae Osloensis* 15/16: 57–85.

Momigliano, A. 1934. "Livio, Plutarcho e Giustino su virtu e fortuna dei Romani; Contributo della riconstruzione della fonte di Trogo Pompeo." *Athenaeum* 12: 45–56.

———. 1935. "La storia di Eforo e le Elleniche di Teopompo." *Rivista di Filologia e di Istruzione Classica* 63: 180–204.

———. 1975. *Alien Wisdom: The Limits of Hellenization.* Cambridge.

———. 1976. "Ebrei e greci." *Rivista Storia Italiana* 88: 425–43.

———. 1993. *The Development of Greek Biography.* Cambridge, Mass.

Moraux, P. 1956. *Les listes anciennes des ouvrages d'Aristote.* Leuven.

———. 1973. *Der Aristotelismus bei dem Griechen.* Vol. 1. Berlin.

Moreau, J. 1964. *Scripta minora.* Heidelberg.

Morr, J. 1926. "Die Landeskunde von Palästina bei Strabon und Iosephus." *Philologus* 71: 256–80.

Movers, F. E. 1841. *Die Phönizer.* Bonn.

Mras, K. 1944. "Ein Vorwort zu neuen Eusebius-Ausgabe." *Rheinisches Museum* 92: 217–36.

———. 1982. *Eusebius Werke².* Vol. 8. 1: *Die Praeparatio Evangelica.* Berlin.

von der Mühll, M. 1942. "Antiker Historismus in Plutarchs Biographie des Solon." *Klio* 35: 89–102.

Müller, C., and T. Müller. 1841–70. *Fragmenta historicorum graecorum.* 4 vols. Paris.

Müller, J. G. 1877. *Des Flavius Josephus Schrift gegen den Apion.* Basel.

Müller, K. E. 1972–80. *Geschichte der antiken Ethnographie und ethnologischen Theoriebildung.* 2 vols. Wiesbaden.

Munz, R. 1929. *Posdeidonios und Strabon.* Göttingen.

Münzer, F. 1900. "Guilelmus Witte, *De Nicolai Damascenai Fragmentorum Romanorum fontibus.*" *Deutsche Litteraturzeitung* 46 (XXI Jahrgang): 2983–84. (Review)

Murray, O. 1970. "Hecataeus of Abdera and Pharaonic Kingship." *Journal of Egyptian Archeology* 56: 141–71.

———. 1972. "Herodotus and Hellenistic Culture." *Classical Quarterly* 22: 200–213.

———. 1973. "The Date of Hecataeus' Work on Egypt." *Journal of Egyptian Archeology* 59: 163–68.

Naber, S. A. 1896. *Flavii Iosephi, Opera omnia (post Immanuelem Bekkerem).* Vol. 6. Leipzig.

Nauck, A. 1886. *Porphyrii philosophi platonici opuscula selecta.* Leipzig.

———. 1964. *Tragicorum graecorum fragmenta.* Suppl., B. Snell. Hildesheim.

Naveh, J. 1996. "On Jewish Books of Magic Recipes in Antiquity." In I. M. Gafni et al., eds., *The Jews in the Hellenistic-Roman World: Studies in Memory of Menahem Stern,* 453–66. Jerusalem. [In Hebrew]

Nebel, G. 1939. "Zur Ethik des Poseidonios." *Hermes* 74: 34–57.

Neher-Bernheim, R. 1963. "The Libel of Jewish Ass-Worship." *Zion* 28: 106–16. [In Hebrew]

Nestle, E. 1907. "Miscellen." *Zeitschrift für die Alttestamentliche Wissenschaft* 27: 111–21.

Nestle, W. 1938. *Der Friedensgedanke in der antiken Welt.* Philologus, Suppl. 31, Heft I. Berlin.

Newell, E. T. 1939. *Late Seleucid Mints in Ake-Ptolemais and Damascus.* New York.

Niehues-Pröbsting, H. 1979. *Der Kynismus des Diogenes und der Begriff des Kynismus.* Munich.

Nikiprowetzky, V. 1984. "'Moyses palpans ve liniens': On Some Explanations of the Name of Moses in Philo of Alexandria." In F.E. Greenspahn et al., eds., *Nourished With Peace: Studies in Hellenistic Judaism in Memory of Samuel Sandmel,* 117–47. Chico, Calif.

Nilsson, M.P. 1906. *Griechische Feste von Religiöser Bedeutung.* Stuttgart.

———. 1955. *Geschichte der griechischen Religion².* Munich.

Noam, V. 2003. *Megillat Ta'anit: Versions, Interpretation, History.* Jerusalem. [In Hebrew]

Nock, A.D. 1944. "The Cult of Heroes." *The Harvard Theological Review* 37: 141–74 (= id., *Essays on Religion and the Ancient World* [Oxford, 1972] 2: 575–602).

———. 1959. "Posidonius." *Journal of Roman Studies* 49: 1–15 (= id., *Essays on Religion and the Ancient World* [Oxford, 1972] 2: 853–76).

Norden, E. 1921. "Jahve und Moses in hellenistischer Theologie." *Festgabe für A. von Harnack.* Tübingen: 292–301 (= id., *Kleine Schriften zum klassischen Altertum* [Berlin, 1966] 276–85).

———. 1923a. *Die antike Kunstprosa⁴.* Leipzig-Berlin.

———. 1923b. *Der germanische Geschichte in Tacitus Germania³.* Stuttgart.

North, H. 1966. *Sophrosyne: Self-Knowledge and Self-Restraint in Greek Literature.* Ithaca.

Norvin, W., ed. 1913. "Olympiodori philosophi in Platonis Phaedonem commentaria." PhD diss., Leipzig University.

Nussbaum, M. 1875. "Observationes in Flavii Josephi antiquitates lib. XII.3–XIII.14." PhD diss., Marburg University.

Obbink, D. 1988. "The Origin of Greek Sacrifice: Theophrastus on Religion and Cultural History." In W.W. Fortenbaugh and R.W. Sharples, *Theophrastean Studies,* 272–95. New Brunswick, N.J.

Oldfather, W.A. 1925. *Epictetus.* 2 vols. Loeb Classical Library. London and Cambridge, Mass.

———. 1933. *Diodorus of Sicily.* Vol. 1. Loeb Classical Library. London and Cambridge, Mass.

Olivieri, A. 1897. *Pseudo-Eratosthenis Catasterismi: Mythographi graeci* 3 (1). Leipzig.

Olshausen, E. 1974. *Prosopographie der hellenistischen Königsgesandten.* Vol. 1. Löwen.

———. 1979. "Zur Frage ständiger Gesandtschaften in hellenistischer Zeit." In E. Olshausen, ed., *Antike Diplomatie,* 291–317. Darmstadt.

Olyan, S.M. 1988. *Asherah and the Cult of Yahweh in Israel.* Atlanta.

Ophuijsen, J.M. van, and M. van Raalte, M., eds. 1998. *Theophrastus: Reappraising the Sources.* Rutgers University Studies in Classical Humanities 7. New Brunswick, N.J., and London.

Oppenheim, A.L. 1956. "The Interpretation of Dreams in the Ancient Near East." *Transactions of the American Philological Association* 46.3.

Ostwald, M. 1996. "Peace and War in Plato and Aristotle." *Scripta Classica Israelica* 15: 100–118.

Owen, G.E.L. 1983. "Philosophical Invective." *Oxford Studies in Ancient Philosophy* 1: 1–25.

Page, D. L. 1934. *Actors' Interpolations in Greek Tragedy*. Oxford.

Pagnet, L. 1975. *Les cyniques grecs*. Ottawa.

Palm, J. 1955. *Über Sprache und Stil des Diodoros von Sizilien*. Lund.

Parker, R. A., and W. H. Dubberstein. 1956. *Babylonian Chronology 626 B.C.–A.D. 75*. Providence.

Paton, R. W. 1907. *Diodorus of Sicily*. Vol. 12. Loeb Classical Library. Cambridge, Mass.

Patterson, C. 1985. "'Not Worth the Rearing': The Causes of Infant Exposure in Ancient Greece." *Transactions and Proceedings of the American Philological Association* 115: 103–23.

Pearson, A. C. 1891. *The Fragments of Zeno and Cleanthes*. London.

———. 1917. *The Fragments of Sophocles*. Cambridge.

———. 1923. *Sophocles Fabulae*. Oxford.

Pearson, L. 1960. *The Last Histories of Alexander the Great*. Oxford.

Pease, A. S. 1955. *De natura deorum liber primus*. Cambridge, Mass.

———. 1963. *M. Tulii Ciceronis, "De divinatione"*². Darmstadt (= id., *Illinois Studies in Language and Literature* 6 [1920]: 161–500; 8 [1923]: 153–474).

Pédech, P. 1964. *La méthode historique de Polybe*. Paris.

———. 1984. *Historiens campagnons d'Alexandre*. Paris.

Pellegrini, A. 1874. *D'una abraxa inedita*. Bergamo.

Perdrizet, P. 1910. "Le fragment de Satyros sur les Dèmes d'Alexandrie." *Revue des Études Anciennes* 12: 217–47.

Peremans, W. 1967. "Diodore de Sicile et Agatharcide de Cnide." *Historia* 16: 432–55.

Perl, J. 1990. *Tacitus: Germania*. Berlin.

Peters, J. P., and H. Tiersch. 1905. *Painted Tombs in the Necropolis of Marisa*. London.

Peters, P. 1865. *Die Quellen Plutarchs in den Biographieen der Römer*. Halle.

Pfeffer, F. 1976. *Studien zur Mantik in der Philosophie der Antike*. Meisenheim.

Pfeiffer, R. 1949–53. *Callimachus*. Oxford.

———. 1968. *A History of Classical Scholarship*. Oxford.

Pfister, F. 1961. "Das Alexander-Archiv und die hellenistisch-römische Wissenschaft." *Historia* 10: 30–67.

Pfligersdorffer, G. 1959. *Studien zu Poseidonios*. Vienna.

Philip, J. A. 1959. "The Biographical Tradition—Pythagoras." *Transactions of the American Philological Association* 90: 185–95.

———. 1966. *Pythagoras and Early Pythagoreanism*. Toronto.

Photiadès, P. 1959. "Les diatribes cyniques du papyrus de Genève 271, leurs traductions et élaborations successives." *Museum Helveticum* 16: 116–39.

Philhopfer, P. 1959. "The Biographical Tradition—Pythagoras." *Transactions of the American Philological Association* 90: 185–95.

———. 1990. *Presbyteron kreitton: Der Altersbeweis der jüdischer und christlichen Apologeten und seine Vorgeschichte*. Tübingen.

des Places, É. 1973. *Numénius, Fragments*. Collection Budé. Paris.

Platthy, J. 1968. *Sources on the Earliest Greek Libraries with the Testimonia*. Amsterdam.

Pohlenz, M. 1948. *Die Stoa*². Göttingen.

Poliakov, L. 1955. *Histoire de l'Antisémitisme*. Vol. 1: *Du Christ aux Juifs de cour*. Paris.

Porten, B. 1968. *Archives from Elephantine: The Life of an Ancient Jewish Military Colony.* Berkeley.

——. 1984. "The Jews in Egypt." *The Cambridge History of Judaism*, 1: 372–400.

Porten, B., and A. Yardeni. 1986–89. *Textbook of Aramaic Documents from Ancient Egypt.* Jerusalem.

Pötscher, W. 1964. *Theophrastos περὶ Εὐσεβείας.* Leiden.

Powell, J. W. 1925. *Collectanea Alexandrina.* Oxford.

Preuschen, E. 1903. *Mönchtum und Sarapiskult².* Giessen.

Pritchard, G. B. 1955. *Ancient Near Eastern Texts Relating to the Old Testament².* Princeton.

Pritchett, W. K. 1974–91. *The Greek State at War.* Berkeley and Los Angeles.

Pucci, M. 1983a. "The Jewish Revolt in the Time of Trajan." In M. Stern, ed., *Nation and History: Studies in the History of the Jewish People*, 125–40. Jerusalem. [In Hebrew]

——. 1983b. "On the Tendentiousness of Josephus' Historical Writing." In U. Rappaport, ed., *Josephus Flavius, Historian of Eretz Israel in the Hellenistic-Roman Period*, 117–30. Jerusalem. [In Hebrew]

——. 1993. "The Reliability of Josephus Flavius: The Case of Hecataeus and Manetho's Accounts of Jews and Judaism." *Journal for the Study of Judaism* 24: 215–34.

Pulleyn, S. 1997. *Prayer in Greek Religion.* Oxford.

Radin, M. 1915. *The Jews among the Greeks and Romans.* Philadelphia.

Radt, S. 1977. *Tragicorum graecorum fragmenta.* Vol. 4: *Sophocles.* Göttingen.

——. 1985. *Tragicorum graecorum fragmenta.* Vol. 3: *Aeschylus.* Göttingen.

Radtke, G. 1893. "De Lysimacho Alexandrino." PhD diss., Strassburg University.

Rajak, T. 1981. "Roman Intervention in a Seleucid Siege of Jerusalem?" *Greek, Roman, and Byzantine Studies* 22: 65–81.

——. 2001. *The Jewish Dialogue with Greece and Rome: Studies in Cultural and Social Interaction.* Leiden.

Ramsay, G. G. 1918. *Juvenal and Persius.* Loeb Classical Library. London and Cambridge, Mass.

Rappaport, U. 1967. "The Hellenistic Cities and the Judaization of Eretz Israel in the Hasmonaean Period." In ΔΩΡΟΝ, *sive commentationes de antiquitate classica, docto viro Benzioni Katz*, 219–30. Tel Aviv. [In Hebrew]

——. 1969. "Les Iduméens en Égypte." *Revue de Philologie* 43: 73–82.

——. 1983. "The Jews in Egypt." In M. Stern, ed., *The Diaspora in the Hellenistic-Roman World*, 21–53. Tel Aviv and Jerusalem. [In Hebrew]

——. 1986. "The Land Issue as a Factor in Inter-Ethnic Relations in Eretz-Israel during the Second Temple Period." In A. Kasher et al., eds., *Man and Land in Eretz Israel in Antiquity*, 80–86. Jerusalem. [In Hebrew]

——. 2004. *The First Book of Maccabees: Introduction, Hebrew Translation, and Commentary.* Jerusalem. [In Hebrew]

Reeg, G. 1985. *Die Geschichte von den Zehn Märtyrern.* Tübingen.

Reesor, M. E. 1951. *The Political Thought of the Old and Middle Stoa.* New York.

Reinach, T. 1895. *Textes d'auteurs grecs et latins relatifs au juifs et judaïsme.* Paris.

Reinach, T., and L. Blum. 1930. *Flavius Josèphe: Contre Apion.* Collection Budé. Paris.

Reinhardt, K. 1921. *Poseidonios.* Munich.

———. 1928. *Poseidonios über Ursprung und Entartung.* Heidelberg.

———. 1954. "Philosophy and History among the Greeks." *Greece and Rome* 1: 82–90.

Reitzenstein, R. 1901. *Zwei religionsgeschichtliche Fragen.* Strassburg.

Rengstorf, K. H., ed. 1973–83. *A Complete Concordance to Flavius Josephus.* Leiden.

Reuss, F. 1906. "Megasthenes." *Rheinisches Museum* 61: 304–5.

Reydams-Schils, G. 1999. *Demiurge and Providence: Stoic and Platonist Reading of Plato's Timaeus.* Turnhout.

Reynolds, L. D. 1965. *L. Annaei Seneca: Ad Lucilium, Epistulae morales.* Vol. 2. Oxford.

Reynolds, L. D., and N. G. Wilson. 1974. *Scribes and Scholars²*. Oxford.

Riginos, A. S. 1976. *Platonica: The Anecdotes Concerning the Life and Writings of Plato.* Leiden.

Rigway, D. 1999. "The Rehabilitation of Bochoris." *The Journal of Egyptian Archeology* 85: 143–52.

Rist, J. M. 1969. *Stoic Philosophy.* Cambridge.

———. 1978. *The Stoics.* Berkeley.

Rizzo, F. P. 1963. *Le fonti per la storia della conquista pompeiana della Siria.* Palermo.

Robert, C. 1878. *Eratosthenis Catasterismorum reliquiae.* Berlin. (Repr., 1963)

Robert, L. 1968. "De Delphes à l'Oxus: Inscriptions grecques nouvelles de la Bactriane." *Comptes Rendus de l'Académie des Inscriptions et Belles-Lettres*, 416–57 (= id., *Opera minora selecta: Epigraphie et antiquités grecques* [Amsterdam, 1989] 5: 510–51).

Rochemonteix, M., and E. Chassinat. 1897–34. *Le temple d'Edfou.* 14 vols. Paris and Cairo.

Roeder, G. 1959. *Die ägyptische Götterwelt.* Zurich and Stuttgart.

Rohde, E. 1871. "Die Quellen des Iamblicus in seiner Biographie des Pythagoras." *Rheinisches Museum* 26: 554–76.

———. 1907. *Psyche: Seelencult und Unsterblichkeitsglaube der Griechen⁴*. Tübingen.

de Romilly, J. 1977. *The Rise and Fall of States According to Greek Authors.* Ann Arbor.

Rösch, G. 1882. "Caput asinum: Eine historische Studie." *Theologische Studien und Kritiken* 55: 523–44.

Rose, V. 1863. *Aristoteles pseudepigraphus.* Leipzig.

———. 1886. *Aristotelis quae ferebantur librorum fragmenta.* Leipzig.

Rosenberg, A. 1921. *Einleitung und Quellenkunde zur römischen Geschichte.* Berlin.

Rosokoki, A. 1995. *Die Erigone des Eratosthenes.* Heidelberg.

Ross, W. D. 1888. *Aristotelis Fragmenta selecta.* Oxford.

Rubincam, C. 1976. "A Note on Oxyrhyncus Papyrus 1610." *Phoenix* 30: 357–66.

Rudberg, G. 1918. *Forschungen zu Poseidonios.* Uppsala and Leipzig.

Rudhardt, J. 1958. *Notions fondamentales de la pensée religieuse et actes constitutifs du culte dans la Grèce classique.* Paris.

Runia, D. T. 1993. *Philo in Early Christian Literature: A Survey.* Assen.

———. 1995. *Philo and the Church Fathers: A Collection of Papers.* Leiden.

Rutgers, L. V. 1995. "Attitudes to Judaism in the Greco-Roman Period: Reflections on Feldman's 'Jews and Gentiles in the Ancient World.'" *The Jewish Quarterly Review* 85: 1–35.

Sacks, K. S. 1990. *Diodorus Siculus and the First Century.* Princeton.

Sadakata, A. 1988. *Buddhist Cosmology: Philosophy and Origins.* Tokyo.

Safrai, Z. 2000. "The Conversion of the Newly Conquered Areas in Hasmonean Judea."

In J. Schwartz et al., eds., *Jerusalem and Eretz Israel, Arie Kindler Festschrift*: 70–88. [In Hebrew]

Sagan, E. 1974. *Cannibalism: Human Aggression and Cultural Form*. New York.

Saletore, B. A. 1958. *India's Diplomatic Relations with the West*. Bombay.

Salomone, E. 1973. *Fonti e valore storico di Pompeo Trogo (Iustin XXXVII.8.2.–XL)*. Genoa.

Sanday, P. 1986. *Divine Hunger: Cannibalism as a Cultural System*. Cambridge.

Sandbach, F. H. 1975. *The Stoics*. London.

———. 1985. *Aristotle and the Stoics*. Cambridge.

Sansone, D. 1997. "Hermippus, Fragment 22 Wehrli." *Illinois Classical Studies* 22: 51–64.

Saunders, T. J. 1966. *Greek and Roman Philosophy after Aristotle*. New York.

———. 2001. "Dicaearchus' Historical Anthropology." In W. W. Fortenbaugh and E. Schütrumpf, eds., *Dicaearchus of Messenia*, 237–54. New Brunswick, N.J.

Sayre, F. 1937. *Diogenes of Sinope*. Baltimore.

———. 1948. *The Greek Cynics*. Baltimore.

Schäfer, P. 1996. "The Exodus Tradition in Pagan Greco-Roman Literature." In I. M. Gafni et al., eds., *The Jews in the Hellenistic-Roman World: Studies in Memory of Menahem Stern*, 9–38. Jerusalem. [In Hebrew]

———. 1997a. *Judeophobia: Attitudes toward the Jews in the Ancient World*. Cambridge, Mass.

———. 1997b. "Die Manetho-Fragmenta bei Josephus und die Anfänge des antiken 'Antisemitismus.'" In G. W. Most, ed., *Aporemata*, vol. 1, *Fragmenta sammelen*, 186–206. Göttingen.

Schalit, A. 1944. *Josephus Flavius: Jewish Antiquities*. 2 vols. Jerusalem. [In Hebrew]

———. 1969. *König Herodes*. Berlin.

———, ed. 1972. *The Hellenistic Age: The World History of the Jewish People*. Vol. 6. New Brunswick, N.J.

Schamp, J. 1987. *Photios historien des lettres: La bibliothèque et ses notices bibliographiques*. Liège.

Schanz, M., and C. Hosius. 1935. *Geschichte der römischen Literatur*, II⁴. Munich.

Schaps, D. 1982. "The Women of Greece in Wartime." *Classical Philology* 77: 193–213.

Scheppig, R. 1869. "De Posidonio Apamensi rerum gentium terrarum scriptore." PhD diss., Halle University.

Schlatter, A. 1893. *Zur Topographie und Geschichte Palästinas*. Stuttgart.

Schmid, P. G. 1947. *Studien zu griechischen Ktisissagen*. Freiburg, Switzerland.

Schmidt, K. 1980. *Kosmologische Aspekte im Geschichtswerk des Poseidonios*. Göttingen.

Schmitt, H. 1957. *Rom und Rhodes*. Munich.

Schneider, G. J. 1880. *De Diodori fontibus*. Berlin.

Schober, L. 1981. *Untersuchungen zur Geschichte Babyloniens und der Oberen Satrapien von 323–303 v. Chr.* Frankfurt.

Schofield, M. 1986. "Cicero For and Against Divination." *Journal of Roman Studies* 76: 47–65.

———. 1991. *The Stoic Idea of the City*. Cambridge.

Schräder, H., ed. 1880–82. *Porphyrii Quaestionum Homericarum ad Iliadem pertinentium reliquiae*. Leipzig.

Schreckenberg, H. 1972. *Die Flavius-Josephus-Tradition in Antike und Mittelalter*. Leiden.

———. 1996. "Text, Textüberlieferung und Textkritik von *Contra Apionem*." In L. H. Feldman and J. Levison, eds., *Josephus' Contra Apionem: Studies in Its Character and Context with a Latin Concordance to the Portion missing in Greek*, 49–82. Leiden.

Schroeder, A. 1921. "De ethnographiae antiquae locis quibusdam communibus observationes." PhD diss., Halle University.

Schürer, E. 1879. *Die Gemeindeverfassung der Juden in Rom in der Kaiserzeit*. Leipzig.

———. 1901–9. *Geschichte des jüdischen Volkes im Zeitalter Jesu Christi*[4]. 3 vols. Leipzig.

Schütrumpf, E. 2001. "Dikaiarchos Βίος Ἑλλάδος und die Philosophie des Vierten Jahrhunderts." In W. W. Fortenbaugh and E. Schütrumpf, eds., *Dicaearchus of Messenia*, 255–77. New Brunswick, N.J.

Schwanbeck, E. A. 1846. *Megasthenis Indica*. Bonn.

Schwartz, D. R. 1996. "On Antiochus VII Sidetes' Parthian Expedition and the Fragmentation of Historical Research." In I. M. Gafni et al., eds., *The Jews in the Hellenistic-Roman World: Studies in Memory of Menahem Stern*, 83–102. Jerusalem. [In Hebrew]

———. 1999. "Antisemitism and Other Ism's in the Greco-Roman World." In R. S. Wistrich, ed., *Demonizing the Other: Antisemitism, Racism, and Xenophobia*, 73–87. Amsterdam.

———. 2003. "Diodorus Siculus 40.3—Hecataeus or Pseudo Hecataeus?" In A. Oppenheimer and M. Mor, eds., *Jews and Gentiles in the Holy Land in the Days of the Second Temple, the Mishnah, and the Talmud*, 2: 181–98. Jerusalem.

Schwartz, E. 1883. "Hekataios von Theos." *Rheinisches Museum* 40: 223–62.

———. 1931. "Einiges über Assyrien, Syrien, Koilesyrien." *Philologus* 40: 373–99.

———. 1956. *Griechische Gesichtschreiber*. Leipzig.

Schwenn, F. 1915. *Menschenopfer bei den Griechen und Römern*. Giessen.

Scullard, H. H. 1974. *The Elephant in the Greek and Roman World*. London.

Seel, O. 1955. *Die Praefatio des Pompeius Trogus*. Erlangen.

———. 1972. *M. Iuniani Iustini Epitoma historiarum Philippicarum*. Stuttgart.

Seibert, J. 1967. *Historische Beiträge zu den dynastischen Verbindungen in hellenistisher Zeit*. Munich.

———. 1969. *Untersuchungen zur Geschichte Ptolemaios I*. Munich.

———. 1983. *Das Zeitalter der Diadochen*. Darmstadt.

Sevenster, J. N. 1975. *The Roots of Pagan Anti-Semitism in the Ancient World*. Leiden.

Shahar, J. 2004. *Josephus Geographicus*. Tübingen.

Shankman, P. 1969. "Le rôti et le boulli: Lévy-Strauss' Theory of Cannibalism." *American Anthropologist* 71: 54–69.

Shatzman, I. 1990. *The Armies of the Hasmonaeans and Herod*. Tübingen.

———. 1992. "The Hasmonaeans in Greco-Roman Historiography." *Zion* 57: 5–64. [In Hebrew]

———. 1995. "Stone-balls from Tel Dor and the Artillery of the Hellenistic World." *Scripta Classica Israelica* 14: 52–72.

———. 2005. "On the Conversion of the Idumaeans." In M. Mor et al., eds., *For Uriel: Studies in the History of Israel in Antiquity Presented to Professor Rappaport*, 215–44. Jerusalem.

Shefton, B. B. 1972. "Götterneid, Gold und Schwarzfirnis." *Antike Kunst* 150: 140–55.

Shulman, D. 2002. "Is There an Indian Connection to *Sefer Yeẓira?*" *Aleph: Historical Studies on Science and Judaism* 2: 191–200.

Shutt, R. J. H. 1987. "Josephus in Latin: A Retroversion into Greek and an English Translation." *Journal for the Study of the Epigrapha* 1: 79–93.

Silberschlag, E. 1933. "The Earliest Record of Jews in Asia Minor." *Journal of Biblical Literature* 52: 66–77.

Simchoni, I. N. 1959. *The Antiquity of the Jews, Against Apion.* Tel Aviv. [In Hebrew]

Simonsen, D. 1912. "Kleinigkeiten." In *Festschrift Herman Cohen,* 297–301. Berlin.

Sivan, R., and G. Soler. 1985. "Discoveries in the Citadel of Jerusalem, 1980–1984." *Qadmoniot* 4: 111–16. [In Hebrew]

———. 1994. "Excavations in the Jerusalem Citadel, 1980–1988." In H. Geva, ed., *Ancient Jerusalem Revealed,* 168–76. Jerusalem. [In Hebrew]

Smith, M. 1973. *Clement of Alexandria and the Secret Gospel of Mark.* Cambridge, Mass.

———. 1978. *Jesus the Magician.* San Francisco.

Smith, M. F. 1998. "Excavations at Oinoanda 1977: The New Epicurean Texts." *Anatolian Studies* 48: 125–70.

Smyth, H. W. 1956. *Greek Grammar.* Cambridge, Mass. (1920; repr. and rev.. 1956)

Sollenberger, M. G. 1985. "Diogenes Laertius 5.36–57: The Vita Theophrasti." In W. W. Fortenbaugh, ed., *Theophrastus of Eresus, His Life and Work,* 1–62. New Brunswick, N.J.

Solmsen, F. 1942. "Eratosthenes as Platonist and Poet." *Transactions and Proceedings of the American Philological Association* 73: 192–213.

———. 1961. *Cleanthes or Posidonius? The Basis of Stoic Physics.* Amsterdam.

Sorabji, R. 1993. *Animal Minds and Human Morals: The Origin of Western Debate.* Ithaca.

Spendel, L. 1856. *Rhetores Graeci.* Vol. 3. Leipzig.

Spoerri, W. 1959. *Spälthellenistische Berichte über Welt, Kultur und Götter: Untersuchungen zu Diodorus von Sizilien.* Basel.

———. 1961. "Zu Diodorus von Sizilien." *Museum Helveticum* 18: 63–82.

Spooner, W. A. 1891. *The Histories of Tacitus.* London.

Staab, G. 2007. "Der Gewährsmann 'Apollonius' in den neuplatonischen Pythagorasviten: Wundermann oder hellenistischer Literat?" In M. Eler and S. Schorn, eds., *Die Griechische Biographie in hellenistischer Zeit,* 195–217. Berlin.

Stählin, F. 1905. *Der Antisemitismus des Altertums in seiner Entstehung und Entwicklung.* Basel.

Stählin, O. 1960. *Clemens Alexandrinus³.* Vol. 2: *Stromata I–VI* (L. Fruchtel ed.). Berlin.

Stanton, G. R. 1968. "The Cosmopolitan Ideas of Epictetus and Marcus Aurelius." *Phronesis* 13: 183–95.

Steidle, W. 1958. *Sallusts historische Monographien.* Historia Einzelschriften 3. Wiesbaden.

———. 1963. *Sueton und die antiken Biographie².* Munich.

Stein, M. 1934. "Pseudo Hecataeus: His Time and the Aim of His Book on the Jews and Their Country." *Measef Zion* 6: 251–71. [In Hebrew]

Stein, O. 1930–31. "Klearchos von Soloi." *Philologus* 86: 258–59.

Steinmetz, P. 1994. "Die Stoa." In *Überweg: Antike,* 4/2: 495–716. Basel.

Stengel, P. 1880. "Entemnein." *Zeitschrift für das Gymnasial-Wesen* 34: 737–43.

———. 1883. "Die Einführung der in homerischer Zeit noch nicht Bekannten Opfer in Griechenland." *Jahrbücher für classische Philologie* 29: 737–45.

———. 1910. *Opferbräuche der Griechen.* Leipzig.

———. 1920. *Die griechischen Kultusaltertümer².* Munich.

Stephens, S. A. 2003. *Seeing Double: Intercultural Poetics in Ptolemaic Alexandria.* Berkeley and Los Angeles.

Sterling, G. E. 1992. *Historiography and Self-Definition: Josephus, Luke-Acts, and Apologetic Historiography.* Leiden.

Stern, E. 1999. "Religion in Palestine in the Assyrian and Persian Periods." In B. Becking and M. C. A. Korbell, eds., *The Crisis of Israelite Religion,* 245–55. Leiden.

Stern, M. 1965. *The Documents on the History of the Hasmonaean Revolt.* Tel Aviv. [In Hebrew]

———. 1973. "Hecataeus of Abdera and Theophrastus on Jews and Egyptians." *Journal of Egyptian Archeology* 59: 159–63.

———. 1974–84. *Greek and Latin Authors on Jews and Judaism.* 3 vols. Jerusalem.

———. 1976. "The Jews in Greek and Latin Literature." In S. Safrai and M. Stern, eds., *The Jewish People in the First Century: Historical Geography, Political History, Social, Cultural, and Religious Life and Institutions,* 2: 1101–59. Assen (= *Compendia rerum Iudaicarum ad Novum Testamentum,* sec. 1: *The Jewish People in the First Century*).

———. 1980. "L. Troiani, Commento storico al 'Contro Apione' di Giuseppe." *Athenaeum* 58: 226–28.

———. 1991. *Studies in Jewish History: The Second Temple Period.* Jerusalem.

———. 1993. "Timagenes of Alexandria as a Source for the History of the Hasmonean Monarchy." In J. Gafni, A. Oppenheimer, and M. Stern, eds., *Jews and Judaism in the Second Temple, Mishna, and Talmud Period, Festschrift for Samuel Safrai,* 3–15. Jerusalem. [In Hebrew]

———. 1995. *Hasmonaean Judaea in the Hellenistic World: Chapters in Political History.* Jerusalem. [In Hebrew]

Stiehle, R. 1849–50. "Die Nosten des Lysimachos." *Philologus* 4: 99–110, 5: 382–83.

Strasburger, H. 1961. "Komik und Satire in der griechischen Geschichtsschreibung." In E. Kaufmann, ed., *Festgabe für Paul Kirn,* 13–45. Berlin.

———. 1965. "Poseidonios on Problems of the Roman Empire." *Journal of Roman Studies* 55: 40–53.

Sudhaus, S., and P. Radermacher. 1895. "Critolaus und die Rhetorik." In S. Sudhaus, *Philodemi volumina rhetorica, supplementum,* v–xlii. Leipzig.

Summers, C. H. 1910. *Select Letters of Seneca.* London.

Susemihl, F. 1891–92. *Geschichte der griechischen Litteratur in der Alexandrinerzeit.* 2 vols. Leipzig.

Syme, R. 1959. "Livy and Augustus." *Harvard Studies in Classical Philology* 64: 25–87.

———. 1965. *Anatolica: Studies in Strabo.* Oxford.

Tabory, J. 1995. *Jewish Festivals in the Time of the Mishnah and Talmud.* Jerusalem. [In Hebrew]

Talbert, R. J. A. 1984. *The Senate of Imperial Rome.* Princeton.

Tannahill, R. 1975. *Flesh and Blood: A History of the Cannibal Complex.* New York.

Tarn, W. W. 1940. "Two Notes on Seleucid History." *Journal of Hellenic Studies* 60: 84–89.

———. 1951. *The Greeks in Bactria and India.* Cambridge.

Tcherikover, V. 1958. "The Anti-Semitism in the Ancient World." *Molad* 16: 361-72. [In Hebrew]

———. 1961. *Hellenistic Civilization and the Jews*². Philadelphia.

———. 1963. *The Jews in Egypt in the Hellenistic-Roman Age in the Light of the Papyri.* Jerusalem. [In Hebrew]

Thackeray, H. S. J. 1926. *Josephus.* Vol. 1: *The Life, Against Apion.* Loeb Classical Library. London and Cambridge, Mass.

———. 1943. *Josephus.* Vol. 7: *Jewish Antiquities, Books XII-XIV.* Loeb Classical Library. London and Cambridge, Mass.

Theiler, W. 1982. *Poseidonios, Die Fragmente.* 2 vols. Berlin.

Thissen, H. J. 1966. *Studien zum Raphiadekret.* Meisenheim.

Thoma, C. 1994. "John Hyrcanus I as Seen by Josephus." In F. Parente and J. Sievers, eds., *Josephus and the History of the Greco-Roman Period,* 127–40. Leiden.

Thomson, J. O. 1948. *A History of Ancient Geography.* Cambridge.

Thraede, K. 1962a. "Erfinder, II (geistesgeschichtlich)." *Reallexicon für Antike und Christentum,* cols. 1191–1278. Stuttgart.

———. 1962b. "Das Lob des Erfinders: Bemerkungen zur Analyse der Heuremata-Kataloge." *Rheinisches Museum* N.F. 105: 158–80.

Tiede, D. L. 1972. *The Charismatic Figure as a Miracle Worker.* Missoula.

Timmer, B. C. J. 1930. *Megasthenes en de indische maatschappij.* Amsterdam.

Toepelmann, P. 1869. "De Posidonio Rhodio rerum scriptore." PhD diss., Bonn University.

Treadgold, W. T. 1980. *The Nature of the Bibliotheca of Photius.* Washington, D.C.

Troiani, L. 1977. *Commento storico al "Contro Apione" de Giuseppe.* Pisa.

Trüdinger, K. 1918. *Studien zur Geschichte der griechisch-römischen Ethnographie.* Basel.

Turner, G. 1861. *Nineteen Years in Polynesia.* London.

Urbach, E. E. 1969. *The Sages; Their Concepts and Beliefs.* Jerusalem. [In Hebrew]

Ussishkin, D. 1994. "The Water System of Jerusalem during Hezekiah's Reign." *Cathedra* 70: 3-28. [In Hebrew]

Uxkull-Gyllenband, Graf W. 1924. *Griechische Kulturentstehungslehren.* Leipzig.

te Velde, H. 1977. *Seth, God of Confusion: A Study of His Role in the Egyptian Mythology and Religion*². Leiden.

Verdin, H. 1983. "Agatharchides et la tradition du discours politique dans l'historiographie grecque." In E. van't Dack, P. van Dessel, W. van Gucht, eds., *Egypt and the Hellenistic World, Proceedings of the International Colloquium Leuven 24–26 May 1982*: 407–20. Leuven.

Verraert, J. B. 1828. *Diatribe de Clearcho Solensi, philosopho Peripatetico.* Ghent.

Vidman, L. 1970. *Isis und Serapis bei den Griechen und Römern.* Berlin.

Viré, G. 1992. *Hygini De astronomia.* Stuttgart and Leipzig.

Virgilio, B. 1972. "Il termini colonizzazione in Erodoto e nella tradizione preerodotea." *Atti della Accademia della Scienze di Torino, Classe di Scienze Morali, Storiche et Filologiche* 106: 345–406.

de Vogel, C. J. 1966. *Pythagoras and Early Pythagoreanism.* Assen.

Vogel, F., and C. T. Fischer. 1888. *Diodorus Siculus*. Vol. 1. Leipzig.

Vriezen, L. 1965. "The Edomite Deity Quos." *Oudtestamentliche Studien* 14: 330–53.

Wacholder, B. Z. 1974. *Eupolemos: A Study of Judaeo-Greek Literature*. Cincinnati.

Wachsmuth, K. 1860. *Die Ansichten der Stoiker über Mantik und Daemonen*. Berlin.

———. 1891. "Timagenes und Trogus." *Rheinisches Museum* N.F. 46: 465–79.

———. 1895. *Einleitung in das Studium der alten Geschichte*. Leipzig.

Waddel, W. G. 1940. *Manetho*. Loeb Classical Library. London and Cambridge, Mass.

Walbank, F. W. 2002. *Polybius, Rome, and the Hellenstic World: Essays and Reflection*. Cambridge.

Walter, R. 1964. *Der Thoraausleger Aristobulos: Untersuchungen zu seinen Fragmenten und zu Pseudepigraphischen Resten der jüdisch-hellenistischen Literatur*. Berlin.

Walton, F. 1955. "The Messenger of God in Hecataeus of Abdera." *Harvard Theological Review* 48: 255–57.

Walton, F. R. 1967. *Diodorus of Sicily*. Vol. 12. Loeb Classical Library. Cambridge, Mass.

Wardy, B. 1979. "Jewish Religion in Pagan Literature during the Late Republic and Early Empire." In H. Temporini and W. Haase, eds., *Aufstieg und Niedergang der römischen Welt*, II, 19. 1: 592–644. Berlin.

Wasserstein, A. 1996. "On Donkeys, Wine, and the Uses of Textual Criticism: Septuagint Variants in Jewish Palestine." In I. M. Gafni et al., eds., *The Jews in the Hellenistic-Roman World: Studies in Memory of Menahem Stern*, 119–42. Jerusalem. [In Hebrew]

Watson, G. 1971. *The Natural Law and Stoicism*. London.

Weber, M. 1920. *Gesammelte Aufsätze zur Religionssoziologie*. Vol. 3: *Das antike Judentum*. Tübingen.

Wehrli, F. 1928. *Zur Geschichte der allegorischen Deutung Homers im Altertum*. Leipzig.

———. 1944. *Die Schule des Aristoteles*. Vol. 1: *Dikaiarchos*. Basel.

———. 1945. *Die Schule des Aristoteles*. Vol. 2: *Aristoxenos*. Basel.

———. 1948. *Die Schule des Aristoteles*. Vol. 3: *Klearchos*. Basel.

———. 1953. *Die Schule des Aristoteles*. Vol. 7: *Herakleides Pontikos*. Basel.

———. 1955. *Die Schule des Aristoteles*. Vol. 8: *Eudemos*. Basel.

———. 1956. *Die Schule des Aristoteles*. Vol. 9: *Phainias von Eresos*. Basel.

———. 1974. *Die Schule des Aristoteles*. Suppl. vol. 1: *Hermippos der Kallimacheer*. Basel and Stuttgart.

Weill, R. 1918. *La fin du Moyen Empire égyptien*. Paris.

Weinfeld, M. 1987. "The Pattern of Israelite Settlement in Canaan." *Cathedra* 44: 3–20. [In Hebrew]

———. 1993. *The Promise of the Land: The Inheritance of the Land of Canaan by the Israelites*. Berkeley and Los Angeles.

Welles, C. B. 1934. *Royal Correspondence in the Hellenistic Period*. New Haven.

Wendland, P. 1912. *Die hellenistisch-römische Kultur in ihren Beziehungen zu Judentum und Christentum²*. Tübingen.

Wendling, E. 1893. "Zu Poseidonius und Varro." *Hermes* 28: 335–53.

Wescher, C. 1874. *Dionysii Byzantii de Bospori navigatione quae supersunt, una cum supplementis in geographos minores*. Paris.

West, S. 1974. "Peripatetic or Alexandrian?" *Greek, Roman, and Byzantine Studies* 15: 275–87.

Whiston, W. 1737. *The Works of Flavius Josephus*. London.

Wilamowitz-Moellendorff, U. von. 1881. *Antigonos von Karystos*. Berlin.

———. 1885. *Euripides, Herakles*, I. *Einleitung in die griechische Tragödie*[2]. Berlin.

———. 1900. "Asianismus und Attizismus." *Hermes* 35: 1–52.

———. 1931. *Der Glaube der Hellenen*. 2 vols. Berlin.

Wilhelm, F. 1915. "Die Oeconomica der Neupythagoreer Bryso, Kallikratidas, Periktione, Phintys." *Rheinisches Museum* 70: 163–223.

Wilk, R. 1987. "Jews in Seleucid Syria." PhD diss., Tel Aviv University. [In Hebrew]

Wilker, J. 2002. "Irrwege einer antiken Bücher-Sammlung, Die Bibliothek des Aristoteles." In W. Hoepfner, ed., *Antike Bibliotheke*, 24–29. Mainz.

Wilkinson, R. H. 2003. *The Complete Gods and Goddesses of Ancient Egypt*. London.

Will, E. 1979–82. *Histoire politique du monde hellénistique*. 2 vols. Nancy.

Will, E., and C. Orrieux. 1974. *Die Schule der Aristoteles*. Suppl. vol. 1: *Hermippos der Kallimacheer*. Basel and Stuttgart.

———. 1986. *Ioudaismos-Hellenismos: Essai sur le judaïsme judéen à l'époque hellénistique*. Nancy.

Willrich, H. 1895. *Juden und Griechen vor der Makkabäischen Erhebung*. Göttingen.

———. 1900. *Judaica: Forschungen zur hellenistisch-jüdischen Literatur*. Göttingen.

Winiarczyk, M. 1981. *Diagorae et Theodori Cyrenaei Reliquiae*. Leipzig.

———. 1984. "Wer galt im Altertum als Atheist." *Philologus* 128: 157–93.

Winston, D. 1979. *The Wisdom of Solomon*. New York.

Wirszubski, C. 1990. *Bein ha-shitin: Kabalah, Kabalah Notzrit, Shabtaut (Sifriyat kinus)* [Between the Lines: Kabbalah, Christian Kabbalah, and Sabbatianism]. Jerusalem. [In Hebrew]

Wissowa, G. 1912. *Religion und Kultus der Römer*[2]. Munich.

Witkowsky, S. 1898/9. "De patria Megasthenis." *Commentarii Societatis Philologiae Polonorum* 5: 22–24.

Wittaker, M. 1984. *Jews and Christians: Greco-Roman Views*. Cambridge.

Wolfer, E. P. 1954. *Eratosthenes von Kyrene als Mathematiker und Philosoph*. Groningen and Jakarta.

Wolff, E. 1934. "Das geschichtliche Verstehen in Tacitus' Germania." *Hermes* 69: 121–66.

Wolska-Conus, W. 1968–73. *Cosmas Indicopleustés: La topographie chrétienne*. 3 vols. Paris.

Yadin, Y. 1962. *The Scroll of the War of the Sons of Light against the Sons of Darkness*. Oxford.

Yavetz, Z. 1993. "Judeophobia in Classical Antiquity: A Different Approach," *Journal of Jewish Studies* 44: 1–22.

———. 1997. *Judenfeindschaft in der Antike*. Munich.

Yoyotte, M. 1963. "L'Égypte ancienne et les origines de l'antijudaïsme." *Revue de l'Histoire des Religions* 163: 133–43.

Zadok, R. 1998. "Prosopography of Samaria and Idumea." *Ugarit Forschungen* 30: 781–827.

Zambrini, A. 1982. "Gli Ἰνδικά di Megasthene." *Annali della Scuola Normale Superiori di Pisa, Classe di Lettere e Filosofia,* serie 3, 12. 1: 71–149; 15. 3 (1985) 781–853.

Zeitlin, S. 1945. "Anti-Semitism." *Crozer Quarterly* 22: 134–49.

Zeller, E. 1923. *Die Philosophie der Griechen in ihrer geschichtlichen Entwicklung*[5]. Vol. 3. Leipzig.

Zimmerman, R. 1888. "Posidonius und Strabo." *Hermes* 23: 103–30.

Zipser, M. 1871. *Das Flavius Josephus Werk "Ueber das hohe Alter des jüdischen Volkes gegen Apion."* Vienna.

Zucker, F. 1937. "Doppelinschrift spätptol: Zeit aus der Garnison von Hermopolis Magna." *Abhandlungen der königlich preußischen Akademie der Wissenschaft zu Berlin, Phil.-hist. Kl.* (6): 3–36.

Zuntz, G. 1965. *An Inquiry into the Transmission of the Plays of Euripides.* Cambridge.

INDEX

Page references in italics refer to illustrations.

cosmology: Aristotle's, 149n59, 536–37; Brahman, 147–50; Chrysippus's, 351; creator god in, 148nn54–56, 152, 155; cyclical theory of, 147n51, 151n71, 153; earth-centric, 150n65, 162; heaven in, 161; Indian, 72n94, 147–50; manager-god in, 148, 151; monotheistic, 148n53; Neoplatonic, 148n54; in Plato, 536n33; Posidonius's, 351, 537–38, 540; pre-Socratic, 147n51, 149n61, 150n65, 159, 161, 162; water in, 150n63, 153–54. *See also* physics
cosmology, Stoic, 149nn58–59, 151, 532–33; *aithēr* in, 527, 532, 540–41; conflagration in, 528n9, 530n13; *ekpyrōsis* in, 528n9; *ouranos* in, 531, 532n22, 533; ruling principles of, 531; in Strabo's excursus, 533–34
cosmos: active aspect of, 151n70; as heaven, 538n35; and *ouranos*, 161n116; role of *pneuma* in, 529; shape of, 147, 153, 161–62
courage: Aristotle on, 496; Stoic view of, 494n77
courage, Jewish: Josephus on, 493, 495; Tacitus on, 492n74
court chronicles, Hellenistic, 6. *See also* Seleucid court scribes
cowardice: charges against Jews, 492–96; Egyptian, 496; and recklessness, 496
Crates of Mallos, 344, 345n29
Crates of Thebes, 68
Cratinus, *Pythagorizousa*, 182
Cratippus, Cicero's use of, 383
Crete: decline in, 376n55; hostile accounts of, 524
Critias, *Sisyphus*, 188n111
Critolaus, embassy to Rome, 346n34
crocodiles, divinity of, 97
Cronus, 151n66; age of, 374
Crotus, Johannes, 481n36
cultic practices: Cicero on, 395; development of, 19–20; Epictetus on, 380; Hellenistic monarchs on, 421; John Hyrcanus and, 335; Stoics on, 396; Theophrastus on, 17–18, 19–20; Zeno on, 379. *See also* animal cults; sacrificial practices
cultic practices, Egyptian, 97; foreign, 114
cultic practices, Jewish: Clearchus's knowledge of, 80; in Hecataeus's excursus, 379; Posidonius on, 523
cultic practices, Roman, 380n75; Varro on, 510–11
culture, Egyptian: degenerate, 395; Hecataeus on, 132; impact on Greek world, 236; pharaonic, 394

culture, Greek: burnt offerings in, 26; dream divination in, 381–82; Egyptian influence on, 236; Oriental influences on, 199
culture, Indian: influence on Greeks, 136
Cumont, F., 232n87
customs, Jewish: Greek knowledge of, 258; in Hecataeus's excursus, 117, 129, 132; Pythagorean similarities to, 198n156, 199
cycles: cosmic, 151n71, 528n9; of power, 66
Cyclopes, society of, 371n47
Cynics: antisocial characteristics of, 70, 71; Clearchus on, 67, 68–73, 518; eating habits of, 68, 69–70, 73; and gymnosophists, 72, 73; Indian origin of, 71n90; *karteria* and, 68, 69, 73, 78n108, 80; lifestyle of, 68; papyri on, 72; and *sōphrosynē*, 69, 70, 73, 80; threat to society, 69; and *tryphē*, 69

Dagon, priests of, 191n122
Damascus, mint of, 407n22
Damocritus: on ass libel, 241; blood libel of, 259–63, 265n44, 279; use of Apion, 262, 266
Danaus, Egyptian descent of, 108, 110, 112, 114
Dandamis. *See* Mandamis
deaths: in battle, 493, 495; strange, 171, 172, 179n76
deisdaimonia: Agatharchides on, 297; Judaism as, 398. *See also* superstition
Demetrius of Phaleron, *On Socrates*, 183
Demetrius Poliocertes, siege of Rhodes, 411n33
Demetrius the Syrian, Cicero's study with, 477
Democritus, 377; in *De natura deorum*, 513n137; inventions of, 503
Dennis, H. G., 28n45
Denniston, J. D., 30n48
Derceto, myth of, 232n88
desert, Oriental romanticization of, 487–88
Diadochi. *See* Successors, Alexander's
Diadochic period: accounts of Jews during, 5; Hellenistic authors of, 7; historiography of, 11; Jews of, 84; wonder stories from, 77n105
Diagoras of Athens, atheism of, 507
Diagoras of Melos, 160
Diamond, F. H., 121n92
diaspora, Egyptian: Idumaeans in, 216–17, 218; Jewish-Greek relations in, 2
diaspora, Jewish: and anti-Jewish attitudes, 520; observance of Sabbath in, 301; Sabbath warfare during, 292–93. *See also* Exodus story
Dicaearchus of Messenia: on ages of mankind,

mals, 18, 39; abstracting of Theophrastus, 39, 100n27; on animal sacrifice, 20n19; on *atheoi*, 508; knowledge of Josephus, 27n41; on Lysimachus, 308; manuscripts of, 23n25; on Molon, 474–75; on plagiarism, 311n24; on pork consumption, 24; on Pythagoras, 183; on siege of Jerusalem, 435n95; use of Diodorus, 410n30; on vegetarianism, 39; view of Jews, 27n41

"Posidonian problem," 338, 348–54

Posidonius of Apamea, 3–4; access to Hellenistic Jewish authors, 392; on Anacharses, 503; on anthropomorphism, 393, 395, 396; anti-Jewish testimonia on, 441–44; on Antiochus Sidetes, 378–79, 427, 428–31; anti-Semitic perception of, 440; Apion's use of, 241, 357–58, 441, 443; and Apollonius Molon, 471, 477, 492–503, 511; and Aristotle, 447; on ass libel, 358, 442–43, 444, 456, 457, 490, 519; Athenaeus's use of, 177, 353, 413n40, 423, 468; on Athenion, 177; attitude toward Jews, 338, 341, 397; attitude toward rhetors, 476–77; attitude toward Roman Republic, 427, 428n77; birth of, 339, 343; and blood libel, 253, 256n15, 279, 456, 515, 519; in Cadiz, 345; on Callanus, 387; Celtic ethnography of, 345, 352, 455–56; Cicero and, 338, 340, 377; Cicero's use of, 4, 377–78, 513n135; on circumcision, 522; cosmology of, 351, 537–38, 540; dates of, 338, 339–40, 348; defense of Euclid, 342n15; Diodorus's use of, 102n31, 104n39, 297n76, 328, 412–13, 415, 416; Diogenes Laertius's use of, 540n38; on the divine, 389; on dream divination, 85n128, 351, 382, 383–88, 390; on Druids, 37; embassy to Rome, 339, 346–47; ethnicity of, 340–42; ethnography of, 4; fame in Rome, 398; fragments of, 348–49, 449; Galen's testimonium on, 349; geographicsl works, 348n41; on god, 529n11, 532, 538; on Golden Age, 271–72, 350, 367, 368, 373–74, 377n59, 393n119, 394; on Hasmonaeans, 392, 393–94; on Hermagoras of Temnos, 351; on Hermogenes of Temnos, 476; historiographic method of, 423; influence on Numenius, 398; influence on Tacitus, 398; on inventions, 377, 500, 501, 502–3; on Jewish *amixia*, 415n47, 432; in *Jewish Antiquities*, 353, 399, 413; on Jewish divination, 343n20; on John Hyrcanus, 431; Josephus's use of, 353, 399, 413n39; knowledge of Agatharchides, 305, 371n47; on later

Judaism, 393, 396, 415n47; letter to Cicero, 339, 347; libel of Jews, 6; life of, 338, 339–42, 431; on luxury, 423–24; in Marseilles, 346; Mediterranean voyage of, 345–46; on Mithridates, 427, 429; on moderation, 385, 387, 426; moral doctrines of, 352; on Mosaic Judaism, 305, 356, 391–97, 432, 440, 452, 492, 495, 506, 518, 523; on nature, 384; omission of Sabbath discussion, 522–23; Oriental influences on, 341; on *ouranos*, 532n22, 538; pacifism of, 377, 494; pan-Posidonian scholarship on, 349, 353; physics of, 530–31; Plutarch's use of, 416; on *pneuma*, 351, 528–33, 538; political ideals of, 463; Pompeius Trogus's use of, 425, 468; Pompey and, 338, 347–48; on Pythagoras, 177n65; on relations between peoples, 454n49; rhetoric of, 352, 353n71, 477; at Rhodes, 341–42, 345, 346; Roman audience of, 396nn122-24; on Roman imperialism, 427; satirical style of, 354; scientific education of, 343–44; scientific theories of, 345; on Seleucids, 426; Seleucid sources of, 449; Senecas's testimonium on, 350, 362n17, 366–67, 371–72, 373, 375, 377, 501; on siege of Jerusalem, 448–49; socio-political views of, 353–54; on the soul, 384; on stages of mankind, 373, 375; state of the wise in, 362–63, 365, 366–69, 377, 503; and stasis theory, 476n17; on statue of Moses, 238, 491; Stoic education of, 342–45; Stoicism of, 343, 423n64, 525–31; Strabo on, 446–47, 539–40; in Strabo's excursus, 355–58, 362, 365, 382, 389, 390–91, 415, 431, 462, 511, 519, 525, 533, 540–41; Strabo's use of, 346, 348, 353, 413; study of tides, 345; study with Panaetius, 340, 342–45; survival of, 5, 338, 348–54; teaching methods of, 393; on *technai*, 353n70; on temples, 380; testimonia on, 348–49, 449; on therapeutic dreams, 388; training in geometry, 342, 343n23; on *tryphē*, 67; use of caricature, 423–24, 432; use of Hecataeus's excursus, 392, 495, 515; use of Olympiad reckoning, 404n19; use of Timochares, 463–64, 468; Varro's use of, 398; on vegetarianism, 375n55

—*Account of Nature*, 351

—*Histories*, 349, 352–53; conclusion of, 416n47; continuation of Polybius, 423; Josephus's unfamiliarity with, 451; philosophical aspects of, 353, 423n63, 437

—*Introduction to Style*, 477

600 INDEX

Posidonius of Apamea (*continued*)
—Jewish ethnographic excursus, 132n120, 354, 355–58, 417; cult in, 523; Exodus story in, 328, 432, 454, 503; Hasmonaean rulers in, 496; Molon's ethnography and, 471, 477, 492–503, 511, 514–16; Moses in, 452, 519, 541; original location of, 448–51; Timagenes' use of, 519
—*On Divination*, 351
—*On General Inquiry*, 351
—*On Gods*, 351, 532n22
—*On Ocean*, 345–46, 348n41
—*On the Cosmos*, 528n10
—*On the Universe*, 351
Pötscher, W., 17n9
potter's wheel, invention of, 502, 503
power, cycles of, 66
Praxiteles of Athens, 230n83
prayer, Jewish: Agatharchides on, 297
pre-Socratics: cosmology of, 147n51, 149n61, 150n65, 159, 161, 162; on divine power, 148n54; on *megalopsychia*, 446; physics of, 145, 146–56, 158–59
Preuschen, E., 381n76
Priapus, conflict with ass, 228, 230
priests, Egyptian, 33n61, 34, 118n73; concept of ruler, 122; preservation of ancient traditions, 314n39
priests, Jewish: authority from Moses, 372; executive powers of, 122; function of, 118; in Hecataeus's excursus, 118, 124–25, 126, 370; leadership by, 101; superstitions under, 440; tyrants, 356, 359, 360, 361, 373, 453
Proclus: commentary on *Politeia*, 55, 56; preservation of Clearchus, 54
prohibitions, Pythagorean, 165, 179, 184–96, 203; against blasphemy, 187–89; concerning asses, 165, 186–87, 190, 196–97; concerning drinking, 189–90; against eating beans, 180; Hermippus on, 184–96, 203; Jewish influence on, 186; Thracian influence on, 186, 190. See also *akousmata*, Pythagorean
prophets, Jewish: on monarchy, 122
Psammetichus (king of Egypt), 98, 132
pseudo-Apollodorus, 32
pseudo-Aristeas, 290, 294
pseudo-Eupolemus, 498n88; on Moses, 500
pseudo-Hecataeus. See *On the Jews*
Ptolemies: despotism of, 281; relationship with Jews, 93, 449, 519; self-deification of, 287
Ptolemy (son of Lagos). See Ptolemy I Soter

Ptolemy I Soter, 46; attitude toward Egyptians, 234; court of, 94, 95; legitimacy of, 142; occupation of Jerusalem, 281, 288–89, 290, 291–98; prestige of, 98; rule of Judaea, 119, 123; ruler cult of, 287; southern expeditions of, 105n42; Tosefta on, 295
Ptolemy II Philadelphus: attitude toward pharaonic tradition, 234, 235; elephants of, 172, 285; military expeditions of, 285; mining enterprises of, 285
Ptolemy IV Philopator, at Jerusalem Temple, 236n100
Ptolemy VI Philometor: and Alexander Balas, 407n22; Aristobulus and, 200, 204; regents of, 282
Ptolemy VIII Physcon, 236n100; expulsion of intellectuals, 342; personality of, 336; reign of terror of, 282, 287; struggle with Cleopatra II, 333
Ptolemy IX Lathyrus, 93, 336
Ptolemy of Mendes, Egyptian ethnography of, 314
Pucci, M., 408n25
Pythagoras: Alexandrian scholarship on, 176; Aristobulus on, 197; Aristoxenus on, 180n80, 183; Athenaeus on, 177; on blasphemy, 165; as charlatan, 175, 176, 178, 179–80, 190, 202, 518; Christian image of, 173; in comedy, 182; communication with spirits, 165–66; controversial character of, 175; cosmology of, 154, 160; in Croton, 174, 177–78, 180; death of, 171, 180, 186n101; deviousness of, 179n72; Dicaearchus on, 179n72, 182, 183; on *euphēmia*, 187; historical personality of, 167; as Hyperborean Apollo, 182; Iamblichus on, 173, 183; on immortality of soul, 179, 184, 185, 198n156; Jewish influence on, 164, 166, 167, 184–85, 193, 194–200, 204; Josephus on, 203; knowledge of Jews, 6; medieval writers on, 205; Molon's *bios* of, 475; on music, 183n89; Neoplatonic image of, 173; Oriental influences on, 167, 180n77, 194n135, 199, 200n159; Origen on, 200–202; as plagiarist, 202; political doctrine of, 177–78, 180; Porphyry on, 183; Posidonius on, 177n65; prohibition concerning asses, 165, 186–87, 190, 196–97; satirical works on, 181–83; Theopompus on, 175n56, 177; Thracian influence on, 166, 184–85, 196; on transmigration of soul, 151n67, 181, 182, 185n99; in underworld, 176, 184, 187; wonderful deeds

TEXT
10/12.5 Minion Pro

DISPLAY
Minion Pro

COMPOSITOR
Bookmatters, Berkeley

INDEXER
Roberta Engleman

CARTOGRAPHER/ILLUSTRATOR
Bill Nelson

PRINTER AND BINDER
Maple-Vail Book Manufacturing Group